D0118998

GREAT HEALTH HINTS & HANDY TIPS

GREAT HEALTH HINTS & HANDY TIPS

MORE THAN 4,000 IDEAS TO HELP YOU LOOK AND FEEL YOUR BEST

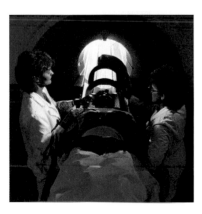

Reader's Digest

The Reader's Digest Association (Canada) Ltd., Montreal

GREAT HEALTH HINTS & HANDY TIPS

READER'S DIGEST STAFF

EDITORS: *Alma E. Guinness*
Sandy Shepherd

GROUP ART EDITOR: *Robert M. Grant*

ART EDITOR: *Judith Carmel*

ART SUPERVISOR: *John McGuffie*

DESIGNER: *Andrée Payette*

SENIOR RESEARCH EDITOR: *Maymay Quey Lin*

RESEARCH EDITOR: *Wadad Bashour*

SENIOR ASSOCIATE EDITOR: *Susan Bronson*

RESEARCH ASSOCIATE: *Christina Schlank*

LIBRARY RESEARCH: *Nettie Seaberry*

PICTURE EDITOR: *Rachel Irwin*

EDITORIAL ASSISTANT: *Elizabeth Eastman*

PRODUCTION MANAGER: *Holger Lorenzen*

PRODUCTION COORDINATOR: *Susan Wong*

COPY EDITOR: *Joseph Marchetti*

INDEXER: *Anita Winterberg*

CONTRIBUTORS

CONSULTING EDITOR: *Genell Subak-Sharpe*

ASSOCIATE EDITOR: *Mary Lyn Maiscott*

WRITERS: *Diana Benzaia,
Rebecca Christian, Jacqueline Damian,
Nancy Gagliardi, Letta S. Neely,
Emily Paulson, Terry Lee Swarts*

RESEARCHERS: *Gabrielle P. Immerman,
Helene MacLean, Brian L. Mitchell,
Paula Phelps, Martha Plaine, Ann Purdy Rafferty,
Anna Sobkowski, Sarah E. Subak-Sharpe*

PICTURE RESEARCHER: *Linda Patterson Eger*

EDITORIAL ASSISTANT: *Troy Dreier*

ART ASSISTANT: *Tomaso Milian*

PRODUCTION COORDINATOR: *Tracey Grant-Starker*

PROOFREADER: *Gina E. Grant*

INDEXER: *Sydney Wolfe Cohen*

TECHNICAL SUPPORT: *Debra Rabinowitz,
Dushan G. Lukic*

CONSULTANTS

EMERGENCY MEDICINE
Malinda H. Bell, M.D., F.A.C.E.P.
Clinical Associate Professor of
Emergency Medicine
Truman Medical Center / University
of Missouri
Kansas City, MO

ENVIRONMENTAL MEDICINE
Robert K. McLellan, M.D., M.P.H.
Medical Director
Center for Occupational and
Environmental Health
Exeter Hospital
Exeter, NH

NUTRITION
Marion Nestle, Ph.D.
Professor and Chair
Department of Nutrition, Food,
and Hotel Management
New York University
New York, NY

PSYCHOLOGY
Herbert Krauss, Ph.D.
Professor of Psychology
Hunter College
City University of New York
New York, NY

INTERNAL MEDICINE
Morton D. Bogdonoff, M.D.
Professor of Medicine
Cornell University Medical College
New York, NY

DERMATOLOGY
Victor J. Selmanowitz, M.D.
New York, NY

PHYSICAL EDUCATION, EXERCISE
Ronald Feingold, Ph.D.
Professor and Chair, Department of
Health Studies, Physical Education
and Human Performance Science
Adelphi University
Garden City, NY

PREVENTIVE MEDICINE
Valerie Ulene, M.D.
New York Hospital-Cornell
Medical Center
New York, NY

TRAVEL AND WILDERNESS MEDICINE
Kenneth W. Kizer, M.D., M.P.H.
Professor, Chair of
Community and International
Health, Professor of Emergency
Medicine and Clinical Toxicology
University of California / Davis
Davis, CA

EMERGENCY RESPONSE SYSTEMS
Margaret A. Wylde, Ph.D.
Vice President, Advanced Living
Systems Division, Institute
for Technology Development
Oxford, MS

ERGONOMICS
Inger M. Williams, Ph.D.
Fairport, NY

LEGAL RECORDS
Joseph W. Mierzwa, J.D.
Highlands Ranch, CO

PEDIATRICS
Barbara C. Kennedy, M.D.
Palo Alto Medical Clinic,
Palo Alto, CA

NATURAL MEDICINE
Rudolph Ballentine, M.D.
Founder and Director
Center for Holistic Medicine
New York, NY

The information, recommendations, and visual material in this book are for reference and guidance only; they are not intended as a substitute for a physician's diagnosis and care. The editors urge anyone with continuing medical problems or symptoms to consult a qualified physician.

The credits and acknowledgments that appear on pages 446–448 are hereby made a part of this copyright page.

Copyright © 1994 The Reader's Digest Association (Canada) Ltd.
Copyright © 1994 The Reader's Digest Association, Inc.
Copyright © 1994 The Reader's Digest Association Far East Ltd.
Philippine Copyright 1994 Reader's Digest Association Far East Ltd.

All rights reserved. Unauthorized reproduction, in any manner, is prohibited.

CANADIAN CATALOGUING IN PUBLICATION DATA

Main entry under title:
Great health hints & handy tips : more than 4,000 ideas to help you look and feel your best.
Includes index.
ISBN 0-88850-242-7
1. Health—Miscellanea. I. Reader's Digest Association (Canada).
RA776.9.G74   1994   613   C94—900443—X

Reader's Digest and the Pegasus logo are registered trademarks of The Reader's Digest Association, Inc.

Printed in the United States of America
94 95 96 97 98 / 5 4 3 2 1

TABLE OF CONTENTS

The workplace will be changing *in the coming years, and more people will find them-selves working at home, as this couple does. While this arrangement offers greater control of the working day, it means learning how to keep work and home life in balance.*

CHAPTER 1

TAKING CHARGE

We make health decisions every day without realizing it. Deciding to spend time with family and friends is a health decision. Eating a salad for lunch and avoiding that second cup of coffee are both health decisions. Even little things like arranging your office for comfort or carpooling to work will affect how you feel. That's because good health is more than a yearly visit to the doctor's office; it's understanding all the little ways you can make your world healthier.

You take charge of your health when you learn that these small changes will pay off big. Learning how to let go of stress at the end of the day can protect you from muscle aches. Making your home safe and quiet will protect your family. You can gain peace of mind simply by putting your insurance forms in order and making a living will. It's important to take care of yourself. If you didn't have your health, it would be impossible to enjoy the good things in life.

Meditation is easy *to learn and will help you relax and release stress.*

TAKING CHARGE OF YOUR LIFE

There are many ways to ensure your own well-being—a mix of common sense, folk wisdom, and up-to-date scientific information. You can start by setting priorities.

FIRST THINGS FIRST

Here are some of the most important things you can do to enhance your health. These hints, which are drawn from topics throughout the book, illustrate how diverse are the ingredients of a healthy life. See the box below for measures that can save your life.

■ Eat not just to satisfy hunger but to be as healthy and vigorous as possible (see "Eating for Good Health," page 38).

■ Pray or meditate, or simply learn how to relax. People who habitually take time for quiet contemplation and spiritual renewal gain the additional benefits of lessened stress and a lowered heart rate.

■ Be sociable. Talking with a friend or relative can do a lot to relieve stress.

■ Install and maintain smoke detectors. Most deaths from fire occur in the home. You can reduce your risk by installing smoke detectors, one outside each bedroom, and an additional detector on each level of the house (see "Fire Safety," page 218).

■ Check the location of the exits whenever you go to a restaurant, theater, hotel, or other public place. Fires create panic and confusion; you can save precious minutes if you have already observed the quickest way out.

■ Learn to control your anger and discharge it appropriately. Venting your anger at your family will only create bad feelings and make your home life worse. Remember that chronically angry people are at greater risk for heart disease than calmer folk. Hiking, jogging, and swimming can help to dispel anger. So can listening to soothing music.

■ If you've never thought of protecting yourself from the sun, it's time to start. Wear a hat and use sunscreen.

■ Learn how to swim or how to perform a technique called drown-proofing (see "Enjoying Water Sports," page 242).

■ Learn your family's health history. Many diseases are hereditary. If you discover that a particular illness "runs in the family," your doctor will be better able to monitor your health (see "The Informed Patient," page 295).

---

6 Ways to Save Your Life

You can contribute to your own longevity with these basic measures. In fact, it is almost impossible to maintain good health without following these rules.

1. If you smoke tobacco, stop. If you don't, don't start. Smoking is the single greatest cause of preventable illness in the country. It is bad not only for smokers but for the people around them.

2. Maintain a healthy weight. Excessive weight is linked to heart disease, high blood pressure, diabetes, back problems, and a host of other ailments. If you need to lose weight, do so gradually (see "Losing Weight Forever," page 52).

3. Exercise. Inactivity puts you at risk for ailments ranging from heart disease to osteoporosis. The good news is that any activity, from walking to gardening, will help you to get started (see "A Lifetime Concern," page 84).

4. Avoid excessive consumption of alcohol.

5. Never drink and drive.

6. Fasten your seat belt every time you drive or ride in a car. Seat belts afford even more protection than air bags do because air bags protect you only from front-end collisions.

- Follow your doctor's instructions. Take all medications as prescribed (see page 296).
- Set up a schedule for any medical tests, including self-examinations, you should have on a regular basis (see "Tests and Examinations," page 300).
- Get immunized. If you're over 65, or if you have certain chronic health conditions, you should get an annual flu shot and a one-time pneumococcal vaccine shot. Check with your doctor to see if you need them.
- Know the warning signs of a heart attack and stroke (see page 418).
- Keep a well-stocked emergency medical kit in an accessible place (see page 384).
- Learn the basics of first aid. These include the Heimlich maneuver for choking. Don't just learn how to help others; find out how to perform the maneuver on yourself as well. (See page 400 for complete instructions.)
- Have your house tested for radon, an invisible gas that can cause lung cancer (see page 208). You should also have your water tested for lead (see page 207 for more information).

UNDERSTANDING HEALTH INFORMATION

Health scares occur when newspapers or television shows misrepresent the results of medical studies. Part of taking charge of your health means knowing what information is useful and what is not.
- Don't jump to conclusions or change your daily habits on the basis of one health study.
- Understand the terms used to describe a study's results. "May" does not mean "will," "in some people" does not mean "in all people," and "contributes to" does not mean "causes."
- Keep a healthy skepticism when reading about medical miracles or breakthroughs. Too often the results of a study have been built up to create reader interest.
- Statements saying that something doubles the risk of a particular disease sound impressive but can be misleading. If the risk was one in a million, a doubled risk may not be that serious. You'll want to pay more attention if the risk was one in a hundred.
- Notice where information comes from. Results based on several studies are stronger than the results of one study. How many were in the study? How much time did it take?
- Use common sense. If an author writes that one nation is healthier than another, realize that there is no single cause that can explain the results.
- Be wary of any studies used to sell a product. The information is likely to be biased.

FINDING TIME

How you manage your time can actually affect your health. No one who is chronically overwhelmed by tasks at home and on the job can operate at peak efficiency.
- Ask yourself what is most important to you. Then schedule your time to satisfy your own priorities.
- Make definite decisions as to how you want to spend your personal time, and resist pressures to sacrifice your time for somebody else's plan.
- Don't overschedule your free time, or you'll make it as stressful as your time at work. Instead, give yourself fewer things to do and enjoy doing them more.

- Think of quick tasks, such as writing notes to friends, that you can do while waiting in line at the supermarket or at your doctor's office.
- Don't wait for "the right moment" to start a project—that moment may never come. This is especially true if you tend to procrastinate. Remember that few tasks have to be started at the beginning. So if the first step seems daunting, start with another part of the project. Once you're in motion, it will be easier to stay with your plan.
- Clear your work area so you won't be distracted either by mess or by another project.

Save time by deciding what not to do. Vacuum once every two weeks, not every week. From time to time, serve your family sandwiches instead of a hot dinner.

DEALING WITH STRESS

When we're in an emergency or a tense situation, we feel stress. Often our heart rate increases as our body prepares us for this new challenge. We all know from firsthand experience what stress is, but how do we beat it?

ABOUT STRESS

When your car skids on an icy road, your body goes on full alert, ready for action. This stress response can save your life because all your faculties are at their highest pitch and your energies are directed toward controlling the car. But more often, stress does not call for a physical response. For example, when you have an argument with a friend, your body may become charged up but there is no physical outlet for your energies. When this happens repeatedly, stress builds, adversely affecting your health.

■ Things that cause stress—called stressors—do not affect everyone in the same way. Much depends on how we perceive and cope with trouble. If every problem is considered a catastrophe, the level of stress is greater. You should think about your problems in the coolest way you can.

> **It is possible to have too little stress. We work better with a certain level of stimulation. If the level is too low, we get bored.**

STRESSFUL SITUATIONS

■ Stress is a normal part of life and usually comes from every-day occurrences. Eliminate as many sources of stress as you can. For example, if crowds bother you, go to the supermarket when you know the lines won't be long. Try renting videotapes rather than going to crowded movie theaters.

■ Clear up the clutter in your life by giving away or throwing away the things that get in your way. A garage sale is one effective way to do this.

■ If you are always running late, sit down with a pencil and paper and see how you are actually allotting your time. Say it takes 40 minutes to get to work. Are you leaving your house on time? You may be able to solve the problem (and de-stress your life a bit) just by being realistic.

■ If you can't find the time for all the activities that are important to you, maybe you are trying to do too much. Again, make a list of what you do during the day and how much time each activity takes. Then cut back.

■ Avoid predictably stressful situations. If a certain sport or game makes you tense (whether it's tennis or bridge), decline the invitation to play. After all, the point of these activities is to have a good time. If you know you won't, there's no reason to play.

■ If you can't remove the stress, remove yourself. Slip away once in a while for some private time. These quiet moments may give you a fresh perspective on your problems.

■ Avoid stressful people. For example, if you don't get along with your father-in-law but you don't want to make an issue of it, invite other in-laws at the same time you invite him. Having other people around will help absorb some of the pressure you would normally feel.

■ Competing with others, whether in accomplishments, appearance, or possessions, is an avoidable source of stress. You might know people who do all they can to provoke envy in others. While it may seem easy to say you should be satisfied with what you have, it's the truth. Stress from this kind of jealousy is self-inflicted.

■ Laborsaving devices, such as cellular phones or computer hookups, often encourage us to cram too many activities into each day. Before you buy new equipment, be sure that it will really improve your life. Be aware that taking care of equipment and getting it repaired can be stressful.

■ Try doing only one thing at a time. For example, when you're riding your exercise bike, you don't also have to listen to the radio or watch television.

■ Remember, sometimes it's okay to do nothing.

■ If you suffer from insomnia, headaches, recurring colds, or stomach upsets, consider whether stress is part of the problem. Being chronically angry, frustrated, or apprehensive can deplete your physical resources.

■ If you feel that stress (or anything else) is getting the better of you, seek professional help—a doctor or therapist. Early signs of excess stress are loss of a sense of well-being and reluctance to get up in the morning to face another day.

DAILY STRESS

Here's how to manage the many small stressful events in your daily routine.

■ Plan ahead for the morning crunch. Set the breakfast table and make bag lunches the night before.

■ Plan what you will wear. Check clothing for rips, runs, or missing buttons.

■ If a child needs help deciding on clothing or gathering books and papers for school, get this organized the night before.

■ Get up before the rest of the family in order to have some time to yourself. Then read the newspaper or do the crossword puzzle in peace.

■ Store plenty of microwavable meals for your family that can easily be put on the table.

■ Too many errands and chores to do? Enlist your children's help, or hire a trusted neighborhood teenager to do some of these tasks.

■ You can use a standard kitchen timer to help manage your schedule. If you don't want a telephone conversation to get too lengthy, set the timer for 15 or 20 minutes. Also use it to time exercising or housecleaning ("I'll do this for just twenty minutes").

■ Get an aquarium. They come in all sizes, for any size room or budget. Watching colorful fish swim gracefully through the water will de-stress you in no time.

■ Spend time with your children. Flying a kite or playing a favorite board game is relaxing and makes the whole family feel closer.

■ Spend time away from your children as well. Occasionally hiring a babysitter can make a big difference in your stress level. To save money, consider forming a babysitting co-op with other parents.

■ Take time out for a hobby you truly enjoy, whether it's knitting, playing the piano, or puttering around the garden.

■ Listen to music. Start with lively music that matches the way you feel, and work into slower pieces. Or do the opposite—start with soothing melodies and end with energizing music.

■ Get enough sleep. Most adults need at least eight to eight and a half hours a night. Your efficiency the next day will more than make up for the extra time lost to sleep. Go to bed at the same time every night and wake at the same time every morning—even on weekends—if possible. This way you won't tamper with your body's rhythms.

■ Try volunteer work. Nothing will take your mind off your own troubles and give you a greater sense of accomplishment than volunteering your time and energy to a good cause (see "The Rewards of Self-Improvement," page 34).

■ Buy cards and gifts throughout the year. Then you won't have to rush around before birthdays and holidays.

■ Keep a record of the things that make you feel stressed. This will help you to become aware of the real stressors in your life.

■ Give yourself permission to be imperfect. Let the dishes go unwashed one night.

■ Getting a pet is another excellent way to reduce stress. Not only will a pet give you warmth and unconditional affection, but merely petting a friendly animal can help lower blood pressure.

THE INSTANT-CALMING SEQUENCE

Many stress-reducing methods are designed to untangle knots after you are stressed. The Instant-Calming Sequence is a technique you can use beforehand, in a potentially stressful situation.

■ Train yourself to continue breathing normally. Most of us stop breathing for a few seconds in a stressful situation. This reduces oxygen to the brain and can fuel feelings of anxiety, panic, and anger.

■ Keep a smile on your face. A positive facial expression, no matter what your mental state, may increase blood flow to the brain and help with the transmission of key nerve impulses for preventing feelings of distress. And even a slight smile will help you stay in a positive mood.

■ Keep good upright posture. Many of us collapse into a slouch when confronted with stress. This restricts breathing, reduces blood flow, and causes muscle tension.

■ Take a tension inventory. Make a quick check for any parts of your body that may be tightening with stress, from your forehead to your toes. Then consciously release

60-Second Stress Busters

Need a quick cure for stress? Look no further.

Close your eyes and make yourself feel a wave of relaxation that starts at your head and goes down to your toes.

Munch on a rice cake, piece of fruit, or other snack in small bites that you take precisely every 10 seconds.

Close your eyes and visualize your greatest achievement.

See if you can point your finger or a pencil at something for 60 seconds without shaking.

Close your eyes and take slow, deep breaths. As you do this, visualize the air coming in and going out.

Try to stand several coins on edge.

Suck on a hard candy and think only of its flavor.

Pick an age between 5 and 25. Try to remember where you lived at that age and who your friends were. What was your daily routine?

Make a paper airplane and sail it across the room.

Listen to the sound of something nearby—the air conditioner, traffic, or similar sound. Close your eyes and try to turn it into a soothing sound.

Give your pet a 60-second scratch.

that tension.

■ Keep your mind calm and clear. Thoughts of blame or helplessness will only contribute to a loss of control of the situation. Simply accept what is happening and choose a wise response.

MAKING FRIENDS

Having friends may well keep you healthier. Some studies show that people with close friends have a greater ability to fight disease than people who are solitary.

■ Make friendship a priority. Find the time to be with your friends even if it means letting the lawn go unmowed or the dishes unwashed for a while. When you can't get together, use the phone to keep in touch.

■ Open up to close friends. Maintaining a deep friendship requires a level of "psychological intimacy." Don't be afraid to express your inner fears and disappointments.

■ Listen to your friends when they have problems, but offer advice only when it's wanted. Help reaffirm friends' self-esteem when they are shaken by a job loss, divorce, or other such event.

■ Have different friends for different activities, such as going to the movies, singing in a choir, and participating in a bowling league.

■ Don't wait for a friend to ask for a favor. When a friend has the flu, offer to go to the store or drive the children to their after-school activities.

■ Never take a friendship for granted. Like a good marriage, friendship needs nurturing and patience.

■ Become a joiner. Find a group that matches your interests. You might look to your church or synagogue for activities. Or try a library, a health club, or an amateur sports group.

■ You can also start a group, such as a discussion group on gardening or books. Place an ad in a community newspaper to find people.

■ Talk to strangers (using discretion and common sense, of course). Conversations started in museums, laundry rooms, or bookstores can lead to firm friendships.

■ Enroll in an adult-education course. A classroom is an ideal place to meet others with similar interests (see "The Rewards of Self-Improvement," page 34).

There are organized support groups for alcoholics, cancer patients, and women with menopausal problems, among others. If you can't find a group that answers your needs, consider starting one.

STRESS IN THE WORKPLACE

The time you spend at the office may be the most stressful part of your day, but it doesn't have to be. You have a greater ability to shape your office environment than you may realize.

■ Take breaks throughout the day. It will help clear your mind and relieve pressure. Something as simple as going to the watercooler for a drink may do the trick.

A STRETCH FOR OFFICE STRESS

If sitting at a desk makes you feel stiff and stressed, head for the nearest doorway for this 30-second stretching routine.

Walk to a doorway *and place your forearms against the frame. Slide your right foot in front of your left and slowly lean forward. You should feel the stretch in your chest and shoulders.*

Keeping your arms *against the door frame, slide your right foot farther forward to focus the stretch on your lower body. The farther forward you slide your foot, the more you stretch your calves and hamstrings and the muscles around your hips.*

Now twist your torso *to one side while braced against the door frame and leaning forward. This will stretch the muscles over the ribs and hips. Hold for a count of three. Ease up, then twist to the other side. Repeat the three steps, this time with your left foot forward.*

■ Enroll in a noontime or an after-work exercise class. This will give you a time to unwind and a way to relieve stress.

■ To help your workday go smoothly, try pacing your activities: do more demanding work in the morning, when your energy level is higher, and easier work later in the day, when you may be tired.

■ Try listening to music, recordings of nature sounds, such as a pounding surf or songbirds, to help you relax. Such tapes are sold commercially. Use headphones if you'll be listening to them in the middle of the workday.

■ Get to work early or stay late once a week. You may be able to accomplish more when you vary your routine.

■ If your stress comes from job insecurity, take stock of yourself. Update your résumé, and remind yourself of your strengths and skills. Also, make sure you keep up with new developments in your field. This will make you valuable to employers.

■ Don't let work rumors, which are usually false, cause you worry. A co-worker may just be thinking out loud about worst-case scenarios.

■ If your office is less structured (or if you are the boss), consider a company mascot. A cat or dog can do wonders for workers' morale.

15

TAKE TIME TO RELAX

You don't have to be on edge with stress to appreciate the various relaxation therapies offered here. Some are ancient and some are modern, but all will help you create a peaceful, reflective space in your daily schedule.

TAKE A NAP

Napping is a simple, effective way to relax. It will refresh you, helping you stay alert during the rest of the day.

■ Don't fight it. The midday drowsiness that used to be attributed to digesting lunch is now recognized as a natural part of our body's rhythms.

■ You'll find that a short afternoon nap is especially restful. Naps taken in the morning are usually lighter sleep. Naps taken in the early evening, on the other hand, will probably only cause you to postpone your regular bedtime.

■ Sleeping isn't necessary for a good nap. Merely lying down and resting can be just as restorative, and might be easier if you work in a busy office.

■ A good nap need only be 15 to 20 minutes long. Make sure you keep your nap to under an hour. Longer naps will leave you groggy.

■ Napping isn't for everyone. People who have trouble getting to sleep at night will find that napping worsens the problem. Others will find it hard to wake completely from a midday nap.

Write out your thoughts at the end of the day. Keeping a journal is an excellent way to relax, and it may help you examine things that have been bothering you.

SOOTHING SITES AND SOUNDS

What is soothing to the senses will soothe the nerves as well. Enjoying beautiful places and sounds is an easy way to calm yourself.

■ Taking a walk in the park will let you look and listen instead of thinking and worrying. Also effective is walking through a local aquarium or taking a stroll in the open countryside.

■ Music hath charms. One way to quiet yourself is to listen to music with a tempo just slightly slower than your heart rate. Classical suggestions include Bach's Brandenburg Concerto no. 4, 2nd movement; Bach's Orchestral Suite no. 2; and Ravel's Mother Goose Suite, 1st movement. New Age stores may also be able to help you find relaxing instrumental music.

■ Wind chimes can be soothing, if you appreciate their gentle, random melodies. Aluminum or copper chimes, tubular in shape and 12 to 18 inches long, produce the most pleasing sounds.

■ Consider a video nature tour. Relaxation has entered the electronic age with the introduction of these videotapes. Large video stores and some direct-mail catalogs offer a wide selection of tours showing national parks and other scenic wonders.

■ Time off—whether a two-week vacation or a weekend trip—is usually very effective in reducing stress. If you are planning time off because you need to unwind, be sure you don't overschedule yourself. Allow for lazy time on a beach or just rambling through the countryside.

PROGRESSIVE RELAXATION

Developed in the 1930's, progressive relaxation uses the mind to overcome tense muscles. Here's how to do it:

■ First, find a quiet place to sit or lie down. Close your eyes and begin by making tight fists with your hands. Hold for five seconds, then relax, paying close attention to the draining of tension. Do this three times, noting the contrast between tension and relaxation.

■ Next, repeat this sequence with various muscle groups: arms, forehead, mouth, shoulders, chest, abdomen, back, hips, thighs, lower legs, and feet. Try to limit each stretch to that particular muscle group. Concentrate on the pleasurable feeling of release as you let go of the flex.

■ At first it may take you 15 minutes or more to go through the routine. But once you become proficient, you can use it as needed, completing the routine in five minutes.

TAKE A BATH

■ A warm tub is a daily oasis for a lot of people. Relaxing in a warm bath will ease the effects of tension and put you in a better state of mind to deal with your troubles. Remember, the bath should be warm, not hot.

■ Some well-chosen herbs in your bathwater could make your soak even more effective. For help in choosing the right herbs, see "Add Spice to Your Bath" (page 123).

■ A whirlpool bath and a steam room are two of the

nicest features that a health club can offer. Before you try either, ask your physician's advice. Both should be avoided by people with cardiovascular problems and by pregnant women. If you do get approval from your doctor, you're sure to enjoy the experience. While whirlpools or steam rooms may seem uncomfortable at first, you'll find that the intense heat can be surprisingly soothing. Use them on their own, or to relax after exercise.

. . . .

Make a joke out of a tense situation and it will immediately lose some of its weight. Humor is now widely recognized to be therapeutic. Fortunately, humor is readily available in books, tapes, and videos.

. . . .

EASTERN WISDOM

Yoga is an ancient practice from India that combines stylized poses, deep breathing, and meditation to produce benefits for the mind and body. When practiced correctly on a daily basis, yoga can help improve posture, strength, and flexibility. It is also a powerful way to beat stress.

■ To get the most from yoga, you must learn to do it correctly. Having a qualified teacher is essential for learning proper technique. Look in the yellow pages to find the yoga schools in your community. There are several styles of yoga. Ask if you can try a class before committing yourself to a course.

How to Meditate

Meditation may seem as far removed as the Himalayas, but this relaxation technique is easy to learn and effective. Try this simple routine for five minutes at the end of the day or throughout the day as necessary. Remember that meditation gets even more effective with practice.

Sit with a relaxed posture. You should feel comfortable without moving. Try sitting either in a straight-backed chair with your feet flat on the floor or on a firm cushion three to six inches thick.

Keep your back, neck, and head upright. Relax your shoulders and find a comfortable place for your hands (usually, on your knees).

Focus your attention on your breathing. Pay attention to your breath as it flows out and in. Whenever you find that your attention has moved elsewhere, just note it and let it go. Then gently bring your attention back to your breathing.

When you are able to concentrate on your breathing without becoming distracted, try to expand your awareness around your breathing, to include a sense of your body as a whole.

■ Zen meditation involves a contemplation of the self through the use of koans, which are riddles or paradoxes. The study of Zen meditation requires a teacher. For help, look for ads in New Age magazines, or ask for advice at a New Age bookstore.

CALLING FOR HELP

The greatest health resource in your home may be your telephone. You can use it in emergencies, to keep track of family members, or to get useful medical information.

EMERGENCY ALERT

For many seniors and people with physical disabilities, having instant access to medical care is crucial. Emergency response systems fill that need.

■ One way to get instant medical help is to buy a phone with speed dialing, and to set one of the buttons to dial a local emergency number. This will help only if you can get to the phone, which may not be possible in an emergency.

■ Emergency response systems are available in all areas. They provide the user with a small transmitter known as a "help button." Transmitters are often worn around the neck. Some may be worn on the wrist like a watch. In an emergency, the user pushes a button on the transmitter, letting the emergency response center know that assistance is needed. The center will usually call a neighbor or family member from a list of phone numbers you have provided.

■ The price for equipment and service varies considerably from company to company. Understand if the company you are dealing with sells or leases equipment. Monthly service fees range from about $30.00 to $40.00.

■ Several systems allow two-way communication. This means that in an emergency you can speak to the emergency response center and let them know what type of assistance is needed, provided you are near enough to your system's console.

■ Shop carefully before you buy an emergency response system. Some companies don't charge for the equipment; at most it should cost a few hundred dollars.

■ Before you choose a system, test several in your home. Make sure the transmitter works from several locations. It's also a good idea to ask for a money-back guarantee.

■ Ask your doctors or friends if they have had experience with emergency response systems, and if so, which ones they would recommend.

■ The American Association of Retired Persons offers a helpful booklet on emergency response systems. Write to AARP Fulfillment (EE0617), 601 E Street, NW, Washington, DC 20049, and ask for publication D12905.

BEEPERS

■ Beepers, or pagers, are also useful ways to get help. While not as fast as dialing an emergency number, beepers offer a way to get assistance from a friend or family member if he or she is not near a phone.

■ When you call someone's beeper number, you usually leave only your own phone number (by dialing it on a push-button phone). Then the other person calls you back. Some beepers, however, do take voice messages and work like a standard answering machine.

■ Working parents can carry beepers; children will feel more secure if they know their parents are always within reach.

■ Parents can also have their children carry beepers so that they can easily get in touch. Parents should know, however, that many schools have banned beepers, which can disrupt classrooms. Find out what the rules are at your child's school.

Hotlines for Health and Safety

Below are listings for some of the most useful numbers. Some of them are toll-free hotlines. Others will give you information, referrals and support group contacts. The abbreviation TDD indicates Telecommunication Devices for the Deaf.

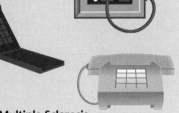

AIDS
Canadian AIDS Society
(613) 230-3580

Alcohol and Drug Dependence
Addiction Research Foundation
(416) 595-6000

Al-Anon Family Groups
National Public Information Canada
(613) 722-1830

Alcoholics Anonymous
Check your local phone directory.

Parents Against Drugs
(416) 225-6601

Pride Canada Inc.
(800) 265-9575

Allergies
Allergy Foundation of Canada
(306) 373-7591

Alzheimer's Disease
Alzheimer's Society of Canada
(416) 925-3552

Arthritis
Arthritis Society
(416) 967-1414

Autism
Autism Society Canada
(416) 924-4189

Cancer
Cancer Information Service
(800) 263-6750

Cerebral Palsy
Canadian Cerebral Palsy Association
1-800-267-6572; (613) 235-2144

Child Abuse
Kids Help Phone
(800) 668-6868

Family Service Canada
(613) 728-2463

Diabetes
Canadian Diabetes Association
within Alberta (800) 272-9607;
British Columbia (800) 972-6526;
Manitoba (800) 782-0715; New Brunswick
(506) 452-9009; Newfoundland
(800) 563-5511; Nova Scotia
(902) 421-1444; Ontario (800) 361-1306;
Prince Edward Island (903) 894-3005;
Quebec (800) 361-3504

Juvenile Diabetes Foundation Canada
(800) 668-0274

Disabilities
Canadian Rehabilitation Council for
the Disabled (416) 250-7490 (TDD)

The Easter Seal Society
(416) 421-8377

Learning Disabilities Association of
Canada (613) 238-5721

Down's Syndrome
Canadian Down Syndrome Society
(403) 241-8158

Eating Disorders
Bulimia Anorexia Nervosa Association
(BANA) (519) 253-7421 (hotline)

Endometriosis
Endometriosis International
1-800-426-2363; or (414) 355-2200

General Health
Canadian Medical Association
(800) 267-9703

Canadian Medic-Alert Foundation Inc.
(800) 668-1507

Headache
The Migraine Foundation
(800) 663-3557; or (416) 920-4916

Hearing
Canadian Deaf-Blind and Rubella
Association (519) 538-3431 (TDD)

Canadian Hearing Association
(416) 964-9595; or (416) 964-0023 (TDD)

Heart Disease
Heart and Stroke Foundation of Canada
(613) 237-4361

Incontinence
Simon Foundation for Continence
(800) 265-9575

Kidney Diseases
Kidney Foundation of Canada
(800) 361-7494

Liver Diseases
Canadian Liver Foundation
(800) 563-5483

Lung Disease
Canadian Lung Association
(613) 237-1208

Lupus
Lupus Canada
(800) 661-1468

Mental Health
Canadian Mental Health Association
(416) 484-7750

Multiple Sclerosis
Multiple Sclerosis Society of Canada
(416) 922-6065

Muscular Dystrophy
Muscular Dystrophy Association of Canada
1-800-465-6322

Neurological Problems
Canadian Neurological Coalition
(416) 596-7043

Organ Donation
Multiple Organ Retrieval and Exchange
Program of Ontario (MORE)
(800) 263-2833

Pain
North American Chronic Pain Association
of Canada (416) 793-5230

Paralysis and Spinal Cord Injury
Canadian Paraplegic Association
(416) 391-0203

Plastic Surgery
Canadian Society for Aesthetic (Cosmetic)
Surgery (800) 263-4429

Rare Diseases
National Organization for Rare Disorders
(U.S.) (800) 999-6673

Safety
Canadian Centre for Occupational Health
and Safety (800) 263-8466

Canada Safety Council
(613) 739-1535

Sexually Transmitted Diseases
Hotlines exist in major centers. Check your
local phone directory.

Stroke
Stroke Recovery Association
(416) 441-1421

Sudden Infant Death Syndrome
Canadian Foundation for the Study of
Infant Deaths (416) 488-3260 (24-hours)

Tuberous Sclerosis
National Tuberous Sclerosis Association
(U.S.) (800) 225-6872

MASTERING PAPERWORK

Do you feel overwhelmed by the amount of paperwork you need to file and save? Getting a handle on paper can make your life simpler and saner. Here's what to keep and what to throw away.

PAPERS TO SAVE

Create file folders for the following and place them in a sturdy box or file cabinet:

■ Insurance policies: Save copies of your life, auto, health, and homeowner's insurance forms, plus all correspondence relating to them. Keep old auto and homeowner's policies for three years.

■ Taxes: Save receipts for deductible items (it's best to have the canceled cheque clipped to each receipt), for seven years' worth of tax returns as well as all supporting data. Keep your tax returns for several years so that you can check them against your statements of contributions to the CPP or QPP plan, which are sent to you every two or three years.

■ Bank accounts: Keep all the information received when the accounts were opened, fee and interest-rate disclosures, monthly statements, the past six months' worth of canceled cheques, passbooks, and statements on the status of certificates of deposit.

■ Credit cards: Keep six months' worth of statements.

■ Debts: Save your mortgage and bank-loan records, and contracts for installment purchases. The mortgage statement that shows how much interest you can deduct belongs with your tax records.

■ Employee Benefits: Keep your current plan description, and keep your statement of the status of your retirement account until you receive the next one and have compared them for possible errors.

■ Investments: Keep mutual-fund, retirement-account, and brokerage-house reports. Save the information you received when opening these accounts.

■ Proof of residence: If you spend extended periods of time out of Canada, keep proof of your departures and returns for pension purposes.

■ Warranties: Save receipts for items under warranty, along with the cards showing what repairs the manufacturer will make and for how long.

HARD-TO-REPLACE PAPERS

You'll want to save important papers in a safe-deposit box at a bank or in a small, fireproof home safe. Here's what to keep in it:

■ A household inventory: This list will help you prove what you owned if your house burns down. It's also helpful to take photos of expensive items or to make a video inventory. Save receipts on expensive items.

■ Personal records: Save birth and marriage certificates, all documents relating to separation and divorce, military records, citizenship or adoption papers, death certificates, original trust agreements, prenuptial agreements, records of money owed you, diplomas, licenses, permits, deeds, contracts, property surveys, and titles.

■ Wills: Put the original in a safe-deposit box only if your province does not seal the box at death. If it does, give the will to your lawyer, and send a copy of it to the will's executor.

■ Life-insurance policies: Again, save these in a safe-deposit box only if your province does not seal the box at death. Otherwise, keep them at home.

■ Records that prove the value of home improvements: Save contractor's bills and canceled cheques. Every cent spent improving your property reduces taxable gain when you sell, so these records can save you a lot of money.

··

If you can't remember your bank card's personal identification number (PIN), disguise it as part of a phone number in your address book, alongside a fictitious name.

··

PAPERS TO TOSS

If your file cabinet is overflowing, here are the papers you can do without:

- Canceled cheques more than six months old, unless they're for tax-deductible expenses, home improvements, or child support.
- Used cheque registers.
- Bank statements that aren't part of your tax or investment records.
- Deposit slips, once you've made sure the bank entered them correctly.
- Tax returns and supporting data more than six years old. After three years a tax return usually cannot be queried or changed. But, if you discover that you should have made a credit claim before that time and did not, the claim might be paid, depending on the reason.
- Paycheque stubs, after you get a T-4 from your employer at the end of the year.
- Receipts for regular bills, like utilities.
- Monthly or quarterly statements on investment accounts, once you have a year-end statement.
- Receipts and warranties for items you no longer own.

TRAF your paper problems away

The question of what to do with papers—mail, faxes, printouts, and notes—can seem so overwhelming that before you know it, you're faced with stacks of clutter. TRAF is an acronym for Toss, Refer, Act on, or File, which are the only four things you can do with a piece of paper. Remember this system, and you'll be sure to keep papers from piling up.

Toss: When in doubt about whether to throw something away, ask yourself if the information is available elsewhere, should you need it. Remember, you can throw the memo away if you write the time of the meeting on your calendar.

Refer: Pass the paper on to someone else who can handle it better. Forward information requests to people who have the information.

Action: Some papers must be personally attended to. When possible, write your reply directly on the letter or memo, then send it back.

File: Save your important papers—the trick is to remember where you filed them.

- All records of investments you no longer own, except those needed to back up your tax returns.

MAKING A LIVING WILL

One of the most important papers you can have in your files is a living will. This document specifies your wishes for medical treatment should serious injury prevent you from communicating them.

- It's best to have both a living will and a durable power of attorney for health care. In a health-care power of attorney, you designate one specific person to be your agent and make health-care decisions for you if you can't.
- A health-care power of attorney is important, as no single document can foresee every health emergency. Sit down with the person you designate and talk about your wishes. It would be helpful to videotape this conversation.
- Assign only one person to represent your wishes, to avoid possible conflicts. You can, however, assign an alternate in case your first choice is unavailable or unwilling.
- For information on getting the right living-will forms for your province, see page 311. If you live part of the year in another province, complete forms for both provinces. You can add to the forms to make them fit your needs.
- Sign the forms as required, usually in the presence of two witnesses who are not relatives, your inheritors, or physicians who will attend you. In some provinces you must sign before a notary.
- In some provinces, living wills or health-care durable powers of attorney are not fully recognized by law. Whether you live in one of these provinces or not, it is a good idea to review your directives every two years. Initial and date them if they still meet your needs.

NOW HEAR THIS

Your home is your castle, and it should be a quiet castle. You can take charge of your environment—and protect your hearing—by learning these tips to control the noise level around you.

YOUR DELICATE EARS

Loud noises can damage fragile hairlike structures in the inner ear, which pick up and transmit sound to the brain. The longer the exposure to noise and the louder it is, the more damage will be done to these cells. Here are ways to protect your hearing:

■ Keep the volume of your radio and TV turned as low as possible. Your hair dryer could also cause hearing damage. Keep it on the middle setting, or shop for a low-noise model.

■ Cover your ears when ambulances go by or when the subway train approaches.

■ When moving, choose a quiet neighborhood. People who live near a source of loud noise—such as an airport—may believe they are used to it, but they are likely to be tense and to have rapid heart rates. Such stress leads to headaches and irritability.

■ Avoid buying children toys that make loud or irritating noises. If you can't tolerate the sound of the toy next to your own ear for 20 seconds, don't buy it.

THE SOUND OF MUSIC

■ Children taking up an instrument should be given a place to practice so that they can play without disturbing the rest of the family.

■ When listening to a portable headset, keep the volume low. If others can hear the music, it could cause you damage.

■ Keep the volume on your car stereo low enough for conversations to be carried on comfortably.

■ Wear earplugs to concerts. If you feel odd doing so, remember that the musicians themselves often wear earplugs.

■ Never sit near the speakers at a concert. Don't assume that only rock concerts can cause damage to the ear. Damage has been reported among rap and country fans, and even among members of high school marching bands.

One simple test to measure high-frequency hearing loss is to rub your thumb and forefinger together near your ear. If you can't hear the rubbing sound, your hearing may be impaired.

Is Your Hearing Impaired?

The din of modern life takes its toll on the delicate workings of the human ear. To find out whether you should take a hearing test, ask yourself the following questions:

Do people complain that you aren't listening?

Do people complain that you turn the TV volume too high?

Do you understand men's voices better than women's?

Do you have trouble hearing birds or the wind in the trees?

Do voices sound blurry—like static?

Do you have to ask people to repeat themselves frequently, even in quiet rooms?

Do you need to turn toward the person speaking or cup your ear to understand what is being said?

Do you find yourself confusing words or making silly mistakes?

Do you sometimes miss hearing common sounds, like the ringing of the phone or doorbell?

If you answered yes to one or more of these questions, it is possible that your hearing is impaired. Make an appointment to see your doctor or a hearing specialist. The problem may not be permanent and could be cured by a simple treatment.

NOISE IN THE HOME

■ Put televisions and speakers on stands. Audio equipment that touches walls or floors will cause sounds to reverberate through your home.

■ Decorate with curtains, carpets, and overstuffed seating to help absorb or muffle existing sounds.

■ Hang a suspended ceiling. Choose fiberglass panels to help soften the noise level within a room or mineralboard panels to stop noise from traveling to the room above.

■ Choose sound-deadening wall coverings as well. Cloth-covered panels or cork panels will help block or absorb sound and are easy to install. They also make great bulletin boards in a student's room or in an office.

■ Consider installing low-noise toilets. These are carried in most hardware stores and cost slightly more than regular toilets.

■ Keep noisy kitchen appliances away from walls and cabinets, which can amplify the sound.

■ When buying appliances and ventilating fans, compare noise ratings. You'll probably have to ask for assistance. A salesperson can help you by finding the manufacturer's specifications.

■ Wear earplugs when doing noisy work around the house, such as mowing the lawn or using power tools.

KEEP OUTSIDE NOISE OUT

Most sound enters homes through the windows—open or shut. If your house has a wooden framework, it can also transmit sound. Keep these hints in mind when you remodel your home:

■ Your first step should be to use caulk and putty to seal gaps around vents and windows—any place where sound can sneak in. More elaborate steps won't do much good unless you do this first.

■ Add whole-house (central) air-conditioning. While a window-mounted air conditioner will let you close windows to block outside noise, central air-conditioning will do the same and is much quieter.

■ Install storm windows. The best results come from exterior storm windows with heavy glass and good weather stripping. But don't overlook interior storm windows, which are inexpensive and easy to install.

■ Install solid entrance doors. A good door that fits tightly, is surrounded by weather stripping, and has a good storm door with it will block four times as much noise as a hollow door with no storm door.

■ Put a damper or a flap on air ducts or laundry vents.

■ Don't let your dog stay outside if it barks; your neighbors don't like noise pollution, either.

STRATEGIC LANDSCAPING

Landscaping for peace and quiet may sound impossible, but there actually are ways to use plants and earth to block sounds.

■ Plants can be used as sound insulation, but they have to be thick. To block unwanted traffic sounds from your house, plant hedges, bushes, and trees on the side toward the road. Hedges should be at least two feet thick.

■ Earth can also be used, if you have the space. Create small mounds (berms) between your house and the source of the noise. For further sound absorption, cover the mound with a dense hedge.

■ A windbreak is useful if your house is downwind from a factory or school yard. A dense evergreen or hedge will provide protection as far downwind as 20 times its height. So, a 9-foot-tall hedge can be planted as far as 180 feet from your house and still offer protection from wind-borne noise.

■ A wall or tight fence covered with dense vines will absorb some sound. An uncovered wall, though, will only make the noise problem worse.

YOU AND YOUR ENVIRONMENT

The science of ergonomics plays a large role in how we arrange our offices and workrooms. By choosing the right furniture, equipment, and lighting, and using it correctly, we cut down on backaches and eyestrain and gain other health benefits.

ERGONOMICS AT HOME

Ergonomics has been used in designing work areas in many homes. You can use ergonomic principles to adjust such rooms as the kitchen and workshop to better fit your needs.

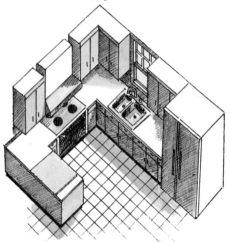

■ Organize your kitchen and workbench areas so that you can get the tools you use the most without having to stretch to reach them.

■ If you are quite tall, talk to a contractor about rebuilding counters or other work spaces so that you don't have to bend when working. Frequent bending can strain the back.

■ When buying kitchen tools, choose ones with ergonomically designed handles. Such items as knives and potato peelers have been redesigned to fit the hand better, so that slicing and chopping are more comfortable. Look for ergonomically designed gardening tools as well.

THE HOME OFFICE

Working at home gives you greater freedom to arrange the office to your own tastes. However, since most people have little extra room for a home office, it's important to set up your space with care.

■ Choose a space that has no other uses (don't, for example, simply take over the dining room table).

■ If you don't have a room to spare, section off part of a larger room. Floor-to-ceiling bookcases will create a feeling of privacy. You could even convert an unused part of a garage or a walk-in closet as long as it has proper ventilation, good lighting, and enough electrical outlets.

■ When you choose furniture, don't settle for card tables and folding chairs. Remember that your productivity will be higher if you are comfortable. Select tables and desks without sharp edges, or cover sharp edges with soft material.

THE WORKPLACE OFFICE

■ Poorly designed office space can be bad for morale and bad for the body. Aching backs, headaches, sore eyes, and irritability are just a few of the more common complaints.

■ If you are having any discomfort related to your work setup, tell your employer as soon as possible; an early change may prevent the dis-

comfort from turning into a real problem. Be clear about what needs to be changed. Many companies will go along with such requests, having learned that improving office space can lead to higher job satisfaction, greater productivity, and fewer sick days.

TONING DOWN NOISE

If noise is bothering you in the office, try to eliminate or reduce it at its source—ask your neighbor to use headphones when listening to the radio, for example. You can also try ergonomic measures.

■ Ask your office manager if it is possible to carpet hard floors and install acoustic-tile ceilings to absorb sound.

■ If printers and facsimile machines are loud, find out if acoustical enclosures can be placed over them.

■ If your office is separated from a noisy neighbor by a waist-high partition, ask for a taller partition, which will block or absorb more sound. Higher walls also provide a greater amount of privacy.

■ Tack memos and mementos on hard wall panels instead of soft office partitions, where they interfere with sound absorption.

■ If the problem is ringing phones, ask co-workers to lower the signal volume on their phones.

■ Place your own phone near

24

a soft partition, which will better absorb the sound.

■ Try listening to soothing music on a tape player with headphones. Or you may want to invest in a white-noise machine, which will help cover distracting sounds.

YOUR OFFICE CHAIR

■ Ask if you can try out a new chair for a day before you or your company buys it. Many vendors will let you do this.

■ Adjustable chairs make the best office chairs, since they can accommodate most people regardless of size.

■ Once you have an adjustable chair—adjust it. Many people go for years without bothering to do this.

■ Your chair's seat should be flat or only slightly contoured, to allow easy adjustments of posture, and wide enough to allow shifts from side to side. Also, the seat should taper downward at the front to avoid pressure on the back of the thighs.

■ The seat cushion should be about half an inch to an inch deep. A hard seat can hamper circulation in the legs.

■ Armrests are not essential, but they can ease back stress, since they allow you to shift weight to your arms. Many armrests are too high, so height-adjustable or removable ones are best.

■ Your chair should offer firm padding and a back support that fits the natural curve of the spine. The backrest should be neither springy nor rigid. Chairs that have a spring adjustment let you control the degree of support.

■ If your chair lacks a contoured backrest, a well-placed cushion could save stress on your back.

■ Your chair should allow your back to angle backward a few degrees to increase blood flow and reduce compression of the spine.

■ Leather chairs are attractive but slippery. Instead, opt for chairs covered with a nonstick fabric to prevent sliding.

■ Maintain good posture, whether you are sitting upright working at a computer terminal or leaning over a desk to write a memo (see "Posture Made Perfect," page 118).

■ Your feet should rest flat on the floor with your knees bent at a 90° angle. If necessary, get a footstool.

■ Be sure to fidget. No chair will keep you comfortable all day, and sitting for long periods of time is bad for your back. Change positions and get up and walk around from time to time.

CUT DOWN ON GLARE

■ The best lighting for most people is a combination of overhead fixtures and a desk lamp. Keep the overhead lighting dim for computer work to reduce glare (perhaps by removing a few fluorescent lighting tubes). Then turn on the desk lamp when working away from the computer.

■ If you have a choice of computer monitors, opt for the flattest screen, which is less prone to glare than a more curved monitor.

■ Another way to cut glare is to tape a piece of cardboard to the top of the computer. It should jut out slightly, shielding the screen from overhead light. Alternatives available in stores include computer hoods and antiglare screens that fit over the front of the monitor.

■ To reduce glare from a window, place your monitor at right angles to the window.

> **If you have to pore over reading material for hours at a time, consider getting a book-holding stand. This allows you to read sitting upright. Hunching over can be bad for circulation, especially for pregnant women.**

TREAT YOUR EYES RIGHT

■ When doing computer or other close-up work, give your eyes a 15-second rest every 15 to 20 minutes. Focus on a distant object, massage the area around your eyes, or walk away from your desk.

■ Remind yourself to blink. Concentrating intently on a computer screen can interfere with the normal blinking reflex. (Staring at a terminal may also speed up tear evaporation, which contributes to dry eyes.) The longer you go without blinking, the drier and more uncomfortable your eyes may become. This is a particular concern for anyone who wears contact lenses.

■ Ask your eye-care specialist about glasses specially designed for computer users. Also, find out about a lens coating that cuts down on light reflection.

■ Consult an eye specialist if you repeatedly experience headaches, blurred vision, stinging sensations in the eyes, or other forms of eyestrain.

■ The visual angle between eyes and monitor should be between 15 and 20 degrees below horizontal. With most monitors, the top of the screen should be at or slightly below eye level. Arrange your chair and monitor accordingly. You may want to tilt the monitor back, unless this creates glare.

■ Spend some time adjusting your screen for image quality, viewing distance, and viewing angle. Have the monitor repaired if the image is blurry, dull, or flickering.

■ When you type or work closely from printed materials, keep the pages on a stand at the same height as your monitor. This will help to minimize the amount of refocusing the eyes must do.

■ Dust your computer screen frequently. Wipe gently with a slightly damp rag.

Buy desks with matte rather than shiny finishes so that they don't reflect overhead light.

TELEPHONE TIPS

■ Never cradle the phone between your neck and shoulder. This can create or intensify neck or back pain.

■ Whenever a phone conversation lasts more than 10 minutes, move around to work your muscles as you talk or listen. Lean back and lean forward; stand up and sit down.

■ Consider getting a headset if you spend a lot of time on the phone, especially if you type or write as you talk. A headset may prevent a stiff neck.

■ For a less expensive alternative, get a shoulder rest. Be sure to switch ears often.

REPETITIVE STRAIN INJURY

The computer keyboard has contributed to the increase in the incidence of repetitive strain injury (RSI). As its name indicates, this disorder can develop when someone does the same movement over and over. A common type of RSI is carpal tunnel syndrome, which affects the hands and wrists (see facing page). Because computer keyboards do not require typists to change positions often, tendons and muscles in the hands and wrists have to bear great stress.

■ To prevent injury, make sure your arms and hands are positioned correctly at the keyboard: Your upper arms should hang vertically, and your forearms should be horizontal (or slightly above that angle). Keep your wrists straight, rather than bending them up or down. You may need to adjust your chair and keyboard height. If your desk is too high, use a keyboard drawer, which attaches to the desk's underside, unless it gives you too little leg room.

■ Use your whole arm to move the computer's mouse; don't just bend your wrist.

■ When you have momentary pauses (as when reading the screen), take your hands off the keyboard and mouse.

■ Take hourly breaks to stretch overused muscles. Exercise the hands, wrists, and fingers (see "Limber Up Your Hands," page 91).

■ Consult a doctor if you have discomfort or loss of sensation in the hand—untreated, RSI's can lead to chronic pain and disability. Do not buy your own hand splint without first seeing a doctor, because an improper splint can cause even more damage.

■ Emotional stress can play a role in developing repetitive strain injuries. See "Dealing with Stress," page 12, and "Take Time to Relax," page 16, for ways to control stress.

Keep your fingernails trimmed. Long nails force you to extend your fingers to hit the keys; this can cause injury.

REPETITIVE STRAIN IN THE WORKPLACE

"I can't control how I feel or how I work. I hurt a lot of the time."
—Susan Harrigan

• • • • • • •

Susan Harrigan seemed to have one of the safest jobs around. As a financial writer for a large daily newspaper, she spent her days typing at her desk. Then in the spring of 1989, Harrigan developed such great pains in her arms and hands that she found herself unable even to hit a typewriter key. Her supposedly safe desk job, she discovered, had left her with a variety of extremely debilitating, repetitive strain injuries.

For more than a year Harrigan couldn't work, cook a meal, or even turn a doorknob. She tied string to her dresser drawers so she could open them with her teeth. "I didn't know I could be in so much pain for so long," she says. Doctors gave her a variety of diagnoses, but it came down to this: three years of typing on a word processor had caused permanent damage to the muscles, nerves, and tendons of her arms.

New dangers. Perhaps the best-known repetitive strain injury is carpal tunnel syndrome (CTS). While it sounds complex, CTS is caused by a simple swelling. The tendons that control the movements of the fingers pass through an area known as the carpal tunnel. In this tunnel, located in the wrist, the tendons are surrounded by bone on all sides. Repeated stress to the hands,

by typing, for example, causes membranes around the tendons to swell, pinching soft nerve tissues against the bones of the tunnel.

Symptoms of carpal tunnel syndrome usually start with a tingling or numbness in the hands. This tingling often begins at night, when people are away from their jobs. Pain, burning, or stiffness in the hands sometimes follows. This is the time to see a doctor. If the symptoms go untreated, CTS can lead to muscle and nerve atrophy, permanent damage to the wrist, and pain that radiates to the shoulder.

Getting medical care. Treatments for repetitive strain injuries vary, depending on how severe the symptoms are. If the pain of CTS is noticed right away, treatment could be as simple as wearing a lightweight, plastic splint when working, or getting a platform that supports the wrists when typing.

A physician's main goal will be to reduce the swelling in the wrists. For that, drugs or injections are often effective. If these measures don't work, patients may need to undergo surgery to open up the tunnel and relieve the pressure. Unless the muscles and tendons have been permanently damaged, patients can then expect a return to normal use.

While this procedure is outpatient surgery, recovery may take as long as seven weeks. New techniques that reduce the recovery time are now being developed.

Susan Harrigan was not able to continue working at her computer keyboard, but her employers found a way around the problem. They bought her a computer program that lets her dictate articles, rather than type them. While the software works too slowly for her to work on stories with daily deadlines, she is able to work on longer features.❑

This headset lets Susan Harrigan dictate, rather than type, into her computer.

THE CHANGING WORLD OF WORK

In the new business climate, where corporations are downsizing and whole industries are shifting, many workers suddenly find themselves out of a job. What's next?

LOSING A JOB

Losing your job can be a shock, especially if you've been with a company for years.

■ If you've been laid off because of corporate downsizing, know that it's not your fault and that you aren't alone.

■ Begin networking at once. This is the process of meeting, helping, and being helped by business contacts. Don't be shy when networking; talk to friends and friends of friends. Many job openings are filled through personal relationships, not through want ads.

■ Get your résumé in order and then call, write, or have lunch with anyone who can help you.

■ If your former employer offers job counseling, outplacement services, or retraining, take advantage of it.

■ Join organizations that are relevant to your job experience or career objectives. Many professional organizations offer phone-in job lines that describe full- or part-time positions available. Most are free to members; nonmembers may have to pay a fee.

■ Find a support group in your community for people who are out of work. Call your local minister, priest, or rabbi. Churches and synagogues often sponsor support groups.

■ Call the Y in your area for information. Check the yellow pages of your telephone directory for "career counseling" or "social service organizations."

■ When you read want ads, don't confine your search to your old title or job description. Take a broad view of your career. Many skills are transferable to other fields. And don't overlook the chance to build a new career on a hobby or special interest.

■ Register at employment agencies; some specialize in particular types of work.

■ You may decide you need more education or training to get the job you want (see "The Rewards of Self-Improvement," page 34). Many employers and employment counselors say that computer skills are an asset. If you don't have such skills, consider signing up for a course.

■ Retraining is often cited as a way to get a new job, but not all retraining results in placement. Before you start training, get the names of companies that are hiring people with the kind of skills you are about to learn.

APPLYING FOR A JOB

■ Your résumé should be reproduced by a quick-print service or by a computer with a clear printer. Have it copied on good-quality 8-1/2-by-11-inch paper in white, off-white, beige, or pale gray. Print on one side of the page only. Include your education, honors you have received, job history, special skills, and personal interests that are relevant.

■ Prepare a list of the names, job titles, and phone numbers of those who will give you references. Have it with you when interviewing.

■ Send a covering letter with each résumé. It should state briefly what job you are interested in and why you are qualified for that position.

■ If you are not responding to a want ad but conducting a general search, call the company you'd like to work for. Find out the name of the personnel manager and, perhaps, the person who heads the department in which you would like to work. Consider writing to both of them.

■ Have business cards printed with your name, address, telephone number, and fax number, if you have one. You may want to include your occupation (such as computer programmer).

■ Overcome any reticence you may have about distributing your business cards. They are especially useful at support groups and meetings of professional organizations. You may also want to leave cards with people whose business you patronize regularly, such as your health club. Ask if the manager will post your card on the bulletin board. Another place for your card may be your local community center.

■ Have interview clothing—a suit or ensemble—clean, pressed, and ready to go at all times. Whenever possible, check out the corporate environment of a potential employer to find out what's appropriate. When in doubt, dress conservatively.

You should have a push-button telephone in order to access job lines and other information systems. You should also have an answering machine or service. Be sure to leave a businesslike, no-nonsense message on your machine.

THE JOB INTERVIEW

■ If possible, read up on the company where you will be interviewing before you meet with them.

■ Plan to arrive at the interview ahead of time so that you won't be late.

■ Project confidence with a firm handshake, a clear tone of voice, good posture, and eye contact.

■ Be ready with a short presentation of your background and experience. When a potential employer says, "Tell me about yourself," have a synopsis of your experiences and skills ready to roll off the tongue. It's a good chance to emphasize your skills. Also, prepare answers to questions that will naturally arise when someone reads your résumé.

■ Ask a friend or your spouse to help you rehearse your interviews by taking the role of an interviewer. This way, you can polish your presentation and become more comfortable with your delivery.

■ If you were fired from a job, be ready to explain briefly why you were terminated. However, never make negative remarks about your previous employer or boss.

■ If there are time gaps in your résumé, be prepared to say how you spent the time.

■ Besides answering questions during the interview, you should ask your own. This gives you a chance to show that you are informed about the organization.

■ Let your interviewer be the first to mention the salary. If the salary has to be negotiated, try to get the interviewer to set a range.

After the interview, send a short thank-you note to the interviewer. If you haven't heard from the company in a week, phone and express your continuing interest.

THE LONG HAUL

Many people are depressed by unemployment. Having invested so much in their jobs, they are deeply troubled to be without the sense of identity, security, and prestige they had in the past. They see themselves as being cut adrift and may feel worthlessness and shame. These feelings, and many practical matters, should be addressed at the outset of unemployment.

■ Realize that it is normal to grieve over the loss of your job. You will most likely go through the same stages of grief as someone who has had a close friend die. First there is disbelief, then anger, then depression, and, finally, acceptance. You are ready to get on with your life.

■ Guard your health. Continue to eat well and exercise (preferably at least one type of aerobic workout, such as a walking program). Exercise stimulates body chemicals that fight depression; it helps your body to fight stress as well. And, in all likelihood, when you exercise, you'll sleep better.

■ Stick with your hobbies and volunteer work, unless they involve too much time or money. No one can or should job-hunt every waking hour. Hobbies and volunteer work provide a good respite by reinforcing your self-esteem and sense of accomplishment.

■ Take stock of your financial assets. If you don't have enough cash in a savings account to pay your bills, contact your creditors. See if they will agree to smaller monthly payments during your period of joblessness.

■ Have family conferences to discuss ways to economize. Include older children in your discussions. You can't shield them from bad news—and most kids are eager to help.

■ Maintain a positive outlook. While you are sure to go through some discomfort and inconvenience while you are unemployed, don't let your situation affect your overall mental health.

■ Be prepared for ups and downs. There will be times when you are sure you could do a particular job and you believe the interviews went well, yet the offer doesn't come through. Being the runner-up often gives rise to second-guessing: "If I had only said this or done that." Don't give in to this impulse. This happens to everyone—just go on to the next interview.

■ Avoid things you find depressing. You'll have enough on your mind when job-hunting, so if you find the late-evening news depressing, opt instead to watch something soothing or amusing.

■ Keep a diary. Writing your thoughts and feelings may help you relax and will certainly help you remember important appointments.

■ Consider career counseling. With the changing economy,

demands for some skills will dwindle. If you must change careers, counselors can help.

■ While you search for a new job, consider working as a consultant or a freelancer. These temporary jobs provide income, add to your work experience, increase your ability to network, and may allow you to be at the "right place at the right time" when a job opens up.

WORKING AT HOME

■ Make a clear division between your personal time and your work time. Answer your phone with a professional greeting when you're working, and ask friends to call only in the evening.

■ Most people who work at home use a computer. You may also want to consider such additions to your office as a modem, a copier, and a facsimile machine.

■ Use one part of your home for your office work and nothing else. For more on creating a home office, see "You and Your Environment," page 24.

■ If you find it difficult to get started, establish an activity to mark the beginning of your workday, such as making coffee or going out for breakfast.

■ If you find it hard to end the workday and often let the job extend into the evening hours, make a practice of turning off your computer and desk lamp at a specified time.

■ You won't need a suit for the home office, but don't be sloppy, either. How you feel about your appearance will come through in your performance and in your phone calls. Keep

in mind: dressing up for an important phone call is a tried-and-true sales technique.

THE AEROBIC COMMUTE

If you have a regular job outside your home and you have a relatively short commute, consider walking, running, biking, or roller-blading to work. You'll take care of two things at once—getting to work and exercising.

■ Commuters who exercise this way are more likely to stick to a routine. Of course, you should have an alternate means of transportation in case of bad weather and for those times when you work late.

■ One consideration when you commute in any of these ways is whether you can take a shower at work or nearby. Some newer office buildings have workout rooms with showers. Having an office with a door is also a plus.

■ Exercising your way to work could help you on the job. You'll find that you will be more alert and ready to start the day. In the evening, exercise will help you to work off job-related tension.

■ You may want to bring your change of clothing into the office ahead of time, perhaps for the entire week. You'll also need a supply of toiletries.

■ If there is a dry cleaner near work, you can avoid bringing clothing home to be cleaned.

COMMUTING BY CAR

Many people spend a substantial part of the day just getting to work. Here's how to make the trip more pleasant:

■ Driving makes some people tense, and in traffic jams, tension often ricochets from car to car. This is a fact of life; it's up to you to keep your cool when other drivers make wrong moves, honk their horns, or generally behave in a discourteous way. Another fact of life is that some of the drivers with short fuses may actually become violent, so don't trade insults.

■ Relieving tension may be as simple as taking a few deep breaths and loosening your grip on the steering wheel. Or tune in to a soothing music station on your radio.

■ Take a break before you drive home, perhaps by going for a brisk walk or stopping at the gym. This will give you time to relax and may allow you to avoid rush-hour traffic.

■ Be aware that when you use a car phone, you are dividing your attention, so that you may miss signals from other drivers or fail to see road hazards. Don't make or receive calls when driving conditions are

hazardous. If a conversation becomes too absorbing, get off the phone. You can tell the other party you will call back.

■ To make your commute more productive, use a dictation machine or portable tape recorder. You can tape ideas or dictate letters as you drive.

■ You can also fill the time by listening to language courses, motivational tapes, or recorded books.

■ Commute with your spouse, if possible. This will give you a chance for conversation. Also, you can help each other relieve stress and unwind after a hectic day.

- -
Before you begin your drive, listen to traffic reports to find out where the problem areas are.
- -

CARPOOL, TRAIN, OR BUS

The simplest way to fight driving stress is to do less of it, either by carpooling or taking public transportation. Mass transit is better for the environment and often cheaper for the rider. It also leaves you with free time in which to work or relax.

■ Members of a carpool save money on fuel and tolls, as well as wear and tear on their individual cars. From an ecological standpoint, carpooling saves a significant amount of fuel and reduces pollution.

■ Many communities encourage carpooling because it relieves traffic congestion. Some cities reserve special lanes for the use of carpools. This gives

a carpooling automobile an advantage over those with just one occupant. If your community isn't doing this, call or write to your local representative to suggest it.

■ If you're in a carpool and you're not the driver, you can catch up on reading or paperwork or take a short nap.

■ Using mass transit helps cut down on pollution. One way to do this is to drive to a train station or bus depot, park, and then take the train or bus the rest of the way to work.

■ Depending on the particular railroad, the train may be a more reliable way to travel than a car. During blizzards and other storms that make roads impassable, trains usually keep going.

■ Mass transit may also be the fastest way to travel in cities. Trains don't get caught in traffic jams.

■ If you hate to give up driving your own car, try taking a bus or train just one or two days a week. Or use your car only when you have errands to run.

■ To unwind and get exercise, leave your carpool, train, or bus 10 to 15 minutes from home and finish your commute on foot.

IMPROVING YOUR BRAINPOWER

Most of us would like to strengthen our memory and increase our creativity. It's easy! Here are practical hints for accomplishing these goals.

BRAIN EXERCISES

Your mind, like the rest of your body, needs exercise in order to function well.

■ Do word puzzles or play games like bridge and chess to help keep your mind sharp.

■ Keep on adding, subtracting, and multiplying. Don't always depend on a calculator.

■ Memorize something—a poem, part of a psalm, or even a joke—daily or weekly.

A CREATIVE STATE OF MIND

Learn to think inventively and let new ideas come forth.

■ Think like a child. Children are full of the wonder, curiosity, and playfulness that lead to creativity. Play games, and allow yourself to daydream.

■ Don't limit yourself to being one type of person. If you see yourself only as the buttoned-down executive or the super-mom, you may find yourself unable to think in other ways.

■ Keep a pen and paper in every room so that you can jot down your ideas immediately.

■ Don't be afraid to make mistakes. Trying new ideas means exposing yourself to pitfalls. If you fail, see what didn't work and try again.

■ Take a notebook or tape recorder along when traveling. New scenery spurs new thoughts. Many people report coming up with their best ideas while driving or when on vacation.

MEMORY TRICKS

■ You're more likely to forget things that don't interest you, so convince yourself of the importance of what you're trying to remember.

■ Talking to yourself might sound silly, but it's a good memory aid. Say out loud where you are putting your car keys or purse. Repeat any instructions or directions you're given.

■ To keep in mind upcoming events, discuss them with friends or family members.

■ Make up odd rhymes or associations to aid your memory—for example, if your friend Helen's birthday is in October, think of Hallowe'en. Or set what you're trying to remember to a familiar tune.

■ Tension can interfere with memory. Learning to relax will help you think clearly and recall things better.

■ Similarly, if something is bothering you, it can keep you from concentrating. Write it down first.

■ Study new subjects or languages before bedtime. New skills seem to be stored in the brain during sleep.

■ Physical exercise is good for the brain. An aerobic fitness program seems to help preserve memory.

■ There's no solid evidence that specific "brain foods" exist. But good nutrition—which benefits the whole body—supplies the brain with what it needs to function well.

■ Don't drink too much alcohol; it can impair memory.

■ Have a set place to put your keys, gloves, and anything else you might easily misplace. Good organization is one of the best memory aids.

REMEMBERING NAMES

Many people find it difficult to remember names. Try these suggestions the next time you meet someone.

■ Stay focused when you are introduced. If you are preoccupied, you may not even hear the name, so clear your mind of other thoughts.

■ Make associations with the name, perhaps with a celebrity who has the same name or with a color, occupation, or thing (Mr. Black, Ms. Carpenter, Mr. Bell). You may be able to associate the name with a striking feature—a woman named Pearl, for instance, has pearly white teeth.

■ Rhyme the name in your mind ("Jones" with "bones").

■ If appropriate, ask the person the origin of his or her family name; this may help you recall it better.

■ Reinforce the memory by using the person's name in conversation as often as seems suitable.

GOOD NEWS FOR SENIOR CITIZENS

When old people have trouble recalling things, many immediately think the worst—that this may indicate Alzheimer's disease. But most memory loss has a treatable cause.

■ It's a half-truth that memory gets worse as you age. Long-term memory shows no significant change, but short-term memory may suffer.

■ Confusion and memory loss may be caused by prescription medicines, especially sleeping pills or drugs for depression or anxiety. Ask your doctor if this could be the cause of impaired thinking. He or she may be able to switch you to a different medication.

■ Depression is often a cause of memory loss. Elderly people are most likely to become depressed if they feel they have no control over their surroundings. If you have family members in a nursing home, talk to the staff about letting them make as many of their own decisions as possible.

■ If you or an elderly family member keeps forgetting something important, try to think of a practical solution.

For example, if you're constantly forgetting to take medication, buy a plastic pill holder or make one out of an ice cube tray.

. . . .

To spur creativity, talk to encouraging, not discouraging, people. A wet blanket can smother another person's ideas. Associate with people who will support your efforts.

. . . .

BRAINSTORMING

Suppose your PTA needs to raise money for new band uniforms. How can you generate ideas? Borrow from the business world a way of stimulating creativity: brainstorming.

■ Ask all participants to throw out ideas, either in turn or as they come to mind—even if they sound silly or crazy. Make it clear: the more ideas, the better.

■ Have someone write down the ideas, or, to save time and keep up the momentum, ask each person to write down his or her own ideas after stating them.

■ Don't stop to analyze, criticize, or argue.

■ Be open to all suggestions. You may be able to "piggyback"—build on someone else's concept. With a wild or impossible idea, look for any positive aspect; a change of some sort may make it useful.

■ When the group has finally run out of ideas, have everyone rate each idea from 1 to 10 (10 being the best). Add up these ratings. The ideas with the highest scores are the most promising.

"STRIKE" for Ideas

Call it a formula for success in creating new ideas. The acronym "strike," which stands for the words below, indicates the steps creative people take, whether they know it or not.

Stew. Start by thinking almost aimlessly about all the things you'd like to do—improvements you'd like to make, problems you'd like to solve, and goals you'd like to achieve. Don't worry if the process takes two hours or two months.

Target. When you are sure of a particular objective, write it down in 10 words or less. For example, if you were stewing about career changes, target your thoughts to one clear career goal.

Research. Find out about the area you've decided to concentrate on. A visit to the library might be helpful. And don't overlook your friends and other contacts as sources of information.

Ideas. Think of ideas that will help you meet your goal. Write them down as they come to you. Keep your mind loose and limber, writing down even the odd thoughts.

Key Idea. Choose the best of all the ideas you have come up with. Make sure the idea is practical and will help you achieve your goal.

Execute. Now that you are prepared, act on your idea. If you have visualized yourself carrying it out, it should be easier to do.

THE REWARDS OF SELF-IMPROVEMENT

Want to feel better about yourself in a hurry? Take a class and fulfill a dream—learn to speak a foreign language or play an instrument. Or become a volunteer and help others.

TAKING CLASSES

There are many reasons to go back to school. You may want to advance your career, learn new job skills, or simply enrich your life.

■ If you never finished high school, consider taking a General Education Development (GED) examination to receive a high school equivalency diploma. The GED exam is offered in all provinces except Ontario. The exam is free, and so are the courses needed to prepare for it. Call your local school board for more information.

■ When looking for specific training, begin at the adult-education office in your local community college. If it does not offer what you want or need, ask someone there to refer you to the continuing-education office at a higher-education institution.

■ If you have a job and the classes you wish to take are work-related, find out if your company will pay full or partial tuition.

■ Be wary of business or trade schools that promise jobs upon completion. Some train for nonexistent jobs, while others duplicate the training an employer will give you once you are hired.

■ Check with your provincial education department or the Association of Universities and Colleges of Canada for the accreditation of a course.

■ Explore an old interest or a new skill. Adult-education programs offer an astounding diversity of courses. You can learn a foreign language, computer programming, or car repair, among other things. You simply pay for the course you want; no credits are given.

■ Take a class so you can become better at your hobby, whether it's writing poetry or refinishing furniture.

■ Combine education with exercise or recreation by signing up for ballroom dance, sailing, calligraphy, cake decoration, jewelry design, magic, or any number of other courses.

■ Strapped for time? Many schools offer one-evening lectures or weekend seminars.

■ Don't let money concerns stop you from going back to college. To see if you qualify for student loans or grants, get two brochures: "Scholarship Programs," and "Canada's universities: Notes for students," from the Association of Universities and Colleges of Canada, 350 Albert, Suite 600, Ottawa, Ont., K1R 1B1. You can also ask a particular school's admissions counselors what type of financial aid is available.

■ If you're a senior citizen, find out if a college near you

Types of Schools

Before heading back to school, know the appropriate one for you.

Four- and two-year colleges confer academic degrees and offer professional and business training.

Vocational education schools offer specific job training in such areas as word processing, secretarial skills, and cooking.

Private business schools offer programs in such subjects as accounting, data processing, and fashion merchandising.

Private trade and technical schools generally teach a single trade, such as cosmetology, real estate, or commercial art.

Home study programs give courses through correspondence, providing training for a specific skill or position, such as travel agent.

Adult education programs offer many types of classes. They may be run by high schools or colleges or exist separately.

offers any free or specially priced classes or programs (often through the association Elderhostel).

■ If you have a computer, check out the many educational software programs available. Or look into home study schools that use computer lines.

You may want to consider teaching a class. Think about the skills, talents, and knowledge you possess, then look through adult-education catalogs. An idea for a course might spring to mind.

THE REWARDS OF VOLUNTEERING

Volunteering does as much for the person who gives help as for the person who receives it.

■ While many know firsthand that volunteering makes you feel better, medical studies are beginning to back this up. People who volunteer seem to stay healthier and live longer than those who don't.

■ Volunteering is more likely to be satisfying if it includes personal contact. Teaching adults to read or tending abandoned babies will be more rewarding than sealing envelopes for an agency's fund-raising campaign.

■ It may help to have something in common with the people you help. A person who was adopted in childhood will take special pride in counseling adoptive parents and their youngsters.

■ You will probably feel more useful if you choose volunteer work that is well suited to your skills. Think about what capabilities you possess, such as being able to teach children, write newsletters, or repair appliances. Whatever they are, some organization would be happy to put them to use.

FINDING VOLUNTEER WORK

Getting started is as easy as picking up the phone and calling an organization you'd like to help.

■ If you aren't sure where to give your time, think about which causes concern you. Nonprofit groups exist for most causes, and hospitals always need volunteers.

■ Before you commit yourself to working at a particular place, talk to current volunteers, if possible. Ask them about the positive and negative aspects of the job.

■ Understand what you're getting into before you start. Be realistic about the time you can give and what kind of work you find satisfying. For certain types of jobs, you may have to go through a training session.

■ There are organizations in many cities across Canada that help volunteers find the type of work that they are interested in. Look them up in the yellow pages and ask for more information.

If you're new to your community, consider volunteering at a charity fund-raiser. It's a good way to meet interesting, active people.

VOLUNTEERING FOR THE YOUNG AND OLD

Teenagers and senior citizens have special opportunities for volunteering. They can often help each other.

■ Many senior citizens find that volunteering is the perfect way to fill their spare time after they have retired. Because of their wisdom and time-tested family skills, elderly people are great choices to work with children in shelters. They are also in demand in understaffed hospital nurseries.

■ Senior citizens interested in volunteering can contact a seniors' employment bureau. There is one in most cities in Canada. These organizations help with job searching, counseling, and placing elderly people in appropriate jobs. Their services are free.

■ High-school students often volunteer, performing such services as visiting nursing homes and cleaning parks. While they often must volunteer to fulfill graduation requirements, many put in extra hours. Young people who volunteer improve problem-solving and critical-thinking skills, which tends to make them more self-reliant and responsible than their peers.

You don't have to give up the foods you enjoy to have healthy meals. The homemade pizza shown here has the characteristic pizza flavor, but with much less fat. Instead of pepperoni or sausage, it's topped with vegetables and a sprinkling of Parmesan cheese.

CHAPTER 2

DIET AND NUTRITION

Does it ever seem like everything you thought you knew about food has been disproved? Information we learned in school on avoiding starches and eating plenty of red meat has been reversed. We've found that other old favorites, like whole milk and cheese, should be limited. These days it's hard to know what to eat and where to look for reliable information. But while it may seem perplexing, taking the time to learn about nutrition will pay off with better health for you and your family.

One of the best places to learn about healthy eating is from a world map. Other countries can teach us a great deal about avoiding fatty foods, cooking creatively with less meat, and using more fresh vegetables in our meals.

Looking to the rest of the world will also add variety to your diet. Plan meals with an international flair and you'll not only get all the necessary nutrients, but you'll surprise your family with zesty new dishes. So eat a variety, for your own good health.

Joseph Bonnano improved his fire station's health by introducing low-fat meals to his fellow firefighters.

EATING FOR GOOD HEALTH

Food is prized not just because it assuages hunger, but for its delicious taste, mouth-watering aroma, and visual appeal. Add to the list the recognition that food can play a crucial role in helping each of us to stay well and to live longer.

NEW WAYS OF LOOKING AT FOOD

Good nutrition is the primary means of realizing your genetic potential. Unless you eat the right amount of nutrients in the right balance, you won't live as long or be as healthy as it's possible for you to be.

■ Past dietary recommendations that promoted eating protein and deplored "starchy" foods (actually, carbohydrates) have been turned around completely. We now know that carbohydrates should form the largest part of your diet, approximately 55 to 60 percent, and that you should hold down the quantity of protein to about 15 percent of total calories.

■ By avoiding foods that are high in fat, you lower your risk of heart disease, obesity, and other disorders. You should aim for a diet that keeps fat to less than 30 percent of your total calories.

■ For foods that may actually help to lower your risk of cancer, see the chart at left.

WHAT PROTEIN DOES

Skin, hair, nails, cartilage, tendons, muscles, and bones are made up largely of fibrous proteins. Protein is essential to metabolism and other bodily processes, and it helps fight disease. Children need protein for growth. Adults need protein to replace tissues that are continuously breaking down.

■ *Myth: You must eat meat to get enough protein.* Generally, there's no need to worry about getting enough protein. Most Canadians eat 50 percent more protein than their bodies can use. Many foods besides meat are rich in protein, including dairy products, beans, grains, and other plant foods. (Eggs were once classified as protein, because egg white is high in protein; however, yolks are high in fat.)

Potentially Protective Foods

Although no food has been shown to prevent any disease absolutely, many foods contain natural substances that experts believe may help prevent some cancers. Foods that contain significant amounts of these substances are listed below.

Beneficial Substance	Associated Cancers	Food Sources
Fiber (insoluble)	Colon, gastro-intestinal, rectal	Wheat bran, whole wheat and other whole-grain cereals and bread products; fruits and vegetables
Antioxidants (vitamins C and E, beta-carotene)	Breast, cervical, gastrointestinal, lung, stomach, prostate	Vitamin C: citrus fruits, dark green leafy vegetables, strawberries, tomatoes, parsley; vitamin E: vegetable oils, wheat germ, soy products, avocados, nuts; beta-carotene: some leafy green vegetables and deep yellow and orange vegetables and fruit
Nonnutritive phytochemicals (chemicals that often give plants flavor and odor)	Breast, colon, gastrointestinal, lung, prostate, stomach	Cabbage, broccoli, Brussels sprouts, cauliflower, and other cruciferous vegetables; soybeans, licorice root, garlic
Folic acid (also known as folacin and folate)	Cervical, colon, rectal	Whole wheat products, wheat germ, dried beans, dark green leafy vegetables, asparagus, bean sprouts, sunflower seeds, cantaloupe, citrus fruit

■ *Myth: Meat contains more protein than any other food.* Meat actually ranks in about the middle of the protein-quantity scale, along with cheese, beans, and some nuts. Only about 25 percent of the calories in a T-bone steak comes from protein; the remaining 75 percent comes from fat. Even a lean cut of well-trimmed flank steak may get 50 percent of its calories from fat. Fish, poultry without the skin, and low-fat dairy products provide a higher percentage of protein per ounce than meat and eggs.

■ *Myth: Adults require less protein as they age.* The need for protein per pound of body weight remains the same, although some researchers suspect that the elderly might require more protein because the body uses it less efficiently over the years. Since calorie needs decrease with age, the elderly need to get low-fat protein.

■ *Myth: Athletes need much more protein than non-athletes.* Athletes may need slightly more during the initial stages of training or competition. But since most Canadians eat more than enough protein, chances are that a normal, balanced diet supplies all that an athlete needs.

> **Growth in the teen years demands higher calorie consumption than in adulthood, but teens need relatively more carbohydrates, not more protein, to fuel their growth.**

WHAT CARBOHYDRATES DO

During the digestive process, carbohydrates are turned into glucose, the body's chief energy source. If glucose is not used right away, it is stored as glycogen. There are two kinds of carbohydrates: simple (some fruits, some vegetables, honey, table sugar, and so on) and complex (beans, grains, potatoes, and other vegetables and fruit). Ideally, complex carbohydrates will comprise about 80 percent of the carbohydrates in your diet.

■ *Myth: Carbohydrates are fattening.* Ounce for ounce, most plant foods have the same number of calories as most meats or far fewer calories. In fact, carbohydrates should be featured in any weight-control program. Whole-grain foods, vegetables, and fruits, which most salad bars offer, not only provide a wealth of nutrients, but fill the stomach and satisfy hunger.

> **A calorie is a calorie, and excess calories, whether from fat, protein, or carbohydrates, will be converted to fat by the body and stored.**

WHAT FAT DOES

Fats provide a ready source of energy. Dietary fats supply the fatty acids necessary for many of the body's chemical activities, including growth in children, and provide cells' membrane linings. Fats carry the fat-soluble vitamins: A, D, E, and K. Fats lend flavor, texture, and aroma to food, and they satisfy feelings of hunger.

■ *Myth: Body fat is bad for you.* Moderate amounts of body fat, about 18 to 24 percent of total weight for women and 15 to 18 percent for men, is consistent with good health. Stored fats regulate body temperature, provide a protective cushion for organs, and aid in hormone production and regulation.

■ *Myth: Cholesterol is bad for you.* The body needs blood cholesterol, a type of fat, for the development of sex hormones, skin oils, digestive juices, and other important functions. As a rule, the body makes all the cholesterol it needs. To avoid raising their blood cholesterol, most people have to follow two dietary rules: limit both high-cholesterol foods and those containing saturated fat. Animal-derived foods, such as meat, poultry, dairy products, and eggs, are often high in cholesterol and saturated fat. Recent studies indicate that saturated fat is more likely to boost blood cholesterol levels than is dietary cholesterol. Excess blood cholesterol contributes to plaque, a substance that can block arteries. The result can be heart disease, the leading cause of death in Canada.

■ *Myth: If you are trying to lose weight, you must ban fat from your diet.* Even people who want to slim down should get about 10 to 20 percent of their calories from fat (unless your physician tells you otherwise).

■ *Myth: If you forgo meat and concentrated fats such as butter and oil, your diet will be fat-free.* Almost all foods contain at least traces of fat, often in the form of oils. Even carrots and celery contain minute amounts of fat.

VITAMINS AND MINERALS

Even though vitamins and minerals are needed in relatively small quantities, their roles in health and well-being are substantial: they stimulate dozens of biochemical reactions throughout the body.

■ Don't worry about deficiency diseases. Few Canadians need vitamin pills to ward off scurvy or rickets. Our concern with vitamins and minerals nowadays is whether or not they can enhance our health.

■ Many health and nutrition authorities believe that people who eat a balanced diet will get all the vitamins and minerals they need without resorting to pills. (The exceptions are pregnant women and persons with particular medical

problems.) For a list of good food sources for vitamins and minerals, see pages 44–45.

■ Other practitioners urge everyone to consume vitamin and mineral supplements. Nobel laureate Dr. Linus Pauling believes that massive doses of vitamin C bolster the immune system and ease colds.

■ Eat plenty of red peppers, squashes, tomatoes, cantaloupes, and other colorful produce because they are rich in antioxidants. In very simple terms, antioxidants repair cell damage. Researchers are investigating whether antioxidants can reduce the risk of cancer, cardiovascular disease, cataracts, and other ailments.

■ If you are prone to the eye problem conjunctivitis, eat plenty of produce high in vitamin A, such as sweet potatoes, broccoli, carrots, and winter squash. This is preferable to taking vitamin A in pill form because you can't get too much in foods, but you can get too much in pills.

■ If you take supplements of vitamin C or E, or beta-carotene (an antioxidant that the body converts to vitamin

A), use moderation. However, recent studies have revealed that supplements of vitamin E and beta-carotene taken by smokers may promote diseases such as lung cancer.

■ Do not take vitamins or minerals in megadoses, that is, far in excess of the recommended levels, where they may begin to function like drugs. Consuming megadoses can put you at risk of side effects.

■ If you take supplements, choose a brand from a reliable manufacturer.

CALCIUM INTAKE

At least one million women over 50 in Canada suffer from osteoporosis, a bone-weakening disease that is caused in part by a calcium deficit. The best defense against osteoporosis is a lifetime of exercising, drinking little or no alcohol, not smoking, and eating calcium-rich foods. How effective calcium supplements are in overcoming bone loss in adults has not been established, but a diet that includes good calcium sources is always sound.

■ Add nonfat milk powder to gravies, soups, and casseroles.

■ Drink skim milk and eat collard greens, Swiss and ricotta cheeses, and canned sardines and salmon with bones. These are among the best dietary sources of calcium.

■ Eat foods that are high in vitamin D, which helps the body absorb calcium. Fortified milk, milk products, and margarine are good sources of added vitamin D (though margarine should be limited, since it is entirely fat).

40

■ Stir a teaspoon of vinegar or lemon juice into soups and stews made with bones, and squeeze lemon juice on broccoli and other calcium-rich vegetables. The acid draws out calcium and helps your body absorb it.

■ Cut back on fat and protein, which may hinder calcium absorption.

FIBER

■ Include in your diet wheat bran and whole-grain cereals, which contain a type of fiber that may guard against colon cancer. Fiber, which is the fibrous part of plants that cannot be digested, is good for you because it helps waste matter to move quickly through the digestive tract.

■ The fiber in such foods as oat bran, legumes, apples, and pears apparently can lower blood cholesterol levels. Experts disagree on whether high-fiber diets can lower the risk of cardiovascular disease.

■ Consuming high-fiber fruits and vegetables, such as potatoes, peas, strawberries, ap-

ples, and pears, plus whole grains and legumes, helps you avoid constipation and various intestinal disorders.

Bypass fiber-poor white bread in favor of 100 percent whole wheat, rye, oat, cracked-wheat, or multigrain breads. If the label lists two or more grams of fiber per slice, you are getting a good source of fiber.

GREAT TASTE, NO CALORIES

■ Call it the world's oldest health drink. Water is essential for good health, good skin tone, and most of the body's functions. While the average person should drink eight glasses of water each day, large or active people should drink more if they need it.

■ If you live in a hot climate or your work is physically demanding, you may need more than eight glasses of liquids daily.

■ Drinking water could actually improve your health. People who drink too little water may be at risk of developing kidney stones. They may also suffer more often from headaches, fatigue, and lack of mental alertness. Continued under-hydration can put stress on the heart, as well as on the vascular and digestive systems.

■ Parents need to be sure that their newborns get enough liquids. Infants, who obviously cannot communicate thirst, can get dehydrated quickly.

■ Seniors should make a habit of drinking water even if they

aren't thirsty. Around age 65, the sense of thirst wanes, which could lead to under-hydration.

■ If you find it difficult to drink enough water, try to follow this schedule: Drink one glass when you first wake up and another with breakfast. Have one when you arrive at the office, one with lunch, another for a mid-afternoon break, and a glass with dinner. Drink one or two glasses of water when you exercise.

■ People who don't like the taste of their tap water or worry about its safety often turn to bottled water. If you drink bottled water, check the source to make sure it's not just tap water. If you're on a low-salt diet, choose bottled water carefully—some brands are high in sodium.

■ Drinking juice can be a healthy way to fill your eight-glasses-a-day quota. Many tomato juices are high in sodium, however, so read labels to find the low-sodium brands.

ORGANIC FOODS

■ The reason for buying organic foods is generally to avoid the pesticides used in commercial agriculture. To be sure the food is, in fact, organically grown, look for a "certified organic" label that lists the name and address of the certifying organization.

■ Don't expect organically grown food to last as long as other produce. Organic foods tend to be more perishable than produce grown for supermarkets, which is often chemically treated to retard spoilage and extend shelf life.

■ If you can't find certified organic foods—or don't want to pay the higher price—you may be able to scrub the produce with a vegetable brush. This works with potatoes and other tubers.

■ Remove the outer leaves from such vegetables as lettuce.

■ Peel fruits and vegetables that have a waxy coating.

■ Be aware that government standards for permissible residue levels include hefty safety margins. This means that even foods that contain pesticides are likely to be safe to eat. However, it may be some time before the questions on safety issues are resolved once and for all.

WHAT IS A SERVING?

Many people wonder how they can possibly eat up to 12 servings of grain products a day or as many fruits and vegetables as the food guide indicates (shown below). But once you consider what a serving is, the problem disappears. A serving is half a cup of cooked or fresh vegetables, one cup of raw leafy greens, a medium-size fruit, or three-quarters of a cup of fruit juice.

■ A grain serving is half a cup of cooked pasta or rice, or a slice of bread. A large bun, a pita bread or a bagel provides two or three grain servings.

■ A cup of milk or ¾ cup (a small carton) of yogurt is a dairy serving.

■ Recognize that foods are seldom simple. A muffin counts as one or two servings of grain, but it may also be high in fat. So if you count calories, note not just the fat that went into the muffin but any calories you put on it, such as cream cheese or jelly.

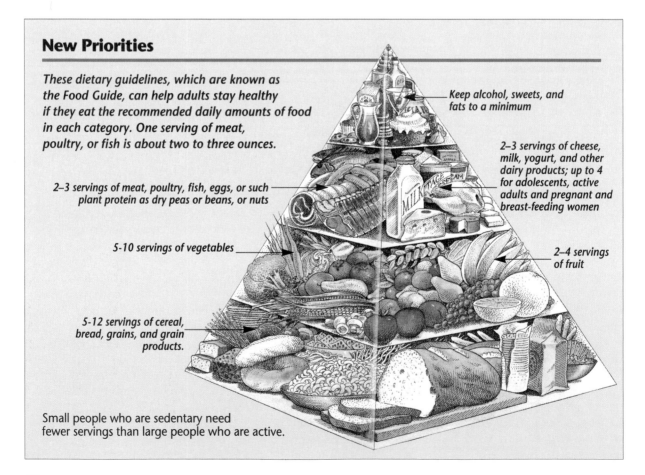

New Priorities

These dietary guidelines, which are known as the Food Guide, can help adults stay healthy if they eat the recommended daily amounts of food in each category. One serving of meat, poultry, or fish is about two to three ounces.

Keep alcohol, sweets, and fats to a minimum

2–3 servings of cheese, milk, yogurt, and other dairy products; up to 4 for adolescents, active adults and pregnant and breast-feeding women

2–3 servings of meat, poultry, fish, eggs, or such plant protein as dry peas or beans, or nuts

2–4 servings of fruit

5-10 servings of vegetables

5-12 servings of cereal, bread, grains, and grain products.

Small people who are sedentary need fewer servings than large people who are active.

BUILDING THE FOOD PYRAMID

*"The general impression of
hygienists [is] that
our diet is one-sided and
that we eat too much
fat, starch, and sugar."*

—W.O. Atwater

• • • • • • •

The above quote is not a new recommendation, but was made by a United States Department of Agriculture employee in 1894.

The USDA first began doing research on the relationship between agriculture and human nutrition in the 1890's. W.O. Atwater was the first director of the Office of Experiment Stations, and the work he did a century ago has a strong influence on how we think of nutrition today. Besides studying the typical American diet, Atwater published tables listing the amount of calories, protein, carbohydrates, and "mineral matters" of different foods.

Atwater also created the first dietary standards, which suggested the amount of food required for different types of people. For laborers he recommended a diet of 3,500 calories, with 15 percent of those calories from protein, 33 percent from fat, and 52 percent from carbohydrates. This advice is amazingly similar to the current recommendations.

The first food groups. The idea of food groups was introduced in *How to Select Foods*, published by the USDA in 1917. This pamphlet advised choosing foods from each of five groups: fruits and vegetables, meats, cereals and other starchy foods, sweets, and fatty foods.

Atwater's advice to limit the intake of fat and sugar was ignored by this publication. Malnutrition was a prime concern for the country at the time, so this guide emphasized eating a variety of foods in order to prevent

*A man ahead of his time:
W.O. Atwater*

vitamin and mineral deficiencies. Since Atwater's suggestions might have limited people's intake of meat and dairy products, which are important sources of vitamins and minerals, they were omitted. Besides, the USDA was in the business of encouraging, not curtailing, purchases of American agricultural goods.

The food-group approach was popular with the public. The number of groups was modified, often as dietary advice changed over the years. Noting that its recommendations meant greater sales for agricultural products, the USDA expanded its list to 12 food groups in the 1930's. Milk, for example, became a separate category. During World War II, people were encouraged to eat daily from eight groups. Eggs were one group, and "butter and other spreads" was another. Later guidelines promoted the Basic Seven food groups, and then the Basic Four.

The controversial pyramid. In the mid-1970's the purpose of food guides changed. Obesity and diet-related illnesses had overtaken malnutrition as public health concerns.

The Food Guide Pyramid (shown on the facing page) was created to illustrate not just food categories but correct proportions for a healthy diet. Breads and cereals form the large base, followed by vegetables and fruits.

Where the guide takes its strongest stand is at the top, advocating fewer servings of sweets, fats, dairy products, and meat products. While the decreased emphasis on foods near the top of the pyramid brought protests from the makers of these foods, the pyramid was eventually released to the public as a way to clarify what constitutes a well-balanced diet. It's interesting to note how close the Food Guide Pyramid comes to W.O. Atwater's original dietary suggestions. ❏

Vitamins

*Fat-soluble vitamins can be stored in the body
and need not be consumed daily.*

Vitamin	Its Functions	Good Dietary Sources	Signs of Deficiency	Signs of Overdose
Vitamin A	Helps maintain skin, hair, nail, gums, bones, teeth; helps ward off infection, promotes eye function	Dairy products, green and deep yellow or orange vegetables, deep yellow or orange fruit	Night blindness, reduced growth in children	Headache, blurred vision, fatigue, diarrhea, joint pain.
Vitamin D	Helps build and maintain teeth and bones; helps body absorb calcium	Egg yolk, liver, tuna, cod-liver oil, fortified milk	Rickets in children, bone diseases in adults	Calcium deposits, fragile bones, hypertension, high cholesterol, diarrhea
Vitamin E	Helps form red blood cells, muscles, and other tissues; preserves fatty acids	Poultry, seafood, seeds, nuts, vegetable oils, wheat germ, fortified cereal, eggs	Rare in humans	Blurred vision, headaches
Vitamin K	Aids blood clotting	Made by intestinal bacteria. Spinach, oats, wheat bran	Excessive bleeding, liver damage	Jaundice in infants

Water-soluble vitamins are stored in smaller amounts than fat-soluble vitamins and need to be consumed more frequently.

Vitamin	Its Functions	Good Dietary Sources	Signs of Deficiency	Signs of Overdose
Thiamin, vitamin B_1	Enhances energy, promotes normal appetite and digestion	Pork, fortified cereals and grains, seafood	Anxiety, hysteria, nausea. Extreme cases: beriberi	
Riboflavin	Metabolism of foods, release of energy to cells	Organ meat, beef, lamb, dark meat of poultry, dairy products, fortified cereals, dark green leafy vegetables	Sores around nose and mouth, visual problems	
Pantothenic acid, vitamin B_5	Needed to convert food to energy, aids digestion	Found in nearly all foods	Weakness, irritability	
Niacin, nicotinic acid	Helps release energy from foods, aids nerve function, digestion	Poultry, seafood, seeds, nuts, potatoes, fortified grains and cereals	Extreme cases: pellagra, a skin disease	Skin flushing
Pyridoxine, vitamin B_6	Aids protein metabolism and absorption, and carbohydrate metabolism	Meat, fish, poultry, grains, cereals, potatoes, bananas, prunes	Depression, confusion, and convulsions in infants	Extreme cases: sensory nerve destruction
Cobalamin, vitamin B_{12}	Builds genetic material needed by cells; helps form red blood cells	All animal products	Deficiency rare except in strict vegetarians, the elderly, and those with malabsorption disorders	
Biotin	Metabolism of glucose, essential for many bodily processes	Made by intestinal bacteria. Meats, poultry, fish, eggs, nuts, seeds	Rare except in infants: scaling skin, fatigue, pain	
Folic acid, folate, folacin	Manufacture of red blood cells and genetic material	Poultry, liver, dark green leafy vegetables, legumes, fortified whole-grain bread and cereal	Anemia, diarrhea, bleeding gums, weight loss, stomach upsets	
Vitamin C, ascorbic acid	Helps bind cells together, strengthens blood vessel walls, helps resist infection, speeds healing of wounds	Citrus fruits, strawberries, cantaloupe, sweet potatoes, cabbage, cauliflower	Bleeding gums, loose teeth, easy bruising. Extreme cases: scurvy	

Minerals

Because the body needs relatively large amounts of these three minerals, they are called macro- (Greek for "large") minerals.

Mineral	Its Functions	Good Dietary Sources	Signs of Deficiency	Signs of Overdose
Calcium	Helps build bones and teeth, promotes proper muscle and nerve function	Milk and milk products, canned salmon with bones, oysters, broccoli	Rickets in children, bone diseases in adults	Kidney stones, lethargy, pain
Phosphorus	With calcium, helps build bone and teeth	Dairy products, egg yolks, meat, poultry, fish	Deficiency is rare	Lowers blood calcium
Magnesium	Helps release energy in body, promotes bone growth	Green leafy vegetables, beans, fortified whole-grain cereals and bread	Muscle weakness, cramps	Nervous-system disorders; overdose can kill people with kidney disease

Trace minerals, which perform a wide range of functions, are needed in very small amounts.

Mineral	Its Functions	Good Dietary Sources	Signs of Deficiency	Signs of Overdose
Iron	Essential for healthy blood	Meat, liver, legumes, fortified breads and cereals, green leafy vegetables	Weakness, fatigue, headache, iron-deficiency anemia	Toxic buildup in liver, diabetes, liver disease
Zinc	Essential to digestion and metabolism	Beef, liver, oysters, yogurt, fortified cereal, wheat germ	Slow wound healing, loss of appetite, slow growth	Nausea, vomiting, abdominal pain, gastric bleeding
Selenium	Helps avoid breakdown of fats and body chemicals	Chicken, seafood, whole-grain breads and cereals	Unknown in humans	Nausea, abdominal pain, diarrhea, irritability, death
Copper	Stimulates iron absorption, helps make red blood cells and nerve fibers	Lobster, organ meats, nuts, legumes, prunes, barley	Rare in adults	Liver disease, vomiting
Iodine	Essential to thyroid gland	Iodized salt, seafood	Goiter, cretinism in infants	Disturbed thyroid function, goiter
Fluoride	Promotes strong teeth and bones	Fluoridated water, tea	Tooth decay	Mottling of tooth enamel
Manganese	Contributes to tendon and bone structure	Tea, coffee, bran, legumes	Unknown in humans	Nerve damage
Molybdenum	Needed for metabolism	Legumes, dark green leafy vegetables, whole-grain breads and cereals	Unknown in humans	Joint pain
Chromium	Aids glucose metabolism	Whole-grain breads and cereals, brewer's yeast	Diabeteslike symptoms	Unknown for food chromium; chromium salts toxic
Sulfur	Helps make hair and nails	Wheat germ, legumes, beef, peanuts, clams	Unknown	Unknown for food sulfur; sulfur salts toxic

Electrolytes are minerals essential to proper body chemistry.

Mineral	Its Functions	Good Dietary Sources	Signs of Deficiency	Signs of Overdose
Potassium	With sodium, helps regulate body's fluid balance	Bananas, citrus fruit, dried fruit, potatoes, legumes	Muscle weakness, cardiac arrhythmias, irritability	Nausea, diarrhea, cardiac arrhythmias
Sodium	Helps maintain body fluid balance	Salt, processed foods, milk, water in some areas	Deficiency is rare in North America	High blood pressure, kidney disease, heart failure
Chloride	Helps maintain acid-base balance	Same as sodium	Deficiency is very rare	Upset in acid-base balance

PLANNING YOUR MEALS

Give some thought to your meals and snacks before you sit down to eat. Whether you dine at home, at work, or somewhere in between, be sure you get the best nutritional value.

BREAKFAST AT HOME

Eating breakfast regularly can help you maintain your proper weight, get your full quota of daily nutrients, do your job well, and possibly even live longer! Take the following suggestions to make this important meal as healthy as possible.

■ Protein stimulates alertness and helps to stave off mid-morning hunger. To get enough protein, you may have to expand your concept of breakfast foods. For example, have cheese or cottage cheese with fruit or toast, or some beans or bean soup with corn-bread.

■ Limit the amount of fat in your breakfast. When having pancakes, waffles, or toast, re-strict the butter or margarine to one teaspoon or skip it en-tirely. For a topping, try a fruit spread like pureed strawber-ries or unsweetened apple-sauce or apple butter.

■ Rather than a doughnut or sweet roll, eat an English muffin or a bagel.

■ When baking muffins, use low-fat dairy products—non-fat buttermilk, nonfat sour cream alternative, low-fat yogurt—instead of the high-fat products.

■ If you would like to make pancakes, waffles, or muffins for breakfast but don't have much time, prepare two bowls the night before—one with the dry ingredients and one with the liquid (refriger-ated). In the morning, you need only blend them togeth-er and cook.

■ Vary your routine. Occa-sionally use peanut butter in-stead of butter as a spread. Have leftover pizza or poultry, a hamburger, or a grilled-cheese sandwich.

■ When buying breakfast ce-reals, check the label to make sure you're not getting too much fat, sugar, and sodium. As a general rule, the shorter the list of ingre-dients, the more nutritious the product.

■ Despite its reputation as a health food, most granola is loaded with sugar and fat. Use it mostly as a garnish on un-sweetened cereal or yogurt.

■ Rediscover hot cereal for cold mornings. In addition to the traditional fare of oat-meal and farina, you might try more unusual grains, such as bulgur, kasha, and couscous.

■ An important nutrient is vit-amin C, easily obtained from many fruits and juices. In-stead of the usual orange or grapefruit juice, have a can-taloupe, strawberries, or the exotic mango or papaya.

■ Here's an easy, nutrient-rich dish: combine brown rice (leftover is fine if you haven't mixed anything with it), dried apricots or other fruit, and skim or low-fat milk.

■ Here's another: toast a slice of bread, spread with low-fat cottage cheese, sprinkle with cinnamon, add sliced fruit, and broil.

Bananas getting soft? Mash them and add them to your French toast or pancake batter for extra flavor and potassium.

BREAKFAST ON THE RUN

■ When you don't have time to eat at home, take a healthy breakfast with you—for exam-ple, low-fat yogurt or cheese and a piece of fruit (perhaps a leftover baked apple), or even a sandwich.

■ For a fast-food meal with good nutrition, choose a small, fat-free bran muffin, or-ange juice, and skim or low-fat milk.

■ Beware of muffins that aren't fat-free or low-fat. Today's soft half-pound vari-ety of muffin has about 500 calories, most of them fat.

■ Steer clear of breakfast "sandwiches" with eggs and ham or bacon. These tend to be high in cholesterol, fat, and sodium.

BROWN-BAG LUNCHES

■ Use whole-grain bread, a good source of fiber and minerals, instead of white bread.

■ Pita bread forms a large pocket that lends itself to imaginative fillings—for example, hummus and chopped carrots; any salad combination; raw or steamed vegetables topped with lemon juice. And pita is widely available in whole wheat form.

■ Bagels, which are low in fat, aren't just for breakfast. Top them with low-fat cheese, cottage cheese (perhaps combined with fruit), or salmon or tuna salad.

■ Forgo processed sandwich meats like bologna, liverwurst, and salami, which are generally high in sodium, fat, and cholesterol. Even turkey bologna and turkey salami tend to be high in fat. Choose, instead, sliced roasted, skinless turkey or chicken breast.

■ When you prepare roast ham, turkey, or other meat or poultry for dinner, get in the habit of freezing what you don't finish. When you need to make sandwiches, defrost one of these packages (see "Cold Storage," page 71, for safe freezer time limits).

■ Remove all visible fat on roast beef, ham, or pork, and limit the quantity of meat you use.

■ Instead of cheese or mayonnaise, use slices of vegetables or fruit to make a sandwich moister and tastier. Try

bananas with peanut butter, and poultry with red peppers, peaches, or mangoes. Or make a chicken or turkey salad using chopped fruit.

■ You can also use herb pestos, low-fat ricotta spreads, and savory marmalades to replace mayonnaise, salad dressings, and butter on sandwiches. Or make your own dressing by blending equal parts low-fat cottage cheese and buttermilk, then season with herbs and spices, mustard powder, horseradish, lemon juice, minced garlic, or ground ginger. Remember that you don't need a lot of dressing on bread.

■ Make sure you include some vegetables in your lunch. You can easily pack carrot sticks, celery, cherry tomatoes, cauliflower or broccoli florets, cucumber or zucchini slices, green or red pepper strips, or a small salad.

■ Pack sandwich trimmings, such as pickles, tomato, and lettuce, separately so that the sandwich doesn't get soggy.

■ Beans provide protein, and their soluble fiber can lower blood cholesterol. Bring a can to work to have with your sandwich or add to your salad.

■ To keep a lunch chilled without a cooler, pack it with a frozen can of juice. By noon, your juice will be thawed and your lunch still cool.

■ The lunch you bring to the office doesn't have to be a sandwich: toss together leftover pasta or rice with vegetables and a few ounces of canned chicken or tuna, or cubes of low-fat cheese and a low-fat dressing.

> **To keep sandwiches fresh and moist, cover them with damp paper towels or a kitchen towel that has been wrung out in cold water.**

YOUR CHILD'S LUNCH BOX

■ If your son or daughter won't eat vegetables for lunch, send extra fruit and offer vegetables at dinner. Cut up fruits for younger children; they'll be more likely to eat them this way. (Treat the edges of apples, bananas, and pears with orange or lemon juice to prevent them from turning brown.)

■ Involve your child in lunch preparations. Kids are less likely to pass up foods they've helped prepare.

■ Use leftovers—for example, spaghetti and meatballs or take-out Chinese food. Put hot foods in a sterile, wide-mouthed vacuum flask that is easy to eat from.

■ If your child objects to mixtures, keep sandwiches simple—sliced turkey instead of turkey salad, for example.

■ Pack 1 percent chocolate milk mixed at home instead of

having your child buy 2 percent chocolate-milk cartons (which contain more fat) at school.

■ Offer grains rather than white bread. Quick breads, such as banana-oatmeal bread, pita-bread wedges, and low-fat crackers may also be good alternatives.

■ If your children resist switching from white bread to whole-grain breads, help them adjust to the new taste and texture. Start by making sandwiches with a slice each of white and whole-grain bread.

For a surprise, add a note or riddle to your child's lunch box .

MIDDAY MICROWAVING

If you have access to a microwave oven, you can use it to prepare quickly many healthy lunches.

■ Place a potato in the microwave for 4 to 10 minutes, depending on the size. Add a topping, such as low-fat yogurt, cheese, cottage cheese, or mock sour cream (see recipe box, page 77). Or try broccoli or other vegetables as a topping.

■ Here's a nutritious Mexican number: Soften a flour tortilla by heating it between paper towels on the high setting for 10 seconds. Spoon 1/4 cup refried beans (flavored with salsa, if desired) onto the center of the tortilla. Top it off with shredded low-fat cheddar cheese, shredded lettuce, and chopped green pepper.

■ You can heat up pasta dishes or just about any other left-overs in the microwave. Keep a set of cutlery in your desk for such occasions.

YOU AND YOGURT

■ Be aware that some commercial yogurts are loaded with fat and sugar. Avoid whole-milk yogurts and any thickened with cornstarch or sugary fruit preserves.

■ To control the amount of sweetener, use plain yogurt. Sweeten it without sugar or honey by stirring in grated, sliced, or whole fresh fruit—grapes, berries, bananas, plums, or peaches, for example. Or flavor it with vanilla, ground cinnamon, or almond or coconut extract. Add almonds for an extra treat.

■ Other good mix-in possibilities include applesauce, apple butter, raisins, and chopped dates, figs, or prunes.

■ Fruit-flavored yogurt drinks vary widely in both sugar and fat content. Still, almost any of these products is better than a milk shake made with whole milk and ice cream.

■ Make your own low-fat shake by blending yogurt with fresh or frozen fruit. You may want to add skim or low-fat milk.

■ For a tangy fruit-salad topping, use a low-fat yogurt like vanilla or lemon.

FAST FOOD

Is it possible to have a healthy lunch or dinner at a fast-food restaurant? Yes, provided you follow certain guidelines.

■ Choose a plain hamburger without cheese, bacon, or sauce, a roast beef sandwich without mayonnaise, a skinless grilled chicken sandwich, or a slice of pizza without meat topping. Be aware that breaded, fried fish or chicken sandwiches have *more* fat and calories than a plain burger.

■ If you do have fried chicken, remove some of the breading before eating.

■ Avoid anything described as extra crispy, which means extra fatty.

■ Many fast-food selections are high in sodium, and it isn't always easy to tell which of the foods provide the largest amounts. If you have a meal at a fast-food restaurant, try to balance it with low-sodium choices the rest of the day.

■ When you place your order, beware of "jumbo" and double burgers. Remember that large sizes of burgers (especially those topped with cheese), French fries, and milk shakes have hundreds more calories than their smaller counterparts.

■ Order a plain baked potato (not cheese-topped) or mashed potatoes in place of French fries.

■ Head for the fresh greens, fruit, and raw or lightly cooked vegetables at a salad bar. By-pass such high-fat additions as eggs, oil-drenched vegetables, cheese, bacon bits, and croutons. And go easy on creamy salads—potato salad, macaroni salad, and coleslaw.

■ Salad dressings are usually high in fat, calories, and sodium. Use them sparingly.

■ Drink milk (skim or low-fat, if available) instead of a milk shake.

■ If you're having your fast-food meal at home, add salad, vegetables, and fruit for nutritional balance.

OTHER DINING TIPS

■ Ask if the restaurant provides nutrition information. If so, use these guidelines to avoid foods that are high in fat, cholesterol, and salt.

■ Sandwiches made at delis, diners, and other eateries are often overstuffed with meat. Ask for yours to be prepared with less meat than usual, or else remove some of the meat from the sandwich, wrap it up, and refrigerate it as soon as possible.

■ Have your sandwich served on whole-grain bread (or bun or roll). When ordering toast, make it whole wheat, rye, or other whole-grain bread.

■ Think twice before having a diet platter if it includes a hamburger patty, hard-boiled egg, and cottage cheese made from whole milk. This high-fat meal is no calorie bargain.

■ If you order a dish that comes with gravy, such as roast turkey, ask for the gravy—usually high in fat—to be served separately, so you can dole it out sparingly.

DINNER

■ Most people think of dinner as the "big meal," but you're somewhat better off having a light evening meal, unless you dine early and remain physically active for the next several hours.

■ When making soups and stews, cut down on meat and add more vegetables.

■ You can also add vegetables, instead of meat, to spaghetti sauce. Roast them first until they're brown and tender to give a more "meaty" texture and flavor.

■ Practice portion control. Rather than eating six or more ounces of meat at a sitting, pare this down to a three- to four-ounce serving—about the size of a deck of playing cards. Instead of having a large amount of meat and small portions of vegetables, reverse this.

■ When choosing a reduced-calorie salad dressing, be aware that many dressings have about 40 calories per tablespoon, which can add up quickly. Many of the dressings are also high in sodium (see "Dressing Your Salad," page 78).

■ When you are in a rush and want to keep dinner simple, buy cut-up, frozen vegetables at the supermarket. Stir-fry them and serve with rice and beans or over pasta.

■ If you or anyone in your family occasionally eats alone, prepare a full recipe for a casserole or other main dish and for rice, potato, and pasta dishes. Then separate into individual portions and freeze.

■ Make your own TV dinners by freezing together single portions of entrées and vegetables. Label them with the date and foods included. If necessary for other family members, include microwaving instructions. (To ensure that you get a good supply of grains, add bread, rolls, or other grain sources when you sit down to the meal.)

■ If you rely on prepared frozen foods from time to time, pick them wisely. Read labels to keep your diet relatively low in fat, cholesterol, and sodium. A rule of thumb: buy commercial frozen dinners or entrées that contain no more than 300 calories and no more than 800 milligrams of sodium per serving (see "Getting the Most from Convenience Foods," page 79).

■ Keep a copy of your favorite cookbook at your office. This way, at the end of your business day, you can decide what to have for dinner, see what ingredients you need, and possibly even photocopy the list of ingredients to take to the store.

Dining alone at home? Make it exciting by trying new foods or a new recipe. Treat yourself like a special guest, with candles and an attractive place setting.

The Right Substitutes for the Wrong Snacks

Snacking has a bad name: it conjures up images of fattening, calorie-laden foods. But snacks can actually add essential nutrients to your diet and be good for you.

Instead of a pepperoni pizza, vegetable pizza.

Instead of potato chips, popcorn.

Instead of a croissant, pita bread.

Instead of a glazed doughnut, angel food cake.

HOW AND WHEN TO SNACK

■ Have two snacks daily, mid-morning and mid-afternoon, in addition to three well-balanced meals.

■ If you like to quantify things, look at your diet this way— your three meals should contribute roughly 75 percent of daily calories, and snacks should account for the other 25 percent.

■ Like the rest of your diet, keep snacks relatively low in fat, high in fiber, and limited in sugar and salt.

■ Eating more often may help you stay svelte. When you dine on small meals frequently, say some researchers, you are less likely to accumulate large deposits of fat.

■ Pay attention when you snack. If you eat as you're driving a car or talking on the phone, you may consume a lot more food than you realize.

■ Snacking can help teenagers get the calcium they need to develop healthy bones. Cheese pizza and cheeseburgers (with extra-lean beef) are good choices. With a blender, teens can make their own milk shakes, another high-calcium snack.

■ Eat pretzels, crackers, and other snacks from a dish, not from the bag or box, so you can monitor your portions. For extra nutrients, choose whole wheat pretzels and crackers.

KIDS' SNACKS: DO'S AND DON'TS

■ Do limit the amount of junk food in the house. While there's nothing wrong with an occasional handful of chocolate-covered raisins, it's better to stock up on such snacks as fresh fruit, nuts, yogurt, and plain popcorn.

■ Do set a good example. How can you expect your children to be satisfied with an apple or a carrot stick if they see you filling up on potato chips and candy bars?

■ Do serve homemade snacks whenever you can. If you make your own cakes, cookies, and other treats, you can control the amount of sugar or fat used, and you can add healthy ingredients, such as grains, nuts, and fruits.

■ Don't use food as a pacifier, giving sweets to quiet children down. Neither should foods be used as a reward.

■ Don't be afraid to set limits. If a child is clamoring for a snack you feel is not good, a parent should determine how often and how much the child is allowed to eat.

■ Don't go overboard on regulations. Banning a food completely will only make it more enticing to most children.

> **Here's a quick way to check how much fat a cracker contains: just rub it on a paper napkin. If the cracker leaves an oily smudge, it's likely to be high in fat.**

PLAN AHEAD

■ Resist the urge for sweets by making tasty low-fat snack alternatives easily available. For example, place a tangerine or an apple on top of your desk as soon as you get to work. When the doughnut wagon comes around, seeing your mid-morning snack ready and waiting can make it easier to say no.

■ Keep the refrigerator at home stocked with tempting packages. Store leftovers—turkey or chicken breast, or a favorite pasta dish, for example—in snack-size portions. Tell family members to help themselves.

■ Be sure to check the label before buying packaged fruit drinks and punches. Some are very high in sugar and corn syrup, a sweetener, and the juice content may be very low.

■ Try homemade yogurt pops to satisfy an ice cream crav-

ing. Combine six ounces of undiluted frozen fruit-juice concentrate with eight ounces of plain low-fat yogurt. Freeze in an ice cube tray or small paper cups. Place a wooden stick in the center of each cup when the mixture is partially frozen.

■ Stock the refrigerator with an assortment of plain soda water and flavored varieties. Get in the habit of making your own punch, combining fruit juices and seltzer.

■ Fill a candy jar with low-fat cereal. It's as crunchy as some popular candy but lower in fat and calories.

■ For an easy snack that supplies fiber and assorted vitamins and minerals, freeze seedless grapes and bananas (whole or chunks). Put peeled bananas in foil or sealed plastic bags.

■ For a snack that can be prepared in a few seconds, take a cup of unsalted pretzels and break them into bite-size pieces. Combine them with a cup of unsalted roasted peanuts, a cup of raisins, and half a cup of unsalted sunflower seeds. Store in an airtight container. Makes 12 servings, approximately 1/4 cup each.

FUEL UP FOR EXERCISE

■ For a reliable energy boost that provides fuel in the form of carbohydrates, eat a hard roll, pita (pocket) bread, a bagel, or other low-fat, low-sodium bread.

■ Everyone who exercises regularly should use the food-pyramid guidelines to get plenty of whole-grain bread and cereals, vegetables, and other complex carbohydrates. The body converts these carbohydrates to glucose, which, stored as glycogen, provides the primary fuel for muscles.

■ "Energy bars" by any name (sports bars, power bars, and nutrition bars) won't boost your athletic performance. As a rule, these bars won't give you more energy than any other high-carbohydrate snack. Some are low in fat, but others contain as much fat as a chocolate bar.

■ It's a myth that eating a sugar snack right before exercising will boost your energy. The sugar in candy bars does raise blood glucose levels, but it provides energy for a relatively brief period.

■ For family members who work out regularly, post on a kitchen bulletin board a list of suggested snacks. Some that are high in iron, which is essential for healthy blood and muscles, are dried apricots, iron-fortified breads and cereals, nuts, and sunflower seeds. For calcium, which is needed for strong bones and muscles, list snacks of cheese (preferably low-fat varieties), custard, pudding, ice milk, and, of course, low-fat milk.

LOSING WEIGHT FOREVER

Permanent weight loss is a slow and steady proposition. Give yourself a year or more to adopt new eating habits. Meanwhile, you may lower your risk of such disorders as heart disease, stroke, diabetes, and some cancers.

LOOK BEFORE YOU LEAP

■ Promise yourself that this diet will be your last. Repeated losses and gains rob your body of muscle tissue, increase your risk of disease, and—most discouraging of all—contribute to the tendency to regain fat.

■ Evaluate whether or not you really need to lose weight. If an extra five pounds isn't causing or aggravating a medical condition, it may be healthier to accept yourself as you are.

■ Forget ideal-weight charts. Think of a weight you were able to maintain comfortably for longer than six months and aim for that goal.

■ Accept the reality that body shape and size are largely determined by genetics. Try to reach the weight that's right for you—not an idealized image—and stay there.

■ If you are obese, discuss a weight-loss plan with your physician. Obesity is commonly defined as weighing more than 20 percent above the desired weight for someone of your height and body type. Risks include high blood pressure, stroke, heart disease, and other illnesses.

■ If you have a health problem that's caused or exacerbated by your weight, such as elevated blood cholesterol or diabetes, losing pounds can bring significant improvements—even if you still weigh well above what is considered ideal.

■ Assess your potential for success in dieting. Do you recognize the need for a nutritional overhaul—not just a diet that you will abandon as soon as you've achieved your weight-loss goals? Can you handle the stresses at home and on the job pretty well? If you answer no to either question, consider postponing your diet.

■ Analyze your own needs. If you lack motivation, you may do best in a program that offers peer-group support.

■ Choose a reducing program that encourages a slow, steady loss (about a pound or less a week for women, two pounds or less weekly for men) and focuses on changing habits.

■ Avoid diets based on one food or food group. Be wary of any eating plan that veers too far from the food pyramid.

■ Recognize the signs of eating disorders. The most common are anorexia nervosa and bulimia. Anorexics starve themselves. Bulimics alternate between binge eating and purging. The disorders often cause serious health problems, so consult a physician if you have developed either disorder—or both of them.

Weight may be an imprecise health gauge. *The man at left, at 240 pounds, has excess fat at the midriff, which poses a risk for heart disease. The other man, a trim, muscular 230 pounds, may have a much lower risk.*

PACE YOURSELF

■ Take a "before" picture of yourself and look at it now and then. Each time you shed 10 pounds, take another picture of yourself. Compare it to the "before" picture and enjoy the new you.

■ Make weight loss your top priority. At the beginning of each week, enter "appointments" on your calendar for exercise and support-group sessions.

■ If you plan to eat at a restaurant, find one that offers low-fat fare.

■ Make a list of nonfood treats, like a new compact disc, flowers, or a manicure. Reward yourself with something on the list each time you achieve a small goal.

■ When anger, boredom, or loneliness makes you want to eat, take a deep breath, hold it for a second or two, and exhale slowly. Repeat this two or three times. Try to identify what sparked the impulse to eat. Let yourself experience the feeling for a few moments to realize that you can survive it without resorting to food.

■ Give yourself time to adjust to a changed diet. After several months of retraining your taste buds, you may actually crave low-fat fare.

■ Be aware of little changes that can make a big difference. For example, if you are in the habit of using bottled Italian salad dressing, by switching to the reduced-calorie version, you may save approximately 100 calories with each two-tablespoon serving of dressing.

• •

Read at least one magazine or newspaper article about nutrition each week. Resolve to learn more about food and how your body uses it.

• •

STAVE OFF A FOOD BINGE

■ Examine your cravings. Identify the food that you yearn for the most.

■ Plan to have the food at a precise time and place. Plan where you will sit when you eat it. Stay in control.

■ At the prearranged moment, indulge in the food craving. Notice if it allows you to avoid an all-out eating binge.

■ If you do go on a binge, forgive yourself. Then get back on track with your next meal.

AVOID FAT TRAPS

■ Choose such low-fat foods as fruits, vegetables, breads, and grains. You can also consume lean meat, some fish and shellfish, and skinless poultry.

■ Add little or no fat to prepared foods. If you must spread something on bread, rolls, and baked potatoes, use olive oil, or reduced-fat tub or squeezable margarines.

■ Select condiments with care. Try to avoid tartar sauce, which is high in fat, and mayonnaise, which is virtually pure fat. Replace mayonnaise with mustard or steak sauce (unless you need to avoid heavily salted food).

■ Have pancakes with syrup (a modest amount) but no butter or margarine.

■ Snack between meals. Keep fresh fruit, unbuttered pop-

---

10 Rules for Dieters

Before you commit yourself to a weight-loss effort, consider these new ways of thinking and dining.

1. Think of yourself as a thin person.

2. Plan your meals and snacks. Know ahead of time exactly what you will eat and how much.

3. Avoid all restaurants for the first week.

4. Do not read or watch television while you eat. Concentrate on your food.

5. Never eat standing up.

6. Put your cutlery down after each mouthful. Don't refill it until you've swallowed.

7. Chew slowly. Taste what you are eating.

8. Fill your plate only with the amount of food you want. Do not eat from platters on the table.

9. Do not take second helpings.

10. Always leave some food on your plate.

---

corn, or a plain bagel within reach in case you get hungry. You'll find that it's easier to resist temptation at mealtime if you're not ravenous.

■ Before dinner, munch on fresh raw vegetables. Be sure to avoid high-calorie dips.

■ Before dessert, go for a walk. It takes several minutes for your mind to catch up with the fact that your stomach is full. If you allow time between your main course and dessert, you'll tend to eat less.

COOK THE LOW-FAT WAY

■ Cook with little or no fat. Steaming, stir-frying, grilling, broiling, baking, and roasting are among the best techniques for preparing meat and poultry. Grill or broil fattier fish, such as salmon. Poach or microwave such lean fish as flounder and haddock.

■ Experiment in the kitchen. Turn favorite recipes into low-fat fare by cutting down on the amount of oil or eliminating it. When possible, try nonstick cooking sprays. Cook with nonstick pots and pans.

Avoid fried shrimp with tartar sauce; try boiled shrimp and cocktail sauce.

Instead of high-fat fettuccine Alfredo, serve pasta with tomato sauce.

■ Use potatoes instead of cream to thicken homemade soups. Boil a couple of peeled, quartered white potatoes, along with an onion if you like, until soft. Puree in a food processor or blender until smooth and stir into the soup.

Drink water before and during meals. It will help you feel full sooner.

WORK OUT OFTEN

■ Find an exercise that appeals to you and do it regularly. Better yet, find two different types of exercises—one aerobic, one strength-building—and do them regularly (see "All About Aerobics," page 92, and "Building Muscles," page 108).

■ Try to include exercise in your schedule daily. The more demanding the workout, the more calories you will burn. Even activities that don't expend many calories can relieve stress, increase energy levels, and give your self-esteem a boost (see "A Lifetime Concern," page 84).

■ Stay active after you've reached your goal. More often than not, the dieters who keep off weight they have lost are those who continue to exercise regularly. A vigorous workout can burn calories for as long as 12 hours after you have stopped exercising.

■ Continue to work out as you age. Not only does exercise help you stay in shape, but such activities as walking and running can help prevent the bone loss that often comes with age.

FOLLOW THE NEW RULES

■ Count grams of fat, not just the calories consumed. The percentage of daily calories from fat is generally more important in determining your weight than your caloric intake. Some diet experts recommend that meals and snacks contribute at most 25 percent fat to your diet.

■ Measure yourself every two weeks during the first month, then once a month. Body measurements may be the best way initially to chart your diet progress. Besides, lost inches are a more tangible sign of success than lost pounds.

■ If you prefer using a scale, weigh yourself no more than once every two weeks at the same time of day and without shoes.

■ Make changes one at a time. Once you've eliminated fried foods, for example, wait until you've adjusted to that dietary shift before eliminating nuts, cookies, or other high-fat foods.

■ Focus on health, not weight. Except for the few people who have medical complications, eating a healthy diet and exercising several times a week will result in your losing weight and keeping it off. Accentuate the long-term benefits of health, instead of merely going on a diet.

■ Avoid very-low-calorie, low-carbohydrate diets that promise quick weight reduction. You may shed pounds quickly from loss of water; however, once you resume eating normally, the water weight will return.

DEVELOP GOOD HABITS

- Find a relaxing place to eat.
- Don't dawdle in the kitchen either before or after a meal.
- Avoid eating late in the day, or within three hours of bedtime.
- Pinpoint the time of day when you're most likely to give in to temptation. Then schedule an exercise class or other activity for that period.
- Set a kitchen timer for 15 minutes whenever you feel famished. Return a phone call or walk around the block. Hunger pangs should pass before the buzzer sounds.
- Don't skip meals or limit yourself to fewer than 1,200 calories daily. If you do, your metabolism may slow down, so that you will burn calories slowly. Fasting may make you more inclined to binge.
- Go easy on yourself. An occasional indulgence is perfectly fine. Vowing never to eat your favorite foods is unrealistic and frustrating.
- Maintain the illusion of a hearty meal with less-than-hearty servings. Serve dinner on a sandwich plate, rather than a dinner plate.
- Avoid alcohol while dieting. The calories from alcohol supply no nutrients, whereas fruits, vegetables, and other high-fiber, nutrient-dense foods are good for you and make you feel full.

Write down everything you are about to eat just before you eat it. Studies have shown that this strategy alone leads to weight loss.

Dieter's Desserts

Going on a weight-loss diet doesn't mean skipping dessert. These low-fat versions offer sweetly satisfying ways to end a meal.

STRAWBERRY DELIGHT

1 16-oz. low-fat or fat-free pound cake
1 container low-fat frozen strawberry yogurt
1–2 pints fresh strawberries, hulled and sliced

Preheat oven to 400°F. Toast pound cake in oven for 8 to 10 minutes. Top with frozen yogurt and sliced strawberries. Makes 8 to 10 servings.

BANANA PARFAIT

1 8-oz. container low-fat banana yogurt
1 ripe banana, peeled and sliced
Coffee liqueur to taste

Mix banana yogurt with sliced bananas. Drizzle with coffee liqueur.

FROZEN PEACH TREAT

6 ripe peaches, peeled and chopped
1 quart plain low-fat yogurt
Juice of 1/2 lemon
Honey to taste

In a large bowl, mash peaches with a potato masher or pastry cutter. Add yogurt, lemon juice, and honey, and stir. Ladle into serving bowls or paper cups. Set in the freezer for at least 2 1/2 hours. Makes 8 to 10 servings.

SESAME-RICE PUDDING

1 3/4 cups cooked brown rice (3/4 cup uncooked)
1/2 cup brown sugar
2 cups orange juice
3 tbsp. ground sesame seeds
Grated rind of one orange
1/2 cup raisins (optional)
1 whole egg plus 2 egg whites, well beaten
1/2 tsp. cinnamon
1/4 tsp. nutmeg
1 tsp. vanilla extract
Garnish: 2 oranges, peeled and sectioned

Preheat oven to 350°F. Combine all ingredients except sectioned oranges and mix well. Put in an oiled baking dish and bake until firm, about one hour. Spoon into bowls and garnish with orange sections. Serve warm or cold. Makes six servings.

EATING OUT, ETHNIC-STYLE

By knowing which ethnic foods are high in fat—and which are not—you can enjoy dining out without compromising on nutritional value, taste, or your good eating habits.

DINNER

■ Have a light snack, such as crackers or fruit, before you leave the house. That way you won't be famished and run the risk of overeating when you dine out.

■ If you're trying a new restaurant, call ahead to see if the chef will prepare special orders. Inquire about specific cooking techniques (such as broiling fish or chicken instead of frying it) and preparing certain dishes without a rich sauce.

■ Be realistic about how much tinkering can be done. Even the finest chef cannot prepare fettuccine Alfredo without using cream.

■ Learn to interpret food descriptions. "Crispy" and "pan-fried" mean "fried." "Sautéed" may mean fried in lots of butter or oil, but it can also mean cooked with minimal butter or oil in a nonstick pan.

■ Recognize items that are high in fat even when the menu doesn't tip you off. For example, potato skins served as an appetizer or side dish at a restaurant tend to be fried and accompanied by high-fat sour cream. Chicken nuggets, which often contain ground skin, are usually very high in fat.

■ Avoid fat-laden gravies and such sauces as hollandaise and béarnaise. Even if a sauce

is described as light, ask whether it's cream- or butter-based; if so, request a substitute of a tomato-, wine-, or broth-based sauce.

■ If certain items on the menu have hearts or other symbols to denote healthier fare, don't let that symbol be the deciding factor in your food selection. There are no organizations that monitor such claims.

■ Ask the waiter to describe how a dish is prepared. Don't be intimidated by the surroundings: the fancier the restaurant, the more willing the chef may be to satisfy a customer.

■ If the restaurant you've chosen serves generous portions, you may want to split an entrée with a companion. Or order an appetizer, soup, and salad, but omit an entrée.

■ Ask for a plain salad with the dressing served on the side. Dip the tines of the fork into the dressing and then spear the greens.

■ Don't be shy about requesting substitutions, like a green

salad for coleslaw and potato salad, which tend to be drenched in mayonnaise.

■ Ask to have your vegetables steamed and served plain or seasoned with lemon juice or herbs. Otherwise, they may be sautéed in butter or oil.

■ If a chocolate-mousse cake, pecan pie, or any other dessert sounds irresistible, order it and share it with others at the table.

A good rule for dining out: don't feel compelled to finish everything on your plate. Most restaurants provide more than enough to satisfy your hunger, and excess calories may end up as excess pounds and inches.

CAJUN

■ *Low in fat*: Red beans and rice (without sausage); greens, meaning kale, mustard greens, or okra; cornbread; shrimp creole (in tomato sauce over rice); jambalaya or gumbo (order the poultry or seafood versions); grilled seafood.

■ *High in fat*: Hush puppies (fried cornbread); dirty rice (fried rice with fatty meats); sausage dishes including *boudin* or andouille; rich soups or stews, such as bisque

56

(cream broth) and *étouffée* (lots of butter); batter-fried seafoods.

CARIBBEAN

Tomatoes and hot peppers figure prominently in this cuisine, along with a wealth of tropical fruits and vegetables—guava, papaya, okra, cassava, plantain, mango, coconut, and many more.

■ *Low in fat*: Black bean soup or pepper pot (spicy vegetable and pork soup), vegetables like calalu (similar to spinach), okra; jerk meats (spicy marinade, usually grilled); curried chicken; seafood in fruit sauces, like lime-garlic prawns, shrimp with garlic and papaya, or red snapper in bananas and rum.

■ *High in fat*: Conch fritters (fried); soups made with cream, like yam bisque, or coconut, such as hot banana soup; fish poached in coconut milk.

CHINESE

Chinese food is very high in complex carbohydrates. Although Chinese restaurants in America tend to use more meat and sauce than those in China, they still serve a relatively low-fat cuisine.

■ Stir-fried vegetables, cooked very quickly in a lightly oiled, very hot wok, retain vitamins better than vegetables cooked the traditional American way. A drawback of Chinese cooking—at least for some people with hypertension—is the sodium in salty sauces (like oyster and black bean sauce) and in monosodium glutamate (MSG). Since some people may be allergic to MSG, many Chinese

restaurants omit it on request.

■ *Low in fat*: Hot-and-sour or wonton soup; steamed dumplings; steamed or braised whole fish or scallops with black bean sauce; chicken or eggplant steamed or braised; stir-fried dishes (ask the cook to go easy on the oil or to use broth instead); dishes made with sliced meat rather than diced (often hides a fatty cut).

■ *High in fat*: Fried egg rolls and dumplings; sesame noodles; fried rice; spareribs; Peking duck; anything "crispy" or "batter-coated" (both terms indicate deep-frying); dishes heavy on nuts, such as *kung pao* chicken.

Pick main dishes with only small amounts of meat, and ask if the proportion of vegetables can be increased. Include a vegetarian dish or two in your order.

EASTERN EUROPEAN

■ *Low in fat*: Rice-stuffed cabbage or peppers; borscht or fruit soups (made with yogurt instead of cream); knishes (pastry filled with spinach, kasha, or mushrooms); poached fish; pierogi, or piroch (pastry filled with meat or vegetables) without sour cream, steamed or boiled instead of fried.

■ *High in fat*: Goulash and *paprikache* (made with cream and fatty cuts of meat); blintzes (lots of cheese); schnitzel (meat breaded, fried, and covered with cream sauce); sausages like kielbasa.

FRENCH

Some French food is loaded with rich ingredients and topped with creamy and buttery sauces. However, there are many dishes that are relatively safe for the fat-conscious diner. As for the truly extravagant desserts and cheeses, the best strategy is to keep the portions very, very small.

■ *Low in fat*: *Salade niçoise*, spinach salad (sans bacon); consommé and other stock-based soups; stews, such as bouillabaisse or ratatouille; poached or steamed fish or seafood; seared or oven-roasted scallops or salmon; dishes with sauces labeled *coulis* (vegetable puree, or reduction); roast chicken.

■ *High in fat*: Cassoulet and gratins (made with lots of cheese or egg), dishes heavy with eggs, such as quenelles and soufflés; hollandaise, beurre blanc, and other dairy-based sauces; fatty meats, such as sweetbreads and duck, and pâté.

GREEK

Greek food is cooked mainly in olive oil and features many vegetables, fruits, lentils, pasta, rice, and fish. When meats are on the menu, they are often grilled or roasted, which reduces the fat.

■ *Low in fat*: *Tarato* (cold soup with eggplant, pepper, and yogurt); grilled fish or octopus; skewered and grilled vegetables and meat dishes, such as souvlaki and shish kebab; grilled lamb chops or roast leg or braised shanks; fish baked with *plaki* sauce.

■ *High in fat*: *Taramasalata* (creamy fish roe dip); meat in *avgolemono* (egg-based lemon sauce); *bourekakia* (cheese-stuffed pastry); moussaka and *pastitsio* (casseroles made with eggs and cheese); *skordalia* (almond-garlic sauce).

INDIAN

This cuisine is rich in vegetables, legumes, and yogurt. But many Indian dishes are soaked in ghee (clarified butter) or coconut oil, one of the few vegetable oils that consist almost entirely of saturated fatty acids (86 percent). It's possible to avoid these fats by asking how each dish is cooked. Some Indian restaurants will also use different kinds of cooking oils on request.

■ *Low in fat*: Baked breads like *chapati, nan, kulcha*; lentil or vegetable-based soups like mulligatawny; chicken or fish prepared in tandoori-, *tikka-, vindaloo-*, or *masala*-style; yogurt-based

curries.

■ *High in fat*: Fried appetizers like *samosas* and *pakoras* or fried bread, such as *poori* and *paratha*; any dishes called *kandhari, malai*, and *korma* (lots of cream or coconut).

INDONESIAN

Rice is the foundation of an Indonesian meal, and there's always a combination of sweet and sour and salty tastes.

■ *Low in fat*: *Rijsttafel*—rice served with a variety of small dishes, such as *ayam panggang* (grilled chicken) and *gadogado* (vegetables—ask for the peanut sauce on the side).

■ *High in fat*: Coconut milk–based dishes like the chicken and nutmeg *opor ayam* or the beef and lemongrass *kalio daging*; fried dishes like *dendeng putri manis* (steak) or *ayam goreng kalasan* (chicken).

ITALIAN

This cuisine, particularly southern Italian cooking, has been called one of the world's healthiest. It is based largely on pasta (which is rich in complex carbohydrates) and olive oil (78 percent monounsaturates), as well as on vegetables, fruit, and fish. Northern Italian cooking tends to be richer, with much more beef, veal, butter, and cream; residents of northern cities suffer from considerably more heart disease than those who live in southern regions.

■ *Low in fat*: Vegetable antipasto (often including roasted peppers and zucchini and

grilled mushrooms); such salads as *panzanella* (with tomatoes and bread); pasta with tomato- or wine-based sauce; linguine with clam sauce; *pasta e fagioli* (shells and beans); *ribollito*, the thick vegetarian stew; grilled game, veal, and fish; chicken cacciatore; snapper in *cartoccio* (baked in parchment); marinated calamari.

■ *High in fat*: Meat and cheese antipasto; *fritto misto* (the "fried mixed" seafood, meat, or vegetable platter); garlic bread; cannelloni, lasagna, and other cheese-filled pasta; pesto; pasta with cream sauces, including carbonara and *Alfredo*; risotto (heavy with butter and cheese); cheesy eggplant, chicken, and veal parmigiana; veal *piccata* and marsala; pizza with sausage, pepperoni, and olive toppings; cannoli or other cream-filled pastries.

JAPANESE

Generally, Japanese cooking is very low in fat. It is based on protein-rich soybean products (such as tofu), fish, vegetables, noodles, and rice.

■ Seaweed used in sushi and Japanese stews is high in calcium, magnesium, and iodine.
■ However, the traditional Japanese diet is high in salted,

smoked, and pickled foods, so if you are on a low-salt diet, consume Japanese food in moderation. Anyone worried about eating raw fish can try sushi made with vegetables and cooked crab or shrimp.

■ *Low in fat*: Miso soup; yakitori (broiled chicken); *sunomono* (cucumber salad); shrimp or chicken teriyaki; tofu and other soybean dishes; *yosenabe*, a seafood and vegetable stew; *shabu-shabu*, a variety of vegetables or meats boiled in broth; broiled fish or chicken served over rice; *sashimi* and *sushi* (except for salmon caviar).

■ *High in fat*: Tempura or anything else under the heading of *age-mono* (deep-fried); pan-fried pork; fried dumplings; sukiyaki; egg dishes, such as *oyako-donburi*.

KOREAN

Bean paste is a staple of Korean cooking. Ingredients are often finely sliced and shredded, then stir-fried in a small amount of oil, and served in small pancakes.

■ *Low in fat*: Soup, like the bean paste and vegetable *doen jang chi gae* or the seafood and tofu *kang doen jang*; pickled vegetables called *kimachi*; *nang myon* dishes featuring cold buckwheat noodles in a spicy sauce with vegetables or poultry; barbecued meats like *bul go ki* (beef) are good—order lean cuts, such as sirloin.

■ *High in fat*: Egg drop soups like *duck kuk*; barbecued ribs, *kal bi*; pan-fried fish dishes like *gul jun* or *sang sun jun*.

MEXICAN-SOUTHWESTERN

The rice, corn, and beans that are staples of the diet in Mexico have little fat and are nutrient-dense. But some of the most popular dishes served in North American Mexican restaurants, such as beef burritos with cheese and sour cream, are quite high in fat.

■ *Low in fat*: Mesquite-grilled chicken, seafood, or lean cuts of beef or pork, especially with fresh salsa; chicken or fish marinated in lime juice; fajitas or tacos *al carbon*, especially seafood (hold the sour cream); corn tortillas; bean or vegetable burritos; rice; soft-shell tacos.

■ *High in fat*: Tortilla chips and nachos; guacamole; fried dishes, such as chimichangas, hard-shell tacos, *flautas, taquitos*; tamales, quesadillas, cheese enchiladas, and chili *con queso*; dishes with *poblano* aioli (chili mayonnaise) or cilantro pesto (nuts, oil, cilantro); refried beans.

MIDDLE EASTERN

Lamb, rather than beef, is featured in Middle Eastern cuisine. Hearty stews, often based on rice or couscous, are enriched by mixtures of nuts, currants, and spices.

■ *Low in fat*: Pita bread; *ful medames* (fava beans and chickpeas); any kind of salads, such as tabbouleh or *fattoush*; lentil soup; rice pilaf; shish kebab; kibbe (baked meat with wheat, onions, and pine nuts); *kofta* (grilled ground beef with parsley and onions).

■ *High in fat*: *Saganaki* (contains fried cheese and butter); falafel (deep-fried); *kasseri* (cheese and butter casserole).

SPANISH

■ *Low in fat*: Tapas, which are Spanish appetizers, such as *chicharron de gallina* (chicken in lemon and pepper sauce), *escabeche* (fish marinated in wine vinegar), gazpacho, a cold vegetable soup; or for entrées, paella, a sort of rice stew with vegetables and seafood, pork, or chicken; fish or chicken baked in *picada* (sweet and sour) sauce.

■ *High in fat*: *Jamón serrano* (fatty ham); *tortillas española* (potato and onion omelette); *chorizo salteado* (pork sausage in oil).

THAI

■ *Low in fat*: Lemongrass soups, such as *tom yum koong* (shrimp and chili paste); stir-fried noodles and sprouts; sautéed ginger beef or chicken (request a light touch with the oil).

■ *High in fat*: Coconut-based soups and curries, peanut sauce, deep-fried dishes, such as royal tofu and hot Thai catfish.

VEGETARIANISM MADE EASY

People who adopt the recommended low-fat, high-fiber diet may discover that they have stumbled into vegetarianism. If you are considering switching to this type of diet, here are some suggestions.

CUT BACK GRADUALLY

■ If you are in the habit of eating meat, poultry, or fish for lunch and dinner, limit such choices to one meal a day, then cut back further.

■ Decrease or forgo the meat in your family's favorite dishes. For example, use more beans and less ground beef in a chili recipe; layer lasagna with ricotta or fresh vegetables instead of meat.

■ When you do eat meat, poultry, or fish, use it sparingly to flavor dishes, such as rice and pasta entrées.

■ If you substitute cheese and other dairy products for red meat, choose low-fat or nonfat varieties whenever possible.

■ Apply the same rules to a vegetarian diet as to any other eating plan: variety, moderation, and balance. Except among very strict vegetarians, deficiencies of vitamins and minerals rarely occur (see chart on facing page).

■ Keep experimenting. Scour cookbooks and magazines to find new recipes using beans, pasta, whole grains, and rice.

GET INTO GRAINS

■ Millet: It's not just bird food. High in protein, millet is an excellent source of B vitamins and several minerals, including iron. Use whole hulled millet in place of rice in stuffings and side dishes. Try puffed millet as an ingredient in breads and puddings.

■ Buckwheat: Its nutty flavor and crunchy texture contribute to entrées and side dishes. Buckwheat can also be eaten for breakfast.

■ Barley: Whole hulled barley is more nutritious than pearled barley, which loses its outer layer in processing. Use barley as a side dish, in soups, or as a breakfast cereal.

■ Quinoa (pronounced KEEN-wa): This ancient Peruvian grain is rich in iron, crunchy, and has a light, nutty flavor. Try it in puddings, stews, and soups or as a hot cereal.

■ Rice: Don't limit yourself to white or brown rice. Try basmati, wild rice, and other types.

■ Boost the flavor of grains by cooking them in wine, vegetable stock, tomato sauce, or with herbs and spices.

■ Stay away from seasoned rice mixes, which generally contain oil, sugar, and sodium.

> **Quick-cooking versions of such grains as barley, brown rice, and bulgur can cut the preparation time by half or more.**

DABBLE IN BEANS

■ Dried peas and beans, which are a staple of vegetarian diets around the world, provide protein, B vitamins, calcium, iron, zinc, and fiber. Red lentils are one of the quickest to prepare, requiring no soaking and less than 20 minutes of cooking. Others, like black-eyed peas and black, fava, lima, navy, and pinto beans, need several hours of soaking before they can be cooked.

■ To shorten soaking time, place beans in a pot, cover with water and bring to a boil. Turn off the burner and let the beans stand, covered, in the pot for an hour or two.

■ Reduce the chance that beans will cause gas and bloating by draining off the water they were soaked in. After soaking them, cook beans in fresh water, then discard that liquid, too.

■ Use canned beans occasionally to save time. Be sure to rinse the beans, which often have added sodium in the canning liquid.

■ Keep dried beans in an airtight container in a cool room; their shelf life is up to a year. Cooked beans can be stored in the refrigerator for five days and in the freezer for six months.

Too much fiber too soon can produce stomach discomfort. Increase your consumption of such high-fiber foods as beans and grains gradually. And be sure to drink plenty of water and other liquids.

A MEAL PLAN

Here's what a healthy lacto-ovo vegetarian diet should include daily:

■ Four or more servings of vegetables

■ Three or more servings of fruit

■ Six or more servings of whole grains (such as bread, cereal, rice, and pasta)

■ Two or three servings of nuts, tofu (a soybean product), and legumes (dried peas and beans)

■ Up to three servings of low-fat dairy foods

■ An occasional egg or egg whites

PUT WORRIES ASIDE

■ Forget the old warning that strict vegetarians, or vegans (whose diet excludes eggs, dairy products, meat, poultry, and fish), must mix and match plant foods carefully at each meal to make sure that they get enough protein. Experts now believe that eating a variety of plant-based foods daily supplies adequate protein. Good sources of plant-based protein include nuts, seeds, dried peas and beans, green peas, tofu, pasta, and rice.

■ To get as much protein from plant foods as you could get from a three-ounce serving of sirloin steak or pork loin, eat a half cup each of green peas, lentils, and soybeans.

■ Iron and zinc deficiencies occur very rarely. In general, if a vegan consumes a good assortment of foods, the only potential nutritional problem will be a vitamin B_{12} deficiency, which is curable when caught early.

■ Vegetarians who avoid all animal foods can help to minimize the risk of a vitamin B_{12} deficiency by drinking fortified soy milk and eating fortified cereals. Also see the suggestions in the box below.

A GUIDE TO VEGETARIANISM

Depending on their food preferences, vegetarians generally fall into one of these three categories:

	What they eat	Benefits	Suggestions
Semi-vegetarians	Eat little or no red meat; eat poultry, fish, and dairy products	May have a reduced risk for some cancers; poultry and fish tend to be less fatty than red meat and contain many of the same nutrients as red meat (although not in high amounts)	Consume plenty of iron-rich foods; use cast-iron pots for cooking foods, boost iron absorption by including foods high in vitamin C with each meal; include foods high in zinc, such as shellfish, seeds, and tofu
Lacto-ovo Vegetarians	Eat no meat, poultry, or fish but do consume dairy products and eggs	May reduce risk of some cancers and heart disease; dairy products are excellent sources of calcium and protein	Follow suggestions above for iron and zinc; choose low-fat or nonfat dairy products; limit egg yolks to 3 or 4 per week to avoid excess dietary cholesterol
Vegans	Eat only plant foods, no animal products	Reduces risk of some cancers, heart disease, adult-onset diabetes, and obesity	Consult a registered dietitian or other nutrition expert to ensure that you are getting enough calories, protein, vitamins, and minerals. Supplements of vitamin B_{12} may be needed

SMART SHOPPING, SAFE STORAGE

Although supermarkets carry some 25,000 different products, most people eat the same 10 to 15 dishes, week in and week out. Here's how to make better use of your shopping opportunities while improving your family's diet.

FIRST THINGS FIRST

■ As you walk down the aisles of your supermarket, repeat to yourself: "less fat, more fiber." That is the essence of the best scientific wisdom where diet is concerned.

■ Think of the departments—dairy, produce, meat, and so on—as separate stores. Some are safe to browse in, others are not. Obviously, it's safe to explore the produce department in a leisurely way, but it's probably best to zip in and out of the baked-goods department as quickly as possible.

■ Organize your shopping so that cold foods go in the cart last. After leaving the store, take cold foods directly home and refrigerate. Never leave food (cold or not) in a hot car.

Never shop on an empty stomach if you can avoid it. A cup of soup or a plain bagel will take the edge off your appetite and reduce the temptation to buy calorie-rich "comfort foods."

POINTERS FOR BUYING PRODUCE

■ Few vegetables are more firmly entrenched in American diets than iceberg lettuce; yet few have less nutritional value. There are, however, many greens that have both interesting flavors and more nutrients. Among them are Romaine (strong taste, used in Caesar salads), watercress (pungent; add to salads or sandwiches), red leaf lettuce (sweet-tasting), spinach (high in folacin and potassium), arugula (high in vitamin A; strong, peppery flavor), Boston lettuce (sweet and delicate in flavor), chicory or curly endive (slightly bitter, mixes well with milder greens; radicchio is a red variety), parsley (a good source of vitamin A, though it's often used as just a garnish), and dandelion (pungent; the youngest leaves make the best-tasting salads).

■ Fortunately, vegetables and fruit not only are cheapest when in season but taste best, too. Nature's ripening, not the hothouse, often provides the fullest flavor. So, however beautiful out-of-season strawberries or blueberries may look, you won't miss much if you pass them by. (However, certain items, such as bananas, broccoli, carrots, cab-

Watercress

Red leaf lettuce

Spinach

Boston lettuce

Romaine

Arugula

bage, and lettuces, are in season year-round.)

■ Avoid vegetables in colored plastic bags. For example, when you buy carrots in orange-colored cellophane, it's impossible to see if they're healthy-looking carrots or not.

■ As soon as vegetables and fruits are chopped up, they begin to lose some of their nutrients. Therefore, it's best to buy them uncut. However, if buying, say, precut carrots helps you to overcome your resistance to these vegetables, precut is better than none.

■ The rule on chopped vegetables and fruits does not apply to frozen foods. Many frozen varieties are as nutritious as the fresh versions.

■ When shopping for frozen vegetables, avoid those drenched in sauces.

■ It's common knowledge that citrus fruits are high in vitamin C, but so are many other fruits and vegetables, including melons, pineapple, strawberries, Brussels sprouts, peppers, kale, and cauliflower.

■ Produce that has deep color is frequently high in vitamins.

Red, yellow, and green peppers, for example, are high in vitamins A and C. With lettuce varieties, the general rule is, the greener the leaf, the higher the nutrient content.

■ Buy dried beans, also known as legumes, that are uniform in size and shape; they'll cook more evenly. Always look for bright colors. Faded color indicates that the legumes have been in storage too long. Also, cracks, pinhole marks, and discolorations are signs that legumes may not be fresh.

Nearly all vegetables and fruits are low in fat. The exceptions are avocados, olives, and coconuts.

SELECTION AND STORAGE OF PRODUCE

■ *Apples*. Firm, unbruised, free of wrinkles, good color. Because apples ripen quickly, they should never be stored at room temperature for more than a day or two. Keep in a plastic bag in the crisper in the refrigerator; they should remain fresh and crunchy for two to four weeks.

■ *Apricots*. Never shipped fully ripe. Select orange-

yellow fruit, relatively soft and plump. Avoid bruised fruit or that with a yellow-green tinge. Firm fruit will ripen quickly at room temperature away from direct sunlight in a well-ventilated place. Store ripe fruit in a plastic bag in the refrigerator, where it will keep for several days. Remember to remove apricots from the refrigerator 15 minutes or so before eating. Like cheese, apricots have a fuller, richer flavor when served at room temperature.

■ *Artichokes*. Compact, heavy, plump globes; large, tightly clinging, fleshy leaf scales, good green color. Baby artichokes can be eaten choke (the core) and all. When the tips of the leaves are hard or are spreading or separating, it's a sign that the artichoke is overripe and likely to be tough and fibrous. Sprinkle fresh artichokes with a little water, seal in a plastic bag, and keep in the refrigerator for up to a week. Do not freeze.

■ *Arugula*. In Italy, it's called rucola or rugala; in California, rocket. Older leaves are pungent. Look for fresh green color. Store in the refrigerator in a tightly sealed plastic bag for no more than two or three days, and wash gently but thoroughly before using.

■ *Asparagus*. Firm, compact closed tips. Select the greenest asparagus; the farther down the stem the green extends, the fresher the vegetable. Avoid angular or flat stalks, which indicate woodiness. Also steer clear of asparagus stored at room temperature or with the ends

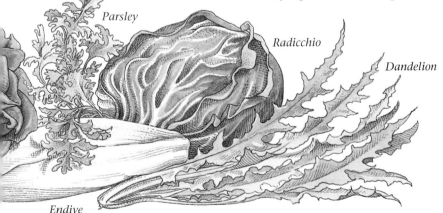

Parsley

Radicchio

Dandelion

Endive

soaking in water. To store, wrap the stem ends in moist paper toweling and refrigerate in a plastic bag for no more than two days.

■ *Avocados*. Heavy for their size, not wilted or bruised. Allow to ripen at room temperature, preferably in a paper bag. When ripe, they may be kept in the refrigerator for up to one week.

■ *Bananas*. Yellow or green, plump, not bruised or split. Avoid grayish yellow fruit, which indicates a chilling injury. Ripen fast at room temperature. When they are at the preferred stage of ripeness, eat immediately.

We are constantly told not to put bananas in the refrigerator, but it is perfectly safe to do so. The skin of a ripened (yellow) banana will turn brown in the refrigerator, but the flesh will keep for two or more days.

■ *Beans* (green). Clear green, pods that are free of scars and discolorations, small seeds; avoid any bulging with seeds. Should feel velvety; snapping does not necessarily indicate freshness. Use promptly or refrigerate in a plastic bag for no more than two or three days. Wash just before using.

■ *Beets*. Firm, with deep red-violet color, sprightly tops. Smaller beets are apt to have the best flavor and texture. Snap tops off after purchasing: they draw water and rob beets of nutrients. Refrigerate unwashed beets in a plastic bag for up to two weeks.

■ *Berries* (all kinds). Choose berries that are dry, free of bruising, molding, or shriveling; no sign of leaking. If you can't eat them immediately, store them, unwashed, in the refrigerator for no more than a day or two.

■ *Broccoli*. Compact, closed bud clusters. Dark green with a purplish cast. No yellow flowers or wilted leaves. To store, wrap in plastic, unwashed; use within five days. If the outer skin is tough (which happens when broccoli is grown in cool weather), remove a thin layer of skin with a vegetable peeler before cooking.

■ *Cabbage* (green, red, savoy). Heavy in relation to size, with three or four green outer leaves on green varieties. Select cabbage that still has some of its outer leaves firmly attached to the stem. Avoid yellowing leaves, splits, softness, and puffiness.

Store in plastic bag in refrigerator. Green and red cabbage will last for a week or more; savoy for several days.

■ *Cantaloupe*. Smoothly rounded; depressed smooth scar at stem end, slight softness at blossom end. Golden color. Under gentle pressure, ripe melon should "give" slightly; distinctive melony aroma indicates ripeness. If not ripe, keep at room temperature, out of direct sunlight, for several days. It can then be stored in the refrigerator in plastic for several days.

■ *Carrots*. Firm, smooth, well-shaped, good orange color. Tops, if still attached, should be fresh and bright green. Remove tops after purchasing. As with beet greens, carrot tops rob nutrients. Avoid carrots that are wilted, flabby, soft, shriveled, rough, or cracked. Small to medium carrots are likely to be sweeter-tasting than the larger ones.

Wrapped in plastic, carrots

keep well in the crisper of the refrigerator for two to three weeks. Flabby carrots sometimes regain firmness when soaked in ice water.

■ *Cauliflower.* White to creamy white, clean, firm, compact, purplish varieties sometimes available. Leaves should be fresh and green. Avoid open flower clusters, spotted curds (they indicate bruising), heads with tops sliced off. Wrap the head in plastic and keep in the refrigerator for up to a week. Wash just before cooking.

■ *Celery.* Green outer stalks, crisp, clean, thick. Soft stalks are a sign of age; excessively hard stalks may be stringy or woody. Wrap celery tightly in plastic and keep in the refrigerator for a week or more. If celery becomes limp, it can often be restored by soaking in ice water.

■ *Cherries.* Firm, highly colored (ranging from bright red to nearly black). Do not buy if soft, sticky, shriveled, or moldy. Cherries should be refrigerated as soon as possible after purchase. Store in plastic bags in crisper; they'll keep for at least two days. Wash just before eating.

■ *Corn.* Yellow or white with fresh green husks. Should be cooked the day it is picked, if possible. If this is impossible, remove the husks and silks, dip corn in a cold water bath, and wrap with plastic wrap. Store in the crisper; use within two days.

■ *Cranberries.* Plump, lustrous, firm, red to reddish black. Reject dull, soft, shriveled, or sticky berries. Cran-

berries may be frozen directly in freezer bags and will keep for up to nine months. Do not thaw before cooking but follow recipe directions using frozen berries.

■ *Cucumbers.* Reject cucumbers that are yellow, large in size, puffy, withered, or shriveled. Do not wash before refrigerating. All varieties keep well in the crisper for three to four days.

· ·

Except in summer, when local produce is available, most cucumbers you buy will be coated with a nontoxic wax, which makes them look shiny and helps to preserve them. If desired, remove the wax with a soft vegetable brush, or peel the cucumber, though peeling will diminish its nutritive value.

· ·

■ *Grapefruit.* White usually has a stronger flavor than pink. Firm, springy; not soft, puffy, or loose-skinned. Heavy fruit has thin skins, more juice. Fruit with somewhat pointed stem ends tends to be thick-skinned. Skin that has russet or brownish markings or greenish tint does not indicate poor quality. Grapefruit will keep at room temperature for up to a week. To store, keep, covered, in the crisper in the refrigerator for up to two weeks.

■ *Grapes.* Green stems with smooth, plump fruit, not sticky. Dry stems indicate old age. Grapes do not continue to ripen after they are picked. The best way to test

for sweetness is to taste one. Grapes are perishable and should be refrigerated as soon as possible after purchase. Store grapes in a plastic bag in the refrigerator, where they will keep for up to five days. Wash gently and serve grapes chilled for best flavor.

■ *Honeydew.* Creamy yellow color and velvety surface show ripeness; blossom end should be soft. It's difficult to know if the fruit will be sweet, but seek out fragrant aroma. Ripen melons at room temperature, away from direct sunlight, for several days. Then refrigerate in a plastic bag for up to a week.

■ *Leeks.* Green tops with medium-size necks; white at least two or three inches from the roots, which should be young, crisp, and tender. Avoid yellowed, wilted tops, which indicate age. Refrigerate in a sealed plastic bag for up to a week.

■ *Lemons.* Rich yellow color, thin-skinned, heavy for their size, moderately firm. Tip should be full. Lemon will keep at room temperature for up to a week when stored away from heat and direct sunlight. For longer storage, seal lemons in a plastic bag and place in the covered vegetable crisper of the refrigerator, where they will keep for two to three weeks.

■ *Limes.* Persians are bright green, heavy for their size. Avoid those with purple or brown irregular-shaped spots. Store at room temperature for a week or in a sealed plastic bag in the refrigerator for three weeks.

To extract the most juice from lemons and limes, roll them firmly on a countertop with the palm of your hand before squeezing them.

■ *Mangoes*. Varying in color from green with yellowish tinge to red. Red and yellow increase as fruit ripens. Reject those with grayish discolorations, pitting, or black spots, or ones that feel mushy. Keep mangoes at room temperature until they are quite soft, then eat promptly. If you have to refrigerate them, mangoes will keep a day or two after they ripen.

■ *Mushrooms*. White or brown, free of open caps, pitting, or discoloration. Caps are more tender than stems. Let any that feel damp dry out at room temperature, but do not wash before refrigerating. Keep mushrooms in a brown paper bag covered with a damp paper towel, which will keep them fresh for four or five days. Clean with a damp paper towel just before using.

■ *Nectarines*. Plump, highly colored, unblemished. Reject hard, dull fruit with signs of shriveling. Ripe nectarines will keep in a plastic bag for several days in the refrigerator.

■ *Onions*. Bright and hard without sprouts; heavy for size. Those with a thick, tough, woody, or open neck will be acceptable, but not the best. Moisture at the neck is a sign of decay. When kept dry and cool, onions will last for three or four weeks.

■ *Oranges*. For juice: firm, heavy, thin-skinned; for eating: slightly thicker skins are best. Color is no guide, as Florida oranges may be dyed. Avoid oranges that are light, puffy, or spongy; they lack juice. Oranges will keep at room temperature for a week to 10 days when stored away from heat and direct sunlight. For longer storage, place oranges in the refrigerator in the covered vegetable crisper. They will keep there for two to three weeks.

■ *Papayas*. Medium rather than large fruit, well colored, at least half yellowish. Smooth skin, unbruised, with no signs of shriveling. Ripen in perforated paper bag at room temperature or, more slowly, in refrigerator, until yellow all over. Refrigerated, ripened papayas will keep for a week.

■ *Parsnips*. Pale, cream-colored. Choose firm, fairly smooth, well-shaped parsnips without soft, straggly rootlets. Flavor is enhanced by cold storage in the refrigerator. Large parsnips are tough. Discard the tops and refrigerate in a plastic bag in the crisper, where parsnips will keep from one to four weeks, depending on the quality of the vegetable.

■ *Peaches*. Yellowish background color and red blush, general absence of greenness. Store ripe peaches in the refrigerator, spread out in a single layer to minimize bruising, for up to a week.

■ *Pears*. Firm, not wilted or shriveled. When ripe, Bartlett is yellow, Anjou green or greenish yellow, Bosc dark yellow with cinnamon-russet overlay. Store in a plastic bag in the refrigerator, where they will keep for up to five days.

■ *Peas (green)*. Uniformly green, long pod, not too full. Because their sugar turns to starch quickly, peas should be consumed promptly. If they must be stored, keep them in a plastic bag in the refrigerator for a day or two and shell just before using.

■ *Peppers*. Firm, bright, thick-fleshed. Color should be yellow, green, green and red, or completely red. Red peppers are ripe and sweet. Store in the crisper in a brown paper bag for up to two weeks. Green peppers generally stay fresh longer than mature red peppers.

■ *Pineapples*. Deep green crown leaves. Fragrance is a

sign of flavor. Pulling out crown leaves is not a reliable test of ripeness. Do not count on ripening a pineapple after it has been harvested. Choose as large a fruit as possible, and one that's heavy for its size—it will be juicier. Refrigeration is not recommended, but, if necessary, a pineapple will keep for several days wrapped in plastic.

■ *Plums*. Plump, full-colored. Choose fruit just beginning to soften. Plums keep for several days in a sealed plastic bag in the refrigerator.

Store such delicate, easily bruised fruits as berries and plums without washing them. Rinse the fruit just before you plan to eat it or cook it.

■ *Pomegranates*. Pink or bright-red rind. Reject hard and dry fruits. Store for several days at room temperature or refrigerate for up to two weeks.

■ *Potatoes*. Firm, relatively smooth, not badly cut or showing green; no sign of wilting or sprouts. Keep cool, dark, and well ventilated; a paper bag is a good storage container. At 7°C–10°C (45°F to 50°F), potatoes will keep well for several weeks, new potatoes for somewhat less time. At higher temperatures, potatoes will not last much more than a week, new potatoes for less time.

■ *Radishes*. Smooth, well formed, firm, crisp, without black spots or pits. Avoid those that are pithy, spongy, or wilted. If tops are on, they should be fresh and green. Remove tops after purchasing, as with beets and carrots. Refrigerate in a plastic bag for up to two weeks. Like celery, limp radishes will perk up after a brief bath in ice water.

■ *Rhubarb*. Firm, crisp, tender, bright, not-too-thin stalks. Younger stems have immature leaves and are the most tender (do *not* eat the leaves; they are toxic). Oversize stalks may be tough. Tenderness, crispness can be tested by puncturing the stalk. Use promptly or store stalks, wrapped in plastic, in the refrigerator crisper for up to one week.

■ *Spinach*. Good green color, though small yellowish-green leaves are okay. Large yellow leaves are not. Store unwashed in the refrigerator in a sealed plastic bag for no more than two or three days. Wash thoroughly just before using.

■ *Squash*. Soft-skin squash should be tender, crisp, and fairly heavy in relation to size. Hard-rind squashes should have no soft spots. Store in the refrigerator in a plastic bag for four to six days.

■ *Strawberries*. Clean, bright, solid red color, caps in place; free of moisture and mold. Discard any that are softened or bruised. Store with caps on in a single layer in the refrigerator. Berries will keep for several days.

■ *Sweet potatoes*. Firm, bright, good coloring. Keep dry; do not refrigerate. If stored at room temperature, use within a week. If stored in a cool, dry place, they will keep for several months.

■ *Tangerines*. Heavy for size, deep orange to almost red. Puffy appearance and feel are normal; softness is not. Store at room temperature for about a week or for several weeks in a sealed plastic bag in the refrigerator crisper.

■ *Tomatoes*. Buy only in season when local harvests are available. Bright red, firm but yielding to pressure. Out of season, buy cherry tomatoes; for cooking, plum tomatoes. For best taste, do not refrigerate and serve at room temperature.

■ *Turnips*. Smooth, firm. If tops are on, they should be green, young, and crisp. Remove after purchasing. Reject those with very large or coarse roots. To store, place in a plastic bag in the refrigerator crisper, where they will keep for about a week.

■ *Watercress.* Young, crisp, tender, rich medium-green leaves. Watercress is quite perishable, so refrigerate immediately in plastic bag. Use within a day or two of purchase. Wash just before using.

■ *Watermelons.* Firm, symmetrical, attractive, waxy bloom, lower side varying in color from somewhat yellowish to creamy yellow. Very hard melons with white or very pale green undersides are probably immature. Avoid those that look dehydrated. Sweetness in whole melons is hard to determine without plugging and tasting; in slices, look for flesh that has deep red color, firm texture, dark seeds, and no streaks. Uncut melons will keep at room temperature or in a cool room for several days. Cut melon, tightly wrapped in plastic, will keep in the refrigerator for several days.

> To get the most nutrients from produce, buy only what you can use in a few days. If fruits and vegetables tend to sit in your refrigerator for a week or more, you're better off with frozen produce—it may retain more vitamin C than fresh produce that becomes wilted or pallid before you can eat it.

CONCERNING EGGS

■ If you notice cartons of eggs sitting in the supermarket aisle waiting to be shelved, don't buy them. Eggs can easily spoil when they are left unrefrigerated.

■ Always open the carton and look at the eggs before you put it in your cart. If even one egg is cracked, select a new carton. Cracked eggs are particularly vulnerable to bacterial contamination, such as salmonella. And once a carton is soiled with raw egg, bacteria can spread to the surfaces of other eggs.

■ Store eggs in their carton on an inside shelf of the refrigerator. Putting them in the little slots on a refrigerator door, which is repeatedly opened and closed, can cause temperature fluctuations; this accelerates spoilage as well as increases the risk of breakage. The carton also prevents eggs from absorbing the odors and flavors of other foods.

THE DAIRY CASE

■ Gradually change from high-fat dairy products to low-fat. For example, if your family drinks whole milk (3.5 percent to 4 percent fat content), switch to 2 percent milk, then 1 percent. Eventually, you may want to buy only skim (fat-free) milk.

■ Don't put milk in your shopping cart until right before you're ready to pay. The less time that milk remains unrefrigerated, the less chance of its being spoiled.

■ Look for varieties of cheese that contain three grams of fat per ounce or less. That means you may have to switch from Cheddar, Swiss, and American cheeses. Fresh goat cheese—often sold at farmers' markets—is a tasty alternative.

STORING DAIRY PRODUCTS

■ Close milk and cream cartons tightly so they do not absorb the odors or flavors of other refrigerated products.

■ Keep nonfat dry milk in a tightly closed container at room temperature to prevent it from getting lumpy or stale.

■ Cover soft cheeses tightly and keep them refrigerated. Hard cheese does fine in a cool, dark place.

■ If mold develops on soft cheese, cottage cheese, yogurt, or sweet or sour cream, discard the entire product. If mold develops on hard cheese, cut off an area an inch in circumference around the mold. The rest will be edible.

BREAD, CEREAL, AND RICE

■ Check the label on the bread packaging. A fiber-rich loaf is one that contains two or more grams of fiber per slice. Also check for sodium. Choose brands with fewer than 200 milligrams per serving.

■ The most nutritious breads are the least refined; however, darker breads are not always more nutritious than highly refined white bread since caramel color is often added to rye, pumpernickel, and whole wheat breads.

■ Select cereals with whole grains—wheat, rye, oat, or corn—listed first on the label.

■ Watch out for granola-style cereals, which are often high in fat because nuts and oils have been added.

■ Know how to read the new cereal and bread labels so you can choose the most nutritious products. For example, a label that reads "high in oat bran" can appear only on

foods that meet the government's standards for "high" fiber or "good source" of fiber. Good sources have 2.5–4.9 grams per serving. High-fiber foods have at least 5 grams.

■ Try brown rice instead of polished, refined white rice or instant white rice. Brown rice contains much more fiber.

STORING GRAINS AND BREADS

■ Keep cereals, rice, and other grains in airtight containers. Exposure to light will destroy their riboflavin, so if the storage containers are glass, keep them in a dark cupboard.

■ Keep yeast breads wrapped in foil or plastic. Store them in a cool, dark place, like a breadbox. In hot, humid weather, place the bread in the refrigerator to protect against mold. If mold does develop, discard any bread, cereal, or grain product.

■ Store whole-grain flours and crackers at room temperature, except in hot weather.

BUYING MEAT AND POULTRY

■ Avoid meat with marbling or visible chunks of fat. Meat or pork cuts labeled round or loin are among the least fatty choices. These include sirloin, tenderloin, pork loin, and top, bottom, and eye round.

■ Choose cuts of meat labeled "select" instead of "choice" and "prime," which are the higher-fat versions.

■ If you buy packages of ground chicken or turkey, ask the butcher if skin or fat was ground into the product. Or

else buy a lean cut of meat, or a chicken or turkey breast, and ask your butcher to grind it without the skin or fat.

■ Avoid self-basting turkeys, which are often injected with oils high in saturated fat. (You can make your own basting liquid with polyunsaturated oils, such as corn or safflower oil.)

■ Try chicken or turkey hot dogs, which have less fat than other varieties. Limit your consumption of these products to twice a week.

KNOW YOUR FISH

■ Buy fish that is refrigerated or placed on thick layers of ice. Beware of stacked fillets or whole fish—the topmost layer may not be cold enough to prevent deterioration. This also applies to fish displayed under hot lights.

■ Sole, haddock, monkfish, pollock, scrod, catfish, and many other species are low in saturated fat and calories.

■ Shellfish, such as shrimp, crayfish, and lobster, are low in saturated fat but relatively high in cholesterol. If you are concerned about your cholesterol level, limit shellfish consumption to twice weekly.

■ Select fresh fish that is clear and shiny, not milky, and without a fishy odor.

■ Whole fish that is fresh will have clear eyes.

If you buy canned tuna, choose water-packed. Oil-packed tuna may have 7 to 13 times as much fat as the tuna in water.

STORING MEAT, POULTRY, AND FISH

■ Loosely wrap meat, poultry, and fish and place them in the coldest part of the refrigerator. The wrapping can be the original packaging, either plastic or butcher's paper. However, if there is a lot of blood on the paper, rewrap the item before storing it.

■ When freezing meat, do not use ordinary plastic wrap, which can make it vulnerable to freezer burn (a result of the loss of moisture from prolonged exposure to air). Instead, wrap it in two layers of plastic freezer paper.

■ If you plan to keep shellfish refrigerated more than a few hours, place it on ice or at below-freezing temperatures. Use it within two or three days.

DESSERTS AND SNACKS

■ Satisfy a craving for sweets with fresh fruit. Some good combinations: a sliced peach, 1/4 cup each of strawberries and blueberries, and 1/2 cup honeydew melon balls; a sliced banana, a sliced orange, and a tablespoon of raisins.

■ Many crackers are high in both fat and sodium. Rice cakes, flatbreads, crispbreads, and graham crackers are among the lowest in fat, and some brands are entirely without salt.

■ For low-fat cookies, choose vanilla-flavored wafers and gingersnaps.

THE DELI COUNTER

■ Choose freshly cooked roast beef, baked ham, or chicken or turkey breast. Avoid such high-fat processed meat as liv-

erwurst, bologna, and salami.

■ Ask to see the meat before it is sliced. If fat is visible, ask if another cut is available. If not, consider an alternative.

■ Steer clear of mayonnaise- and oil-based salads. If you prefer the convenience of ready-made salads, ask if they can be prepared with light mayonnaise, which has half the fat of the regular variety, or with fat-free dressing.

FOOD BY MAIL

Mail-order food has become a popular gift for friends and family members. Common sense demands that certain safety precautions be observed. Here are some facts to remember when sending or receiving food over long distances.

■ Be sure that the food is labeled properly. The packaging must indicate clearly that the item is perishable and the need for refrigeration, if any.

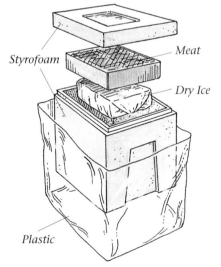

Styrofoam
Meat
Dry Ice
Plastic

■ Ask the supplier if the food will be shipped insulated or with a cold source. Dry ice is preferred. This may apply even to smoked, canned, or

vacuum-packed meat or poultry products.

■ Alert the recipient to expect a delivery, to ensure that someone is there when it is due to arrive. Neither the mail-order company nor the delivery company is responsible for the product if there is no one there to receive it.

■ When you receive a mail-order food product whose label says "Keep refrigerated," use it only if it arrived well chilled. Otherwise, you may be courting danger.

Follow handling directions carefully for dry ice. Do not touch it or inhale the fumes.

IF YOU LOSE POWER

Normally, set the refrigerator below 4°C (40°F) and the freezer at or below -18°C (0°F). If your power goes off, a full upright or chest freezer or a freezer compartment will keep food frozen for about two days. A half-full freezer will keep food frozen a day. Here's what to do if there is a sudden power outage.

■ Keep the freezer door shut as much as possible if you expect power to be restored fairly soon. Without power, the refrigerator section will keep food cool between four and six hours, depending on the kitchen temperature.

■ Add dry ice to the freezer unit; block ice can keep food on refrigerator shelves cool.

■ Refreeze food that still contains ice crystals or that feels refrigerator-cold when the power returns.

■ Take food to friends' freezers or a commercial freezer, or else use dry ice if you expect a prolonged power outage.

■ Discard any thawed food that has reached room temperature and remained there two hours or longer.

■ Throw away foods with a strange color or odor.

■ Don't smell moldy food— some molds can cause respiratory problems. Wrap up moldy food and discard it. Clean the refrigerator where it was sitting. Inspect foods nearby in case the mold has spread.

STORING LEFTOVERS

■ Transfer cooked food into shallow containers. Cover them tightly, and label, date, and refrigerate them promptly. Bacteria multiply rapidly in warm food: the bacterial content of unrefrigerated foods can double in 20 minutes.

■ Remove leftover stuffing from poultry and refrigerate separately.

■ Use refrigerated leftovers within a few days (see chart at right).

■ Reheat leftovers thoroughly in a microwave oven or double boiler to retain most of their vitamins, color, texture, and flavor. Wrap large pieces of meat in foil and reheat in the oven at 177°C (350°F).

■ Discard any food that is questionable in smell or appearance. Bacteria can grow readily in meats, poultry, fish, stuffing, gravy, cream sauce, and cream or custard desserts.

■ Foods that cause food poisoning often show no signs of spoilage, so don't rely entirely on taste, smell, or appearance.

COLD STORAGE

These short but safe time limits will help keep refrigerated food from spoiling or becoming dangerous to eat, and will keep frozen food at top quality.

Product	Kind	Refrigerator (4°C)	Freezer (-18°C)
Eggs	Fresh in shell	3 weeks	Don't freeze
	Raw yolks, whites	2-4 days	1 year
	Hard-cooked	1 week	Don't freeze
	Liquid pasteurized eggs or egg substitutes,		
	opened carton	3 days	Don't freeze
	unopened carton	10 days	1 year
Deli and Vacuum-Packed Products	Store-prepared (or home-made) egg, chicken, tuna, ham, macaroni salads	3-5 days	These products don't freeze well
	Store-cooked convenience meals	1-2 days	
Soups and Stews	Vegetable or meat added 	3-4 days	2-3 months
Hamburger, Ground, and Stew Meats	Hamburger and stew meats	1-2 days	3-4 months
	Ground turkey, veal, pork, lamb	1-2 days	3-4 months
Hot Dogs and Lunch Meats	Hot dogs,		In freezer wrap, 1-2 months 
	opened package	1 week	
	unopened package	2 weeks	
	Lunch meats,		
	opened package	3-5 days	
	unopened package	2 weeks	
Bacon and Sausage	Bacon	1 week	1 month
	Sausage, raw from pork, beef, turkey	1-2 days	1-2 months
	Smoked breakfast links, patties	1 week	1-2 months
	Hard sausage, pepperoni, jerky sticks	2-3 weeks	1-2 months
Ham, Corned Beef	Corned beef, in pouch with pickling juices	5-7 days	Drained, wrapped 1 month
	Ham, cooked whole	1 week	1-2 months
	Ham, cooked half or slices	3-4 days	1-2 months
Fresh Meat	Steaks, beef	3-5 days	8-12 months
	Chops, pork	3-5 days	4-6 months
	Chops, lamb	3-5 days	6-9 months
	Roasts, beef	3-5 days	6-12 months
	Roasts, lamb	3-5 days	6-9 months
	Roasts, pork and veal	3-5 days	4-6 months
Meat Leftovers	Cooked meat and meat dishes	3-4 days	2-3 months
	Gravy and meat broth	1-2 days	2-3 months
Fresh Poultry	Chicken or turkey, whole	1-2 days	1 year
	Chicken or turkey pieces	1-2 days	9 months
Cooked Poultry, Leftover	Fried chicken, plain pieces	3-4 days	4 months
	Cooked poultry dishes	3-4 days	4-6 months
	Pieces covered with broth, gravy	1-2 days	6 months

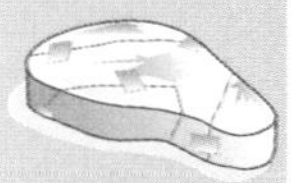

The cardinal rule: when in doubt, throw it out.

■ Exclude air when packing food for the freezer to reduce oxidation and loss of nutrients, flavor, and color. Fill containers of solid food to the top; containers of liquids, to within half an inch of the top.

■ When freezing leftovers, seal packages with freezer tape, label contents with a felt pen or wax pencil, and date them.

■ Once the food packages are solidly frozen, arrange them within the freezer to allow for circulation of air.

The smaller the container, the more quickly—and more safely—food will freeze and thaw.

NUTRIENT INTAKES

■ Health Canada has set guidelines for nutrition called Recommended Nutrient Intakes (or RNI's). They differ for men, women, and children of different ages. For example, a man aged 50-74 needs 9 mg of iron; a woman the same age needs 8 mg; a younger woman, who is menstruating, needs more—13 mg.

■ RNI's refer to intake over several days. So if your intake of a particular nutrient drops slightly below the suggested amount for a few days, your diet will still be adequate.

■ The Recommended Daily Intake (RDI) given on food labels refers only to vitamins and mineral nutrients. These are micronutrients, unlike nutrients such as protein, carbohydrates and fats, which are macronutrients.

Food labels list their vitamin and mineral content as a percentage of RDI.

CALCULATING FAT

■ Know how much fat you consume daily so that you can guard against heart disease and some types of cancer and control your weight.

■ For a general idea of your daily limit of fat grams, take your ideal body weight and divide it in half. For example, if you would like to weigh 130 pounds, aim for a limit of 65 grams of dietary fat daily. Consult a dietitian or physician for further guidance.

■ Read nutrition labels and use a guide listing the dietary fat in common foods.

The New Food Label

Prepared- and processed-food labels have been redesigned to make it easier to choose healthy products.

Serving sizes have been standardized, as shown on this box of cereal.

Knowing how many of the total calories come from fat can help you identify low-fat items.

The Recommended Daily Intake tells you what percentage of your daily requirements of vitamins and minerals this food product provides.

The ingredients list gives the ingredients used in the product, listed in the order of the amount used. The amount is based on the weight of the ingredient, not the volume.

NUTRITION INFORMATION
PER 30 g
SERVING CEREAL
(175 mL, 3/4 CUP)

ENERGY	Cal	100
	kJ	420
PROTEIN	g	3.0
FAT	g	24.0
CARBOHYDRATE		4.4
SUGARS	g	16.6
STARCH	g	3.0
FIBRE	g	265
SODIUM	mg	168
POTASSIUM	mg	

PERCENTAGE OF RECOMMENDED DAILY INTAKE

THIAMIN	%	46
NIACIN	%	6
VITAMIN B$_6$	%	10
FOLACIN	%	8
IRON	%	28

INGREDIENTS
WHOLE WHEAT, WHEAT BRAN, SUGAR, SALT, MALT, THIAMIN HYDROCHLORIDE, PYRIDOXINE HYDROCHLORIDE, FOLIC ACID, REDUCED IRON, BHT

FOOD-LABEL GLOSSARY

The Food and Drug Regulations require standard descriptions in food labels that do not mislead or deceive the consumer.

■ *Free or without.* An amount that is nutritionally trivial and unlikely to have a physiological consequence.

■ *Low or little.* Follows specific limits set for foods labeled as low-calorie, low-sodium, low in cholesterol, etc.

■ *More.* Contains a higher proportion of a particular nutrient (say, dietary fiber, potassium, protein, or an essential vitamin or mineral, such as calcium) than the reference food that it resembles.

■ *High in.* Has a protein rate of 20 percent or more, or 15 percent or more of the RDI for vitamins and minerals.

■ *Excellent source.* Has a protein rating of 40 percent or more.

■ *Light (or lite).* These terms must qualify a calorie or nutrient content. If they refer to calories, for example, the product must contain 50 percent or fewer calories per serving than the original product, and provide no more than 15 calories per average serving. If used for sodium content, they should mean that there is 50 percent less sodium in the product than if the food were not described as low-sodium.

■ *Calorie free.* Fewer than 1 calorie per serving.

■ *Low calorie.* At least 50 percent fewer calories.

■ *Calorie-reduced.* At least 50 percent fewer calories per 100-gram serving than the reference food.

■ *Sugar free.* 0.25 percent or less available carbohydrate.

■ *Reduced sugar.* At least 25 percent less sugar per serving than the reference food.

■ *High in fiber.* 4 grams or more of dietary fiber per serving. (Foods making high-fiber claims must meet the definition for low fat, or the level of total fat must appear next to the high-fiber claim.)

■ *Source of fiber.* 2 grams or more of dietary fiber per serving.

■ *More or added fiber.* At least 25 percent more fiber per serving than the reference food.

■ *Fat free.* Less than 0.1 gram of fat per 100-gram serving.

■ *Free of saturated fats.* Less than 0.1 gram of saturated fat per serving and the level of trans fatty acids does not exceed 1 percent of total fat.

■ *Low fat.* Contains 3 grams or less of fat per serving.

■ *Reduced or less fat.* At least 25 percent less fat per serving than the reference food.

■ *Low saturated fat.* 2 grams or less per serving and not more than 15 percent of calories from saturated fatty acids.

■ *Source of, or contains, polyunsaturates.* At least 2 grams of polyunsaturated fats per serving.

■ *Cholesterol free.* 3 mg or less of cholesterol and 2 grams or less of saturated fat per serving.

■ *Low in cholesterol.* 20 mg or less of cholesterol and 2 grams or less of saturated fat per serving.

■ *Reduced or less cholesterol.* At least 25 percent less cholesterol and 2 grams or less of saturated fat per serving than the reference food.

■ *Sodium free.* 5 mg or less of sodium per serving.

■ *Low sodium.* 40 mg or less per 100-gram serving.

■ *No added salt.* No salt (NaCl) or other sodium salts.

■ *Reduced or less sodium.* At least 25 percent less per serving than reference food.

■ *Light in sodium.* Contains at least 50 percent less sodium than the reference food.

■ *Lean.* This term can be used to describe the fat content of meat, poultry, seafood, and game meat. For ground beef and ground pork it must refer to a fat content of 17 percent or less. For other meats, poultry and fish, the fat content should be 10 percent or less.

■ *Extra lean.* The term can be used to describe meat, poultry, seafood, and game meats that have less than 5 grams of fat, less than 2 grams of saturated fat, and less than 95 mg of cholesterol per serving and per 100 grams.

COOKING KNOW-HOW

You don't have to be an experienced cook to prepare appetizing dishes that are low in fat. But everyone who cooks and stores food does need to be fully informed of how to guard against food poisoning.

PREPARING MEAT, POULTRY, AND FISH

Animal foods contribute a substantial amount of fat to the diet. Here are ways to compensate.

■ Techniques that are good for cooking meat, poultry, and fish without adding calories from fat include broiling, braising, poaching, and roasting. Avoid frying.

■ Stir-frying and sautéing, which require adding fat, are fine periodically if you use oil cooking sprays or a small quantity of oil. Choose a non-stick skillet or a wok.

■ Heat the pan before adding oil when preparing to stir-fry. Heat makes the oil go further, so you can use the smallest possible quantity. Be careful when adding the oil, so that you avoid getting spattered.

■ When roasting chicken or turkey, elevate the bird on a roasting rack. Baste the fowl with wine, fruit juice, or broth instead of drippings.

■ Chill drippings, then skim off the fat before making gravy.

· · · · · · · · · · · · · · · · · · · ·

Remove the skin from chicken *after* cooking, not before, to reduce fat content. Skin locks in moisture, flavor, and heat-sensitive vitamins.

· · · · · · · · · · · · · · · · · · · ·

MICROWAVE SAFELY

It's easy to undercook foods in the microwave and leave dangerously high levels of bacteria alive. Proper cleaning and maintenance are also important to ensure safety.

■ Heed your manual's recommendations for both cooking and standing times. Also follow the instructions for operating procedures and safety precautions.

■ Be sure that children who use the microwave know the rules for its operation.

■ If there are signs of rusting inside the unit, have the oven repaired.

■ Clean the oven cavity and the door with water and a mild detergent. Do not use scouring pads or other abrasives.

■ Cover food to keep heat from dissipating before the center is cooked. While microwave ovens cook the surface of food rapidly, the center may not be cooked until minutes after the microwave has shut off.

■ If the microwave does not have a turntable, turn the dish several times during cooking for even heating.

■ Stir such foods as casseroles and soups.

■ Don't let food come in contact with plastic wrap in the microwave. Chemicals from the plastic can "migrate" into the food, with possibly harmful results.

■ Check for thorough cooking at the center of salty dishes, such as prepared dinners. Salt makes it tougher for microwaves to penetrate food. Salt may also produce dark

---

Implements for Low-fat Cooking

Most cooks already have on hand the basic equipment for preparing healthful meals. For foods items to stock up on, see page 80.

Nonstick skillet or wok, for stir-frying and sautéing meats and vegetables with minimal oil or other fat

Vegetable steamer, for retaining vitamins and minerals during cooking

Two heavy-gauge stainless steel saucepans: a medium or large one for pasta, a smaller one for soups and sauces

Skimmer/strainer to remove congealed fat from chilled soups and stews

Several sharp knives

Wire whisk

Wooden spoons and plastic spatula to avoid damaging nonstick cookware

Measuring cup and measuring spoons

Microwave cookware (if you own a microwave)

spots on vegetables during microwaving.

■ Stay close by the oven if you are using a microwave for popping corn. Some ovens can scorch popcorn in two minutes, and heat buildup can cause a fire.

BARBECUE SAFELY

■ Marinate meats to be grilled in the refrigerator, not on the counter, so bacteria won't have a chance to grow.

■ Place meat that has been parboiled or partially cooked on the grill immediately after removing it from a microwave, stovetop, or oven.

■ If you have to precook meat well ahead of serving time, cook it at a temperature high enough to destroy all bacteria, then refrigerate it.

■ Wash all utensils and plates that have come in contact with raw meat before using them for cooked foods.

■ Cook meat medium to well-done.

■ Keep vegetables or fruits that are intended for grilling separate from raw meat to avoid contamination.

■ Choose the leaner cuts of meat for grilling. Chemicals suspected of causing some types of cancer may be activated when fatty foods are smoked or grilled. However, most researchers feel that occasionally eating barbecued meat poses little hazard to your health.

■ To be on the safe side, keep fat from dripping onto the coals and producing chemical-laden smoke. Use a drip pan, wrap meat in foil, or place the meat over to the side, not directly over the coals. Raise the grill so it's farther from the heat source.

■ Cut away any of the meat that has been charred. Chemicals that are suspected of causing cancer accumulate on charred surfaces, so try to avoid eating such meat.

■ Use regular charcoal. Soft woods, such as mesquite, burn at a higher temperature than regular hardwood charcoal, which increases the risk of creating cancer-causing chemicals.

■ Serve food immediately if possible. When the outdoor temperature is 27°C (80°F) or more, serve within an hour. Otherwise, food should be served or refrigerated within two hours of cooking.

■ Practice environmentally friendly barbecuing: avoid lighter fluid and self-igniting briquets, which can create smog-forming emissions. Instead, use electric or other fire-starter devices, or switch to a gas grill.

■ If dripping fat causes the fire to flare up, douse it with a lettuce leaf. Place it over the flame.

● ●

If you want to use some marinade for a dip or basting sauce, reserve a portion in advance. Don't reuse marinade that's touched raw meat: it may be contaminated.

● ●

CHOOSING A CUTTING BOARD

■ Contrary to expectations, microbiologists at the University of Wisconsin at Madison have found wooden cutting boards to be more sanitary than plastic ones for cutting raw meat and poultry.

■ On some of the boards that were tested, nearly 100 percent of the bacteria were dead, or at least gone, in three minutes. (One theory: wood cells absorb and trap bacteria.) Old woods performed even better than new ones.

■ When contaminated boards were stored overnight, the wooden ones were bacteria-free the next morning, while the population soared on the plastic boards. And it wasn't easy to wash off the plastic, especially if the surface was scratched.

■ Whatever you use to cut poultry and meats, wash it afterward with soap and hot water. Be especially thorough if the board is covered with grease. Researchers suggest putting plastic in the dishwasher and using bleach on it.

VEGETABLES

■ Wash vegetables quickly when preparing to cook them, then drain or pat dry. Do not soak them. Vitamins and minerals dissolve in the soaking water.

■ The best way to eat most vegetables is raw or slightly cooked so they retain the maximum nutrients, color, and texture. Aim to cook vegetables just long enough to be softened but still remain somewhat crisp or crunchy. (Exceptions to this rule include potatoes, turnips, and acorn and butternut squash.)

■ Techniques recommended for cooking vegetables to the crisp-tender stage are steaming in a steamer basket or microwaving in a small amount of water.

■ Cook farm-fresh produce from a roadside stand for slightly less time than the same produce purchased at a supermarket, which is likely to be "older" and to have traveled farther.

■ For even cooking, cut to uniform size any vegetable that can't be prepared whole.

■ Preserve any liquid that remains after steaming or boiling vegetables: it contains vitamins and minerals that leached out during cooking. Use the liquid as soup stock, in casseroles, or in a sauce.

■ When cooking fruits and vegetables, consider a microwave oven. Fruits and vegetables are the best dietary sources of vitamin C—the vitamin most easily destroyed by heat. However, microwaves do not affect vitamin C.

LOW-FAT TRADE-OFFS

■ Substitute plain low-fat yogurt for sour cream or mayonnaise in dips and sauces. At 16 calories per two-tablespoon serving, it has one-third the calories of sour cream. It is also higher in protein and calcium and lower in fat. Or make Mock Sour Cream (see recipe on facing page).

■ For scrambled eggs, combine one whole egg with the white of a second egg. You'll have half the fat, calories, and cholesterol of two whole eggs. In many dessert recipes, you can often substitute two egg whites for one whole egg.

■ Use ground turkey or extra lean ground beef for chili, casseroles, or spaghetti sauce.

■ Increase the protein, fiber, and minerals in dishes by adding chickpeas, navy beans, lima beans, and other dried beans and peas, which are known as legumes. They add nutrients but relatively little fat to soups, stews, salads, and other dishes.

■ Chill soups and stews after cooking, then skim off any fat that congeals on top. Do the same with canned bouillon before cooking, or run an ice cube over the top to remove fat.

■ Rinse legumes carefully and remove any dirt or debris.

■ Soak dried peas and beans at least four hours in a large pot of water. For a speedier method, place the dried peas or beans in a saucepan, cover with an inch of water, and boil for two minutes. Remove the pan from the heat and let the legumes sit, covered, for an hour.

■ Substitute mashed cooked legumes for cheese and mayonnaise in dips and sandwich spreads. Not only are dried peas and beans lower in fat, but they also may help lower your LDL cholesterol, which is the so-called bad cholesterol.

■ Instead of drenching pasta with a cream sauce, try tossing the noodles with a lentil soup or other bean soup, either canned or homemade. You'll cut the fat content and boost your fiber intake.

■ Squeeze fresh lemon or lime juice onto steamed vegetables for zip without calories. If you can't do without the flavor of butter, use just enough to add the taste (less than a teaspoon) immediately before serving.

■ Add tofu to stir-fried vegetables and casseroles. Tofu—also known as bean curd—is made from soybeans. Rich in protein and minerals, cholesterol-free tofu is a soft cheese-like product that makes a good substitute for meat.

■ Refrigerate fresh bean curd submerged in water in a covered jar or bowl. Change the water daily to keep the bean curd fresh for several days.

■ If the bean curd is too soft and waterlogged when you want to use it, rinse out a piece of cheesecloth and line a strainer with two or three layers of it. Place the strainer over a bowl and let the bean curd drain there for several hours, or until it feels firm and the excess liquid is gone.

■ Purée bean curd in a food processor and use it in place of cream in soups.

Eat dried peas, dried beans, and nuts with rice, barley, bread, or other grains to get the most benefit from their protein.

OILS

■ Select olive, peanut, soy, canola, sesame, and walnut oil for cooking and salad dressings. These monounsaturated fats are considered healthy for the heart (except by those who advocate an extremely low-fat diet for persons with heart disease).

■ To cut calories and fat by

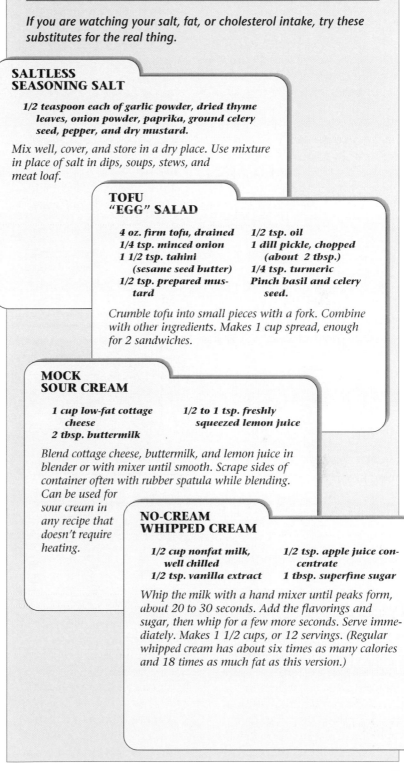

Tastebud Teasers

If you are watching your salt, fat, or cholesterol intake, try these substitutes for the real thing.

SALTLESS SEASONING SALT

1/2 teaspoon each of garlic powder, dried thyme leaves, onion powder, paprika, ground celery seed, pepper, and dry mustard.

Mix well, cover, and store in a dry place. Use mixture in place of salt in dips, soups, stews, and meat loaf.

TOFU "EGG" SALAD

*4 oz. firm tofu, drained
1/4 tsp. minced onion
1 1/2 tsp. tahini
   (sesame seed butter)
1/2 tsp. prepared mustard*

*1/2 tsp. oil
1 dill pickle, chopped
   (about 2 tbsp.)
1/4 tsp. turmeric
Pinch basil and celery
   seed.*

Crumble tofu into small pieces with a fork. Combine with other ingredients. Makes 1 cup spread, enough for 2 sandwiches.

MOCK SOUR CREAM

*1 cup low-fat cottage
   cheese
2 tbsp. buttermilk*

*1/2 to 1 tsp. freshly
   squeezed lemon juice*

Blend cottage cheese, buttermilk, and lemon juice in blender or with mixer until smooth. Scrape sides of container often with rubber spatula while blending. Can be used for sour cream in any recipe that doesn't require heating.

NO-CREAM WHIPPED CREAM

*1/2 cup nonfat milk,
   well chilled
1/2 tsp. vanilla extract*

*1/2 tsp. apple juice con-
   centrate
1 tbsp. superfine sugar*

Whip the milk with a hand mixer until peaks form, about 20 to 30 seconds. Add the flavorings and sugar, then whip for a few more seconds. Serve immediately. Makes 1 1/2 cups, or 12 servings. (Regular whipped cream has about six times as many calories and 18 times as much fat as this version.)

about a third, choose whipped butter or margarine rather than stock versions. Diet margarines can save you about half the calories of margarine and butter, which both have 100 calories per tablespoon.

■ When sautéing onions, garlic, or other vegetables or herbs, substitute vegetable-oil spray for oil or butter. One tablespoon of oil has 125 calories and 14 grams of fat; 1 tablespoon of butter has 100 calories and 11 grams of fat; 1 1/4 seconds of spraying adds up to 7 calories and less than 1 gram of fat.

> **Introduce new foods to your family in small amounts, then ask for a verdict. For example, add a few slices of kiwifruit to a dessert dish, or try mustard greens in a salad.**

DRESSING YOUR SALAD

To whittle down the fat and calorie content of your salad dressing, replace half the oil—or more than half—in dressing recipes with low-fat ingredients, or expanders.

■ In noncreamy dressing, substitute lemon or tomato juice, water, ketchup, or broth for part of the oil.

■ For a creamy dressing, use low-fat yogurt, buttermilk, tofu, or cottage cheese instead of mayonnaise, sweet cream, and sour cream. For a smooth texture, swirl the dressing in a blender or food processor for a few seconds.

■ Wash, drain, and dry salad greens well. Consider a salad-spinner device. Dressing sticks best to dry greens, so by drying greens, you'll be able to use less dressing for the same flavorful taste.

> **Sharpen kitchen knives regularly. You are more likely to cut yourself using a dull knife than a sharp one.**

BAKING

■ When baking cakes, try reducing the amount of sugar by one-third. You'll save 258 calories per one-third cup. You can also cut back the sugar in many cookie recipes by a third to a half without sacrificing much taste.

■ As tempting as it may be, don't taste cake or cookie batter that contains raw eggs. The eggs may be contaminated with salmonella bacteria (which are killed by cooking). Save your spoon-licking for the cake frosting if it is egg-free.

■ Add sweetness to baked goods and other foods with such spices as cinnamon and ginger. Vanilla and almond extracts are good sugar substitutes.

■ Replace half the white flour called for in most recipes with whole-wheat flour. You will get a bonus of more fiber, vitamins, and minerals, plus richer color and taste.

■ Bake crustless pies. For example, baked pumpkin-pie filling gives you a smooth, tasty dessert that is high in vitamin A and low in fat.

■ Be aware that carob desserts have virtually the same calories and fat content as the chocolate versions. The chief benefit of using carob when baking for children is that carob, unlike chocolate, has no caffeine.

WHEAT GERM, BROWN RICE, AND SPROUTS

■ Wheat germ, which is rich in protein, zinc, several B vitamins, and vitamin E, is great for sprinkling on cereals and salads and as a breading for fish and meat. But because it contains fat (polyunsaturated), wheat germ goes stale quickly, so keep it refrigerated.

■ Brown rice, which is high in fiber and minerals, is more nutritious than white. Soaking brown rice in water reduces the cooking time from 45 minutes to 25 minutes. If you cook the rice in the soaking water, you will preserve nutrients that may have leached out into the water.

■ Mung-bean and alfalfa sprouts are rich in nutrients, especially vitamin C. Use them in salads and stir-fry dishes, or in sandwiches.

REDUCING SALT

■ Give your favorite dishes a sodium-free makeover. Substitute dried or fresh herbs and spices, or a salt-free blend (see recipe on page 77). A good herb assortment includes basil, dillweed, rosemary, oregano, tarragon, and thyme. Recommended spices are allspice, cardamom, chili powder, cinnamon, cumin, curry powder, ground ginger, dry mustard, and nutmeg.

■ To cut down on salt, fill your pepper shaker with salt. Fewer and smaller holes make it flow slower and more sparsely than from a saltshaker. Eventually, you may want to get rid of the shaker to avoid adding table salt.
■ Soak salty foods like corned beef and sauerkraut in cold water for at least 15 minutes before cooking or eating. Change the water several times if you wish.
■ Reduce the salt in soup or other liquids heated over the stove by adding raw sliced potatoes. Remove the slices when they begin to turn soft.
■ Salt can be eliminated from any recipe except baked goods made with yeast, in which it is necessary to control the rising of the dough.

· ·
Read labels to avoid seasonings that are high in sodium. Many combination seasonings, such as lemon pepper and salad seasoning, include liberal amounts of salt.
· ·

AVOIDING FOOD POISONING

The keys are good hygiene, proper cooking temperatures for animal protein, and the rule "Keep hot foods hot and cold foods cold." Remember proper storage, too (see "Smart Shopping, Safe Storage," page 62).
■ Keep utensils, working surfaces, and your hands clean. Rinse your hands in warm, soapy water for 20 seconds before preparing food. Wash them thoroughly with soap and warm water after you've handled raw meat.
■ When canning foods, follow instructions carefully to avoid botulism, a potentially fatal form of food poisoning.
■ Thaw frozen meats—especially ground meat—in the refrigerator, and cook them as soon as they have defrosted.
■ Cook steaks, roasts, ribs, and chops until no pink remains. Cooking to "rare" may not kill the bacteria that can cause illness.
■ Cook poultry until there is no red in the joints and juices run clear when you prick it.
■ Cook fish so that it flakes with a fork, and it looks firm and opaque, not shiny.

Getting the Most from Convenience Foods

Perk up frozen, quick-cooking, or store-bought dishes by adding vegetables, cheese, and other foods. You can get nearly the same texture, flavor, and nutritional quality as home-cooked meals.

Add fresh mushrooms, onions, and peppers to bottled or canned spaghetti sauce.

Top frozen pizza with fresh tomatoes, peppers, and onions.

Add a single-serving can of tuna to a pasta salad from a salad bar.

Thin mayonnaise dressing on coleslaw with low-fat yogurt.

Spice up frozen or canned corn with lemon juice and salsa.

Add fresh onions, peppers, beans, chicken bouillon or tomato sauce to quick-cooking rice.

Add steamed zucchini, mushrooms, and a bit of grated cheese to a microwave "baked" potato.

Mix sliced yellow squash, broccoli florets, or green peas into a flavored rice-and-noodle casserole.

Add diced mushrooms, celery, carrots, and onions to prepared poultry-stuffing mixes.

Increase the calcium in instant mashed potatoes. Follow package directions but reverse the quantities of milk (use skim) and water called for.

■ Don't prepare or serve steak tartare or other raw-ground-meat dishes. These are among the type of foods most likely to cause food poisoning. Grinding equipment may harbor contaminants, and ground meat offers microorganisms more surfaces on which to multiply.

■ Cook ground meat until it is well-done. The center should look gray or brown and the juices should run clear, not pink or red.

■ When dining out with your family, check the food served to young children and the elderly before they eat. Make sure that they do not eat rare or undercooked hamburgers. The very young and the elderly are especially vulnerable to food poisoning.

■ Don't depend on the sniff test. Meat that has been contaminated with *E. coli* bacteria, a major cause of food poisoning, does not necessarily smell bad.

■ If you travel abroad, be cautious about what you eat (see "Eating and Drinking Here and Abroad," page 282).

■ Do not eat raw fin fish or shellfish if you have an immune disorder or are on chemotherapy. Although most fish you buy has been commercially frozen and thawed, freezing does not kill bacteria (it does kill most parasites).

STOCKING YOUR PANTRY AND REFRIGERATOR

When you have the ingredients within easy reach, preparing meals with balance and variety will not be hard. As a rule, use fresh herbs and spices rather than dried or powdered versions.

■ *Greek:* Olive oil, red and white wine vinegars; lemon juice; orzo (rice-shaped pasta), rice, short macaroni; cannellini beans, gigandes, lentils, dried yellow split peas; plain low-fat yogurt; canned and fresh tomatoes, eggplant, zucchini, carrots; garlic, oregano, rosemary, and parsley.

■ *Italian:* Balsamic and red wine vinegars; dried cannellini beans and chickpeas; extra-virgin olive oil; various types of dried pasta; coarse cornmeal; dried porcini mushrooms, canned and fresh Italian plum tomatoes, artichokes, asparagus, broccoli, cabbage, carrots, leeks, red peppers, spinach; Parmigiano-Reggiano cheese in chunks for grating; part-skim ricotta cheese; garlic, basil, oregano, rosemary, and sage.

■ *Mexican:* Corn tortillas, dried pinto and black beans, rice, white cornmeal; avocados, tomatoes, corn on the cob, zucchini and pumpkin squashes, jicama, cilantro; limes, apples, mangoes, papayas, pineapples; fresh and dried chilies.

■ *Chinese:* Short- or medium-grain rice, egg noodles; soy sauce; corn or peanut oil, sesame oil; fermented black beans, fresh ginger, scallions, garlic, and red-pepper flakes.

■ *French:* Olive oil, red wine vinegar; red wine, cognac, and port for sauces; Dijon mustard; defatted chicken stock; shallots, garlic, chervil, chives, parsley, and tarragon.

■ *Low-fat:* Chicken or beef bouillon; pasta, brown rice, and other types of grains; an assortment of whole-grain breads, rolls, pita, and bagels, which can be frozen; fresh fruits and vegetables (frozen produce as a backup); dried peas and beans.

MAKING FOOD TASTE BETTER

■ Choose foods for each meal that give you the maximum textural variety of chewiness and crunchiness, smoothness and roughness.

■ Use less fluid in soups or sauces to increase flavor intensity.

■ Use the greatest possible variety of spices. Fresh herbs are often more flavorful than dried herbs. Vary spices with different dishes.

■ Chew your food thoroughly to release all the taste- and scent-bearing molecules each bite contains.

■ Alternate bites of one type

of food with bites of another type. The olfactory receptors in your nose, which detect scents, adapt to a smell by roughly 50 percent in the first second or so after stimulation. This means that you will savor the most taste with the first bite, and then only half the taste sensation with the second bite.

■ Drink water to clear your palate as you eat.

■ Check your medications. Ask your doctor if one of them may decrease taste sensation. If so, have him or her suggest alternative medications that do not diminish taste.

■ Stop smoking, if you do smoke, for the sake of good taste, as well as for all the other benefits that come with quitting (see "Dealing with Addiction," page 378).

Cooking in iron pots adds iron to foods, which is a plus for nearly everyone, but especially for pregnant women and people who eat no meat, poultry, or fish. Foods high in acid, such as tomatoes, cause the most iron to leach out from the cookware.

COOKING SHORTCUTS

■ Don't stint on nutrients just because you don't feel like cooking. For a well-balanced meal with almost no effort, bake a potato (or two), and top it with leftover side dishes, for example, cooked broccoli, spinach, chili, or spaghetti sauce. Sprinkle some grated cheese on it.

■ Add a small amount of chopped nuts to ground meat for hamburger or meatloaf. Nuts are a delicious meat extender and, since they are relatively high in protein and vitamin E, more nutritious than most bread crumbs.

■ To help your family stoke up on beta-carotene, a health-enhancing substance found in orange vegetables (and some leafy green vegetables), grate a carrot or two into tomato sauces for spaghetti, lasagna, and other casseroles and pasta dishes.

■ It's easy to boost the protein content of vegetable and fruit salads, which tend to be loaded with carbohydrates but light on protein. Add ground toasted sesame seeds or toasted sunflower seeds.

■ Prepare a snack or appetizer quickly by slicing some raw vegetables and making a dip in the blender. Use cottage cheese with chopped onion and canned minced clams that have been drained. Or substitute chopped fresh parsley and garlic cloves for the clams.

■ To save time and effort in cleanup, boil pasta and cut-up stalks of broccoli, cauliflower, or other vegetables in the same pot.

■ For an easy first course or dessert, halve a grapefruit, drizzle some honey on top, and place on a baking sheet in the oven. Broil six inches from the heat for one to two minutes. Serve warm or cold.

■ When berries are in season, buy more than you need. Freeze the extra berries on a cookie sheet, then transfer them to a closed container for use throughout the year.

■ When preparing dishes to freeze, undercook slightly so that the food will retain its texture when reheated. Season the dishes with a light hand, then correct seasonings before serving. Freezing causes some spices to turn bitter or intensify in flavor.

■ Never place food on a paper towel or napkin for microwaving. Recycled paper products contain chemicals that may promote cancer.

■ When baking muffins, banana cake, or other recipes that call for two whole eggs, replace one of the yolks with a tablespoon or two of milk. You will halve the cholesterol content of the baked goods.

■ For a nutrient-packed breakfast or snack, place in a blender a large peach that is peeled, pitted, and quartered, 1/2 cup low-fat vanilla yogurt, 1 teaspoon honey, 1 ice cube, and a dash of cinnamon. Process until well blended.

After a big meal, pop a few fennel or anise seeds into your mouth. Italians and Greeks use these sweet herbs as an aid to digestion.

Soccer is a good exercise for young people, as it provides more aerobic benefits than many other team sports and is fairly safe. At this age children should sample a variety of activities and choose the ones they enjoy, playing for fun rather than competition.

CHAPTER 3

EXERCISE AND FITNESS

Whether they're weekend bicyclers or mall walkers, league bowlers or avid gardeners, people are learning to bring exercise into their daily routines. They're playing on company softball teams and training for triathlons, recognizing that fitness has to be a regular part of a healthy life, as standard as working and sleeping. And people are realizing that fitness needs to be a lifelong commitment, from childhood games to senior activities.

The key is to choose exercises you like, and to make sure they are convenient to your routine. Organize an after-work tennis group or jog around the park. Join a high-energy aerobics class or buy a set of barbells. Anything, as long as it gets you moving and you enjoy it. You'll see the results in all the areas of your life. So get out there and exercise—you've got nothing to lose but a few spare pounds.

Most marathon runners don't expect to win; their satisfaction comes from competing against themselves.

A LIFETIME CONCERN

Fitness has come a long way since the days of morning calisthenics. You might be surprised at how much fun exercise can be and how easy it is to fit regular workouts into your schedule.

ON YOUR MARK...

■ Consult your doctor before starting an exercise program if you are over 35, if you have any medical problems, or if any of the following risk factors apply to you: inactivity, overweight, high cholesterol, diabetes, family history of heart disease, smoking, or hypertension.

■ Muscles need time to adjust, so begin whatever activity you choose at a low level.

MAKING A PROGRAM

■ Structure your routine around two types of activity: aerobic exercise, such as walking, jogging, or swimming, which improves the cardiovascular system; and weight training, which builds the strength and endurance of specific muscles.

■ Perform aerobic exercises three times a week for approximately 20 to 30 minutes, including a warm-up and cooldown, depending on the intensity of the workout. Weight training can be done two to three times a week, also for 20 to 30 minutes each day.

■ Decide on your fitness goals. If you are working out to lose weight and gain endurance, jogging, swimming, and cross-country skiing are ideal choices. Those who want to gain weight should go easy on aerobic exercise, focusing instead on weight training. If meeting new people is important to you, consider team sports.

STAYING WITH IT

■ Setting goals is a useful way to measure your progress. Set weekly goals, which are more flexible and easier to meet than daily goals.

■ If you find workouts boring, try listening to music on a portable tape player. You can also listen to books on tape, now available in many libraries. However, you should do this only in safe areas—such as along the beach—and never in areas of heavy traffic.

■ Varying your exercise program will help you achieve a complete workout, prevent repetitive strain injuries, and fight boredom (see "Cross Training," page 110).

WHAT EXERCISE CAN DO

■ There's strong evidence that regular exercise can reduce the risk of coronary heart disease, high blood pressure, and sudden death from heart attack. It can also help fight obesity.

■ There are some indications that regular exercise may lower the risk of cancer and help lower high cholesterol levels.

■ Though there is no evidence that exercise will help prevent arthritis, gentle exercise—especially when done in water—may help relieve stiff joints.

Your Exercise Heart Rate

During aerobic workouts, your heart rate should stay within its training zone, defined as 60 to 85 percent of its maximum level.

   Here's how to find your training zone: Subtract your age from 220. Multiply that figure by .6 to find the low end of your zone, and by .85 to find the high end.

   Different levels of activity will require different heart rates. For low-level activities, such as walking, keep your heart rate at 60 to 70 percent of its maximum for 40 to 60 minutes. Jogging will require a heart rate of 70 to 85 percent for 18 to 25 minutes. And when running, keep your heart rate near its maximum for only 12 to 18 minutes.

HOW IT WORKS

■ Exercise helps with weight loss by raising the metabolic rate, not only during exercise but for hours afterward. A more rapid metabolic rate, which burns more fat, also increases your lean body mass. (In contrast, dieting without exercising will lower the metabolic rate. Low-calorie diets make the body work slower and result in the loss of lean body mass as well as fat.)

■ Exercise helps clean the arteries. It induces an increase in the amount of a protective cholesterol (HDL cholesterol) that is thought to clean the arteries by removing damaging cholesterol (LDL cholesterol).

■ Exercise may help prevent osteoporosis and fractures by increasing the calcium content of bones. Actually, not all exercises do this, only those that work against gravity (running or walking are effective; swimming is less so). Tennis players, for example, have thicker bones in their playing arms.

> **Diabetics should know that exercise helps make the body more sensitive to insulin. Exercise reduces fat, which interferes with the work of insulin. Type II diabetics may then be able to reduce their insulin requirements.**

FITNESS FOR THE MIND

■ Because exercise releases the hormone beta-endorphin, which has an effect similar to that of morphine, it is a natural tranquilizer and antidepressant. It may also help ease anxiety and stress.

■ Many who take up exercise report feeling more self-confident than when they were sedentary. They also experience heightened creativity and better moods.

> **Read up on your chosen sport. This will give you confidence by teaching you proper technique and helping you avoid common pitfalls.**

MEALS AND EXERCISE

What you eat and when you eat it will affect your endurance and, ultimately, your performance. So give your body the right fuels to run on.

■ Complex carbohydrates, also called starches, are your body's most important source of energy. They supply glucose, which is stored in the muscles and liver as glycogen. During a typical workout, it is glycogen that is used first as fuel. Glycogen is crucial for high-intensity activities, such as weight lifting. After 10 to 20 minutes of moderate exercise, the body will rely more heavily on fat stores for energy. Pasta, bread, cereal, fruits, and vegetables are all excellent sources of complex carbohydrates.

■ Before a workout, avoid simple carbohydrates, found in candy bars and sweetened sports drinks. Rather than giving you a quick energy boost, they trigger the release of insulin, which takes sugar out of the blood. This drop in the level of blood sugar may actually hinder sports performance for up to an hour.

■ Protein, which is needed to maintain and repair the body's cells, is the last substance the body draws on for energy. Protein is tapped once the available supplies of carbohydrates and fats have been used up.

■ While you should avoid a heavy pre-exercise meal, it is important to drink water before, during, and after exercise.

■ If you think you can improve the timing of your meals but aren't sure how, keep a log. Write down what you eat, the amount of food, and when it was eaten. Record how you felt before, during, and after exercise. Once you discover a pattern, you'll be able to plan your own training schedule and pre-workout meals.

■ Don't wait until you're thirsty to drink water when exercising; by then you may already have lost two to four pounds of fluid. During a workout, even mild dehydration can lead to reduced strength and endurance.

WARMING UP, COOLING DOWN

How you begin and end your exercise routine is just as important as the exercises themselves. Warming up and stretching will help you prevent injuries, while cooling down, stretching, and massage will keep your muscles limber.

You'll feel the Hamstring Stretch in the back of your thigh.

START WITH A WARM-UP

■ You'll find it's easier to stretch "warm" muscles than "cool" ones. If possible, run a few easy laps around a track, or jog in place, to warm yourself up.

■ A few minutes of jogging will increase blood flow to the muscles, making them easier to stretch and less likely to be injured.

A GOOD STRETCH

Stretching is convenient: you can do it at home or as a break from work or while waiting for the bus—anytime at all.

■ Stretch the muscles that you use in exercise or that you regularly use while you are at work.

■ Neck and shoulder stretches are especially good stress relievers. You may want to use this type of stretch while at work to relieve the tensions of a busy office day (for more stretches to do in the office, see "Workouts at Work," page 90).

■ When you begin a stretch, you should feel a slight tension in your muscles, but the stretch shouldn't hurt.

■ Stretch slowly, holding the position for 10 to 30 seconds. The tension will slowly diminish. If the tension intensifies or the stretch becomes painful, you're overstretching and should ease off.

■ After this slow stretch, increase the tension by moving a fraction of an inch farther. Hold this position for about 10 to 30 seconds. The tension will stay the same or gradually lessen. Perform each stretch three to five times.

■ Stay relaxed when you stretch; breathe deeply and be sure not to clench your teeth or hold your breath. Don't carry anxiety into your workouts.

■ Try to perform some mild stretching every day, or at least every other day. If you don't, muscle fibers will creep back to their original state.

■ Slow and steady stretching is easier on your body—never arch your back or bounce during a stretch.

STRETCHING BEFORE OR AFTER A WORKOUT?

■ As long as you start out slowly, you may not need to stretch before exercising. When done at a moderate pace, bicycling, jogging, swimming, and walking put few demands on your muscles and joints.

■ On the other hand, such sports as baseball, basketball, golf, tennis, downhill skiing, and racquetball require quick movements, putting more immediate demands on your muscles. If you haven't stretched beforehand, you will be vulnerable to muscle tears or more serious injuries.

The best way to build long-term flexibility is by stretching after a workout. Post-exercise stretching can also reduce the muscle aches you might feel the next day.

AVOIDING INJURIES

■ Make sure that all equipment you use is in good condition. Shoes should fit snugly and have sufficient cushioning.

■ Get advice from a trainer or physical therapist if injuries recur. Improperly hitting a

To do the Single-Knee-to-Chest Pull, grab your leg below the knee and behind the thigh.

backhand is a common cause of "tennis elbow," and poor running form can cause knee or back injuries.

■ Don't overdo stretching; take it easy on the days you don't feel your best. And keep in mind that injuries can be caused by overstretching as well as understretching.

■ Notice the warning signs that precede an overuse injury. Excessive fatigue, a tingling sensation, or a localized, light throbbing may signal an injury in the making.

■ Recurring injuries are often caused by too little recovery time. If you do sustain an injury, give it plenty of time to heal (see "Exercise Injuries," page 114).

■ Consider cross training to prevent injuries. Doing the same exercise too often could put you at risk for repetitive strain or overuse injuries (see "Cross Training," page 110).

The Calf Stretch is excellent for runners and walkers.

A Stretching Routine

Stretching before exercise is a great way to warm up your muscles and prevent injuries. Stretching is also valuable on its own: after doing these stretches for a week or two, you will be surprisingly more flexible all the time.

Hamstring Stretch (Above left): Sit on the floor with your legs positioned as shown. Reach forward along the extended leg until you feel a gentle stretch in your hamstrings, the muscles in the back of your thigh. Flex from the hips and keep your back straight. Hold, then repeat with the opposite leg.

Single-Knee-to-Chest Pull (Below, far left): Lie on your back with both knees bent and both feet flat on the floor. Grip your right leg and pull your thigh toward your chest, then extend the knee toward the ceiling. Hold, then repeat with the opposite leg.

Calf Stretch (Below, near left): Stand about two feet from a wall. Step forward with your right foot, bend your right knee, and extend your left leg behind you. Keep your back straight and aligned with the extended leg. Put your hands on the wall and lean forward, keeping both heels on the floor, until you feel your left calf muscle stretch. Hold, then repeat with the opposite leg.

Trunk Twist (Below right): Sit on the floor, with your legs crossed as shown. Rotate at the hips and look behind you. Keep your back straight and point the toes of the extended foot toward the ceiling. Hold, then switch leg positions and repeat.

Shoulder Stretch (Pictured in "Workouts at Work," page 90): Stand up straight, with your shoulders relaxed. Put your arms behind your back and clasp your hands. Lock your elbows and lift your arms until you feel a stretch in your arms, chest, and shoulders. Keep your shoulders down and as relaxed as possible. Hold. This stretch should be done without bending forward, and it should be avoided by those with shoulder problems or stiffness.

Hip and Thigh Stretch : Squat down so that your right leg is in front of you—forming a 90° angle, with your right knee directly above your right ankle—and your left leg extends behind you, with your left knee touching the floor. Press your pelvis forward and downward, holding the stretch for several seconds. Repeat with your left leg bent and your right leg stretched back.

Side-to-Side Neck Stretch : Gently push your right ear toward your right shoulder, then bring your head back to an upright position. Next lower your left ear toward your left shoulder. Repeat, without rolling your head from side to side.

Keep your back straight when doing the Trunk Twist.

RELAX WITH A MASSAGE

Massage not only feels great but can enhance your exercise program. You can use massage (or self-massage) before exercise to warm up and loosen your muscles or after exercise to help prevent stiff muscles and relieve muscle cramps.

PRE-EXERCISE MASSAGE

■ If it isn't possible to get a whole-body massage, concentrate on the main muscles you will be using. Most sports put a demand on the leg and back muscles, so massage these areas thoroughly.

■ Use fast movements for pre-exercise massage. Rapid pummeling or kneading will stimulate your muscles and increase the blood supply.

POST-EXERCISE MASSAGE

During exercise, metabolic waste products, such as lactic and carbolic acids and urea, are released into the muscles. The accumulation of these wastes can cause stiffness and pain. While the lymphatic system drains waste out of the cells, the process can take several hours or even days. Massage, with its pumping and stroking action, may speed the process.

■ It is essential to keep muscles warm after exercise, so make sure that you are in a well-heated room, or that you are warmly dressed.

■ If you have time, massage the whole body. Begin by massaging firmly, with movements going toward the heart. Finish with gentle, stroking motions.

■ If there is any sign of injury, avoid the area until you have consulted a doctor.

SPORT-BY-SPORT MASSAGE GUIDE

Every sport stresses particular muscles, and these are the ones you should focus on with pre- or post-exercise massage.

■ Skiing: Major leg muscles (hamstrings, quadriceps) and back muscles; cross-country skiers should also massage their shoulders.

■ Cycling: Muscles of the legs, back, and shoulders.

■ Tennis: Shoulder muscles (deltoids), the back, biceps, triceps, forearms, and legs.

■ Golf: Same as for tennis.

■ Running: Muscles of the legs and back, including the upper back and neck.

PROFESSIONAL MASSAGE

Swedish massage and Japanese shiatsu are the most common types of professional massage. Sports massage, a comparatively new technique, combines elements of the two.

■ Swedish massage is a deep, muscle-kneading treatment that stimulates the soft tissues, ligaments, and tendons. Swedish massage helps induce relaxation and relieve muscle soreness.

■ Shiatsu is also known as acupressure. Guided by the ancient belief that the body's life energy (called *qi*) runs through 12 major meridians, a shiatsu practitioner applies pressure to points where energy may be blocked. Because pressure is applied firmly, this type of massage may be uncomfortable, but the overall effect is invigorating.

■ Sports massage is vigorous and focuses on muscles that may have been stressed during a workout. Anyone who exercises regularly or suffers from a sports-related injury can benefit from this therapeutic massage.

FINDING A MASSAGE THERAPIST

■ How can you tell if massage therapists are competent? Ask what training they have received and check their references. If you live in a province that requires licensing, make sure the therapist is licensed. The Canadian Massage Therapist Alliance in Toronto (416-968-6487/2149) will put you in touch with your provincial organization for references.

■ A responsible massage therapist will ask about your medical history before beginning. People with diabetes, cardiac problems, varicose veins, high fever, cancer, or infectious diseases should avoid massage or should get the advice of a physician first.

Shiatsu uses pressure points on the body to stimulate and unblock energy pathways.

A MASSAGE PRIMER

You need to know only a few basic movements before you can give a complete body massage. Use oil—preferably a natural vegetable oil—to minimize contact with bare skin and provide a smoother surface. Also, position your partner on a table that is at a comfortable height for your back, or work on a pad on the floor, kneeling next to your partner. A bed, even with a firm mattress, is too soft a surface.

1. STROKING

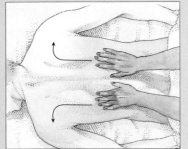

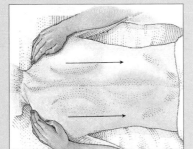

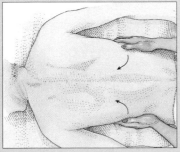

The rhythmic, flowing movements of stroking form the basis of a massage. You can do a whole-body massage using only stroking movements, giving variety by changing the speed and pressure of the strokes. Slow movements are calming, while brisk movements are stimulating.

2. KNEADING

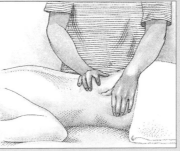

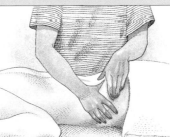

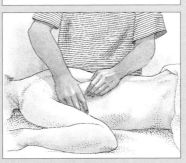

Named for its resemblance to kneading bread dough, this movement is useful on such fleshy areas as the shoulders, hips, and thighs. Light kneading will affect only the skin and the top layer of muscle, while firm kneading will stimulate deeper muscles.

3. PRESSURE

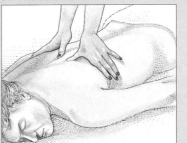

Use deep, direct pressure to release tension in the muscles on either side of the spine. Apply pressure steadily, working from the lower back to the shoulders. You'll want to use little oil when doing this, to keep your hands from sliding.

4. PERCUSSION

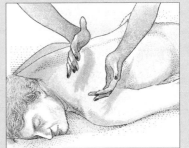

The movements of percussion should be light and springy and are useful on fleshy, muscular areas. Done quickly, percussion is stimulating, so use it at the end of a session to wake the subject up. Never use percussion over the kidneys or over bones or bruises.

WORKOUTS AT WORK

You spend one-third of your day at work, but that doesn't mean you have to spend that time without exercise. Knowing a few simple tips will help you fill your days with efficient workout breaks that not only keep you fit but relieve stress, too.

WORKDAY HINTS

Anyone who has tried to start a new exercise routine knows that half the battle is just getting yourself to stick with it. Try these suggestions to keep yourself on track.

■ Let your first step be two minutes of walking. Get off the bus one stop earlier.

■ Use small holes in your schedule—between meetings or appointments, for example—to stretch your limbs or do simple exercises.

■ Join a gym. Working out after work gives you an excuse to leave the office at a reasonable hour.

■ When traveling on business, consider staying in hotels that have exercise rooms.

USE ACTIVITY CUES

People exercise regularly when reminded to do so. Maybe you need to find the right reminder.

■ Wear a watch with a beeper.

■ Write a reminder on your desk calendar.

■ Put a note to yourself in your in-basket.

■ Ask a co-worker to remind you at a certain time.

BREAK FOR EXERCISE

Think of your exercise time as a break from your workday, not as a chore. The following exercises outline a simple routine that you can do at your desk to stretch out those stiff muscles. Add or delete exercises to tailor the program to your own needs.

■ Clock Stretch: This neck stretch is excellent for relieving the day's tensions. Imagine you are facing the hands of a huge clock. Turn your head to the left to look at 9 o'clock, then look to the right, to 3 o'clock. Look up to 12 o'clock and then down to 6 o'clock. Do the movements slowly, feeling the stretch in your neck muscles.

■ Shoulder Shrugs: Hunch your shoulders, moving them upward. Then rotate them forward, down, back, and up to your ears again. Do this slowly three times and then rotate them backward, down, forward, and up to your ears three times.

■ Apple Picker: Stretch your arms as though you were picking apples from a tree. Stand or remain seated as you reach up with your left arm, then with your right, stretching as far as you comfortably can.

■ Shoulder Stretch: While standing, reach behind you, grasping your hands behind your back. With your hands joined, lift your hands up as far as they will comfortably go. You should feel a stretch in the front of the shoulders.

■ Simple Massage: With your fingertips, massage the muscles between your shoulder blade and spine. Use firm, circular movements, paying attention to any tenderness or knots you might feel.

■ When doing any of these exercises, move only as far as is comfortable for you. Stop if you feel pain or great discomfort.

Any exercise counts. The benefits of simple routines, such as stretching or taking short walks, will add up when they are done often throughout the day.

COMMON OFFICE AILMENTS

Some aches are so common to office workers that doctors have labeled them "execupains." Most are caused by a mix of tension and poor posture. Here are the most common office aches, and hints for avoiding them:

■ Head and neck aches may be caused by cradling the phone with your shoulder or craning your neck to see the computer screen. Ease these aches with some gentle neck stretches, such as the Side-to-Side Neck Stretch, as described in "Warming Up, Cooling Down," page 87. You can also try the Isometric Neck Press: Press the palm of your left hand against the side of your head while resisting the pressure and holding your head steady. Repeat with the other hand. This will build neck strength, perhaps making future neck aches less common.

■ Sore jaws are often the result when people under pressure grind their teeth. Ease tension by opening your mouth halfway and gently swiveling your jaw left and right for 30 seconds.

■ People who sit all day are vulnerable to backaches, as the back muscles do most of the work of supporting the body of a seated person. Get a good, ergonomically designed chair; change position and move around often.

LIMBER UP YOUR HANDS

If you work at a computer or typewriter, your hands may feel tense and stiff at the end of the day. Use these simple techniques to relax them.

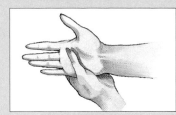

Massage the inside and outside of one hand with the thumb and fingers of the other.

Grasp the fingers of one hand and gently bend back the wrist. Hold this position for five seconds.

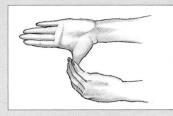

Gently pull your thumb down until you can feel the stretch. Hold this position for five seconds.

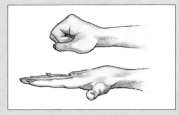

Clench one fist tightly, hold the clench, and then release, fanning out your fingers. Do this five times.

■ Stress often leads to shoulder pains, which in turn may cause pain along the arms. Try this stretch (pictured at left) to reduce tension: Bring your right arm in front of your body, across your chest. Hook your left arm under your right elbow and pull your right arm across the chest. Hold for 30 seconds, then release. Repeat this with your left arm.

■ Leg pains often result from back pains, when aches in the lower back move downward. To stretch your gluteal muscles, sit in a chair and place your left ankle on your right knee. Hold your left knee with your left hand and your left ankle with your right hand. Si-multaneously pull your left ankle and knee toward your right shoulder until you feel a stretch. Hold this position for 30 seconds, then release and repeat with the other side.

STRESS RELIEVERS

If you can't change the stress, change the way you react to it.

■ Aches and stiffness can be caused by sitting at computers or typewriters too long. Move around if you have been sitting longer than an hour.

■ Make a point of taking a 10-minute break every day.

■ To relax quickly, take four deep breaths, inhaling for seven seconds and exhaling for eight seconds.

ALL ABOUT AEROBICS

While aerobic dance, step aerobics, and water fitness will appeal to different people, all these exercises offer great cardiovascular workouts. They can help with weight loss and will make you feel more energetic all day long.

AEROBIC DANCE

Dance classes are a popular way to get the benefits of aerobic fitness. At their best, they combine energetic music, a knowledgeable instructor, and a fast-moving, friendly environment.

■ You can do aerobic dance at home or at a local gym. If you attend aerobics classes, you'll find that having a good

instructor is crucial to getting a good workout. Most gyms use several trainers, so if you aren't comfortable with one, try a different class.

■ Aerobic dance classes can vary greatly in how vigorous a workout they offer. You will find classes divided into the following three categories.

■ Non-impact aerobics require no jumping and exercise the large muscles of the thighs, rather than those of the feet and calves. Non-impact aerobics also use more arm movement than high-impact aerobics. As this type is the least stressful on the joints, it has the lowest rate of injury.

■ Low-impact aerobics are designed so that your feet stay close to the floor and only one foot leaves the floor at a time. It offers a brisk workout while keeping jerky movements to a minimum.

■ High-impact aerobics are best suited for the fit and experienced participant. Both feet leave the floor with frequent jumping. Classes use faster and more strenuous movements.

■ While you may see people using hand weights while doing aerobics, they are not recommended; their use could cause arm or shoulder strain.

CHOOSING A CLASS

■ For your own safety, check that the instructor has a CPR certificate and is certified by a recognized aerobic dance organization. Look for at least two years of experience.

■ You should have enough room to extend your arms in all directions and to move around freely. Ideally, each participant should have about six feet by six feet of space.

■ Check the floor in the aerobics area. You're better off exercising on floors of cushioned hardwood. Don't do aerobic exercises on concrete floors, even if they are carpeted.

■ Check that the workout includes a warm-up and a cool-down phase.

■ Check your pulse rate before and after an aerobics class. The instructor should also stop class once, giving you time to check your pulse.

■ For a good overall workout, look for aerobics classes that exercise the large muscles of the legs, hips, and back. Classes that tone specific areas are also available.

■ Make sure that all exercises are explained fully, so that you know the right way to do them. At least 20 minutes of the class should be a vigorous aerobic workout.

■ The music should be upbeat to motivate you, but it shouldn't be so loud that you can't hear the instructor.

If you enter an aerobics class in progress, don't try to keep up; go at half the pace or at whatever level you are comfortable with. Better still, wait until the next session begins and start fresh.

STEP AEROBICS

While it's one of the newest aerobic sports, step aerobics classes are already popular. Step classes widen the possible range of movement by letting you step on and off a low, cushioned bench.

■ Beginners may want to keep their hands on their hips, concentrating first on the basic steps. Leg movements should provide the basis of any aerobic dance exercise. Once you have mastered them, it will be easier to add arm movements.

■ If you plan to do step aerobics at home, you will need to buy a special bench designed just for that purpose. Pick a model that can be adjusted to different heights and that offers a large, stable platform to step on.

■ Beginners should keep the bench at a lower height, about 4 inches, while those who are more experienced

can set it at 8 to 12 inches. But don't try to do too much—setting the bench too high could put you at risk for knee injury or back strain.

■ To minimize possible stress to your Achilles tendon and the arch of your foot, stand no farther than one foot length from the bench.

■ When you step off the bench, place your foot on the floor toe first. Then lower your heel to the floor before taking the next step. Doing this will distribute your weight over the whole foot and reduce stress.

■ You need to know only a few basic steps to develop your own routine, and many gyms offer instructor-taught classes. If you prefer, home videos are available that teach step aerobics workouts.

■ Stop exercising if you feel pain. Be especially cautious if you've had a previous knee injury; a mild workout might be better for you.

. . . .

Look straight ahead when you bench-step. Staring down at your feet can cause neck and back pain.

. . . .

WATER AEROBICS

Many people are discovering that aerobic exercises are more fun when done in a pool. Besides offering the potential for a total-body workout, water aerobics are non-impact, so they are easy on the muscles and joints.

■ You'll find it easier if you join an existing water aerobics class. But if you decide to create your own routine, be sure to work out your upper body, midsection, and legs. Use the following four exercises to build a routine.

■ Arm Swirls: Stand in shoulder-deep water, then bend your knees slightly so that your arms and shoulders are fully submerged. Extend your arms on each side and rotate them forward in a circular motion, then backward. You can increase the intensity by flexing your wrists up and down; by cupping your hands to increase resistance; by making larger, more vigorous circles; or by walking or jogging as you move your arms.

■ Jumping Jacks: Stand in shoulder-deep water with your arms at your sides and your feet together. Rotate your hands so

Start with a few simple steps or with an instructor-taught class. *Once you have learned the basics, you can vary your routine by creating your own steps.*

that your palms face forward and then outward. Keeping your arms straight, force them up out of the water and touch them overhead. At the same time, jump up, spreading your legs in an inverted "V" position. Then turn your palms outward and bring your arms back to your sides as you bring your legs back together.

■ Leg Swings: Stand in the corner of the pool, with one hand on each ledge. Lift your left leg so that it is perpendicular to your body. Swing your leg from side to side, then repeat this action with your right leg. If that's too difficult, try doing the exercise with your knees bent.

■ Leg Lifts: Stand in water that is waist deep, with your back against the pool wall. Keeping your legs straight, lift them one at a time as high as they'll comfortably go. For an easier workout, bend your knees.

JUMPING ROPE

You haven't done it in years, right? Well, this simple exercise is more valuable than you may know.

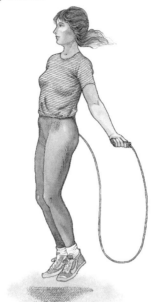

■ A piece of clothesline is all you need to get started. Or you can buy a specially made jump rope that has weighted handles and comfortable grips.

■ To measure the right length, stand with the jump rope running under both feet. The rope should be long enough to reach the level of your armpits on both sides.

■ Jumping rope puts stress on your feet, knees, and thighs. Aerobic dance shoes will provide stability and cushioning, as will good tennis shoes. Never jump rope on concrete floors.

■ Jumping rope can be especially rigorous for beginners; you may jump too high or overemphasize the arm movements. Instead, jump slowly at first. Wait until your breathing is comfortable and your

rhythm is smooth before you pick up the pace.

■ When you begin, aim for 30 to 50 turns per minute.

■ Most people who jump rope find it tiring, so they jump in intervals, or sets. Jump for one to two minutes, then rest for 30 seconds. Continuing this for 15 minutes will provide an excellent aerobic workout.

■ If you are jumping rope indoors, you'll quickly find that a high-ceilinged room is essential. Also, be sure the room has good ventilation.

■ Try skipping one foot at a time or even using fancy arm work if you get bored with ordinary jumping.

> **When jumping rope, you don't have to jump high to get a good workout. In fact, jumping only an inch or two off the ground will reduce your risk of injury.**

THE VCR WORKOUT

There is no reason to join a gym if you're comfortable exercising to an aerobics tape on your VCR.

■ Your local video store will have several tapes to choose from. If you are new to working out, choose a tape meant for beginners. It should teach non-impact aerobics.

■ A good beginner's tape will have spots where the instructor stops and tells you to check your heart rate. There should also be rest periods. If you are just starting, don't make the mistake of following the tape too closely; rest when you need to rest.

KICK UP YOUR HEELS AND DANCE

"Country-western dancing is a dance of community. And that's what a lot of people are looking for these days."

—Nancy Sheppard, owner, Satin 'n Denim dance studio

• • • • • • •

The country dance floors are filling quickly, as people from all walks of life enjoy the boot-stomping popularity of country-western dancing. Although not new, this latest wave of popularity has earned it a wide following. People can socialize and exercise while enjoying the latest country music.

There's a great variety to country dance. Two-stepping is the more traditional form, and this dance requires a partner. But it's line dancing that is responsible for the current wave of interest. You don't need a partner or even fancy clothes—just a few lessons (often provided free or at low cost by dance clubs) and a little enthusiasm.

Joan Messina took up country dancing at a friend's suggestion, after her husband passed away. She decided to go, despite her depression and painful arthritis. She received some wonderful benefits from dancing.

"My depression lifted, and I found that the dancing kept me limber. There are some nights I feel I might be too stiff and sore to dance, but I just take a hot shower, put on my boots and go. As soon as the music starts, I'm on the floor, and as far as I'm concerned, the pain is gone," says Joan. She also credits dancing with helping her keep off the 50 pounds she lost through dieting.

Strictly ballroom. For those who prefer the timeless elegance of Fred and Ginger, ballroom dancing is another great way to get an aerobic workout. While you might expect interest in this activity to have died down, ballroom dancing is more popular than ever.

This continued support might be because ballroom offers something for dancers at any level. Those who are out of shape can start with slower dances like the fox-trot and waltz.

Ballroom dancing provides a good workout as well. Exercise specialists say that vigorous ballroom dancing can raise your heart rate just as much as running or cross-country skiing.

Honor to your partner. Also popular is the energetic country group dance known as square dancing. Here dancers follow the instructions of a caller, listening for the next steps to be announced. A square dance is colorful: women wear full ruffled dresses, and men wear western shirts and boots. What sets square dancing apart, and what may be its greatest strength, is that it is a group activity. Here people dance in sets of four couples, changing partners often, as the steps dictate. This dance is a terrific way to overcome shyness. Once-timid people report finding new inner confidence with the friendly group support offered.

These three dances provide only a sampling of the ways you can kick up your heels for good health. Check for local dance classes if you are interested.❑

Line dancing is all the rage, as people scoot, dip, turn, and kick their way across the dance floor.

WALKING WORKOUTS

Walking could be the best way for couch potatoes to become active. Of all your fitness options, walking is the easiest, safest, and cheapest (you need no equipment except for comfortable shoes). It's also gentle on your ankles, knees, and back.

STARTING OUT

■ Beginners can benefit from as little as three 40- to 60-minute walking sessions each week. Once you have got used to the exercise, you may want to burn more calories by walking the same amount of time five times each week.

■ An easy way to add variety is to walk on both hills and flat terrain.

■ When walking on flat surfaces, keep your posture upright and relaxed. Your shoulders should be aligned over your hips.

■ When walking uphill, try leaning forward slightly—it's easier on your leg muscles.

■ Walking downhill, contrary to what you might think, is harder on your body. It places extra stress on your knees, so it's a good idea to slow your pace and take shorter steps.

■ Briskly walking one mile at 3.5 to 4 miles per hour burns nearly as many calories as running the same distance at a moderate pace.

■ Walking uphill burns more calories than walking on flat surfaces. The steeper the hill, the more calories you walk off.

■ You can also burn extra calories by walking on grass or a gravel trail.

■ Walking along the beach is great exercise, too: keeping your normal pace on sand will burn more calories because of the extra resistance.

If you have trouble sticking to your walking routine, think about getting a dog. You can trust a dog to get you up and walking at least twice a day.

RACEWALKING

■ Racewalking is a great calorie burner. The objectives are to get your body moving forward as quickly as possible without running, and to avoid the up-and-down motion of regular walking. Instead of a regular stride, you thrust your hip forward and swivel it around. This propels you more efficiently than the normal side-to-side swing of the hips.

■ Think of racewalking as walking a tightrope. Normally your feet make parallel tracks, but in racewalking you put one foot down in front of the other almost in a straight line. Because of anatomic differences, this may not be completely achievable by everyone. Come as close to it as you can.

■ Your feet should stay close to the ground, with no wasted motion. Let each foot strike the ground solidly on the back of the heel, with the toes pointed slightly upward.

■ Use long strides. Your motion should be efficient and smooth.

■ Bend your arms at a 90° angle and pump your arms. When you bring your arm back, your hand should come about six inches behind the hip, while on the swing forward the wrist should cross the center of your chest.

■ Keep your hands above your hips. The vigorous arm pumping counterbalances your leg/hip motion, allows for a quick pace, and provides a good workout for your upper body.

■ Keep your torso, shoulders, and neck relaxed. Don't bend from the waist—this can lead to back strain. Some racewalkers angle their whole bodies forward slightly.

■ Technique is important, so practice. Get advice from an experienced racewalker, if possible.

POLE WALKING

■ Think of pole walking as cross-country skiing without the skis. Instead of ski poles, use lightweight, rubber-tipped poles, sold in many sporting-goods stores.

■ Find the right-size poles by testing them in the store: you should be able to grip the pole and keep your forearm nearly level as you walk.

■ When you step forward with your left foot, bring your right arm forward and plant the pole on the ground, about even with the heel of your left foot.

■ Pole walking exercises the legs, chest, and arms, and some abdominals as well.

WATERWALKING

Waterwalking started as rehabilitative therapy for people with injuries. It wasn't long, however, before it was recognized as a boon for everyone.

■ You can waterwalk along a lake shore or a beach—in water ankle- or calf-deep—without ever getting your hair wet. Walking at a steady pace will burn 300 to 500 calories per hour.

■ Deep water provides more resistance, but you may prefer waist-high water, since you won't tire so easily. Walking in shallow water is fine, too—just walk faster and longer.

• • • • • • • • • • • • • • • • • • • •

Because of the water's resistance, you don't have to walk as fast in water as you would on land to burn the same number of calories. Walking two miles per hour in thigh-high water is the equivalent of walking three miles per hour on land.

• • • • • • • • • • • • • • • • • • • •

RETRO WALKING

■ Walking backward has a lot to offer: It strengthens the abdominals, the back muscles, the quadriceps, and the hamstrings. It also makes for a fun change of pace.

■ If you are recovering from a leg or ankle injury, you'll find retro walking less stressful than regular walking.

■ Take precautions. Do retro walking only on a smooth surface, like a track, and never do it around automobile or pedestrian traffic.

■ It's helpful to do retro walking with a partner. This way one of you can walk forward while the other walks backward. Do this for a while, then switch.

■ Start off slowly to keep your calves from getting sore. Be sure not to walk more than a quarter of a mile backward your first week.

■ Use retro walking only for variety, as it doesn't provide as good a workout as brisk forward walking.

DON'T FORGET THE ARMS

■ By swinging your arms, you'll burn 5 to 10 percent more calories, and you'll get an upper-body workout as well.

■ Your arms should move in opposition to your legs—swing your right arm forward as you step forward with your left leg. This arm motion helps counterbalance the motion of your legs.

■ As you increase your pace, switch to pumping your arms: bend your elbows at 90° angles and pump from the shoulder. Keep your wrists straight and—to reduce fatigue—keep your hands unclenched. Swing your arms in a small arc across your chest; your elbow should come to about the middle of your chest and as far back as your buttock. (This is similar to the arm motion of racewalking.)

GET A RUNNING START

*Jogging is a popular exercise for a good reason—
it's great for the heart and lungs, for weight loss, and for
allover conditioning. Here are a few tips to help you
start (and stick to) a jogging routine while getting
the most out of your workout.*

GOOD JOGGING FORM

While professional joggers
have a characteristic grace
and smoothness to their
stride, there is no one right
way to jog. Keeping good
form, however, will help you
jog efficiently and cut down
on foot and hip injuries.

■ Keep an upright posture
when you jog. Your back
should be straight, and your
eyes should look forward to
the road ahead rather than
down to your feet.

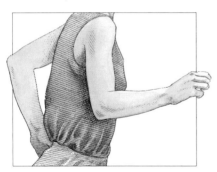

■ Carry your arms at about
waist level. Your elbows should
be bent at a 90° angle, so that
your forearms are parallel to
the ground. Swing your arms
freely while you jog.

■ Your fingers should be
curled loosely instead of
clenched into a tight fist,
which would have the effect
of tensing up all your muscles.

■ Jogging on soft surfaces will
help cut down on injuries.
Golf courses or high school
tracks are ideal. Whenever
you jog off the pavement,

make sure the surface is
smooth and regular so that
you don't turn an ankle or trip
and fall.

■ Concentrate on landing on
your heel and then rolling forward to push off with the ball
of your foot and big toe.

■ If you feel pain in your feet
when jogging, consider having
an experienced jogger evaluate your stride. You may be
rolling your foot outward or
inward as you jog. Checking
how the treads on your shoes
wear down can also reveal
these problems.

· ·

**You can use your arms to
adjust the stride of your
legs. When you pump
your arms more, you get
extra power for hills or
for speed.**

· ·

FINDING THE RIGHT SHOE

■ Jogging shoes are lightweight and are designed with
certain features in common.
They have durable, deeply
patterned outer soles, thick
heel wedges to tilt the body
forward, and shock-absorbent
midsoles. The top of most jogging shoes will be made of a
light, breathable material.

■ Since jogging—or walking—
will cause your feet to expand, jogging shoes should be
more flexible than other
shoes. Lace them snugly to

prevent slippage. Women who
have a hard time finding shoes
that are wide enough might
do better shopping for a man's
jogging shoe.

■ When you are ready to buy,
wear the socks or foot covering that you normally wear
when jogging. Buy your shoes
late in the day, when your feet
are most swollen.

CARING FOR YOUR SHOES

■ After a workout, take off
your shoes, loosen the laces,
pull back the tongues, and remove the insoles. This will
allow more air to circulate and
hasten drying.

■ Stuff shoes with cedar shoe
trees or bags of cedar shavings. A porous wood, cedar
not only soaks up moisture
but also absorbs the odor,
salts, and acids from perspiration. Wads of newspaper will
do if cedar is not available.

■ Think about replacing your
jogging shoes after 6 to 12
months of active wear, even if
they don't seem to be worn
out. Loss of cushioning will
occur long before the outsides
of the shoes show significant
wear and tear.

GOING THE DISTANCE

■ Are you jogging too hard? A rule of thumb for judging effort is the "talk test." You should be able to talk to a partner while you jog without gasping for air. If you can't, slow your pace.

■ If jogging three days a week isn't enough of a workout, add a fourth day. Add a fifth day only if you are sure you aren't overdoing it. People who jog six or seven days a week are taking a risk; the likelihood of injury outweighs the potential for improvement.

■ Never increase the number of times you jog per week and the distance you jog at the same time.

■ When you're ready to jog faster, concentrate on lengthening the back of your stride: push off harder and lift your legs higher behind you.

■ On a long jog, go slower than normal. It's easier on your legs and will help your heart and lungs handle the extra effort.

■ Drink water before, during, and after your jog, especially if it's warm or humid out.

Add an occasional long jog to your schedule. This will force your cardiovascular system to work more efficiently and will give you a well-earned sense of accomplishment.

WEATHER CONCERNS

■ Avoid jogging in extreme heat. If the weather is too warm, try cutting down on your mileage or jogging at dawn or dusk. Dress lightly and drink plenty of water.

■ Midday is the best time for winter jogging: you can take full advantage of whatever warmth the sun provides.

■ Wear a wool hat in cold weather, as you can lose a great amount of body heat through an uncovered head. Also, it's better to wear three to five layers of lightweight clothing than a layer or two of heavy clothing.

■ If possible, move against the wind on your way out and with the wind going home. This will cut down on the windchill factor when you're perspiring most.

Dress for the second mile of a jog. If you dress to be comfortable in the first few minutes of a workout, you'll probably find yourself overheated the rest of the way.

EASY DOES IT: A RUNNING PLAN FOR BEGINNERS

Don't expect to start off jogging for 30 minutes at full tilt. Begin with an easy rhythm, mixing jogging with walking. If you follow this plan, which takes no more than half an hour a day, two to four days a week, you will work up to a 30-minute jog in 12 weeks.

Week No.	Run-Walk Schedule
1	Walk 20 minutes.
2	Walk 30 minutes.
3	Jog 2 minutes; walk 4 minutes. Complete the sequence 5 times.
4	Jog 3 minutes; walk 3 minutes. Complete the sequence 5 times.
5	Jog 5 minutes; walk 2 1/2 minutes. Complete the sequence 4 times.
6	Jog 7 minutes; walk 3 minutes. Complete the sequence 3 times.
7	Jog 8 minutes; walk 2 minutes. Complete the sequence 3 times.
8	Jog 9 minutes; walk 2 minutes. Complete the sequence twice, then jog 8 minutes.
9	Jog 9 minutes; walk 1 minute. Complete the sequence 3 times.
10	Jog 13 minutes; walk 2 minutes. Complete the sequence twice.
11	Jog 14 minutes; walk 1 minute. Complete the sequence twice.
12	Jog 30 minutes.

PEDAL POWER: BICYCLING

Whether you're a novice or a serious athlete, you'll enjoy the scenery as you tour the countryside on your bicycle—and your body is sure to enjoy the aerobic workout. Whatever your fitness level, these tips will help you get more out of your routine.

GETTING IN GEAR

Bicycling has enjoyed several waves of interest through the years. One reason for its popularity is that it can be enjoyed by just about anyone, regardless of age or level of fitness.

■ This sport can be enjoyed in groups or solo, on the roads or with a stationary bike. You can also vary your pace, from leisurely touring to intense training.

■ Incorporate bicycling into your schedule. Bike to work or when running errands.

■ The beginning bicyclist may need only a three-speed bike, but many will prefer to have 10 or 12 speeds. This will make it easier for you to go over hills and allow you to increase the resistance on the straightaways.

■ Biking at a fast speed is excellent for weight control. Pedaling one hour at 13 miles per hour—a brisk pace—will burn about 650 calories.

■ Bicycling is especially good for building the quadriceps (a group of four large muscles in the front of the thigh). Toe clips are useful if you have problems with your feet slipping off the pedals, but they also help you to work your calf and shin muscles. You may want to consider toe clips with a quick-release mechanism if the clips are especially snug-fitting.

A BICYCLING ROUTINE

Beginners will do fine riding for 20 to 30 minutes at a moderate rate. Try the following routine for a more disciplined approach.

■ First week: Work on getting comfortable with the bike and experimenting with gears. Try to ride 2 to 5 miles during the week and 5 to 10 miles on the weekend.

■ Second week: Include a few short periods of faster riding in your routine. This is called interval training and will help you develop strength and endurance. Aim for 4 to 7 miles during the week and 10 miles on the weekend.

■ Third week: Include five-minute periods of faster riding, separated by five minutes of easy riding. Ride 6 to 9 miles during the week and 15 miles on the weekend.

■ Fourth week: Try doing one day of three-minute intervals, instead of five-minute intervals. Ride 8 to 11 miles during the week and up to 20 miles on the weekend.

Spare your tires. Storing your bicycle near appliances that give off ozone can age your tires, causing cracks and other damage to the rubber. Keep your bike away from refrigerators, freezers, and electric heaters.

THE RIGHT POSTURE

■ Getting the right-size bike is important. When you straddle your bike, with both feet on the ground, there should be one to two inches between the front tube (the bar that runs from the handlebars or the front fork to the seat) and your crotch.

■ When you are seated, your leg should be only slightly bent when it reaches the bottom of the pedaling movement.

■ Bend forward at the hips—not at the waist—when you ride. Keep your back straight and your neck and shoulder muscles relaxed.

■ When gripping the handlebars, keep your elbows slightly bent. This will give you better leverage and shock absorption when going over potholes or bumps.

■ Ease the stress of a long ride by changing your hand position often.

DRESS FOR COMFORT, DRESS FOR SAFETY

■ You can bike in just about any clothing, but serious bikers prefer a pair of chamois-lined shorts. These reduce chafing and pressure in the groin. A padded seat will also help you stay comfortable.

■ Gloves are useful for reducing pressure on the palms that comes from leaning on handlebars. Gloves will also protect your hands in case you fall.

RIDING WITH CAUTION

■ Inspect your bike before every ride. Check the tires, brakes, gears, and headlight.

■ Practice sudden braking techniques. Always squeeze both brakes, the front harder than the rear, and let up on the front brake if you feel yourself skidding. Sliding back in the saddle will also help stabilize the bike.

■ Attach a loud horn to the handlebars and use it whenever necessary.

■ Don't ride at night unless you have no choice, and then use reflectors and headlights and wear reflective clothing.

■ Secure flapping pant legs with rubber bands to avoid having them get caught in the bike's wheels. Also, tuck in loose shoelaces.

■ Rearview mirrors should be mounted on your handlebars, not on your helmet.

■ A water bottle can come in handy, either to fight off dehydration or to squirt at overly interested dogs that may chase you.

> **Bicyclists are safest when wearing neon pink. It's easy for motorists to spot this uncommon color.**

BIKING IN ANY WEATHER

■ Windchill rapidly becomes a factor when you're traveling at 15 miles per hour. Consider wearing a mask to stay warm.

■ Hypothermia can occur in temperatures as high as 16°C (60°F) on wet and windy days. Cyclists should wear gloves, leg coverings, long-sleeved shirts or sweaters, and a close-fitting hat when it's cool outside.

■ In wet weather, brakes don't hold very well. Use caution when your hubs become wet.

■ Take along something to drink when biking in warm weather. If you ride in isolated areas, equip your bike with two quart-size water bottles.

Helmet Protection

Bicycle helmets are a good idea whose time has finally come. When you consider the lifelong damage that one head injury can cause, you'll see how important it is to wear a sturdy helmet every time you bike.

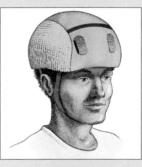

Buy only helmets that are approved by the Canadian Standards Association (CSA) or the American National Standards Institute (ANSI).

A properly fitting helmet should touch your head at the crown, sides, front, and back. Choose the smallest size that fits comfortably, and use the sizing pads included with most helmets to fine-tune the fit.

Put the helmet on and try to push to the sides, front, and back. If it moves enough to create a gap between your head and the pads, use thicker pads. If it's still loose, get a smaller helmet.

Adjust the straps. With the helmet level across your forehead just above your eyebrows, the front strap should be close to vertical. The back strap should lie straight, just below the ear, without any slack. The chin strap should feel tight when you open your mouth.

Think of a helmet as a one-shot purchase. Once it's been damaged in an accident or in any other way, you're better off replacing it—even when the damage isn't obvious.

IN THE SWIM

Swimming is thought by many to be the perfect exercise, combining a vigorous aerobic workout with muscle development and posing little risk of injury. And besides—swimming is fun. No wonder so many turn to the pool to get in shape.

GETTING YOUR FEET WET

■ Take a shower to warm up your muscles before a swim. Also, beginning your workout slowly is easier on your heart.

■ Maintain a slower pace until your breathing is comfortable and your heart rate has risen. Vary your strokes in the first few laps to get all your muscles working.

■ After your workout, do a few easy laps or tread water to cool yourself down.

■ Some people seem to have trouble losing weight when swimming. Although one theory suggests that swimming promotes fat storage as an insulating mechanism, this probably isn't the culprit for those swimming in heated pools. More likely, people simply find it difficult to sustain a rigorous pace when swimming and take breaks more frequently than they realize.

It's important to drink water periodically when swimming. You won't notice it, but your body will lose water from the exercise.

DIFFERENT STROKES

There's no reason to let your swim routine get boring when there are so many ways to cut through the water. Besides, using a variety of strokes will give you a better workout. Illustrated here are the four main swimming strokes. For more complete swimming instruction, consider taking a swim class or hiring an instructor.

THE CRAWL

■ Also referred to as freestyle, this is often the stroke swimmers learn first.

■ Most of your propulsion will come from the arms. Once your hand enters the water, pull downward and then outward, tracing an "S" in the water.

■ One common mistake is to kick solely with the lower leg, but experienced swimmers know this kick should be done with the whole leg, from the hip to the toes. The heel of the kicking foot should just break the surface, and the other should be no more than a foot deep. Kicking two to three times per stroke is standard, but use whatever rhythm works best for you.

THE BACKSTROKE

■ Keep your back and neck straight, but not rigid. Also try to keep your head straight. Tilting your head too far back will raise your hips; tucking your chin in too much will cause your hips to sink.

■ The arm movements of this stroke can be difficult to master. Reach back with your arm extended. Once your arm is above your head, bend the elbow in a 90° to 105° angle, then straighten your arm again as it passes your hip.

■ The kick is similar to the kick for the crawl. Try for two to three kicks per stroke.

Backstrokers take note: the strip of colored flags often hanging above pools is there for your benefit. These flags hang five yards from the end of the pool and tell backstrokers to be careful not to hit the edge.

THE BREASTSTROKE

■ You may find the breaststroke to be the least complicated and least strenuous of all. But it's still a great workout, firming the chest, arms, and thighs.

■ The arm movements aren't tricky; just make a large arc, moving your arms in unison. Start with your arms stretched in front of you, then pull back in a large circle.

■ You may have learned to do a frog kick with the breaststroke, but the whip-kick is more efficient. With your feet together, bring your legs upward until your feet almost touch your buttocks. Then snap your legs out in a "V" shape, and bring them together again while you glide.

■ While the movements are simple, it takes some practice to combine the stroke and kick correctly.

THE BUTTERFLY

■ The butterfly is the most difficult of the basic strokes, requiring greater muscle strength and coordination.

■ Sometimes called an hourglass movement, the arm pull for the butterfly is similar to that of the crawl, the difference being that both arms work simultaneously.

■ The kick presents a greater challenge. It's called the dolphin kick because both legs kick as one in a quick, flicking movement. This provides a good workout for the legs and abdominals.

■ Breathe every two or three strokes, whichever way you find easier. Time it so that you inhale during the last part of your arm pull and exhale—into the water—as your hands reach shoulder level.

■ Putting the stroke and kick together may be a challenge. Many swimmers perform two kicks for every stroke.

SET SWIMMING GOALS

■ Make a schedule. If this is your primary exercise, swim 20 to 30 minutes a day, three to five times a week.

■ Because of the cooling effects of water, you won't know if you're working up a sweat. Try to gauge how your body feels. Push yourself hard enough to get a good workout, but not so hard that you end up exhausted.

FINDING A POOL

■ Standard pools are either 25 yards, 25 meters, or 50 meters long. However, you can still get a good workout in a smaller pool—just do a few more laps.

■ The water temperature should be between 26°C (78°F) and 28°C (82°F). Warm pools are more appropriate for slow swimming and practicing stroke technique. Cooler pools are better for

competitions, as well as rigorous workouts at faster speeds.

■ If you swim in a busy health club or college gymnasium, you will likely have to share your lane with other swimmers. Pool etiquette says to swim in a counterclockwise pattern, keeping as close as possible to the right side of the lane at all times.

■ To help swimmers time themselves, many pools have large, easy-to-read poolside clocks.

■ Don't solo. All swimming workouts should be done under the supervision of a qualified lifeguard.

TOOLS OF THE POOL

■ Swim fins: While these froglike fins may look funny, don't laugh at people who use them. Fins let you get more from your kick, helping swimmers to achieve a full-body workout. Also, fins help beginners swim longer before they tire.

■ Pull buoys: These are canister-shaped flotation devices that attach to your legs. Use them when you want to rest your legs and concentrate on your arm movements.

■ You can minimize drag (the force of the water pushing against you) by wearing tight-fitting competition-style suits during your workouts. Synthetic fabrics have the advantage of drying quicker.

■ Some pools require both men and women to wear a cap. Racing caps may cut down on drag, helping you to speed through the water. They may also help protect your hair from the chlorine in the pool.

BETTER BREATHING

For the beginning swimmer, even taking breaths can be a chore. If swimming a few laps leaves you gasping, learn these breathing tips.

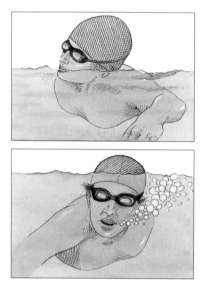

■ When doing the crawl, don't hold your head too high; the water level should be at your hairline.

■ Exhale completely into the water before you turn your head to breathe again.

■ To inhale, turn your head just far enough to breathe, rather than lifting your whole head out of the water.

■ Breathe once every two or three strokes.

■ Learn to breathe on alternate sides. This will make you feel more in control and will reduce shoulder tension.

Get a good push off from the wall. You're at your fastest when pushing off, so use your momentum to glide at least a full body length before starting your stroke.

WATER WEAR AND TEAR

■ Chlorine is notorious for damaging hair. Before you swim, try putting a small amount of creme rinse or conditioner in your hair and then wearing a latex swim cap.

■ A post-swim shampoo with products designed to remove chlorine residue will also help keep your hair soft.

■ Thoroughly dry your ears after swimming. Shaking your head vigorously to one side may do the trick.

■ Those especially prone to ear infection should consider earplugs. Puttylike plugs that mold to the shape of the outer ear canal are the most effective.

■ For longer wear, rinse your swimsuit with tap water after each use. This will help wash out the chlorine residue.

SORE EYES? GET GOGGLES

The chlorine in pools can be irritating to your eyes, causing burning, redness, and tearing. You can protect your eyes with well-fitting goggles.

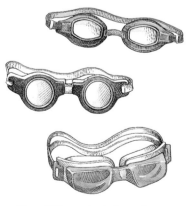

■ Try different styles of goggles until you find the pair that fits best. If they leak, adjust the strap.

■ Wear goggles that fit tightly over the eyes; smaller racing goggles should be seated within the eye socket.

■ To prevent fogging, wet the inside of your goggles with water or a wetting solution before you put them on.

■ Prescription goggles are available, although they can be expensive.

CONTACT LENS TIPS

Swimming with contact lenses demands a few precautions.

■ It's easier to swim with soft contacts; their larger circumference helps them to stay on in the water.

■ If you wear soft contacts, insert them at least 30 minutes before entering the water. Apply one or two drops of saline solution to reduce the risk of losing a lens. If saline is unavailable, use sterile distilled water. When you are done, wait 30 minutes before removing the contacts.

■ If you can see sufficiently well without them, avoid swimming with hard contact lenses. Hard and gas permeable lenses are more likely to be washed away.

■ Always wear goggles when swimming with contacts. This will not only prevent your losing the lenses but prevent infection from acanthamoeba, an organism commonly found in pools, hot tubs, or any other body of standing water.

■ After swimming with contacts, be sure to disinfect them that night—even if they are extended-wear lenses. If they are disposable contacts, throw them out and wear a new pair the next day.

FIT FOR LIFE

"If exercise could be packed in a pill, it would be the single most widely prescribed and beneficial medicine in the nation."

—The National Institute on Aging

• • • • • • •

In 1920, at the age of 14, Aileen Riggin Soule won her first gold medal. Here, at age 85, she shows the form and grace that come from a life of fitness.

Exercise has accomplished more for Olympic medal winner Aileen Riggin Soule than just keeping her in remarkable condition. She took up swimming at the age of 11 in 1917, on her doctor's recommendation.

"I wasn't a very healthy child," she says. "I had anemia, I was very stoop-shouldered, and I had suffered a terrible bout of Spanish influenza." She stood 4'10" tall and weighed only 65 pounds. Yet despite great odds, she went on to win the gold medal for three-meter springboard diving only three years later in the 1920 Antwerp Games. (She was almost denied a spot on the Olympic team because she was only 14 years old.) Four years later she won two more medals in the 1924 games in Paris.

Aileen has barely slowed down over the years. She still makes two or three half-mile swims each week, in the ocean off Oahu, Hawaii. In 1991, at the age of 85, she won a dozen gold medals in her age division at two different U.S. Masters swim championships.

Never too late. Exercise may be the world's greatest medicine and a natural antidote to the effects of aging. Regular fitness is one reason why Aileen Riggin Soule and many others are able to stay in top condition throughout their lives.

"Exercise will prevent most age-related deteriorations through age 60," says Jim Graves of the University of Florida Center for Exercise Sciences. But the advantages don't stop there. Seniors benefit from exercise more than any other age group. Studies have found that elderly men and women, even those in their nineties, can double their muscle strength by working out with weights.

One piece of the puzzle. But this increase in senior fitness is only a part of a larger movement—letting exercise play a greater role in our lives. The benefits are amazing: Exercise tones and conditions the muscles, increases flexibility, and helps you avoid putting on weight. It will boost your heart and lung capacity and may lower your chances of developing heart disease, diabetes, and certain types of cancer. It even seems to brighten your mood, helping keep your spirits high.

The key is to understand that good health doesn't mean devoting all your spare time to workouts; it means bringing exercise into your life. Avoiding labor-saving devices is a good way to start. Try climbing the stairs instead of taking the elevator. Use a manual instead of an electric lawn mower.

And, of course, make fitness a lifelong commitment. For Aileen Riggin Soule that means spending her life around water.

"It's very relaxing," she says. "Swimming is a great sport for women, and it's something you can do all your life. I'm afraid to stop—if I did, I'd fall apart."❑

CROSS-COUNTRY SKIING

This winter workout combines snowy meadows, quiet wooded paths, and elegant gliding movements. It's also a great aerobic exercise that uses most of the major muscle groups.

STARTING OUT

■ Think of cross-country skiing as a balancing act. It takes some practice to get used to the long, skinny skis and the fact that the boots are secured at the toe only, leaving the heel free to rise and fall.

■ Before you begin, get the feel of the skis. Walk in them. Bend your knees just enough to keep yourself stable over the center of the ski. Your weight should rest a little more on the balls of your feet than on the heels.

■ Use your poles for balance. Push off with them, gliding forward first with one ski and then the other.

Start off with a lesson, if you've never tried cross-country skiing before. Otherwise, you probably won't get a complete workout.

THE RIGHT EQUIPMENT

■ If you're going to hit the trails only a few times each season, consider renting skis and poles; it would take years to get your money's worth purchasing good equipment.

■ When you are ready to buy, be willing to spend a little more for better equipment. Bargain prices aren't a bargain if the skis are unusable.

■ Find a knowledgeable person to help you fit your skis.

You can choose between waxless or waxable: waxless skis require less care and generally perform well for noncompetitive skiers.

■ If you are going to create your own trails, choose off-track skis, which have metal edges that grip ice and hardened snow. If you follow trails, track skis are your best bet. Off-track boots are warmer and sturdier than track-skiing boots. Besides handling well on hardened snow, off-track skis also provide the extra control you need for gliding through fresh snow.

■ Choose poles that are made of aluminum or fiberglass. They should reach to the underside of your outstretched arms or nearly to the top of your shoulder.

■ Pole straps should be adjustable and should be wide where they wrap around your wrist. The poles' grips should be made of porous plastic, cork, or leather.

KICK AND GLIDE

■ There are two steps to cross-country skiing: kicking and gliding. Kick by pressing the center section of the ski into the snow for grip and pushing off. Then let yourself glide, balancing your weight between the skis.

■ As the right ski moves forward, the left pole goes back.

Once you've pushed off, relax your grip on the pole so that your arm is free to move forward and plant the pole again.

■ Remember that when done correctly, cross-country skiing has little in common with walking. While this sport's stride may look like a typical strolling gait, the emphasis should be on smooth kick-and-glide movements.

Although using a ski machine offers many of the same benefits as cross-country skiing, doing well on a machine doesn't translate into proficiency on snow. The skis on machines are too short for kicking and gliding, and the poles are pulled rather than pushed.

TIPS ON TECHNIQUE

■ Going up hills is easier if you know the "herringbone" technique. Think of making a fish skeleton in the snow with your skis. Point your toes outward one at a time and use poles for support.

■ When slowing or stopping, do just the opposite. Point your ski tips inward with the tails apart and the inside edges of your skis on an outward angle.

■ Whether going uphill, downhill, or skiing on level ground, stay relaxed. Lean over your skis and keep your eyes looking forward (one sure way to fall is to watch your skis). Even with falls, though, cross-country skiers generally suffer few injuries.

As a beginner, it's best to avoid hills. But if you can't, don't ski down them. Instead, take your skis off and walk down.

WHAT TO WEAR

■ It's important to dress resourcefully when cross-country skiing. When it's -23°C (-10°F), your body temperature may be pushing 37°C (98.6°F) plus, as your muscles burn enormous quantities of energy, much of it for heat production. Cross-country skiing generates as much heat as competitive running.

■ Use layering to keep cold out and remove sweat. Clothes nearest the body should be snug, but not tight. Natural fibers, such as silk, wool, or cotton, work well. Polypropylene is a favorite because it carries sweat away from the body.

■ Middle-layer clothing is usually wool or down.

■ Outer clothing should be both waterproof and breath-

able. A windbreaker would be a good choice.

■ The tights that are popular with runners and cyclists can also be used for skiing. Depending on the temperature, tights may be worn alone or under pants.

■ Windpants are favored by many skiers as protection from the cold. Pants with a full side zipper allow you to put them on and take them off without removing your skis.

■ Always wear a hat—the head is the source of most heat loss. Consider wearing earmuffs or a headband, too.

■ Mittens are warmer than gloves and easier to remove, but gloves will give you more flexibility.

■ Sunglasses that reflect the snow's glare are a must. Avoid metal frames, which can blister your cheeks on a cold day.

Things to Bring

Stay safe and warm on the trails. Carrying the following items won't add much weight and will keep you prepared for nearly any situation.

1. A plastic water bottle
2. Some high-calorie snacks
3. Sunscreen (with a protection factor of 15 or higher) for your skin and lips
4. Sunglasses
5. A trail map
6. Matches
7. Small first aid items
8. A trusty knife
9. A windbreaker
10. Windpants
11. A wool hat

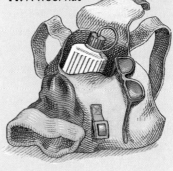

BUILDING MUSCLES

Weight training is not just for the bodybuilders on Muscle Beach. This type of exercise can help you with such everyday tasks as carrying groceries and shoveling snow, and can even help stop the loss of muscle tissue that comes with age. It's also extremely versatile and will complement any routine.

POINTS FOR BEGINNERS

■ Weight training is useful at any age. It has helped even people in their nineties build muscle mass and stay mobile.
■ Experienced lifters often wear four- to six-inch training belts to protect back and stomach muscles. Beginners with a history of lower-back problems may also use a belt.
■ Dress in clothing that won't restrict your movements. If handling weights gives you calluses, wear padded gloves.

CHOOSING EQUIPMENT

When designing a muscle-building program, you can choose from free weights or weight-training machines.

■ Weight-lifting machines have several advantages for the beginner: they don't require much instruction, and they are easy to set up.
■ Using weight-lifting machines often means belonging to a gym. Home gyms are available for a price. Check the want ads for good deals (for tips on buying equipment, see page 112).
■ All weight-lifting machines have changeable settings, so adjust them to fit your body.
■ Free weights (such as dumbbells and barbells) can be intimidating to the novice. However, because they require more control and balance and stress muscles in a greater range of motion, they offer a more versatile workout than weight-lifting machines.
■ Ultimately, a well-balanced bodybuilding routine will require the use of both types of

weights in a combination that best serves your body.

A BASIC ROUTINE

While the best routine is one that you have customized to your own needs, the six exercises on the bottom of these pages will get you started.
■ Begin with a warm-up set, completing 5 to 10 repetitions at 50 to 60 percent of the weight you will lift.
■ Next, complete 2 to 3 sets of 8 to 12 repetitions at the full weight that you are lifting. Either rest one minute between sets or use that time to exercise a different area.
■ Whatever order you find works best, be sure to save the abdominals for last.

Lat Pulldown: *Take a grip three to five inches wider than your shoulders, pulling the weight down slowly.*

Bench Press: *Grip the bar, your hands spaced three inches wider than your chest. Push it up without arching your back.*

Seated Pulley Row: *Keep a narrow grip with your hands, and pull the weight toward your abdomen.*

BUILDING MUSCLE

You can use weight-training to create either a toned or a muscular physique. These tips will help develop muscle size.

■ Exercise big muscles before small ones. When you work the back, chest, or shoulders, you're actually working groups of muscles. It's more efficient to work from large to small. For example, do bench presses, to exercise the chest area, before doing exercises that isolate the triceps.

■ Use heavier weights. Exercising at a higher level and doing only four to six repetitions is more effective for building muscle. This advice isn't for beginners, who should use lower weights and higher repetitions during their first weeks.

■ Stay with it for six months. If you work out two to three times per week, you'll see the fastest gains in this period. After six months, you may need to lift weights only once or twice a week to maintain what you've built.

Women worried about "bulking up" can relax. Because they have less of the hormone testosterone, women don't gain as much muscle mass as men.

TONING MUSCLE

■ If your goal is to firm and tone your muscles, do more repetitions at a lower weight. This will also build endurance.

■ Start with 60 percent of the maximum amount you can lift. Complete 10 to 20 repetitions, doing 3 to 5 sets.

■ Traditional non-weight-bearing exercises, such as knee push-ups and seated leg lifts, are also effective for muscle toning. They may be right for those too frail to use even light weights.

LIFTING TECHNIQUE

■ Breathe steadily; don't hold your breath. Exhale during the lifting part of the exercise, and inhale during the recovery.

■ Go slowly: fast, jerky repeti-

tions won't give you as good a workout and may injure muscles and joints. Be sure to lift through a full range of motion.

■ Technique is more important than weight at the outset. Learn the correct way to do each exercise. Consider hiring a personal trainer to instruct you on proper form.

■ Whatever areas you build, also develop the opposite muscle group. For example, if you stress your chest muscles, also work the upper back. Other pairs include triceps and biceps, as well as quadriceps and hamstrings.

■ Try to do strength training for 30 minutes two or three times each week, with a day's rest between sessions.

Pound for pound, muscles burn 40 to 50 more calories a day than fat does. Putting on just three pounds of muscle will consume an extra 120 to 150 extra calories every 24 hours—even while you sleep.

Military Press: Starting with your hands near your shoulders, lift the weight directly up.

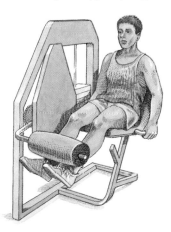

Leg Press: Push up with your feet until your knees are nearly locked. Then let the weight down gently.

Abdominal Crunch: Press apparatus forward with your chest, contracting your abdominal muscles.

CROSS OVER TO CROSS TRAINING

Bored with the same old routine? Mix it up! Cross training is fairly new, but it's already a big hit. It lets you challenge your body with new workouts while increasing the benefits of exercise.

KEEP IT VARIED

■ Cross training simply means combining two or more activities to achieve a well-rounded fitness program.

■ Choose activities that you enjoy and you'll be more likely to stick to your routine.

■ There are two ways to cross train: First, you can choose exercises that work the same parts of the body (such as running and bicycling to exercise the legs), thereby enhancing your performance of each activity by strengthening the muscles used in both. Second, you can choose exercises that work different areas (such as swimming and aerobic dance) to develop an all-over conditioning routine.

■ Cardiovascular benefits gained from one sport carry over to other activities. Endurance achieved by walking or running, for example, will let you bike or swim farther.

Vary your sports to lessen the chance of injury. By spreading the stress among different muscles and joints, you lower the wear on any one area.

TYPES OF ACTIVITIES

It will be easier to plan a cross training routine if you think of all exercises as being divided into the following four categories. Make sure your exercises don't all come from the same group.

■ Aerobic activities should be the foundation of any cross training routine. Many excellent examples are covered in this chapter, such as aerobic dance, walking, running, swimming, biking, and cross-country skiing. You might also try rowing, roller skating, or canoeing. Aerobic exercises help you develop endurance and cardiovascular health.

■ Strength training is extremely adaptable and will complement nearly any other exercise (see pages 108–109 for more information). Building muscle offers more benefits than you may think, as it can lessen your chance of injury and help slow the natural deterioration of the body that comes with aging.

■ Leisure activities, such as gardening, bowling, or golf, also have a place in cross training. They make an enjoyable break from more strenuous exercises.

■ Sports (such as softball, volleyball, tennis, or basketball) offer aerobic conditioning when played vigorously. Their most important role in cross training, however, is in helping you enjoy your routine.

PLANNING A PROGRAM

■ Move into a new sport gradually. Warm up beforehand, and keep the initial workouts short so muscles and tendons can adjust to new movements.

■ Invest in the right gear. Good shoes are essential to any exercise involving running, walking, or jumping.

■ Alternate the intensity and duration of workouts: Follow a long, slow workout with a shorter, more intense session the next day. Avoid doing high-impact activities two days in a row; give your body a rest in between.

■ It's easy to overdo it when cross training, so be sure to pencil rest days into your schedule.

If your legs become sore, switch to an upper-body activity for a few days. If your arms ache, exercise your lower body.

Choose Your Sports

The four goals of any exercise program are cardiovascular fitness, muscle strength, muscle endurance, and flexibility. Because no one exercise will give your body a complete workout, this chart will help you pick varied activities. It will also help you avoid common injuries and will pair up compatible sports.

	Body Parts Worked	Advantages	Injuries to Avoid	Complements
Swimming	Upper body (chest, arms, shoulders, upper back), cardiopulmonary system	Non-impact, so there's no great stress to the joints. A good maintenance activity when nursing an injury	Shoulder and neck strain due to overuse, eye and ear infection and irritation	Bicycling, running, walking, climbing
Running and walking	Back of the legs (calves, hamstrings), buttocks, stomach. Excellent for cardiovascular fitness	Can be done anywhere. Forces many of the larger muscle groups to be used. Easy to attain target heart rate	Strain to lower tendons and ligaments due to bad form or overuse	Swimming, weight lifting
Aerobic dancing	Legs and waist. Very good cardiovascular activity, depending on the rate	Much depends on the instructor or the program being followed. Variety. Convenience	Overuse injuries	Weight lifting for strength. Volleyball for coordination
Stretching/yoga	All parts, depending on the particular stretches	Decreases chance of injury in other sports. Helps promote a full range of motion	Hyperextension, and muscle tears when cold. Torn connectors (ligaments and tendons)	All cardiovascular activities and weight lifting
Downhill skiing	Front of legs, hamstrings, buttocks. Helps maintain toned stomach and hips	Maintains endurance and strength. Demands that the legs and aerobic capacity be in excellent shape	The sport on this list most liable to cause injury due to falls, exhaustion, hypothermia, and natural hazards	Bicycling, running, swimming with kickboard, and weight lifting
Cross-country skiing	Entire upper and lower torso; the best cardiovascular workout available	This exercise works more muscles than any other activity. Low impact	Shoulder and hip strain due to overuse or bad technique	Swimming or weight lifting
Racket sports	No real fitness benefit, unless extended, high-paced volleys are maintained	Increases flexibility and agility. Builds muscle endurance if played at advanced level	Strains to hand, forearm, and elbow tendons, ankles, and knees. Back muscle strain	Running, weight lifting, aerobic dancing, bicycling
Bicycling	Lower torso, hips, thighs, calves. If a vigorous pace is kept, it's also an excellent cardiovascular activity	Non-impact. Less strain and pounding on muscles. Changes in scenery. Variety	Damage to knees due to pedaling in too low a gear. Falls due to traffic hazards	Swimming, weight lifting, racket sports
Weight lifting	Any muscle group	Builds muscular strength, size, and endurance. Lets you isolate and work specific areas of the body	Muscle strain if too much weight is attempted or technique is wrong	Any aerobic activity (such as running, bicycling, and cross-country skiing)

WORKING OUT AT HOME OR AWAY

Finding the right place to exercise is important. If you like your environment, you're more likely to keep exercising. Some enjoy the convenience of an at-home workout, while others like the variety of equipment health clubs can offer.

THE AT-HOME WORKOUT

The advantages of an at-home gym are many: no crowds, no lines, and no membership fees (although you will need to invest in your own equipment).

■ Another advantage of working out at home is that you can read, watch television, or listen to music while you condition your body. Where's the best place to put your equipment? Right next to your home entertainment system.

■ Working out at home can also benefit people who enjoy seasonal sports. If you have a cross-country skiing machine, for example, you don't need to rely on snow.

BASIC EQUIPMENT

Buy the following for a good general conditioning routine:
■ An exercise mat for stretches and floor exercise.
■ Dumbbells or free weights for building strength.
■ Weight cuffs to increase resistance during leg work.
■ A jump rope.

YOUR OWN WEIGHT ROOM

The price of a home weight room is comparable to that of a one-year membership at a good gym. The following is what you'll need to start.

■ A 45-pound Olympic bar (this is 7 feet long, 2 inches wide, and sturdy enough to handle any amount of weight) with about 110 pounds of weights. Or buy a good set of barbells, with about the same amount of weights.
■ A curling bar (for arm curls).
■ A pull-up bar (which can be wedged into doorways for chin-ups).
■ A free-weight bench.
■ As you build more, you'll need more weights. These are sold by the pound at sporting-goods stores.

....

When buying weight lifting equipment, be willing to pay for quality. A poor free-weight bench, for example, could collapse underneath you.

....

TIPS ON BUYING MACHINES

Buying exercise machines for the home can be pricey; here's how to get your money's worth.
■ Try out equipment before buying to make sure it is comfortable and easy to use.
■ Check the machine's construction. Avoid lightweight, flimsy models that may rock or wobble when you use them.
■ Shop at a reputable sporting-goods store with a knowledgeable staff.

■ Cross-country Skiing Machine: Some models allow you to move your arms and legs independently; others require synchronized movements. Pick whichever one you are comfortable with.

The machine should have a base long enough for a smooth stride and adjustable leg and arm resistance. Models that have cords rather than poles may give an especially strenuous upper-body workout.
■ Exercise Bicycle: Most models work only the lower body, but some have pumping handlebars for arm and shoulder work. Some machines can simulate biking uphill.

Look for smooth pedaling motion, a comfortable seat, and handlebars that adjust to your height. Pedal straps will keep your feet from slipping and force your legs to work on the upstroke, too.

Recumbent models let you sit back in a chairlike seat with your feet in front of you. This puts less strain on the back, neck, and shoulders.

■ Bicycle Trainer: Cheaper than an exercise bike, this stand lets you convert your regular bike for indoor use. The rear wheel usually rests on a roller.

■ Treadmill: Some treadmills have adjustable inclines to simulate hills and make workouts more challenging. Some can be programmed for preset workouts. Monitors on the front of most machines display calories burned, miles covered, and speed.

Choose a treadmill that has a running surface wide and long enough for your stride and that absorbs shock well. You'll also appreciate having front or side handrails, which will help you keep your balance.

■ Rowing Machine: Some rowing machines have hydraulic pistons to provide variable resistance; many larger models use a flywheel attached to a bar by a chain. Piston-type models are cheaper and more compact than flywheel models, but flywheels have a smoother action that's more like real rowing.

CHOOSING A HEALTH CLUB

Ask yourself these questions when looking at a health club: Is it convenient to my home or office? Do I like the ambience? Do its hours of operation fit my schedule? If the answer to any of these is no, this isn't the club for you. Here are some other points to consider:

■ Most clubs will offer you a trial membership of a few days in which you can get your money back if the club doesn't suit you. In some provinces health clubs are required by law to offer trial periods.

■ If you aren't familiar with the machines, you will need help to develop the proper form. Ask if new members get an orientation or free sessions with a trainer.

■ New members should also receive a health and fitness assessment. This will help the trainer customize a program.

■ Don't overlook the other members when judging a gym. Are you comfortable around them? Is the atmosphere relaxed and friendly? If you're a beginner, you may feel intimidated in a club full of serious bodybuilders.

■ The club should offer a variety of equipment in good working order. If you only want to use free weights, however, you should be able to find a smaller and less expensive gym.

■ Water fountains should be accessible in exercise areas.

■ The club's safety rules should be posted. Club policies, procedures, and safety guidelines should be distributed in writing to members.

■ Check that the staff instructors are certified by the National Fitness Leadership Advisory Committee, or an organization approved by it, and are certified in CPR by the Canadian Red Cross or the St. John Ambulance.

■ Are the exercise areas monitored by staff who can answer questions and otherwise assist members? If the staff is not accessible, you may not get advice when you need it.

■ Check that the locker rooms are clean, well ventilated, and secure, and provide towels, shampoo, soap, and hair dryers.

. . . .

Before joining, visit health clubs during the hours that you will most often work out. This will alert you to any overcrowding problems.

. . . .

EXERCISE INJURIES

Sprains and strains may happen even after a good warm-up. Knowing how to treat exercise injuries is important; you'll get back to your routine faster and prevent the injury from recurring.

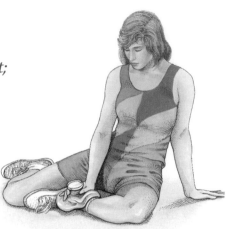

ACT QUICKLY

Don't put off treating a sports injury. Fast action will speed recovery time.

■ For minor discomfort, try changing your technique or position; for example, bad form could cause back pain in joggers or swimmers. Also, rotating your foot slightly in or out may relieve knee pain that develops while bicycling.

■ Runners may find that breathing deeply helps relieve painful cramps in the abdomen, especially in the beginning of a run.

■ Wait several hours, or even a day or two, before applying heat to an injured area. Heat may increase swelling and interfere with healing.

■ Recognize the signs of a fracture or dislocation (see "Fractures and Dislocations," page 412).

■ Consult a physician if you suspect a fracture or dislocation or if there is numbness or tingling. Call also if an injury doesn't respond to treatment within a day or two.

■ Consider pain a warning sign. While the pain may not seem serious, it could indicate a more serious injury.

COMMON INJURIES

■ Women, who have wider hips than men, suffer more problems with knees and ankles because of their leg-muscle alignment. Men tend to have more shoulder injuries because they participate more often in sports that require upper-body strength.

■ Test yourself for knee problems. Runner's knee is the most common knee problem affecting women. To see if this is the cause of your knee pain, do the following: sit on the floor and stretch your legs out in front of you, relax them, and see if it hurts when you wiggle your kneecap with your hand.

■ Building the quadriceps (in the front of the leg) and the hamstrings (in the back of the leg) through weight training will help protect your knees from injury. For treatment of other common injuries, see the chart on the facing page.

- - - - - - - - - - - - - - - - - - -

If you rub a pain-relieving balm into a sore muscle, don't cover the area with a heating pad or bandage. Doing so could produce a serious burn.

- - - - - - - - - - - - - - - - - - -

R.I.C.E. for an Injury

The next time you get a sports injury, remember R.I.C.E. The term stands for Rest, Ice, Compression, and Elevation, and it's the first thing you need to know when pain strikes.

Rest means taking a break from exercise or any movement that might stress the injured area. Minor injuries should be rested for a day or two, and more severe injuries need even longer. Returning to your exercise routine too soon will only cause the problem to worsen.

Ice the affected area. Ice reduces pain, limits the swelling and bleeding, and encourages quick healing. Wrap an ice pack (or even a bag of frozen peas) in a towel to avoid direct contact with the skin.

Compress the injury with a stretch bandage. Wrap it just tight enough to support the injured area comfortably.

Elevate the limb. Keep the injured part above the level of the heart, if possible, or at least higher than the hips. This will limit the swelling and also prevent movement of the injured area.

Be patient, and give your body time to heal. After the pain has gone, work out at a low level of exertion. This stimulates blood flow, thus warming the muscles and making you feel better.

SELF-CARE FOR COMMON SPORTS INJURIES

Problem	Possible Causes	Symptoms	Treatment	Tips
Leg cramps	Strained muscles from stretching too hard or too much. Loss of water, salt, and potassium through sweating	Painful, involuntary muscle contractions	Gently stretch the cramped muscle by walking, then massage it	Drink plenty of fluids. Restore lost potassium by eating an orange or a banana. Do not take salt tablets
Shinsplints	Running or jumping repeatedly on hard surfaces	Pain in muscles around the shin	R.I.C.E. (see opposite page)	Wear shoes with adequate heel support and shock absorption. Run on softer surfaces, avoid hills, and adjust your stride so that you run farther back on your heel
Sore muscles	Overexertion from strenuous exercise	Muscle aches that develop a day or two after exercise	Warm up and stretch carefully. Return to initial intensity only after the pain disappears	Moderate exercise is better than inactivity for boosting circulation and easing the soreness
Sprains	Injury to the ligaments, the connectors between two bones, from a sudden, wrenching movement	Joint pain and swelling that is sometimes disabling	R.I.C.E.	When resuming activity, tape joint to prevent reinjury. Strengthen with resistance exercise
Strains	Pulls or tears in muscle fibers from sudden changes in tension through bursts of activity	Pain and swelling with some loss of power and motion. Soreness usually vanishes in a few days	R.I.C.E.	Avoid exercising when muscles are stiff, cold, or overtired
Tennis elbow (also associated with bowling, canoeing, and pitching)	Excessive strain on the muscles of the forearm from gripping and rotating motions	Tenderness below the outer part of the elbow, with pain radiating to the forearm	R.I.C.E.	Correct your technique. Tennis players may want to change their backhand stroke or try a lighter, more flexible racquet or one with a smaller grip. If you wear a brace, don't fasten the strap too tightly. You should feel its pressure only when the forearm muscle contracts and expands

Grooming is only one facet of good looks. *The better you feel about yourself and your relationships, the more attractive you will appear to others. Conversely, knowing that you look your best most certainly contributes to your sense of well-being.*

CHAPTER 4

LOOKING YOUR BEST

The first step to looking your best is feeling good about yourself. People with healthy self-esteem stand straighter, smile more, and project a sense of friendliness and confidence that is naturally attractive. A push in the right direction is treating your body right—giving it gentle, natural cleansings, avoiding the damaging effects of excess sunlight, and using exercise and a sensible diet to keep it in top condition.

Feeling your best also means accepting yourself as you are. There are attributes that you couldn't, and shouldn't, change—after all, they make you unique. Stop worrying about your height, bone structure, skin tone, or age; they are facts of life. You don't need to live in a beauty salon or plastic surgeon's office to be attractive. Grace and self-confidence will make you stand out far more than will dyed hair or cosmetic surgery.

Youngsters who tend to scrutinize themselves for flaws should be encouraged to recognize that they have many good points.

STANDING TALL

Good posture can make you look and feel younger, taller, thinner, and more self-assured. Bad posture not only detracts from your appearance but may also strain muscles and ligaments and inhibit normal breathing.

ABC'S OF GOOD POSTURE

■ When standing, make sure that your body is in straight vertical alignment, from the top of your head, through the center of your body, to your feet. Try to imagine a plumb line extending through your ear, shoulder, hip, knee, and ankle. Examine yourself, in profile, in a full-length mirror.

■ In this position, your back should curve slightly in three spots: a forward curve at the neck, a backward curve at the upper back, and a forward curve at the lower back. A slumping posture (below right) distorts these natural curves and puts a strain on the lower back.

Correct   *Incorrect*

■ When viewing yourself from the front, make sure that your shoulders are level with each other. The same applies to your hips. If you can't align them, you may have a postural problem; consult your doctor.

. . . .

Check the curves in your spine by pressing your back against a wall, with heels about three inches away. Place your hand behind your neck and lower back. If it doesn't fit comfortably, without much excess space, try adjusting your posture.

. . . .

POSTURE MADE PERFECT

Many people literally forget what good posture feels like. If this is your problem, try this easy exercise a couple of times each day to remind you.

■ Stand with your heels a few inches from a wall and about six inches from each other. Make sure your weight is evenly distributed.

■ Let arms hang at your sides with palms forward. Your kneecaps should also be facing forward.

■ Keep your lower back near the wall as you straighten your upper back. Lift your chest upward and bring your shoulders down and against the wall.

■ Bring your head to rest against the wall with the chin tucked in slightly.

■ Concentrate on flattening your lower abdomen by pulling the muscles up and in. Breathe normally as you keep the muscles tight for about 10 seconds. Release and repeat several times.

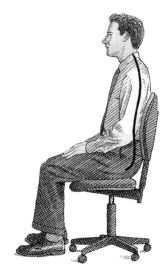

■ You should be able to maintain good posture throughout the day, whether standing, sitting, or moving. To achieve the perfect sitting posture, sit up tall and keep your spine straight against the back of the chair, your head erect, and your chin parallel to your lap.

RELAX AND BREATHE DEEPLY

Here's a mental exercise that dancers sometimes use. It combines deep breathing with visualization exercises to help relax constricted muscles and improve posture.

■ Stand at ease and imagine slipping a tiny air pillow

between each of the vertebrae in your lower back, from the base of the spine to the rib cage. Concentrate on giving each of them a little more "breathing space." Focus your attention on each in turn, as if you were opening and extending the distance between your pelvis and rib cage. Keep your shoulders down as you inhale deeply. You should begin to feel lighter and more relaxed as your lungs expand fully and begin to release the oxygen that your body needs to function smoothly. Exhale and repeat.

STRENGTHENING EXERCISES

Flexibility and strength are crucial to good posture and overall fitness. Devote between 5 and 10 minutes daily to the following exercises or others like them.

■ The Crunch (for abdominal muscles): To do this sit-up, keep your knees bent. Place your arms across your chest, and lift your upper body slightly off the ground, keeping the neck and head in line with the spine.

■ The Pelvic Tilt (for abdominal muscles): Lie on your back with your knees bent and your feet on the floor. Press the lower back against the floor, tighten the abdominal muscles, and squeeze the buttocks as you raise your hips off the floor. Hold for three to five counts, lower, then repeat.

■ The Push-up (for upper back and shoulders): If the military version—on the toes—is too tough, push up from the knees. Or do the standing version—lean against a wall and push.

· ·
To keep tabs on your sitting posture, place large mirrors on walls near your desk and table.
· ·

MAKE SOME ADJUSTMENTS

■ When you're working at a desk or table, move your chair close enough so that you don't need to lean over. Your feet should touch the floor comfortably; if they don't, use a small stool or a phone book to support them (see "You and Your Environment," page 24).

■ If your kitchen sink is too high to work at comfortably while standing, sit on a stool.

■ Have groceries loaded into two bags, rather than one, if you intend to carry them any distance. Always try to carry an equal weight on either side.

■ Whenever you carry a single heavy suitcase, briefcase, grocery bag, or other package, switch the load from side to side frequently.

■ The best sleeping position is on your side with one or both knees pulled up toward your chest. If you must sleep on your back, place a pillow under your knees to relieve muscle stress. If you must sleep on your stomach, put a pillow under your waist.

■ When driving a car, adjust the seat so that your knees are bent and you aren't stretching to reach the pedals. Otherwise, you put unnecessary strain on lower-back muscles. Use a pillow if necessary.

BEYOND POSTURE

■ Be conscious of your body language. How you hold yourself affects how others see you—and how you feel, too. If you move with purpose, energy, and pride, you will internalize those qualities.

■ Choose clothes that tell the world you care about yourself. Train your eye to recognize what works well. Changing your wardrobe periodically will help you look and feel young, but beware of trendy styles that don't suit your body type.

■ Be meticulous about hygiene, and get your hair cut and styled regularly.

· ·
Pretend that someone is about to take your picture. Relax your shoulders, elongate your neck, straighten your back—and smile. Make that posture a habit.
· ·

SKIN: HANDLE WITH CARE

For skin care, simpler is often better. For instance, you'll find that wearing protective clothing to shield yourself from harsh elements is a better method of skin care than using very expensive beauty creams.

ENEMIES LIST

■ Baking in the sun may feel good, but it's the worst thing you can do to your skin. The sun's ultraviolet rays can cause wrinkling and skin cancer (see "Sun Sense," page 126).

■ The wind dries and toughens the skin. Cover up on windy days—wear a ski mask or scarf to protect your face—and use a moisturizer regularly as a preventive measure.

■ Dry air, whether hot or cold, robs the skin of moisture. In winter, use a humidifier or put an open pan of water on the radiator. Plants are also good humidifiers, since they emit water vapor. See page 206 for information on humidifiers.

■ Smoking is bad for your skin. Nicotine constricts blood vessels, interferes with the flow of oxygen and nutrients to skin cells, and can emphasize crow's-feet.

■ Hot tubs and baths can take moisture out of your skin. The longer the soak, the more moisture you lose. Go easy on these, as well as hot showers.

Shorter and cooler showers are better for your skin, especially when the weather is cold.

■ Saunas will make your skin feel tight not because its texture is improved but because it's dried out. Don't take saunas too often.

■ Diuretics are water-reduction pills sometimes used by dieters. They work by stealing water from body tissue, essentially drying the skin from the inside out.

■ Poor nutrition affects the whole body, but the skin may show it first.

■ Inactivity means sluggish skin. Exercise increases blood flow and bathes the skin in its natural moisturizer—sweat. It may also help reduce the tension and stress that eventually etch the face with lines and creases.

■ If you sleep under an electric blanket, make sure that you're not turning it up any higher than necessary. The heat promotes loss of water from the skin surface; the higher the setting, the greater the loss. See page 207 for other safety precautions.

. . . .
Facial exercises designed to fight wrinkles may instead actually produce them, since they tend to crease the skin into set patterns.
. . . .

KNOW YOUR SOAPS

■ True soaps are composed of alkaline salts and fatty acids. Oils, scents, coloring, and antibacterial agents may be added to true soaps.

■ Synthetic soaps are less alkaline and are made from detergents (a term that does not necessarily indicate harshness), fatty acids, and other sources. They lather better in hard water and don't leave a bathtub ring. They're also called beauty bars, soap-free cleansers, and nonsoaps.

■ Transparent soaps contain 10 percent more glycerin, a substance that helps the skin hold moisture. However,

some contain alcohol and are therefore drying.

■ Superfatted soaps have extra fats or oils, such as cocoa butter and mineral oil. They work well for dry skin.

■ Antibacterial soaps have ingredients that kill bacteria on the skin's surface. Older formulas, which tend to dry the skin, can sometimes help alleviate shaving irritation. The new formulas are non-drying and so are especially good during winter and for older people.

■ Abrasive or exfoliant soaps, with tiny particles meant to slough off dead cells, can be harsh and drying. People with extremely oily skin may find them helpful when used occasionally (and gently).

■ Acne or medicated soaps contain topical drugs in addition to the cleansing agent. Although they can be helpful, they also tend to be drying and can be irritating. If you experience irritation, stop usage until the skin recovers.

■ Liquid soaps are usually synthetics and have the same cleansing ability as the bars. Some people find them convenient. More important, they may be less likely to attract bacteria than bar soaps.

■ Unscented soaps have little or no added fragrance, so they are a wise choice for those with sensitive skin or allergies.

■ Specialty soaps may have added vitamins, minerals, perfumes, wheat germ, or vegetable or fruit juices. (The additives aren't on your skin long enough to have any effect.) They possess the same cleansing power as other soaps and should be selected based on skin type.

GENTLE FACE CLEANSING

Cleaning your face improperly may do more harm than good. Many of us assault the face with harsh products that can injure skin cells.

■ Wash your face once a day with warm—not hot—water and a mild cleanser. Don't massage soap into your skin because this may clog your pores. Rinse thoroughly to remove all traces of soap.

■ Use a soft washcloth to help remove dead skin cells and dirt. Be sure to rinse the cloth after each use.

■ You needn't worry too much about the pH (the numerical indication of acidity or alkalinity) of a soap. Your skin will return to its normal pH level soon after washing.

■ If you live in a heavily polluted area, clean your face a second time each day using a cotton ball moistened with a nonalcohol toner.

■ For a gentle massage, stimulate your face with a dental irrigator. This will also flush out pores. Avoid your eyes and ears.

NUTRIENTS FOR THE SKIN

■ Vitamin C helps produce collagen, the substance that gives skin some of its elasticity. Citrus fruits, green peppers, and tomatoes are high in vitamin C.

■ Vitamin E, an antioxidant, helps to counter the effects of pollution and ultraviolet rays. Among foods high in vitamin E are wheat germ, whole-grain breads, oatmeal, and vegetable oils.

■ Beta-carotene is also an antioxidant. It is found in various fruits and vegetables, including carrots and broccoli. You may also want to take a multivitamin supplement containing beta-carotene.

■ Drink eight glasses of fluids a day to make sure your skin is getting enough moisture from within. Besides plain water, you can meet this quota with mineral water, seltzer, diluted fruit juices, herb teas, decaffeinated tea and coffee, and artificially sweetened beverages. (Drinks containing alcohol, caffeine, sugar, and salt, on the other hand, are dehydrating.)

If you have tiny facial surface veins, avoid alcohol and hot or spicy foods; they aggravate flushing.

IF YOUR SKIN IS SENSITIVE

■ Remember that the term *hypoallergenic* means only that the most common allergens—fragrance, cocoa butter, cornstarch, cottonseed oil—have been removed from the product. There is no guarantee that you will not be

allergic to one or more of the remaining ingredients.

■ The terms *unscented* and *fragrance-free* can be misleading. Masking scents may be used to cover the odor of some antiperspirant ingredients.

■ If you react badly to commercial antiperspirants and deodorants, try a mixture of equal parts of vinegar and water (the vinegar smell will disappear). Or wash twice a day with an antibacterial cleanser. Other options include using talcum powder, baking soda, or witch hazel. If none of these measures work, consult a doctor, who may provide an antiperspirant solution.

■ If you're allergic to makeup, try a little beet juice for color. Apply it with a soft sponge or cotton ball.

■ If you have pierced ears and tend to get infections, try dipping the back of the steel posts in an antibacterial ointment before wearing them. And don't wear earrings containing nickel; this highly allergenic metal can cause dermatitis.

KEEPING THE MOISTURE IN

■ There are two types of moisturizers. Emollients, such as petroleum jelly and mineral oil, work best on dry or chapped skin. Humectants—glycerin, sorbitol, lactic acid, and urea—are good for oily or sensitive skin.

■ The best time to put on moisturizer is right after washing, when your skin is still damp. Apply a light coating to seal moisture in.

■ For extra moisture in your face, wring out a washcloth and drape it over your face for a few minutes. Then apply moisturizer.

■ Makeup helps reduce water loss from the skin, so if you don't wear makeup, be sure to use a moisturizer.

■ Don't assume that expensive products offer special advantages. Cheaper creams and lotions may be just as effective.

■ Let a moisturizer set for 10 minutes before applying makeup. Most foundations are oil-based and don't mix well with the water in moisturizers.

> **To make your own bath pillow, fill a hot-water bottle with warm water, or roll up a big bath towel and seal it inside a plastic bag.**

TUB OR SHOWER?

■ Your limbs become slightly buoyant in bathwater. This causes a drop in muscle tension, making the bath a good way to relax. A shower is more invigorating, probably because of the temperature disparity—part of your body is exposed to hot water and the rest to cooler air—and the fact that you're standing instead of reclining.

■ Taking baths can ease arthritis, muscle injuries, skin maladies, and poor circulation. Combining baths and massage therapy will often alleviate stress.

■ Before entering a bath or shower, always test the water temperature at the tap with your elbow, which is more sensitive to heat than your hand. Heaters in some homes can bring the water to a scalding 62.8°C (145°F).

■ If you feel flushed or sweat profusely within a couple of minutes of getting into the tub or shower, lower the water temperature.

■ People with heart trouble should take cool or warm—but never hot—baths. When the water is hotter than normal body temperature, the body tries to compensate by expanding the blood vessels near the surface of the skin. This can cause a drop in blood pressure.

■ Every few days, stay in the bath or shower long enough to soften dead skin on your feet, elbows, and elsewhere. Then rub those areas with a wet pumice stone, loofah, or abrasive puff. After removing

rough skin, rinse off and apply body lotion.

■ No talcum powder? You can substitute cornstarch (unless you're allergic) if you like a dusting after your bath.

■ Avoid bath oils. They don't add moisture to the skin, and they can make the tub dangerously slippery. Instead, dissolve 1/2 cup salt in your bathwater; it helps to prevent drying and "winter itch."

SMOOTH SHAVING

■ Most people need to warm the skin and hydrate facial hair so that it's erect and easier to shave. The hot, wet towels of the old-fashioned barbershop are ideal, but the next-best thing is to shave immediately after a shower, bath, or sauna.

■ You can also shave *in* the shower; fog-free mirrors are now available. Those who like to use a razor but suffer from neck irritation or ingrown hairs will especially benefit from this method. Don't stay in the shower longer than 15 minutes—oversoaked skin prevents a smooth shave and may cause nicks.

■ If you use a softening agent, consider the traditional shaving brush for lathering. It makes the beard stand up more than foams and gels do. To preserve the brush, stroke up and down rather than in a circle.

■ Aftershaves are a matter of personal preference. All you really need is a warm-water rinse. If you have sensitive skin, use an aloe lotion.

■ Forget "the perfect shave." If you move the razor both in and against the direction

---

Add Spice to Your Bath

Different herbs provide subtly distinct sensations when added to bathwater. Place one type of herb or a mixture in a cloth or net bag, and then toss the bag into the tub or hang it on the faucet as the tub fills. Use the guide below to help you choose.

    Stimulating, for a refreshing early-morning bath: lovage, mint, rosemary, sage, orange, pine, thyme

    Tranquilizing, for an end-of-the-day bath: chamomile, sandalwood, lavender, marjoram, marigold, mint

    Relief for sore muscles or joints: sassafras, wintergreen, lavender

    Relief for itchy skin: parsley, sage, rosemary, basil

    Antidote to fatigue or stress: pine, sage, fir (plus a cup of cider vinegar)

---

of the hair, you're literally shaving your skin, promoting irritation and ingrown hairs.

■ Those who do become irritated (redness, small bumps) should use an antibacterial soap twice a day to help avoid infection. After the first wash—right after shaving—apply 1/2 or 1 percent cortisone cream (but avoid the eye areas). This will have an anti-inflammatory effect.

■ To prevent dulling, never run a razor blade across a towel.

■ Shave in the direction the hair grows—downward, except on the neck (for most men).

■ Women shaving their legs should do the opposite: shave against the grain so that the razor can lift up the hairs before cutting them. Use long, even strokes, and moisturize your legs afterward.

■ Never use deodorant right after shaving under your arms. If possible, shave underarms at night, pat on witch hazel, and then give your skin an

---

overnight rest.

■ If you plan to use a bleaching or depilatory cream on facial hair, test it first on your forearm or the inside of your wrist to see if your skin can tolerate it.

To treat a shaving nick, apply a tea bag moistened with cold water.

AFTER-SHOWER STRETCH

Hold on to your towel after each warm bath or shower. In only a few minutes, you can do exercises involving the shoulder, arm, and chest muscles for improved upper-body flexibility. Stretch until you feel a slight pull in the muscle, and then hold for 10 seconds. You should feel some tension, but not pain.

■ Hold the towel above your head with your hands about two feet apart. Pull backward until you feel a stretch in your armpits.

■ Then gently pull your right hand straight up in the air as you pull to the side with your left hand. Reverse.

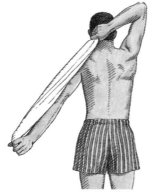

■ Next, drop the left end of the towel behind your back and use your left hand to pull down on the towel. Repeat on opposite side.

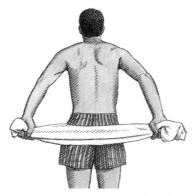

■ Finally, grasp both ends of the towel behind your back and try to lift your arms up and back. Do not arch your back.

DEALING WITH ACNE

■ In treating acne, start with the mildest medication, such as a 2.5 percent solution of benzoyl peroxide. Check the label to make sure the product does not contain lanolin or mineral oil. If the skin tolerates this mild solution but the acne does not improve, try 5 percent strength. When using any benzoyl peroxide, avoid the area around the eyes. Persistent acne may require a prescription medication; consult a dermatologist.

■ Check your medications. Dilantin, cortisone, and other steroids, and hormone preparations, including birth control pills and estrogen, commonly trigger acne. If you're taking any of these drugs, pay extra attention to skin care.

■ Iodides and fluorides—found in kelp, spinach, seaweed, shellfish, and iodized salt—may worsen problem skin.

■ Although some foods can aggravate acne, chocolate isn't one of them. Numerous studies show that even large amounts of chocolate will not provoke outbreaks.

■ Working out may also mean breaking out, especially at the start of an exercise program, when the skin isn't used to the increased sweat and oil. Remove makeup before exercising, change out of damp clothes afterward, and spritz your face with water or toner if you can't shower right away. Wipe off a communal gym mat—with alcohol, if possible—before using it.

■ Cosmetics may contribute to acne problems. Buy products labeled "noncomedogenic,"

which means that they are free of oil and other ingredients that can clog pores.

■ Noncomedogenic moisturizers and sunscreens are also available. Always use moisturizers sparingly.

■ Certain hair-care products—mousses, conditioners, sprays—may lead to skin outbreaks. Stay away from those that list oils among the ingredients.

■ Dirty makeup brushes can harbor bacteria and germs. At least twice a month, soak brushes for 10 minutes in a dish of warm, soapy water (use a liquid, antibacterial soap). Then rinse them thoroughly and blot them dry with a clean towel. Stand brushes, handle ends down, in a glass until they're completely dry.

■ Does your chin, cheek, or forehead break out? Notice whether you tend to rest it in the palm of your hand (or, with the chin, against a telephone receiver). If so, change this habit.

■ Lip balm can cause acne or blackheads around the mouth. Check your brand; if it contains mineral oil, buy another kind without that ingredient.

■ Men with acne should shave as seldom as possible and always use a sharp blade. A translucent, rather than opaque, shaving gel will help you to see sensitive areas.

ITCHY SKIN

Treatment varies according to the underlying cause, but here are some all-purpose remedies.

■ Try a soothing bath. Tie about a cup of oatmeal in a

cheesecloth bag, and swish the bag through warm bathwater until the water looks somewhat milky. Or add 1/2 cup salt to a tub of tepid water. Soak in the tub for 10 minutes.

■ For temporary relief, calamine lotion—*without* added antihistamines, which may cause allergic reactions—or a nonprescription hydrocortisone cream may help. You can also try a product containing pramoxine, which is somewhat anesthetic and can give rapid relief; use it alone or along with the hydrocortisone cream. Don't apply any of these, however, if you have an infection, and consult a doctor before treating a rash in this way. Also limit use to four or five days. After this, see a doctor—persistent itching may indicate a serious condition.

■ Experiment with different fabrics. Many people cannot tolerate wool; others react badly to dyes and synthetics. Your detergent may also be the culprit; try putting clothes through an extra rinse cycle. Wear plain white cotton, which seldom provokes a reaction, next to the skin.

■ If you tend to have itchy skin, watch what you eat and drink. Coffee, alcohol, and spicy or steaming-hot foods cause the blood vessels in the skin's outer layer to swell and can trigger itching.

. . . .
Find relief for itchy skin in your freezer: apply crushed ice wrapped in a towel to the area.
. . . .

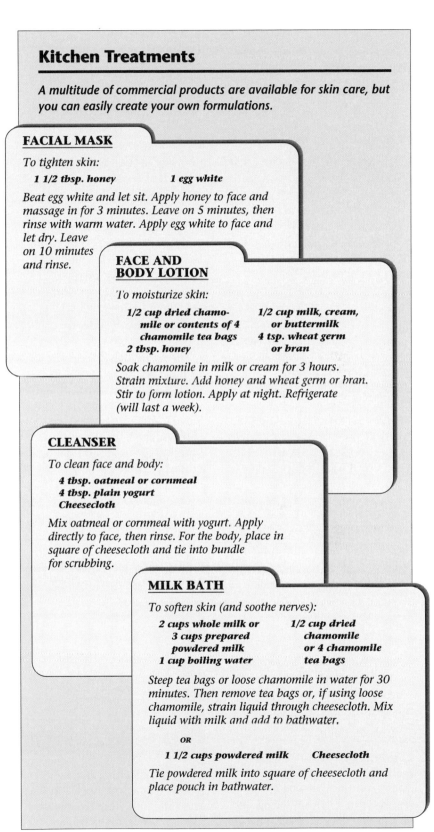

Kitchen Treatments

A multitude of commercial products are available for skin care, but you can easily create your own formulations.

FACIAL MASK

To tighten skin:

1 1/2 tbsp. honey   **1 egg white**

Beat egg white and let sit. Apply honey to face and massage in for 3 minutes. Leave on 5 minutes, then rinse with warm water. Apply egg white to face and let dry. Leave on 10 minutes and rinse.

FACE AND BODY LOTION

To moisturize skin:

1/2 cup dried chamomile or contents of 4 chamomile tea bags
2 tbsp. honey

1/2 cup milk, cream, or buttermilk
4 tsp. wheat germ or bran

Soak chamomile in milk or cream for 3 hours. Strain mixture. Add honey and wheat germ or bran. Stir to form lotion. Apply at night. Refrigerate (will last a week).

CLEANSER

To clean face and body:

4 tbsp. oatmeal or cornmeal
4 tbsp. plain yogurt
Cheesecloth

Mix oatmeal or cornmeal with yogurt. Apply directly to face, then rinse. For the body, place in square of cheesecloth and tie into bundle for scrubbing.

MILK BATH

To soften skin (and soothe nerves):

2 cups whole milk or 3 cups prepared powdered milk
1 cup boiling water

1/2 cup dried chamomile or 4 chamomile tea bags

Steep tea bags or loose chamomile in water for 30 minutes. Then remove tea bags or, if using loose chamomile, strain liquid through cheesecloth. Mix liquid with milk and add to bathwater.

OR

1 1/2 cups powdered milk   Cheesecloth

Tie powdered milk into square of cheesecloth and place pouch in bathwater.

125

SUN SENSE

Most of us enjoy being out in the sun, and sunlight does have its benefits. Unfortunately, too much exposure to its ultraviolet (UV) radiation can cause wrinkles, skin cancer, and other problems.

BE WARY

■ The summer sun is the most hazardous, but you need sunscreen protection year-round. (For information on treating sunburn, see page 424.)

■ The sun's rays are most intense from 10:00 A.M. to 2:00 P.M. (11:00 A.M. to 3:00 P.M. daylight saving time). Plan your outdoor activities for early mornings or late afternoons.

■ Glare from sand, snow, and water reflects the sun's rays, greatly increasing their effect. Cement also reflects the sun. Be sure to use sunscreen and sunglasses when glare is present, and walk on the shady side of the street. Place your child's sandbox in a shady area.

■ The closer you are to the equator, the stronger the sun's rays. When in the tropics, limit any first-day exposure to direct sunlight to 15 minutes at a time, for a total of one hour or less, and always use sunscreen.

■ High altitudes are also a hazard. Because the atmosphere is thinner, more UV radiation reaches your skin. Be particularly careful when working or vacationing in mountain regions.

■ The longer the horizon, the more vulnerable you are to harmful rays. Someone standing on an open plain is at more risk than a person whose view of the horizon is blocked by trees or buildings.

■ Don't be fooled into reserving your sunscreen for bright days. Most of the sun's UV rays penetrate clouds, so that even hazy, overcast days can damage your skin.

■ Tanning salons provide sunlamp radiation that carries all the risks of real sunlight, including skin cancer. Unless the user wears goggles, the radiation may also cause serious eye damage.

■ Fluorescent lights emit small amounts of radiation, especially some newer fixtures (shaped like egg crates) that leave bulbs unshielded. Use incandescent lighting wherever possible. Uncovered halogen bulbs also present a risk, but a double-envelope halogen bulb provides its own shield.

PROTECT YOURSELF

■ Use sunscreens (see "Buying and Applying Sunscreen," on the facing page).

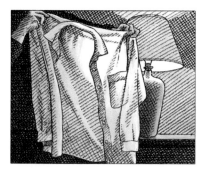

■ Choose clothing that will sufficiently come between you and the sun's rays. To get an idea of how much a piece of clothing will shield you from the sun, hold it up to a lamp and see how much light it lets through. Clothes with thick, tight weaves and ample coverage work best. Some T-shirts offer good protection, but they lose up to 25 percent of their effectiveness when wet. Lightweight clothing made especially to provide sun protection is now available. However, any clothing is better than none, and is better than most sunscreens. Avoid clothing that is supposed to allow an allover tan; that means it lets in too much UV radiation.

■ Put on a hat with a brim, preferably about three inches wide. Baseball caps and visors shade the face, but they leave the ears and back of the neck exposed.

■ Wear gloves when gardening or playing golf.

■ Guard your eyes with sunglasses. Over the years, exposure to UV rays can harm the lens, retina, and cornea and can lead to cataracts (see "Protecting Your Eyes," page 148).

■ Seek out shade, but remember that beach umbrellas do nothing against rays reflected off sand and sea.

■ Be aware that glass windows block some UV rays, but not all.

The safety glass in windshields has an inside layer of plastic, which adds more protection, but car interiors are still not completely free of UV radiation.

■ Never use a sun reflector or metallic reflector blanket. They can cause serious burns very quickly.

Children's skin is especially vulnerable to the sun; childhood sunburns mean a greater risk of skin cancer, including melanoma, in later life. Make it a family routine to put on sunscreen and hats before going out. Teach children this rule: If your shadow is shorter than you are, stay out of the sun.

BUYING AND APPLYING SUNSCREEN

■ Sunblocks are barriers that reflect and scatter rays. Unlike the "white stuff" lifeguards use, many new blocks disappear on your skin. Sunscreens work differently, with chemicals that absorb specific sun rays, preventing them from penetrating to the skin.

■ Sunlight consists of two types of harmful rays—UVB and UVA. UVB rays are the primary cause of sunburn, but both UVB and UVA rays play a role in causing skin cancer, and UVA rays also promote premature wrinkling. Sunblocks protect against both types of rays. If you buy a sunscreen instead of a sunblock, make sure that the label indicates protection against both UVA and UVB rays.

■ If your skin or eyes are sensitive, look for products that are hypoallergenic, fragrance-free, and nonstinging (won't irritate eyes). Be leery, however, of such claims as "waterproof" and "sweatproof." The most effective way to use all sunscreens, despite the manufacturers' claims, is to apply them after swimming, perspiring, showering and toweling dry.

■ Certain medicines increase sensitivity to the sun (and sunlamps). These include antihistamines, oral contraceptives, some antibiotics, and antidiabetic and high-blood-pressure drugs. Check with your doctor if you are taking any medications. You may want to use a sun product made with titanium dioxide, which also blocks infrared light (sometimes a problem for photosensitive people).

■ Choose the type of sun product that works best for you: A spray of mist showers every inch of skin quickly and easily. A lotion that goes on white lets you see where you've missed. Ready-made sunscreen-soaked towelettes ease the task.

■ Test for sensitivity by dabbing some of the product under your chin or on the back of your hand, then seeing if any redness develops after about two hours outside.

■ Choose a PABA-free sunscreen. PABA sometimes causes allergic reactions.

■ Apply sunscreen to unclothed areas of your body and those covered only by thin fabric. Don't forget your head, especially if your hair is thinning. Other areas to remember: hands, hair part, tops of ears, top of brow, neck, and neckline. When going barefoot or wearing sandals, cover the tops of feet as well.

■ Put on sunscreen 15 to 30 minutes before going out, to allow time for it to penetrate the skin. Slather it on liberally, but don't rub it in any more than necessary. Reapply every two hours if you stay outside.

■ Even with sunscreen protection, no one should stay in the sun for long periods. Be aware that sunlight may interfere with the immune system's normal workings, and sunscreen ingredients do not entirely prevent this.

■ Ultraviolet rays can penetrate at least three feet of water, so swimmers aren't exempt from sun damage.

Put on sunscreen before going into the water, and reapply after swimming. Wear a white or pastel bathing suit to reflect rather than absorb the light.

■ Toss out any sunscreens that are past their expiration dates. If no date is given, don't keep them longer than a year and a half.

■ It's never too late to start using sunscreen, even if you've already racked up years of exposure.

> **Sun exposure is responsible for vitamin D production in the skin. Those who use sunscreen regularly—particularly the elderly—should consume at least 400 IUs (international units) of that vitamin daily. Foods rich in vitamin D include salmon, tuna, eggs, and milk.**

WHAT'S YOUR NUMBER?

■ The SPF (sun protection factor) number tells you how long a sunscreen will protect you from burning; multiply the SPF by the amount of time it normally takes you to get red. Those with fair complexions burn fastest (usually in about 15 minutes), but even olive-skinned people can burn within 30 minutes. No matter what your complexion, be sure to use sunscreen.

■ A tan actually serves as a natural sunscreen; however, even the deepest tan gives only limited protection—estimated as the equivalent of an SPF of only 4. Thus, regardless of how deeply you tan, you still need sunscreen.

■ Your skin's best friend is a sunscreen with an SPF of at least 15, applied daily—even when it's cloudy or you're going to be out only a few minutes. If you work outdoors, apply again every two hours; for office workers, one application is enough.

■ For lips, you can purchase a balm that contains SPF-15 sunscreen.

■ Protection does not increase proportionally as the SPF numbers rise. An SPF of 2 indicates 50 percent blockage of burning rays, while an SPF of 15 indicates 93 percent. But an SPF of 30 increases the blockage only a small amount, to 97 percent. Certain people, however, may want to use an SPF between 20 and 30—for example, someone with a history of skin cancer or a fair-skinned person in the tropics.

■ Don't use sunscreen on infants under six months old. Instead, keep them under wraps and use shading devices on strollers. After six months, apply a sunscreen with SPF 15. Special sunscreens for children are unnecessary, but you should choose creamy, alcohol-free, nonstinging, unscented types.

> **Perfume can make your skin especially sensitive to sunlight, causing brown spots. When heading into the sun, coat your skin with a thin layer of petroleum jelly before dabbing on any fragrance. Better yet, save the scent for later.**

THE MAKEUP CONNECTION

■ For day-to-day protection, consider moisturizers and makeup (including lipstick) that contain sunscreen, but make sure that the SPF is at least 15; otherwise, use a separate sunscreen as well. SPF protection is not cumulative; when products are layered, the protection you get is equal only to that of the highest SPF product used.

■ Apply sunscreen under your foundation or over your daytime moisturizer.

■ Because the sun dries your skin, you need moisture replenishment along with a sunscreen. Some sunscreens contain moisturizers.

THE SUNLESS TAN

■ A self-tanning lotion will give your skin color but may offer little or no protection. Unless it has an SPF of 15, top it off with sunscreen.

■ Choose a product without artificial dyes. If you have oily skin or acne, buy a lotion without mineral oil. Colors differ, so don't mix brands.

■ Test the shade inside your elbow a day ahead.

■ Apply the product evenly over freshly scrubbed skin—missed spots or heavy dabs result in streaks or splotches. Avoid hair, eyebrows, and eyes, but include the neck and under the chin.

■ Be sparing on thick-skinned areas, such as elbows and knees, which tend to absorb more and become darker.

■ Wash the palms of your hands as soon as you've finished so they don't stain. Wait at least 10 minutes before putting on any clothes that will touch the lotion.

■ Be patient while awaiting results—it takes up to six hours for color to emerge.

■ If you do end up with streaks, cover the lighter patches with a dark foundation, blending it into the tanned-looking areas.

■ To maintain your "tan," you'll need to redo it in a few days, but remember that too-frequent applications may result in blotches.

TANNING: LESS IS BETTER

Overexposure to the sun is now the leading cause of skin cancer, so protecting yourself is more important than ever.

• • • • • • •

Is this the look of the future? North Americans are starting to take their fashion cues from the desert, where people have been covering up for centuries.

In 1985 President Ronald Reagan was diagnosed with basal cell carcinoma, a form of skin cancer that is common but usually not dangerous. Reagan conceded that it was the result of too much sun and too little protection, starting at a young age. In 1990, Quebec Premier Robert Bourassa was diagnosed and treated for malignant melanoma—a less common and more serious type of skin cancer also associated with overexposure to the sun.

In fact, the number of cases of skin cancer has nearly doubled over the last decade, making it the most common cancer in Canada. Tens of thousands of Canadians are diagnosed with skin cancer each year, and some 500 die from malignant melanoma.

Despite the growing numbers, scientists can't seem to agree on whether the problem stems from the depletion of the ozone layer or simply from an increase in the amount of time we spend basking in the sun. However, they do agree that limiting the body's exposure to the sun's dangerous ultraviolet (UV) rays is the only way to prevent skin cancer.

Early detection. Most skin cancers can be treated if caught in time. Get in the habit of examining your body monthly for:

- ☐ A persistent patch of irritated skin
- ☐ A small growth
- ☐ A sore that doesn't heal but forms a crust and bleeds
- ☐ A new mole
- ☐ A mole that changes in any way
- ☐ A mole that itches or hurts

The changes mentioned occur with basal and squamous cell carcinomas. The early warning signs of malignant melanoma are:

- — a darkening of an existing mole
- — an increase in its size
- — irregularity of its margins
- — an increased elevation of the mole
- — bleeding in the later stages of development.

If you are in doubt, have a doctor examine a suspicious area of skin.

Self-test. To perform your own examination you will need a full-length mirror, a hand mirror, and a brightly lit room. Examine your body, front and back. Raise your arms, and turn to the right and then to the left. Look carefully at your forearms, upper inner arms, and palms. Pay attention to the backs of your legs, the soles of your feet, and the spaces between your toes.

Use the hand mirror to examine the back of your neck and your scalp. You may want to part your hair (or use a blow dryer to lift it) so you can get a better look. Check your back and buttocks as best you can by using both mirrors. Of course, see your doctor immediately if you detect any changes, but also have a dermatologist examine your skin once a year.☐

THE BASICS OF HAIR CARE

Healthy, good-looking hair is not just a matter of luck. Even "uncooperative" hair can shine if given the proper care—protection from sun, wind, rough handling, and the wrong hair products.

BE GENTLE

■ Protect your hair against the sun and wind by wearing a hat or scarf whenever you go outdoors. Not only can the sun burn your scalp, but if your hair has been treated with rinses or dyes, the sun can change its color. Ingredients added to hair products to block ultraviolet rays provide some protection, but not enough.

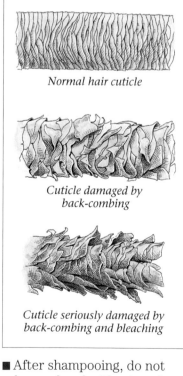

Normal hair cuticle

Cuticle damaged by back-combing

Cuticle seriously damaged by back-combing and bleaching

■ After shampooing, do not rub your head with a towel. Hair is at its most vulnerable when wet, and rubbing can damage it. Instead, blot excess moisture with a towel. Then gently comb it out, using a wide-toothed comb (not a brush). Rubber or tortoise-shell combs are better than plastic or metal.

■ Blow-dryers, hot rollers, and curling irons can burn and dry out hair. Try to choose a hair-style that can be air-dried.

■ If you prefer a blow-dryer, don't use it when your hair is sopping wet: you will need too much heat, which will create split ends. Don't use a blow-dryer when the hair has completely dried, either, as this can also cause damage. The best heat settings are low and medium.

■ Brushing hair when it's dry can impart a healthy-looking fullness. It will also distribute the oils from the scalp along the shafts to the ends of your hair. Natural-bristle brushes are recommended. To keep from harming hair cuticles, don't brush too vigorously. Use only 15 to 20 strokes; more can be damaging.

■ To tame static electricity, apply a drop of hand cream to your palms, rub well, and run your hands over your dry hair. You can also lightly rub your hair with a fabric-softening sheet, or put hair spray on your hairbrush before brushing gently.

■ If you're thinking of getting a permanent, keep in mind that this process can cause both structural damage to the hair (though this is only temporary) and allergic dermatitis of the scalp, forehead, and neck.

■ Eat a well-balanced diet so that your hair will get the protein, vitamins, and minerals it needs to stay healthy.

■ After swimming in the ocean, rinse your hair in fresh water to remove salt water. Rinse, too, after swimming in a pool to remove the chlorine. If chlorine turns blond hair green, rinse your hair with a mixture of four crushed aspirins and one to two ounces of water; leave on your hair for 10 minutes.

A SHAMPOO SAMPLER

■ Rotate several brands of shampoo. After two or three washes with conditioning shampoos, or rinsing with a separate conditioner, switch to a plain cleansing shampoo.

■ Conditioning shampoos have ingredients to provide shine, body, and manageability or to improve the look of damaged hair. Most shampoos contain about 15 ingredients; those that also condition may have as many as 25.

■ If you use a conditioning shampoo, you don't need a separate conditioner. Rinse your hair well—for at least 60 seconds—after washing to remove any residue.

■ The best shampoos are those with a neutral or acidic pH. They'll shrink the cuticle (the hair shaft's outer layer), smoothing it and thus making the hair shaft stronger and shinier. A pH of seven is neutral, which means the shampoo is fine for normal or oily hair. Look for a lower (acidic) pH for damaged, weathered, or chemically treated hair.

■ Many shampoos are alkaline, with a pH above seven. These products can swell and weaken the shaft, leaving even normal hair looking dull.

■ If a shampoo label doesn't list the pH, you can test the product yourself with a sensitive litmus paper (available at many drugstores).

■ Hair often benefits from rest; try washing every two or three days instead of daily. However, if you do prefer daily washing, use a gentle—nonfragrant, nonmedicated—shampoo.

■ Much of the need for daily shampooing comes from the overuse of conditioners and styling products, which weigh down and flatten the hair as well as attract dirt and oil. Try to style your hair with just one or two products.

■ If your hair is fine-textured and oily, condition it before (rather than after) shampooing to give it more body.

Hair Recipes

Follow the recipes below and on the next page to make your own hair products. You'll sometimes need a fine strainer or cheesecloth to strain herbs from liquid.

SETTING LOTION

To make a fresh-smelling holding lotion:

> **1 large lemon**
>   **or orange or 2 limes**
> **2 cups water**

Cut the fruit into quarters, and squeeze juice into water. Bring the mixture to a boil, then let cool. Strain and store in spray bottle. Spritz on before setting hair.

RESIDUE RINSE FOR LIGHT HAIR

To remove residue from light hair:

> **1/4 cup concentrated lemon juice**
> **2 cups lukewarm water**

Mix lemon juice and water together and pour over hair. Leave on 10 minutes, then rinse with warm water.

RESIDUE RINSE FOR DARK HAIR

To remove residue from dark hair:

> **2 tbsp. apple cider vinegar**
> **2 cups lukewarm water**
> **1 tsp. oil of cloves (can be purchased at drugstore)**

Mix vinegar, water, and oil of cloves together. Pour over hair, leave on 10 minutes, and rinse.

GRAY HAIR DYE

To color graying sections of dark hair:

> **1 tbsp. fresh**   **1 tbsp. fresh**
>   **or dried sage**   **or dried rosemary**
> **1 cup boiling water**   **3 tea bags (regular)**

Put tea bags in water and let steep 15 minutes. With bags still in water, add sage and rosemary. Let stand 3 hours (or overnight), then strain mixture. Pour liquid over hair, or spray it on, after shampooing; cover thoroughly. (Wear old clothes, as tea stains.) Blot with towel or use hair dryer—do not rinse out. May take several applications to produce color change.

Hair Recipes

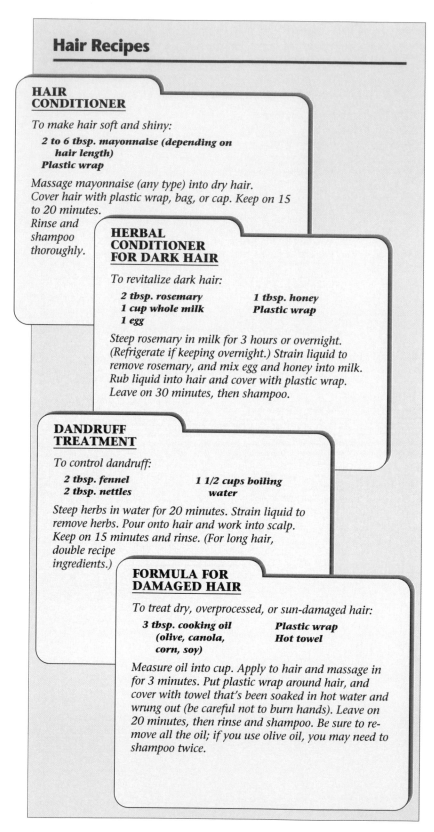

HAIR CONDITIONER

To make hair soft and shiny:

2 to 6 tbsp. mayonnaise (depending on hair length)
Plastic wrap

Massage mayonnaise (any type) into dry hair. Cover hair with plastic wrap, bag, or cap. Keep on 15 to 20 minutes. Rinse and shampoo thoroughly.

HERBAL CONDITIONER FOR DARK HAIR

To revitalize dark hair:

2 tbsp. rosemary   **1 tbsp. honey**
1 cup whole milk   **Plastic wrap**
1 egg

Steep rosemary in milk for 3 hours or overnight. (Refrigerate if keeping overnight.) Strain liquid to remove rosemary, and mix egg and honey into milk. Rub liquid into hair and cover with plastic wrap. Leave on 30 minutes, then shampoo.

DANDRUFF TREATMENT

To control dandruff:

2 tbsp. fennel   **1 1/2 cups boiling**
2 tbsp. nettles   **water**

Steep herbs in water for 20 minutes. Strain liquid to remove herbs. Pour onto hair and work into scalp. Keep on 15 minutes and rinse. (For long hair, double recipe ingredients.)

FORMULA FOR DAMAGED HAIR

To treat dry, overprocessed, or sun-damaged hair:

3 tbsp. cooking oil   **Plastic wrap**
(olive, canola,   **Hot towel**
corn, soy)

Measure oil into cup. Apply to hair and massage in for 3 minutes. Put plastic wrap around hair, and cover with towel that's been soaked in hot water and wrung out (be careful not to burn hands). Leave on 20 minutes, then rinse and shampoo. Be sure to remove all the oil; if you use olive oil, you may need to shampoo twice.

Dilute your shampoo and conditioner by pouring half into empty bottles and topping both bottles with water. Diluted products work just as effectively and cut down on residue buildup.

PROPER CONDITIONING

You probably need a conditioner, at least occasionally, to promote shine and health, even if your hair is in good shape.

■ There are three major types of conditioners:

Creme rinses help manage tangles. Keep in mind, however, that creme rinses can make oily hair limp, and some are alkaline and thus drying. To avoid a sticky film on the hair, rinse for a full two minutes.

Instant conditioners should be left in for one to two minutes after shampooing and then rinsed out. They flatten the cuticle and coat the hair shaft, creating shine and volume.

Deep conditioners are thick emulsions that should be left in the hair for 30 minutes. They restore moisture and protect the hair shaft, making damaged hair less brittle and frayed. As a preventive measure, use a deep conditioner a few days before you color or perm your hair. Remember that deep conditioners tend to flatten normal hair and to make oily hair limp and dull.

■ When conditioning your hair, place most of the product on the bottom half of your hair, especially the ends. This is the oldest hair; it's had the most abuse and needs the most enhancement.

■ Though conditioners can help damaged hair look better, they can't rejoin split ends. The only way to get rid of split ends is to cut them off.

Before taking a sauna or steam bath, put conditioner on your hair: the heat will help it penetrate.

PRODUCTS FOR HARD-TO-MANAGE HAIR

■ For thin or thinning hair, use protein shampoo and conditioner, as well as body-building products containing resin, plastic, or balsam.

■ For broken hair, usually associated with bleaching and permanents, try a low-pH shampoo, a protein conditioner, and a warm-oil treatment.

■ For naturally dry hair, use a rich emollient shampoo with film-forming agents, such as protein and balsam. Then apply a creme rinse. If you use gels or mousses, buy those that are alcohol-free.

■ For processed dry hair, you need a shampoo rich in protein, oil, and moisturizers, and with a low pH. Styling products should have hydrolyzed protein, balsam, and other film-forming agents.

To clean hairbrushes, mix 2 tablespoons baking soda and 2 tablespoons colorless mouthwash in enough water to cover bristles (don't submerge wooden handles). Soak for 15 minutes, scrub with an old toothbrush or nailbrush, and rinse.

IS IT REALLY DANDRUFF?

■ A lightly flaking scalp could be caused by residue from shampoo or another hair product. To eliminate this possibility, rinse after shampooing three times as long as usual and skip conditioners, setting lotions, mousses, gels, and sprays for two weeks. If your scalp is still flaky, you probably have dandruff, which occurs when the normal process of shedding skin speeds up.

■ Most dandruff is caused by too much oil, not too little. Before using an antidandruff shampoo, clean your scalp with 1 part clear mouthwash or antiseptic to 4 parts water. Part your hair in one-inch sections

Herbal Helpers

Fresh infusions of certain herbs can be excellent for the hair. Clover blossom, cornflower, chamomile (for blonds), and orange pekoe or Red Zinger tea (for redheads) can brighten and soften. Fennel, which is slightly antiseptic, and nettle are good for dandruff. For brunettes, rosemary is an old standard for shine. To make an herbal infusion:

1. Steep 1 tablespoon of herbs in 8 ounces of boiling water for 30 minutes. Strain and cool.

2. Pour onto the hair and work into the scalp; leave on for 15 to 20 minutes.

3. Rinse out with lukewarm water for a full minute.

and apply the mixture with a saturated cotton ball. Cover your hair with a shower cap, leave it on for an hour (or overnight), then shampoo.

■ Another quick fix: Saturate a cotton ball with witch hazel and apply to your scalp at half-inch intervals. The best time to do this is after you wash your hair, while it is still wet.

■ Shampoo frequently. Leave shampoo on five minutes, then rinse thoroughly to avoid leaving a residue; repeat. Medicated shampoos are sometimes more effective than others, but they should be used less often to avoid skin irritation. The best contain pyrithione zinc, sulfur, salicylic acid, or resorcinol. Tar shampoos, while strongest, may discolor hair or irritate scalp. Your scalp can become resistant to one brand, so you should alternate. The strongest shampoos are available only by prescription.

■ Dandruff shampoos are not very gentle, so use sparingly if your hair is permed or colored.

■ If your "dandruff" occurs only in winter, it may be the result of dryness caused by central heating. Use a humidifier or turn the thermostat down low at night.

Lemon juice, if used regularly as a rinse, helps to prevent dandruff.

COLOR CUES

■ Streaking, frosting, and hair painting are relatively trauma-free. The alkaline chemicals of coloring products don't touch your scalp, and not all your hair is subjected to the processing.

133

■ Hair dyes, on the other hand, are not without hazards. Coal-tar dyes, the most common type of dyes, cause severe skin allergies in some people, while lead is an ingredient of "progressive" hair dyes (those that require several applications to cover gray). Also, studies have suggested an association between some hair-dye chemicals and certain cancers, but as yet the evidence is inconclusive.

■ If you want color that fades gradually and evenly (thus eliminating the need for frequent retouching), consider using henna, a plant extract.

However, the results are unpredictable, so if you're planning a big color change, use traditional coloring agents.

■ Don't use a henna rinse if your hair has been permed or colored, and never perm or color over henna.

■ Don't use shampoos containing sulfated castor oils, which can strip color.

HAIR REMOVAL

■ Increased hair production may occur for several reasons, including menopause (because of a drop in estrogen production), certain diseases (such as multiple sclerosis and encephalitis),

certain medications (such as phenytoin, minoxidil, and some contraceptives), and tumors that produce androgen (a male hormone). If you experience this condition, called hirsutism, consult a doctor. If necessary, tests can help determine the cause and provide a direction for treatment.

■ Facial shaving is acceptable for women. Contrary to conventional wisdom, shaving does not make the hair grow back thicker; the hair that grows back is initially shorter and therefore stubbier-looking than the hair that was removed. For information about

How to Read a Label

Here are 10 common shampoo and conditioner ingredients and what they can and cannot do for your hair.

Aloe	This plant extract interacts with living skin cells but is thought to have little effect on the dead cells of hair
Balsam	This natural resin stiffens the hair, adding volume and body
Eggs	The protein in egg does not break down into a form that hair can catch and hold
Herbs	These are so delicate that their intended benefits are usually lost in the blend of other ingredients
Lemon	Citric acid, not lemon juice, is usually the active component of these shampoos. They're designed to remove film from oily hair to make it shiny and soft
Moisturizers	Urea, lactic acid, lecithin, and others help the hair shaft hold water, which is useful for dry or damaged hair
Oils	Coconut, avocado, wheat-germ, and other oils shield against evaporation and slick down the surface of the cuticle, adding shine
Proteins	Hydrolyzed proteins, keratin, amino acids—the hair has an affinity for these proteins and others, which fill in cracks in the cuticle
Silk	Tiny parts of fibers added to shampoo act as reflecting particles, causing the hair to look shiny
Vitamins	Panthenol, a form of vitamin B_5, penetrates and restructures the hair shaft. However, hair cannot absorb other vitamins—such as A, D, and E—from shampoo

shaving, see page 123.

■ Tweezing is fine for removing stragglers—like those between the eyebrows or on the upper lip—but you risk inflammation if you use this technique for large areas. To dull the sting, apply a cold or ice compress before or after tweezing. Never tweeze hair from a mole or mark on your skin.

■ Because they can irritate sensitive skin, bleaching and depilatory preparations should be tested on a small sample of skin the day before each application. To minimize irritation, apply a moisturizer afterward. For facial hair, use a product made specifically for the face.

■ The sun, chlorine, salt water, and sweat can all irritate skin when a depilatory or waxing product has been used. Don't stay out in the sun too long, engage in vigorous activity, or swim in chlorinated or salt water for 24 hours after using these hair-removal methods.

■ If you do experience inflammation, apply Burow's-solution compresses followed by a hydrocortisone cream, or try witch hazel or both antibiotic and cortisone creams. Do not squeeze any bumps, as this can lead to infection and scarring.

■ The only permanent way to remove hair is by electrolysis. This expensive, somewhat uncomfortable process involves killing the hair roots with an electrified needle. Don't use it if you're prone to keloids or have suffered from ingrown hairs. Because this method can cause infection or scarring, it should be done only by a licensed or certified operator

(not all provinces license electrologists). Ask your dermatologist for a referral, and look for the initials CPE (Certified Professional Electrologist) or CCE (Certified Clinical Electrologist). You can help prevent infection and scarring by applying an antibiotic cream and a cortisone cream twice daily for five days after the procedure.

....

Skin irritation may cause more hair or thicker hair to grow under a plaster cast. The hair will return to normal, however, soon after the cast is removed.

....

HAIR LOSS AND BALDNESS

■ If your hair is thinning, don't go on crash diets (a bad idea for anyone) and don't take large doses of vitamin A; they can both cause hair loss. Also avoid teasing, back-combing, using tight rollers, and anything else that can pull hair out at the roots.

■ Both coloring and perming will dry your hair, but they won't damage the roots or exacerbate hair loss.

■ If you have experienced sudden hair loss, see your doctor. Round or oval bald patches may indicate alopecia areata, a common hair-loss condition that can be treated. Sudden hair loss may also be a symptom of a more serious problem, such as an inactive thyroid gland.

■ Certain medications for ulcers, arthritis, and high cholesterol can also cause sudden hair loss. If this is the case, your doctor may be able to

provide alternatives.

■ If you have had recent surgery or have been under extreme stress, hair loss may be due to these circumstances.

■ If you have a bald spot, be especially careful to use sunscreen and to cover your head while outside. The sensitive skin on the scalp is especially susceptible to the adverse effects of ultraviolet rays, and exposure to the sun may hasten hair loss in some men.

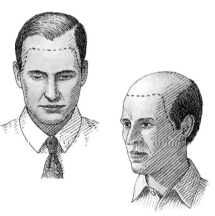

■ Most men eventually experience a receding hairline. With some, the process slows after the crown has thinned out. With others, it continues, affecting the back and sometimes the sides of the head. For those who want to cover bald spots, there are new hairpieces that are anchored to natural hair with wires; however, the constant tug on the natural hair promotes its loss. Other alternatives include plastic surgery, such as hair transplants and scalp reduction, and topical minoxidil, which can stimulate hair growth. Minoxidil, an expensive drug, must be used daily to maintain new hair growth, and the results are often disappointing.

HELP FOR HANDS

The skin on your hands is subject to similar aging processes as facial skin, but hands that are cared for can remain supple, move gracefully, and look attractive. The fingernails are an important part of your hands' appearance.

PAMPER YOUR HANDS

■ Wash your hands with luke-warm water and only a small amount of soap. Concentrate on the palms, which have the most contact with dirt and are less vulnerable to dehydration than the backs of hands. Apply moisturizer while hands are still slightly damp.

■ When using a hot-air dryer, hold hands at least six inches from the nozzle and rotate them frequently.

■ Rub on a moisturizer in the morning and evening, especially after bathing, and any time in between that you can. Carry a small tube or bottle of hand cream in your purse or briefcase for this purpose; don't wait until your hands feel dry to apply it.

■ If you have very chapped hands, cover them with petroleum jelly and wear cotton gloves overnight.

■ When the weather is cold, protect your hands from dry air with gloves.

■ Wear rubber gloves when doing work that puts your hands in contact with water, cleaning products, or soil. Gloves should be lined with cotton to absorb perspiration. If they're not, wear cotton gloves underneath.

■ The sun promotes development of brown spots on backs of hands. Put on sunscreen (SPF 15 or higher) before spending any time outdoors.

Keep a bottle of hand lotion next to every sink in your home.

SPECIAL TREATMENTS

■ Simple hand "facial": Use your moisturizing face mask on your hands after bathing. For deep cleaning, try a mud facial.

■ Supple-hands treatment: Melt paraffin wax (found in hardware stores) in a double boiler. Apply a coat of moisturizing cream to your hands. Test the now-liquid wax on your inner wrist for a comfortable temperature; then paint it on your hands with a clean, narrow paintbrush. Let the wax harden, then remove it in large pieces, lifting dirt and debris from the skin. Rinse with cool water.

■ Grit removers: For ground-in dirt, wet hands with warm water and lather with baby shampoo; leave on for one minute, then rinse. Use a fine pumice stone on roughened, dirt-filled skin, but don't do this too often.

■ Grit preventer: If you have a dirty job in store and can't use gloves, first scratch your nails several times across a wet bar of soap. The dirt won't have room to penetrate.

■ To remove stains, soak nails in a bowl containing one pint of warm water and one table-spoon of lemon juice.

CHOOSING A NAIL SALON

Getting your nails done professionally can be a health risk. Before sitting down to a manicure, be certain you have chosen a reputable salon.

■ Check if the salon or manicurist has a certificate from the province; some provinces require salons to meet specific hygienic standards and manicurists to pass exams.

■ Ask about sterilization procedures. The only effective procedure is heat sterilization with an autoclave machine (used in hospitals to clean medical instruments).

■ Be sure that emery boards are discarded after each use. You may prefer to simply bring your own file and other implements.

■ Watch for one sure infection spreader—the wooden orange stick. Wood traps moisture, permitting fungal and bacterial organisms to thrive.

Many nail products are highly flammable. Don't smoke or leave products near the stove or any flame when giving yourself a manicure.

ARTIFICIAL NAILS

Artificial nails and nail wraps can cause such serious problems as infected, swollen fingers and permanently distorted nails. Because of these

THE HOME MANICURE

*If you borrow professional techniques, a regular manicure is simple and speedy.
To avoid overuse of nail polish remover, which can be drying, give yourself a manicure only every two weeks; in between, touch up your polish. For your manicure, you'll need a good, focused work light. No time for a full manicure? At night, do the steps through the first coat of nail polish. Next morning, apply the second coat. Later in the day, put on the top coat. This has the added benefit of giving the enamel plenty of drying time.*

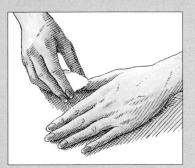

Saturate a cotton pad about halfway with nail polish remover. Press down on the nail, using a rocking motion of your thumb on the pad to take up all the old enamel; then whisk it off quickly. If necessary, repeat to remove every trace of polish.

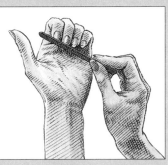

File dry nails with an emery board or diamond-cut metal file. File toward the center of each nail in one direction only; don't saw. Shape nails into slightly blunted ovals. For the best filing position, make a fist, uncurl your fingers slightly, and file with your fingers facing you. Do the thumb last.

Soak fingertips briefly in warm, sudsy water to soften cuticles. Rinse and dry hands. Smooth cuticle remover into the base and sides of each nail. Let it work for a minute or two. After covering your fingertips with a linen towel, push back cuticles gently; don't use orange sticks or "cuticle pushers."

Dip fingers into warm, sudsy water, and clean nails with a soft brush. If you have a hangnail, use a cuticle clipper to remove the torn skin, but don't clip into the cuticle itself. Massage cuticle conditioner (or moisturizer) around the base and sides of each nail. Rinse off excess, and dry nails thoroughly.

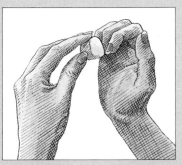

If you choose not to use polish, buff your nails to a natural shine with a dry paste and a chamois-covered nail buffer. (Limit buffing to once a month if your nails are thin.) If you are using polish, first apply a base coat. Hold the brush so that it spreads out flat against the nail. A thin, even coat adheres best.

Apply polish in two thin coats. Use three strokes from base to tip: up the center, then each side. Let the first layer dry for three minutes and the second for five, then brush on a top coat. If you can't wait for your nails to air-dry, dip them into ice-cold water to dry the top layer, but be careful for another half hour.

hazards, some experts advise against using them at all. If you do intend to use these products, be certain to take the following precautions:

■ If there is any question about sensitivity to the materials, have one nail done as a test and wait a few days to see if any reaction develops.

■ Never apply an artificial nail if the natural nail or tissue around it is infected or irritated; let the infection heal first.

■ Read instructions for do-it-yourself nails before applying them, and follow the directions carefully. Save the ingredient list for your doctor in case of an allergic reaction or other problem.

■ Treat your artificial nails with care so that they don't break and separate, creating a space vulnerable to germs. Keep the nail areas clean and protect them from harsh detergents.

■ If a nail does separate, dip the fingertip into rubbing alcohol to clean the space between the natural and artificial nails before reattaching the artificial one. Never use household glues for home repairs. Only use products intended for such use, and follow the instructions and heed all cautions on the labels.

■ Choose nail tips instead of products that cover the entire nail surface.

■ Give your nails a month's rest after each three-month period of being covered.

■ Keep artificial-nail removers out of the reach of children. Cyanide poisoning has occurred in children who ingested the solvents.

• •

Before opening a bottle of nail enamel, shake it well so that air bubbles won't form.

• •

NAIL PROBLEMS

■ See a dermatologist quickly if a nail becomes infected. Signs are swollen, red surrounding skin; discoloration of a nail; and a thickened, whitish nail that partially falls off. Nail loss may result without prompt treatment. Do not polish the nail—enamel can seal in the infection.

■ Nail problems can be clues to medical conditions. Consult the chart below, but do not attempt a diagnosis yourself; leave this to your physician.

HEALTHY HABITS

■ Break the nail-biting habit with regular manicures. Not only will the manicures keep the area smooth, but your attractive hands will give you an incentive not to chew.

■ Certain medications can make nails sensitive to sunlight, possibly causing

FINGERNAIL DISORDERS

These nail maladies are among those that may be linked with illnesses.

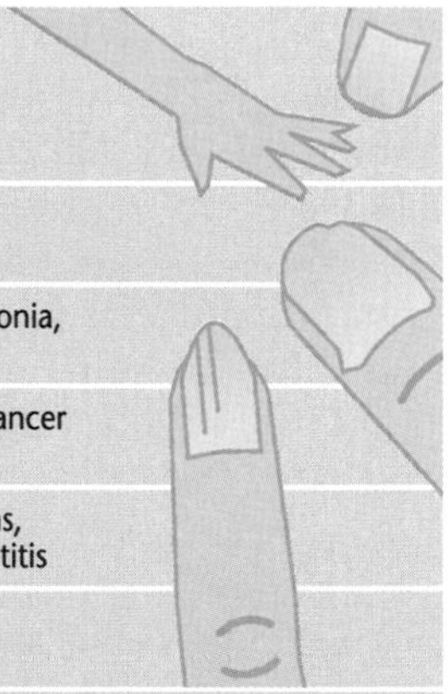

Disorder	Appearance	Possible Cause
Beau's lines	Indentations running across nail	Heart attack, measles, pneumonia, or other severe illness; fever
Clubbing	Widened and rounded fingertips; curving nails	Lung disease, heart disease, cancer
Onycholysis	Nail separated from nail bed	Injury, psoriasis, drug reactions, fungal disease, contact dermatitis
Pitting	Small pits or depressions	Psoriasis, alopecia areata (hair-loss condition)
Spoon nails	Soft nails that look scooped out	Iron-deficiency anemia
Terry's nails	Opaque, white nail; nail tip has dark pink to brown band	Cirrhosis, congestive heart failure, adult-onset diabetes, cancer, aging
Vertical ridges	Narrow ridges running the length of nails	Aging, kidney failure
Yellow nail syndrome	Yellow or green nail; cuticle and "moon" disappear	Swelling of hands and feet, respiratory diseases such as chronic bronchitis

brittleness and ridges (see page 127). To help prevent this damage, apply sunscreen from the first joint below each cuticle to the tip of the nail. Nail polishes that are opaque or contain sunscreen also act as shields against ultraviolet rays.

■ Be careful when cleaning under your nail tips. If you're too vigorous, you may create space that allows fungi or bacteria to grow.

■ If a hangnail develops between manicures, soften it with cuticle cream, then cut it off with sharp scissors.

TOUGH AS NAILS

The suggestions below will help you to develop or keep strong nails.

■ Apply a nail-hardener, but don't use products containing toluene-sulfonamide formaldehyde resin, which can cause rashes.

■ To prevent cracking, splitting, and injury, don't let nails grow longer than a quarter-inch past the nail bed.

■ Avoid polish removers containing acetone, which may dry nails. If you must use acetone remover, add olive oil or unscented castor oil to it.

■ Repair splits or tears with nail glue or clear polish.

■ Unless you're deficient in protein (rare among North Americans), no change in diet will strengthen your nails. Gelatin, for example, has no effect on weak nails.

■ Fingernails are not nature's screwdrivers. Don't use them to assemble bookcases, pull out staples, or open boxes. Pick things up

with your fingertips, not your nails. Push telephone buttons with the fleshy pads of fingers, and use a pencil to turn rotary dials.

■ If you have fragile nails, practice this regimen nightly: Submerge your nails in lukewarm water for 10 to 15 minutes. Gently pat them dry and immediately apply a moisturizer directly over them. You can also try an occasional soak in warm olive oil, a horsetail infusion, or cider vinegar.

■ Clipping can weaken nails, so don't trim them unless they're very long. Cut nails while they're wet; they're more flexible and less susceptible to splitting. File nails, however, only when they're dry.

■ Don't pick at polish, especially if nails are weak. When you peel off a layer of polish, a layer of the nail itself may come with it.

- -

A dark streak running lengthwise under the nail may indicate melanoma, a dangerous type of skin cancer. Unless you're dark-skinned and such marks are normal, have a dermatologist check it immediately.

- -

HAND MASSAGE

Massage is a good way to release tension and keep the hands limber. You may want to use lubricants: Massage cuticle cream into each nail base with the thumb and first finger of the opposite hand. Warm hand lotion by placing it in the palm of your

hand, and then spread it over the back and fingers of the opposite hand. (You can also have someone else massage your hands.)

■ Massage the hand and wrist with circular movements with the tip or ball of the thumb. To relax the wrist and finger joints, use kneading movements of the thumb and fingers. Massage each finger gently from the knuckle to the tip.

■ Using very little pressure, pull each finger from the knuckle to relax the joint.

■ Make several clockwise circles in the air with each finger. Then massage the hand with circular movements from the base of the fingers down to the wrist.

■ Put the palms of the hands together, entwine the fingers, and make several clockwise circles with the wrist. Finish with light stroking movements over the whole hand.

GO EASY ON YOUR FEET

A complex jigsaw of 26 bones, 19 muscles, and over 100 ligaments and 31 tendons, the foot is an engineering marvel that combines the best features of beanbag, lever, and concrete.

BE CREATIVE

■ Slip off your shoes to give feet a breather during the day. Enhance this pleasure with a refreshing foot spray.

■ Go barefoot when you can, but protect your feet from sharp, craggy surfaces and during sports.

■ If, from time to time, you have to stand for hours at a stretch, try shifting your weight to the outer edges of your feet to reduce stress on the usual weight-bearing points.

■ Use feet instead of hands to turn the TV dial, pick up marbles, open a drawer. Rotate and flex your feet. Drop a pencil on the floor; pick it up with your toes.

. . . .
To strengthen your arches, stand pigeon-toed and rise up on your toes. Repeat four times in succession. Do this several times a day.
. . . .

FOLLOW A REGIMEN

Daily: In the shower or bathtub, remove dry skin with a pumice stone (both pumice and skin must be damp). Rub gently over soles, heels, and sides of toes.

■ Dry feet thoroughly, especially between the toes.(This is very important if you have diabetes. For more informa-

tion on foot care for diabetics, see page 363.) If feet perspire a lot, sprinkle them with talcum powder.

■ Feet need daily moisturizing. The skin on your feet is coarser than that on your hands, so use richer lotions.

Weekly: Give your feet a 15-minute soak in warm water to which you've added sea salt or plain table salt.

■ For problem feet, alternate soaks in warm and cold water; be sure to end with cold water.

■ Use a pumice stone; abrasive creams can be used as well.

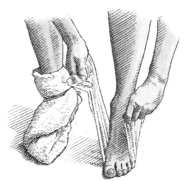

■ To relieve dryness (caused partly because the soles of the feet have no oil glands), apply a rich cream: Wrap feet with plastic wrap, and cover with towels that have been dipped in hot water and wrung out. Wait 10 minutes; then remove wrappings and smooth cream into skin.

Monthly: Do a complete pedicure. If you walk a lot or participate in foot-pounding sports—like running and racquetball—give yourself a pedicure every two to three weeks.

SAVVY SHOE SHOPPING

■ Most foot problems are caused not by disease but by improper footwear. Comfortable shoes tend to be on the squarish side, with wide toe areas and room for your feet to spread out.

■ Buy shoes at the end of the day, when your feet are a bit swollen.

■ Remember that no two feet are the same—including the pair that belongs to you. Buy length to fit your longer foot, width to fit the wider one. Allow no less than half an inch between your longest toe and the front of the shoe. If necessary, have the shoe for the smaller foot adjusted by a shoe repair shop, which can add inserts.

■ Don't assume your shoe size is forever. As you age (or during pregnancy), your feet get bigger. The next time you shop for shoes, have the clerk measure both your feet.

■ Buy a shoe with a slight heel for added arch support. Avoid heels that exceed two inches.

■ If you like high heels, try to limit the time you wear them to three hours at a stretch. Walking in three-inch heels greatly increases the pressure on the balls of the feet, which can lead to bunions, corns, and problems with knees, hips, and back.

■ The proper positioning of the foot within the shoe depends upon the area around the instep. If this area fits properly, it will feel snug and close to the foot all the way around.

■ Alternate between heels and flats on different days.

■ Make certain new shoes have adequate cushioning. If possible, try them on both rugs and hard surfaces; the carpeted area in a shoe store may give you a false sense of comfort.

■ Look for rubber heels, which absorb shock better than leather or synthetic heels.

■ If you have flat feet or high arches, you may be especially prone to heel pain. Shoe inserts can bring relief.

The weight of the body is divided on each foot at approximately 50 percent on the heel, 30 percent on the big-toe area, or ball of the foot, and 20 percent on the little-toe area. Therefore, a wide toe box with sufficient wiggle room is important. A narrow toe area squeezes the toes together, diminishing your balance.

FOOT EXERCISES

These stretching exercises will help the muscles in your feet and lower legs. Do each of the following sequences, except the last, five times.

■ Ankle Stretch: While sitting down, cross your left foot over

SELF-MASSAGE

When you massage the thousands of nerve endings in the foot, you can feel relaxation throughout your body. Regular massage keeps the foot flexible and healthy.

DEEP MASSAGE

Grip the foot in your hands, with fingers on the sole and thumbs on top. Work the bones by pressing outward with the heels of the hands, and up and in with your fingers. Then move one hand up the length of the foot while moving the other hand down.

THUMB PRESS

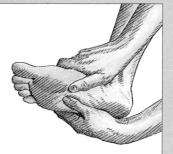

Hold your foot with your thumbs on the sole and fingers on top. Press in hard, firm circles over the sole. Repeat over the top of the foot. Be thorough, making sure to cover the entire area. Use your fingers to press near the ankle and heel.

TOE STRETCHES

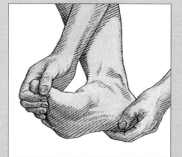

Hold the heel firmly with one hand. With the other hand, push the toes forward and backward (omit the little toe if you wish). Hold the stretch for several seconds each way, then repeat.

TOE TUGS

Gently tug each toe with your index finger and thumb. Then, starting with the big toe, twist each toe from side to side; let the thumb and forefinger slide off the end. Don't crack the toe knuckles.

your right knee. With your right hand, hold the foot under the heel. With your other hand, gradually push the top of the foot away from your heel so that you're pointing your toes. Hold the stretch, then pull the top of the foot back. Repeat with the other foot.

■ Inchworm: While standing and keeping your weight mainly on one foot, move your other foot forward—curl your toes and arch your foot; then, keeping the heel in the same position, extend your toes to flatten the foot once again. Repeat until your foot has moved forward four to six inches, then reverse: by pressing your toes, slowly push your foot back to the start.

■ Total Foot Flex: Lie on your back with your feet apart. Extend your foot upward by flexing your ankle so that you feel a stretch at the Achilles tendon. Hold for 10 to 15 seconds. Next, point your foot downward, then outward. Hold each position 15 seconds. Finally, rotate your feet in ankle circles, four times in each direction. End by shaking your feet.

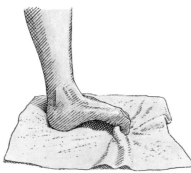

■ Towel Challenge: While sitting or standing, place your foot on top of a towel on the floor. Spread your toes and grab the towel with them so that you can pull it along the floor. Get your arch into the action, but not your heel. (It may take a while before you can do this; these muscles have been hibernating inside your shoes for years.) Now try it with the other foot.

■ Toe Tricks: Sit on the floor so that you can easily reach your bare feet. Keeping your foot flat, flex your toes up. Now curl your toes back down one at a time, if you can, from your little toe to the big one. (If the little toe lies limp, help it along with your hand.) Do the same with the other foot.

■ Achilles Tendon Stretch: This easy exercise will make your feet less vulnerable to fatigue if you do it twice a day. While holding on to the handrail, stand on a step with heels extended two inches off the edge. Rise up on tiptoes and hold 10 seconds. Then lower heels as far as they can comfortably go and hold 10 seconds. Repeat 15 times.

Avoid medicated corn pads. Most contain an acid that can burn the thinner areas of skin.

SOOTHING FOOT BATHS

■ Foot-bath salts may provide excellent relief for tired, aching feet. The alkali in the salts also help soften the outer layers of skin, facilitating the removal of dirt and possible sources of odor.

■ There are alternatives to commercial foot-bath preparations: A little lemon juice or a few drops of lavender oil in tepid water can feel good. So can Burow's solution (one powder packet to one pint boiling water) or full-strength cider vinegar. The last two can also eliminate itchiness caused by athlete's foot.

■ Feet may burn and sting because of irritating fabrics, poorly fitted shoes, or athlete's foot. Soothe them by soaking them in cold—not icy—water for 15 minutes twice a day.

■ Relieve soreness with hot-water soaks, which promote circulation.

A pedicure differs from a manicure in one important way: the toenails should always be cut straight across.

HELP FOR PROBLEM FEET

■ To avoid blisters and athlete's foot, choose socks made of polypropylene or other special synthetic materials that wick perspiration away from the feet.

■ Only wear shoes made from natural materials that "breathe," such as leather and canvas.

■ Before you suit up for a workout, put a large glob of petroleum jelly over any area that regularly blisters.

■ To combat foot odor, reduce sweating by wearing light, airy shoes in the summer and minimizing the use of rubber boots in the winter. Change your shoes daily to let each pair air out.

TEN COMMON FOOT PROBLEMS

Problem	Cause	Remedy	Prevention
Aching arches	Walking, running, or standing more than usual	Change from flat to low-heeled shoe (1 to 1 1/4 inch)	If weak arches are a chronic problem, use arch supports
Athlete's foot	Contagious fungus that flourishes in dark, humid environment	Wash feet daily with soap and warm water; dry carefully, especially between toes; use antifungal powder on feet and antifungal creams around toenails	Change shoes and socks often to decrease moisture. Don't go barefoot in locker rooms, public showers, and pool areas
Blisters	Friction from ill-fitting shoes or socks; moisture	Try not to break blister. Instead, place moleskin or bandage over it. If blister does break, follow instructions on page 423	Wear shoes that fit properly, and change socks that become damp. Socks should be snug (not tight) with no extra fabric to create folds
Bunions	Enlarged, misaligned big-toe joints are caused by heredity and sometimes aggravated by narrow-toed shoes	Cover with moleskin or foam pad. Physical therapies, such as whirlpool massage, and use of innersoles, arch supports, or orthotic inserts may reduce pain; however, surgery may be necessary. For inflamed bunion, apply ice for 15 minutes, then soak in warm water for 15 minutes; repeat three times a day. (Diabetics should check with a physician first)	You may be able to delay bunions by avoiding badly fitting shoes. Exercises to strengthen the middle of the foot—such as pointing toes and rising onto balls of feet—can also help
Calluses	Repeated friction	Soak feet in warm water for 5 or 10 minutes, and rub calluses with pumice stone. Moleskin or cushioned innersoles can reduce pressure from shoes	Keep feet well lubricated with moisturizing lotion
Corns	Friction	For hard corn, use nonmedicated corn pad with opening slightly larger than corn's diameter. To soften corn, soak in warm water and rub top layer with pumice stone; then apply lotion or petroleum jelly. Repeat once a week. For soft corn between toes, keep toes separated with lamb's wool or sponge	Eliminate source of friction; keep feet well lubricated
Hammertoe	A bent, clawlike toe, usually the second, is caused by muscle imbalance, bunions, tight shoes or socks, or heredity	Surgery to straighten may be necessary. For inflamed hammertoe, use ice-and-warm-water treatment described for bunions	Wear properly fitting shoes and socks
Ingrown toenail	Toenail cut too short; tight-fitting shoes; excessive curvature of toenail (inherited)	If infected, see a doctor. If not, soak foot in warm water. Then, using nail file, insert small wad of cotton to lift nail away from sore spot. Repeat twice a day	Cut toenails straight across, no shorter than end of toe. Wear shoes with sufficiently wide toe box
Plantar warts	Flat, spongy warts on the soles of the feet are caused by a virus	Warts sometimes disappear spontaneously. Otherwise, a podiatrist or other physician can remove them	Avoid going barefoot, especially on dirty surfaces or in communal bathing areas
Thickened, yellowish nails	Fungal infection that can spread from athlete's foot or occur after a trauma that damages nail bed	Requires prescription medication. If desired, file nails for comfort, but clean hands and feet afterward to control spread of fungus	Keep feet clean and dry; treat athlete's foot promptly

TOOTH-CARE TACTICS

The key to keeping your teeth in top shape is regular brushing and flossing. Awareness of proper tooth care has helped to bring about a new generation of young people who are virtually cavity-free.

DAILY TOOLS

■ Think of your toothbrush as a disposable item. Replace it every few months or even sooner if the bristles become worn or splayed.

■ Because the moist environment of the bathroom is ideal for microorganisms to survive, it's a good idea to keep your toothbrush (uncovered) in your bedroom, which is typically a drier area.

■ When you have a cold or the flu, replace your toothbrush while you are sick and again once you have recovered.

■ People undergoing chemotherapy should replace their toothbrushes as often as once every three days. Patients recovering from a major operation, such as bypass or transplant surgery, should replace their toothbrushes every day.

■ Before brushing, soften the toothbrush bristles by soaking them in warm tap water.

■ For sensitive teeth, try a desensitizing toothpaste. If the

---

BETTER BRUSHING AND FLOSSING

Brush your teeth at least twice a day and floss once; you should spend a minimum of five minutes daily (total) on these routines. Make sure you're brushing and flossing correctly, as shown below.

Hold the brush at a 45° angle, pointing toward the gum line. Use a gentle, circular motion—almost a wiggle.

Tilt your brush vertically and use up-and-down strokes to clean the inner surfaces of upper and lower front teeth.

To floss properly, use a gentle sawing motion as you bring the taut floss to the gum line. Then carefully slide the floss up and down, following the shape of the tooth. Move the floss under the gum line, but be careful not to cut into the gum. Be sure to do each tooth with a clean section of floss.

Use short, angled strokes to clean the outer and inner surfaces of back teeth. Close your mouth slightly to make brushing the back teeth easier.

With a light back-and-forth motion, scrub the chewing surfaces of back teeth with the brush held flat.

paste lacks fluoride, use a flu-oridated mouthwash as well.

■ Unless your dentist recommends one, avoid toothpastes that claim to whiten your teeth. These often contain harsh abrasives; prolonged use can damage or wear away the enamel of the tooth.

■ Remove minor stains on teeth by gently brushing with a paste made of baking soda and water.

■ Advertisements frequently show a toothbrush covered with a large dollop of toothpaste. Actually, you need only a pea-sized amount of toothpaste for each brushing.

Unless you're having dental problems, you'll need a complete set of X-rays only every five years, and bitewings (X-rays that show the molars and premolars) every two years.

THE RIGHT TECHNIQUE

■ Overzealous scrubbing with a toothbrush can cause the gums to recede and can even damage the tooth's exposed root. If you tend to brush too vigorously, try holding the brush as you would a pencil—between your thumb and first two fingers. This will automatically make your strokes shorter and lighter.

■ Floss after you brush rather than before. Besides removing plaque (a bacterial film), you'll also be working the toothpaste down between your teeth.

■ If your floss shreds, you may simply need to use a thicker, waxed floss, or you may have a filling that needs smoothing.

Check with your dentist.

■ If you have fixed bridgework, use a toothpick to help control plaque buildup and gum bleeding. Insert the toothpick at a 45° angle down into the gum groove in front and in back of each tooth. Scrape very gently.

If you notice a smooth, opaque white patch inside your mouth or on your lip, see your dentist or dermatologist. This may indicate a precancerous condition.

GUM DISEASE

Plaque and tartar (a hard mineral deposit) can cause periodontal, or gum, disease—called gingivitis in the early stage and periodontitis in the more advanced stage.

■ To prevent a buildup of plaque and tartar, brush and floss regularly and properly, and have professional cleanings at least twice a year. Bacteria flourishing on dental surfaces can affect your body as well as your teeth.

■ Avoid cigarettes and chewing tobacco; they can irritate gums and can also lead to oral and other cancers.

■ Eat healthy, balanced meals; a diet low in nutrients can diminish your body's efforts to fight infection.

■ Persistent bad breath and red, tender, or easily bleeding gums may be signs of gum disease. If you experience any of these, see your dentist. Remember that gingivitis is usually reversible.

■ Toothpastes that claim to be

antiplaque are effective, but they remove plaque only from the exposed surfaces of teeth, so you still need to clean between your teeth with floss or special cleansers your dentist can recommend.

IF YOU'RE PREGNANT

■ There is no direct link between tooth decay and pregnancy; calcium is not absorbed from the mother's teeth for the benefit of the developing child. However, hormone levels do make pregnant women's gums more sensitive to the effects of plaque and more hospitable to certain bacteria. Routine dental cleanings are important.

■ If you need dental work, be sure to tell your dentist that you're pregnant. Avoid X-rays, if possible, but take care of any cavities. Extensive treatment involving general anesthesia could put the fetus at risk.

Keeping your spouse awake? Dentists can solve some snoring problems with custom-made orthotic appliances.

CHILDREN'S TEETH

■ Start good habits early. Teach children not to bite hard objects—such as ice, pencils, and popcorn kernels—that can damage teeth.

■ Clean a toddler's teeth with a moistened washcloth or gauze pad. A small child should use a toothbrush, with soft bristles, made for children.

■ Do not put your baby or toddler to bed with a bottle of juice or milk. This practice exposes the teeth to sugars for long hours. Fill the bottle with water instead.

■ Check with your dentist to make sure your preschooler is getting the proper amount of fluoride. An overdose of fluoride supplements can lead to fluorosis—white blotches on developing tooth enamel. Young children, who may lack control over the swallow reflex, are also prone to ingesting too much toothpaste, which usually contains more fluoride than children need. Be sure your child uses only a tiny amount of toothpaste.

■ When your child's permanent molars come in, consider protecting them with sealants—clear plastic coatings the dentist applies to the chewing surfaces of back teeth. Sealants form a barrier that keeps food and bacteria out of tiny grooves in the teeth. Cavity-prone adolescents and adults may also want this protection, which is nearly completely effective in preventing decay in back teeth.

Some people grind their teeth during sleep, which can cause facial and jawbone pain, headaches, and abraded teeth. If you suffer from nighttime grinding, ask your dentist about a splint—a plastic or rubber device that protects the teeth.

KEEPING BREATH FRESH

■ More than 300 species of bacteria inhabit the human mouth, causing bad breath, often in

CDA Seal of Recognition: What It Really Means

To get the Canadian Dental Association's Seal of Recognition on a product, a manufacturer must submit convincing research—often clinical studies conducted at universities—to demonstrate that its product is effective. The company must also follow CDA rules for advertising and packaging.

the form of "morning breath."

■ Causes of bad breath other than bacteria include:

Smoking, chewing tobacco, and drinking alcohol

Aromatic compounds in certain foods, such as garlic and onions, which enter the bloodstream and are carried to the lungs, then exhaled

Gum disease, especially when accompanied by bleeding

Localized respiratory-tract infections, such as chronic bronchitis or sinusitis with postnasal drip

■ After you brush your teeth, brush your tongue to help freshen breath.

■ Don't count on a mouthwash to affect your breath for very long. Tests with garlic found that bad breath returned between 10 and 60 minutes after rinsing. Another potential problem with most mouthwashes is that they contain alcohol, with content ranging from 6 to nearly 27 percent. Alcohol in high concentration creates a

burning sensation in the mouth, and regular use can dry out the mucous membranes and aggravate any existing inflammations.

■ Since chronic bad breath may be a symptom of dental or other disease, a person with this condition should be examined by a dentist and possibly by a doctor.

■ For a natural breath freshener, try parsley, clove, cinnamon sticks, or the seeds of cardamom, anise, or fennel.

DENTURES

■ Be sure to store your removed dentures in water; otherwise, they may warp. If your dentures have a metal base, however, don't soak them in a cleaning solution for more than 15 minutes.

■ Clean dentures over a basin filled with water; this way, if you should drop them, the water will cushion the fall. You may also want to put a folded towel around the rim of the sink.

■ If your lower dentures hurt or feel loose, they may need adjusting. Have your dentist perform this work rather than doing it yourself with denture adhesives—an improper fit can lead to increased irritation and more serious problems.

■ Ask your dentist about alternative ways to floss if you have a hard time with your new fixtures.

If canker sores are bothering you, try rinsing with a weak solution of sodium bicarbonate.

DENTAL WIZARDRY

New techniques make beautiful teeth easier to attain and offer an alternative to dentures

•••••••

Remarkable advances in the field of dentistry have given us new options for improving or replacing defective teeth.

Better braces. Not so long ago, only children wore braces, and those who did risked taunts of "tinsel teeth" and "metal mouth." But today more than 20 percent of orthodontic patients are over 18 years old, and the braces or other tooth-straightening appliances they wear are hardly noticeable. Metal braces now have fine wires and tiny brackets. Even less obtrusive are tooth-colored wires and brackets. Lingual braces, placed on the inside surface of the teeth, can't be seen at all. "Braceless" orthodontics, better for minor adjustments, lets patients wear a plastic-and-wire retainer molded to fit the roof of the mouth.

Improvements in orthodontics affect more than a patient's appearance. Treatment time is shorter than in the past because of a super-elastic material used to make wires.

Brighter smiles. Cosmetic dentistry has developed several ways to help people troubled by stained or flawed teeth; these include bleaching, bonding, and applying veneers. Bleaching removes stains from teeth with a peroxide solution. Bonding

uses a puttylike plastic resin to restore chipped, cracked, or crooked teeth, filling in gaps between teeth and whitening badly stained teeth. These problems can also be solved with porcelain veneers—thin, custom-made shells that the dentist affixes to the surfaces of teeth after removing some of the natural tooth enamel.

Truer false teeth. Artificial roots to hold false teeth date back to ancient times; some Egyptian mummies have crude implants set in the jawbone and splinted to adjacent teeth with gold wire. Until fairly recently, however, artificial roots would not anchor firmly enough to last long, and they often caused infection. What was needed was a substance that would bond with bone tissue—finally discovered in the metal titanium. This breakthrough meant that implants were at last a viable option for those who could not (or would rather not) wear dentures.

Today the most common type of implant is the endosteal (see illustration). In this procedure, a dentist inserts a titanium fixture into the jawbone; then, several months later, the dentist attaches a metal

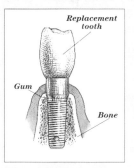

An endosteal implant

post and finally a replacement tooth. This procedure requires sufficient bone for support. Those who have lost too much bone might instead have a subperiosteal implant, in which a metal frame (holding the necessary number of artificial roots) is placed on top of the jawbone, under the gum tissue.

Implants can be used to replace any number of missing teeth and generally last at least 10 years. Not everyone is a candidate, however, and there can be complications if the procedure fails. But the vast majority of implants—now numbering in the hundreds of thousands—are successful, providing artificial teeth that look natural and feel secure. As one 77-year-old says, "You really forget your teeth aren't your own."❏

PROTECTING YOUR EYES

Here are some simple measures you can take to guard and soothe your eyes, as well as the delicate skin around them. They include guidelines on using makeup and selection and care of glasses and contact lenses.

BASIC PRECAUTIONS

■ Over the long term, sun exposure can damage the eye's lens, retina, and cornea. It can also cause cataracts. Wear sunglasses on sunny days, even in winter. A large-brimmed hat will further help to protect your eyes (see "Sun Sense," page 126).

■ To rest your eyes when reading or studying, occasionally look out a window and focus on distant objects.

■ Don't work in bad light. While it's a myth that reading in dim light will ruin your vision, you'll be less likely to get a headache when you work in an adequately lit, glare-free setting.

■ When working with power tools or dangerous chemicals that might splash, wear goggles with side shields. Put on helmets with face masks before playing hockey and football, and safety glasses before playing racquetball and other high-risk sports.

■ Be wary of flying objects, such as twigs from a lawn mower or a cork from a champagne bottle.

■ Tanning booths and sunlamps can cause irreversible eye damage, including blindness. Anyone getting an artificial tan in this way should be certain to wear opaque goggles. The radiation involved can also cause skin cancer, so it's best to avoid artificial tanning entirely.

■ If you have dry eyes, humidify your house and avoid arid environments. Taking these two steps can reduce the need for artificial tears.

THE SURROUNDING SKIN

The fragile skin around the eyes is twice as thin as the skin on the rest of the face. It has fewer oil glands, weaker internal support, and gets the most exercise. Therefore, it's important to take steps to protect it.

■ Use a sunscreen (SPF 15 or higher) whenever you go outside. Be careful, however, to keep it out of your eyes.

■ Use a moisturizer—heavy on the eyelid, lighter underneath the eye—night and day. Dry skin wrinkles more quickly and more deeply than moisturized skin. A moisturizer specifically designed for the eye area will provide more antibacterial protection.

■ Don't smoke. Smoking cuts down on peripheral blood circulation, dries your skin, makes you squint (thus imprinting crow's-feet), and robs your body of vitamin C.

■ Get enough sleep. The skin around your eyes is so delicate that it responds immediately to fatigue and stress.

■ Don't rub your eyes. Rubbing stretches the thin skin around the eyes; this encourages bags to form.

■ You may be able to reduce chronic puffiness under the eyes by drinking at least eight glasses of water a day.

Cataract prevention? Studies suggest that people who consume plenty of fruits and vegetables containing antioxidants, such as beta-carotene and vitamins C and E, are less likely to have cataracts.

SAFE USE OF EYE MAKEUP

■ Remember that cosmetics are foreign substances capable of causing eye irritation.

■ Replace mascara three or four times a year. Through contact with airborne bacteria, the wands can become contaminated and cause infections.

■ Throw away other types of eye makeup after a year. If your eyes tend to become red or infected, replace these items even more often.

■ Never use saliva to moisten cosmetics.

■ Never share eye makeup.

■ Never apply eye makeup while in a moving vehicle.

■ Use your ring finger or little finger to apply products; the index finger tends to move the skin rather than the cosmetic.

■ Pat gels and creams lightly on the skin. Apply only a tiny amount of the product, moving from the outer corner inward.

■ For eye shadow, use a cotton swab or an applicator. Dispose of cotton swabs after use, and change applicators at least twice a year—three times if your eyes are sensitive.

■ Don't line the inside of your lower eyelids with pencil—the wax can block glands. Stick to the outside of your lids.

■ If your eyes are puffy and irritated and you're not sure why, try this test: Choose a place behind your ear, under your arm, or along your inner arm or thigh. Wet the skin with cool water, then stroke on one of the eye products you use daily. Circle the area with a pencil and check it in 24 hours. If redness develops, you're allergic. If there's no reaction, leave it and check again in another 24 hours and, if necessary, after a third full day. If there's still no reaction, wash and repeat the process with another product.

■ If you suspect that the culprit is your iridescent eye shadow, there's a quicker method to test for an allergy: Dab some of the product just inside your nostril. If your nose starts running, you're allergic. (This also works with pearlized powder blusher.)

■ As you age, your skin becomes drier and gets irritated more easily. You therefore may develop an allergy to an eye product that you've used comfortably for years.

■ Wear waterproof mascara only when swimming or attending an event that may bring on tears, such as a wedding. Otherwise, stay with water-soluble mascara, which is easier to remove.

■ Use a gentle eye makeup remover every night, wiping the area, from the outside in, with cotton balls. (Tissues are too harsh for this area.)

■ Don't color your eyelashes or eyebrows with permanent or semipermanent dyes. You risk severe eye injury and even blindness.

■ Make sure that your nail polish is dry before you put makeup on your eyes. Ingredients in the polish can irritate and cause allergic reactions.

You can remove eye makeup with baby oil, mineral oil, or petroleum jelly. Then splash well with water.

IF YOU WEAR GLASSES

■ Don't try on other people's glasses or let them try on yours. This practice can spread diseases and infections.

■ Tired of having your bifocals slip down your nose? Bifocal contacts now come in soft lenses, but not everyone can tolerate them and fitting fees are expensive. A much less

How to Adjust to Bifocals or Trifocals

Let your eye doctor know all the tasks you do both on and off the job that require clear vision. This information will help in the correct placement of the lens segments.

Make sure that eyeglass frames are always adjusted for your face so that the lenses are properly positioned.

Don't look down when you walk.

Hold reading material close to your body, and lower your eyes, not your head, so that you are reading out of the lowest part of the lens.

Fold the newspaper in half or quarters and move it, rather than your head, to read comfortably.

Wear the lenses continuously for the first week or two, until you are accustomed to them, even though you may not need them for all situations.

Choosing Frames

A dark-toned bridge will make a wide nose look narrower.

Frames with light tones in the center that darken at the edges will make close-set eyes appear wider, as will decorations on the outer edges of frames.

Frames should complement your face, not overpower it. Choose frames that are the same width as the widest part of your face, or slightly longer than that.

Frames with shapes different from the shape of your face are the most flattering. If your face is square, for example, round or oval frames will look good; if your face is round, those that are square or rectangular will be more attractive.

Basic metal frames look good with all hair and skin tones.

Different colors complement different hair and skin tones. Consult the chart below for your best colors.

Frame	Blond Hair / Pale Skin	Brown Hair / Olive Skin	Red Hair / Tawny Skin	Black Hair / Black Skin
Rose	✔	✔		✔
Blue	✔	✔		
Green	✔		✔	
Tortoise	✔		✔	
Plum		✔		
Brown		✔	✔	
Coral			✔	
Amber			✔	✔
Purple				✔

costly alternative is to fit one eye with a contact lens for near vision and the other with a lens for distance vision—an approach called monovision.

■ Wearing clear prescription glasses in the sun may make dark circles under your eyes even darker. The clear glass allows sun rays to beat down on your under-eye area, where the skin is very thin. The best solution to this problem is to get a prescription for sun lenses—preferably medium to dark gray—to filter out the rays. The second-best solution is to apply sunscreen to the area, taking care not to get it in your eyes.

■ Pink lenses may help reduce the glare of fluorescent lights in an office.

■ Can't find your glasses without your glasses? To keep them on hand, attach an eyeglass case near the place where you normally take off your glasses—taped to your nightstand or tacked to the wall near the sink where you wash your face.

AGING EYES

Virtually every middle-aged person develops presbyopia, an inability to focus on close objects. Here are some suggestions for those who are holding reading material farther and farther away.

■ First have an eye examination to rule out cataracts or an underlying disease.

■ Change your lighting: try reading in an otherwise dimly lit room with a spotlight shining directly on your book.

■ Buy or borrow large-print books and magazines.

■ Consider ready-to-wear glasses, available at drugstores and other outlets in most provinces. To choose the correct pair for you, use the guide mounted on the display case. However, keep in mind your usual work distances when trying the various lenses. If you do word processing, for example, you may need a different pair from those you'll use for reading.

■ Choose ready-to-wear glasses with metal temples so that you can bend them, if need be, to make them fit better. If they have plastic pads in areas that you need to bend, immerse those portions in hot water for five minutes before bending them to keep from cracking the plastic.

■ For a pretty but practical fashion accessory, buy a lorgnette—a pair of glasses on a wand. (You may find one in an antique shop.) Have your optician put magnifying lenses in the frames.

CAN YOU WEAR CONTACTS?

While most people can wear contacts happily, some shouldn't wear them or should limit their use.

■ Diabetics tend to have fragile eye tissue and may be more prone to infections.

■ People with chronically dry eyes, low-grade eye infections, or eyelid problems should avoid contacts.

■ Those who work in dirty environments or around noxious fumes should not wear contacts while on the job.

■ Those with allergies have an increased risk of complications—such as lens coating, eye irritation, and conjunctivitis—from wearing contacts.

■ Some drugs—including antihistamines, diuretics, and some antidepressants—dehydrate the eyes, which may make wearing contacts uncomfortable.

IF YOU WEAR CONTACTS

■ Don't use oily soaps or hand creams before you handle your lenses.

■ If your eyes stay red, irritated, or sore for more than 24 hours, seek medical advice. You could have an infection or scratched cornea needing immediate attention.

■ Never use saliva to lubricate or clean your lenses.

■ Keep a pair of glasses with a current lens prescription on hand, just in case.

■ If you use disposable contacts, wear them for no more than six days, clean them properly if you're going to reuse them, and be sure to have regular checkups.

■ To improve your success with soft contacts, insert a drop of saline into the eye to make removal easier, but don't force the lens out if it's stuck to the eye. Never wear a torn or dirty lens. Replace daily-wear soft contacts every 18 to 24 months; replace extended-wear lenses every 6 to 9 months.

■ Soft and gas-permeable contact lenses can absorb chemical vapors that could damage your eyes. Before using paints, chemicals, or solvents, put on well-sealed protective goggles. Better yet, switch to your glasses.

■ Use a pressed eye powder rather than a liquid or cream shadow. Never use pearlized or frosted types, which contain a chemical that can stain contacts. Choose a soft pencil eyeliner instead of a liquid or powdered version that may flake off. Buy a mascara designed specifically for use with contact lenses or for people with sensitive eyes.

■ Insert contact lenses before applying makeup, and remove them before taking the makeup off. Put in lenses after using hair spray, which clings to lenses and cannot be removed. With extended-wear lenses, close eyes tightly when using hair spray, and walk out of the area immediately.

■ Use any other aerosol products, such as deodorant or cologne, before lens insertion.

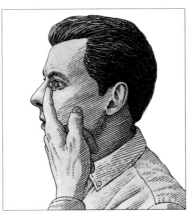

■ After you've put in your contacts, alternately cover each eye to make sure both lenses are in correctly.

■ Avoid swimming with contact lenses in place because of the danger of bacterial contamination from pool or ocean water.

■ If you use extended-wear contact lenses, prevent them from drying out during winter nights by running an ultrasonic humidifier in your bedroom.

■ Wondering if tinted contact lenses are safe? Yes, they are, if they have US FDA approval (which ensures that the dye won't leak). Opaque types should not be worn at night, however, as they may interfere with night vision.

• •

Traveling to a dry area? Your lenses may shrink temporarily. Rewetting drops can help make your eyes more comfortable.

• •

SHOPPING FOR SUNGLASSES

■ Look for lenses that block 99 or 100 percent of ultraviolet rays, or check for a "use category" label (see page 153).

■ The best sunglasses are large, curved to fit the face, and snug-fitting, with opaque or ultraviolet-blocking side shields. If you're going to use the glasses for driving, however, make sure the frames don't block your peripheral vision.

■ The color of the lens is significant. Gray lenses provide the least distortion of colors. Amber lenses may define distant objects better, especially in haze or snow (hence their popularity among skiers); however, they do distort colors—including green traffic lights—so you shouldn't wear them while driving.

■ Glasses that properly block light are dark enough that your eye is not clearly visible through the lens. Avoid glasses that are too dark, however, as they can cut your vision too much and contribute to falls or other mishaps. Ask the clerk if you can step outside

Home Remedies for the Eyes

A quick way to refresh eyes bothered by everyday irritants, such as air pollution and pollen, is to splash them with plain water. Below are other easy treatments for eye complaints.

BAGS AND DARK CIRCLES

To reduce bags and lighten dark circles:

2 slices potato or pear

Place a thin slice of pear or potato beneath each eye and lie down to rest. Keep on for 15 minutes and then rinse off residue.

REDNESS AND PUFFINESS

To soothe red, puffy eyes:

2 slices cucumber

Lie down and place thin slices of cold cucumber over closed eyes. Relax for 15 minutes. For a cool, clean feeling, rub slices over face. Rinse.

DRY SKIN IN EYE AREA

To moisturize skin around eyes:

1 tbsp. castor oil, mineral oil, or oil from vitamin E, A, or D capsules (break open)

Being careful to keep it out of eyes, gently rub oil on surrounding skin. Use before going to bed for all-night treatment.

TIRED EYES

To soothe tired eyes:

2 chamomile tea bags
2 cups boiling water
Cheesecloth

Steep tea bags in water for 30 minutes. Remove bags. Let water cool, then freeze it in ice cube tray. Tie ice cubes into square of cheesecloth. Rub bundle around eyelids and under eyes. (Also refreshing for entire face, especially on hot days.)

for a moment to test the glasses in bright light.

■ Before you purchase non-prescription sunglasses, check for distortion. Hold them at arm's length, and, with one eye closed, look through each lens at something with a rectangular pattern, such as a floor tile. Move the glasses slowly toward you and away from you, then up and down. If the lines wiggle, try another pair.

■ Mirrored lenses reflect light, while traditional dark-colored lenses absorb it. But don't assume that any dark or mirrored sunglasses will fully protect against ultraviolet radiation. Look for a label that says they will. Also keep in mind that mirror coatings will scratch easily, unless they're scratch-resistant.

■ Gradient lenses let in varying amounts of visible light while blocking ultraviolet rays evenly.

Single-gradient lenses are darker on top and lighter on the bottom. They're good for driving because they don't block out the dashboard, but they let in too much glare when snow or sand is present.

Double-gradient lenses are dark on the top and bottom, light in the middle. They're good for outdoor activities but not so good for driving.

■ Polarizing lenses are good for driving, because they're treated to reduce glare.

■ No matter what the fancy name of the material, no plastic lens is truly unbreakable. Still, plastic is safer than glass because it's less likely to shatter. It's also better at blocking ultraviolet light. However, glass is less likely to scratch and tends to have somewhat better optical quality.

■ See an eye-care professional for sunglasses if you've had cataract surgery, which removes the eye's ultraviolet-absorbent lens, or if you're taking a drug (such as tetracycline) that increases sensitivity to ultraviolet rays.

■ To save money on frames for prescription sunglasses, buy a good pair of regular sunglasses at a drugstore. Then have your optician insert new lenses made to your prescription.

■ Don't wear sunglasses indoors or when it's dark; they'll temporarily impair your vision.

Any sunglasses are better than none. It's not true that sunglasses cause the eyes to dilate and thus may admit more ultraviolet rays.

"USE CATEGORIES" OF SUNGLASSES

The Department of Health and the Canadian Standards Association are developing a labeling system for sunglasses. It will define levels of protection appropriate for different outdoor environments:

■ Cosmetic: lightly tinted lenses for use in nonharsh sunlight.

■ General Purpose: medium to dark tinted lenses for use in most outdoor activities, such as boating and hiking.

■ Special Purpose: heavily tinted glasses for use in very bright environments, as when skiing or mountain climbing or at tropical beaches.

REDUCING EYESTRAIN FROM COMPUTER SCREENS

If you work at a VDT (video display terminal), make the following adjustments to help prevent eyestrain.

■ Inform your eye specialist that you use a VDT. Glasses and contacts worn for other activities may not be effective for computer work. You may need a special prescription.

■ To cut down on glare, keep your VDT away from any windows, turn off or shield overhead lights, and place a glare-reducing filter over the screen.

■ Place your paperwork close enough that you don't have to keep refocusing when switching from the screen to the paper. You may want to use a paper holder.

■ Position the screen so that your line of sight is 15° to 20° (about 1/3 of a 45° angle) below horizontal.

■ Clean dust off the screen frequently.

■ Blink often to keep your eyes from getting dry.

■ If the image on the screen flickers or becomes blurred or dull, have the VDT serviced right away.

EYEDROPS AND OINTMENTS

Treatment for eye problems usually consists of eyedrops or ointments.

■ Before inserting eyedrops, wash your hands thoroughly. Carefully remove the bottle's top and place it on a clean tissue. Keep the tip of the bottle from touching your fingers, lashes, or anything else.

■ To insert eyedrops, gently pull the lower lid down and slightly out with the index finger of one hand. Hold the bottle between the thumb and index finger of the other hand, bracing the other fingers against the side of your nose. Tilt your head back, look up, and put one drop in the pouch between the lid and the eyeball. If you think you've missed, put in another drop. (Don't worry about putting in too many drops; any excess will be blinked away from the eye.)

■ Inserting ointment is similar to the above, except instead of a drop, place a ribbon of ointment in the lower pouch, look down, and then gently close the eyes.

■ Never use eyedrops or ointment that has been prescribed for someone else.

■ Throw away eye medications that have been opened for 28 days, as the preservatives may no longer be effective.

■ Avoid excessive use of over-the-counter eyedrops. They whiten eyes by constricting blood vessels but may eventually cause vessels to become dilated and eyes to redden more.

Spending a summer day *working outdoors on a project is one way to bring family members closer. The three generations of men in this family are building more than a stone wall; they're building bonds of friendship and trust that will last a lifetime.*

CHAPTER 5

YOUR FAMILY'S WELL-BEING

Whether you have good news or bad news, it's your family that you turn to first. They're the people you call when the job promotion comes through, when the wedding date is finally set, or when the car breaks down and you need a ride home. In these and other ways, your family plays a vital role in your physical and emotional health; they help keep you healthy just by being there, giving support and affection.

The face of the Canadian family is changing, and we should make the most of these changes. Whether they're blood relatives, in-laws, step-relatives, adopted family, partners, or special friends, we can never have too many people who care about us. Make time for them; spend moments together and let them know you care. Even in the rough times, keep in mind that these are the most important people in your life.

This family gets the day off to a happy start by playing *before doing anything else. For them, this shared time is well worth waking up a half hour earlier.*

THE STRONG FAMILY

A strong marriage and a caring family will provide a refuge from the stresses of daily life. But even the best relationships take time, patience, and commitment.

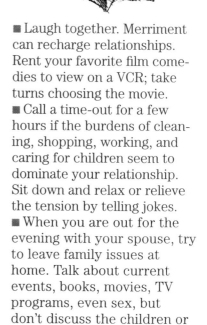

ENRICHING YOUR MARRIAGE

■ Don't keep your feelings to yourself. Say "I love you" to your partner often.

■ Make physical gestures part of your relationship. When you sit on the couch together, exchange hugs, hold hands, and enjoy the closeness.

■ Surprise your spouse with little gifts that say "I was thinking of you today."

■ Compliment your partner's looks.

■ Make your spouse feel appreciated. Say "Thank you" for the little things he or she does for you.

■ Carry a photograph of your spouse in your wallet or purse. It will help you feel connected when you're apart.

LISTEN TO EACH OTHER

■ Your tone of voice when speaking to your spouse or any family member sets the tone for the relationship. Civility begins at home and is the single most potent peacemaking element in a marriage.

■ When you arrive home with all the freight of a hard day at the office or a frustrating drive in heavy traffic, don't take it out on the family. Try to shift gears for them.

■ Couples are often advised to set aside time to talk, but this isn't always practical. A better plan is to have conversations while you are working around the house or getting ready to go out—in short, at every opportunity.

■ When your spouse has something on his or her mind, listen attentively. Nothing encourages communication more—or encourages a sense of closeness to a greater degree—than a sympathetic ear.

■ Talk about your future and pay attention to each other's ideas. What goals would you like to achieve? Keep in mind that your marriage changes with time and experience, and so will your objectives.

■ Everyone needs personal time and space. Make sure you and your spouse respect each other's need to read, to take a solitary walk, to pursue special interests and hobbies.

> **The early evening hours are important in many families; it's when everybody is home and together. Make it "prime time"—don't try to iron out problems until dinner is over and everyone has had time to unwind.**

LOOSEN UP

■ Don't wait for fun to happen by chance: plan picnics, supper parties, outings of all kinds. And keep a deck of playing cards and assorted board games handy.

■ Laugh together. Merriment can recharge relationships. Rent your favorite film comedies to view on a VCR; take turns choosing the movie.

■ Call a time-out for a few hours if the burdens of cleaning, shopping, working, and caring for children seem to dominate your relationship. Sit down and relax or relieve the tension by telling jokes.

■ When you are out for the evening with your spouse, try to leave family issues at home. Talk about current events, books, movies, TV programs, even sex, but don't discuss the children or problems at work.

■ Change your routines. Take turns driving the car, making dinner, paying bills, and planning vacations. It will help to make your marriage a little less predictable.

HEALTHY SEX LIFE

■ Always make some time for intimacy. Teach your kids to respect your time alone when you are in your bedroom. Install a lock on the door if needed. Frequent sex may not be absolutely essential for a healthy marriage, but emotional intimacy is.

■ Be realistic. Too often people think that in a good relationship sexual desire should be as strong after several years as it was at the beginning. Even among happily married couples, desire will wane occasionally. But this needn't be a problem. In fact, many happily married couples find greater emotional depth and satisfaction in sex as time goes on.

■ If your lovemaking begins to get routine, try new approaches. Indulge in sexual fantasies. Or use such techniques as sensual massage.

■ Alternate which partner initiates sex.

■ Keep all of your battles out of the bedroom.

TROUBLESHOOTING

A certain amount of conflict is normal in a healthy marriage. However, if you find that fighting has become the only way you and your partner communicate, take a closer look.

■ When you are angry, attempt to define the issue, stay focused on the topic of discussion, and try to understand each other's positions.

■ Fight fair. Because you know each other so well, it's all too easy to dredge up something hurtful from the past. Stick to the present.

■ When you argue, avoid phrases like "You always" and "You never," which put your spouse on the defensive. Also avoid such psychological words as *paranoid* and *projecting*. A layman's use of these terms usually makes things worse.

■ When you criticize, offer a possible solution. For example, if you believe your spouse is playing favorites with one child over another, suggest an action or activity that may redress the balance.

■ Before you get worked up at your partner for, say, being disorganized or messy, ask yourself what you really can expect. In all probability, he or she was messy when you first met and will continue to be messy for life. Maybe it's time to accept at least some of it. Or work around it.

■ Figure out what time of day is best for a discussion with your spouse. Many people are decidedly morning types (larks) or night people (owls). Larks rise early, do their best work in the morning, and prefer to go to bed early. For owls, the pattern is reversed. If you and your spouse are opposites, take this into account. Don't initiate a serious discussion when he or she is not yet fully awake or is ready to go to sleep.

■ Don't be afraid to tell your spouse that you are having a problem—either within yourself or within the relationship. No one, not even a loving husband or wife, is a mind reader.

MAKE TIME FOR UNITY

Most of us are inundated with demands from the outside world, but don't let this become an excuse for neglecting your family—and yourself. With a bit of creative tinkering, even the busiest schedules can yield a little more family time.

■ Eat your evening meal to-

gether as a family as often as possible—at least four times a week. And make it convivial. Save any gripes for later.

■ Keep one big calendar where everyone can pencil in individual activities for the days and weeks ahead. Mark an X on blocks of time reserved for family activities.

■ If family time seems to get crowded off the calendar all too often, juggle schedules or shave time off other commitments.

■ Collect ideas for family activities on a bulletin board. Post announcements of upcoming events. When a family day approaches, you will have a lot to choose from—auctions, fairs, exhibitions, bike races, and so forth.

■ Use the bulletin board as a family information center: pin up cartoons, clips from magazines and newspapers, and recent photographs.

■ Household chores are less bothersome and are finished sooner when they are done as a team. Have the children fix a salad while you cook dinner; sort clothes or fold laundry together as a family.

■ Post a chores chart so that everyone knows what's expected of him or her.

FINDING SOLUTIONS

It's unrealistic to expect your family to agree all the time and never argue.

■ Encourage family members to write down problems as they arise. Children too young to write can make drawings. Toss the notes and sketches, if any, into a cookie jar. Hold a weekly meeting to brainstorm solutions. If a suggestion doesn't resolve a problem within a week or so, try something else.

■ Hold your meeting at the kitchen table—or on the living room floor, where grown-ups won't loom over kids. Children open up more when an adult's head is level with theirs.

■ Limit these meetings to a half hour or less if your children are young.

■ How to hold down the shouting at your family councils? Make your own version of a Native American sacred stick, which is passed from speaker to speaker. Whoever holds the stick has the right to speak, and no one else may talk. A small hourglass can set the amount of time for each speaker.

RITUALS WORK MAGIC

Create your own family rituals. Families with the most rituals—major and minor,

serious and silly—generally have the strongest ties.

■ Plan special events and seasonal outings to enjoy every year—a fishing trip in the spring, berry-picking in the summer, visiting a pumpkin patch in the fall to choose your Halloween pumpkin, and reading aloud *A Child's Christmas in Wales* in December.

■ Establish weekly activities, such as baking bread together on Saturday mornings and playing board games on Sunday nights.

■ Make special foods to mark special occasions, for example, chocolate-chip cookies for celebrating the last day of the school year.

■ On each child's birthday, plant a shrub or perennial that the child has chosen.

■ Keep a family journal in which you record milestones as they happen.

■ Tell your kids stories about the people they know—how Mom and Dad met, how Grandpa and Grandma started their own business, what happened when Uncle Hal tried to teach Dad to drive.

A homemade calendar makes a great stocking stuffer for every member of the family. Each month pinpoints important dates—birthdays, anniversaries, special events, and upcoming family outings. Decorate the calendars with family photos and write in amusing family anecdotes.

THE EXTENDED FAMILY

For many of us, grandparents are a source of special affection and reassurance. They tend to love their grandchildren unconditionally, and they know fascinating things about the past—for example, how well Mom or Dad did in school when they were kids. Grandparents (and in these long-lived days, great-grandparents as well) often have stories to tell about faraway places, wars, and adventures.

■ Encouraging a close relationship with grandparents—and aunts, uncles, and cousins—will give your kids an enhanced sense of their own identity.

■ Because grandparents are usually more lenient with kids than parents are, it's important to establish a few ground rules. If a child asks Grandma to intervene in an argument between himself or herself and the parents, Grandma should gently decline. Instead, she should listen to the child and suggest ways for the child to present his or her own case to the parents.

■ Consider maintaining two sets of standards, such as allowing children to stay up later when visiting grandparents but adhering to the regular bedtime at home.

■ Grandparents can stay close while far away by telephoning frequently and by making audio- or videotapes for the kids—perhaps reading a favorite children's story.

■ Remind grandchildren to write back and send photos.

■ Celebrate birthdays and holidays with cards or letters. You can make up your own red-letter days, such as celebrating the day a grandchild got his or her driver's license.

■ Visit whenever you can.

MONEY MATTERS

For many couples, marital fights focus more often on money than any other issue. To get a marriage off to a solid start, it's best to discuss the subject candidly from the outset. But there's no time like the present to halt spats over family finances.

■ Speak up. This is the key to all healthy financial relationships. Without open discussion, small differences over the handling of finances can turn into major problems.

■ Respect how your partner feels about money. Accepting differences is the first step toward finding common ground.

■ Go shopping together so that both partners know what things cost. Ignorance of prices may create unrealistic expectations.

■ Starting in the first year of marriage—or as soon as possible—have planning sessions. Schedule them at least once a year. Ask your partner about his or her needs.

■ Get the facts. Sit down and review the household bills jointly every month.

■ Prepare a budget. Treat it as a spending plan to help you achieve your goals. Once decisions have been made, the budget should be firmly adhered to. However, it should be reviewed periodically and adjusted as circumstances change.

■ In addition to budgeting for food, rent or mortgage, utilities, and other essentials, each spouse—and children old enough to handle money —should have a set amount to spend as he or she pleases.

■ Discuss only the subject at hand. Don't let a finance session escalate into a free-for-all about the kids, the dog, or the in-laws.

■ Tackle one financial chore at a time. Don't try to establish a budget and make investment decisions all at once.

■ Consider what-if scenarios: What would you do if you lost your job? What if a family member piled up huge dental bills? By planning ahead, you'll feel less anxious.

■ Have regular dream-sharing conversations: "If I had an extra $10,000, I would . . ." "If I could be anywhere I wanted to be, I would go to . . ." Then, if you have a sudden windfall, you will know what to do with it.

■ Recognize the breadwinners as well as those who do unpaid work. A husband in school or a wife raising children at home should feel that these contributions are just as vital as a salary.

■ It may be a truism, but it's worth reminding yourself that money can't buy happiness. To feel really free, secure, loving, and powerful requires emotional maturity, not dollars in the bank.

■ If you find that money battles threaten your relationship with your spouse, consider hiring a professional financial planner. Getting advice from a reliable, neutral outsider can defuse tension, smooth out financial hurdles, and maybe boost your net worth.

For newlyweds: Vow not only to love and honor each other but to salt away the extra cash you get with each pay raise. Put it into a savings account or other money-building resource. For remarried couples: Keep chequing and savings accounts separate until you adjust to each other's money-management style.

EFFECTIVE PARENTING

Helping youngsters develop positive feelings about themselves and respect for others is among a parent's most demanding—and rewarding—jobs. Here are some strategies for raising healthy children.

SETTING AN EXAMPLE

■ Children learn more from parents' behavior than from their words. Knowing how to handle your own anger and frustration is a good beginning.

■ Keep criticism to a minimum. Most children try very hard to please.

■ Show your children respect. Knock at their closed bedroom door and wait for an invitation to enter.

■ Let all family members contribute to running the household. Even a three-year-old can pitch in, for example, by picking things up or putting clothes in the hamper.

■ Kids love to do real jobs that have genuine value to the family. Let them help you with home repairs. Young children can safely handle the smaller parts of fix-it tasks, like holding the end of a tape measure or handing you tools. Or start a simple project together, such as building a toy box, a dog

house, or a bird feeder. Draw up the plans, then let the kids do as much of the hammering, painting, and sawing as they want, under your supervision.

■ When friends come over for dinner, let the children sit with the grown-ups rather than at their own table. Children love to listen to adults talk—particularly adults who aren't their parents.

■ Make a practice of introducing your children to others as you do with adults. This demonstrates that the basic elements of respect and recognition apply to children as well as grown-ups.

■ Don't let TV viewing take over your whole evening. Let children choose what they want to watch (within reason), but then turn the set off.

■ Find physical activities you can all enjoy together: biking, hiking, swimming, skating, softball, or bowling.

■ Explore your own area with your children. Using public transportation, visit different neighborhoods. Take a tour of a local firehouse, factory, or waterworks, eat at ethnic restaurants, and attend street fairs and cultural festivals.

Take classes with your children—cooking, drawing, whatever. Learning side by side is fun for both parents and kids.

GUIDING YOUR CHILDREN

Self-esteem is considered by many the foundation for healthy emotional growth. It flourishes when parents give children love, support, and a chance to take responsibility.

■ Give your children options whenever possible. This tells them you have confidence in their ability to choose. For example: "Do you want to do your homework before or after dinner?"

■ When your children make mistakes, don't just correct them. Reassure youngsters that everyone makes mistakes now and then and that the important thing is to learn from them.

■ It's hard to teach children self-discipline, but there are ways you can encourage them to stop and think before they act. For example, if your children accept an invitation to a friend's party, don't allow them to change their minds at the last minute and stay home or go somewhere else. The lesson is: you have incurred an obligation, and you must honor it.

■ Don't help your children too much. For example, it's all right to provide some assistance when they get stuck on a homework assignment, but the actual work should be theirs. Too much help can undermine children's confidence in their ability to handle their school assignments.

■ Foster self-reliance so that even younger children can manage without constant help from an adult. Build a sturdy box that will enable small children to reach the faucets at the bathroom sink; they can then wash their hands and brush their teeth by themselves. Add a bathroom towel rack at the child's level. Put cereal boxes and bowls on a low kitchen-cabinet shelf.

■ Give praise immediately, preferably while the child is still engaged in an activity or as soon as it is finished: "Nice job straightening up the kitchen" or "Thanks for keeping the baby quiet while I was on the phone."

■ Compliment a child for specific behavior or success—an improved report card or learning a new piece on the piano.

■ Avoid such vague generalizations as "You're the greatest!" Overly praised children can develop oversized egos.

■ Don't spoil a child's enjoyment of praise by adding a negative comment, such as "Well, you've finally done it right."

■ Let your children know

about the realities of the family's economic situation. You really can't shield children from money troubles—if they don't know what to expect, they may imagine the worst.

■ Enlist their help in managing family affairs. You can encourage thrift in everything from the use of electricity to returning bottles for the deposit money.

■ Don't underestimate the importance of encouraging children to earn their own money to buy toys or clothes.

■ Be sure to reward notable examples of obedience, thoughtfulness, and generosity. For young children, gold stars on a wall chart will do the trick. For older children, a compliment or a warm hug may be the best reward. And young and old alike appreciate a small bonus in the allowance department.

■ Ask your children's opinions on matters that affect them, but make it clear that your decision will be final. Even if they don't get their own way, they will appreciate having an opportunity to be heard.

■ Provide a place where it is acceptable for a child who is furious to vent frustrations. Encourage such vigorous activity as pounding a pillow or a punching bag.

■ Remind yourself that everyone gets angry sometimes. Tell that to your child, too.

■ If your child seems prone to hostility, you may need to limit his or her television viewing. Studies show that TV violence can exacerbate hostile behavior in children with aggressive tendencies.

- - - - - - - - - - - - - - - - - - - -
Try to see a conflict through your child's eyes. Perhaps you can recall a similar situation from your own childhood.
- - - - - - - - - - - - - - - - - - - -

MAKING RULES

■ Set clear rules of behavior with appropriate disciplinary consequences. For example, many parents set a specific time for youngsters to return home in the evening. If the kids fail to follow the rules, they can expect to be "grounded."

■ Avoid power struggles with your children. Discipline should not be a game with winners and losers.

■ If a child consistently fails to complete a task, such as cleaning his or her room, try dividing the job into several small parts. For example, start with putting toys in the toy box, then hanging up clothes, and so on, until the room is clean.

■ Avoid making rules sound too negative. Saying "I want you to stop roller-skating in the house" pits you against your child. Try, instead, "Use your roller skates outdoors, not in the house." Or say "Speak quietly" rather than "Don't shout."

■ If your children complain that they are always being "bossed," point out that everyone has to live with rules and limits—adults as well as children.

■ Periodically review the rules together. As children grow older, they should need fewer rules.

■ Be flexible. Consider making an exception to the rule if there's a special occasion, such as letting a child stay up later than normal for a weekend party.

■ Take a child's feelings into account, but do not cave in to outside pressure or a child's protest that "Everybody else's parents let them do it."

■ Let children contribute to making family rules. If they help formulate the rules, they are less likely to break them.

EXPRESSING AFFECTION

■ Show love and affection often. In the long run, nothing is as highly valued by a child as being hugged and hearing a parent say "I love you."

■ Make it plain that your love is not contingent on achievement. You will always love your children whether or not they bring home prizes.

■ Time alone with a parent is very important to youngsters. If you have several children, plan individual excursions—just you and one child—at regular intervals. Do this weekly, if you can. However, the point isn't the frequency of the event—whether a trip to the zoo or dinner at a restaurant—but the certainty that the child will have some time alone with a parent.

■ Urge children to invite a friend to dinner occasionally. This is a good way to get to know your children's friends and their friends' parents.

• • • • • • • • • • • • • • • • • • •

Set aside a drawer, shelf, or box to collect your children's treasured works—art, cards, notes, and such. Display some and save the rest to decorate the family photograph album.

• • • • • • • • • • • • • • • • • • •

THINK BEFORE YOU SPEAK

Offhand remarks can damage a child's self-esteem. Here are a few to avoid:

■ "Why can't you be more like . . .?" Comparisons hurt, make your child resentful, and feed sibling rivalry. A better course is to compare a child's present behavior with what he or she has done in the past. For example, "You were a very good sport yesterday when you lost the game. Why not be a good sport about this now?"

■ "Why don't you act your age?" Consider whether you are asking the child to perform beyond his or her level of maturity.

■ "Must you always look like a slob?" Criticism won't improve a child's grooming. A compromise that often works is to allow children to dress as they like when they are with their friends and to insist on higher standards only when they are with you.

■ "How could you be so stu-pid?" It is all right to tell children you are angry about their behavior or disappointed, but you should never resort to calling them names. If you, of all people, say they are stupid, after a while they may begin to believe it.

■ "Do it, or else!" Though menacing, a threat of this kind is too vague to motivate. Instead, state the punishment you will impose, such as "If you don't stop yelling now, I'll send you to your room until dinner."

■ "Either you come now or I'll leave without you." Don't play on a dawdling child's fear of separation. Instead, give him or her advance notice of your departure. "You have five more minutes to play before we leave."

■ Don't give a direction by asking a question, for example, "Would you like to come in now?" The child's answer would probably be no, which sets up a conflict. If the child has no choice in the matter, be direct about it by giving a clear order, not by making a request.

LISTENING TO YOUR CHILDREN

■ Talk less to be heard more. Few things shut down a dialogue more quickly than a lecture, which is, by definition, a monologue. If you are always preaching, your children will probably not try to talk to you about things that really matter to them.

■ Get into the habit of listening to your children without passing judgment. Fight the impulse to hurry them along, feeding them words and finishing their sentences. And don't interrupt when a child is speaking.

■ Children receive information every day at school and elsewhere that is really worth listening to. In many households, for example, the most ardent recyclers are the kids.

■ When a child makes you furious, the less said, the better. Usually, a quiet, thoughtful response leaves a positive, lasting impression on a child.

■ If you do occasionally erupt in anger at a child, don't stew about it. An outburst signals clearly how strongly you feel about an issue. Sometimes that's what it takes to get your point across.

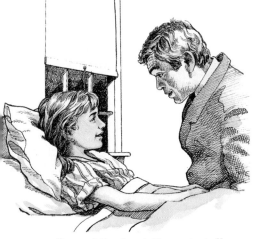

■ One of the best times to talk with your children is when they are tucked into bed. They are more likely to feel relaxed. Ask if anything special happened that day. You may learn a lot.

LET THE PUNISHMENT FIT THE CRIME

■ Warnings and penalties should be administered to your child as privately as pos-

sible. No one likes to be criticized in public, and we react with open or hidden resentment when it happens. In accord with the golden rule, treat children as you would like to be treated yourself.

■ If things begin to get out of hand, call a time-out. Send your child to a quiet room or corner with a warning that if this cooling-off period does not help him or her to calm down, there will be other consequences. For example, television time may be cut back.

■ Act quickly when a child misbehaves (but be sure you have the facts). Delaying discipline dilutes its impact.

■ Deal with the problem yourself. Never say "Just wait till your father (or mother) gets home!" It isn't fair to make one parent the "heavy" in matters of discipline, and, besides, this postpones the reckoning.

■ Choose appropriate punishments for rule-breaking or repeated carelessness. If a child loses his or her lunch box, pack school lunches in brown paper bags. If one toddler hurts another in a fight over a toy, separate them.

■ Be fair: Is this the first time your child has misbehaved in this way? Was the misdeed planned or was it impulsive? Were there any extenuating circumstances? If, for example, your child was influenced by an older kid, the solution (as well as the punishment) could well be to prohibit your child from playing with the older one.

■ Don't assign as a penalty something you want your

child to enjoy, such as reading a book or playing the piano.

■ Make sure that you do not punish a child twice for the same offense. For example, if the teacher has punished the child, the parent should not, and vice versa.

■ Avoid corporal punishment. It may seem reasonable at the time to slap a child for hitting a younger sister or brother, but you are sending the wrong message. You cannot teach children that it's wrong to hit by hitting them.

■ Heed the results of your disciplinary efforts. If your child persists in unacceptable behavior, try to discover why. If the child is cutting up just to get your attention, let him or her know that there are much better ways of doing this.

■ If you are feeling overwhelmed by your child's misbehavior, get professional help. See a trained counselor or enroll in a parenting class.

Keep your sense of humor. It can help you to put transgressions in proper perspective.

CALMING FEARS

■ Treat all fears seriously and consider how to alleviate them. For example, if a small child is afraid of shadows on the bedroom wall caused by passing traffic, move the bed or get an opaque shade. Or teach the child to make shadow animals, perhaps a bunny or a bird.

■ Tell the child that sometimes parents are afraid, too.

■ Encourage your child to put

his fears into words. Talking can sometimes make them vanish.

■ Help your child face a fear by exposing him gradually to what scares him. For example, if he's frightened of dogs, periodically drop by a pet store or visit a neighbor's puppy. Reassure him all the while, and recognize even the smallest improvements. However, do not push too hard or overwhelm a child who is not ready.

■ Don't discourage your child if he or she needs a security blanket or other favorite object to feel safe. He or she will outgrow it in time.

■ Be sure that a child who has had a nightmare is fully awake, so that he or she won't slip back into the same dream. Emphasize that dreams can't hurt you. Let the child fall back to sleep with a light or a radio on.

■ Occasionally, children become so fearful of bad dreams that they dread the approach of night. Parents should provide relaxing bedtime routines and regular sleep schedules. If these approaches don't work, parents may want to seek professional advice.

■ A child who has night terrors (which are different from nightmares) will awaken abruptly, crying and screaming. The child may not recognize familiar faces and indeed may still be semiconscious. Though the child may resist attempts at comforting, parents can try. Night terrors are

alarming, but they have no serious effects and usually vanish by age eight.

■ If a child has persistent nightmares or fear of the dark, try putting a lighted fish tank in the bedroom. Watching fish is soothing, and the aquarium doubles as a nightlight.

SIBLING RIVALRY

Parents need to understand and accept the fact that rivalry among siblings is perfectly normal. It is as deep in the human psyche as an infant's fear of abandonment and is based on the child's need to get all the attention he or she needs to survive. What parents have to do is set civilized limits on this impulse.

■ Not every argument among children should be considered sibling rivalry. When kids fight, there may be a good reason for it, having nothing to do with sibling one-upmanship.

■ On the plus side, fighting within the family setting gives children experience in resolving conflicts and practice in making up—saying "I'm sorry" or "I didn't mean it."

■ But when children are constantly picking on one another—teasing, prodding, and ridiculing—it may be time

to seek professional help. An atmosphere of hostility can interfere with the development of friendly, enduring relationships.

RIVALRY-REDUCING RULES FOR PARENTS

Although rivalry is natural, you don't want to exacerbate it.

■ Be aware that even comments that seem positive can foster rivalry. Say what you have to say about one child's behavior without reference to any other child.

■ Forget the 50-50 split. Children have different needs, so don't try to treat them exactly the same. Focus on each child as an individual, meeting special needs as they occur, and strive for an overall fairness.

■ Rotate chores so one sibling doesn't feel he or she has a harder job than the other.

■ If your children constantly complain to you about each other, give them "gripe books," personal notebooks in which they can write or draw whenever they are angry.

■ Hold the labels. When parents say "Lisa's the artist, and Pete's a real athlete," they may make their children (whose interests often change from one day to the next) feel locked into roles. Though this would *seem* to be giving each child his or her own special niche, it implies that there's room for only one artist or athlete in the family. The "artistic one," for example, may suppress her athletic abilities. And a child who has been labeled "the smart one" may feel pressure never to fail. Those with less complimentary labels—such as fresh, fat, or lazy—may find themselves shackled to an unflattering image, one that has a way of sticking with them all their lives.

■ You can point out the advantages of sharing, but don't try to force it. With time and tolerance, children learn that they usually enjoy themselves more when they share toys and games.

■ Don't get locked into "teams." If you're the one who always brings your son to his guitar lesson while your spouse shepherds your daughter to soccer games, play "musical parent" and rotate.

■ Don't let others overlook a sibling. Well-intentioned but insensitive friends and relatives can incite rivalry. If someone gushes over the new baby or compliments only one child, help out by steering the conversation the other youngster's way.

WHEN CHILDREN FIGHT

■ Obviously, you must stop a fight when there's danger of one child's inflicting injury on the other.

■ When you intervene, don't spend a lot of time trying to find out who started the fight.

You'll hear "He said," "She said," and so forth, but there is seldom a single, true answer to the question.

■ Separate children until they are calm enough to talk sensibly. Tell them they can disagree all they want, but they can't hit one another or throw things and they must be civil. Their fight can't be allowed to disturb the rest of the family. In other words, they'll have to keep it down.

■ Aside from that, it's best to remain vigilant but invisible, letting squabbling siblings settle things for themselves. After all, you don't want to play referee all the time.

■ Then, too, when parents intervene in a conflict, it almost always ends with one child as villain and the other, victim.

■ A villain-versus-victim showdown can easily transform an ordinary fight into sibling rivalry. The children now begin to compete for the coveted Victim Award, which only a parent can hand out.

■ Discourage tattling, a bad habit for a child to get into. The exception is if a child does something dangerous.

· ·

Remember that the worst rivalry occurs in the presence of a parent and is often staged to push parents into taking sides.

· ·

TWINS: A SPECIAL CASE

■ Parents of twins should expect sibling rivalry at its most intense, since neither twin ever has the parents' exclusive attention.

■ Be especially sensitive to

the feelings of older siblings. The birth of not one but two rivals who demand parents' time can cause resentment.

■ During the twins' infancy, alternate routines to ease the workload. Instead of bathing both daily, for example, bathe them on alternate days.

■ As twins develop, support the emergence of individual identities. Encourage them to dress differently, have different friends, participate in different sports.

WHEN SIBLING RIVALRY GOES TOO FAR

Unhealthy rivalry may require professional help. Be alert to the following behaviors, especially if they tend to recur:

■ A child takes delight in a sibling's feeling bad.

■ A child talks about hurting a sibling.

■ A child resorts too often to physical or emotional abuse or humiliates the sibling in front of others.

■ Both children consistently

avoid each other.

■ A child shows signs of depression or withdrawal—plummeting grades or changes in such daily routines as sleeping and eating. This may indicate that the rivalry has gone too far and is cutting into the child's self-esteem.

ADULT SIBLING RIVALRY

Childhood competition isn't always outgrown. It can remain a potent ingredient in relationships throughout life. However, there are ways to get beyond it.

■ If you were the favored child, realize that your sibling suffered. If you were the less-favored, know that it wasn't your sibling's fault.

■ Be aware of the need for tact in situations that can easily revive old rivalries—such as holidays.

■ Meet your sibling on neutral turf instead of in your parents' house, where childhood roles are often perpetuated.

■ Discuss any long-concealed feelings, such as anger or jealousy, but also talk positively about improving your relationship. You might first try putting desired changes in a letter to help clarify your thoughts.

■ Show your affection. A hug, a compliment, or a thoughtful gift can heal many wounds.

If your spouse quarrels with a brother or sister, be supportive but remain emotionally neutral; you want to help your mate to be more objective, rather than inflaming feelings any further.

HANDLING LEARNING DISORDERS

Certain learning disorders, such as dyslexia and attention deficiencies, can severely impair a child's ability to perform in school. However, with proper diagnosis, these conditions can be treated effectively.

■ Dyslexia is characterized by difficulty in recognizing words and letters. Children with this disorder have trouble learning to read, write, and spell. However, many have normal to superior intelligence and some are above-average in art, music, dancing, or sports.

■ Parents of dyslexics should seek out teachers trained to deal with the problem. With the right kind of help, many such children overcome their disability. Nelson A. Rockefeller, who was dyslexic, became governor of the state of New York. The important thing is not to avoid the problem. If left untreated, learning disabilities can become more difficult to cope with, particularly in the teen years.

■ Children with attention deficit disorders generally exhibit a short attention span, difficulty listening, an inability to complete tasks, impulsive behavior, moodiness, and distractibility. Many of them are also hyperactive. Medication can lessen symptoms in up to 80 percent of these children, who are predominantly male.

■ Take care not to overstimulate a hyperactive child, especially at bedtime.

■ Be skeptical of claims that link hyperactivity to a diet

high in sugar and artificial colorings and low in vitamins. Clinical studies have failed to prove any such link.

■ Consider family counseling if relationships between the hyperactive child and other family members have become strained.

A PLACE TO STUDY

Good study habits are the cornerstone of a solid education, so it's important to start your school-age children off well. Begin by providing a quiet area for homework. With minimal effort, you may be able to transform a relatively small space, even a closet, into a study area that your children can call their own.

■ Consider using a canvas shower curtain, bookcases, or a folding screen to partition off the homework area from the rest of the room for times when children really need to concentrate.

■ Take a look at your children's study habits. Do they naturally seek out a quiet place to study, or do they prefer to be with the rest of the family, for example, at the kitchen table? Are they able to tune out noise, or are they easily distracted? Do they like to spread out their materials, or are they more comfortable in a smaller, more organized space? Asking these questions of your children and yourself will help you to create the best work environment for your child.

■ Ask your children to help choose and organize their own space. Their involvement will ensure its success.

HOMEWORK AIDS

Although children have very different studying styles, there are some basic necessities for any work space.

■ Adequate lighting: Strong direct illumination is the most important element; it reduces eye fatigue and helps children to concentrate.

■ Comfortable seating: A chair that encourages good posture is a must, especially if your children work for extended periods. Choose one that allows the feet to touch the floor and arms to rest comfortably on the desk. Adjustable chairs are your best bet, since they will accommodate your children as they grow. Alternatively, an adult-size chair with a cushion and footrest will work well.

■ Work surface: Almost any desk or table can be equipped for a child's use—the kitchen table, a desk made from a piece of plywood atop two file cabinets, an antique writing desk.

■ Storage: Encourage order with painted wooden crates or wire or wicker baskets. Even color-coded cardboard boxes will serve as storage devices for books, folders, pens, and art supplies. A hanging pegboard with small storage compartments is a good way to take advantage of wall space.

TEENAGE ISSUES

In adolescence, youngsters strive for greater autonomy, often asking for more freedom than they are able to handle. It's the parents' job to help them gain independence and to develop a sense of responsibility.

■ The issue of teenage sexual behavior is one that parents need to discuss frankly with their children. It's not enough to hope they are not active sexually or to get angry if you think they are. Teenagers need to know what you consider responsible sexual behavior, including a discussion of your views on safe sex.

■ Teenagers need to hear, clearly and often, why teenage pregnancy is a disaster for all concerned—for the baby

and for the youngsters themselves, both female and male. Adolescents are not equipped emotionally or economically to rear a child.

■ Ultimately, young people make their own decisions. Make sure your youngsters know where they can get reliable information about disease prevention and birth control. The source of the information can be a doctor, their school, or the parents themselves.

■ Teenage drinking—often exacerbated by peer pressure— is a problem that won't go away on its own. Talk to your teenagers about the hazards of drinking, particularly when driving.

■ Let your kids know about the designated driver—the person in the group who agrees not to drink so that he or she will be able to drive. They should never get into a car with a driver who has been drinking. Be sure they have money with them to take a taxi, or tell them to call you to come pick them up.

■ Examine your own use of alcohol, nicotine, and even prescription drugs. What kind of example are you setting? If you have (or had) trouble quitting smoking or you have an alcohol problem, for example, a frank discussion with your children may help them avoid these pitfalls.

■ Like alcohol, drugs are a grave danger to the life and well-being of teenagers. (For signs of drug abuse, see page 379.) If your son or daughter has this problem, it is important to get professional help at once.

FINDING GOOD CHILD CARE

Entrusting your child to a sitter or day care center can be a difficult decision. Here are some guidelines for ensuring the best care for your child and peace of mind for yourself.

HIRING A SITTER

■ Check the applicant's personal references. Ask the former employer if the sitter was reliable, whether the children liked her, if she ever faced an emergency, and, if so, how she handled it. (Though sitters are most often female, boys and men sometimes take on the job. The hints given here apply to both male and female sitters.)

■ Ask the job-seeker what she likes most and least about babysitting, what activities she enjoys doing with children, and how she would handle such problems as an infant who wakes up with a fever.

■ If the sitter is fairly young, try to gauge whether she is mature enough to handle problems. If the sitter is elderly, make sure that she is energetic enough to keep up with your baby or toddler.

■ Spell out clearly your views on discipline. No one should be allowed to strike a child. Make sure that you tell the sitter that physical punishment is grounds for dismissal.

■ Discuss whether you allow smoking (health experts advise against smoking in the presence of infants and children), your policy on alcoholic beverages, and whether the sitter is allowed to have visitors to the house.

■ Invite her to spend an hour or so with you and the child, and watch how they interact. Does she seem comfortable with the child? Does she appear to like him or her?

■ Trust your instincts. If the sitter has all the right answers but something about her bothers you, don't hire her.

> **Arrange for your sitter to get a complete physical examination. This should include a TB test, especially if she has recently lived or traveled abroad.**

TRAINING YOUR SITTER

Once you've chosen a sitter, schedule a get-acquainted session in which you give her a tour of the house and detail your child's habits and needs. Of course, the sitter should be paid for the time she spends in this meeting.

■ Emphasize the location of exits to be used in the event of a fire. Review the family's evacuation plans (see "Fire Safety," page 218).

■ Show her where you keep your flashlight and first-aid kit (see page 384). She should also know where to find the fuse box and other essential items.

■ Outline rules on use of the phone, TV, stereo, and VCR.

■ Specify what snacks you will provide. Note that you will expect the sitter to clean up after snack time.

■ Show her where you keep diapers, extra clothing, bottles, formula, food, and other baby supplies.

■ Review the proper way to pick up, hold, feed, and diaper the baby, as well as instructions on sterilizing bottles and serving baby food.

■ Describe your child's special pre-sleep habits, such as crying, rocking, sucking on a finger, thumb, or pacifier. Older sitters may object to thumb-sucking, but current thinking is that it fulfills a baby's needs for sucking and rhythmic motion and may even be an early sign of self-sufficiency.

> **Treat your sitter as a professional. If you anticipate a long-term relationship, write up a job description and an agreement detailing working hours, salary, overtime pay, and benefits.**

■ Explain the sleeping positions you want for your infant. Be sure that the sitter knows that the baby should sleep on his or her back or side. Recent studies indicate that a child who sleeps on the stomach is more vulnerable to sudden infant death syndrome than a child who sleeps on the back or side. To prop an infant on his or her side, place a rolled-up towel against the back.

■ Leave one or two extra pacifiers in the crib. If a pacifier falls out of the baby's mouth, he or she can find one to replace it.

■ Every now and then, make an unannounced stop at your home. It's an effective way to learn what's happening in your absence, especially if your child is too young to talk.

■ When you leave for the day, bid your child a cheerful good-bye, then leave promptly. The longer the farewells, the more likely the child will become upset.

COPING WITH EMERGENCIES

■ Post important phone numbers: home, office, pediatrician, police, fire, ambulance, nearest hospital, poison control center, a neighbor or relative to call in a pinch.

■ Leave an abbreviated medical history—your child's allergies, medications, immunizations, and illnesses.

■ Review first-aid procedures. Better yet, have the sitter take a course at a hospital, YMCA, or Red Cross chapter.

■ Supply a signed release form authorizing emergency medical services in your absence. You can obtain the form from a doctor or an attorney. Without it, doctors can treat a child only if withholding care would be life-threatening.

■ Leave enough money in an envelope to pay for cab fare to the nearest emergency room. Write on the envelope the phone number of a taxi service, the address and phone number of the hospital, both parents' offices during the day, and where they may be reached at other times.

■ Go with the caregiver to the nearest medical center to show her the route.

■ Combine emergency information with other instructions on how to care for your child—favorite toys, the bedtime routine—in a small loose-leaf binder. That way, everything is in one place and information can easily be added or updated.

JUDGING DAY CARE

■ Inquire whether the center is licensed, which means it must meet minimum standards of safety, hygiene, and staffing. Although not all provinces require it, ask if the center conducts a criminal-history background check on its employees.

Ask about employee turnover. A fairly stable staff often indicates a well-run center with experienced, dedicated caregivers.

■ Check social service agencies to find out if any reports have been filed on the center.

■ Whether home- or center-based, day care facilities should be warm and inviting places. First, look at the physical facility. Is it neat and free of safety hazards? Do you see toys, books, and play equipment appropriate to young children? Is the kitchen clean and large enough for adequate meal preparation?

■ Is the bathroom clean? Is there a place for changing diapers safely? How are soiled diapers disposed of? Antiseptic procedures for handling soiled diapers are crucial to keeping young children healthy.

■ Ask to observe a provider changing a diaper. Ideally, she should wear thin plastic gloves, wash her own and the baby's hands afterward, turn the water off with a paper towel, and sanitize the changing area.

■ Inquire about how the staff handles diaper rash. Common practice is to wash the affected area with mild soap or disposable wipes and dry it after each diaper change. For mild rashes, a cream containing zinc oxide or another protective ointment may be used.

■ Ask about immunization requirements for the child and other health policies.

■ Observe interactions between the provider and the

169

children, and among the children themselves. Do the kids look happy? Do the staff seem to know how to handle conflicts among children?

■ Arrange to meet everyone who will have contact with your child, including bus drivers and janitors.

MORE POINTERS

■ Check out the activity schedule. See if snack time, lunch, and naps are always at the same hours, so the day has a pleasant, predictable rhythm to it. Young children need a regular routine.

■ Ask if you may visit during the day, unannounced. The center may not encourage this, because it has schedules to maintain, but you should be able to drop in occasionally to see how your child is faring.

■ Make sure that the ratio of staff to children meets the legal requirement. It varies from one province and territory to another—check first what the ratio should be.

■ Try to avoid overcrowded facilities. The amount of children in any age group as well as the number allowed in the day care center is set by the province or territory. Check what the numbers should be.

■ Find out how much TV is allowed, if any. An hour of *Sesame Street* is fine as long as there are lots of play activities the rest of the day.

■ When you drop your child off at day care, do so in the same cheerful, brisk manner you use at home when you leave him or her with a sitter. Otherwise, the child is likely to hang on and cry.

If you're going to be even a little late at the beginning or end of the day, call in advance to say so.

PLAYING OUTDOORS

■ If the day care center offers a playground with swings, seesaws, and other equipment, look at their condition. They should be sturdy and well maintained, standing on earth or sand rather than concrete; when children fall, as they inevitably will, they should land on a relatively resilient surface.

■ Swings should be lightweight but sturdy. Rubber or plastic seats are preferable to wood, which can splinter or cause serious injury if they accidentally hit a child. The swing area should be fenced off to prevent toddlers from running in front while the swing is in use.

■ On a slide, there should be guardrails or barriers on the elevated platform. The chute should have a smooth surface with no protruding seams. The sides of the chute should be about four inches high.

■ Trampolines, trapeze bars, and swinging exercise

rings are not recommended for children's playgrounds.

■ If there is a sandbox, check on its cleanliness. Is it covered when not in use? Unprotected, it is an open invitation to neighborhood cats and dogs. Is it in a shaded location or does it have a sunroof over it? The glare of the sun on sand can be just as intense in a sandbox as at the beach and the likelihood of sunburn just as great.

■ If you expect your child to play outdoors for any length of time, be sure to put sunscreen on him or her before the child leaves home. Apply sunscreen to the child's face year-round, winter or summer. Cover any other exposed skin as well (see "Sun Sense," page 126).

WORKPLACE DAY CARE CENTERS

"My whole face lights up when I see the children going to the center."
—Nancy Platt, Time Warner, Inc., executive

• • • • • • •

One morning, Andrew Alper, a partner at the investment firm Goldman, Sachs, was presented with a problem: what to do with his two daughters, ages 4 years and 20 months, on the sitter's day off. His wife, a lawyer, had planned to stay home with the kids but was called to make a court appearance at the last minute. Instead of calling a babysitting agency and leaving the girls with a total stranger, he simply brought them to work with him.

This would not have been possible in the past, but his company had recently opened an on-site child care center for just this kind of emergency. "They loved it," Alper says. "The girls had art projects and toys and areas to play in and climb over. I went down to see them a couple of times during the day."

The baby business. Across North America, institutions like Goldman, Sachs, best known for their mergers and acquisitions, are getting into the baby business. In this still small but growing group of firms, stroller sightings are frequent, peanut butter and jelly sandwiches have made it onto cafeteria menus, and books such as *The Cat in the Hat* sit alongside company prospectuses in corporate libraries.

These changes have come about because businesses recognize the frailty of most child care arrangements and are trying to help. Of course, it's not pure altruism on the part of companies; they're still ruled by economic matters. As one business owner puts it, "Each employee turnover costs the company about $50,000. Once you've trained someone and put all the time and effort into their training, you can't afford to lose them."

Companies are being forced to recognize that work and family profoundly affect each other. If a child is sick at home, a parent either misses work or spends the day at work worrying. Statistics Canada has shown that, on average, Canadian women take 7.9 days a year off work to deal with family issues

A helping hand. Some corporate day care centers are designed for short-term crises. They fill the gap when a babysitter gets sick or when a school is unexpectedly closed for the day. Generally, companies limit the number of times an employee can use the center, for example, 20 days a year. Of course, there

The on-site day care center at Goldman, Sachs is a children's paradise, filled with colorful toys and games.

are exceptions. A secretary at Time Warner, Inc., the media and entertainment company, used the center for five weeks while her husband, who had been caring for their three-year-old son, recovered from a heart attack.

Children pass the day at corporate day care centers under the guidance of trained educators. Parents can check in on their kids throughout the day and even take them to lunch. Kids get to see where their parents work, and parents get the comfort of knowing that their children are well cared for.❏

LATCHKEY CHILDREN

Youngsters who return from school to an empty house or apartment may suffer anxiety and stress. Here are ways to help such children cope with boredom, loneliness, and fear—and also stay out of harm's way.

ARE YOUR CHILDREN READY?

Some provincial and local laws regulate the age when a child can be left alone. The Canada Safety Council recommends that no child under 10 should be left alone. The decision to leave your children by themselves should not be taken lightly, even for older children. When considering it, it's important to assess their physical, social, and emotional maturity.

■ Can your children lock and unlock the door? Can they dial the phone and write messages? Can they tell time? Are they comfortable with being home alone? Can they recognize dangerous situations and react appropriately? Can they communicate with adults?

■ Is there an adult living or working nearby whom your children know and can depend on in case of an emergency?

PREPARE YOUR CHILDREN

■ Before leaving children alone on a regular basis, make a trial run. Leave them at home a few times while you shop or visit a neighbor. Afterward, ask about the experience and listen carefully.

■ One way to teach kids how to cope is to rehearse what they should do or say in various situations. "What would you do if . . . ?" Review this strategy often.

■ Don't overpraise youngsters for staying home alone. If you do, they may try to keep any problems that arise to themselves for fear of losing their parents' respect.

■ Establish a phone-in routine so that children call you or another trusted adult as soon as they arrive home from school each day.

■ Phone latchkey children at least once a day. Such calls are very reassuring.

■ Post a list of emergency numbers (police, fire, ambulance, doctor, neighbors, your office) near every phone in the house.

■ Make sure that your children memorize important phone numbers—even if you have a phone that is programmed for speed-dialing. Youngsters may not have access to that particular phone when they need to make an emergency call.

■ Teach children how to use a pay phone, including dialing the operator or an emergency number, without having to deposit money.

■ Children home alone should tell callers "My mom (or dad) is busy right now. May I take a message?" They should not say that you are not home.

■ Have your children bring in the mail after school. Most break-ins occur during the day, when no one is home; a mailbox that has been emptied indicates that someone is there.

■ If your children are left by

Parents can give a child a sense of self-confidence by carefully going over safety rules and discussing fears openly before leaving him at home alone.

themselves because of your job, make sure they understand why you are working. They should be reassured that you would rather be there with them but that the family needs the money.

If possible, take your kids to visit your workplace so they will know where you are during the day.

AN INVITING PLACE

■ Welcome your children home even when you can't be there. Leave an affectionate or funny note or homemade card for them to find when they get home from school.

■ Leave some lights on so your children won't walk into a dark house. Have a radio tuned to a station that they enjoy.

■ If you don't get home at the usual time, your children may worry. Be sure to call if you're running late.

SAFETY FIRST

■ Ask your local police or fire department to inspect your home. Investing in double locks, a smoke detector, and other recommended safety and health features will help reduce children's fears.

■ If your children wear the house key on a string around their necks, make sure that it's out of sight.

■ Hide an extra key outside or leave one with a neighbor, in case a key is lost. If you leave a spare key outside, never put it near a door, under a doormat, or in a flowerpot—those are the first places an intruder

might look. Change the hiding place every so often.

■ Tell your children to ignore the doorbell or a knock at the door. Otherwise, children are forced to decide for themselves whether or not the person at the door is safe to admit, which is too much responsibility. Exceptions to this policy should be spelled out precisely.

■ Get a large dog, such as a Labrador retriever, which can provide a certain amount of protection.

■ Devise a fire-escape plan (see "Fire Safety," page 218), teach basic first aid (see page 380), and explain how to use appliances safely.

■ Often just knowing how to handle a scary situation defuses fear. For example, if your children know where to find a working flashlight, they won't be as frightened in a blackout.

SIBLINGS: ALONE TOGETHER

■ Specify if an older child is to be in charge of a younger one or if they're each responsible for themselves.

■ Define how you expect

siblings to resolve conflicts or report problems.

■ Consider assigning household chores, ones that need no adult supervision.

■ Chores should be divided up so that each child knows what's expected.

ANTIDOTES TO BOREDOM

■ Pets can provide entertainment, companionship, and affection. While dogs may be "man's best friend," a kitten or even a gerbil is nice to come home to.

■ To control the quantity and quality of the TV programs your children watch, sit down with your kids on Sunday night and review their television schedule for the week ahead.

■ If possible, set up visits or activities outside the home. A midweek break—for instance, spending Wednesday afternoon at a friend's house—makes the time alone more manageable.

■ Suggest activities to help your children keep busy. Put together a puzzle; build a model; make puppets; set the dinner table; prepare dessert for dinner; collect baseball cards, photos, maps, coins, or dolls; write a letter; keep a scrapbook on current events or sports.

Stock the kitchen with healthy snacks like applesauce, pre-popped popcorn, fresh and dried fruit, nuts, vegetable sticks, yogurt, low-fat cheese, peanut butter, and wheat crackers.

PROTECTING YOUR KIDS

When children are kidnapped, it's often by someone they know. Rather than merely warning your children to beware of strangers, tell them about situations they should avoid and suspicious adult behaviors they should watch out for.

BASIC LESSONS

To minimize the chance of your child's being abducted, experts recommend that you teach your child the following as soon as he or she is old enough:

■ The child's full name, address, and phone number, including area code (because kids may be taken to another province). The child should also know his or her parents' names, and, if possible, their work addresses and phone numbers.

■ How to dial the local police, emergency services, and a neighbor or relative.

■ How to make a long-distance call, both directly by using the area code and by dialing "0" for operator.

. . . .

Tuck an ID card into your children's backpacks, book bags, or coat pockets. Tape a few quarters to the back of the card so they will always have spare money.

. . . .

RULES FOR YOUNGSTERS

Parents should also instruct kids on the following points:

■ Never leave your apartment or house, or leave the yard, without asking a parent's permission. Older children should phone home to inform a parent where they are, especially if they change locations. For

example, if they go from one friend's house to another or are going to a baseball field.

■ Never leave a schoolyard during school hours or leave a playground without first getting a parent's or babysitter's permission.

■ Never hitchhike.

■ If you become separated while shopping or in any public place, don't wander around looking for a parent or guardian. Instead, go to the nearest checkout counter, security office, or lost and found. Tell the person in charge that you have lost Mom and Dad and need help finding them.

■ Never tell anyone over the phone that you are home alone.

■ Never answer the doorbell when you are home alone.

RULES FOR PARENTS

■ Never leave a child unattended in public, including in a parked car.

■ When you enroll a child in a day care center or school, make sure the policy is not to release children to anyone but their parents. Ask the school to call you whenever your child is absent.

■ Know your child's friends and their parents. Be involved in your child's activities.

■ Pay attention when your child tells you he or she does not want to be with someone;

ask why not. Be sensitive to changes in your child's behavior or attitudes.

■ Observe when an adult lavishes a great deal of attention on your child; find out why.

■ Devise a plan so your child knows what to do if you become separated while away from home.

■ Having several up-to-date photos of the entire family around the house or in your wallet or purse can come in handy if instant identifications are needed.

. . . .

Do not buy clothing or other items bearing your child's name. Such apparel permits an abductor to address your child directly and start a "friendly" conversation.

. . . .

WHEN A CHILD IS OUT AND ABOUT

■ If your child walks to school, have him or her walk with other children. A child is most vulnerable when alone.

■ Children should be leery when adults ask them for travel directions. Adults should ask directions from other grown-ups, not from kids.

■ If someone is following a child on foot or in a car, the child should not try to hide. He or she should stop at the nearest house or store for help.

■ When your child is playing outdoors with friends, have him use the buddy system.

■ Children should refuse a stranger's request for help of any kind. Sometimes children can be tricked by an appeal to look for a "lost puppy" or a "lost kitten." In all likelihood there is no puppy or kitten.

■ Children should avoid adults who wait around a playground, particularly an adult who wants to play with children.

■ A child should not believe a stranger who says that a parent is in trouble and offers to take him or her to Mom or Dad. If such an approach is made to a child when he or she is leaving school, the child should return to the school immediately to report what has happened. (A teacher or other school official can call the child's home or the parent's work number to reassure the child.)

■ A child should yell "Help!" and make as much noise and commotion as possible to get attention if someone tries to abduct him or her.

Families should have a secret code word that only they know. Any adult who makes a nice-sounding offer to a child but does not give the code word should be considered suspicious.

IF YOUR CHILD IS MISSING

■ Act immediately. Search your house thoroughly, including closets, piles of laundry, in and under beds, old refrigerators, or wherever a child might hide, fall asleep, or get trapped.

■ If you still have not found your child, think of where he or she could have gone. Check with your neighbors, your child's friends, and school; if you are divorced, place a call to your ex-spouse.

■ If you still haven't found your child, call the police and start procedures immediately. Provide as much precise information as you can, including the clothing the child was wearing when he or she disappeared. Be sure to advise the police if your child is on medication, has any special health needs, or is mentally incapacitated.

■ Ask your local police to ensure that your child is registered as missing with the databank of the Canadian Police Information Centre (C.P.I.C.). Also request that they register your child with the RCMP's Missing Children's Registry, a unit specialized in dealing with all aspects of missing children.

■ After notifying the police,

you could ask the police for the name of a local nonprofit organization that deals with missing children.

■ Check your child's room for notes, letters, missing clothing.

■ Review your phone bill. Are there any unfamiliar long-distance calls that may indicate where your child may be?

■ Canvass local people, distant relatives, and friends.

■ Search locked areas in your neighborhood, such as garages, roofs, and basements.

■ If your child calls, communicate love and concern for his or her safety.

■ Check with the police that you may publicize your child's disappearance. If they agree, contact the media with a description. Make flyers with the child's recent photo, and a detailed description of what he or she looks like, with details of clothing when last seen. Give the flyer a heading such as "Missing" or "Have You Seen This Child?" Give the name and phone number of a law enforcement office that can receive calls around the clock. Post flyers in groceries, malls—everywhere you can.

175

SEPARATION AND DIVORCE

Marriages can be undone legally in weeks, months, or years, but breaking the emotional bond may take much longer. Here's how to ease the process for all concerned.

SEPARATION

■ A separation can actually save a marriage by giving the parties concerned enough time to reconsider their feelings and goals. After cooling off and, ideally, getting professional counseling, the couple may be able to set new ground rules for a better relationship.

■ Many people look at separation as a defeat, a failure to make their marriage work. It is almost always painful for those concerned. Nevertheless, separation may be the wisest course to take in certain circumstances. No one should stay in a relationship where there is physical or emotional abuse. And if addiction to drugs or alcohol has taken over one partner, the other should most certainly get out and take the kids.

■ In abuse cases, the abuser frequently resists a spouse's efforts to separate. Often, the abuser will promise to reform; evidence indicates that unless there is counseling, this is an empty promise. In all likelihood the abuse will get worse. Enlist the support of family and friends, get legal help, call social agencies, and, if necessary, call the police.

■ In cases of marital infidelity, long-standing lack of affection, or what is termed irreconcilable differences, the separation can take place in a more rational atmosphere. This doesn't mean that the parting will not be acrimonious. But both partners can usually manage to communicate—via their lawyers. If there are children in the marriage, parents should make every effort to spare the children's feelings.

■ If possible, children should be told about a separation and impending divorce with both parents present. Often kids will try to get their parents to reconsider. With both parents there, the firmness of the decision is reinforced.

■ Children often feel guilty when parents separate and assume that something they said or did caused the marital breakup. Assure your children that this is not true.

■ Be ready to explain to your children—again and again—what decisions have been made about custody, living arrangements, and other issues that affect them.

> **Try to maintain established routines. Keeping the same times for meals, homework, and going to bed can help lessen the impact of separation on children.**

DIVORCE

Feelings of grief are natural in a divorce. You have, after all, suffered a great loss. But do not confuse grief with guilt. Indulging in self-reproach will accomplish nothing. Remind yourself that you did your best during the marriage and that no one can do more. And no matter how earth-shattering it seems at the time, you can and will survive the dissolution of your marriage.

■ Don't let divorce lawyers prolong the battle over financial arrangements. You may want to seek the advice of a divorce mediator to settle the details.

■ Expect to be on an emotional roller coaster for a while. It's a typical experience for divorced people.

■ If your anger does not subside after a reasonable time, or if you begin to feel hopeless or helpless, you may find therapy useful. Consider a psychotherapist or a support group affiliated with a community center or church. If money is a problem, contact a private or public family-service agency.

■ Take one day at a time. Be pragmatic: don't expect that you can immediately resolve all your problems.

TRANSITION AND RECOVERY
■ Remember that it can take a year or two after the divorce is finalized for you to adjust to your new life.
■ Take care of yourself: eat right, get enough sleep, and exercise daily.
■ Overcome anger and depression by keeping busy. Accept invitations from friends and extend invitations to them to come over for coffee or dinner or just to watch TV. Consider taking classes, doing volunteer work, or taking up a new hobby.
■ Pamper yourself occasionally. Spend a day in bed watching football games. Get a professional massage. Buy tickets to a concert or play.

THE CHILDREN'S WELFARE
■ Shield the youngsters from disputes between you and your ex-spouse. Such conflicts are often more damaging than the breakup itself.
■ Do not bad-mouth the other parent to the children.
■ Allow your children to express their anxieties, anger, and other emotions. If you feel hard-pressed to deal with their emotions or the children show signs of stress, such as sleeplessness or aggression, consider professional help.
■ Don't deprive yourself of clothes, entertainment, or other amenities in order to shower your children with extras. You will begin to feel resentment, which only adds to

your (and their) problems.
■ Do not expect your children to function as your support system. Rely on friends, get counseling, or join a support group, such as Parents Without Partners.

■ Don't be surprised if your children get clingy or show off to get your attention: it signals their insecurity. Remind them that parents never divorce children, so you'll always be there for them.
■ Develop new family rituals. Have dinner each Sunday with other single-parent families, for example.
■ Encourage cooperation among your children. Once they realize how much stress you feel as a single parent, particularly if you're a working parent, they may readily pitch in with chores.
■ Forget about being both mother and father to your children. If your son can no longer go fishing regularly with his dad, find another

adult who enjoys fishing—an uncle, cousin, grandfather, or a family friend.
■ If your children were young when the divorce occurred, discuss it more candidly when they are teenagers. Explain what was good about the marriage. Help the children avoid feeling doomed to repeat their parents' mistakes.
■ Discuss with your children the possibility of remarriage and, perhaps, your financial status. If you clam up, your children may imagine situations more worrisome than what is really happening.

• •

Reassure children when you begin dating that it does not mean you love them less, nor will you ever abandon them.

• •

HOW TO HANDLE YOUR EX
■ Keep your emotional distance. Do not get involved in your ex-spouse's personal problems or tell about yours. Do not expect your ex-husband or -wife to be suddenly understanding or helpful.
■ Ignore criticism from your ex-spouse, rather than trying to respond to it.
■ Support your spouse's efforts to fulfill parenting obligations. Children who do the best after a divorce have both parents actively involved in their upbringing.
■ Work at becoming more self-reliant. For example, if your ex-husband was a natural handyman, find someone else who can fix a leaky toilet or install window screens. Or try doing it yourself.

177

STEPFAMILIES

Stepparent and single-parent households with children of divorced or widowed parents can be more tumultuous than traditional households. These families often require an extra degree of compromise, flexibility, and patience.

STEPPARENTING

When a parent remarries, it may take a year or more for the children and new spouse to adjust to one another, and even longer for the stepfamily to blend. Here are some tactics that may ease the process for all involved.

■ Don't try to force close relationships. Instead, start by encouraging stepfamily members to respect one another, much as they would a houseguest.

■ Start off with small gestures, such as driving the kids around, appearing at hockey games, offering to help with homework.

■ Expect ups and downs. It's normal for children in an intact family to have mood swings; such feelings may be intensified in stepchildren.

■ Leave discipline to the biological parent, especially early in the marriage. One study found that the more active a disciplinary role the stepparent played, the worse the children's behavior problems, especially in the first two years of marriage. However, the biological parent should support the stepparent's role as the authority figure in the household in his or her absence. Of course, it's best to discuss household rules and personal values early on with your spouse.

■ Treat the children equally. Don't play favorites. Don't compare your stepchildren to your biological children.

Leave the words *stepson* and *stepdaughter* out of introductions. These reinforce the distance in your relationship. Just say, "I want you to meet David" or "This is my son David." If the specifics are important, explain them later.

YOURS, MINE, OURS, THEIRS

■ Give all children, resident or visiting, a place in the house that is their own—if not a room, then a drawer or shelf for personal belongings.

■ Set aside time at least once or twice a week to be alone with your biological child. Ride bikes, cook, or go to a store. Such attention can reassure him or her that, despite your remarriage, he or she is still an important part of your life.

■ Look for activities—hobbies, school projects, even chores—that you and your stepchildren can do together.

■ Schedule a movie outing, a sporting event, or other family get-together once a month. Give each family member a turn deciding what the activity will be.

■ Get away by yourself once in a while.

ESTABLISHING HEALTHY COMMUNICATION

■ Look for your stepchildren's good qualities and let them know you appreciate them.

■ Express angry feelings honestly but tactfully. Tell your spouse that you are having problems getting along with your stepchild, for example, not that your spouse's child acts like a brat. Ask the biological parent for help with the problem.

■ Criticize the stepchild's behavior, not the child: "John, in this house we keep our rooms clean," not "You're a bad boy for leaving your room so messy."

■ Let the children express feelings, fears, and concerns. The more readily youngsters can convey their emotions, the less need they may have to misbehave.

■ Don't put children in a "loyalty bind." Confine negative comments about the absent parent to private conversations with your spouse.

■ Reassure children that loving a stepparent doesn't mean

that they are giving less love to their biological parent. They should also know that they don't *have* to love the stepparent. However, they do have to show respect.

Daughters have a harder time adjusting to remarriages than sons, especially when they have a new stepfather. Studies show that stepdads should talk more—girls respond best to praise and verbal affection—but hug less. Physical gestures cause discomfort.

MAKE IT LEGAL

■ If you have stepchildren who are minors, ask your spouse to grant you limited power of attorney over them. Otherwise, you can't authorize emergency medical care, get school records, or sign important documents.

■ If there are adult stepchildren, make wills now and explain the provisions to avoid creating disagreements over inheritance later on.

KEEP IN TOUCH

Children of divorced parents often shuttle between Mom and Dad. To help these visits go smoothly, parents need to set up a schedule, communicate with each other, and focus on the children's needs.

■ The noncustodial parent—usually the father—should see his children at least once a week, if possible. Frequent, routine visits are best for both parent and child.

■ Make your children feel at home when they come for a visit. Keep toys, clothes, toothbrushes, and other essentials at your place. Provide a space they can decorate with their artwork or posters.

■ Devote time and attention to your children; don't turn them over to grandparents, a new spouse, or babysitters when they come to visit.

■ Avoid the temptation to overindulge your children with gifts or entertainment.

■ If possible, abide by the same rules—on snacks, bedtime, TV, and so on—that prevail in the custodial parent's home.

■ Help children remember when they will be with each parent by marking their visiting days on a calendar that is displayed prominently. Whenever you have a schedule conflict, let the children know well in advance.

■ Have your children subscribe to a magazine that is sent to your residence. Receiving mail there will help them feel at home.

EXTENDED STAYS

■ Don't schedule a flurry of activities as soon as the children arrive; after a separation, they need time to warm up and get to know you again. Initially, share such low-key activities as making dinner, taking a walk, or reading a bedtime story.

■ When planning holidays and summer vacations as the noncustodial parent, defuse the young child's travel anxiety by showing him on a calendar the exact dates of his departure and return.

■ Explain to the children how and where their time will be spent and who else (including stepfamily members) will be there.

■ Emphasize that they can call home any time.

■ If children who spend their summer vacation with you can find no one nearby to play with, sign them up for such activities as hockey games, music lessons, or day camp.

■ Investigate local historic sites, go camping overnight, or attend a concert. Help your children create a scrapbook for the mementos they gather on these expeditions.

■ When you and your children are apart, keep in touch with frequent letters and phone calls. Make videos and tape recordings to exchange.

Reassure your children that you are fine while they are gone and that you want them to enjoy visiting the other parent. Some youngsters need to be told that it's all right to feel close to the noncustodial parent.

PRESSURE POINTS

A disabled person in the house, grown children who return home, aging parents in need of care, in-laws from a previous marriage—all pose special challenges to the family.

HELPING A DISABLED PERSON

First and foremost, a disabled person is a person; no one should be defined by his or her disability. Most disabled people want to achieve as much independence as possible. Even if they do not actively seek independence, it is best for all concerned if their care in the home is undertaken with this objective in mind. They should be assisted in doing things for themselves and consulted about decisions that affect them.

■ If the disabled person is a child, parents and other family members should resist the temptation to wait on him or her. If a child has a muscular weakness, it's easier to dress him or her than to watch a struggle. But the child needs both the experience of dressing himself or herself and the sense of accomplishment—no matter how long it takes.

■ Don't overlook gadgets that can make life easier for the disabled person. For example, a wire basket mounted on a walker can be a great convenience.

■ For some, having a disability is so frustrating that they become depressed and resentful. Of course, this is extremely painful for everyone. However, in many cases, the family is actually being manipulated by the disabled member. Don't allow anyone to make you feel guilty because he or she is disabled and you are well. It's bad for you and bad for the disabled person. If possible, discuss the problem openly. If this doesn't work, it might be wise to seek counseling.

BOOMERANG KIDS

Adult children may move back home for a variety of reasons. Often, it's because they have lost a job or have just ended a marriage or other relationship. It's easy to distinguish between a nice long visit and a case of moving in—in the latter instance, the "visitors" generally bring all their goods and chattels.

Communicating With a Disabled Person

Here are some simple and tactful ways to approach people with specific problems.

Wheelchair: Don't lean on the wheelchair; it's part of the user's "personal space." Sit in a chair if your conversation lasts more than a few minutes. That way you'll be eye to eye and the person won't have to crane his or her neck to see you.

Hearing problems: Speak slowly. Keep your hands away from your mouth. Stand in the light so the person can watch your expressions and movements. Don't shout. Speak at a low pitch—it's easier to understand than a high-pitched voice. If you are having trouble in the midst of a group, take him or her aside. This is especially helpful for those with hearing aids. A hearing aid magnifies all noise—clanking dishes, the TV, phone conversations—so it's harder to discern individual sounds.

Vision loss: Identify yourself when approaching and ask family and friends to do likewise so the person doesn't have to guess who's there. Use a normal voice. You'd be surprised at how many people shout at the blind.

Speech problems: Be patient; stroke victims often speak very slowly. Resist the temptation to finish every sentence. Don't pretend to understand when you really don't. Ask the person to repeat the statement.

Severe memory lapses: Display clocks and calendars prominently.

■ It's fine for parents to give their children an affectionate welcome, but they should state plainly at the outset that living at home cannot be a permanent arrangement.

■ Set a definite date of departure or a specific goal—such as getting a job. Be willing to modify the plan, however, if there are extenuating circumstances. For example, when an adult child becomes a single parent, grandparents often become a source of financial and emotional support. Be sensitive to the needs of your child and grandchildren, but try not to become an essential part of their daily lives for an extended period.

■ Remember that you can't solve your children's problems for them. In fact, you might find that your child's true strength emerges when you stand at a distance.

■ Remember, too, that it's your house, so as a parent, you get to set the rules on visitors, smoking, loud music, and the like.

■ Resist the urge to treat a returning adult child like a youngster. Do not tell him or her what to wear or eat. Do not try to choose your son's or daughter's dates or friends.

■ Don't give an older child his or her old room back if it has been taken over by someone else. A young sibling shouldn't be displaced because an older brother or sister has returned.

■ If there's enough space, set aside a room to which the adult child can retreat in the evening. A basement room or an empty guest room may be suitable.

■ Respect one another's privacy. You can test whether you're invading your child's privacy by asking yourself if you'd do the same thing to a friend who was staying at your house.

A good housekeeping rule: whoever makes a mess cleans it up.

MONEY ISSUES

■ If you expect your child to pay rent, help with the cooking, walk the dog, or do yard work, explain this clearly. You may want to list the agreed-upon services and payments in writing in some type of contract.

■ Instead of lending money to adult children, suggest they go to a local bank.

■ If you choose to lend money, put the terms in writing. List the total amount, rate of interest, repayment schedule, and cancellation conditions. This will help prevent misunderstandings.

■ Try to make financial assistance a temporary or one-time gesture. You might consider subsidizing your child's rent on his or her own apartment, for example, until the first pay raise.

Consider putting in a separate phone line billed to your adult child. Otherwise, parents should set up a log for long-distance phone calls and get reimbursed.

PROBLEM PEOPLE

Most families have in their ranks persons who are hard to deal with—the parent who is always right or grandparent who consistently looks on the dark side of things or sibling who is aggrieved over the real or imagined inequities of life. There are no magic formulas for defusing the problems created by such attitudes. The important thing is not to waste your energies fighting losing battles.

■ Relatives who are always finding fault with, say, the gifts they receive for their birthday or Christmas are probably unpleasable. Just give what you consider appropriate, then forget it.

■ People who cherish grievances can seldom be persuaded to give them up. The best thing you can do is tune them out.

■ Family troublemakers who set one person or branch of the family against another can be held in check if everyone agrees not to pass on the gossip.

■ "If I were you . . ." is one of the opening lines of the relative who wants to run your life and, usually, wants to know too much. Except for parents, who have a duty to advise underage children and to know what they are doing, most of such "helpfulness" is unwarranted. As tactfully as possible, cut short the discussion.

■ Then there is the crisis-prone relative who tries to involve everyone in his or her problems. Many people feel guilty when they withhold assistance. The real question is,

Does going to the rescue really help, or does it perpetuate a dependency? If the latter, then grit your teeth and refuse.

HELPING AGING PARENTS

■ Be realistic about what your parents need. Don't go overboard doing things for them if they can still handle most tasks themselves.

■ Get your kids to pitch in. If they're not old enough to drive to a doctor's appointment or mow their grandparent's lawn, they can do small chores, such as carrying in the groceries or walking the dog.

■ Let everyone have a say—shared decision-making is likely to produce the best results.

■ Schedule regular meetings around holidays or other family get-togethers. Discuss how to divide up responsibilities among the children and other close relatives. Arrange a conference call for close relatives who can't be there in person.

■ Make contingency plans before an emergency occurs. Hasty decisions like inviting a parent to move in with you after a hospital stay can backfire badly (see "Alternatives to Hospitals," page 316).

■ Make a large-print directory of your parents' support system for their use. List the names and phone numbers of family members, close friends, doctors, hospitals, and ambulance and rescue services for emergencies. List separately neighbors who will drop by, supermarkets that deliver, cleaning services, and the like.

■ Be pragmatic about what you can—and cannot—do. Caring for a seriously ill or disabled parent is draining. Women who juggle a job, the needs of a

family, and the care of an elderly parent may develop health problems themselves.

■ Consulting a geriatric counselor can help a family choose the best course of action. Get referrals from a teaching hospital, nursing home, senior citizens' center, or physician.

> **Don't decide what's "best" for Mom and Dad without consulting them. Parents may get angry or depressed when they feel their children are controlling their lives.**

LIVING WITH ELDERLY PARENTS

■ Most elderly people prefer to remain where they've been living as long as possible. When parents need assistance in daily living tasks, suggest that they get a home aide, who can help with housekeeping, meal preparation, and other necessities.

■ If a parent does move in, try to ensure his or her independence. Create a small apartment, if space allows; otherwise, take such steps as declaring Grandma's or Grandpa's room off-limits to other family members.

■ Take disabilities into account. Rearrange commonly used items if a parent's arthritis makes it difficult to reach things stowed away in closets or on shelves. Install handrails or wheelchair ramps, if needed.

■ Enlist outside help. Check the community's public and private resources for adult

---

Caregiver's Burnout

These are warning signs. If any of these statements accurately describes your feelings or behavior, it may be time to seek professional help.

I've gained or lost an appreciable amount of weight in the past few months.

I feel boxed in by my responsibilities and see no way out.

I feel there's no one to turn to, that I am my only resource.

I've been drinking more heavily and/or depending on drugs to help me get through the day.

I frequently lose my temper with my friends, spouse, or children.

My sex life has suffered because of the stress I feel.

I cry for no apparent reason.

CELEBRATING THE FAMILY

*"The reunion gives us a chance
to come together in
a time of joy, not sadness."*
—*James Peter Lowry*

• • • • • • •

A Lowry family gathering is no small affair. Since their first reunion in 1962, this annual event has grown to a 100-person, 3-day get-together. Relatives come from across the country each year to share good times and talk about the family's past, present, and future. As Lowry family matriarch Annie Boyd put it, "Our family gatherings are a celebration of life."

The Lowrys are one of a growing number of families who have discovered the joys of big family reunions.

The modern family. Today's family is more complex than ever, ranging from single parents to extended households. Some families are so scattered across the country that they rarely see each other—perhaps only on major holidays. As a result, the traditions and stories of the past are forgotten. Today, however, family reunions are proving to be a powerful antidote to isolation and family fragmentation.

Reunions bring together different branches and different generations of the family. This is a perfect setting for older members to offer youngsters a glimpse of their family history through storytelling and family photo albums. Knowing where their family came from will help children take pride in their history.

Getting everyone involved in the reunion is the most important thing. This may mean discovering people's skills and then getting them to lend a hand—perhaps by cooking, decorating, or even organizing a pickup soccer game (kids versus adults). Consider having a talent show or family skit night. And always keep in mind that reunions are occasions to have fun, share memories, renew old friendships, and build new ones.

Including family heirlooms and mementos is a surefire way to create enthusiasm. You might think about bringing a diagram of the family tree (to which everyone can add information), a specially designed T-shirt, or a cookbook featuring favorite family recipes. Give out a family directory listing addresses and phone numbers. This will help everyone keep in touch between reunions.

Your own reunion. Planning a family reunion takes time, organization, and hard work, but participants will tell you it's well worth the effort. So, whether your family numbers 50 or 500, here are some basic guidelines for planning a reunion:

Choose someone who has the time and energy to act as the chief organizer.

Hold the event in a community hall, city park, hotel, or family home.

Develop a plan at least a few months ahead of your target weekend. Take even longer if you have a large family.

Keep everyone up-to-date. Send an introductory letter. Later, follow up with chatty newsletters giving further details and inviting suggestions.

If cost is an issue, ask participants to contribute to a reunion fund.◻

Pictured here are three generations of Quanders. This family of 2,000 has been holding reunions since 1926.

day care, free or cut-rate transportation, and other services.

■ Encourage friendships. Surveys show that older people who have relationships with their peers are more satisfied than those whose lives are entirely tied up with family.

■ Let your parents participate in running the household— most families cope best when the elderly members play an active role. Even someone in a wheelchair can make a salad or stitch a hem.

■ Make time for yourself. Researchers say that those who live most amicably with their live-in parents are people who pursue their own interests.

■ Don't shut a parent out of the problems in your life in the belief that you're shielding him or her. It might well be understood as rejection.

> **Buy a lightweight back-pack or hip pack for a parent with arthritis in the hands. It's an easy way to tote things and keep the hands free.**

SPOUSES AS BUSINESS PARTNERS

Being in business with your spouse means that when you get home from the office you never have to ask, "How was your day, dear?" You already know. Here are a few things to remember if you are considering an all-in-the-family business.

■ Share your vision and objectives. A strong business plan helps resolve differences that may surface later.

■ Acknowledge that you can't reach a consensus on all things; be prepared to compromise.

■ Choose or create a separate area of expertise and responsibility for each spouse. Of course, you should both have ideas about the other's area.

■ Partner-spouses must not feel threatened by each other's professional competence.

■ Try not to eat, sleep, and breathe business. In some partnerships the combination of long hours, hard work, and closeness can be unbeatable. But many spouses do better with less pressure. You may decide not to talk about the office in the evening or, say, on Sundays—giving yourselves a rest from stress.

■ Place your personal relationship first. Ask yourselves, If worse came to worst, would you drop the business for the marriage?

■ Don't exclude the rest of the family from discussions about the business.

IN-LAWS

Although the parents of a bride or groom are often told that they're not losing one child, they are gaining another, that's far from the complete story. Each generation of in-laws brings with it unspoken beliefs and assumptions that may get a new marriage off to a poor start. Here are a few pointers to prevent conflict.

■ Parents should respect the fact that their adult children have a right to marry as they choose. If you disapprove of the match—even for sound reasons—you may do better to withhold comment than to argue. Many a marriage has taken place because parental opposition made it seem an assertion of independence.

■ Parents should not assume that the holidays will be the same after a child marries as before. Often there is another set of parents equally eager to have the young people at their house. Discuss this fully before the holidays arrive; be prepared to take turns from one year to the next.

■ Be sure that all grandparents get to spend time with their grandchildren.

■ Parents often fear loss of affection and influence when children marry. As a result, they may be quick to take sides in disputes. When there is a conflict, avoid making one spouse choose between the other spouse and a parent. That's a no-win situation.

■ Mother-in-law jokes, a staple of TV and movies, are not funny in real life. Spouses should avoid such humor.

Never undermine a parent's authority by criticizing them in front of your grandchildren. If something upsets you, discuss it in private.

FORMER IN-LAWS

Sometimes, the unfortunate consequence of a divorce or the death of a spouse is that one set of grandparents loses contact with their grandchildren. This can be an extremely touchy situation. The custodial parent may be glad of the break from the past, and the ex- or deceased spouse's parents may be deeply resentful of the loss. But what should be considered first and foremost are the interests of the children. Children should have the benefit of knowing both sides of their family. This is a situation that calls for diplomacy on both sides, but it's well worth the effort.

■ As the custodial parent, you should think about reaching out to the grandparents and other relatives of your former spouse. Call or write to discuss possible visits.

■ As "displaced grandparents," your best course is to concentrate on your grandchildren. Promise yourself that you will not stir up old debates or offer unsolicited advice. You can express your concern for your grandchildren's well-being with your supportive presence and unconditional love.

■ If the adults—parents and former in-laws—have a major disagreement, hold a family conference (excluding very young grandchildren). Use the time to explore each other's positions and examine the underlying assumptions. If the discussion gets too warm, enlist the good offices of some relative or friend to help bridge the gap.

■ Try to work out a compromise on conflicting issues.

■ Consider asserting yourself only when you suspect there's a threat of abuse or neglect. Otherwise, let the parent have the final say.

MAKING A WILL

Inheritances bring out strong emotions in families. They raise several uncomfortable issues: death, money, and how survivors are perceived by the important people in their lives. If a parent's will specifies that one son receives less than another, does this mean the parent loved one child less? Perhaps it expresses greater faith in the other son's abilities or simply indicates differences in the children's needs. Whatever the case, such issues should be addressed while the parent is still alive.

■ Many people find making a will upsetting; often children are disturbed by the mere suggestion that a parent will die. But making a will is a responsibility that should not be put off. In fact, it is best attended to while parents are young and enjoying good health. Wills should then be amended as the family grows and situations change.

■ A case can be made for one or many family conferences on the subject of inheritance. You may discover that small possessions have great symbolic value. It's not just how real estate will be divided but who will inherit the family Bible and assorted clocks, lamps, silver, and photo albums. Discussion can defuse jealousy and resentment.

A fresh coat of paint creates *more attractive surroundings, as well as giving do-it-yourselfers a sense of accomplishment. If possible, leave windows open for ventilation while painting, then close off the room until the paint odor is gone.*

CHAPTER 6

AROUND THE HOUSE

On a basic level, a house is a shelter—something our bodies require for protection against the elements. For that it need only be sturdy and warm. For most of us, however, our house is much more; it is our *home*. Whether you live in a ranch house, mobile home, apartment, mansion, condominium, or other structure, you probably think of your house as special—a retreat where you can relax with the people you love.

Most of us put a great deal of thought into what fills our homes; our furnishings and decorations reflect our taste, personalities, and interests. However, we are often unaware that many of our house's components actually affect our health, both mental and physical. For example, color scheme and lighting can influence mood, and improper air and water quality can cause illness.

Knowing how to recognize and address such issues will help you to make your home safe and inviting for everyone who lives and visits there.

Children can help with household tasks, but be sure to stress safety when tools are involved.

COLOR AND LIGHT IN YOUR HOME

Most people give little thought to health when decorating their home, but such factors as wall color and lighting can have an impact on the way you act and feel.

COLOR IT HEALTHY

Some colors make us smile; others make us cringe. Although favorite colors are highly subjective, there are some choices that can actually improve the way you feel and perform routine tasks.

■ Light colors tend to open up a room, creating a feeling of space and airiness, whereas dark colors make a room seem smaller. Paint small rooms with light colors or whites, and make a large room cozier by painting it a darker shade.

■ In rooms that rely mostly on artificial light, choose pale wall colors, which spread the light evenly around the room.

■ Bright wall colors make some people restless and nervous. If you like bright colors, consider painting the walls a neutral color and using pillows, furniture, or throw rugs to add splashes of color.

■ Grays and browns are believed to inspire efficiency, so use them in a home office or other work area.

■ Use cool, relaxing colors, such as blues and greens, in rooms where you rest after a busy day. These colors have been used in hospitals to establish a sense of calm and enhance recuperation.

■ Blue may discourage flies and other insects, making it a good choice for kitchens and porches.

■ Babies are stimulated by bright colors, so primary colors, instead of pastels, are a good choice for a nursery.

SUNLIGHT

Light plays an important role in regulating mood, hormone production, and other body functions. The average person spends more than three-quarters of daylight hours indoors, so it's important to take full advantage of natural daylight.

■ Rooms with southern exposure are perfect for family gathering areas and children's playrooms. With this type of exposure, light comes directly from the sun, creating a warm, cheerful atmosphere. In the summer, use window shades and ventilation to keep these rooms from getting too hot.

■ A room with southern exposure is not a good choice for a home office or reading room, because glare can make concentration difficult and computer work uncomfortable. If possible, choose a room with northern exposure for its more indirect light.

■ Use light-colored shades or curtains on windows to reflect the sun and keep rooms cool in warm weather. Make sure that curtains can be opened fully to let in the maximum amount of light.

LET THERE BE LIGHT

A well-lit room is bright enough to navigate easily and safely, but not so bright that it is uncomfortable.

■ To control the amount of light, install rheostats, which allow you to brighten or dim lights, on the light switches. They usually require little or no rewiring.

■ In the kitchen, make sure adequate light shines on counters and other food-preparation areas. Position downlights over the sink and other kitchen work areas to help prevent accidents. A range-hood light should be able to accommodate two 75-watt bulbs; alternatively, mount reflector downlights in the ceiling over the stove.

LIGHT SAFETY

Faulty light fixtures are a common source of household fires and electric shocks, and certain lights cause physical symptoms in some people. Here are ways to avoid such problems.

■ Check older light fixtures for loose sockets and frayed cords. Rewire any that are damaged.

■ Place floor and table lamps out of the reach of toddlers, young children, and pets.

■ Bathroom lights should not

be exposed to water. Choose recessed ceiling lights with watertight coverings.

■ Incandescent and halogen lightbulbs give off a tremendous amount of heat. Lampshades, especially the metal ones on desk lamps, should have ventilating holes that allow heat to escape. Most desk lamps call for 60- or 75-watt bulbs; don't try to increase lighting by resorting to higher-watt bulbs. If you need more light, use extra lamps.

■ Try to limit fluorescent lighting, which gives off rays that vibrate, causing headaches and eyestrain in some people. If you do use them, make sure they are properly screened and located at least four feet away from a work area.

. . . .

Some people, particularly those with blue eyes, are sensitive to certain colors of fluorescent lights, such as cool-white. If your eyes are being affected by these lights, try switching to a warm white, daylight fixture.

. . . .

PICKING THE RIGHT LIGHTS

■ Before buying light fixtures, think about the particular room—the way it's used and any special lighting needs.

■ Select lightbulbs according to the time of day a room is used most. Incandescent bulbs emit light high in reds and oranges, which is similar to that of afternoon sunlight— good for rooms in which you spend the late-afternoon and evening hours.

■ New quartz-type incandescent bulbs are smaller and last longer than conventional lightbulbs. They are also safer because they don't produce as much heat. However, you will need to buy special fixtures designed for compact incandescent bulbs.

■ A halogen light can illuminate an entire room if it is directed toward a white ceiling.

■ Full-spectrum lightbulbs have a wider range of wavelengths than other bulbs, so they more closely mimic natural light. Some people find that they improve mood and alertness when placed in an area where much time is spent, such as an office or kitchen.

CLEAN BULBS

Grime from kitchen vapors, smoking, and dust reduces effective output of light. Fluorescent tubes are even more affected because of their larger surface area.

■ Dust bulbs frequently. If you need to wash them, first remove them from fixtures; dry thoroughly before replacing.

■ Never put a hot bulb in water.

■ Make sure fixtures holding the bulbs are clean, especially their reflective surfaces.

Placing Your Light Fixtures

Choosing the right type of lighting isn't all you need to think about. Where you put the fixtures can be just as important.

Space recessed fixtures 6 to 8 feet apart for general lighting, and use flood bulbs. For task lighting, install them 15 to 18 inches apart.

Hang a pendant light or chandelier with the bottom about 30 inches above the table. However, if the fixture has a bare bulb and open bottom, make it low enough to avoid harsh light in diners' eyes.

At a chair or bed, position a hanging light so that its lower edge is about 4 feet from the floor. Site a fixture so that its lower edge is about 15 inches above a desktop.

Short floor lamps—40 to 42 inches high—should line up with your shoulder when you're seated. Taller lamps should be set about 15 inches to the side and 20 inches behind the center of the book you're reading.

The bottom of a table lampshade should be at eye level, about 38 to 42 inches above the floor, when you're seated. For tasks, the ideal light source is 10 to 12 inches below the user's eye level.

CLEANING HOUSE

A clean, fresh home contributes to your family's health and happiness, but many of our most common household products are highly toxic. Here are ways to make cleaning safer—and easier, as well.

GETTING ORGANIZED

Much of the drudgery of housecleaning can be eliminated by getting rid of clutter and approaching the task in an orderly fashion.

■ Periodically go through rooms and closets, gathering what you don't use or don't want. Donate items to a local charity (many organizations will come to your house to pick items up), or offer them to friends.

■ Resist the temptation to stack paper items in the attic, basement, or garage, where they can attract pests and create a fire hazard. A community hospital, senior-citizen center, or nursery school may welcome magazines and other items that can be used for craft projects.

■ Reserve a shelf or closet for cleaning products. Pick one that can be locked if there are children or pets in the household—even nontoxic cleansers can be harmful if ingested.

■ To save steps and to keep from lugging cleansers and other supplies up and down stairs, keep frequently used items—including a broom, vacuum cleaner, and mop—on each floor.

■ To prevent dirt from building up in places that are used often, such as the bathroom sink, keep a sponge nearby so that family members can wipe off the area after each use.

RECYCLING

Recycling is widespread throughout the nation, and it should be a natural part of your housecleaning and organizational efforts.

■ One of the most important contributions you can make is to reduce the amount of waste you produce. To reduce excess packaging and toxic waste, substitute nontoxic solutions (made from ingredients you may already have in your kitchen cabinet) for prepackaged household cleansers (see box, page 193).

■ Other waste-reducing techniques include buying products in containers that can be recycled, buying refillable and reusable products, and bringing your own canvas bag to the grocery store in place of plastic bags.

■ After you've done what you can to prevent unnecessary waste, focus on recycling methods. In most cases, recyclables are broken down into two categories: One receptacle holds plastic bottles, glass bottles, glass jars, metal cans, and aluminum-foil wrap and trays. The second stores newspapers, magazines, catalogues, telephone books, and flattened cardboard boxes. (In some areas these groupings are broken down further.)

■ Though the disposal of hazardous-waste products is not regulated, the dangers are many. Be sure to dispose of such products as aerosol cans, pesticide containers, smoke detectors, and swimming-pool chemicals properly. For more information, see "Hazardous Products," page 240.

■ Collect all recyclable items in receptacles at home and then transfer them to official recycling bins as often as possible. Food waste should be disposed of separately.

Recycling laws vary with building size and location, so if you're in doubt about what can and cannot be recycled, contact your municipal recycling center.

BASICS FOR A CLEAN AND HEALTHY HOUSE

In today's world it is almost impossible to create an entirely nontoxic environment; however, you can take steps to minimize the number of toxic products you have in your home.

■ Start by getting rid of aerosol sprays. Many contain

methylene chloride, a suspected carcinogen, which is dispersed into the air in large quantities when sprayed.

■ Limit the number of cleansers you have in the house. You don't need a different product for everything you clean.

■ The following ingredients form the basis of many natural, effective cleansers: white vinegar, baking soda, borax, salt, and lemon juice. If you want to use nontoxic alternatives to commercial products, keep these items on hand (see box, page 193).

■ If you choose to use commercial products, handle them carefully and follow any instructions on the labels.

■ Never mix chlorine bleach with ammonia—this releases deadly chlorine gas. Also be cautious when using common household cleansers simultaneously. Many cleansers contain chlorine bleach, while glass and floor cleaners may contain ammonia. To avoid inadvertently mixing potentially dangerous chemicals, use separate sponges, scrub pails, and mops.

FOR A CLEAN WASH

■ Choose oxygen bleaches, white vinegar, baking soda, or borax to whiten and brighten laundry. Borax also disinfects and deodorizes laundry and inhibits mold growth. Avoid chlorine bleaches—the fumes can irritate the eyes, nose, and throat, and splashes can cause skin irritation. If you do use chlorine bleach, wear rubber gloves and make sure the area is well ventilated.

■ If you should spill chlorine

Safe Stain Removers

Commercial spot and stain removers often contain sodium hypochlorite, perchloroethylene, or trichloroethane—all of which can cause liver and kidney damage. Dry cleaning fluid (tetrachlorethylene) is a suspected carcinogen. Try these nontoxic alternatives to remove tough stains.

BLOOD

1/4 cup borax
2 cups cold water

Rinse with cold water before blood dries, then scrub with warm water and soap. If stain remains, dip in solution of borax and cold water.

CHOCOLATE AND COFFEE

1 tsp. white vinegar
1 quart cold water

Mix white vinegar with cold water, sponge on stain, and wash as usual. Or try borax solution described for blood stain.

INK

Cream of tartar
Lemon juice

Make paste of cream of tartar and lemon juice, apply to stain, and leave on for one hour. For delicate fabrics, sponge paste off immediately; then repeat procedure until stain is removed.

GREASE

Baking soda or cornstarch
Water

Make paste of water and baking soda or cornstarch, cover spot with it, let dry, and brush off. For rough-textured fabric, use cornmeal instead. For polyester, try talcum powder; for double-knit fabrics, club soda. Or rub spot with wet cloth dipped in borax.

bleach on your skin, rinse the area thoroughly with plain water until it no longer feels slippery.

■ For very dirty laundry, soak the articles in a solution of one tablespoon borax in one gallon water for an hour, then wash as usual.

■ For an alternative to synthetic laundry detergents, try soap flakes. After collecting leftover scraps of soap in a jar, add water and liquefy in a blender. Soap flakes are nontoxic and biodegradable. You may want to add some washing soda (sodium carbonate), available at the grocery store, for extra whitening.

To give your ironed clothes a crisp look without using aerosol starches, make your own starch spritzer. Mix one to two tablespoons cornstarch in one pint water. Put the solution in a spray bottle and shake before using.

LIVING SPACES

■ Instead of using rug shampoos, sprinkle dry cornstarch or baking soda on the carpet before vacuuming. These powders help remove deep dirt, and baking soda also removes odors.

■ Instead of buying aerosol furniture polishes, which are laden with chemicals, choose those made from beeswax, lemon oil, or vegetable oils. Or make your own (see box on facing page).

■ To clean and restore leather furniture, apply a mixture of equal parts vinegar and

linseed oil with a soft cloth. Saddle soap also works well.

■ To clean windows, mirrors, and other glass surfaces, mix white vinegar in water. Wash the surface using a soft cloth, then wipe it dry with crumpled newspaper for a sparkling shine and no streaking.

■ Clean drapes and curtains, which harbor dust and other bacteria, on a regular basis. It's best to avoid dry cleaning, since the solvents used can release harmful fumes. If possible, wash curtains in cold water instead. If you do dry clean them, air them out, preferably outdoors, for at least six hours.

■ If a family member has asthma or another respiratory disorder, consider installing a central vacuum system to cut down on dust in the air after vacuuming.

Instead of a dry cloth, try a silicone-treated dust cloth. Dust and dirt stick better to this cloth, which means that you inhale less dust.

BATHROOM AND KITCHEN

Bathroom and kitchen products should disinfect and deodorize as well as clean. Here are some nontoxic alternatives and other methods for cleaning these rooms safely and thoroughly.

■ Borax disinfects as it cleans. Add 1/2 cup to a gallon of warm water for a good all-around kitchen and bathroom cleanser.

■ To prevent clogged drains, use a strainer to trap hair and food particles. Never pour grease down the drain; instead, pour it into a used can or other container, let it cool, and discard it with your kitchen garbage.

■ To unclog a grease- or hair-filled drain, skip the harsh commercial products. They usually contain lye, which can cause serious burns to eyes and skin. Use a plunger instead, or make your own nontoxic solution (see box on facing page).

■ Use a baking soda rinse as an alternative to ammonia to make metal appliances and tile shine.

■ If you do use ammonia, dilute it first. In a well-ventilated room or outdoors, mix 1/2 cup household ammonia (never use commercial-grade ammonia—it is much too strong), 1/2 cup washing soda, and a gallon of warm water. Be sure to wear rubber gloves—even diluted ammonia irritates skin.

■ Use equal parts baking soda and water to make an effective air deodorizer. Fill a spray bottle with the mixture, and spray in a fine mist to dissipate offensive odors.

■ To remove refrigerator odors, an open box of baking soda will do the trick. Or try soaking a cotton ball in vanilla extract and putting it on a saucer in your refrigerator. Replace the cotton ball every couple of days.

■ Empty trash cans as frequently as possible. To keep them germ-free and clean-smelling, sprinkle some borax or baking soda in the bottom of each can.

■ Avoid using commercial oven cleaners—even those that claim to be safe contain aerosol propellants and chemicals that can burn eyes and skin and damage lungs. Place a cookie sheet or aluminum foil on the bottom of the oven to catch spills. If a spill does occur, sprinkle it with a mixture of equal parts salt and baking soda while the oven is still warm. Then remove with steel wool or an abrasive sponge.

■ To loosen a baked-on oven spill, pour 1/4 cup household ammonia into a shallow bowl (do not use aluminum), and place it in the closed oven overnight. By morning, the stain should come off easily with a damp cloth. Take care, however, not to inhale the ammonia fumes.

Waterproof gloves are always a good idea when cleaning, especially if you have sensitive skin. If rubber gloves cause a rash or irritation, try vinyl gloves, which tend to be less irritating.

Environmentally Sound Cleansers

Here are some easy-to-make, easy-to-use recipes using nontoxic and environmentally friendly ingredients from your kitchen pantry. Most of these cleansers work best when freshly mixed.

FURNITURE POLISH

1 tbsp. lemon juice or white vinegar
1/2 cup olive or vegetable oil

Mix lemon juice or white vinegar with olive or vegetable oil. Apply and polish with a clean, soft cloth.

TOILET BOWL CLEANER

Baking soda
Borax
White vinegar

To clean toilet bowl, sprinkle equal parts baking soda and borax around bowl, add white vinegar, and clean with toilet brush. For stubborn stains, leave mixture in overnight.

DRAIN CLEARER

Vinegar
Salt
Baking soda

To clear a drain clogged with grease or hair, try a mixture of equal parts vinegar, salt, and baking soda. Let stand for 15 minutes, then pour boiling water down drain.

MILDEW REMOVER

1/2 cup vinegar
1/2 cup borax
2 cups water

To remove mildew from bathtub, tile, or shower curtain, wipe affected areas with mixture of vinegar, borax, and water. Or dip half a fresh lemon in borax powder and rub it over mildewed areas.

SAFE PEST CONTROL

No one wants to share their home with flies, bugs, mice, and other pests. But before resorting to commercial pesticides to get rid of these pesky invaders, try nontoxic alternatives—many work just as well, and they're a lot safer than poisons.

PREVENTION, THE BEST CURE

Some of us unwittingly put out a welcome mat for household pests. Take the steps below to make your home less attractive and accessible to them.

■ Block off common points of entry. Keep window and door screens in good repair. Plug cracks and crevices with caulk or weather stripping.

■ Even tiny crumbs and sugar grains attract insects and rodents. Store food in insect- and rodent-proof containers.

■ Clean up spills promptly with soap or another cleanser.

■ Wipe off kitchen counters and other food-preparation areas with vinegar water.

■ Make sure your garbage can has a tight-fitting lid. Rinse out cans and jars before putting them in a recycling bin.

■ Many household pests prefer paper to organic food. Put newspapers and other wastepaper in a plastic bin with a tight lid while awaiting a recycling pickup.

■ Like humans, insects and rodents need a steady supply of water. Repair plumbing leaks and dripping faucets. Have your basement waterproofed.

■ Pour dish detergent into puddles around your house to kill mosquito eggs and larvae. (You can use a similar tactic to kill household pests; simply set out a shallow pan of soapy water, which is lethal to insects that use it to drink or lay eggs.) Change pet water daily, and place it and pet food dishes in a shallow pan of water, forming a deadly moat against ants and other crawling insects.

■ Be careful not to bring in pests with groceries. Before buying, inspect flour bags for holes, a possible sign of weevils. Be wary of bulk grains, legumes, and other foods—they may be less expensive than packaged foods, but they are also more likely to harbor insect eggs and larvae. Remember that paper bags are favorite hiding places for cockroaches.

■ Vacuum frequently to get rid of larvae and eggs deposited in rugs and upholstered furniture. Add pyrethrum or salt to the vacuum cleaner bag to kill those trapped in the bag.

■ Store firewood off the ground. Don't keep it in the basement or any other indoor place; instead, bring in only what you will burn that day. Otherwise, your home may end up with carpenter ants, spiders, and other insects that nest in wood.

Temperature extremes kill most insects. Pumping liquid nitrogen into the infested area to lower the temperature to -29°C (-20°F) kills termites, ants, and many other insects. Alternatively, covering your house with a plastic tent and blowing in hot air to heat it to 65.5°C (150°F) will kill virtually every bug.

NONTOXIC PEST KILLERS

There are a number of natural pest killers that you can use instead of poisonous pesticides. You may already have many of them in your kitchen cabinets or herb garden. If they don't do the job, experiment with biological controls, such as nematodes (tiny parasites that kill termites, ants, and other insects). Pyrethrum, a natural pesticide made from chrysanthemums and related flowers, kills many insects and repels others. Diatomaceous earth, a type of mineral dust available in nurseries, kills insects by shredding their outer coating. The following sections contain

KNOW YOUR PEST

The more you know about household pests, the easier it is to control them.

Pest	Warning signs	Finding the source
Ants	Swarms of ants on bits of food	Look for nests under kitchen or bathroom sink or along floorboards; if ants are coming from outdoors, find entry holes by putting food near some ants and following their trail to it
Carpenter ants	Large dead ants on sills or in light fixtures; piles of fine sawdust; tapping damaged wood produces hollow sound	Find where the ants are attacking your home, then follow them to their main nest, usually in a dead tree or woodpile; also track down their source of water
Cockroaches	Scurry of roaches when you turn on light at night; roach feces and egg sacks in kitchen and bathrooms	Roaches usually nest in walls; place sticky tape near likely entry points around plumbing, air vents, cracks, and crevices
Fleas	Pets scratching themselves; suspect fleas if you develop unexplained itchy, red welts	Inspect pets for tiny, jumping insects or small, black larvae and pupae; rub masking tape over rugs and pet beds to see if you pick up fleas or their pupae
Flies	Black specks on walls, dead flies on sills and in light fixtures	Look for holes in screens and other openings; cluster flies nest in walls, especially around windows
Mice and other rodents	Rodent droppings in cabinets or other places where food is stored	Look for entry holes around plumbing, floorboards, windowsills, and foundation cracks
Mosquitoes	High whiny buzzing, especially at night; itchy, red welts	Look for puddles of water where mosquitoes can breed, especially around plants or in basement; also look for holes in screens and other entry points
Moths	Small holes in woolens; adult moths fluttering around a lightbulb at night	Look for silken mat or tube of moth eggs attached to woolens in closets and other dark places
Termites	Soft, crumbly wood riddled with tunnels; shed termite wings; small fecal pellets near damaged wood	Call in a professional who uses trained beagles to sniff out termite nests
Wasps	Dead bodies on sills	Look for nests near windows or in walls
Weevils	Insects (both dead and alive) in flour, cereals, and other grain products	Check flour bags for small holes; look for spilled flour and cereal on pantry or kitchen shelves

remedies you can try for specific pests.

FLEAS

■ Groom your pet regularly with a fine-tooth metal comb to remove fleas, eggs, larvae, and pupae. Do this outdoors, and resist killing the fleas with your fingernails—some carry diseases and parasites. Instead, dip the comb in a glass of water that contains rubbing alcohol.

■ Groom your animal over a sheet, then gather up the sheet and wash it immediately in hot, soapy water to kill any larvae and pupae.

■ Bathing your pet will get rid of many fleas by drowning them. Use a mild soap or shampoo, or a flea shampoo containing pyrethrum or citrus oil. Although they also must be used with caution, these are much less toxic than flea dips and pesticide shampoos.

■ To make your own flea-killing potion, cut up two lemons and pour two cups of boiling water over them. Let this stand overnight, then sponge it on your pet. It should kill the fleas instantly. Or sponge on a cooled solution of the skins of three or four oranges and three cups boiling water that have been processed in the blender.

■ To get rid of fleas in the house, try placing a heating pad, set on low, atop a low cushion on the floor. Cover the pad with a piece of flannel sprinkled with diatomaceous earth or boric acid. The fleas will jump on the warm flannel and soon die.

COCKROACHES

■ Boric acid is one pesticide for which roaches have not yet developed resistance. To get roaches to eat it, mix a cup of borax (a form of boric acid sold as a laundry product) with 1/2 cup flour, 1/4 cup powdered sugar, and 1/2 cup cornmeal, and spread the mixture in the back of your cupboard, under your sink, and in other places where roaches look for food and water. Don't put it where children or pets might find it, however, since it is toxic when ingested.

■ If high humidity is not a problem, use a bulb duster or turkey baster to blow boric acid into cracks and crevices, between walls, under sinks, and along baseboards. Spread it around under refrigerators, stoves, and other appliances. (Wear a dust mask while doing this to keep from inhaling the pesticide.) Roaches that have walked through the boric acid will later ingest it during grooming. For further deterrence, add boric acid to water and mop the floor with it, or dip a sponge in it to wipe down walls and counters.

■ Bay leaves, cucumbers, and garlic are said to repel cockroaches. Garlic cloves, peeled and split to release their odor, may also do the job in drawers, under cabinets, and along baseboards. Replace cloves when they lose their fragrance—about once every two weeks.

ANTS

■ If you have only a few ants and you're sure they're not the type that can destroy houses, try to tolerate them. They may even help you, since ants will eat flea and fly larvae and attack termites.

■ If the ants are out of control, such household products as window cleaners, furniture polish, and heavy-duty spray cleaners will destroy them. But the cheapest, easiest, most effective method is putting a teaspoon of liquid dish detergent into a pint spray bottle of water and zapping the ants with it. A solution of blended citrus peels and water (or citrus rind oil, which you can buy from herbal-supply and health food stores) also kills ants.

■ Track down the ants' point of entry and block it with something the ants abhor. Boric acid, powdered charcoal, turmeric, black or cayenne pepper, citrus oil, lemon juice, and a line of chalk make excellent ant barriers. Squirting undiluted dish detergent into their point of entry also keeps them out.

■ Crushed mint leaves, oil of clove, and camphor are natural insect repellents. Leave handfuls of crushed mint where you see ants. Or pour oil of clove or camphor oil onto a piece of cloth and rub the doorsill with it.

MOSQUITOES

■ Rub a little pennyroyal or citronella oil on the headboard of your bed to keep mosquitoes from buzzing around your ears as you sleep.

■ To keep mosquitoes from biting you, dilute pennyroyal or citronella oil with olive oil and rub it into your skin. Or apply vinegar to your skin with a cotton ball.

■ Set your own mosquito trap by putting water in a bucket or other container and adding a good dose of soap. The mosquitoes are attracted to the water, but the oily soap drowns the female mosquito; if she does manage to lay her eggs, the soap will destroy them.

■ Be sure to get rid of all other reservoirs of stagnant water, including plant saucers. A single pint of water can nurture 500 mosquitoes.

MICE AND OTHER RODENTS

■ Trapping is the best way to kill rodents. Set traps where you find their droppings. If you suspect that there are a lot of rodents, set traps every couple of feet. Traps should be placed with the baited end closest to the wall.

■ When setting traps, wear heavy rubber gloves so as not to leave a human smell behind. Before using the gloves again, scrub them with soapy water; then, after dipping them in boiling water, rub them with vegetable oil.

■ Sometimes mice and rats are suspicious of traps, especially if they've had a previous near-catch. To get the mice used to eating food on a trap, bait it without setting the spring for a few days.

■ Bait materials include cheese, walnuts, peanut butter, bread, raw bacon, gum drops, and dried fruit. Or instead of food, try a piece of fluffy cotton, string, or twine. Rats and mice collect such items to use for nesting material. Whatever you use, anchor it firmly to the trap; otherwise, mice quickly learn to steal bait without springing the trap.

■ Glue traps are an alternative to the old-fashioned spring traps. If you use these, place a little bait in the middle to make them more attractive. Check the trap several times a day. If you find a live rodent in a trap, pick it up with tongs or two sticks and drop it in a bucket of soapy water to kill it quickly.

■ Never touch a dead rat or mouse. Use gloves, along with tongs or two long sticks, when handling the animals. Place them in sealed plastic bags to trap the parasites, and discard the bags.

■ If possible, enlist the help of natural predators, such as cats and dogs. Often the mere presence of a cat is sufficient to convince some rodents, especially chipmunks, not to stay around.

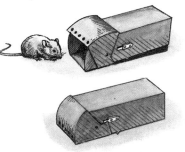

■ If you want to get rid of rodents but do not want to kill them, look into "live traps," which can be ordered from the United States by catalog. Some models allow more than one animal to enter; you can trap the entire family and take them elsewhere to live. Pick a barn or some other unoccupied building—house mice have evolved to live indoors and most cannot survive outside.

■ You can make your own live trap with a large stainless steel bowl. To do this, smear the sides of the bowl with oil or butter and place the bait in the bottom. Fashion a couple of outside ramps leading to the bowl rim. Once the mouse is in the bowl, it cannot climb up the slippery sides, and you can easily release it later. (This trap also works for gerbils that have escaped from their cage.)

CHILDPROOFING YOUR HOME

Making your home safe for children means it will be a happier place for both adults and youngsters. But it's not a one-time task—plan to make necessary changes with each stage of a growing child's life.

GET A CHILD'S-EYE VIEW

As you begin to childproof your home, inspect each room from your youngster's viewpoint. Look beyond the obvious things—get down on your hands and knees, and imagine how a toddler might approach each object. Here are specific things to look for and what to do about them.

■ Are there sharp corners? If so, blunt them with padding and tape.

■ Are there objects a child can pick apart and choke on? If so, put them well out of reach.

■ Can the child be injured by falling lamps, books, and other objects? Put away or firmly secure anything that a toddler can pull over or knock off a shelf or table. Also, place all breakable knickknacks in a closed display cabinet, or replace them with unbreakable objects.

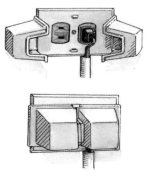

■ If there are open electrical outlets that a child can reach, install safety plugs.

■ To prevent burns, install covers on radiators, floor registers, and other heat sources.

■ Arrange furniture so that a child cannot use various pieces as stepping stones to reach a dangerous height. For example, children often use a stool or an ottoman to reach an armchair, and then the chair to reach a high shelf.

■ If possible, put the television set, stereo, and other electronic equipment in a cabinet that you can lock, protecting both the child and the equipment.

■ Secure drapery and blind cords out of children's reach. Young children can become entangled in these cords.

■ Lock doors to rooms or closets where you don't want children to go unattended, but make sure that bathrooms can be unlocked from the outside. If this isn't possible, remove the lock or cover the bolt with duct tape to prevent a child from getting locked inside.

■ Install guards on any windows that can be opened, especially those on upper floors. Even so, never place beds and other furniture in front of windows.

■ A purse or briefcase is often filled with common objects—such as cosmetics, paper clips, and small change—that are potentially harmful to youngsters. Don't leave either where a child can get into it.

KITCHEN DANGERS

The typical kitchen presents a fascinating place to children; there they can learn, explore, and observe adults in action. However, it's also filled with such potentially dangerous objects as knives, breakables, and toxic substances.

■ Install safety latches on all kitchen cabinets except one that is for children only. Use it to store child-size pots, pans, and other objects they can play with.

■ Unplug toasters, mixers, and other appliances. Wrap their cords around them when they are not in use.

■ Encourage young children to help with cooking and other tasks, but emphasize possible hazards. Buy special covers to prevent a child from turning on stove burners. Make sure they understand that stoves can burn, knives can cut fingers, and so forth.

■ Don't leave bowls of pet food and water on the kitchen floor; otherwise, a young child is likely to help himself or herself.

> **Iron pills are one of the most common causes of childhood poisoning. Make sure all vitamin pills are in bottles with childproof caps and stored with other medications, not left out on a kitchen counter or table.**

BATHROOM SAFETY

■ Young children should never be left unattended in the bathroom. This is especially true of the bathtub—a child can drown within minutes in only a few inches of water.

■ When putting away hazardous substances, don't overlook cosmetics and toiletries, such as shampoo, toothpaste, and nail polish remover. These substances often don't have child-resistant packaging, and they can be toxic when ingested.

■ Use plastic cups instead of glasses and breakable bottles in the bathroom.

■ Keep a separate, covered garbage can to dispose of razor blades and other dangerous waste.

■ Set your hot water thermostat at 49°C (120°F) instead of the standard 60°C (140°F). Even so, always test bath temperature before allowing a child to get in. Conceal the bathtub faucet with a cushioned cover and have your child face away from the faucet knobs when in the tub to keep him or her from turning on the water.

■ Keep the toilet lid down, and install Velcro strips to keep a toddler from opening it and drinking or playing with the toilet water. Young children have also drowned after tumbling into a toilet.

STAIRWAYS

Learning to climb stairs is an important developmental milestone, but you need to protect babies, toddlers, and even older children by following these safety measures.

■ If you have a crawling baby or a toddler, install a safety gate at both the top and the bottom of stairs and at each landing. Check gates to see that they are securely latched at all times, except when you are supervising stair climbing with a toddler.

■ Once children are old enough to navigate the stairs on their own, make sure that all stairs have handrails that they can reach. The rails must be sturdy, not loose. If their slats are more than four inches apart, secure netting along the rails to prevent the children from falling or getting their heads stuck between the slats.

■ Never place scatter rugs near the top or bottom of staircases.

■ Secure stair carpeting with carpet nails, and be sure to check it periodically for loose edges that might trip a child (or adult).

■ Never leave anything on stairs or landings.

■ Never leave anything on floors near stairs. Similarly, keep all floors clear of clutter.

BEDTIME

■ Place a "Child Alert" decal on the window of a nursery or child's bedroom for the fire department to see in the event of a fire.

■ Before accepting a hand-me-down crib, check it carefully to make sure that it is safe. The mattress should fit snugly, there should be no sharp hardware or edges, and the slats should be no more than 2 3/8 inches apart. The rails should be at least 26 inches above the mattress, and the side that drops should have a secure lock.

■ Make sure the crib mattress is firm, and don't cover it with a feather bed or any other soft cushions.

■ Keep plastic bags and sheets out of the crib—they are a smothering hazard.

■ Never lay a baby down for a nap on a regular bed. When placed in the middle of a bed, even a tiny baby can roll off or get caught between the mattress and the frame or wall. And putting pillows around a baby can lead to suffocation. If a crib is not available, it is far safer to lay the baby on a firm pad on the floor than on a bed.

To determine if a mattress is safe for an infant, place a 10-pound weight (a large bag of flour or sugar will do) on it. If it makes a deep depression, the mattress is probably soft enough to restrict a child's movement and increase the chance of suffocation.

PREPARING YOUR HOME FOR THE ELDERLY

When older relatives come to visit or live with you, you may have to make some adjustments to your home. Fortunately, a few relatively simple changes can make any residence safer for the elderly.

BASIC SAFETY

■ Go through each room looking for possible hazards, much as you would in childproofing. Reduce clutter and pay particular attention to removing anything that might cause a fall, such as objects that an older person might trip over.

■ Have light switches near the entrance to each room and near the bed so that older people do not have to navigate dark rooms.

■ Install a telephone that can be reached from the bed. Choose a phone that has a programmable memory for police, doctor, ambulance, and other important numbers.

■ Put in night-lights and make main switches accessible in case the older person must go to the bathroom or kitchen during the night.

■ Set the thermostat between 18.3°C (65°F) and 20°C (68°F). Older people often have reduced circulation, and those who do not move around a lot are especially susceptible to cold, even though they may not feel chilly. Have plenty of throw blankets around the sitting areas so that getting warm is easy and convenient.

■ Make sure the bed has enough blankets. Flannel sheets and a down comforter are excellent choices because they are warm but lightweight.

■ Dabs of fluorescent paint around keyholes, outdoor steps, house numbers, and driveways make them more visible at night and can be especially helpful to an older person with dimming vision.

STEP BY STEP

Stairs and steps are a common trouble spot for older people, so pay special attention to making them safe.

■ Attach bright or contrasting nonskid treads or mats to stairs, especially on the edge of each riser. This not only makes steps less slippery but also helps older people see where each step begins. In addition, make sure stairs, hallways, and other pathways are well lit to compensate for diminished eyesight.

■ Avoid putting thick-pile or heavily patterned carpets on stairs. They decrease the amount of surface area on each riser and make it difficult to see the edge of each step. If you do have stair carpeting, make sure there are no holes, snags, or other irregularities.

■ Install rounded handrails wherever there are three or more steps, preferably on both sides of the stairs, making it easier to maintain one's balance between them. Handrails should extend beyond the top and bottom stairs.

■ Whenever possible, install ramps in place of steps. However, even ramps can be treacherous to walk on if they are wobbly or slippery. Make sure the ramps have a sufficiently gradual incline, and attach nonskid treads to them. Ramps, like stairs, should have sturdy handrails.

■ If a person finds it difficult to negotiate broad outdoor steps, provide a portable half step with its own railing.

■ Remove raised thresholds to rooms to prevent tripping.

There have been many cases of visitors tumbling down basement stairs after mistakenly opening the door in the dark. Lock the basement door or place a large, illuminated sign on it. Also consider installing a warning alarm that will sound if the basement door is opened.

IN THE KITCHEN

■ Keep frequently used utensils, foods, and plates in a low, easy-to-reach cabinet, shelf, or drawer. Purchase long-handled tongs, similar to those used in grocery stores, for reaching lightweight items on higher shelves. A similar device is useful for picking up fallen objects from the floor.

■ Look for tools to make cooking tasks easier. For example, a French-fry basket can be used for cooking pasta, vegetables, and other foods that require draining. When the food is cooked, simply lift the basket—and the food—out of the water.

■ Keep a long-handled mop nearby for quick cleanup of spills. A wet floor makes falls more likely.

■ Make sure the "off" positions on the stove and oven are clearly marked and the "on" light works properly so that an older person can quickly see if he or she has left the heat on.

IN THE BATHROOM

■ Put nonskid mats at the edge of the tub or shower as well as inside. As an alternative, attach safety strips to the tub or shower floor. A foam pad serves as a good nonslip bath mat for outside the tub.

■ Install grab bars in the bathtub or shower as well as beside the toilet. If there is no wall near the toilet, install a toilet-safety rail, which attaches directly to the toilet seat. An elevated toilet also makes rising easier.

■ Consider installing a handheld shower head. This, combined with a bath bench or shower chair, allows the older person to sit while washing.

. . . .

Buy a pair of shower slippers or water shoes with nonskid soles. These ensure a nonskid surface throughout the bathroom.

. . . .

GETTING AROUND

A sense of independence is important at any age, but especially for an older person living in someone else's home. Here are ways to foster independence and ensure safety.

■ Provide a comfortable chair with sturdy arms that can aid the person in getting up. If the person has arthritic or weak knees, the chair seat should be elevated with a cushion to make sitting and standing easier on the knees.

■ If the person has difficulty getting around, furnish his or her room with an eye to saving steps. Provide a remote control for the television set and bedside light switch. A cordless phone allows the person to carry it to a chair or elsewhere.

■ Getting out of bed can be difficult, especially if there is no side rail.

Rig up a rope or overhead monkey pole to allow the person to pull himself or herself into an upright position.

FREQUENT FALLS

■ If an older person is having trouble with frequent falls, check his or her medications, both prescription and nonprescription. A drug interaction may be causing dizziness, vision problems, or other symptoms that contribute to falls.

■ Get rid of scatter rugs. If wood floors are slippery, install a carpet runner; be certain that it is securely taped to the floor. Use nonslip polish on waxed floors.

■ Encourage an older person to get up slowly from a sitting position. Standing suddenly can lead to a temporary drop in blood pressure, which causes light-headedness, increasing the chances of a fall.

■ If the person tends to lose his or her balance when standing up, suggest this technique: Place both feet firmly on the floor. Then bend forward from the hips, rise to an erect posture, and take one sideward step to gain balance.

■ Install a two-way intercom communication system so that the elderly person can immediately contact a family member or neighbor in case of a fall, an accident, or another emergency. Alternatively, look into a personal alert system that allows an older person to summon help with a device he or she wears at all times.

201

LIVING WITH PETS

The companionship of pets adds a new dimension to family life, but remember that pets need care and affection. The more you understand animals, the better your relationship with them will be.

KEEPING YOUR PET SAFE AND HEALTHY

■ Take a new pet to a veterinarian for a complete checkup. All animals should be tested for parasites. Also have cats tested for feline leukemia and dogs for heartworm. Healthy pets should have annual checkups; old or sick pets may need more frequent visits to the vet.

■ Don't feed animals human food. Pet food contains all the nutrients your dog or cat needs. Give supplements only if recommended by your veterinarian. And don't forget to have a bowl of fresh water available at all times.

■ Exercise your pet regularly. Dogs should be walked at least twice daily. Even a cat who sleeps most of the time needs regular exercise, so provide a scratching pad, climbing posts, and toys to keep it active.

■ If your pet goes outdoors, have it checked regularly for worms and other parasites.

■ Never leave an animal tied up outside, where it can be seen and snatched.

■ If you worry about your pet being abducted, an SPCA-endorsed electronic identification system can be handy to identify a stolen pet. A 10-digit alpha-numeric code is planted painlessly under the animal's skin and can be picked up by scanners at shelters.

■ If you live in a high-rise building, make sure your windows have screens to prevent a cat or dog from falling out.

■ Keep your pet clean and well groomed. Empty cat litter boxes daily, brush both dogs and cats frequently, and bathe dogs regularly.

> **Even healthy pets can transmit certain diseases to humans. Wash your hands after handling an animal and especially after changing a cat's litter box.**

PET-PROOFING YOUR HOME AND YARD

No matter how domesticated an animal is, it never completely loses its instinct to hunt and to explore by sniffing, scratching, and chewing. So you need to make sure your home offers a safe environment for a pet.

■ Keep pesticides, cleansers, and other toxic substances locked away where a curious pet cannot get to them.

■ If your pet develops such symptoms as drooling, vomiting, lethargy, weakness, bleeding, convulsions, or bowel problems, it may have ingested poison or a dangerous object (for example, a string or rubber band). Take the animal to a veterinarian immediately.

■ Cats have an uncanny knack for getting into cozy hiding places, such as clothes dryers, drawers, and cabinets. Check appliances before turning them on. When closing a cabinet or drawer, look first to make sure a pet is not inside.

■ Cover all trash containers with animal-proof lids.

■ Both dogs and cats love to chew grass and plants. If you or a neighbor uses lawn or garden pesticides, keep your animals indoors until you're sure the poisons have dissipated. Similarly, fence off poisonous outdoor plants, and put any poisonous houseplants out of your pet's reach. (As an alternative, tempt your cat with a pot of catnip or cat mint.)

BRINGING HOME A NEW BABY

The arrival of a baby can be traumatic for a pet, but with certain precautions, most pets will accept the newcomer.

■ Take your pet for a checkup early in (or even before) your or your wife's pregnancy to make sure it's in good health and all vaccinations are up-to-date. If your pet is not neutered, consider having this done, because neutering often improves an animal's temperament. However, if your cat is not declawed, don't use the arrival of a baby as a reason for having the procedure done. Declawed cats often become more defensive and resort to biting.

■ If your dog is not used to babies, try to get it accustomed to youngsters before your baby arrives. Dogs can be especially upset by an infant's crying. Make a recording of a baby crying, and play it occasionally before your dog is exposed to the real thing.

■ Acquaint your pet with the baby's smell. Before the newborn comes home from the hospital, give the animal a blanket or piece of clothing with the infant's scent on it. When you bring the baby home, have the mother spend a few minutes with the pet before introducing the baby.

■ Do not exclude or ostracize the animal. Many dogs are fascinated by watching a baby nurse, and cats often like to cuddle up beside a mother feeding her baby.

■ If you don't want the animal in the baby's room, put up a screen door so it can see what's going on. If a cat has access to the nursery, keep it from sharing the baby's bed by covering the crib with a tent-shaped safety net that can be zipped open and shut.

■ Never leave a dog alone with a baby, even if the dog is ordinarily protective of the child. By squirming and squealing, the child may trigger the dog's attack response.

AVOIDING DOG BITES

More than three million North Americans are bitten by dogs each year, but most dog bites could be prevented by understanding a dog's behavior and warning signals.

■ Teach children the proper way to interact safely with dogs. Many animal-welfare organizations and animal-control offices offer free seminars to schools or social groups.

■ Use extra caution when approaching a chained dog. Tied-up dogs are often angry and likely to attack if you come within reach.

■ Don't assume you're safe just because you're not on the dog owner's property. Territory is the dog's perception, not yours. A dog may claim not only its owner's yard but also the driveways on each side and the street and sidewalk in front, as well.

■ Learn the correct way to greet a dog. Let the animal take the initiative; extend your hand and let the dog sniff it. Never lean over a strange dog, gaze into its eyes, smile, and pat it on the head. To the dog, these are threatening gestures—dogs lean over each other, stare at each other's eyes, and bare their teeth to show dominance. And dogs often dislike being patted on the head. If the dog is small, try squatting so that you're at its level.

A wagging tail isn't always a friendly signal. A dog whose tail is up, stiff, and switching back and forth may be feeling aggressive. A friendly dog wags its tail in a relaxed way, with its whole back half in motion.

IF A DOG ATTACKS

Given the right provocation, any dog will bite or attack. If a dog appears ready to attack, your natural instinct is to run, but unless you can dive into a nearby doorway or car, stay put and follow these guidelines.

■ Try to act like a subordinate dog. Avoid eye contact, stand sideways, and look off to the side. If you stay still, the dog will probably lose interest, giving you a chance to slowly back off. But don't turn your back on the animal.

■ Speak to the dog in a medium-pitched, soft voice, using long, extended syllables, as in "staaaay, boy." In doing so, you're creating the calming sound trainers use. If you shriek or yell, the dog may become more aroused.

■ If a dog springs at you, try to meet its mouth with a rolled-up jacket, a purse, or even a shoe. This action may give you time to retreat to safety.

INVISIBLE DANGERS IN THE HOME

Our houses often harbor contaminants that we can neither see nor smell—among them, poisonous gases, radon, and lead. Fortunately, there are ways to detect and rid your home of such hazards.

UNHEALTHY GASES

Household products are often doubly hazardous because they give off dangerous fumes in addition to containing toxic compounds. Fortunately, you can avoid many of these products.

■ When storing woolens, use dried lavender or pieces of cedar instead of mothballs, which emit a chemical that has been linked to neurological damage and cancer. These natural substances repel moths and have the added advantage of making your clothes smell fresh.

■ Avoid using solid air fresheners, which also emit a chemical suspected of causing cancer. Instead, use herbal sachets or a spray made by mixing four teaspoons of baking soda in a quart of water.

■ Before putting dry-cleaned clothing in your closet, remove it from the plastic bags and hang it up outside for a few hours. This allows gases from the cleaning chemicals

to disperse more quickly than they can in your closet.

■ Choose natural fabrics for curtains, bedding, and upholstery, especially if the fabrics are exposed to direct sunlight or a source of heat. Cotton and wool are less likely to emit allergy-provoking chemicals than polyesters and other synthetic fibers.

HOW CLEAN IS YOUR AIR?

If you suspect that the air in your home is contaminated with asbestos, lead, or other harmful substances, have it professionally tested. Otherwise, you may want to simply rely upon your own senses or use home testing devices to monitor air quality.

■ Take a good sniff. If the air smells musty or unpleasant, try to track down the source.

■ If you have recently moved or renovated, be alert to the onset of new, unexplained symptoms, such as headaches, nausea, wheezing, and fatigue. They may be due to exposure to new or higher levels of chemicals. Try this test to be sure: Leave your house for a few hours. If your symptoms disappear while you are away but recur when you return, suspect that the air in your home is the irritant.

■ You can test your home for specific contaminants, such as formaldehyde and carbon monoxide, with special

sensors that you hang for a certain time and then send to a lab for analysis. Before buying these sensors, however, check with your local Environment Canada office or provincial public health department to make sure that the manufacturer is reputable.

THE HEAT IS ON

All heating systems can emit hazardous gases and particles. Here are measures to help minimize these dangers.

■ Have gas appliances and heating systems serviced and inspected regularly. Heating systems should be inspected by a qualified repair company or utility at least once a year to ensure that they are running efficiently and without leakage. All gas systems should be adequately vented to the outside.

■ If you prefer gas to electricity for cooking, choose a stove with an electronic ignition, which is safer and also more energy-efficient than a pilot light. Install a hood over a gas oven, and have it properly vented to the outside. If the flame from a burner is tipped with yellow, rather than blue, even when it is on low, the stove needs maintenance. Never use a gas oven as a source of home heating.

■ Make sure the chimney is clean and the flue open before building a fire in a fireplace or woodstove. A woodstove should be an EPA/CSA-certified model that meets safety standards. Its doors, gaskets, and joints should be closed tightly when the stove is in use.

■ Do not use a charcoal or propane grill indoors or in an enclosed area; this can result in carbon monoxide poisoning.

■ Do not burn wrapping paper, magazines, or other colored or glossy paper in a fireplace or woodstove. These papers may be printed or manufactured with potentially harmful chemicals that are released in the heat of the fire.

■ If you must use a kerosene space heater, choose a model vented to the outside. If that's not possible, use it for short periods only, keep the doors to the room open, and do not use it overnight.

■ Clean the filter for your central heating or cooling system every month by vacuuming it and its housing. Make sure the drip pans are properly drained to prevent a reservoir of standing water. If water does accumulate in a drip pan, empty the pan weekly and clean it with a mixture of 1 part vinegar to 8 parts water to retard mold growth.

■ Heat prompts some building materials and fabrics to emit gases. For example, new wall-to-wall carpeting or shelving made out of pressed wood (also called particle board) may emit formaldehyde and other hazardous chemicals. Try to install such materials in the summer, when you can keep windows open to allow the gases to dissipate.

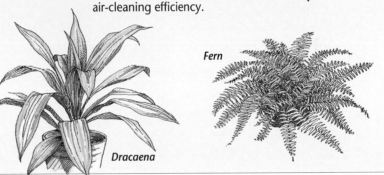

Grow Your Own Air Cleaners

Some common houseplants can reduce the amount of formaldehyde, benzene, and other toxic chemicals in the air.

For optimal air cleaning, have at least one of the plants shown here for every 100 square feet of a room.

Make sure the plants get enough light and water, but be careful not to overwater—too much moisture can cause mold or mildew.

Occasionally cut back the lower branches. The real benefits of houseplants may lie in the root system and the microorganisms in the soil. Exposing these parts of the potted plant to air increases its air-cleaning efficiency.

Philodendron

Fern

Dracaena

KEEP YOUR AIR CLEAN

Today's super-insulated homes save energy, but they must be properly ventilated to prevent a buildup of chemicals and other irritants in the air. You should try to minimize pollutants through ventilation and in other ways.

■ Do not allow smoking in your home. Cigarette smoke contains more than 4,000 substances, including formaldehyde, carbon monoxide, and many other toxins.

■ Keep at least one window of your home open, if only a crack, to improve indoor ventilation. Alternatively, install an air-to-air heat-exchange system. These systems range from window units, which ventilate just a small area of the house, to whole-house systems that require ducts. They use heated air from inside the house to warm fresh cold air from outside, providing ventilation without wasting energy.

■ When buying an air-cleaning (air-purifier) appliance, consider one that uses activated carbon or a high-efficiency particulate arrestance (HEPA) filter; these are more effective than electrostatic or ionizing appliances. The carbon should be at least one-inch thick and must be cleaned every six months—or more often, depending on the level of air pollution. HEPA filters need to be changed every year or so.

■ Humidifiers moisten overly dry air, but they can release harmful mineral particles into the air. Choose one that uses an HEPA filter and heats the water.

■ Install exhaust fans in bathrooms, kitchens, and attics to help remove moisture and pollution from indoor air.

■ If there is a garage attached to your house, make sure that cars, lawn mowers, and other gas-powered vehicles are not run inside the garage.

ELECTROMAGNETIC RADIATION

Electricity, central to modern life, constantly courses through the walls of our homes; however, it may not be as safe as we have assumed. Numerous population studies link electromagnetic fields, the magnetic radiation given off by electrical power lines and appliances, with an increased risk of brain tumors, leukemia, and other cancers. Although scientists disagree over possible electromagnetic hazards, it's prudent to reduce unnecessary exposure, at least until more is learned.

■ Unplug appliances when they are not in use. Even when turned off, some appliances give off low-frequency electromagnetic radiation.

■ Keep a safe distance between you and electrical appliances. Don't be lulled into thinking that small appliances are safer than large ones. Small electric motors actually give off a wider magnetic field.

■ If you have an older microwave oven, consider replacing it with a newer model that has tighter seals to reduce microwave leakage. Even so, microwave ovens should be checked by an appliance repair service once a year to make sure the seals are tight.

■ To keep children from sitting directly in front of a television set, mount it on the wall. They will then have to sit farther away to see the screen.

■ Electric clothes dryers give off large amounts of electromagnetic radiation. Avoid working in the laundry room when one is in use. If you use a commercial laundromat, put your clothes in the machines and then do an errand while they wash or dry to minimize time spent near the machines.

■ Switch from fluorescent lightbulbs to traditional tungsten lightbulbs. Although fluorescent lightbulbs use less energy, they give off more electromagnetic radiation.

■ If you have an ionizing smoke detector, replace it with one with a photoelectric device. They cost more but give off far less radiation.

PERSONAL APPLIANCES

Electric razors, hair dryers, and cellular phones are potent sources of electromagnetic radiation because they have small motors and are used close to the body.

■ If you use a plug-in electric razor, switch to a battery operated model or, better still, a blade razor.

■ Use hair dryers on a low setting for the shortest time possible. Towel-dry your hair first to reduce exposure to your hair dryer.

■ If you need a cellular phone, select one with an antenna on its base instead of the headset. Car phones should have outside antennae.

Cellular phones have been linked to an increased risk of brain cancer. Although more studies are needed, some experts advise reserving the phones for emergency use and keeping conversations short.

IN THE BEDROOM

Because you spend more time in your bedroom than any other room, this is an especially important place for minimizing your exposure to electromagnetic fields.

■ Don't place beds, especially those of children and infants, against a wall that has an electrical appliance in use on the other side. Walls do not shield against low-frequency magnetic fields. Similarly, don't put a bed or crib near electric baseboard heaters.

■ If you use an electric alarm

clock, don't put it on a night-stand next to your bed. This is much too close to your head, and you will be constantly exposed as you sleep. Move it across the room or switch to a battery-operated clock.

■ Do not sleep under an electric blanket, especially if you are pregnant. Both the heat and the electromagnetic radiation are potential hazards to a fetus. If you want a toasty bed, use the electric blanket to warm it for half an hour before bedtime. Then unplug the blanket, and cover it with a thermal blanket or down comforter to retain some heat.

KEEPING VDT'S AT ARM'S LENGTH

Video display terminals are no longer confined to the workplace. They are also common household appliances. Here are suggestions for reducing VDT electromagnetic exposure at home and in the office.

■ To minimize the electromagnetic radiation absorbed by your body when you're working at a computer, sit at least three feet away from the VDT. If your computer has a detachable keyboard, you can increase the distance even more. If you have trouble reading the screen, use eyeglasses adjusted for the appropriate distance (see "Reducing Eyestrain From Computer Screens," page 153).

■ To further minimize electromagnetic exposure from your VDT, place a grounded conductive micromesh filter in front of the screen.

■ If you have more than one VDT in a room, arrange them to allow at least three feet between machines, and never place them back to back.

■ When working at a VDT, schedule a 15-minute break at least every two hours. This not only reduces electromagnetic exposure but also protects against repetitive strain injuries, eyestrain, and other such problems.

■ If your child uses a computer in school, find out how old it is. Businesses often donate old computers to schools, and although they are still usable, those manufactured before 1983 tend to give off more radiation than later models.

A detachable keyboard can help you to sit at a distance from your VDT.

LEAD IN YOUR WATER

Drinking water is a major source of lead. When water leaves a treatment plant, it is virtually lead-free. But it can pick up dangerous amounts of lead on its way to your tap—from lead connector pipes and lead solder in copper plumbing.

■ Have your water tested for lead. Many cities now offer free or low-cost testing; contact the nearest Environment Canada office for information. When testing water, submit two samples—a first-draw sample taken after a tap has been off for several hours, and a second, purged sample after the tap has run for several minutes.

■ Hot water leaches more lead than cold, so use cold water for drinking and cooking.

■ Let the cold water tap run until it reaches its maximum coolness, especially if it has been off more than six hours, to clear out any accumulation of lead. To save water, draw an extra gallon or two of water and keep it in the refrigerator.

■ Consider switching to bottled water or installing a water-purification device if your lead level is 10 or more parts per billion even after the water has run until it is cold. A distiller or reverse-osmosis system removes the most lead and should be used if your lead tests higher than 10 parts per billion. Other filtration devices are probably sufficient for lower lead levels.

■ Check whether your electrical lines have been grounded to your plumbing pipes. The electrical grounding increases metal corrosion, allowing more lead to escape into your water. Hire a licensed electrician to change the ground system.

■ Ask your municipal utility whether your water connector lines are made of lead. (If they are more than 50 years old, they probably are.) Many utility companies are now replacing these connector lines; if yours is not, you may want to have it done yourself.

SHOULD YOU TEST FOR RADON?

Radon, an odorless gas produced by decaying radium, is the largest single source (40 percent) of radiation exposure in Canada. It may be responsible for 5-15 percent of all lung cancers each year. Fortunately, it is fairly easy to detect radon and eliminate it from your home. Check with your provincial authority responsible for radiation-related problems to see if your house is in a known radon hot spot. Testing is especially critical if:

■ Your home is in a radon area—it could have a problem even if a neighbor does not.

■ Your home contains an earth wall, floor, or crawl space.

■ Your home contains large amounts of exposed brick, stone, or concrete—common building materials that are likely to give off radon.

■ You have an indoor groundwater sump pump or your water comes from a well drilled into bedrock.

PRELIMINARY TESTING

Before calling professionals, you can screen for radon yourself by using a home testing kit. Such kits are widely available, easy to use, and quite reliable.

■ One type of home test uses a canister of activated charcoal granules, which absorb radon gas. After placing it in your home for seven days, you send it to a laboratory for analysis. Don't use these charcoal-absorption kits for long-term testing or if the area being tested is damp.

■ For humid areas or long-term measurement, use an alpha track test kit. This is made up of canisters of small plastic strips, with microscopic etching, that record the alpha particles emitted by radon. They are left in place for at least a month and can accumulate data for more than a year.

■ To get the most accurate results, test your home during the heating or cooling season, when the house is closed and ventilation is reduced.

■ Test the basement (or ground floor if you have no basement) first. Place the device two to four feet off the floor, away from windows and sources of dampness.

■ If your home has more than 800 becquerels per cubic metre, it may be time to call a professional for further testing. Make sure the tester uses special instruments, such as smoke tracers, to find the radon entry points and pathways the gas travels along. You will need this information to remedy the situation.

Well water is a common source of radon. Have a professional test the water itself.

REDUCING RADON

These are a few of the many steps you can take to reduce radon levels in your home and thereby reduce your own exposure to it.

■ Radon and other soil gases are drawn into the house through every crack or space in contact with the soil. Seal the obvious paths of gases from the soil to the basement.

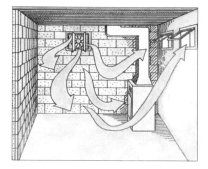

■ A forced ventilation system of fans in the basement, which balances the air exchange between the inside and outside of the house, can lower radon concentrations, but it is not a permanent solution.

■ Limit the time you spend in the basement or other areas with high radon levels. If possible, seal off such areas from the rest of the house.

■ Don't allow smoking in the house; cigarette smoke increases the danger of radon.

■ Make sure that furnaces and woodstoves are properly vented and have outside air supplies. Avoid using the fireplace, attic fans, or kitchen exhaust fans—all of which draw radon gas through the house—until levels are lowered.

■ Depressurize the soil under the floor slab by venting the gases through a pipe to the attic where a fan expels them.

TESTING FOR RADON

*"Simply inhaling the air
in our home was
the equivalent of smoking
260 cigarettes a day."*
—*Stanley Watras*

• • • • • • •

On December 2, 1984, Stanley Watras, a senior construction engineer for Bechtel, Inc., went to work at a nuclear power plant under construction in southeastern Pennsylvania. Radiation detection stations were set up in certain areas of the plant, which was not yet operating. As Stanley passed through one station, he set off an alarm heard nationwide.

Watras himself seemed to be the source of the radiation. After two weeks of searching, he discovered the cause. His home had a frighteningly high level of radon, a gas that occurs as uranium deteriorates in rocks and soil. Investigators found the level of radon to be at least 1,000 times higher than what is considered safe. The state ordered the home evacuated, and efforts were begun to get rid of the radon.

Natural causes. Although the dangers of radon to uranium miners were well known, the Watras house was the first in the United States in which a radon hazard was traced to the ground underneath. As it turned out, the problem was not unique —the Environmental Protection Agency now estimates that 1 in 15 homes in the United States harbors unsafe radon levels. The presence of radon is not a haz-ard outdoors, but radon raises the risk of lung cancer when trapped inside a house.

Older homes built on stone foundations or with dirt crawl spaces are especially vulnerable, but newer homes are also at risk, especially if they are well insulated.

Completely treatable. Technology has come a long way since 1984, when it took more than six months to lower radon levels in the Watras home. Now, with a relatively small investment of time and money, homeowners can detect and eliminate the problem.

Self-tests for radon are available at most hardware stores for $20 to $50 and are easy to use (see facing page). Safe levels of radon are placed below 800 becquerels per cubic metre (Bq/m^3). If you find your house has higher levels, don't panic. Repeat the test in two living areas of the house. You could start by testing the living room and, if the house has more than one floor, a second-floor bedroom. If you continue to find elevated levels, it's time to contact a contractor who is licensed to do radon abatement.

Stanley Watras has taken a minor setback and turned it into an opportunity by starting his own radon-cleanup business. He says that nearly all of his cases can be taken care of in one day by installing fans, sealing cracks in foundations, and identifying other sources of radon contamination.

The problem of radon can be highly localized. Although levels in some parts of the Watras home exceeded 160,000 Bq/m^3, a similar ranch house less than 100 yards away tested at less than 80 Bq/m^3. As Watras points out, radon is one environmental hazard that has no boundaries or predictability. "Testing is the only way you can learn whether your home is radon-safe," he advises.❏

The Watras family has its radon problem under control.

RENOVATIONS AND REPAIRS

As every homeowner knows, something always needs to be fixed up around the house. Doing it yourself saves money and provides satisfaction. But take care when using tools, and guard against flaking paint, asbestos, and other potentially dangerous materials.

GENERAL SAFETY

■ Dress for safety. Never wear scarves, loose sleeves, dangling jewelry, neckties, or other clothing that can get in the way of power tools. Tie your hair back so that it doesn't fall in your eyes when you're leaning over your work. Always wear sturdy shoes or work boots when using heavy tools.

■ Wear the appropriate protective gear, especially when using power tools: a dust mask for tools that produce shavings; ear protectors for loud machinery; and a face shield, safety glasses, or goggles for all power tools. Don't scrimp when buying safety equipment—if it's comfortable and efficient, you are more likely to use it.

■ Concentration and full alertness are crucial when working with sharp tools and dangerous materials. Keep your eyes on the work area at all times. Don't try to talk to someone while using a sharp tool.

■ Don't be afraid to ask for help. Moving heavy or oversize materials may require two people to avoid accidents or injury.

■ Alcohol and power tools definitely do not mix. The same goes for many over-the-counter cold and allergy pills and other medications that can cause drowsiness. If you don't feel your best, put off working until another time.

■ Keep children out of the work area except for special, child-oriented tasks. Although children are fascinated with tools and are eager to watch adults working with them, their presence can be distracting and lead to accidents.

■ Set aside a time to work with your child on a simple project that requires manual tools. Look at the project as an opportunity for fun and a hands-on safety lesson.

Even a simple project has a way of getting out of hand. Start with small, easy tasks and work your way up to those that are more complicated. If possible, apprentice yourself to an experienced hobbyist or take a woodworking or other crafts class.

DESIGNING A SAFE AND EFFICIENT WORK AREA

■ Choose the location for your work area carefully. It should be dry and adequately heated. A damp area can cause tools to rust and may make power tools hazardous. A space that is too cold can chill and stiffen hands, making accidents more likely to happen.

■ Make sure your workshop is well ventilated and away from living areas of the home, especially if you plan to work with paints or solvents.

■ Install cabinets and drawers for keeping tools organized. Do not stack tools or overload storage space. Label all cabinets and put locks on those that hold power tools, solvents, paints, sharp tools, and other hazardous materials, especially if there are children in the household.

■ Keep tools with sharp blades covered when not in use. Pieces of old garden hose make fine blade protectors. Cut a piece as long as the blade edge. Slit the hose and fit it over the sharp edge of a saw, knife, or other tool.

■ Install good overall lighting, as well as auxiliary lights, near the workbench and other work areas. The area where you do most of your work should be three times as bright as the rest of the room.

■ Make sure your workbench is sturdy and stable. Place it close to electric outlets and consider installing extra outlets at the work level every three feet to minimize the need for extension cords. If your workbench is in the middle of the room, install overhead electric outlets.

■ All electric outlets in the work area should be properly grounded. Do not use overhead lamp outlets to plug in power tools.

■ To prevent falls, keep the floor clear of debris. Tape extension cords to the floor or ceiling.

■ Keep your work area clean. Brush sawdust from materials after each cut so you can see what you're working on. Sweep sawdust from the floor after each work session. Not only is sawdust slippery, but it is also a fire hazard.

■ Keep a fire extinguisher nearby. Never smoke or use an open flame in an indoor work area.

POWER TOOLS

Keep safety in mind when buying new tools. At the very least, check for the CSA-approved seal, which means that the tool has met minimum safety requirements.

■ Look for new, double-insulated tools that have built-in protection against electric shock. If you buy a secondhand tool, make sure it has safety features.

■ Read the instructions carefully before using a new tool. Keep the operator's manual nearby and refresh your memory if you haven't used that tool in a while.

■ Before using three-pronged power cords, be certain that your electrical system is properly grounded and that you have attached the ground wire to the screw on the wall outlet.

■ Before buying a circular saw, test that the blade guard moves smoothly and releases easily. The lever that opens the guard should be readily accessible so that you do not accidentally touch the blade when opening the guard.

■ Choose a router with the on/off switch on the handle. This will make turning the tool on and off much safer because both hands can remain on the handle.

■ Before sawing into wood, check for knots, nails, and other defects that may cause the power tool to kick back. If possible, remove these obstacles or choose another piece of wood.

■ Use guides to ensure that a tool stays on the path you intend. Any straight edge will do if it is as long or longer than the cut you want to make. A pencil mark, however, is not enough.

■ Secure the material you are working on to a sturdy work-

bench with one or more clamps. When sawing, make sure the weight of the tool rests on the part of the material that is on the workbench, rather than the part being sawed off.

■ Always plug your power tools into an outlet equipped with a ground fault circuit interrupter (GFCI), which automatically turns off the electricity if there is a possibility of electric shock. An existing outlet can easily be refitted with a GFCI, available at most hardware stores.

■ Don't operate power tools in damp or wet conditions, even if you are using a ground fault circuit interrupter. Before the GFCI has a chance to block an electric current, you may have already received a serious electric shock.

■ Make sure the power tool has stopped moving before you set it down. Always unplug the tool when it is not in use and whenever you adjust the setting or blades.

■ Keep your power tools in good working order with regular maintenance and repairs. Make sure that blades are sharp, safety features are functional, and electric cords are not frayed or worn.

Before turning on a power tool, do a test run with the power off. This will alert you to potential hazards, such as a tangled cord or an awkward position, that can lead to accidents. Correct the problems before actually using the tool.

LADDERS

Ladders are one of the most common sources of injuries during home repairs. Follow these guidelines for safe ladder use.

■ When shopping for a ladder, note its grade number, which corresponds to the weight it can safely support. For example, grade 1 ladders, which are commercial grade, sup-port up to 250 pounds per rung, grade 2 ladders support up to 225 pounds per rung, and grade 3 ladders, intended for domestic purposes, sup-port 200 pounds per rung. Any of these grades should be adequate for most household uses.

■ When doing electrical work, choose a wooden or fiber-glass ladder. Aluminum lad-ders conduct electricity, so there is a risk of electric shock when they are used around power lines.

■ Use a stepladder instead of a chair to reach a high shelf. For extra stability, select a one- or two-step model that has flat steps instead of nar-rower rungs.

■ A five- or six-foot steplad-der will enable you to reach

LADDER SAFETY

Always be very careful when using a ladder for renovations or repairs. Besides taking basic safety measures, follow the advice below to avoid accidents and to make your work easier.

To remind yourself *never to stand on the top two steps of a tall stepladder, paint them a very bright color, such as yellow or red.*

If you must place *a ladder in front of a door, make sure the door is locked (or tie it completely open) so no one will open it and hit the ladder.*

When painting a ceiling, *use two stepladders to hold a long plank for you to stand on. Make sure the plank is strong and the ladder legs rest squarely on the floor.*

the ceiling of most houses. However, do not stand on the top or the step just below it—the ladder may become top-heavy and topple over. A model with steps on both sides may save you from moving the ladder frequently during some jobs.

■ For high, outside work, choose an extension ladder. Because these ladders need a three-foot overlap for safe operation, buy one that is at least three feet longer than the height you want to reach. For example, if you want to reach 13 feet, you need a 16-foot ladder to extend that far.

■ To ensure the stability of your ladder, make sure the space between the ladder and the wall is one-fourth the height from the ground to the point where the ladder leans against the wall.

WET PAINT

Paint contains a number of chemicals that can cause headaches and eye irritation. Prolonged exposure to wet paint can result in more serious problems, including kidney, lung, liver, and nerve damage. Fortunately, there are several ways to reduce such risks.

■ Although oil-based paint creates a better seal and is more durable than water-based latex paint, it contains more volatile toxins, requires paint thinner or turpentine for cleaning up, and takes longer to dry. Reserve oil-based paint for the outside of your house, especially if the wood is old and dry.

Also, recent improvements in latex paints make them a better option for many newer houses.

■ Consider having a professional paint the outside of your house, especially if it is more than one story. If you choose to paint it yourself, use scaffolding, or arrange several sturdy stepladders and boards to fashion a substitute for scaffolding.

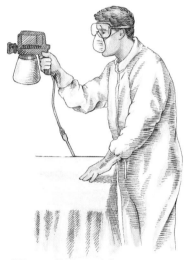

■ Wear a lightweight, protective jumpsuit (available at most paint stores) to reduce the amount of paint that gets on your skin. This will also make cleanup a lot easier.

■ Do interior painting when the weather is warm and dry so that you can leave the windows open for ventilation. Paint one room at a time. If possible, close off that room from the rest of the house until it is odor-free—up to two weeks for water-based paint and at least a month for oil-based paint.

■ To help eliminate paint odors quickly, add a pound of baking soda to each can of paint. Stir until bubbling

stops. Do one can at a time, and test with a small amount first to make sure that the baking soda does not interfere with the paint's adherence to the walls.

■ Here is another trick that may reduce paint odors: Place a handful of hay in a bucket, and add warm water. Put the bucket in the painted room overnight.

■ Look into alternatives to standard commercial paints. These paints, such as casein-based "milk paint," do not contain fungicides or other chemicals that many people find irritating. However, they are not good choices for damp rooms—such as basements, kitchens, and bathrooms—because they do not deter mold growth.

■ Follow Tom Sawyer's example and use whitewash, a mixture of water and hydrated lime. Experiment with the portions—the recipe varies somewhat according to the surface and whether it is indoors or outdoors. You can even add pigment for colored whitewash. Whitewash is a good choice for a translucent finish and for basements and cinder block walls.

Choose custom-mixed latex paints. Premixed colors often contain tetrafluoroethylene, a toxic chemical.

WOOD FINISHES

■ Varnish, polyurethane, and other wood finishes may contain formaldehyde, ethanol, benzene, and other toxic

213

substances that cause headaches and nausea in most people. Use these products outdoors or in a well-ventilated room. Even so, wear a facial mask that filters out fumes. Shellac may be a better choice than the other finishes; although it can emit alcohol vapors for up to six months, the odor is not as irritating as that of the others.

■ Consider using a water-based wood finish for furniture and wood flooring. Most of the toxic fumes from these finishes are released within a few minutes of application and are quickly dissipated.

■ Paint, varnish, and other finishes contain solvents that are flammable. Do not smoke while applying finishes, and keep cans, brushes, and freshly painted materials away from flames, stoves, and electrical circuits.

CLEANUP

■ For a safe, fast, and easy cleanup, use water-based latex paint. Rinsing with plain water removes any paint residue.

■ Instead of using commercial paint removers to loosen old paint, try mixing four ounces of trisodium phosphate (TSP, available at most hardware stores) with one quart of hot water. Apply with a brush, leave on for 30 minutes, and then rinse with plain water. Always wear gloves when working with TSP.

■ Commercial paint thinners and removers may contain a variety of toxins, including methylene chloride, a known carcinogen. When using them,

always wear a protective mask, goggles, and gloves, and work in a well-ventilated space. Don't use these products at all if you have a lung, liver, or kidney disorder.

■ When working with paint strippers and other toxic substances, keep a bucket of warm water nearby to quickly rinse accidental splashes off your skin.

Paint remover, paint, and other substances containing solvents are hazardous waste and should not be thrown away with the regular garbage. Ask your local recycling center, health department, or environmental agency how to dispose of cans and leftovers.

LEAD PAINT IS STILL A THREAT

Lead has been banned from interior house paint since 1977, but millions of homes built before then still have lead paint on their walls, often under coats of more

recent lead-free paint. As the paint chips or deteriorates, the lead is released into the atmosphere. Lead paint is the most common source of lead poisoning among young children.

■ Use extra care when scraping or stripping old paint, whether from walls or furniture. The best alternative is to call in a professional. But if you decide to do it yourself, wear gloves, goggles, and a facial mask. A combination of using chemical strippers and scraping is the safest removal method. Avoid heat guns and blowtorches—which vaporize the lead, making it easy to inhale—and sanders, which create lead dust.

■ Work on one room at a time and seal it off from the rest of the house to keep lead dust from permeating the air. Even so, children and pregnant women should stay elsewhere until the work is complete. Change out of your work clothes and shoes immediately upon leaving the room, and wash them separately.

■ Keep pets out of the work area. They can carry lead to other parts of the house on their paws and in their fur.

■ Don't eat or drink in the room where you are working. Ventilate the area by opening windows and using an exhaust fan. Minimize dust by mopping the floor, walls, ceiling, and woodwork between work sessions; use water that contains a trisodium phosphate solution. Shower and shampoo your hair before coming in contact with other household members.

■ Pick up flaking paint or chips and mop the area often to keep children from eating the chips or inhaling dust contaminated with lead.

■ The disposal of leaded paint requires that you take special precautions. Contact your local board of health for information about proper disposal of leaded debris.

■ As an alternative to removing the paint, consider covering the walls with paneling, plasterboard, or plywood.

■ Interior paint is not the only source of lead—old paint flaking off the outside of the house may also contain lead. When repainting the house exterior, use the same protective measures as when removing interior lead paint.

Lead paint is no longer used on children's toys and furniture, but be cautious about passing down your childhood toys and cribs. If they were made before the 1970's, they may well be covered with lead paint. If in doubt, strip and repaint them, or have a professional do this.

ASBESTOS

Asbestos is a group of naturally occurring minerals that was widely used in public buildings for insulating and fireproofing until the 1950's. At that time, it was linked to certain cancers among asbestos workers. The asbestos used in homes and schools is just as dangerous as the type used by asbestos workers, especially if it is disturbed or if it flakes and peels, releasing its fibers into the air.

■ Before buying or renovating a house that predates 1950, consider having it inspected for asbestos by a qualified professional. Asbestos (see micrograph above) was occasionally used in the past to insulate boiler pipes and the pipes of steam and hot water systems. However it is not a common problem in houses in Canada and is generally not a cause for alarm. If you have any doubt, contact the Canada Mortgage and Housing Corporation.

■ Look in your basement for covered pipes and water heaters. If the insulation is in good shape, there probably is little reason for alarm, even if it does contain asbestos. Removing it may cause more harm than good. Check it periodically, however, for signs of damage.

■ If asbestos is flaking or damaged, take care not to stir up the air in the area. Do not dust, sweep, vacuum, or use a fan or ventilation system until the area is professionally checked and the asbestos is removed or sealed off.

If you believe you have been exposed to asbestos in the home or in the workplace, it is even more important that you are not exposed to cigarette smoke. The combination of these two carcinogens increases your risk of lung cancer 50 to 90 times.

ASBESTOS REMOVAL OR SEALING

■ If airborne asbestos in your home is confirmed, do not let children or pets in the area until the source has been eliminated. If you do go into the area, wear a protective mask and remove your clothes and shoes before entering other parts of the house.

■ Don't attempt to remove asbestos yourself—this requires safety equipment, including an asbestos approved respirator and special protective clothing. In some cases, it may be better to seal off the asbestos rather than remove it. This task also should be left to a licensed professional.

■ If you choose to have asbestos removed professionally, monitor the air after the abatement has been completed. Take several samples to ensure that no asbestos fibers are still airborne.

■ If you collect test samples yourself, wear gloves, goggles, and a facial mask. Carefully extract a few of the flaking fibers and put them in a glass of water. If the fibers don't dissolve, they may be asbestos.

Send the samples to a testing laboratory or your local Environment Canada office for confirmation.

FORMALDEHYDE

Many common building and house materials, ranging from carpeting to particleboard, contain significant amounts of formaldehyde resins. When these materials are exposed to water or heat, they give off gases that can cause fatigue, headaches, and respiratory problems.

■ Be especially wary of formaldehyde if you live in a mobile home or small, well-insulated home. Many common household products—such as paper towels, cleaners, and permanent-press fabrics—contain small amounts of formaldehyde, and gases from them can mount up in an airtight space.

■ Some blown-in insulation installed in the late 1970's and early 1980's contained large amounts of urea-formaldehyde. Inspect the outside for telltale round plugs in the siding, especially around windows and near the roof. A professional can then determine if the insulation is the type containing formaldehyde.

■ In mobile homes, paneling, cabinetry, shelving, flooring, carpeting, and insulation may all contain urea-formaldehyde. Check whether your local or provincial health department offers free formaldehyde testing. If not, ask for a referral to a qualified professional.

■ In many instances, maintaining moderate temperatures and humidity levels in your home is sufficient to reduce formaldehyde emissions. You may be able to do this by using dehumidifiers and air-conditioning.

■ If you find that the walls or other wood products in your home are contaminated by formaldehyde, you can choose from a number of ways to remedy the problem. They include ventilation, sealing, and removal of the source.

■ If you are considering removing the source of formaldehyde, be aware that this is the most complicated and expensive method but that it is also foolproof.

PICKING SAFE MATERIALS

If you are planning major renovations or repairs, you can reduce exposure to hazardous gases through careful product selections.

■ Avoid cabinets and other items made of particleboard. The urea-formaldehyde resin that is used in particleboard is much more potent than the phenol-formaldehyde resin in plywood. Instead, choose solid wood or metal.

■ Plastic laminated cabinets and countertops usually contain particleboard as well. Tile or synthetic marble is a better choice for counters.

■ If you are considering putting up wall coverings, avoid vinyl wallpaper and self-adhesive wallpaper, which contain formaldehyde. Instead, choose paper or foil wall covering (not Mylar) with a starch-based wallpaper glue.

■ If you must use products containing formaldehyde, try sealing in the vapors with at least two coats of polyurethane, wax, or latex-based paint. Alternatively, you can speed up the release of formaldehyde gas by sealing off the room and turning the heat up to 26.7°C (80°F). Stay out of the house at least 12 hours. Then open all the windows and doors and turn on fans to ventilate the house.

■ When buying carpeting and rugs, look for natural fibers, such as cotton and wool, that have not been treated with stain repellents, biocides, or other chemicals. Jute backing is recommended over polyurethane.

■ Draperies and upholstery should also be made from untreated, natural fibers, such as cotton, wool, and linen. Clean them often to avoid buildup of dust and soot.

■ When choosing tiles or other floor covering, be aware that soft-vinyl, no-wax tile and self-adhesive tiles contain petroleum products that give off toxic fumes. Opt for ceramic tile, hard vinyl, or wood flooring instead.

■ Asphalt shingles are a good choice for roofing. Slate, galvanized or painted steel, aluminum, cement or concrete, clay, or metal tiles are also good but they tend to be more expensive.

■ For interior wall and ceiling coverings, the best materials are plain plaster, brick, and hardwood paneling. With softwood paneling, apply a lacquer sealer, since some tree resins provoke allergies. Avoid plastic brick veneer, interior plywood, and pre-finished interior paneling.

CHOOSING GOOD WOOD

Although wood is not as dangerous as particleboard and plywood, some types may be treated with harmful chemicals. In fact, some woods are known to cause allergic reactions, such as rashes and respiratory problems. Pay attention to the following when choosing your wood.

■ For indoor use, avoid woods that are treated with chemicals—such as creosote, pentachlorophenol, and water-soluble salts—to make them more durable outdoors. Of these, pentachlorophenol is probably the most dangerous and should never be used.

■ If you are considering building a deck or outdoor structure, beware of green-tinted wood. This wood has been preserved with water-soluble salts that produce compounds, similar to arsenic, that can leach into soil or collect as a white, poisonous dust on the wood surfaces.

■ Never use pressure-treated wood for picnic tables, near vegetable gardens, or where children play. Instead, use redwood or cedar.

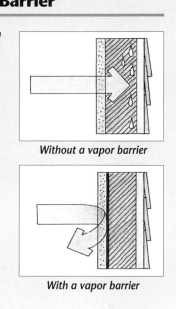

Why You Need a Vapor Barrier

When you install insulation, build in a vapor barrier on the warm side of the wall or ceiling.

During cold weather, the warm air inside your house has more moisture than outside air. This moisture finds its way to cooler, drier air, such as that in wall spaces.

When condensation then occurs in these spaces, water soaks into the insulation, diminishing its effect. Condensation can also lead to mold, mildew, and deterioration of the insulation material.

A vapor barrier prevents the moisture from penetrating the wall.

Without a vapor barrier

With a vapor barrier

■ If you must use treated wood, avoid making unnecessary cuts, which can release dangerous chemicals into the air. Wear gloves and a filter mask while working with the wood, and do not work with it indoors.

INSULATE FOR SAFETY

■ Choose yellow fiberglass batting or fiberglass board insulation over other types of roll or board insulation. Fiberglass fibers can be irritating, and the resin used in the board insulation contains some formaldehyde; however, these substances can be safely sealed off from living areas with foil or plastic sheathing. Wallboard covered with latex paint forms an additional sealant. Take extra precautions around electrical outlets and ceiling fixtures to ensure that they are

properly sealed.

■ As a nontoxic alternative, consider cork sheeting and cotton/polyester insulation. If you need blow-in insulation, look for foam insulation made from magnesium oxide, which is nontoxic.

■ Choose pure, clear silicone caulking, and ventilate the space thoroughly during and after the job. Although silicone caulking emits strong odors and fumes during application, once the odor has dispersed and the substance has thoroughly dried, it is considered safe.

Use felt or hard-vinyl weather stripping instead of a plastic or neoprene type. Neoprene rubber strips contain chlorinated hydrocarbons and should not be used.

FIRE SAFETY

Hundreds of Canadians die in home fires each year, but most of these deaths could be avoided. Make sure your family knows simple fire-prevention rules and what to do if fire does strike.

START WITH A PLAN

Many fire deaths occur because the victims did not know how to get out of their burning home safely. Don't wait for an emergency to locate fire exits—by then it may be too late.

■ Make a list of all possible exits from your home, and check that they are all accessible and clear of obstacles. For example, see that windows are not bolted or painted shut.

■ Draw a floor plan of the house, indicating all windows and doors (see illustration). Locate two exits from each bedroom. In most cases, this means that a window may serve as an emergency exit. Mark all primary and alternate exits on the plan.

■ Go over the plan and rules of survival with each family member, and walk everyone through the escape routes. Can everyone reach and operate latches, bolts, and locks? Climb out windows?

■ Agree on a predesignated outside meeting place and make sure the entire family knows to go there immediately after escaping from a fire. This way, you can "count noses" to be sure everyone has made it out safely. Include this location on your plan and mark it with a large X.

■ Tack up the plan on a bulletin board or refrigerator door where family members, visitors, and babysitters will see it easily and frequently. Write the fire department number on it in large red numerals.

■ Consider buying portable escape ladders for bedrooms on second and third floors.

■ Remember "EDITH," meaning "Exit Drill In The Home." Call a family fire drill at least once every six months and include even young children in discussions. Try to plan a few fire drills for the middle of the night, since this is when most fires occur.

AN OUNCE OF PREVENTION

All fires require three elements—oxygen, fuel, and heat. Most fires start when people or man-made devices supply the heat.

■ Heating equipment is a major cause of home fires. Have your heating system inspected by a professional at least once a year.

■ If you use a coal or wood stove, make sure it rests on a fireproof floor protector, such as a metal sheet or ceramic tiles, and is a safe distance from walls, furniture, and other combustible materials. Even so, ask for a fire department inspection to make sure it is properly installed.

■ Allow ashes to cool, and then dispose of them in a tightly covered metal container, not a box or bag.

THE IMPORTANCE OF SMOKE DETECTORS

Contrary to popular belief, the smell of smoke may not wake a sleeping person. The poisonous gases produced by a fire can numb the senses quickly and put you into a deeper sleep. By sounding an alarm and alerting you to a fire in time to escape, a smoke detector can save the lives of all family members.

■ Be sure the smoke detector bears the label of approval from an independent testing laboratory. Both ionizing and photoelectric devices give adequate

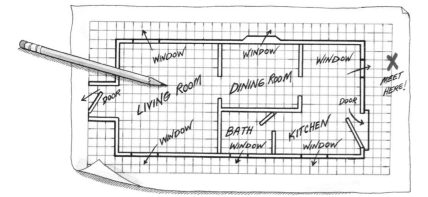

protection, but photoelectric devices are preferred because they don't emit as much radiation as ionizing models.

■ If you select a plug-in smoke detector, add a restraining device so the plug cannot be pulled out. Never connect a detector to an electrical circuit that can be turned off at a wall switch.

■ Install smoke detectors outside bedrooms, and make sure they can be heard inside the rooms when the doors are closed. In addition, install detectors on every level of your home, including the basement. For added protection, consider putting detectors in the dining room, furnace area, utility room, and hallways. Smoke detectors are not recommended for the kitchen, attic, and garage; instead, install heat detectors in these areas.

■ If a family member is hearing-impaired, install an additional detector inside the person's bedroom. Smoke detectors specially made for the hearing-impaired flash a light in addition to sounding an alarm.

■ Clean your smoke detectors according to the manufacturer's instructions; dust and cobwebs can reduce a detector's sensitivity to smoke. Never paint a smoke detector.

■ Test all smoke detectors every week or so, and replace batteries as needed (at least once a year) or according to the manufacturer's instructions. Don't allow family members to "borrow" batteries from a smoke detector.

INSTALLING A SMOKE DETECTOR

When putting up a smoke detector, follow the manufacturer's directions, as well as these recommendations.

■ Because smoke rises, each detector should be high enough to detect the first traces of smoke. Install wall-mounted units 4 to 12 inches from the ceiling. Place a ceiling-mounted detector at least 4 inches from the wall.

■ In a room with a high-pitched ceiling, mount the detector on or near the highest point.

■ Along a stairway, install the detector in the path where smoke would travel upstairs.

■ Locate a basement detector close to the stairway but not at the top of the stairs. Dead air space near the door may prevent smoke from reaching the detector.

■ Don't install detectors near windows, doors, or air registers, where drafts can reduce their sensitivity.

RULES OF SURVIVAL

Most fire victims die from inhaling smoke and poisonous gases, not from burns. If you know how to recognize danger signs and how to act appropriately, you will increase your chances of getting safely out of a burning building.

■ If a smoke detector goes off, act immediately. To waken anyone who may still be asleep, shout, "Fire! Everyone out!" Don't waste time getting dressed or searching for valuables.

■ Sleep with bedroom doors closed. Doors offer protection

from heat and smoke and slow a fire's progress. If in your escape you must go from room to room, close each door behind you.

■ Feel every door before opening it. Place the back of your hand on the crack between the door and the door frame; if it's hot, do not open the door. Even if the door is cool, open it cautiously. Stay low in case smoke or toxic fumes are seeping around the door. If heat and smoke come in, slam the door tightly and use your alternate way out.

■ If you use a window for your escape, be sure the door is tightly closed. Otherwise, the draft from the open window may draw smoke and fire into the room.

■ If you must go through smoke, crawl under it on your hands and knees. However, do not crawl on your belly, because some heavier toxic gases settle in a thin layer on the floor.

■ If you are unable to escape from a room because of a fire on the other side of the door, stuff clothing, towels, or newspapers in the door's cracks to keep smoke out of your refuge.

■ Remember "STOP, DROP, ROLL" if your clothing catches fire. The moment it happens, stop where you are. Drop to the ground, and cover your mouth and face with your hands to protect them from the flames. Then roll over and over to smother the flames.

FIRE EXTINGUISHERS

In addition to smoke detectors, a home should have at least one portable fire extinguisher. Remember that these small extinguishers are designed for small fires only.

■ Use an extinguisher only if you know you have the right one for the type of fire and you already know how to use it.

■ A multipurpose fire extinguisher, marked "ABC," is probably best because it is effective against all types of fire: those fueled by wood, paper, rubber, and most plastics; those fueled by flammable liquids; and those ignited by live electrical equipment, such as televisions, radios, and other appliances.

■ Try to extinguish a fire only after calling the fire department. Even then, keep your back to an exit, and leave immediately if the fire threatens your escape route. If the fire persists for more than 30 seconds, get everybody out of the house.

■ Remember "PASS"—for "Pull, Aim, Squeeze, Sweep"—when using a fire extinguisher. Pull the pin or other releasing mechanism. Aim low, pointing the extinguisher nozzle (or its horn or hose) at the base of the fire. Squeeze the handle to release the extinguishing agent, then sweep from side to side until the fire is out. Watch the fire area. If fire breaks out again, repeat the process.

■ Extinguishers require routine care. Read your operator's manual, and ask your dealer how often your extinguisher should be inspected and serviced. Disposable fire extinguishers can be used only once, and reusable fire extinguishers must be recharged after every use.

SMOKING HAZARDS

■ Careless smoking is the number one cause of home-fire fatalities. If you smoke, use a large, heavy ashtray, and don't let it become so full that hot ashes overflow. Before emptying an ashtray, make sure that its contents are cool. Even so, check the trash to see that nothing is burning.

■ Before you go to bed after a party, check for any smoldering cigarettes under all cushions and chairs. A cigarette that falls into an upholstered chair can smolder for hours before bursting into flame.

■ Never smoke in bed or anywhere else that you are likely to doze off.

■ Store matches and lighters out of the reach of small children.

KITCHEN FIRES

Your kitchen stove can both start fires and inflict serious burns. Cultivate these safe cooking habits to prevent either from occurring.

■ Don't leave something cooking unattended. Turn pot handles in so they can't get knocked off the stove or pulled down by a child.

■ Keep broilers, ovens, and vents free of grease, which can easily ignite.

■ Don't wear flowing sleeves while cooking.

■ Don't hang spice racks or potholders over stoves, as they can easily catch fire. If you

have to reach over the burners to get to them, you also risk catching your clothing on fire.
■ If a pan on the stove catches fire, slide a lid over the pan to cut off the supply of oxygen. Turn off the burner. To avoid fanning the flames, don't carry the pan away from the stove.
■ If flames are coming from an oven, broiler, or microwave oven, close the door to the unit and turn off the heat source.

If you have a kitchen grease fire, water will only spread the flames. Likewise, throwing salt, flour, or baking soda on a fire is not recommended. Flour products can actually explode.

ELECTRICAL HAZARDS
■ Never overload electrical outlets, and use only one appliance per extension cord.
■ Don't run extension cords under rugs or across doorways, and never hang them over nails. This may cause the insulation to deteriorate, exposing a wire that can cause a fire or electric shock.
■ Check electrical cords for cracks, fraying, broken plugs, and loose connections. Replace them immediately. Also replace cords that become hot when in use.
■ If a fuse blows, try to find out why it blew before you replace it. Fuses are designed to protect against fire; if you use the wrong amperage, you lose this protection.
■ If fuses blow or circuit breakers open frequently, your wiring may not be

adequate. Shrinking television pictures and slow-to-heat irons and toasters are tip-offs that your wiring may not be adequate. Call a licensed electrician to check and update your wiring.
■ Portable space heaters account for a large number of house fires every year. Use only electrical space heaters that have a tip-over shut-off switch and protective grills around the heating elements.

HAZARDOUS MATERIALS
■ Never store gasoline inside the home.
■ Store paints, thinners, and other flammables in their original containers, away from heat, sparks, or flames. Keep oily rags in a closed glass or metal container.
■ Take a heater or its tank outdoors to add fuel, but never move a heater or add fuel when the heater is still hot.
■ Aerosols are highly flammable. When using hair spray or other aerosols, make sure that you are not near a heat source or open flame.
■ Never dispose of aerosol cans in trash that is to be burned. They can explode with great force.
■ Keep the attic free of combustibles, such as old newspapers and magazines.

HIGH-RISE FIRES
■ Learn your building's evacuation plans. Know the location of fire alarms, and learn how to use them. Post emergency fire department numbers near all telephones.
■ If you hear instructions on

your building's public-address system, listen carefully and do as you're told.
■ Never take an elevator when leaving a burning building. Instead, go directly to the nearest fire- and smoke-free stairway.
■ If you cannot get to a fire stairway, go to a room with an outside window.
■ If there is a working phone, call the fire department emergency number and tell the dispatcher where you are. Do this even if you can see fire trucks on the street below.

■ Stay where rescuers can see you through the window, and wave a light-colored cloth to attract their attention.
■ If possible, open the window at the top and bottom. Be ready to shut the window quickly if smoke rushes in.
■ You may need to be patient; the rescue of occupants of a high-rise building can take several hours.

KEEPING INTRUDERS OUT

A burglary or other break-in violates both your home and your peace of mind. Although no lock, home security system, or other form of protection is foolproof, there are ways to discourage intruders.

LIGHT IT UP

A well-lit house is intimidating to intruders. You can use well-placed lights to protect your home.

■ Install outdoor lamps on both sides of the front door. If one bulb blows out, the other will probably still be working.

■ Install low path lighting and floodlights that automatically come on when motion is detected. If an intruder approaches your house, the lights will go on, putting the person in the spotlight and letting you know someone is out there. They are also useful for lighting your way should you return home after dark.

■ Attach a timer device or a photosensor to your front-door light and one or two low-volt indoor lights so that the lights will come on when you are not there. Choose timing that reflects your normal daily movements through the house—for example, a living room light may come on at 7:00 P.M. and go out at 11:00 P.M., a kitchen light may go on at 6:00 A.M. and off at 8:00 A.M.

> **In addition to good lighting, visibility from the street makes a home more secure. Prune low branches on trees so that windows and entrances can be seen.**

LOCK IT UP

■ Choose secure door locks. A doorknob lock is flimsy and easy to break. Install a dead-bolt in addition to the door-knob lock on every entrance.

■ The best lock in the world won't do any good on a hollow or flimsy door. Choose a solid wood or metal door that opens in, not out, so that the hinges are on the inside. If there are windows near the door, install grills that make it impossible to break the glass and reach the doorknob.

■ If you live on the first floor or near a fire escape in an apartment building, install security gates on the windows. These are available in decorative patterns that make them less prisonlike.

■ For sliding glass doors, use a security bar as well as a door lock. A broomstick or board (at least one inch thick) will work, or buy a specially made bar equipped with a light and an alarm.

■ If the garage is attached to your house, keep its doors closed and locked at all times. If you have an automatic garage door opener, unplug the unit and padlock the garage when you go away for more than a day or two.

■ Windows should also have secure locks. On double-hung windows, make your own lock by drilling through the top of the bottom window into the bottom of the top window and inserting a nail or bolt through the hole.

PLAY IT SAFE

■ Do not leave valuables out in plain sight, especially near a large window. Choose an unlikely place, such as a food freezer or flour bin, to hide irreplaceable items. Avoid predictable places, such as under the bed, in the underwear drawer, or in a closet.

■ Never open your door unless you know who is knocking. Install a peephole so that you will not need to crack the door to see who is there.

■ If you don't recognize the person, do not open the door until you have seen proper identification. Don't be fooled by a uniform—ask the person to pass an ID card under the door or through the mail slot.

■ Even if the person has a uniform and an ID card, it's a good idea to telephone the company involved before opening the door. If the company cannot confirm that your caller is legitimate, phone the police.

When recording a message for your answering machine, never say that you are out or when you will be home. Simply state that you are not able to come to the phone. Turn down the ringer on your phone so that it cannot be heard from outside the house.

SECURITY SYSTEMS

Home security is a major growth industry. If you decide to buy a security system, shop carefully.

■ Choose a system that fits your needs and is not overly sensitive. Some systems can be set off by a draft, a pet, or even a ray of sunlight coming through a window.

■ Look for a system that offers a relay station to notify the police or fire department of a break-in or fire, as well as setting off an audible alarm. If you have this notification feature, be extra careful to eliminate false alarms. In some areas, the police will not respond after a house has had three or more false alarms.

■ Don't buy a system unless it comes with a maintenance contract and money-back guarantee in case it is faulty or not suited to your home.

■ Make sure the system is well concealed. If a burglar can look in the window to see how the system works, he or she may figure out how to disable it.

KEEP IN TOUCH

■ Keep a memory telephone by the bed. Program in numbers of the police and fire departments, a neighbor, and other important telephone numbers in case of an emergency.

■ Get to know your neighbors, and let them get to know you—especially if they are home when you are not. The best security system is a neighbor who knows your normal routine and is able to notice when things are amiss.

■ Join your neighborhood or block association. If there isn't one, then start it yourself.

■ Acquaint yourself with your police or security patrol officers. Some precincts have crime-prevention programs that residents can join. Others offer home security checks and advice.

IF YOU HEAR AN INTRUDER

Although you may not want to think about it, it's a good idea to have a plan for what to do should you hear a burglar in your home.

■ If possible, make a hasty exit. You can call the police from a neighbor's house.

■ If you are alone, shout as if you are warning other family members. If possible, stomp around in different rooms and slam doors to make it sound as if there are several people in the house. Few burglars want to rob a full house.

WHEN YOU GO AWAY

To help keep your house secure while you're away, make it look as though someone is there.

■ Don't close all the curtains and shades. If you were there, you'd want some light.

■ Cancel newspaper and mail delivery or have a neighbor pick up your papers and mail each day. Ask a friend to check the house regularly, perhaps turning some lights on or off or moving papers around inside to show signs of activity.

■ In addition to light timers, attach a timer to a radio in the kitchen and living room. Set them to go on at various times during the day.

■ Find someone to maintain your yard. An unmowed lawn and unshoveled walk or driveway indicate that you've gone away.

■ Leave your car in the driveway, or have your neighbors park their car there while you're gone. If you park your car at the airport or train station, remove from it all receipts and materials that list your address.

Leave a rake or other garden tool out when you are away. This makes it look as though someone has been around recently.

For most people, enjoying the waters of Havasu Falls *would be part of an exotic vacation, but for these teenagers, it's a common experience. They live near the falls, in the Grand Canyon, with other members of the Havasupai society of American Indians.*

CHAPTER 7

THE GREAT OUTDOORS

We are all attracted by the beauty of nature. Its forests, mountains, rivers, lakes, deserts, and other wonders invite exploration. They can make us forget the powerful forces that should command our profound respect—for nature, of course, can be dangerous.

You're already familiar with some of these dangers. If you grew up near the ocean, for example, you learned how to avoid rip currents and undertows. But you may not have learned how to avoid snakes and bears when in the wilderness. New situations require new information.

Human beings have created another hazard—environmental pollution. Each of us must try to counteract this problem; by keeping the great outdoors as pristine as possible, we can continue to delight in its riches.

Stay on the trail *when you hike: you'll protect both yourself and the surrounding land, which may be vulnerable to erosion.*

AROUND THE YARD AND GARDEN

Backyards and patios are personal oases where families can relax and enjoy the outdoors. Make sure that yours are safe for everyone.

BACKYARD BARBECUE

■ Place the barbecue grill on a sturdy surface, away from the house, shrubs, branches, and other flammable objects.

■ To avoid the noxious fumes and dangers associated with lighter fluid, use a charcoal chimney—available at most hardware stores—to ignite your coals. Never spray lighter fluid on a lit fire, even if the fire appears to have gone out.

■ Keep a continuous watch on the barbecue-grill fire, and make sure children and pets remain at a safe distance.

■ Don't wear loose clothing that can catch fire. To keep your fingers from getting burned, use long-handled tools and a flame-resistant fireplace mitt.

■ Keep buckets of sand or dirt beside the grill, especially when barbecuing meat—fat dripping from the meat can cause flames to shoot up. If any flames become dangerously high, smother them with the sand or dirt, or use a fire extinguisher.

■ When you're finished barbecuing, make sure the fire is completely extinguished; to be on the safe side, use both water and sand.

■ Don't attempt to barbecue when it's windy—a gust of wind can spread sparks and start a fire.

■ If you use a propane barbecue, check the gas orifices and air-mixing chambers before lighting. These often become plugged with insects or debris, leading to a flare-up or an explosion.

GARDEN AND POWER TOOLS

A hoe or spade left lying about can easily cause an accident. Proper storage of tools not only makes them last longer but can also prevent injuries.

■ If there are children around, store garden knives and other hazardous tools and materials in a locked cabinet.

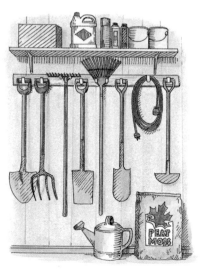

■ Otherwise, hang tools up whenever possible. For small tools, use a pegboard and hooks or a row of nails hammered into the wall. Use a barrel or sturdy hooks to store rakes and other large tools. When hanging large objects, make sure the nail is fastened securely into a stud, not just dry wall. Turn any pointed or sharp objects, such as pitchforks, toward the wall. Make sure anything hanging on the wall is out of the line of traffic.

■ Before using a power tool, read the instructions carefully. Some tools come with several different blades; pick the right one for the task at hand, and check that it is properly attached.

■ Never refuel gas-powered equipment while the engine is hot. If the engine has been running, let it cool for at least 10 minutes before refueling.

■ Don't use electric gardening tools—such as mowers, post-hole diggers, and hedge trimmers—after a rainfall or heavy dew. The wetness increases the chance of electrocution. For extra protection, even on dry days, make sure your tools are plugged into an outdoor outlet equipped with a built-in circuit breaker; use a three-pronged extension cord designed for outdoor use.

■ Wear the proper clothing and protective gear—sturdy shoes, gloves, long pants, and safety goggles—when using power garden tools. Do not wear loose clothing that can get caught in spinning parts. Also use earplugs when working with noisy equipment.

■ Always use two hands when operating a hedge trimmer. Don't trim where you can't see—if you hit metal or another object, a fragment could come flying back at you. If you are on a ladder, make sure it is steady and secure before turning on the trimmer.

■ When using a brush cutter or weed whip, wear heavy boots or shoes to protect your feet. Don't operate the machine close to fences or other objects.

LAWN MOWING

■ Before you mow the lawn, clear it of toys, rocks, garden hoses, sticks, and debris. Keep children and pets away from the mower while it is in use. (The same goes for power rototillers.)

■ Check the age of your power mower. Recent models have a special safety feature that stops the blade when you release the mower control bar. Make sure that this safety feature, called a dead man's switch, is working, and have the mower serviced on a regular basis.

■ When using a walk-behind mower, mow across slopes and keep all four wheels on the ground at all times. When using a riding mower, mow up and down slopes. Avoid starting, stopping, or turning your riding mower while you are on a slope.

■ The blades are not the only dangerous part of a mower; the muffler gets extremely hot. Stand directly behind the mower to avoid the line of fire

---

Understanding a Pesticide Label

All pesticide labels in Canada contain important information that conforms with the Pest Control Products (PCP) Act. Make sure that you read the label carefully before using the product:

Principal Display Panel. The most visible label, it shows the product name in large letters, as well as the product's designated use (domestic, commercial, restricted, or manufacturing). It also displays the appropriate precautionary symbols (for a poison, a flammable substance, an explosive, a corrosive or an irritant). If you see the words *danger* or *poison*, the product is potentially lethal. *Caution* denotes a less toxic substance that is still capable of causing injury or death. A product labeled "warning" falls somewhere in between.

Directions to read the label before using the pesticide are given, and a Guarantee statement. Each active ingredient is listed by its common name, or its chemical name when it has no common one.

In addition, the registration number, the product's net contents in metric units, and the name and address of the company registering the product are given.

Secondary Display Panel. This label is printed in smaller type. It gives detailed directions for the use of the pesticide, including the pests it kills and the plants it should be used on. It also contains precautionary information about storage and handling, and details of the hazards to people, wildlife, or the environment that may result from the use of the product.

First aid instructions are given, in the event of poisoning, intoxication or injury by the product. Toxicological information is provided, for the treatment of anyone harmed by the product.

A notice to the user declares that the product must be used in strict accordance with the directions on the label, and that not to do so is an offense under the Pest Control Products Act.

---

from the discharge chute.

■ Try not to leave power mowers, tillers, and other such equipment outdoors. Rain and heat can damage motors, making them less safe to use. If you don't have a toolshed or garage, cover the equipment with a waterproof tarpaulin or sturdy plastic.

PROPER USE OF PESTICIDES

No pesticide is 100 percent safe; even common products like 2,4-D, malathion, benomyl, and diazinon have been linked to a wide range of disorders in sensitive individuals, including an increased risk of cancer. Pesticides also kill beneficial insects and so, over time, may actually make your garden more susceptible to disease. If you must use pesticides in your yard or garden, take the following precautions to be as safe as possible.

■ Avoid overkill. Identify the

pest or disease you want to eradicate, and then choose a product designed for that problem. Ask your local authority or a garden-supply dealer for advice.

■ Read the label carefully before buying a pesticide. Make sure it bears the manufacturer's phone number for emergency information.

■ Buy only the amount you think you'll use in the next month or two. Long-term storage of pesticides is not recommended because even a well-sealed container can leak, and any evaporation alters the pesticide's strength. If you must store a pesticide, put it in a locked cabinet in an area away from food, first-aid supplies, and cleansers. Leave it in the original container; for extra protection against leakage, place the entire container inside an airtight plastic container. Save all instructions and warning labels.

■ When transporting a pesticide home from the store, put it in the trunk of your car and make sure that it can't be knocked over if you should make a sudden stop.

■ Be certain that you use the proper formulation for diluting a concentrated pesticide.

■ Apply pesticides on a still day to lessen the chance that the wind will carry the chemicals elsewhere. Warn your neighbors that you will be using the chemical, and ask them to notify you any time they plan to use pesticides in their yards.

■ Remove toys, lawn furniture, and barbecue grills from the area, or carefully cover them with plastic. Also cover pools or ponds, especially ponds that contain fish.

■ Keep children indoors or send them elsewhere to play when the pesticides are applied. Check the instructions to see when the area will be safe for humans and pets— some products require only a few hours, but others are not safe until after it rains.

■ Close the windows of your house or car if they are near the area to be treated. Avoid spraying near a well or other water supply.

■ Use only the amount needed, and apply it just to the area affected by the pest or disease. Make a special effort to avoid bird's nests and flowering plants frequented by bees and other beneficial insects or birds.

■ Wear rubber gloves, a long-sleeved shirt, long pants, and a hat while applying pesticides. Choose rubber or vinyl shoes rather than those made of canvas, leather, or other permeable materials. Wearing a mask and goggles may also be a good idea. If possible, remove outer clothing and shoes before entering the house, and wash them separately from other laundry. An extra rinse cycle will remove any residue from the washer. Discard clothing that is doused with the chemical.

■ After applying the pesticide, thoroughly rinse the tools you've used. Then take a shower, carefully washing your skin and hair.

■ Be cautious when disposing of pesticides, even if the container is empty. The label will give you instructions, or you can contact your local health department. Some neighborhoods have a designated pickup area for pesticides and other hazardous chemicals. Never pour leftover pesticides down the sink or toilet, and never burn pesticide containers or place them in an incinerator.

If you use a lawn-service company, find out what chemicals it uses. Also ask if a chemical-free service is available—one based on natural pest-management methods.

PESTICIDE ALTERNATIVES

Here are ways to reduce infestations of common garden pests and plant diseases.

■ Choose grass seed and plant varieties designed for your climate and altitude. These are more likely to produce healthy, disease- and pest-resistant plants.

■ Try companion planting. Certain herbs and flowers have a protective effect on vegetable plants. For example, marigolds planted near carrots may protect them against carrot rust flies. Basil, coriander, thyme, and other kinds of herbs repel other pests.

■ Cut the grass by only one-third of its length each time. This inhibits weed growth and promotes a healthier lawn.

■ Don't overwater; many pests and plant diseases thrive on extra moisture. Let your lawn or garden become moderately dry before watering.

■ Test your soil every few years to find out what nutrients and minerals are lacking. The proper balance of soil nutrients renders lawns and gardens less susceptible to pests and diseases.

■ Make sure your vegetable seeds are virus-free. If you had a problem with any plants last year, buy new seeds for this year's garden. Some seed companies offer disease-resistant strains; choose these whenever possible.

■ Plant a bit more in your vegetable garden than you think you'll need. Then if bugs or animals get some of the vegetables, your garden won't be a total loss.

■ Attract beneficial bugs and animals. Bees, ladybugs, fireflies, spiders, lacewings, and other insects prey on less desirable bugs. Frogs and toads also eat bugs. Although releasing beneficial insects into a garden is rarely effective, you can encourage the bugs that are already there by not using pesticides.

■ If destructive bugs become a problem, try sprinkling baking soda, garlic juice, hot pepper, or soapy water (use phosphate-free soap) in the area. These ingredients discourage many pests and are not harmful to plants or people.

■ Bugs avoid areas where others of their kind have died. Try collecting dead pests, mashing them with some water, and brushing the paste onto leaves to discourage other bugs from preying on your plants.

■ Make your own traps for slugs and earwigs with jar lids filled with stale beer; sink them into the ground near your plants. Trap whiteflies by smearing a board with sticky molasses.

■ To remove Japanese beetles from your plants, flick them into a wide-mouthed glass jar containing bleach, soapy water, or another household cleanser.

■ For problem areas, try an organic solution, such as microbial insecticides (*Bacillus thuringiensis*, or BT, for example) and nematodes (microscopic worms). These products are available through garden stores and catalogs. BT is especially effective against cabbageworms, and nematodes are recommended for cutworms.

Plant at the right time of year for the particular type of plant. A healthy start is the best defense for any growing thing.

DISCOURAGING ANIMAL RAIDERS

Deer, rabbits, raccoons, and other animals are notorious for ruining yard and garden plants. Try these methods to keep them at bay.

■ Many animals are repelled by the smell of blood. Sprinkle dried blood, which is sold as a fertilizer in garden and farm stores, around the edge of your garden and around favorite plants.

■ To keep deer from munching on your shrubs, cover the plants with fine netting. Many garden stores carry barely visible dark-green netting that does not interfere with the plant's appearance.

■ Enlist mock predators. A rubber king snake or blacksnake deters rodents and rabbits, as does a life-size, plastic great horned owl.

■ Hinder, a product made from ammonia esters, has an odor that discourages deer, rabbits, and raccoons from eating plants. Spray it on new plants before the animals acquire a taste for them. The product, available in most garden stores, is nontoxic and safe for plants and pets.

■ To keep chipmunks and squirrels from raiding your tulip or hyacinth bulbs, try planting cloves of garlic in the same hole as the bulbs. Or plant daffodils, which are repellent to animals, nearby. If these measures fail, cover the bulb garden with chicken wire; the mesh allows the plant shoots to grow but prevents animals from digging up the bulbs.

POISONOUS PLANTS

Most people are familiar with poison ivy, but they often don't know about poison oak, poison sumac, and other toxic plants that may be growing in their yards or nearby. Learn how to spot these plants and what to do about them.

POISON IVY, OAK, AND SUMAC

Poison ivy, which grows mainly east of the Rockies, is one of the most common poisonous plants. Poison oak, found mostly in the West, and poison sumac, found mostly in the American Southeast, are less common. All contain urushiol, an oily resin in the plant sap that causes an itchy rash.

Poison oak

Poison sumac

Poison ivy

■ "Leaves of three, let it be" is a common admonition for avoiding poison ivy, but it's not quite that simple. Poison ivy blooms in springtime and bears white berries in the late summer. Depending on the time of year, it may have more than three leaves, and they may be shiny or dull, red or green. In winter, when the vines have no identifying leaves, the plant is still poisonous.

■ Poison oak also has three leaves together, but they are lobed at the edges, and the plant usually grows as a shrub rather than a vine.

■ Poison sumac is a small tree or shrub that has pairs of pointed leaves. Apart from the American Southeast, it also thrives in freshwater wetlands in northern areas.

■ There is a wide range of sensitivity to urushiol; some people can handle plants that contain it without having any reaction, while others have a severe reaction at the slightest contact. Even if you haven't had problems in the past, don't assume that you're immune. Remember, too, that a reaction may occur immediately or take up to 25 days to develop.

■ If you suspect that you have come in contact with poison ivy, oak, or sumac, wash the affected area thoroughly with cold water and a strong soap or detergent, such as dishwashing liquid. After you have cleaned the skin in this way, apply rubbing alcohol to the area to remove any remaining sap.

■ You can spread urushiol to other parts of the body not by scratching the affected area but by touching the sap on pets, clothes, garden tools, or other objects, often long after the initial exposure.

Immediately after any possible contact with poison ivy, wash tools and launder clothing in hot, soapy water. Make sure children change clothes after hiking or playing in an area that might have poison ivy. Shampoo pets that may have touched the plant.

GETTING RID OF POISON IVY

■ The safest way to kill poison ivy is with a systemic herbicide that contains triclopyr. It may take several days and several applications for the vine to die. Follow the directions on the package, and make sure you apply it only to the poison ivy.

■ Even when the poison ivy plant is dormant in winter, or dead, the rash-causing urushiol persists. Whenever you remove vines that you haven't positively identified as safe, take precautions, as if they were poison ivy.

■ Large poison ivy vines that climb up a tree or building should be cut at the bottom and treated with an herbicide. Wear gloves when cutting the vines, and be sure to wash all tools and clothes thoroughly after you are finished.

■ Never burn poison ivy or any other urushiol-containing plant. If you do, you may inhale the poison in the smoke, which can cause a severe lung reaction. Instead, seal the plants in a plastic bag and discard the bag with other trash headed for a landfill.

● ●

Mango rind, ginkgo nut, cashew shells, and poisonwood branches contain oleoresins similar to urushiol. For some people, contact with these may cause a rash similar to that of poison ivy.

● ●

TREATING A RASH

■ If a rash appears, use cold compresses and calamine lotion to relieve itching. Most cases clear up by themselves in one to two weeks.

■ You can also use nonprescription hydrocortisone creams for a rash; apply five or six times a day, including after washing or bathing. Don't use antihistamine lotions, and be careful about using over-the-counter analgesic creams—some may actually make a poison ivy rash worse. Products containing menthol, camphor, or alcohol may burn if the rash has developed into sores.

■ If the rash becomes severe or infection develops, see a doctor; a prescription cortisone preparation or oral steroids may help.

CHILDPROOFING YOUR YARD

■ Teach children not to eat any plant or berry without first checking with you.

■ If you have young children (or pets), plant only nontoxic flowers. If you already have poisonous plants or flowers, remove them from the children's play area and transplant them in a fenced-off section of the yard.

■ Remove stinging nettles by pulling them up. Be sure to wear long pants, a long-sleeved shirt, gloves, socks, and work shoes to avoid contact with the plant.

PLANT POISONING

■ Since many plants are poisonous, be cautious when making your own herbal teas, especially from wild plants. Many plants look alike, so that what you think is a harmless herb may actually be toxic.

■ Don't store poisonous bulbs, such as daffodils or narcissi, in the refrigerator or root cellar. They may be mistaken for onions or shallots, with dire consequences.

■ The symptoms of plant poisoning range from a burning sensation in the mouth to abdominal pain, vomiting, rapid heartbeat, and, in severe cases, hallucinations, coma, and death.

■ If you know or suspect that someone has ingested a poisonous plant, call your local poison control center or hospital for guidance immediately; see page 421 for further instructions. If you go to the hospital, take along a sample of the plant, if you have it.

Common Poisonous Plants

Poison ivy, oak, and sumac are not the only poisonous plants found in yards and gardens. Some plants are poisonous when touched; they include four o'clock, sagebrush, stinging nettles, and yew. The following plants or plant parts are toxic when ingested, and those marked with asterisks are especially dangerous.

Apple seeds (in quantity)

Caladiums

Cherry pits (in quantity)

Daffodil bulb

Delphiniums

*Dumbcane (or Dieffenbachia)

Elephant ears

*English ivy

Foxglove

Holly leaves and berries

Jack-in-the-pulpit leaves

Jerusalem cherry

Lily of the valley

Mistletoe berry

Morning glory seeds

*Nightshade (or Belladonna), especially berries

Oleander

Philodendron

*Poinsettia

*Poisonous mushrooms, especially *Amanita*

Poppy berries

Potato sprouts, roots, and vines

Rhododendron

Rhubarb leaves

Spider plant

LIVING WITH INSECTS AND ARACHNIDS

Insects, the most numerous of the world's creatures, play a vital role in maintaining our environment. Since insects and arachnids can also be annoying (and even harmful) to humans, here are some suggestions for dealing with them.

STINGING INSECTS

Bees, wasps, hornets, yellow jackets, and some stinging ants are members of the Hymenoptera order of insects. Their venom causes pain and itching in most humans, and some people are so sensitive that a single sting can be fatal (see "Allergic Reactions," page 391).

■ If you are hypersensitive to bee venom, wear a medical identification bracelet (or pendant or card) and ask your doctor about getting an emergency kit for insect stings.

■ If you are hypersensitive but must work around bees, talk to your doctor about desensitization. This involves weekly shots of small amounts of bee venom to help your body build up a tolerance for it.

■ A honeybee can sting only once, but wasps, yellow jackets, and other bees can sting repeatedly. If you are stung, move away as quickly as possible. The bees may follow for a short distance, but they usually do not go far.

....

Don't try to blow away a bee that has landed on your skin. Bees are more likely to sting when agitated by moving air. Just remain still until it leaves.

....

■ Be very wary of disturbing a nest of fire ants, which are common in the southern United States. A species called red imported fire ants builds dirt mounds up to two feet high. An angry swarm of these ants can sting thousands of times in a matter of seconds. If stung, seek immediate medical attention.

■ For treatment of stings, see page 390.

MOSQUITOES

Bites from most mosquitoes native to Canada are simply itchy and annoying—unless an allergic reaction occurs (see page 391). Although it may be difficult to rid your property of mosquitoes, you can reduce the population.

■ Mosquitoes require stagnant water to lay their eggs. Try to eliminate water that collects in the yard, trash area, and other places near the house. Store wheelbarrows and planters on end, empty wading pools regularly, and fill in ruts in grass and concrete that collect water.

■ Put goldfish or other small minnows, which eat mosquito larvae, in ornamental pools.

■ Make sure your roof and gutters are draining water properly; flat roofs are a particular problem in this regard. Clean leaves and other debris out of gutters to keep the water flowing.

■ Install screens on all windows in your house, and make sure they do not have any holes or gaps. Use screens with a very fine mesh. Make sure that doors and windows close tightly to prevent mosquitoes and other insects from finding their way inside your house.

■ If you have enough open land, put up a purple-martin birdhouse. Each bird eats thousands of mosquitoes every day. Swallows are also voracious mosquito predators.

■ Light citronella candles or lanterns around your patio or porch to ward off mosquitoes.

■ Eating a lot of garlicky foods

may ward off mosquitoes; however, it may keep people away as well!

■ For treatment of mosquito bites, see page 390.

REPELLING INSECTS SAFELY

■ Check the label before using an old bottle of insect repellent. Registration of the ingredient R-11—also known as 2,3,4,5-Bis (2 butylene) tetrahydro-2-furaldehyde—has been canceled, since studies suggest it may be a carcinogen. If you find a bottle containing this ingredient, return it to the supplier. Dispose of any opened bottle with your household waste. Wrapping it in layers of newspaper beforehand is not necessary.

■ DEET is a highly effective insect repellent. However, it commonly causes an allergic reaction and can, when overused or misused, cause neurological harm to children. If you choose to use a DEET repellent, select one with a low concentration of the chemical (35 percent or less) and apply the preparation to your exposed skin. For added protection, apply a permethrin product, which will not stain, to clothing. After coming indoors, wash the DEET off your skin.

■ You can use DEET products of less than 35 percent sparingly on a young child, but do so only when necessary. Apply it over another cream, such as a sunscreen, for maximum protection and minimum absorption. To protect the head and neck, you can spray a head net with permethrin and drape it over a brimmed

hat. Skip the hands, which may end up in the mouth.

■ Try natural repellents, such as oil of citronella, peppermint, pennyroyal, or spearmint. Don't rub full-strength oils on your skin, because they can be quite irritating. Instead, dilute them in a vegetable oil or apply the essence to your clothing.

■ You can also try rubbing vinegar or a whole onion plant (if you and your friends can stand the smell) on your skin.

■ Avoid insect electrocutors—those purple lights that attract and then kill insects. Studies have shown that people who have them suffer no fewer bites from insects than those who don't have them. The ultraviolet light may actually cause more bugs than usual to fly into your yard, and, once there, the bugs are attracted more to you than to your insect electrocutor. These devices also kill beneficial insects.

■ Try Skin-So-Soft (by Avon). This bath oil is not manufactured to prevent insect bites and contains no known repellent ingredients. Nevertheless, it has gained a reputation as an excellent bug repellent among outdoors enthusiasts. Researchers speculate that it may work for some people because of an element in their skin chemistry that combines with the oil to prevent bites.

· ·

Never apply insect repellents to broken or irritated skin. You will be more likely to have an adverse reaction to the chemicals.

· ·

AN OUNCE OF PREVENTION

You may be able to prevent insect infestations and bites by making yourself and your property less attractive to the creatures. Try the following suggestions.

■ Remember that where there are fruit trees, flowers, clover, or food, there are bound to be bees. Be extra careful after a rainstorm or in summer, when bees are most prevalent.

■ Avoid wearing bright colors and prints, as well as scented lotions and perfumes, when outdoors. Hair spray, scented soaps, and aftershave lotion also attract insects.

■ Wasps and other stinging insects are attracted to sweet liquids, such as juice and soda. Keep drink cups covered and use a straw. Always check the cup before you drink—a bee sting in the mouth is dangerous because swelling can block your airway. Also keep food covered at picnics.

■ Always wear shoes when you are outdoors, especially when walking in grass.

■ Keep insects away from your house by installing barriers of sand or concrete around the foundation of the building. On the other side of the barrier, plant different shrubs and plants to attract a variety of insects, rather than an infestation of one type.

■ Avoid using chemical pesticides, which kill beneficial insects just as easily as detrimental ones and can also be harmful to humans (see "Proper Use of Pesticides," page 227).

■ Many plants help repel insects. Put a stand of tansy near doors and windows to deter mosquitoes from flying inside. Basil, placed in windowboxes or around a deck or patio, may also ward off biting bugs.

SPIDERS

These arachnids help control the mosquito, roach, and cricket population, so it's usually best to let them be. Very few species are dangerous, and most spiders will not bite unless they or their webs are disturbed. You can therefore take measures to keep from being bitten by a spider.

■ Check shoes and clothes that have been kept in storage before putting them on.

■ Wear gloves when rummaging through boxes, especially those in the garage and attic. Also wear gloves when doing yard work.

■ Be careful around tree stumps and woodpiles.

■ If you must get rid of spiders, use a broad-spectrum insecticide. It's best to spray spiders directly, but if you cannot do this, spray the area where you frequently see them.

■ For information on the symptoms and treatment of spider bites, see page 389.

SCORPIONS

Scorpions have stingers at the end of their tails, and some species have a potentially lethal venom. If you visit an area with scorpions, such as the American Southwest, take the suggestions below.

■ Be careful when in or near such damp, cool places as basements and woodpiles.

■ Remember that since scorpions tend to be nocturnal, they are most likely to sting in the evening.

■ Check the insides of your shoes before putting them on.

■ If you are not sure whether you have been stung by a scorpion, be aware of the following symptoms (you may have one or more): burning pain at the site, numbness and tingling in the area, stomach pain, nausea, vomiting, muscle spasms, blurred vision, slurred speech, difficulty breathing or swallowing, shock, convulsions, and coma.

■ If you are stung, keep the area lower than the heart, put a cold compress on it, and get medical help at once.

TICKS

Ticks are parasites that live on the blood of mammals. Their bites are relatively painless, but the diseases ticks carry—such as Rocky Mountain spotted fever and Lyme disease—can be serious. Find out what ticks live in the area you are traveling in, and what diseases they may transmit.

■ Cover up when venturing into tick-infested areas, especially woods, grassy meadows, and anywhere that deer are prevalent. Wear long-sleeved shirts and pants; tuck pant legs into your socks; and put on a hat. Light-colored clothes make it easier to spot ticks.

■ When outdoors, check yourself, your children, and your pets frequently for ticks. Ticks may wander about on clothing or skin before finding a spot (often on hair-covered or moist skin) to settle in.

■ When you come inside or back to your campsite, examine yourself and your children more carefully. Use two mirrors to inspect your back and head; these are two favorite spots for ticks.

■ If you find a tick, carefully remove it with tweezers; see page 390 for instructions. Specially designed "tick tweezers" are best, but any type will do.

Ticks require several hours to become firmly attached, so take a shower and shampoo your hair as soon as you come indoors. This will wash away any ticks that are not yet affixed to your skin.

THE HIKER'S DISEASE

"Lyme disease is a complex topic that has raised a lot of anger, hostility, resentment, and anxiety."
—Leonard H. Sigal, M.D.

• • • • • • •

Being an avid outdoorsman and wilderness lover made Roger Payne a prime candidate for Lyme disease.

When Roger Payne, a 33-year-old real estate appraiser, began waking up with stiff joints and sore muscles, he blamed his hard, lumpy mattress, which he promptly replaced. Weeks later, though, he was still waking with aches and stiffness. More troubling, he had difficulty concentrating and was tired by midday. "At that point," he recalls, "I went to see my doctor." His doctor was also mystified until Payne described his fondness for hiking and camping in upstate New York—a high-risk area for Lyme disease.

A disease of many faces. Payne's experience parallels that of many patients with Lyme disease, a bacterial infection spread by deer ticks in the American East and Midwest and black-legged ticks in the West. (The disease is rare in Canada.) A classic case of Lyme disease begins with a bite by an infected tick, followed a few weeks later by flulike symptoms and a red bull's-eye rash spreading outward from the bite. At that point the patient usually takes oral antibiotics, which wipe out the bacteria, leaving no residual symptoms. Without further treatment, however, the disease may progress, causing arthritis (often of the knee), numbness, tingling, facial paralysis, and other neurological disorders. Rare cases can even cause heart problems.

The trouble is that a number of Lyme patients fail to notice or even develop early symptoms, and treatment is more difficult—and controversial—if arthritis and other later symptoms develop. Some doctors recommend intravenous antibiotic therapy, which is costly and carries a high risk of adverse side effects. Other doctors advocate oral antibiotics. Symptoms may linger for several weeks after treatment. As the body heals, however, these symptoms should disappear. This is what happened in Roger Payne's case. After eight weeks of oral amoxicillin, he felt better and declined to undergo intravenous therapy for lingering aches and fatigue. Within a few months he was symptom-free.

A few patients, however, continue to experience severe, sometimes debilitating symptoms. These patients argue that, contrary to the opinions of infectious-disease experts, they have a chronic Lyme infection that requires prolonged intravenous therapy, a treatment only a handful of physicians now prescribe.

Focus on prevention. The issue of who does—and does not—have Lyme disease may soon be put to rest with the development of improved diagnostic tests. Or the disease may be prevented entirely by vaccines, two of which are being tested in volunteers living in areas with high rates of the disease.

In the meantime, researchers emphasize that the threat of Lyme disease should not discourage people from enjoying the outdoors, even in high-risk areas. Infection can almost always be prevented through simple precautions (see the facing page for ways to protect yourself).❑

ANIMALS IN THE WILD

Spotting wildlife is surely one of the great pleasures of being outdoors. However, some wild animals carry diseases that can infect humans, and others are danger- ous themselves, so enjoy them from afar.

BEAR FACTS

As we encroach more and more on the natural habitat of bears, we increase the likeli- hood of coming into contact with them. Use the following advice to protect yourself should you ever encounter a bear in the wild or elsewhere.

■ When hiking in bear territo- ry, make plenty of noise. This will let the animals know that you're coming. Bears are nat- urally shy creatures; they will generally attempt to stay out of your way.

■ If you're in a national or state park, check in with park rangers. They know where bears are likely to be, and they can give you safety pointers.

■ Bears, who are always hun- gry, know that campsites are good foraging grounds. Never keep food in your tent; instead, put it in the trunk of your car. If you must leave food anywhere else in the car, make sure all windows are tightly sealed; a bear can get its claws into even a tiny slit and tear out a window to get at the food. You may want to purchase bear-proof containers (available in some camping-goods stores).

■ Conventional wisdom says to hoist your food out of reach in a tall tree, but expert campers scoff at this advice. Black bears can climb trees— so can raccoons and other camp raiders. If you can't stow food in a car, seal it in plastic to eliminate odor, and take it away from the campsite. (Bears are used to foraging around camps but are unlikely to hunt for a food pack that they can't smell.) Some parks provide high racks for storing food out of bears' reach; you can also hang food containers from a rope suspended be- tween trees at a height of at least 15 feet.

■ Bear cubs may look cuddly and playful, and they often approach humans. But be wary—cubs always have a watchful mother nearby, and she'll attack if she thinks her young are in danger. Sows often send their cubs up a tree for safety, so if you see a cub in a tree, be sure to keep your distance.

■ If you surprise a bear, don't panic. Bears don't see well, so they may come close sim- ply to satisfy their curiosity. Talk to the bear in an author- itative tone while slowly backing away. Don't make eye contact, and don't turn your back on the bear. Above all, don't run away. Running invites a bear to give chase, and you can't outrun a bear.

■ If the bear is holding its ground or becoming menac- ing, plan your next move carefully. Bears are very un- predictable, but if the animal is making clacking, woofing, or hiccuping sounds, the situation is getting dangerous. If you see a tall tree nearby, you might try climbing it, but be aware that a black bear can come after you and a grizzly might try to shake you out of the tree.

■ If you are charged by a griz- zly bear, drop to the ground and roll into a fetal position with your head tucked in and your hands clasped behind your neck. Play dead, even if the bear sniffs you. Most times, the grizzly will check you out and then look for something more interesting. This is not true, however, of a black bear, so don't use this tactic with this type of bear.

OTHER ANIMALS

Although bears are probably the most dangerous animals you may encounter in the wild, you should avoid certain others as well.

■ Almost all mother animals will fight to protect their young. Enjoy watching fawns and other baby animals at a distance, but be sure not to block the mother's view of her offspring.

■ In cougar country, travel in groups and never leave chil- dren alone. Cougars rarely attack adults, but several children have been mauled in the West in recent years.

■ Be wary of a wild animal that approaches you or appears sick or hurt. If an animal is injured, send for a park ranger or veterinarian.

■ Aside from hanging a bird feeder, resist the temptation to feed wild animals. Doing so encourages them to rely on humans for food, instead of foraging on their own.

For the most part, wolves, coyotes, foxes, deer, and other wild animals do not make good pets, since they are highly unpredictable and impossible or difficult to train. Stick with dogs, cats, and other truly domesticated animals.

RABIES ALERT

In recent years, an epidemic of rabies, especially among raccoons, has moved steadily northward into southern Ontario and Quebec. Rabies is a deadly disease, but there are steps you can take to keep yourself and your pets from contracting it. (For additional information, see page 389.)

■ Have all pets, as well as horses and other domesticated animals, immunized against rabies. A single shot, followed by yearly boosters, confers immunity.

■ If your pet gets into a fight with a raccoon or other animal that might have rabies, use extra caution in treating it. Even if your pet is immune to rabies, you can contract it from the attacker's saliva. Wear heavy rubber gloves to handle

the pet. Wrap it in a sheet or blanket, and take it to the vet.

■ Be alert to any unusual animal behavior, a common sign of rabies. For example, raccoons and bats are nocturnal animals, so one that is out during the day may be infected. Be especially leery if a raccoon tries to follow you or if it is staggering or appears disoriented.

■ If you are bitten by a raccoon or other wild animal, seek immediate medical attention, even if the wound is minor. If rabies is suspected, get preventive shots as soon as possible. Rabies is nearly always fatal once symptoms begin, usually two or three weeks after exposure.

■ If you can safely corner the animal, do so, being careful not to destroy it. Contact your local health department; it can study the animal to determine whether it is rabid.

Anyone who is frequently exposed to wild or stray animals should be immunized against rabies. The shots are similar to those given to animals, but they are formulated for human beings.

SNAKES

There is only one type of poisonous snake in Canada—the rattlesnake, which belongs to the family of venomous snakes called pit vipers. Almost all snakebites occur when people are careless and inadvertently step on a snake

or try to pick it up.

■ The three species of rattlesnake found in Canada are the Massasauga, the timber and the prairie rattlesnakes. They are normally shy, so you probably won't see one even in snake country. Nevertheless, keep a sharp eye out and listen for the warning rattle, especially in grassy, sandy, and desert areas.

■ If you do run into a rattlesnake and it coils, it's in striking position. Back away slowly and give the snake a chance to escape in the opposite direction. Snakes don't want to waste their venom on targets that are too big for them to eat, but they will strike to defend themselves.

■ If you are bitten, do whatever you can to get out of the snake's range. Most bites are on the hands or legs, and usually little or no venom is injected on the first bite. But you don't want to risk a second bite from an already frightened snake.

■ If venom has been injected, the area will burn and begin to swell almost immediately. Try to stay calm fear prompts the body to release extra adrenaline, which sends your heart racing, spreading the venom more rapidly. Get medical help as quickly as possible (see page 388).

POLLUTION CONCERNS

Despite the growing number of antipollution laws, environmental pollution remains a major problem throughout Canada. Still, there are measures each of us can take to protect ourselves and the environment.

AIR POLLUTION AND YOUR HEALTH

Air pollution comes in many forms—smog, acid rain, and toxic industrial emissions, among others. Follow these suggestions to minimize its effects on your health.

■ If you live in an area where smog is common, listen for pollution alerts on the radio and stay indoors as much as possible when levels are high. This is especially important for the elderly, people with heart or lung disorders, and young children. If you fall into one of these groups and must venture out, wear a facial mask specially designed to filter out ozone and other harmful pollutants (see box on facing page).

■ Refrain from exercising outdoors when there is heavy smog or during a pollution alert, especially if you have asthma, chronic bronchitis, or any other lung condition. Even when the air is clear, do your outdoor exercising before or well after rush hour to avoid exposure to heavy traffic pollution.

DRIVING CLEAN

Cars are a major source of air pollution, so it makes sense to start your conservation efforts by paying strict attention to your driving habits.

■ If you're buying a car, choose a fuel-efficient model.

To find out how a car rates, write to Transport Canada, Energy and Emissions Fuel Guide, 13th Floor, Canada Building, 344 Slater Street, Ottawa, Ontario K1A 0N5. The best performance noted in the guide is 5.4 litres/ 100 km. Small, lightweight cars use up to half the fuel of large, heavy models.

■ Decide whether you really need such options as air-conditioning and power steering, which add to your car's weight and fuel consumption. If you opt for air-conditioning, have it serviced regularly by a qualified technician. Many new cars sold now have CFC-free air-conditioning systems. The conversion to non-CFC systems will be completed in 1994 for models to be sold in the following years.

■ Select a light-colored car with tinted glass. It will stay cooler in hot weather.

■ Use radial tires, which improve fuel economy. For long-distance driving, inflate them

three or four pounds above the recommended pressure; this can save you up to 10 percent on gas. A word of caution, however: Overly inflated tires reduce traction and control, so don't go above your maximum pressure—check your car owner's manual. Also, let out some air when driving in the mountains or on slippery roads. Use a pressure gauge, checking while the tires are cold, not hot from driving. Make sure all tires are equally inflated.

■ When filling your gas tank, heed the pump's automatic shut-off signal—topping off the tank adds to air pollution as the spillage evaporates.

■ Use a high-quality multi-grade oil.

■ Keep your car properly maintained. Have it tuned every 5,000 to 10,000 kilometres or every six months— whichever comes first. Make sure brakes are properly adjusted, since dragging brakes will diminish fuel efficiency.

■ Turn off the engine if the car is idling for more than a few minutes. A car engine uses about a litre of gas for every half hour it idles.

■ To further increase fuel savings, avoid city driving and always select the shortest, least congested route to your destination. For neighborhood errands, consider walking or cycling—you'll both save fuel

PROBLEM POLLUTANTS

Environment Canada bases its air-quality standards on the first five common pollutants. The last, lead, may be a problem in homes built before the mid-1970s.

Pollutant	Where it comes from	What it does
Carbon monoxide	Odorless toxic gas from car exhaust and other combustion engines	Interferes with blood's ability to carry oxygen; can cause death
Ozone	Colorless, harmful gas in smog that is produced when gases of organic chemicals (hydrocarbons) combine with nitrogen dioxide	Causes lung inflammation, coughing, and chest pains
Nitrogen dioxide	Gas produced by burning of fossil fuels	Contributes to ozone production; forms acidic particles that irritate lung tissue
Sulfur dioxide	Gas produced by smelters, burning of coal, diesel fuel, and other fuels containing sulfur	Irritates lung tissue; can precipitate asthma attack
Particulate matter	Microscopic particles and liquid droplets produced by diesel engines, industrial furnaces, and earth-moving equipment	Irritates nasal passages and airways
Lead	Fumes from vapors and dust from paints and other materials that contain lead	Accumulates in body, resulting in mental impairment and damage to nerves, blood, and internal organs

and benefit from the exercise. If mass transit is available, use it whenever you can.

■ Joining a car pool could be your most efficient way to save fuel. Officials estimate that adding one passenger to each commuting car could save 125 million litres of gas each day.

OTHER WAYS TO CLEAR THE AIR

■ Avoid using aerosol consumer products. Even though they no longer contain CFC's, they are often a flammable hazard and can cause respiratory ailments. An added disadvantage of aerosols is that their containers are not recy-

clable. A common source of CFC's today is foam insulation (use cellulose fiber, gypsum, or foil-laminated board instead).

■ Have your air conditioner regularly cleaned and maintained by a qualified service technician. When buying a refrigerator or freezer, consider new models that do not use CFC's, which will be phased out by the year 2000. But also check on the safety of the replacement refrigerant because some refrigerants still damage the ozone layer.

■ If you are buying a fireplace or woodstove, choose one that meets EPA/CSA B415 smoke-emission standards. Such

stoves are efficient and clean. The fuel efficiency of these stoves comes from a catalytic combustor or advanced combustion device, which burns smoke. In British Columbia, avoid using stoves and fireplaces during No-burn Day alerts. However, EPA/CSA B415 stoves are exempted.

■ To help save forests, buy paper products (especially toilet and facial tissues) made from recycled paper. If your local market does not stock such products, ask the manager to order them, and let him or her know you are willing to shop elsewhere.

■ If possible, plant a tree. Trees absorb carbon dioxide and air pollutants and give off oxygen. If you are an apartment dweller without a plot of land, join a group that plants trees on streets and other public property, such as a block association or highway-beautification program.

■ Ask your provincial and federal representatives to support programs that promote clean air. Write letters and report violations to your provincial environment department.

WATER POLLUTION

Our water sources contain both natural and man-made contaminants, such as nitrates, chlorine compounds, pesticides, and industrial and agricultural chemicals. Some of these contaminants are dangerous; however, you can take steps to make sure your drinking water is safe (see "Lead in Your Water," page 207). You should also be careful about the water you swim in, bathe in, and cook with.

■ If you have a well or old plumbing, have your water tested by your local health or sanitation department. An on-site inspection by a sanitary engineer may also be advisable, especially if you have your own well and septic system. Wells should be upgrade and at least 50 feet from a septic tank and 100 feet from a cesspool.

■ Both septic tanks and wells should be properly constructed, with complete concrete liners and tight covers.

■ Avoid putting hazardous materials like paint and solvents down your drain; they may find their way into the water supply.

■ When camping or hiking, never drink directly from a stream, pond, or lake. To purify such water, boil it for 20 minutes or use iodine tablets or a micropore filter.

■ Be careful about swimming or boating in a freshwater pond or lake. Even if the water looks clean, it may be contaminated by bacteria or hazardous waste.

■ Always heed "no swimming" signs—they are there for your protection. If you see indications of hazardous waste, such as used hypodermic needles and other medical items, report them to your local health department. This type of refuse sometimes washes up along swimming beaches after being dumped illegally at sea.

HAZARDOUS WASTE

Each year, some 8 million tons of hazardous waste are produced in Canada. Unfortunately, much of this eventually turns up in lakes, streams, underground waters, and landfills.

■ If you live near what appears to be a hazardous-waste area, check to see if it is registered as an authorized facility. If not, call your provincial environment department and request that it inspect the site.

■ Lead finds its way into the soil from such sources as peeling paint. If you are concerned, have the soil where children play tested for lead. If levels are dangerously high, the area should be off-limits to children. Alternatively, you can reduce the lead contamination: Remove 6 to 12 inches of surface soil, replace it with low-lead soil, and plant new grass or vegetation. Or you can cover the area with a hard-top surface.

HAZARDOUS PRODUCTS

Potentially hazardous products include anything flammable, toxic, explosive, or corrosive—for example, paint, weed killer, and many household cleansers. Inappropriate use and disposal of these products cause environmental pollution, and injury and poisoning can also result from mishandling.

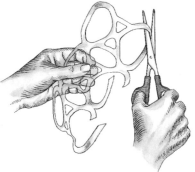

■ Cut plastic holders for six-packs of beverages before throwing them away. Birds and other animals can strangle if their heads get caught in the loops.

■ Buy liquid, paste, or powder forms of products instead of aerosols.

■ Choose water-based paint, glue, and similar items instead of solvent-based products.

■ Always read hazardous-product labels; the manufacturers are required to describe the hazards involved and tell you how to avoid them. Follow instructions carefully.

■ Never combine hazardous products with other materials; they may ignite or explode.

■ If you're not sure how to recycle or dispose of a hazardous product, call your municipal recycling center or provincial environment department.

■ Find a service station that will recycle used motor oil and old car batteries. An auto-parts store may also take a battery, and a dealer should take your old battery when you're buying a new one.

■ Rinse out empty pesticide containers three times, and then use the rinse water as a pesticide.

■ If you find that you have paint or any other hazardous product left over, offer it to a friend or neighbor, or to a school or church. Do not store it indoors—the toxic fumes can cause serious ailments.

■ Do not burn treated lumber; it will release toxic fumes.

■ Many common items pose a threat to the environment once they are in landfills. These include nail polish, nail polish remover, and disposable batteries. If you do throw away nail polish, remove the cap and let the polish dry first. Use rechargeable batteries.

RECYCLE, RECYCLE

Almost everything can be reused or recycled once you get the hang of it.

■ Bring your own bags to the store, and reuse any bags that you do take away. Whenever possible, avoid packaging; for example, buy a whole cantaloupe rather than a plastic container full of cut pieces.

■ Look for products made from recycled materials, and note whether plastic or glass containers can be recycled.

■ Be aware that the term *recyclable* does not mean a product has been recycled—only that it might be at some time in the future. Also, "degradable" plastics are not biodegradable. They break down into smaller pieces but still leach toxic chemicals and harm animals that eat the pieces.

THE COMPOST HEAP

A compost heap is an excellent way to recycle various organic materials and enrich your garden soil. You can use such potential garbage as leaves, dead flowers, yard clippings, vacuum-cleaner fluff, and kitchen scraps. However, don't use woody materials, diseased plants, perennial-weed roots, annual-weed seeds, protein and dairy foods, or anything containing grease.

Begin the compost pile on bare soil. Make the first layer about 5 feet square and about 1 foot deep. Press down and water well. Sprinkle on a handful of ammonium sulfate. Cover with a 2-inch layer of soil.

As you build up the pile using 9- to 12-inch layers, contain it within wire netting secured to wooden stakes. If soil is acidic, add lime to each alternate layer. Sprinkle each layer with complete organic fertilizer. Cover the top with plastic.

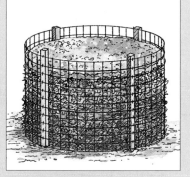

Stop when the heap is about 4 feet high; cover it with soil. Keep it moist. When it has shrunk to about 1 foot high, move the top layer to the inside of the pile. After a few months, the material will become dark and crumbly—ready to use.

ENJOYING WATER SPORTS

Water—whether it be a backyard pool, a pond, an ocean, or a river—provides many recreational opportunities, but it can also be hazardous. Take the following precautions to enjoy it safely.

BASIC WATER SAFETY

■ No matter how good a swimmer you are, never swim alone. Even the best swimmer can get tired or injured and need help. If you don't have a companion to swim with, choose a pool or beach where others are swimming. Better yet, choose one with a lifeguard on duty.

■ Children and nonswimmers should wear life jackets when playing in the water, including at the shore or the shallow end of a pool. However, life jackets are not a substitute for know-how—if you can't swim, sign up for lessons at your local Y or a swim club. You should also learn "drownproofing," a simple breathing technique that keeps bringing you back to the water's surface; this is especially important for children.

■ Always watch small children when they are around water, even if lifeguards are nearby. A lifeguard cannot be expected to keep a constant eye on every child, and a drowning can happen very quickly.

■ Never dive into a pond, pool, or other body of water unless you know the depth. Diving into shallow water can result in a paralyzing or fatal neck injury (see page 406).

■ Do not swim during an electrical storm, when there are small-craft warnings, or when you feel tired or overheated.

■ Avoid swimming near piers, pilings, wrecks, and other objects in which you may become entangled.

■ If you get in trouble while swimming or feel unable to reach shore, wave your hands or call for help. Never fake a call for help, and instruct your children in the importance of this rule.

■ If help is not forthcoming, don't panic. Roll onto your back and float until you are again able to swim.

■ For rescue methods and revival techniques, see page 406.

POOLSIDE SAFETY

■ Remove the pool cover completely when the pool is in use, but make sure the pool is covered when not in use. The cover should support at least 30 pounds per square foot, and there should be no gaps when it is in place. Remove standing water from the cover whenever it collects.

■ Install a phone extension near the pool and post emergency numbers close by.

■ Keep doors from the house to the pool locked at all times; consider installing a door alarm. This is particularly important if there are young children in the house.

■ Fence off a backyard pool to prevent unsupervised children and animals from wandering into the area. The fence should be at least five feet tall and have a latch and lock out of the reach of small children. Make sure that the fence does not obscure the view of the pool from the house, so that you can see if a child does slip through (or over) the fence.

■ Install a removable ladder on aboveground pools. When the pool is not in use, remove the ladder and store it where children cannot get to it.

■ Keep a first-aid kit and lifesaving equipment near the pool at all times. Equipment should include a life-ring with a rope attached. All family members over the age of six should be acquainted with basic rescue procedures, and at least one person should be trained in CPR (cardiopulmonary resuscitation).

■ Maintain your pool according to the recommendations of the local health department or the manufacturer. To ensure clear and clean water, see that your filtration system is working properly. Keep the chemicals used to clean and sanitize the pool locked in an area away from children; always follow the precautions listed on the label.

■ Mark both the deep and

shallow ends clearly with actual depths.

■ Make rules clear to both children and adults: no running, pushing, or roughhousing near the pool. Ban sharp objects and glass objects, such as beverage bottles, from the pool area.

Even small plastic wading pools pose a hazard if small children are allowed to play unsupervised. Always empty and flip over a small pool after use. To avoid waste, use the water on your lawn or garden.

PONDS

■ Check water regularly before and during the season to be sure that it is safe for swimming. A buildup of algae and insect larvae in stagnant water may make it unsafe during late-summer months. Check with your local health department for water-testing procedures or any health warnings.

■ Have debris—bottles, old tires, sharp objects that may cause injury—removed from the bottom of the pond. Submerged hazards that cannot be removed should be marked with a sign.

■ Wear water shoes when swimming in a pond or any other body of water in which you cannot see the bottom.

■ Make sure that docks and floats are sturdy, especially if you are not a strong swimmer.

AT THE BEACH

■ Pay attention to any warning signs or flags near beach entrances, lifeguard towers, and the water.

■ Also ask the lifeguard if there are any special conditions—currents, undertows, jellyfish—that you should be aware of. Conversely, if you notice any unsafe conditions or a swimmer who appears to be in trouble, report it to the lifeguard immediately.

■ Do not swim in areas with boats or water skiers.

■ When swimming, stay clear of boogie boarders and other surfers who may not be in total control.

■ When distance-swimming, swim parallel to the shore, rather than out toward open water. You'll get the same amount of exercise without the danger.

CURRENTS

Even if you know how to swim, a strong or unexpected current can mean trouble. When swimming in an ocean, bay, or river, keep the current in mind.

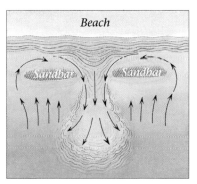

Beach

■ Rip currents, caused by water flowing to the sea through a gap in a sandbar or reef, can be dangerous; they are sometimes unpredictable and unnoticeable. Even calm waters can harbor a strong

current that can very quickly pull swimmers away from shore. For signs of a rip current, look for breaks in the wave pattern or water clouded by sand in the current.

■ If you get caught in a rip current, don't try to swim against it toward shore. Instead, swim parallel to the shore or diagonally across the current. Once you are out of its grasp, head back toward shore. If you feel tired or are unable to get out of the current, wave your hands to alert lifeguards or others on shore.

■ Also pay attention to the undertow—the force of water rushing back into the ocean after a wave hits the shore. A strong undertow can quickly pull an unsuspecting wader or swimmer into deeper water, and it can be very dangerous for a small child.

■ Before plunging into a river, check with local authorities to determine if it is safe for swimmers. Remember that river currents are constantly changing—even from week to week during high-flow times.

BODY SURFING

■ Attempt body surfing (riding a wave without a board) or boogie boarding (riding a wave while holding a small board) only if you are a strong swimmer and the water is not too rough. If they're available in your area, take lessons.

■ Learn how to recognize safe waves. Waves that roll in are generally safer, while waves that curl under and crash on the shore can be dangerous.

■ Surprisingly, body surfing in shallow water—on waves close to shore—creates the highest potential for injury. Since body surfing is done headfirst, you chance being thrown into the sand head-down by a wave, which could cause a paralyzing or even fatal neck injury.

■ Wear fins for better control.

SURFING

■ Take lessons to learn how to surf properly and safely. When you first begin surfing, select an area with slow-breaking, rolling waves. Avoid areas frequented by experienced surfers; you'll be in their way. If you're not sure where to go, ask a veteran surfer.

■ Never surf alone. You may need someone to help you or go for help.

■ Do not surf near swimmers, especially if you're inexperienced. Surfboards can injure swimmers.

■ Lobster traps near shore pose a danger because surfboard leash lines can become

tangled in the traps' buoy lines. If you must surf in waters used by lobster fishermen, watch out for the buoy lines and use breakaway surfboard leashes.

■ Do not "grab a wave" that another surfer is riding; it's not proper surfing etiquette and it's not safe.

• • • • • • • • • • • • • • • • • • • •

When engaging in any water sport, have a first-aid kit handy in case of an accident.

• • • • • • • • • • • • • • • • • • • •

SCUBA DIVING

"Scuba" is an acronym for "self-contained underwater breathing apparatus." A scuba diver wears a tank containing compressed air on his or her back.

■ This sport requires formal instruction and certification. When shopping for a course, make sure that the instructors are certified. Have a medical checkup before starting.

■ Never dive alone. The buddy system makes two divers responsible for each other's safety.

■ Know the standard scuba diving signals (see box).

■ Like driving, diving doesn't mix with alcohol. Refrain from drinking prior to a dive, and don't dive with a hangover.

■ Do not dive when you have a cold or lung congestion.

■ Breathe continuously and never hold your breath; this will prevent lung-expansion injuries, which can be serious.

■ Diving causes excess nitrogen to form in the body. Dive tables are available to help you keep this under control by following safe time and depth limits. Otherwise, you risk getting decompression sickness ("the bends").

■ If you have unexplained pains after scuba diving, see a doctor. Tell him or her that you've dived recently—you may have a diving-related injury.

SCUBA DIVING SIGNALS

The following are a few of the standard signals that enable scuba divers to communicate with their boat operators and with their "buddies" underwater.

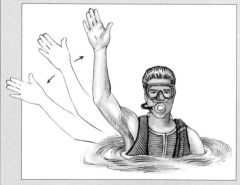

Distress, help

Attention (strike your tank)

Go up, going up

SKIN DIVING

The skin diver (or free diver) goes deep into the water using very little equipment—usually mask, snorkel, fins, and safety vest.

■ Before you can dive safely, you have to learn to equalize the pressure in your ears. For this safety reason and others, you need instruction before pursuing this sport. You also need to be a good swimmer.

■ Before beginning instruction, have a medical checkup.

■ Do not dive if you have an ear, nose, or throat ailment.

■ Never dive alone. Use the "one up, one down" buddy system: while one is underwater on a breath-holding dive, the other remains at the surface, watching the diver.

■ Do not wear earplugs or goggles when skin diving. Wearing earplugs may lead to rupture of the eardrums. Water pressure can push goggles hard against the eyes, causing injury.

■ Wear a safety vest on every dive and a wet suit when diving in cold water.

■ Find out about dive flags. You'll need one to warn boaters of your presence when diving.

■ When ascending from a dive, place your hand over your head, look up, and rotate so you can get a complete view of the surface.

■ Do not dive in stagnant or polluted water; you may get a skin, ear, eye, or gastrointestinal infection.

■ Avoid very long and deep dives. Holding the breath for too long can cause anoxia (oxygen starvation), a dangerous condition.

STINGERS AT SEA

■ Before swimming or diving in unfamiliar waters, find out about plants and creatures common to the area. Some animals are equipped with tentacles containing stinging cells, called nematocysts. This way, you will know what to look for.

■ Keep an eye out for brightly colored jellyfish when swimming—and swim the other way if you see one. The tentacles of many jellyfish extend 5 to 20 feet from their bodies. If the water is infested with jellyfish, stick to the beach or find another place to swim.

■ The Portuguese man-of-war has clear tentacles that can trail many feet behind the body. Even a piece of tentacle that washes up on shore can cause a reaction if you touch it.

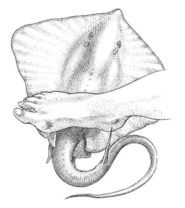

■ When diving into deep waters, watch out for other creatures that can sting or cause puncture wounds (from spines), including sea anemones, sea urchins, and stingrays. Also be careful not to touch fire coral, which causes an intense burning sensation; you can recognize it by its mustard color.

■ You may want to wear a wet

suit or other type of exposure suit to help protect you from stings and scrapes.

AFTER A STING

■ For treatment of jellyfish and Portuguese man-of-war stings, see page 391.

■ Wash out a stingray wound completely with salt water. Then soak the area in hot water—43.3°C to 46°C (110°F to 115°F)—for 30 to 90 minutes to deactivate the venom. (Since the poison may numb the area, check water temperature with an uninjured part of the body to avoid scalding.) Stingray wounds carry a high risk of infection, so you should see a doctor.

■ Carefully remove the spines of a sea urchin with tweezers. Then deactivate the venom as described above. If you think a broken spine remains in the skin, see a doctor.

FISH THAT BITE

Most sharks, barracuda, and other fish would prefer to avoid human contact. Attacks usually occur in self-defense or because the animal has mistaken a person for its natural prey.

■ Do not wear shiny, dangling jewelry that might attract barracuda or other fish.

■ When swimming near fish, do not dart at them or move your hands toward them.

■ With most fish bites, the bacteria from the fish's mouth pose the most danger. Wash a bite wound immediately and thoroughly with salt water. Then wash with soap and water promptly. See a doctor if the wound is more than superficial.

STORMS AND NATURAL DISASTERS

The weather and other natural phenomena can create many dangerous emergencies—from tornadoes and hurricanes to earthquakes and floods. Learn how to safeguard yourself, your family, and your property.

IN GENERAL

■ Tune in to a weather report and forecast both morning and evening. Pay particular attention to such words as *watch* and *alert*, meaning that conditions are right for a weather emergency, and *warning*, which means the storm has developed and may be headed your way.

■ For information and instructions during a storm watch or warning, tune in to Weather Radio Canada, operated by Environment Canada on the PSB high band on a portable FM radio. If you don't have this type of radio, find a local station that broadcasts emergency information. Use this station in the event of other disasters as well; stay tuned for advisories.

■ List the common emergencies in your area, and pick the best places to seek shelter from each. Many public buildings, factories, and malls have emergency shelters, if needed. Go over the list with the entire family, then do a trial run to make sure each member knows where to go

and what to do during an emergency.

■ Before storing water (see box on facing page), treat it with chlorine bleach to prevent the growth of microorganisms. Use liquid bleach that contains 5.25 percent sodium hypochlorite and no soap. Stir in 4 drops per quart of water (or 2 teaspoons per 10 gallons). You can disregard any "not for personal use" warnings if sodium hypochlorite is the only active ingredient and you use only the small quantity just described. Label the water containers and keep them in a cool, dark place.

LIGHTNING AND THUNDERSTORMS

During a thunderstorm, your chances of being struck by lightning are slim, but lightning does not need to strike you directly to kill or cause injury. You should always take precautions.

■ Seek shelter immediately with the approach of a thunderstorm. If possible, go to a building that has an electrical ground, but avoid isolated barns, sheds, and huts.

■ If you're outdoors, get off high ground, such as the brow of a hill, and away from tall trees, electric fences, and telephone wires and poles. If you're part of a group, spread out. Do not lie flat—this would allow an electrical current to travel more easily through your vital organs. Instead, squat down on the lowest level ground you can find. Put your head between your knees, and hug your knees.

■ If you're on a golf course, don't carry your clubs; they act as lightning rods, as do fishing rods, guns, backpack frames, aluminum bats, and tennis rackets. Remove any metal objects that you're wearing, such as cleated shoes, helmets, hearing aids, jewelry, and hair barrettes.

■ Water also conducts electricity. If you're boating or swimming, try to reach shore immediately or take shelter under a bridge or cliff. In a large boat, the crew should go below the deck and the person at the helm should avoid touching metal objects. At home, don't bathe, wash dishes, or handle wet objects.

■ When hiking or climbing, don't take cover in rock-face overhangs, cave mouths, or recesses under boulders. Lightning can arc across the gaps on its way to the ground.

■ If you're in an automobile, stay there. The car's shape deflects and harmlessly grounds even a direct hit. Keep the windows closed.

■ Do not handle electrical appliances during a lightning storm, and stay away from stoves, metal pipes, and parts of the plumbing system, all of which can act as electrical conductors.

■ Avoid using the telephone during a thunderstorm. Unplug the phone and all other appliances; this may protect them from being damaged if lightning strikes the house.

■ See page 409 for instructions on treating someone struck by lightning.

TORNADOES

Tornadoes are violent, twisting windstorms that form when a mass of warm, moist air collides with dry, cold air. They can occur at any time and in any place but are most common in southwestern Ontario from May to September. Most tornado injuries and deaths are caused by flying glass and other debris, collapsing buildings, and downed power lines. Here's what to do before and during a tornado.

■ If thunderstorms are forecast, watch the sky in the southwest for a tornado funnel. If you see one, report it immediately to the local police, radio station, Environment Canada, or telephone operator.

■ If there's time, turn off the electricity and gas.

■ Go to a tornado cellar or other shelter. If you can't reach your predesignated spot, get as low to the ground as possible in a basement, first-floor center hallway, closet, or bathroom. Take cover under a heavy table, or crouch in a bathtub. In schools, duck under a desk or other sturdy piece of furniture. Always tuck your head down and cover it with your arms to protect it from any flying debris.

■ Stay away from windows and doors. Stay out of gymnasiums, auditoriums, and other structures with large, free-span roofs.

■ If you are outside and cannot reach a suitable shelter in time, lie flat in a ditch, ravine, culvert, or under a bridge. Do not crouch under a tree or structure that can topple on you. Do not try to outrun a tornado—it moves faster than the fleetest runner and takes erratic turns.

■ If you are in a car, mobile home, or trailer, get out and follow the instructions that are given above.

AFTER THE TORNADO PASSES

■ Stay in your shelter for at least 10 minutes. A series of twisters often develops from a storm cloud, so another may be right behind.

■ Stay tuned to the emergency radio station for information on medical care and emergency procedures.

Stocking Up for an Emergency

If you live in an area where storms or natural disasters are common, you should stock enough emergency supplies to last at least four days. Check your supplies monthly so that you can replace water and any other items as needed. Use this checklist of basics:

Battery-operated radio and flashlight; extra batteries for both

First-aid kit

Canned or dried foods (include any special foods, such as infant formula, that may be needed)

Can opener, paper plates and cups, and eating utensils

Water—at least three gallons per person stored in clean, tightly closed, durable containers, such as plastic milk bottles (see facing page for how to treat water)

Canned juices

Fire extinguisher

Candles

Matches in a waterproof container

Blankets or sleeping bags

A camp stove or other nonelectric cooker that can be used indoors, along with extra fuel

Necessary medications (e.g., insulin, heart medications)

A pail with a cover or large plastic garbage bags (which can double as a portable toilet)

■ Proceed with caution. Be especially alert for broken glass, fallen power lines, and weakened structures.

■ Check your home for structural damage, especially gas and water leaks, electrical problems, and broken sewer lines. Don't light a match or smoke around gas lines. Don't even switch on a flashlight in a hazardous area; get well away before you turn it on.

If you're going to a public shelter, you won't be able to take your pets. If you can't find a temporary home for them, put them in the safest part of the house with plenty of food and water.

HURRICANES

Hurricanes are tropical storms with winds that spin counterclockwise at a speed above 120 kilometres per hour. Generally, they affect coastal areas between June and November. There is usually at least 12 hours' notice before a hurricane hits, giving you time to prepare.

■ Pack up family medicines, emergency supplies, important documents, protective clothing, and necessary personal items. Stow them in your car to save last-minute preparations.

■ Familiarize yourself with evacuation routes in advance. If evacuation is ordered, go immediately, especially if you are in a low-lying coastal area, where roads may flood before the hurricane hits. Listen to the radio for instructions, and avoid back roads—you may find your way blocked by a washout or downed power lines and trees.

■ Even if evacuation is not ordered, don't attempt to sit out a hurricane if you live in a mobile home, no matter how well it's anchored. Before leaving, however, check all tiedowns to make sure that they're securely anchored. (Homes 10 to 14 feet wide should have four sets of over-the-top and frame ties; double units need only frame ties. Install anchors with a holding power of 4,800 pounds in four to five feet of soil, and use wire rope or rust-resistant steel straps.)

■ Set your refrigerator and freezer on their coldest settings; if the power goes out, your food will keep longer.

■ Board up, tape, or put storm shutters on windows and glass doors. Close drapes, which can help prevent injury from flying glass. Securely lock windows and doors to prevent them from blowing open.

■ Tie up awnings or bring them inside. Put away all loose outdoor objects, such as garbage cans and lawn furniture. Tie down what you can't move indoors.

■ If you do not have storm-proof door sills, place a folded towel under the bottom of the door to keep out water.

■ Wedge sliding glass doors to keep them from lifting out of their tracks.

■ Clean the bathtub and fill it and other large unbreakable containers with water. Before the storm hits, turn off the water so that it will be safe to use what is in the pipes.

■ Make sure drains and drainspouts are not clogged. If time permits, cut down loose tree branches or palm fronds and drain the swimming pool.

■ Fill your car's gas tank; if the power goes off, you will not be able to get gas from an electric-operated pump.

■ If possible, park your car in a garage or shelter; if not, move it to high ground and away from trees in an easy-to-reach area in case you need to evacuate. Be sure to set the emergency brake.

■ Haul any small boat out of the water and put it on a trailer. Remove accessories, let the air out of the trailer tires, and lash the boat down securely. Alternatively, remove the engine and sink the boat, mooring it securely. It is safer underwater during high winds.

■ If you can't remove the boat from water, moor it on an inland creek or canal away from docks, pilings, or overhanging trees.

BLIZZARDS

A storm is a blizzard when the temperature drops to -6.7°C (20°F) or lower and winds of at least 56 kilometres per hour blow snow into drifts for three hours or longer. If possible, head for home when a blizzard is forecast. Make the following preparations in advance.

■ Winterize your car (if you haven't already done so). Have snow tires put on, and let out some of the air to further improve traction. Keep the gas tank filled to prevent water from getting into the fuel and stalling the engine.

■ Check your supply of heating fuel. If it's low, request a delivery before the snow hits. If your heat depends upon electricity, arrange for an alternative (fireplace, wood-stove, camp stove, or kerosene heater) that you can use if the power goes off.

■ Check all battery-powered equipment, emergency cooking facilities, flashlights, and lanterns so that you won't be without heat or light.

DURING A BLIZZARD

■ Stay indoors, especially if you have a condition aggravated by the cold, such as heart disease or asthma. If you must go out, dress in several layers of loose-fitting, lightweight, warm clothing. Outer clothing should be tightly woven and water-repellent. Wear a hood or hat, and cover your mouth and nose with a scarf or ski mask to protect your lungs from cold air.

■ Overheated stoves and furnaces are major causes of winter fires. To reduce the pressure on your heating system, heat only the rooms you must use. Stuff towels or cloths under doors, and cover windows at night. Stay warm by wearing extra layers of clothing, but remove layers if you begin to feel overheated.

■ If you're trapped in your car, stay in it unless you're certain that you're within a few minutes of shelter. Remember, you can become quickly disoriented when trying to walk in blowing snow.

■ Keep fresh air in your car by cracking a downwind window. Run the motor only if you're sure the exhaust pipe isn't blocked by snow. With more than one person, take turns sleeping, if necessary.

■ To stay warm while in a car, clap your hands and move your arms and legs every few minutes. Be sure to keep a hat on; it will greatly improve your body's ability to heat itself.

■ Keep a flashlight turned on to make the car visible to rescue crews. You can also tie a colored cloth to your antenna or door.

■ If you're without a car and can't find shelter, dig a hole in the snow next to a tree—trees give off a little heat and offer protection from wind. Cover the top of the hole with branches, cardboard, or anything that will help protect you from the cold. For ventilation and to avoid being trapped, shake snow from covering periodically. Generate body heat by moving your arms and legs frequently. Build a fire outside the snow hole (*not* inside), and place rocks around the fire to absorb and reflect heat; the fire may also attract attention. Do not eat snow unless you melt it first; otherwise, it will lower your body temperature.

Winter-Survival Car Kit

Besides the items suggested on page 266, carry the following in your car if there is any possibility of a winter storm:

Blankets or sleeping bags and a box of newspapers to use for insulation

Matches and candles

Extra clothing, especially caps, mittens, and overshoes

High-calorie, nonperishable food

Compass and road maps

Knife and hatchet or ax

Two tow chains

Catalytic heater

Transistor radio and flashlight, with extra batteries

After the blizzard stops, dig yourself out of your home slowly; overexposure and overexertion in cold weather increase the risk of a heart attack. It's better to stay put for a day or so to allow power and highway crews to clear the way.

FLOODS

A broken dam, an earthquake, or a torrential downpour can cause flash floods. Unfortunately, there's not much you can do except flee to higher ground. More commonly, floodwaters rise slowly, allowing time for warnings and preparation. But don't wait until it's too late to develop a plan.

■ During flood season, do not allow children to play near culverts, drainage ditches, and creeks. A flood can turn normally safe streams into raging torrents. Every year, a number of children are carried off by floodwaters, often from their own backyards.

■ If you live in a river floodplain, ask your county engineer to estimate how many feet the river would have to rise to endanger your home. Locate the nearest safe, sheltered area, and determine the best route to it, such as a high road without bridges.

■ If annual flooding is the rule rather than the exception, consider moving your house to higher ground or putting it on a stilt foundation.

■ Install check valves in building sewer traps to prevent floodwater from backing up into the drains of your home.

■ Stockpile materials for emergency flood control, including plastic sheeting, sandbags, plywood, and lumber.

■ Basements flood first, so if time permits, empty your basement of anything that should not be submerged. Turn off the fuse box and disconnect electrical wiring. Remove lightbulbs, telephones, and electrical cords, and then seal all sockets and outlets with waterproof tape to prevent silt from entering.

■ Seal all openings into your home, such as windows and sliding glass doors, with plastic sheeting, garbage bags, towels, or weather stripping.

■ Cover all air vents under your home with plywood, brick, or sandbags to prevent water leakage.

■ If possible, move rugs, furniture, and appliances to a high floor. Carefully pack in boxes dishes and other items that can withstand water; put bedding and clothing in plastic bags. Place important documents, valuables, and personal treasures in plastic bags and stow them in your car in case of evacuation.

■ If you can, move farm animals, equipment, and outdoor furniture to higher ground.

■ When sandbagging around your home, don't place the bags directly against the outer walls—the added weight may put additional strain on the foundation. Some experts recommend leaving a space of between one and two feet.

■ Check your automobile to see that it is fully fueled.

ESCAPING A FLOOD

■ If there's time, do a final check to make sure electricity, gas, and water are turned off. Leave the basement windows open to equalize pressure and allow water to flow out when the flood recedes.

■ Wear a life jacket, and make sure that each other family member also has one, regardless of how you're traveling. If you have an inflatable raft, rowboat, or other small craft, tie it to your car roof or tow it in a trailer. Then if you are caught by floodwaters, you have an alternative means of escape.

■ Avoid driving on a flooded road; parts of it could be washed out, and the depth of the water is not always obvious. If your car stalls, leave it immediately and head for higher ground—only two feet of water will carry away most automobiles.

■ When walking, stay on firm ground. Even six inches of moving water can knock you down. Standing water may be electrically charged from underground or downed power lines, and floodwater and debris may hide animals and broken glass.

■ If you cannot reach high ground, climb whatever appears to be the sturdiest structure within reach, such as a big tree or building roof, and wait for help.

RETURNING HOME

Receding floodwaters do not necessarily mean all danger is gone, so always proceed with caution.

■ Assume that floodwater is contaminated by disease-causing organisms. Do not eat food that has come in contact with it. Drink bottled water and boil tap water for washing and bathing until health officials say the water is safe.

■ You can keep food that's in airtight metal cans, except for aluminum beverage cans. However, the cans must be disinfected: Wash in soap and warm water, then immerse for two minutes in a solution of two tablespoons of 5.25 percent sodium hypochlorite laundry bleach per gallon of water. Rinse immediately with clear water. Discard any cans that bulge.

■ If your house is seriously damaged, wait for a building inspector before entering.

■ If you do go into your home, use only a flashlight; explosive fumes may be present. Stay out of a flooded basement until a utilities inspector tells you it's free of electrical currents.

■ Be wary of electrical appliances until they have been thoroughly checked by

an electrician. Even if they appear to be dry, they may be damaged and able to electrocute someone or start a fire.

■ Watch out for slippery floors and for animals, especially snakes, seeking shelter. Use a stick to turn items over.

■ Small children, pregnant women, elderly persons, and those with health problems should generally stay out of flooded areas until cleanup is finished.

EARTHQUAKES

Most earthquake deaths stem from falling debris and fires. An earthquake lasts only seconds, but knowing what to do when you first feel a tremor can save your life. You can also

take measures well in advance to help ensure your safety.

■ If you're indoors when an earthquake occurs, stay there but take cover in a doorway, under heavy furniture, or in a corner away from windows. Stay clear of anything that might fall on you, especially brick walls or chimneys and glass objects. Crouch down and wait until the shaking ends.

■ If you're outdoors, stay in the open—away from trees, power lines, and glass buildings or large windows. If you can't get into an open area, crouch in a sturdy doorway if one is nearby.

■ If you're in a car, slowly pull to the side of the road. Do not stop abruptly or swerve into

---

Making Your House Earthquake-Safe

Go through your home room by room to see that appliances, heavy furniture, and other items are firmly secured.

Use L-shaped metal braces to connect cabinets, bookcases, and other freestanding units to wall studs.

Secure water or gas heaters by means of metal strips that are anchored to wall studs.

Make sure that gas stoves and dryers are connected to gas outlets with flexible metal tubing.

Lock the wheels of movable appliances in place, and use braided wire to affix refrigerators, washers, dryers, and other heavy appliances to wall studs.

Use heavy-duty, closed-eye hooks fastened to wall studs to hang heavy mirrors and pictures. Substitute thin plexiglass sheets for picture glass.

Put heavy objects on low shelves. If you have precious items on shelves or in display cases, wire them in place. Don't stack glasses or other breakable objects.

Use flexible wire to secure overhead lighting fixtures, as well as any hanging plants.

Place your bed in the middle of the room, well away from tall chests, bookcases, and other furniture that could topple on you.

another lane. Do not park on or under a bridge or under an overpass, sign, or tree. Stay in the car; its springs deflect tremors and the car body protects you from debris.

■ When buying a home in an earthquake-prone area, check with the Geological Survey of Canada, or the federal Department of Natural Resources. There are seven earthquake hazard zones in Canada, ranging from a minimum hazard in zone 0 to the greatest hazard in zone 6. Ask for a seismic zoning map for your region.

■ Wood-frame homes with diagonal bracing and foundations bolted to the house frame can best withstand earthquakes. Don't consider unreinforced brick houses—their rigid construction of many small pieces makes them vulnerable.

AFTER THE QUAKING STOPS

■ If you're indoors, move calmly to an outside open area. Most earthquakes are followed by aftershocks, some as powerful as the original quake. Don't use an elevator; its cables may be damaged.

■ If you live near the coast, listen to the radio for advisories and consider going to higher ground; tidal waves may follow earthquakes.

■ Don't return to a damaged building until safety inspectors give their okay.

■ If you return to a seemingly undamaged building, don't turn on gas or electrical appliances. If electrical wiring is shorting out, turn off the electricity at its source. If water pipes have been damaged, shut off the main valve and use bottled water until health officials say the tap water is safe.

■ If you smell gas, open the windows, shut off the main valve, and evacuate the house at once. Don't return until your utility service tells you it's safe. Even if you don't smell gas, refrain from lighting candles or matches; the sparks could set off an explosion.

■ If you can do so safely, douse any small fires. However, if the fire is beyond your control, leave the house immediately.

■ Open closet and cupboard doors carefully, and watch for objects falling from shelves.

■ Don't drive on bridges or other structures that could be damaged until they're cleared by the authorities.

■ If you're in a car and a power line has fallen on the car, don't try to get out; wait for help.

■ Don't touch downed power lines or objects in contact with downed lines.

> **After any disaster that leaves debris, wear heavy shoes to avoid injury to your feet.**

WILDFIRES

Wildfires, such as forest and brush fires, have various causes, including lightning and human carelessness. If you live or are camping in or near a wooded area, take these steps to protect yourself and your property from fires.

■ If you're building a home in a remote wooded area, pick a level site, because fire travels more rapidly uphill. If possible, invest in a two-way road that allows for quick evacuation and access by fire crews.

■ Ask your local fire department to inspect the property for adequate water and other fire-safety measures. Consider an outdoor radio or cellular phone so that you can summon help from outside if the house catches fire. Make sure that your address is clearly visible to firefighters and other rescue crews.

■ Select a home built with fire-resistant building materials. Wood should be treated for fire resistance, and a roof made of tin, tile, slate, asphalt, or fire-retardant shingles is safer than one of ordinary shake shingles.

■ Before buying a home with balconies, porches, or decks, consult the local fire department or another expert concerning fire safety. The house you choose should have screened overhangs, balconies, and vents to keep sparks from igniting combustible materials.

■ Consider a permanently installed roof sprinkler system that can cover the entire roof by opening one valve. The system need not be expensive

AFTER THE FLOODS

"People who cope best with a natural disaster are those who admit they are helpless in the face of what's going on."
—Margie Conrad, American Red Cross

• • • • • • •

When the floods of 1993 swept through Iowa, Steve and Sandy Belluchi were set on an emotional roller coaster that continued long after the waters receded. It began with dismay and apprehension as the rising waters came ever closer to their home.

Steve, a mail clerk for a Des Moines publishing company, had spent six years remodeling their modest home to make it accessible for his wife, Sandy, who uses a wheelchair. They were assured that levees would prevent any flooding, but no one had anticipated the endless rains of that summer.

"When the river crested at two feet below the levee, I took my wife to my mother's house, and family members came to help me save what I could," Steve recalls. "I was in the basement when my relatives started yelling to get out. The levee had broken, and by the time I reached the front door, the water was chest deep. I just made it to my truck, but it was too late to load it."

As Steve outraced the rising waters, Sandy was engulfed in near-paralyzing fear. "When I heard the levee had broken, I was terrified that Steve would drown," she remembers.

The Belluchis' collection of clown figurines was left covered with mud.

After the waters had receded, all the Belluchis' possessions, including Sandy's beloved collection of 500 clown figurines, were covered with mud.

"We both just fell apart," Steve recalls. "We talked a lot, we prayed a lot, we cried a lot, but we didn't know where to start to reclaim our lives."

The kindness of strangers. The Belluchis regained their footing thanks to an outpouring of generosity from their friends and neighbors, and even from strangers. Their story was told by a radio station in Alabama, and soon much-needed contributions began to arrive. Eventually, between donations, government disaster aid, and a helping hand from Steve's employer, the couple made a down payment on a new home that is even more accessible for Sandy than the one they lost.

The Belluchis' method of coping—admitting how sad they felt, comforting each other, and keeping the lines of communication open—was a healthy one, says Margie Conrad, of the American Red Cross in Des Moines. "People going through post-traumatic stress reactions need to be patient and gentle with themselves."

Typical reactions. Normal reactions to a natural disaster include sadness, apathy, fear, anxiety, anger, memory loss, sleep disorders, and difficulty making decisions.

Despite the many manifestations of post-traumatic stress, most people manage to prevail, and some emerge stronger than before.

"A sense of humor is the number one asset," says Margie Conrad. "If you can still joke and laugh, even when everything seems bleak, you're on the way to recovery."❏

CAN YOUR HOUSE SURVIVE A WILDFIRE?

If you live in a wildfire-hazard area, you need to create a 30-foot zone around your home that is free of risk factors.

1. *Make sure any highly flammable vegetation—cedar, cypress, or pine—is at least 30 feet away. Reduce density of any surrounding forest.*

2. *Thin tree and brush cover and dispose of debris left from thinning. Remove dead limbs, leaves, and other litter.*

3. *Mow grass and water outdoor plants.*

4. *Prune tree branches to 10 feet above the ground.*

5. *Clean roof and gutters. Don't allow trees or branches to overhang the roof.*

6. *Stack firewood away from home and any other structures.*

7. *Install a fire screen on your chimney.*

or complex; most roofs can be covered with one or two agricultural-type sprinkler heads.

■ If you have a fireplace, burn the deadwood and brush from the immediate vicinity of your house before using commercial firewood (which contributes to deforestation). This will help clear the area.

■ Space your vegetation, and don't plant trees or shrubs in front of the windows; they might hamper a quick escape.

■ If you are caught in a wildfire while in your car, stay in the vehicle. Roll up your windows and close air vents. Drive slowly with the headlights on as you watch for other vehicles and pedestrians, but do not drive through heavy smoke. If you have to stop, park away from brush and the heaviest

trees. Keep headlights on. Get on the floor and cover up with a blanket or coat.

■ When camping, use extra caution during droughts. If you go into a public forest, heed fire-danger postings.

■ If campfires are permitted, learn how to make a safe one. Rangers advise digging a pit and lining it with stones. Lay your firewood in the pit, and watch it at all times. Make sure you have water and loose dirt nearby. To extinguish a fire, sprinkle it with water, stir it with a stick, and sprinkle again. Repeat until the remaining charred coal or wood is cool.

. . . .

Make sure your chimney has a fire-safe flue. Clean it of soot and creosote at least once a year.

. . . .

MUDSLIDES AND LANDSLIDES

Rain can bring disaster to those who live on hillsides, for with the water comes the possibility of major threats to their property—mudslides and landslides. These occur when hillsides become saturated with water, causing the soil to move downhill. (Landslides involve deeper strata of the earth than mudslides.) The danger is worse when vegetation has been destroyed by wildfire; in such cases, the storm water may carry rocks, brush, and trees.

■ Before building a house or other structure in a hilly area, have soil engineers excavate loose and porous soils by cutting steplike benches to expose firm earth. And be certain that foundations are set far enough back from the top of a slope to allow for any future erosion.

■ To help prevent a mudslide or landslide, plant deep-rooting trees that will anchor the top-soil of slopes. Avoid plants with shallow root systems that need a lot of watering. Be careful not to overwater plants and trees.

■ Keep gutters and down-spouts well maintained and clear.

■ Use paved drains and ditch-es to carry excess water from the slope. Be sure to keep them clean.

■ Create a mid-slope terrace, which will carry runoff away from the slope above.

■ Fill in depressions or low spots in the ground, where water can accumulate.

■ Build a retaining wall two to four feet high. It will help con-fine soil flow from the hillside above. Clean away debris periodically.

■ When threatened by a mud-slide or landslide, cover win-dows and sliding glass doors with plywood. Direct water flow away from structures by using sandbags, sand, or lum-ber; however, do not confine the flow more than is neces-sary—do not create a dam.

AVALANCHES

Although avalanches generally occur in mountainous areas between January and March, they are hardly confined to winter. Some of the worst avalanches occur during spring thaws.

■ If you intend to venture off regular ski trails, check first with the ski patrol. Let them know where you're headed, and ask specifically about avalanche activity in the area. Equip yourself with avalanche cords and a rescue beacon, which can help guide rescue groups to you.

■ Don't go out alone, and let someone at your base camp know when to expect you back. Then if you don't show up, a rescue squad can be sent.

■ Remember that making loud noises or throwing stones can set off an avalanche.

■ Wait a complete day after a heavy mountain snowstorm before going into potential avalanche terrain. Be espe-cially wary of steep slopes with a pitch of 30 degrees or more. Bowls or gullies above the tree line and patches of damaged and missing trees are also signs of avalanche territory.

■ When camping in the moun-tains, pitch tents as far away from avalanche terrain (see above) as possible. Be sure to pack a folding shovel and a collapsible probe stick in your backpack.

■ If you are caught in an avalanche, fight to remain up-right. If you fall feet first, flip on your back and tread the snow, much as you would tread water. Get rid of back-packs and other cumbersome, heavy gear that weighs you down. Use swimming strokes to stay on top of the upper-most layers of snow. The backstroke works best, but any swimming motion that in-volves the arms will help.

■ Avalanche snow packs tightly and can suffocate you if you are caught under it.

If you still have a sense of direction when you feel the avalanche slowing down, attempt to burst through to the surface by thrusting your body upward with swimming motions. Simply getting an arm or hand to the surface will increase your chances of being spotted by rescuers or passersby.

COMMUNICATING AFTER A DISASTER

■ Do not use the telephone immediately after a disaster except for lifesaving or other critical reasons; otherwise, you may be hindering such calls from getting through. However, you may want to designate a friend or relative outside your area as the person family members should contact as soon as they can.

■ If your neighborhood is vul-nerable to any natural disas-ter, establish an alert system. For example, you can use colored ribbons to let neigh-bors and officials know whether you need help. A red ribbon on your door can signify that you need help im-mediately; a yellow ribbon, that you would like help soon; and a green ribbon, that all's well. Or you can use colored construc-tion paper displayed in your windows to give these same signals.

A spirit of adventure *can carry you to places you never knew existed, perhaps to the storybook-perfect Castle Neuschwanstein in western Germany. However, you don't need to travel hundreds or thousands of miles to get the benefits of a vacation.*

CHAPTER 8

VACATION AND TRAVEL

While it may surprise you, a change of scenery can do wonders for your health. We all need to "get away from it all" and break from our usual routine. Travel gives us the chance to forget our everyday stresses while seeing new sights, tasting new foods, and meeting new people. The best vacations let us return to our daily lives rested, refreshed, and with a new perspective on the world.

Before you go, consider all your options to ensure that your holiday is a success. Do you need a relaxing trip, or do you crave the excitement of adventure travel? Would you enjoy a leisurely car drive, or is going by plane more practical? Also, take any necessary health precautions to make your vacation as pleasant and safe as possible. Then, whether you camp out under the stars, eat exotic foods in faraway places, or hike along remote mountain paths, you'll be sure to come home with only great stories to tell.

Your choice of traveling companion is important. Make sure that you enjoy not only each other's company but the same activities, as well.

HAVING A GREAT VACATION

Memorable vacations often require planning and advance preparation, especially if you travel to a different climate. Here are some hints for getting off to a smooth start and for staying fit while having a good time.

DESTINATION DECISIONS

■ When considering where to go on vacation, consult relatives, friends, and co-workers, as well as travel books, travel agencies, and tourist information bureaus. If you have a chronic medical condition, talk to a knowledgeable physician before you firm up your plans. People with heart conditions, for example, should probably avoid high altitudes.

■ Work out an itinerary and route. You may decide to diverge from your plan, but at least you'll have a framework.

■ If you're going to a place that may be crowded, such as a lakeside resort, make reservations for your lodging.

■ If you're trying something new, do a trial run. For example, if you've never camped out, start with a weekend at a provincial or national park.

■ Never embark on a wilderness trip or exotic adventure travel unless you have acquired some expertise through prior experience.

> **Give a copy of your itinerary to a friend or family member in case there's an emergency.**

CLIMATE CHANGES

A change of climate, such as going south in the winter, may provide a welcome change, but your body may need a while to adapt to it. You can take steps to help yourself adjust more rapidly.

■ For a warm climate, pack loose-fitting, lightweight clothing, preferably in white or light colors, which reflect the sun.

■ If you're heading into the cold, you'll need layers of warm clothing. Pack long underwear made of silk or polypropylene; wool or polyester sweaters; wool socks; down-filled overgarments; waterproof, lined boots; a waterproof and windproof shell; a warm hat; and perhaps a face mask.

■ Take it easy for the first day or two of your vacation. In a hot climate, spend the hottest hours of the day indoors or in the shade; schedule exercise for the early morning or late evening (see also "Sun Sense," page 126).

■ Drink extra fluids in hot climates, even if you don't feel thirsty. Water and fruit or vegetable juices are best. Avoid drinking a lot of beverages with caffeine and avoid too much alcohol, which can increase the risk of dehydration.

> **While on vacation, especially in a harsh climate or at a high altitude, start out slowly with any sport or exercise routine.**

GETTING IN SHAPE

Vacation activities—even just walking—can be tiring. If you're not used to exercise, get into better condition before you leave.

■ About a month before your departure date, start an exercise routine to prepare your muscles and ligaments for physical activity. You may want to seek advice from a health-club trainer.

■ If you plan to do a lot of touring on foot, start a walking program. An hour a day of brisk walking can help you avoid fatigue on your vacation, and it gives you a chance to break in new walking shoes.

■ If you are preparing for a ski trip, try step aerobics or working out on a stair or skiing machine. These exercises work the thigh and buttock muscles, which are important for skiing.

For scuba diving or snorkeling, spend some time at a local pool, swimming laps and perfecting your form. A strong stroke can make these water activities more enjoyable.

If you intend to do any other activities that require considerable exertion, start an exercise routine between six and eight weeks prior to departure. You may want to consult a fitness trainer so that the conditioning exercises you perform are geared to your planned travel.

MAINTAINING YOUR FITNESS ROUTINE

Daily exercise is one of the best ways to stay healthy and energetic when away from home. Even the most hectic travel schedule should allow time for a short workout or a brisk walk each day.

Before leaving on a trip, find out about the facilities at your hotel. Many hotels have fitness rooms; even more have pools. Others have agreements with nearby gyms or health clubs.

If you belong to a franchised health club, check if there's a branch you can use at your destination. Or ask if your club has reciprocity with out-of-town facilities.

Take advantage of fitness classes and facilities on cruises and at resorts.

Look for portable exercise equipment. A jump rope can provide an excellent workout for people with sturdy knees. A cassette player and workout tape fit easily into a suitcase, and they can inspire you to keep up with your exercise routine on the road.

Even without equipment,

Exercise in Transit

Sitting for hours in a plane, train, car, or bus can leave you tired and listless. By exercising along the way, you can reach your destination feeling more refreshed. Here are a few techniques to try.

Seated isometrics. Sit with your shoulders back, stomach in, knees together, and feet flat on the floor. Starting with your shoulders and working down, contract each major muscle group, holding it for the count of five and then relaxing. This can be especially effective for the buttock, stomach, and back muscles. Car drivers: Be sure to keep your eyes on the road and both hands on the wheel.

Seated flexing exercises. Keep your body moving to prevent stiffness and fatigue. At least once an hour, wiggle, bend, or rotate all movable parts. Start with your toes and ankles. Next, bend your knees and straighten them. (Be careful not to kick the seat in front of you.) Stretch your arms and shoulders by reaching up to the ceiling. Bend your arms over your head to get a good back stretch. End by shrugging your shoulders and rotating your head.

---

you can do calisthenics, sit-ups, leg lifts, and other flexibility exercises in your hotel room.

Walking is the best way to get to know most cities and towns. Get a good map from your hotel or the local tourist board and take off exploring.

To relieve foot pain from a day of city touring or museum-going, soak your feet in cool water for 10 minutes. Then massage them (or have your travel companion do it).

Elevate your feet to help ease swelling caused by walking or standing (see "Go Easy on Your Feet," page 140).

When vacationing at the beach, don't just relax on the sand. Get in the water and swim—it's one of the best forms of exercise. Bring a mask, snorkel, and flippers to explore the underwater landscape as you exercise. (Using flippers has the added benefit of working the upper thighs.)

AND DON'T FORGET...

If you wear glasses or contact lenses, bring an extra pair and a copy of your prescription in case you lose the original pair. Contact-lens wearers should bring glasses in case eyes get irritated or tired.

If you wear a hearing aid, carry along the brand name and model number, as well as extra batteries.

YOUR TRAVEL MEDICINE KIT

A well-stocked medicine kit can mean the difference between comfort and discomfort while traveling—and it can be a real lifesaver in emergencies. Here's what to include in yours.

PACKING MEDICATIONS

■ Include over-the-counter preparations as well as prescription drugs if you are traveling abroad. Some medications available without a prescription in Canada require one in other countries (and vice versa).

■ Choose a waterproof container that fits in your hand luggage. A clear container will make finding medications easier and will be handy if your luggage is searched by customs or during a security check.

■ Clearly mark all medicine containers with your name, the contents, and expiration dates. If possible, carry medicines in their original containers (see exceptions below).

■ Replace glass containers with plastic ones. Cotton balls or fine plastic bubble wrap will prevent pills from rattling in their bottles.

■ When buying creams, choose tubes (if available) rather than jars.

■ Suppositories do not travel well in hot climates, since they are designed to melt at body temperature. Talk to your doctor or pharmacist about other options.

■ If you take any medication regularly, pack two to three times the amount you expect to use on the trip. Divide it between at least two bags— including one that you keep with you—in case one bag gets lost, stolen, or damaged. Also ask your doctor for extra prescription forms.

■ In Canada, a pharmacist may be able to call your home drugstore (you pay for the call) for prescription information, and will give you a prescription refill if the prescription allows for it. However, for more than one refill you will have to see a local doctor.

■ Ask your pharmacist if you need to take any special precautions when traveling. For example, some drugs lose their potency in extreme heat or cold.

■ If your medication requires refrigeration, ask your doctor if you can take a different drug while traveling; if you can, begin the new medicine well before your trip to make sure that there are no complications.

■ If you are taking prescription medication while flying to a different time zone, consult your physician. In some cases, the dosage schedule will change.

What to Include in Your Kit

Ease minor discomfort quickly by having supplies on hand.

1. Antacid to treat minor gas or indigestion
2. Antibiotic tablets in case you go to any remote areas
3. Antidiarrhea medication
4. Antihistamine to treat allergies, mosquito bites, and other skin reactions
5. Antiseptic for minor wounds
6. Aspirin, acetaminophen, or ibuprofen to treat headaches and muscle pains
7. Baby powder to relieve prickly heat
8. Bandages, adhesive tape, gauze, and moleskin to dress wounds and protect blisters
9. Decongestant
10. Elastic bandage for strained or sprained joints
11. Feminine-hygiene products, especially important when you travel overseas and find supplies limited
12. Fiber tablets for constipation
13. Insect repellent
14. Motion sickness medication
15. Multipurpose pocket knife
16. Thermometer
17. Tweezers to remove splinters, thorns, and ticks

OTHER PROTECTIVE MEASURES

■ Have several plastic bags in various sizes for storing medications and other items that should not get wet.

■ Carry a medical identification card, or wear a bracelet or pendant if you have allergies or other chronic conditions. In an emergency, health-care personnel will know how to treat you.

■ Those with other medical problems should carry a letter from their doctor explaining their condition and the prescriptions necessary.

■ Even if you are not going to a sun-drenched or snow-covered spot, it's wise to pack sunglasses, sunscreen, and a wide-brimmed hat (see "Sun Sense," page 126).

Carry with you your immunization history, health-insurance card, claim forms, and family doctor's name and telephone number.

PRECAUTIONS FOR TRAVEL ABROAD

■ Have a checkup before your trip, especially if you plan to visit a remote locale, if you will be away for a month or more, if you have a chronic illness or are recovering from a recent illness, or if you are on a special diet.

■ You may want to go to a travel medicine clinic. Get a referral from your family doctor, or ask an experienced traveler to recommend a clinic. Travel medicine clinics at hospitals or universities are usually good choices (see box below).

■ Check with the Canadian Society for International Health, 170 Laurier Avenue West, Suite 902, Ottawa, K1P 5V5, for current information on vaccination requirements, and antimalarial treatment.

■ If you need immunizations, plan to get them at least six weeks before your departure so you have enough time to complete them and to recover from side effects, if any.

■ Make sure your vaccinations are up to date, even if you do not plan to travel far (see immunization schedules, page 341).

■ Ask your doctor for new prescription forms for medication you will carry with you. Keep these (or photocopies) in a wallet or another safe, accessible place. If a customs agent questions a drug, you can show your prescription. Also, if you lose your medication, you may be able to get a new supply.

Pack toilet paper and moist towelettes in case you must use public facilities of questionable cleanliness.

Travel Medicine Clinics

These are a few of the travel medicine clinics in Canada. For a more complete list, ask for the brochure Health Information for Canadian Travellers, *from the Canadian Society for International Health, address above.*

McGill University Centre for Tropical Diseases, Montreal General Hospital, Room B7-153, 1650 Cedar Ave., Montreal, Que., H3G 1A4.

Clinique Santé Voyage, Hôpital Saint-Luc, 1001 rue Saint-Denis, Montreal, Que., H2X 3H9.

Infectious Diseases Clinic, Ottawa General Hospital, 501 Smyth Road, Ottawa, Ont., K1H 8L6.

Infectious, Tropical and Parasitic Diseases, 795 Eglinton Ave. East, Toronto, Ont., M4G 2K9.

The Travel Counselling and Immunization Services, St. Michael's Hospital, 61 Queen Street East, Toronto, Ont., M5B 1WA.

Vancouver Travel and Immunization Clinic, 705-1160 Burrard Street, Vancouver, B.C., V6Z 2E8.

UBC Tropical Diseases Clinic, Division of Infectious Diseases, Room 452 D, Heather Pavilion, VGH, 2733 Heather Street, Vancouver, B.C., V5Z 3J5.

PREVENTING MOTION SICKNESS

Getting there may be half the fun of traveling, but not if motion sickness strikes. Whether you go by air, sea, or land, you want to avoid that queasy feeling. Here are some suggestions.

AVOIDANCE, ANTIDOTES

Motion sickness is caused by conflicting signals: your inner ears tell your brain that you are moving, but your eyes say you're not. Most methods of prevention involve straightening out those mixed messages or avoiding them altogether.

■ Both seasoned and inexperienced travelers can be afflicted with motion sickness; even naval captains (including the famed British admiral Lord Nelson) and astronauts have contended with the symptoms on occasion. Children over the age of 2 are the most susceptible, and people over age 50 are the least so. Women are more susceptible than men, especially during menstruation or pregnancy.

■ If you are susceptible to motion sickness, do not eat a heavy meal or drink alcoholic beverages before setting off. Have toast or crackers about a half hour before leaving. Consider taking a nonprescription pill for preventing discomfort.

■ Ask your doctor about prescribing a skin patch that is worn behind the ear. Be aware that side effects may include blurred vision for several days after the patch is removed.

■ Watch for early warning signs: pallor, drowsiness, headache, excessive salivation, intestinal gas, a cold sweat, and rapid, shallow breathing. Preventive measures at this time can usually stop a progression downward to light-headedness, sweating, nausea, and vomiting.

■ Try deep breathing and relaxation exercises. Concentrate on something besides impending queasiness. (A fishing boat captain observes that his passengers are never seasick when fish are biting!)

■ Don't face backward or look at a sick passenger.

■ Keep your eyes on the horizon, preferably in the direction you're moving.

■ Try natural remedies, such as sucking on a lemon or taking a tablespoon of powdered gingerroot, available in health-food stores.

■ Try a technique known as acupressure. This entails pressing a sensitive point on the inside of your wrist. You can also buy an acupressure bracelet, which has a button that does the pressing for you.

■ If you start feeling sick, one of these positions may help: Sit down with your head back, keeping it as still as possible. Or put your head between your knees. Or lie down with your eyes closed.

....

Nibbling a few dry crackers and sipping a flat soda can help to settle a queasy stomach.

....

BY LAND

■ In a car, sit where you can see what lies ahead so you can anticipate the vehicle's movements. If possible, do the driving. Focusing on the road will help prevent car sickness. The front passenger seat is the next-best position after the driver's seat.

■ If you must sit in the backseat, move toward the middle so you can look out the front window without blocking the driver's rearview mirror.

■ Open a window at least a crack when possible. With air-conditioning, open the vents rather than recirculate air, unless you're in heavy traffic or following a truck or bus.

■ Ask the driver to maintain a consistent speed and go easy around curves. Abrupt or frequent acceleration and braking increases car sickness.

■ On a train, try to sit toward the front, facing forward (next to an open window, if possible). In a bus, make sure you can see the driver or out the front window.

■ Avoid reading, which adds to the problem of conflicting

eye messages. If you want a diversion, listen to music or a recorded book.

BY SEA

Modern cruise ships are more stable than in the past. And the bigger the ship, the less likely you are to become sick. Remember, however, that seas are more likely to be rough in fall and winter than spring and summer.

■ Choose a cabin as close to the middle of the ship as possible.

■ Stay on deck whenever you can, and take advantage of on-board activities (other than overeating and drinking). The fresh sea air should ward off most queasiness, and when you are busy, you are less likely to get seasick.

■ Avoid the back of the ship, even if you don't feel sick. The fumes from the engine can make anyone queasy. Similarly, avoid the smoking section of the on-board restaurant.

■ If you start feeling sick and you can't get up on deck, lie down, close your eyes, and try to relax. Move out on deck as soon as you can.

■ Stick to low-fat, high-carbohydrate foods. And be patient—most people become accustomed to the ship's constant motion in a day or two. By that time, you may be in calm seas.

■ If you do get seasick, don't let it spoil your cruise. Ask the ship's doctor for medication, which can be given as an injection or suppository. Several medications are very effective in combating motion sickness, but they tend to produce drowsiness.

BY AIR

Of all modes of travel, flying in a jet plane is the least likely to cause motion sickness, unless the plane hits turbulence.

■ If you tend to suffer from motion sickness, choose a seat over the wings, where the plane is most steady.

■ Also try to book nonstop flights. The fewer takeoffs and landings, the better.

■ Direct the air vents above your seat toward your face. (Avoid the back of the neck, which can cause stiffness.)

PREPARING YOUR BODY FOR MOTION

Exercises used to prevent dizziness can also help prevent motion sickness. Try these methods to accustom your body to motion before embarking on your trip.

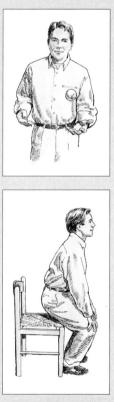

Toss a tennis ball *from hand to hand. Follow the arc of the ball's motion with your eyes. This exercise can also be used while in transit to help prevent motion sickness.*

Look up, then down. *Repeat, starting slowly but rapidly picking up speed. After 20 up-and-down motions, look from side to side 20 times—again going from slow to fast. Repeat several times a day for two or three days and again just before setting off.*

Sit in a chair *with your feet flat on the floor. Stand up straight, then sit down. Repeat several times. Then try the same exercise with your eyes closed.*

Clear a 10-foot path *next to a wall or the back of a sofa. Walk back and forth several times. Repeat the exercise with your eyes closed, holding on to the wall or sofa for balance, if needed.*

GOING BY CAR

Car travel is by far the most popular way to get away, but it is also one of the most dangerous forms of travel. To help ensure a safe vacation, take these precautions and use these hints whenever you're on the road.

SEAT BELTS AND AIR BAGS

■ Always wear your seat belt when traveling by car, including when you are riding in the backseat. Not being belted in when you are in the backseat poses a danger not only to yourself—if an accident should occur, other passengers could be injured by the impact of your body against the front seat.

■ Combination shoulder-lap seat belts offer maximum protection. Make sure that each belt fits tightly and properly. Wear the lap belt slung low on your lap. The shoulder belt should extend across the chest and over your shoulder.

■ Pregnant women should wear a lap belt below the abdomen, over the pelvic bone. This is one of the strongest bones in the body. There is no evidence that safety belts increase the chance of injury to the fetus in an accident.

■ If you are in a car with air bags, you still need to wear your seat belt. Inflated air bags can injure motorists riding with no seat belt. And air bags offer protection only in severe head-on crashes, not in low-severity frontal collisions, side or rear impacts, or rollovers.

■ Keep your seat upright, with the middle of the headrest at ear height. This maximizes the efficiency of seat belts and reduces the risk of whiplash.

■ After a severe crash in which the air bag has inflated or you have sustained bruises from impact against the seat belt, replace both the air bag and the seat belts.

■ With babies and small children, car safety seats take the place of seat belts; they are extremely important—and required by law. For information about car seats, see page 288.

AVOIDING FATIGUE BEHIND THE WHEEL

■ To make sure you stay alert, have a light meal and do not drink alcohol before driving.

■ Warm temperatures can make you sleepy, so keep the car slightly cool. You may also want to turn the vents toward your face and turn up the fan.

■ Put on a tape with lively music, or turn on the radio. Sing along if you wish, but don't let yourself get distracted by the song.

■ Don't drive for more than two or three hours without a break. Stop at a rest stop and walk around for a few minutes. Movement encourages good circulation, which helps fight fatigue. Drink a cold soda or cup of tea or coffee.

When you drive in unfamiliar territory, in bad weather, or at night, take breaks more frequently than you ordinarily do. You have to concentrate so hard in these situations that you may tire more quickly.

AVOIDING COLLISIONS

■ Drive with your low-beam headlights on during daylight hours. Studies show that low beams increase your visibility to other cars, thereby reducing collisions.

■ Constantly be alert to possible trouble: flashing lights and sirens, cars ahead with their brake lights on, children playing near the side of the road, or cars pulling out from driveways or side streets. If you see a potential hazard, immediately take your foot off the accelerator and prepare to brake or veer to avoid a collision.

■ Unless there are pedestrians on the side of the road, it is best to veer to the right rather than the left to avoid an on-the-road hazard. If necessary, drive onto the shoulder or even the grass to the right of the shoulder. Don't brake too hard; instead, steer yourself to safety as you stop gradually.

■ If a collision is inevitable, choose the least dangerous option. Aim for the protective railing, which is designed to absorb impact. Hitting a stationary car or sideswiping one going in the same direction is less likely to cause a serious injury than a head-on collision or hitting a wall or tree.

■ Heed road signs that indicate deer- and other animal-crossing areas, especially at night. Slow down, and watch for the reflection of eyes along the roadside. Hitting a deer is especially dangerous because it may try to jump over your car and come through your windshield instead.

If you feel that another driver has threatened you in any way, or if you get "bumped" and you feel it was not an accident, do not stop. Instead, drive to the nearest police station to report the mishap.

IN THE EVENT OF AN ACCIDENT

According to the Canada Safety Council, these are the steps to take if you are in a collision:

■ Stop your vehicle as soon as it is safe and legal to do so. If injuries or death have resulted, cars should not be moved. But use your judgment. The

vehicle should be moved out of the way of oncoming traffic.

■ Check for injuries among all drivers and passengers. If necessary, call an ambulance or apply first aid.

■ Call the police to report the accident.

■ While you are waiting for the police, mark the accident scene with flares or other highly visible markers.

■ Take the names of the people in the accident and the license numbers of the drivers. Insurance information should also be gathered at this time. If there were any witnesses, take down their names as well.

■ Do not assign blame or argue with the other drivers. Wait until the police get there to make your statement.

■ If you have a camera with you, take several pictures of the scene. Otherwise, draw a diagram of what you saw when the accident occurred. The police will also do this after a serious accident.

■ After giving your statement to the police, arrange to get a copy of the police report from the local precinct.

DEALING WITH DARKNESS

■ After being outside in bright sunlight or inside a brightly lit building, it may take time for your eyes to adjust to the relative darkness of your car. Try to allow enough time that you can sit in your car for a few minutes before starting to drive. This way, your eyesight will be at its best.

■ Wear sunglasses to cut glare on a very bright, sunny day. Do not wear sunglasses once the sun has set.

■ Make sure your car's headlights and windows are clean inside and out. This helps both your vision and your visibility at night.

■ Have your mechanic check periodically to see that your headlights are aimed correctly to maximize your field of vision when driving at night. (This may be part of your province's annual safety inspection.)

■ Night vision decreases with age, so older people should consider avoiding night driving when possible. A driver over 50 may need twice as much light to see as well as a 30-year-old.

■ Turn on your headlights at dusk. You may not need them to see the road, but it will help other drivers to see you more clearly.

The reduced light at twilight (either early morning or late afternoon) decreases the amount of contrast between objects. If you must drive at twilight, be extra vigilant.

Equipping the Car for Road Trips

Accidents occur on rural roads more often than elsewhere, but travelers should prepare for all situations. Have these items handy for emergencies:

Fire extinguisher, either a three-pound dry powder type or two-pound gas type. The fire extinguisher should be easily accessible

Flashlight and spare batteries

Blankets

Battery-powered radio

Drive belt or fan belt

Extra fuses, spark plugs, and lightbulbs

Duplicate ignition key (stored in a concealed spot)

Tools: regular and Phillips screwdrivers, wrench, and spark-plug wrench

Tire-changing equipment and spare tire

Compressed-air tire inflator (Although changing a tire is much better for the tire, this product can be a lifesaver in certain situations.)

Jumper cables (Check your owner's manual in case you shouldn't use jumper cables.)

Windshield-wiper fluid

Flares or reflectors

A sign saying "Call police" to put in your rear window

Bar of plain soap (for temporarily repairing a leaky gas tank)

Drinkable water

In winter, add a flat-blade shovel, a bag of sand or cat litter, a snow brush, an ice scraper, and spray de-icer

SNOW, SLEET, RAIN, OR FOG

■ Even if you are driving only a short distance, make sure you have good visibility before setting out in bad weather. Clean snow off windows and use the defroster to eliminate fog or condensation.

■ Adjust your driving for the conditions. On wet or icy roads, drive more slowly to account for the greater distances required for braking. In heavy rain or other low-visibility conditions, turn on your lights and reduce your speed. Avoid sudden turns or stops; remember that a slow, smooth pace is safest.

■ When driving in fog, make sure that your headlights are clean. Mud and dirt can dim the lights and make it more difficult for other cars to see you.

■ Drive with a window open when it's foggy so you can hear cars that you cannot see.

■ To keep your windows from fogging, turn on the heater or air conditioner for a few minutes before you start the defroster.

■ Do not use high-beam headlights ("brights") when driving in fog. Turn on regular headlights or fog lights instead. Put the windshield wipers on the intermittent setting to remove moisture from the windshield.

■ When visibility is limited, use the white line (if there is one) on the side of the road as your guide. If possible, follow a large truck at a safe distance; high-clearance vehicles sometimes have better visibility than passenger cars. Do not, however, follow another car's red taillights—you may end up repeating the driver's mistakes.

■ Before winter arrives, have an auto mechanic thoroughly check your car. The battery should be fully charged; otherwise, it may fail in cold weather.

■ To reduce the ice and frost on windshields on winter mornings, cover them with an old blanket at night. Or coat the glass with a homemade antifreeze. Mix three parts vinegar to one part water, put the mixture in a spray bottle, and apply to the car windows.

■ If your car gets stuck on snow or ice, don't push down on the gas pedal. The spinning tires will only dig you in deeper. Instead, find something to put under the wheels (front ones for front-wheel-drive cars, rear ones for rear-wheel-drive). Sand, cat litter, an old piece of carpeting, or some twigs will do the job. Then gently accelerate, and let the wheels grip the surface.

If people are helping you by pushing your car as you accelerate, make sure they are not directly behind the car—you may roll back and hit them. Also, they should watch out for sand, twigs, or other materials shooting out from under the spinning wheels.

OTHER SAFETY TIPS

■ If a car is approaching you in the wrong lane, first flash your headlights or sound your horn to alert the driver to the danger. Start braking and scanning the area for a shoulder or side road on the right. Once you can determine which direction the other car is going, turn away from it. Sideswiping one or more cars is less dangerous than colliding head-on.

■ Slow down on curvy roads, especially on hills. Be sure to stick to your side of the road when you can't see what's around the corner.

■ Trucks speed up on downhill stretches. If a truck is behind you going downhill, change lanes, if possible.

■ When making turns on busy city streets where visibility is blocked by other cars and trucks, make use of reflections in store windows and other vehicles. They may help you to see what's around a corner or how close you are to other cars when you're parallel parking.

■ Get your eyes checked every two years to make sure you don't need glasses or a stronger prescription. This is particularly important for drivers who are over the age of 55.

■ At railroad crossings, obey all signals. Check carefully for oncoming trains before driving over the tracks.

■ When driving in the country near farms and grazing land, look for mud, hay, or animal droppings on the road. They may indicate livestock or a slow-moving tractor ahead. Be prepared to slow down or stop.

■ When renting a car, make a safety check before leaving the parking lot. Check that the lights, wipers, turn signals, horn, and other equipment are in proper working order. Determine how to use the radio and air-conditioning system. Make sure there is a spare tire, jack, and other tire-changing equipment.

■ When buying a new car, look for one that offers a mirror on the right side, which reduces the blind spot on the passenger side. For other safety features, see the box on page 269.

■ If you feel anxious, frustrated, or angry, take time to calm down before getting behind the wheel. Practice deep breathing or walk around the block.

DRIVING UNDER THE INFLUENCE

Alcohol and drugs are implicated in nearly half of all traffic fatalities. Just one drink can slow reaction time and reduce vision. Even some over-the-counter drugs can impair driving performance.

■ Follow this simple rule: Don't drink and drive. For parties, choose a designated driver who abstains from alcohol.

■ When you're the designated driver, adopt the European practice of keeping your car keys in your glass to indicate to a host that you should not be served alcohol.

■ If you are planning to drive a long distance, do not drink for at least 24 hours before setting out. A few drinks on Thursday night can increase your fatigue while driving Friday night.

■ Check with your doctor about possible side effects whenever he or she prescribes a new medication. If you don't feel your best, you are probably better off not driving.

■ Read the labels on antihistamines, cold preparations, and motion-sickness drugs, all of which can cause drowsiness.

Be aware of cars that are weaving and moving erratically. Stay well behind them, and do not try to pass a weaving vehicle.

PETS AND CARS

■ Before taking your dog on a long trip, try short drives. This will accustom your pet to being in the car and will give you a chance to train it to behave in the car.

■ Make sure your pet is up to date on all vaccinations, especially rabies. Be aware that some inoculations require a few weeks to take effect. Tell the vet where you are traveling (in case any diseases are prevalent in the area), and ask for a document stating that your pet has been vaccinated.

■ Your dog or cat should wear a collar with identification information when traveling.

■ If you don't keep your dog in a carrier or cage while driving, train it to sit in one place and to obey your commands. Even so, it is best to install a gate between the front and back seats to prevent the dog from climbing into the front or otherwise distracting the driver.

■ Attach your pet's leash before getting out of the car. Keep your pet on a leash or in a pet carrier when not in your hotel room or car.

■ Stop every two hours to walk your pet for 10 or 15 minutes. Offer the animal some water, but don't feed it until you've stopped for the

night to decrease the likelihood of car sickness.

■ Many tourist attractions offer an on-site kennel for pets. Reserve space ahead, if possible.

■ Don't leave your pet alone in a car. The temperature inside a car can soar very quickly, making the animal vulnerable to life-threatening heatstroke.

• •

Make sure your pet is flea-free before you take it on a trip. Fleas can easily infest your car upholstery, not to mention any hotel accommodations you might use.

• •

PREVENTING CARJACKING AND OTHER CRIMES

■ When getting into your car, have your keys ready so that you can enter quickly.

■ In a dark, secluded, or underground parking lot, have someone accompany you to your car.

■ Give your car a quick inspection for tampering before you enter it. Check the door handles, locks, and the backseat. Be wary of people coming toward you as you get into your car.

■ When approaching your car, take a quick look underneath to make sure no one is lurking there. Carjackers sometimes hide under the car and then grab their victim's legs as he or she unlocks the car.

■ Be especially wary when getting in and out of a car in a mall parking lot. Try to park near a store entrance or security patrol; if this is not possible, drive around until you

come to an area where there are several people. Carjackers prefer to attack without a crowd of onlookers.

■ Safety experts recommend cellular car phones for anyone who does a lot of night driving and, especially, for women who drive alone. If you have a programmable phone, list the number of the police or emergency services.

■ Don't sit alone in your car when waiting for someone else. Arrange to meet in a store, restaurant, or other building, and then approach your car together.

■ When using a self-service filling station, take your keys out of the ignition and lock the car while you are pumping gas and paying for it.

■ Consider installing an electronic alarm that you can activate from both inside and outside the car. There are now electronic lock and alarm systems that allow you to stop or disable the car as it is being driven away. If you have such a system, be sure to carry its key on a chain separate from your other car keys; otherwise, the carjacker can make off with it, too.

■ Lock your doors and close windows when possible. If necessary, leave windows open only an inch or so.

■ When you stop at traffic lights, leave enough room between your car and the one in front of you so that you can pull out if necessary.

■ Carry your car registration and any other documents that include your address in your purse or wallet, rather than leaving them in the glove compartment.

■ Be careful when using a drive-up teller machine or when getting into your car after using an automatic teller machine.

■ Choose well-lit, heavily traveled roads whenever you can. Be familiar with your route before driving. If possible, let someone know where you are going, what route you are taking, and when you expect to arrive.

■ Whenever you can, find out where safe havens are along your route. If you sense that trouble is brewing, do not hesitate to get assistance or head for the nearest phone.

■ If you get lost, be cautious when asking people for directions. You may be better off finding a police station, a pay phone, or a well-lit gas station.

■ Don't accept assistance from strangers if your car has broken down. If someone approaches the car and you have been able to use a call box, inform the person—speaking through a closed or nearly closed window—that help is

---

Safety Features to Look for in a New Car

When buying a new car, pay special attention to the safety features listed below. Also look for favorable ratings from the Vehicle Information Centre of Canada (which publishes the pamphlet Choosing your Car) *and Transport Canada, which assign ratings based on highway statistics and crash tests. Other sources are the Insurance Bureau of Canada, which produces a pamphlet called* Play it Safe, *and the Automobile Protection Association (APA).*

Air bags on both the driver's and the passenger's side for protection in head-on collisions

Antilock braking system (ABS), which prevents wheels from locking in sudden stops

Comfortable and adjustable safety belts

Four-door models, whose extra metal between the doors provides additional roof support

Headlamp cleaners

Reinforced side walls for passenger compartment

Side mirrors on both the driver's and the passenger's side to reduce blind spots, and automatic day/night mirrors to improve visibility for night driving

---

on the way. If you have not been able to call for assistance, ask the stranger to drive to the nearest pay phone and call the police.

■ If your "gut reaction" to the stranger is not good, tell him or her that you have already contacted the police and that help is on the way—whether or not you've been able to call for help.

■ If an unmarked patrol car signals you to pull over, nod to acknowledge that you have seen the signal. Slow down and gesture for the car to follow you. Stop in a well-lit, populated area. Keep your car doors locked. Ask to see identification to confirm that you are dealing with the police, not impostors.

■ Obvious though it may

seem, do not leave your keys in the ignition when you leave your car.

■ Buy a steering wheel lock or car alarm, or both.

■ To avoid theft and rolling, leave a standard car in gear and an automatic in park; with both, put the parking brake on.

■ To deter a thief with a tow truck, park with your wheels turned toward the curb.

■ Keep valuables—even spare change for tolls—out of sight.

■ Instead of placing items in your trunk when you stop somewhere (a restaurant, for example), do so when you first set out; otherwise, someone may see you stowing away the items and try to break into the trunk to get them.

CAMPING: OUTDOOR SAFETY

Camping has been the great Canadian family vacation since long before the first theme park was built. Take the kids and head to the countryside, but be sure to keep safety in mind.

BE PREPARED

■ If you spend a lot of time camping and hiking, consider taking a first-aid course. St. John Ambulance, the Red Cross and the Y's offer such courses.

■ When you take a day hike or other trip away from the campsite, put a small first-aid kit in your backpack. Include bandages, a water-purification chemical, sunglasses, sunscreen, a hat, and insect repellent (see "Your Travel Medicine Kit," page 260).

■ Plan to arrive early if you are using a public camping ground. The choicest sites are usually gone by midafternoon.

SET YOUR SITES

■ To ensure that your tent stays dry, sew a waterproof ground cloth inside the tent before setting off. This is much more effective than pitching your tent on top of a ground cloth. However, you will need to waterproof the seams where needle holes allow leakage.

■ Never pitch your tent where there is evidence that the ground has been underwater (a waterline, less vegetation, patterns in sand or soil). Even if the skies look clear, weather changes may occur upstream or while you're sleeping.

■ Avoid meadows and flat mossy areas as campsites. Water collects in meadows, and moss acts as a sponge.

You may wake up in a puddle.

■ If a lightning storm is possible, make sure your tent is not the highest object in the immediate area. Camp within the protection of the tallest trees or some other tall object (see "Storms and Natural Disasters," page 246).

■ To reduce exposure to insects, choose a site away from ponds or lakes. Near the top of a hill, you'll usually get a good breeze and sun, which will discourage gnats and mosquitoes, though it may be chillier than elsewhere.

■ Use insect netting in areas that have large numbers of biting insects. This is particularly important when sleeping outside your tent.

■ To guard against such crawling insects as fleas and ticks, choose a tent with a "floor."

■ Don't pitch a tent over rodent holes or in thick brush.

■ To minimize the bugs around your campsite, pitch your tent and set up your sleeping bag before evening, when insects are most active. If possible, finish dinner, including washing dishes, before the evening onslaught.

■ Before retiring, you need to

Camping Checklist

Once you have the basics (sleeping bag, tent, camp stove), these items will help make you comfortable and prepare you to cope with an emergency:

All-weather blanket

Battery-powered radio

Compass

Damp-proof matches

Emergency provisions (water, high-carbohydrate bars, powdered drinks)

Flashlight with extra batteries

Insect repellent

Net bags (for dirty laundry or hanging up food to keep it away from animals)

Plastic bags

Rescue whistle

Signal mirror

Thermal sleeping pad

Toilet paper

Towelettes

Travel medicine kit

Waterproof tarpaulin

Water-purification device or tablets

take care of any leftover food or garbage. Discard it in the proper campground receptacle, bury it at least 500 feet from the campsite, or stow it inside your car to discourage nighttime visits from raccoons, skunks, and other scavengers (see "Animals in the Wild," page 236).

CAMPFIRES

Cooking, cleaning, warming up, storytelling—all take place around a campfire, making it an integral part of the camping experience. But campfires, as well as camp stoves, do pose a risk.

■ Keep tents, sleeping bags, and other flammable materials away from the camp stove or campfire. Never set a camp stove on a sleeping bag or tent floor. If you must cook under shelter because of bad weather, make sure the shelter is sufficiently ventilated and away from your sleeping tent.

■ Don't run your camp stove at full power for more than a few minutes. Stoves can explode if they overheat.

■ Wait until a camp stove has been turned off and had time to cool down before trying to refill the fuel tank.

■ Refuel and light stoves and lanterns outside a tent.

Never walk away and leave a campfire smoldering. To test it, hold your hand about six inches above it. If you feel heat, douse it with more water and cover it with dirt.

CLEANING UP

■ Take a liquid soap, rather than a bar type. A biodegradable, concentrated liquid soap is easier to use than bar soap. Most of these soaps will clean not only hands but also hair, dishes, and clothing.

■ Avoid perfumed soaps; they may attract insects.

■ In camp or on a trail, carry water at least 200 feet from lakes, streams, and springs before you wash. That will help keep soap from getting into open water, where it may harm plants and wildlife.

■ Use a large pot or a collapsible washbasin for cleanups. Boil the water on the camp stove or campfire, and let it cool down.

■ Campers who pack light and travel long need a laundry kit. Carry a net bag to store dirty clothes, a clothesline, and plastic clothespins. Use concentrated liquid soap or other biodegradable laundry soap. A small brush will help get out stains and dirt.

■ Insect repellents are more likely to cause skin reactions in children than adults since children's thinner skin absorbs chemicals faster. Apply preparations to clothing rather than to skin to help prevent rashes.

HOW TO SIGNAL FOR HELP

If you ever get lost, stay put and await rescuers. Make yourself very visible.

■ Fly a bright-colored flag, sleeping bag, or blanket from a tree.

■ Sweep the horizon with a mirror or a bright can lid that an airplane pilot can see.

■ Use the universal distress signal: any signal repeated three times. Or send the S-O-S Morse code of three dots, three dashes, three dots with a flag, flashlight, lantern, mirror, or whistle.

GROUND-TO-AIR RESCUE SIGNALS

To send a message to planes flying overhead, find an open area near your camp. Form the appropriate letter (see below) by lining up rocks, by using parts of tents, ground cloths, or clothing, or by stamping the shape in snow or sand.

V	N	X	Y	↑
Require Assistance	No or Negative	Require Medical Help	Yes or Affirmative	Proceeding in this Direction

BOATING AND WATERSKIING

Whether a river, lake, ocean, or just a small stream, water inspires relaxation and peacefulness. But water is also one of nature's most powerful forces, demanding good judgment and respect.

SAFETY FIRST

■ The Canadian Coast Guard requires all boats to be outfitted with approved Personal Flotation Devices (PFDs)—for pleasure craft—or life jackets, for other vessels. Even if you know how to swim, wear your PFD whenever you are out in a small craft.

■ Make sure that children always wear PFDs while on board, even when sleeping.

■ Besides PFDs, you should have the following safety equipment on board: throwable rescue device, first-aid kit, signal kit, whistle or air horn, bilge pump, fire extinguisher, knife, extra paddle, anchor, and anchor line.

■ Before you throw a rescue device, make sure the other end of the line is securely tied to the boat. Rescue throw bags, which are easy to throw, are preferred over life rings or seat cushions for rough, white-water conditions.

■ Maneuvering any kind of boat requires training and practice. Before setting off on your own, get appropriate instruction. The nearest Coast Guard office can suggest a reliable course or instructor.

■ Do not cast off without a chart of the waters you are on, such as a river map or a nautical bay or ocean chart.

Study it beforehand, and waterproof it with clear, moisture-proof paper.

■ If you are on a bay, ocean, or other tidal water, carry a tide chart. During tidal changes, currents can wreak havoc on boaters, especially those under sail.

■ Listen to a marine forecast before taking a boat out. Even when skies are blue, stay ashore if Environment Canada issues "small-craft warnings." A change in the weather can occur quickly.

■ Water reflects sunlight upward, exposing you to more ultraviolet rays. Wear protective clothing, sunglasses, a hat, and water-resistant sunblock when you are on the water, even if it's cloudy (see "Sun Sense," page 126).

■ Never operate a boat while under the influence of alcohol or other drugs. A designated driver is as good an idea on the water as it is on the road. Exercise caution if you are taking tranquilizers, painkillers, antihistamines, or other drugs. Both prescription and nonprescription drugs can decrease a driver's alertness and increase risks of an accident.

■ Be alert to "boater's hypnosis," or fatigue, caused by prolonged exposure to noise, vibration, sun, glare, wind, and the boat's motion. It can slow

reaction time almost as much as if you were legally drunk.

If you are involved in an accident—even one that involves no other boats— you should report it to the appropriate authority. Check with the nearest Coast Guard office for instructions on how to file an accident report.

CANOEING AND KAYAKING

■ Buy or rent a canoe or kayak that is suitable for the type of water you will be on. For white water, you will need a boat designed to stay dry and one that is easily maneuvered.

■ To increase stability, paddlers should sit low in the canoe. A good position is kneeling while resting the buttocks on a low seat. Distribute weight evenly.

■ Remember that kayaking requires more skill than paddling a canoe, even though new models for sea kayaking and touring are designed for stability. Before setting out, take a basic course; most stores that sell kayaks offer some instruction. Practice capsizing and righting a kayak in calm water, such as a pool or pond, before tackling rougher water.

■ To add stability to a kayak in rough water, carry an inflatable paddle float or sponson float system.

■ When canoeing or kayaking on white water, wear a safety helmet designed for on-the-water use. These lightweight, quick-draining helmets can save lives in the event of a flip.

■ To protect your hands from blisters and increase your gripping power when paddling, always wear boating gloves.

■ Secure gear so that it does not shift or go overboard in rough waters. To keep its contents dry, line a bag (even if it's supposed to be waterproof) with a plastic bag.

SAILING AND BOARDSAILING

■ As with other forms of boating, learning to sail requires training and practice. The Coast Guard, provincial sailing associations and sailing schools offer courses. Make sure you know how to handle your boat before setting out.

■ If you are sailing on a small boat in cold water or cold weather, wear a wet or dry suit, depending upon the temperature. A person can survive only a few minutes in very cold water. The combination of cold water spray and wind can cause hypothermia.

■ If you capsize and cannot right the boat, stay with the vessel until help comes. Even if it looks like the shoreline is close, you may not be able to reach it on your own.

■ Boardsailing can be exhausting. While you're learning, stay close to shore and don't go out in a brisk wind. A gentle breeze is best for novices.

Always sail upwind first. Sailing downwind (in the direction of the wind) is much easier. Many novice sailors have sailed with the wind a long distance only to find that getting back requires more skill than they have.

WATERSKIING

■ Waterskiing requires three people: the driver, the skier, and an observer to watch the skier and alert the driver to any problem.

■ Skiers should learn waterskiing hand signals, such as those shown below. These can be essential if problems arise.

■ Choose a boat equipped with a rearview mirror, which enables the driver to see the skier.

■ Wear a Canadian Coast Guard-approved PFD or life jacket. It should fit snugly so that it does not slide up. If you are uncertain as to how snug it should be, remember that too tight is safer than too loose.

■ Plan the general path in advance. Avoid the shoreline, other boats, and any obstacle. Allow a safety area of 100 feet on either side of the boat, as well as 2,000 to 3,000 feet of obstacle-free waterway.

■ In a heavily trafficked area, follow the general pattern of other boats. Avoid swimming and mooring areas and marina channels. Give more room than usual to fishing boats (to account for lines that may be out) and slow-moving boats, such as canoes.

■ Once the path is settled, do not change it unless absolutely necessary.

■ Before turning, check both sides to see that there are no oncoming or stationary boats that could cause trouble.

■ Approach a fallen skier so that he or she is on the driver's side of the boat and so the driver can see the skier at all times. Before the skier climbs back on board, turn off the motor.

Waterskiing signals *from left: Skier wants boat operator to go faster, slow down, stop, and turn off the boat engine.*

GOING BY PLANE

Some simple measures can help you compensate for jet lag, low air pressure in the cabin, and extended periods of sitting still. Just knowing the right way to eat can ease the stress of air travel.

SAFETY IN THE AIR

Overall, air travel is one of the safest transportation methods—25 times safer than car travel, some experts estimate. However, there are measures passengers can take to further ensure their safety in case of an accident.

■ Transport Canada grounds a plane if it doubts its safety record. But check with the Travel Information Line of the Department of Foreign Affairs for warnings about overseas flights.

■ Keep valuables out of sight when waiting in airline terminals to avoid theft.

■ Most accidents that befall air travelers occur on the ground rather than in the air. Watch your step while hurrying through airports, and be careful carrying heavy luggage (check it, if possible).

■ Do not put heavy items in the overhead baggage racks on a plane. If they fall out when the compartment is opened (by a passenger or accidentally during turbulence), they may cause injury.

■ If you have a chronic illness, be sure to bring your medication on board in your carry-on bag. (For more information on flying with various medical conditions, see the box on the facing page.)

> **After a long flight, it's best to rest before driving in an unfamiliar place. This is especially important if you have had any alcohol or taken such medications as antihistamines or sleeping pills while airborne.**

COMFORT IN THE SKY

■ Choose loose clothing for travel. Wear layers of light clothing so that you can easily adjust to cabin temperature. Be sure to bring something warm with you because cabin temperatures can get quite chilly.

■ Feet tend to swell while in the air, so wear loose shoes. If you must wear tight shoes, don't slip them off during the flight because if your feet swell, you may not be able to get the shoes back on.

■ Sitting in cramped quarters for long periods on airplanes can reduce circulation and increase the chance of blood clots. Pregnant women and people with heart conditions, circulation problems, and other ailments are most vulnerable, but even healthy people can suffer adverse effects. Get up and move around, and try some of the exercises on page 259.

■ If you're tall, ask for an aisle or bulkhead seat, which usually allows for more leg room. It's also easier to get up and walk around if you don't have to climb over other passengers.

■ Aspirin may help reduce the chances of blood clots and other circulation problems in the air. Consider taking one a day beginning on the day prior to your departure, but be sure to check with your doctor first.

■ Smoking is barred on all domestic flights in Canada, and from July 1994 was banned on all Canadian international flights. However, smoking is still allowed on many foreign airlines, usually in and around only a few rows of seating at the back of the aircraft.

■ Avoid smoking areas of airports and especially airport bars. On flights where smoking is allowed, sit in the non-smoking section, preferably several rows away from the smoking section.

■ Even if you ordinarily smoke, abstain while in the air. Both smoking and inhaling secondhand smoke increase the chance of blood clots. They also decrease the amount of oxygen taken in with each breath, adding to the fatigue of travel.

■ If you have asthma or another medical condition aggravated by smoke, ask about the location of the smoking section when reserving a flight on a foreign airline. Reserve a seat as far away from the smoking section as possible.

THE EFFECTS OF LOW AIR PRESSURE

■ The air pressure in airplanes is similar to that of elevations of between 7,000 and 10,000 feet. That means there is less available oxygen, which can lead to fatigue. To reduce these symptoms, arrive at the airport well rested and try to keep stress levels low.

■ Low-pressure air has a relative humidity of about 10 percent—much lower than at sea level. To compensate for the dry air, drink plenty of nonalcoholic fluids in flight, bring along saline drops for your eyes and nose, and apply moisturizer before and during the flight. An atomizer filled with water can help moisten your skin before you apply the moisturizer.

■ If you are congested and must fly, take a decongestant at least an hour before departure, preferably taking the first dose the night before the flight. On a long flight, you

---

Special Cases

Certain medical conditions and circumstances create special needs while flying, or they may mean not flying at all. If any of the following apply to you, talk to your doctor before taking off:

Asthma, emphysema, and other lung disorders. These conditions are exacerbated by the reduced amount of oxygen in pressurized airplane cabins. Make sure that the airline can supply extra oxygen if you need it (physician's prescription required).

Colostomy. During long flights, use a larger bag than usual. For patients who use ether to clean the stoma, another cleanser must be used on airplanes.

Diabetes. Extra vigilance in controlling blood-sugar levels may be needed, especially when traveling across time zones. Be sure to pack a glucometer in your carry-on luggage.

Epilepsy. Dosage of anticonvulsant medication may need to be increased before flying; check with your doctor.

Newborn babies. Lungs are not fully expanded until 48 hours after birth. For the first month, babies are readily susceptible to infections, which may be spread by recirculated cabin air.

Pacemakers. Let the airline and airport security officers know that you have a pacemaker. Request a hand check rather than going through a metal detector at the security check-in site.

Plaster casts. On long flights, air trapped in casts may expand and squeeze underlying tissue. A split cast allows air to escape.

Pregnancy. Discuss travel plans with your doctor. Generally, flying after the 34th week of pregnancy is not recommended, and flying is not advisable at all for women with high-risk pregnancies.

Recent heart attack or stroke. Wait at least two weeks to fly. A rule of thumb is that people who are able to walk 150 feet and climb 10 to 12 stairs without symptoms are generally able to fly.

Recent surgery or accident. Change in air pressure may cause intestinal gases to expand, which can produce pain. Wait one to three weeks before flying, especially if surgery or an injury involved the ears, jaw, abdomen, skull, lungs, or chest.

Sickle-cell anemia. People with this disease often experience bone pain during air travel or at altitudes above 8,000 feet. If you must fly, request oxygen to help reduce symptoms.

---

may need to take another dose before landing. You can also use a nasal spray.

■ Congestion is more likely to cause ear discomfort on landing than takeoff. Forcing a yawn is the best way to open drainage tubes and unblock ears. Another way to clear your ears is to pinch the nostrils slightly, close your mouth, and gently breathe out through your nose. You can also suck on hard candy or chew gum.

When you hear a click in your ears, they are clear.

■ You can also request two Styrofoam cups and steaming hot towels (paper or cotton). Wring towels of excess water, put them in cups, and hold cups over ears. The heated moist air will make your ears "pop."

■ If you have ear pain on landing that intensifies and then suddenly stops, you may have ruptured an eardrum. Check for drainage from the ear and loss of hearing. If you do have drainage, place a cotton ball or tissue against the ear opening to soak up the fluid. See a doctor as soon as possible.

FEELING YOUR BEST WHILE FLYING

■ To promote good circulation, prop your feet up on a piece of carry-on luggage instead of crossing your legs. Walk up and down the aisles periodically.

■ Place one pillow at the small of your back and another behind your neck.

■ If you wear contact lenses, use saline solution or other mild eyedrops to moisten eyes. Wearing glasses on the flight may help prevent irritation.

IN-FLIGHT FOOD AND DRINK

■ Airline food is sometimes high in fat, salt, and calories. Call ahead for a special meal if you prefer a low-fat, low-salt diet or another type of menu.

■ Consider bringing your own food and water. Sometimes airline water tastes stale; bottled water will help ensure that you drink enough during the flight. Also, a sandwich, fresh fruit, or other healthy snack comes in handy in case of airline delay.

■ Avoid drinks containing alcohol or caffeine. Not only do these beverages exacerbate the effects of jet lag, but they also increase urination.

■ Some people who are prone to digestive problems should skip carbonated drinks. Combined with changes in air pressure, drinking sodas and sparkling water can cause flatulence and other intestinal discomfort.

- -

To avoid decompression sickness, scuba divers should not make decompression dives the day before a flight or within 12 hours of a scheduled departure.

- -

JET LAG

Jet lag occurs when you fly across several time zones, causing such symptoms as headaches, insomnia, difficulty waking up, stomach upset, concentration problems, impaired coordination, and mild anxiety. There are several ways to minimize jet lag.

■ Allow a day per time zone to recover fully from jet lag. Eastward travel is harder on

your internal clock than westward travel because it pushes your clock ahead.

■ Take jet lag into account when scheduling your flight. If you are flying east, choose a departure early in the day. When heading west, fly in the late afternoon or evening.

■ Begin preparing for a time change a few days before your departure by getting up a half hour to an hour earlier or going to bed later (depending on what time zone you are going to).

■ When you get on the plane, adjust your watch to the time of your destination. If it is nighttime at your destination, turn off the overhead light and rest your eyes. Better still, put on an eye mask and try to nap.

■ A good night's sleep on a long flight or once you reach your destination helps to readjust your biological clock.

■ If you feel you might have trouble sleeping, ask your physician about a short-term sleeping pill. Some experts recommend a sleeping pill to ensure rest on a flight more than six hours long.

■ Take it easy for the first day or two after your arrival, but don't curtail all activity just because you feel tired. Activity helps ease the transition to a new time zone.

■ Sunlight is a powerful ally in overcoming jet lag. After flying west, spend a few hours outdoors in the afternoon. After heading east, take a half-hour walk outside in the morning. This technique can be effective even on a cloudy day. Some pilots find that exposure to very bright indoor lights can counter jet lag.

ON TOP OF THE WORLD

"When you go by helicopter, you get views that you can't possibly get any other way."
—Carol Livezey

· · · · · · ·

After exploring a mountain glacier, travelers have a helicopter waiting to ferry them back to their hotel.

No way!" That was the initial response from Carol Livezey, a retired hardware-store owner, when her husband, Paul, suggested taking a helicopter to explore the majestic Columbia Glacier.

"I felt I had already had my share of adventures," she explains. In the past few weeks she had floated down the rapids of Alaska's frigid Nenana River, taken a stern-wheeler to an Indian village, and flown to the Arctic Circle. Still, she conceded that each trip had been enjoyable and had shown her another part of the glorious north. Finally, after gentle coaxing from her husband, Carol decided to give it a try.

Sheets of ice and barking seals. After flying over Prince William Sound and the glacier, the helicopter flew into a deep crevice. The pilot landed on the rocky ice and soil at the edge of the glacier, allowing Carol and Paul to wander about.

"Hearing the seals barking from their ice floats, and listening to the glacier's snapping and crackling from cracking ice—it was truly wondrous," she recalls. Just as the tour group was taking off, there was a thunderous roar as a huge sheet of ice broke away—a glacier calving—which sent waves of water rushing toward them. "We were never in any real danger," Carol says, "but it certainly was an awesome experience."

Carol Livezey's adventures may be tame compared to diving for lost treasure, skydiving, climbing Mount Everest, and other challenges that appeal to adventure travelers. But with the aid of experienced guides and modern modes of travel, such outings are no longer the exclusive province of the young and superfit.

According to the American Society of Travel Agents, most adventure travelers are over 40. For example, Elderhostel, which specializes in travel for the 50-plus set, has such varied itineraries as archeological digs, trekking in the Himalayas, and cross-country skiing in the backcountry of Montana and Idaho.

A love of nature. Much of the interest in adventure travel stems from concern for the endangered environment. "People hear about the rain forest," says Chris Doyle of REI Adventures, an organizer of adventure travel tours, "and they want to see it." Most travel companies now abide by strict standards to ensure that their trips do not endanger fragile wilderness areas.

Travel counselors work with prospective travelers to choose a suitable destination. Fitness training and a medical checkup may be recommended. Those with chronic conditions may be given less rigorous alternatives.

Carol Livezey agrees with this policy. "Our pilot made sure that we were in reasonable health before taking off. Anyone who might have breathing problems at a high altitude was cautioned to avoid flight-seeing, and instead visit the glacier by boat. They might not get to experience the inside of a crevice, but they wouldn't get in trouble, either." ❑

ADVENTURE TRAVEL

Once reserved for the risk-taker, adventure travel is now a popular way to vacation. Offerings range from alpine trekking to windsurfing. While this type of travel can be appealing, being prepared for it is essential.

GENERAL ADVICE

■ Consider taking an organized trip rather than heading out on your own, especially if you're trying adventure travel for the first time. Tour companies have a vast array of excursions, from light hiking to mountain climbing. These trips offer a good opportunity to get out in the wilderness with expert guidance.

■ Get recommendations from other travelers on guides and outfitters. Most are knowledgeable and reputable, but be sure to ask for references from clients when checking out a tour company. Inquire about the leaders' equipment and training for handling emergencies.

■ Before investing in gear, ask veteran travelers what they recommend. A knowledgeable sporting-goods salesperson can also help.

■ Before you head out for the backcountry in a national park for one night or longer, you must register and leave your complete itinerary at a park warden's office. Be sure to check in again at a park warden's office when you have completed your trip. If you don't show up on schedule, a rescue team may be sent out.

■ Rescue insurance may be essential in the United States and other foreign countries. It is not yet required in Canada, although in British Columbia it is possible that you could be billed for a search and evacuation if you were negligent about safety and following directions.

PREPARING FOR ADVENTURE TRAVEL

■ If you'll be on the water, in the snow, or at high altitudes, purchase high-glare sunglasses. A special coating cuts glare and promotes eye comfort in extreme conditions.

■ Pack two pairs of shoes: one for the activity you'll be participating in and another for times around the campsite. For the latter, choose lightweight shoes, such as sneakers, that are comfortable and allow air to circulate.

■ Take clothing that dries quickly, such as lightweight cotton, wool, and synthetics.

■ Pack rain gear. A two-piece suit offers the best protection and can be a lifesaver in cold weather. Make sure the suit is big enough for warm clothing underneath, yet not cumbersome. Self-adhesive ankle and wrist fasteners on foul-weather gear improve mobility.

■ Whenever possible, choose items that you can use for more than one purpose. A lightweight shirt can be worn alone on a hot day or as a first layer on a cold day.

■ Choose the smallest backpack you can get away with.

To waterproof it, line the pack with a plastic bag and then a light stuff sack or other liner.

TAKE A HIKE

■ On smooth terrain, sturdy, low-cut shoes with a treaded rubber sole will do. On rocky, steep, or wet trails, wear ankle-high boots to protect your ankles and feet from injury.

■ When trying on boots, wear the same socks you will be wearing when hiking. For most situations, two pairs of socks are recommended: a lightweight wool or polypropylene liner to draw moisture away from your foot and a thick wool outer sock. With these thick socks, you may require a larger shoe size than usual.

■ Unless you're going to be carrying a heavy pack or hiking in winter, you don't need a heavy boot. In fact, such footwear may increase the risk of injury by causing fatigue. Instead, choose a lightweight, flexible boot.

■ If you'll be doing a lot of walking in water, such as traversing streams, choose a high, fully waterproof boot.

■ Before going on a long hike, break in new boots by wearing them an hour or so every day for a week before you leave. Even so, tuck bandages and moleskin into your backpack in case you develop any blisters.

■ To avoid blisters, wear your lightweight inner socks inside out, so that the seams are on the outside. Change these socks every day (or wash them out each evening). In most cases, outer socks can be worn for two or three days without washing.

■ Before setting out on a trail, get a good map from the park ranger's station or a local sporting-goods store. Maps should show not only the trail but also topographic features and landmarks.

■ When possible, walk around rocks, logs, and other hurdles to avoid injury. Take inclines slowly, especially when going downhill. (People with knee problems have more difficulty going downhill than uphill.)

■ If you're carrying a heavy pack, consider using a walking stick to take some of the weight off your legs. You can make one from a relatively straight stick or you can buy one. If you purchase an adjustable model, shorten it for climbing up hills; lengthen it for descents.

■ On long hikes, take frequent breaks to rest your feet. Some people like to take their boots off while resting to let their feet air out. However, never walk barefoot; going without shoes puts you in danger of getting cuts and parasites.

If you wear bifocals, replace them with two pairs of glasses when hiking: one for walking and one for reading maps. Looking down at an out-of-focus trail through bifocals increases the risk of an accident.

CLIMBING SAFETY

Rock climbing may look easy when done by experts, but it requires strength, coordination, and patience.

■ Before setting out on your own, take a course or go on a guided outing for novices. For lists of guides and other information, contact the Association of Canadian Mountain Guides, Box 1537, Banff, Alberta T0L 0C0.

■ Your equipment is literally your lifeline when you're doing technical climbing. Check each line and fitting carefully

before undertaking a climb.

■ Buy the shoes appropriate for your type of climbing and level of skill. Consult a salesperson experienced in fitting climbing shoes.

■ Make sure you have adequate medical and rescue insurance.

NEW HEIGHTS

■ When traveling to a high-altitude destination (over 5,000 feet, but especially over 8,000 feet above sea level), prepare your body by drinking plenty of fluids (at least 10 eight-ounce glasses a day) and avoiding alcoholic beverages for a few days before departure.

■ Plan a gradual ascent. If you are going to a city 5,000 to 7,000 feet above sea level, remain at that level for a day or so before continuing up.

■ Take it easy the first day above 5,000 feet. Many travelers experience headache, nausea, and fatigue during the first few days—especially if they overdo it.

■ If possible, plan to stay at about 8,000 feet, climbing up to higher altitudes during the day and returning to 8,000 feet at night. This can help ease the symptoms of altitude sickness.

■ If altitude-sickness symptoms persist, descend 2,000 to 3,000 feet as quickly as possible to avoid serious danger.

An aspirin a day to thin the blood or a diuretic to ease fluid retention may help minimize the effects of altitude sickness. Discuss these with your doctor before you try them.

GETTING MEDICAL CARE ABROAD

Before departing for a foreign country, make certain that you have adequate insurance and know how to locate a doctor. You may also want to learn about local health-care customs and facilities.

TRAVEL INSURANCE

■ Check your provincial health plan in advance to see what type of foreign care (if any) it covers; check in particular to see if it covers evacuation to a hospital. Provincial health plans impose limits on insurance coverage during travel outside Canada. For example, they may cover emergency care but not routine doctor visits.

What Is a Medical Emergency?

If you are injured in an accident, you need medical help. Here are other situations that warrant emergency treatment anytime, anywhere, according to the Canadian Association of Emergency Physicians.

1. Chest or upper abdominal pain or pressure
2. Difficulty in breathing or shortness of breath
3. Fainting or feeling faint
4. Sudden dizziness, weakness, or a change in vision
5. Any sudden, severe pain
6. Severe or persistent vomiting
7. Coughing up or vomiting blood
8. Bleeding that won't stop
9. Suicidal or homicidal feelings

■ Check with your supplementary health and life insurance plan at work. Some health benefit plans provide full travel insurance for the employee and her family. If yours does not, consider extra insurance.

■ Some tour operators offer health insurance. Compare such a policy with those you can buy yourself to find the best value.

■ Know what you are buying. Find a policy that covers hospitalization and emergency surgery. You may also want doctor fees and drugs included. Other health-related expenses to consider are evacuation to a hospital and travel expenses to allow a family member or friend to assist the patient.

■ If your travel plans include such high-risk pursuits as mountain climbing or visiting areas affected by terrorism or war, expect to have a hard time getting insurance.

■ If you have a chronic illness or disability, check that the insurance will cover it while you are traveling.

■ Look for companies that offer policyholders a toll-free number to call with questions or concerns while traveling. Some companies can refer you to a doctor when you are more than 100 miles from home.

■ Even with good coverage, you will probably have to pay for medical expenses and then submit an itemized bill for reimbursement.

BUYING MEDICATIONS

■ Bring your regular medications with you (see "Your Travel Medicine Kit," page 260). Ask your pharmacist or physician to write down the generic names of the drugs you take (including over-the-counter preparations) so that pharmacists in foreign countries can help if you should lose your medications.

■ If your regular dosage is not available, you may have to improvise a bit. For example, if you normally take a 100-milligram dosage but the medication is available only in 200-milligram tablets, ask the pharmacist if you can split the pill in half. Do not take more than your normal dosage.

■ When you patronize a pharmacy abroad, be sure that you know what you're getting. Medications that can be dangerous may be sold without a prescription in countries you plan to visit. Do not assume that every nation has a national agency that determines whether medications are safe and effective.

MEDICATIONS TO AVOID ABROAD

The following preparations were found to be ineffective or unsafe by the federal Department of Health:

■ Aminopyrine is sold in some European countries as a cold remedy. Studies show it destroys white blood cells, with possibly fatal consequences.

■ Chloramphenicol, a powerful antibiotic, is sold in some countries for traveler's diarrhea and colds. Side effects include bone marrow depression and aplastic anemia.

■ Iodoquinol, a drug to prevent diarrhea, is ineffective and may cause serious neurological side effects. The Department of Health does not recommend it.

When buying a pocket dictionary in a foreign language, make sure it has phrases for handling medical problems—such as "I have pain here" and "Call an ambulance."

FINDING A DOCTOR

■ Before you go abroad, contact the International Association for Medical Assistance to Travelers (IAMAT), 40 Regal Road, Guelph, Ontario, N1K 1B5. This nonprofit organization provides lists of English-speaking doctors around the world who accept travelers as patients.

■ The International Red Cross can supply names of physicians. Check the telephone directory for the nearest office.

■ In major foreign cities, the American, British, or Canadian consulate may be able to refer you to an English-speaking doctor or a translator to assist you with a doctor who doesn't speak English. Carry the consulate telephone number with you in case of emergency.

■ In an emergency, the nearest hospital is usually the best bet. Look for the international symbol for a hospital—a white "H" on a blue background. If you need help finding the hospital, ask a cab-driver to take you. Hospitals in rural areas can generally handle common illnesses and accidents.

■ Don't insist on going to a big-city hospital for all medical problems. A small-town or rural doctor may be better able to diagnose a local disease, such as a parasitic infection, than a city doctor.

■ If you're staying at a hotel or resort, ask the management to recommend a local doctor for minor ailments.

■ If you have travel health insurance, ask the insurance company for names of foreign doctors.

■ Medical schools abroad usually have English-speaking physicians on their faculties. If you need a specialist, call the nearest medical school.

MEDICAL TRADITIONS

Knowing about the diverse approaches to medical care worldwide can be helpful. The same clinical signs may lead physicians in different countries to different diagnoses and treatments.

■ Before you travel, make sure you know what blood pressure reading is normal for you. Blood pressure seen as high enough to warrant hypertension medication in Canada might be considered normal in England, for example. Only you can determine whether there has been a change from your usual blood pressure reading.

■ If you find yourself undergoing surgery in Great Britain, take heart: British anesthesiologists are highly regarded worldwide, and the country's medical profession pays close attention to pain relief.

■ If a French doctor diagnoses your problem as anemia, you will most likely be given vitamin B_{12}, a vitamin originally isolated from liver extracts, or liver extracts themselves. In Canada, however, the recommendation would probably be iron supplements.

■ The French prescribe far more drugs—everything from aspirin to antibiotics—in the form of suppositories than Canadian doctors do.

■ German doctors prescribe six or seven times as many digitalis-like drugs as doctors in England or France but far fewer antibiotics. Some German doctors maintain that antibiotics should be used only when a patient is sick enough to be hospitalized.

EATING AND DRINKING HERE AND ABROAD

Don't miss out on local cuisine because of fear of intestinal problems—but don't throw caution to the wind, either. Simple precautions will enable you to partake while staying healthy.

HEALTHFUL EATING

Advance meal planning can remove the temptation to rely on fast foods while traveling and ensure that you won't return from your vacation pounds heavier.

■ Consider eating your main meal at midday. Among the advantages: it can fuel the day's activities, it provides a break during the hottest part of the day, and restaurants generally charge less for lunch than for dinner.

■ Bring plenty of water, fruit juice, and other healthy beverages with you while traveling. Also pack such low-calorie snacks as pretzels and low-fat crackers. If you're driving, you can stop at local farm stands and produce markets (but see "Food Poisoning" on the facing page).

■ Boredom often breeds hunger. Bring along something to occupy your mind when riding in a car, plane, or train. Read, listen to a book on tape, or play word games.

■ Look for healthful local specialties. For example, high-fiber beans are the basis of many meatless meals in the Southwest United States and Central America, and coastal towns usually have excellent seafood.

■ To avoid overeating, share with your travel companions.

Order one dish less than the number of people, ask for an extra plate, and divide the food among everyone at the table.

■ If you are on a low-salt diet, carry a small packet of herb flavoring. Ask that your food be prepared without salt, and then season it yourself. Also, if you use an artificial sweetener, bring your own along.

■ If you want to try a local dish that is high in fat or calories, don't deny yourself completely. Order a small portion (many restaurants offer appetizer portions of main dishes), or share with a friend. Adjust your next meal to compensate for the extra calories.

■ If you enjoy sampling the local wines and beers, do so in moderation.

WATER, WATER EVERYWHERE

Most travelers to underdeveloped countries know that it's not wise to drink the water. Besides carrying bacteria that cause traveler's diarrhea, contaminated water can transmit diseases, such as typhoid, cholera, and hepatitis. Travelers to South America, Central America, Asia, the Middle East, Africa, and some Caribbean islands should be very cautious about water.

■ Stick to sparkling water,

soda, other carbonated drinks, and beer in areas where drinking the water is risky. Look for well-known brand names; these companies are likely to follow sanitary bottling practices. Carbonation adds acid, which creates a hostile environment for bacteria; it also ensures that a bottle has not been filled with tap water and resealed.

■ Ask for soft drinks and sparkling water without ice. To be extra safe, open the bottle and pour the drink yourself.

■ Coffee and tea are usually safe if they are made with boiling water and served hot. Canned fruit juices that have not been diluted are also generally safe.

■ Use boiled or bottled water for brushing your teeth. Some hotels provide boiled water for this purpose. If you can draw tap water that is too hot to touch, it is probably safe. Wait for it to cool, then use it to brush your teeth.

■ *Giardia lamblia,* a protozoan parasite that lodges in the top of the small intestine, produces giardiasis—persistent diarrhea, along with stomach pain, cramps, gas, and sometimes nausea and vomiting. This organism is endemic to many areas of the world, especially the tropics but, surprisingly, also colder places, such as Russia. Other protozoan parasites, including *Cryptosporidia,* cause illness similar to giardiasis; they, too, live mainly, but not exclusively, in warm climates. Be especially careful to purify water and to cook foods rinsed in water that may harbor these parasites.

■ Most people swallow a bit of water while swimming, so avoid plunging into fresh water in unfamiliar areas, especially if the water is stagnant, slow-flowing, or inhabited by beavers, which may carry the parasite that causes giardiasis. (For other swimming precautions, see "Enjoying Water Sports," page 242.)

■ Make sure the hotel pool has adequate chlorine and that the water is frequently changed. If the hotel maintains high standards in other areas, the pool is probably also well kept.

PURIFYING WATER

■ Boiling is the most effective way to purify water because heat kills disease-causing organisms without affecting the taste. Bring the water to a high boil for five minutes, cover, and let cool before drinking.

■ If boiling is not possible, use water-purification tablets, available at camping-goods stores. Follow the directions carefully.

■ Another way to purify water is filtration, using kits that are sold at sporting-goods stores. However, check with your local health department or travel medicine clinic before buying a device, since not all of them are effective.

■ For do-it-yourself types, add five drops of iodine or two drops of chlorine bleach to disinfect a quart of water. Wait at least 30 minutes before drinking. If you cannot taste the chlorine or iodine, add one or two more drops and wait another 30 minutes. Cold or cloudy water may require twice the normal dosage. People with thyroid problems should not drink iodine-treated water without consulting a doctor.

Even clear water from a stream or river should be purified before drinking. Pollution, animal wastes, runoff from farms, and other contaminants can cause problems.

FOOD POISONING

■ Most food poisoning and traveler's diarrhea is caused by an intestinal bacterial infection. As a precaution, you may want to ask your doctor to prescribe antibiotics to take with you (see box, page 285).

■ Don't taste any food that looks or smells bad.

■ Avoid food sold by street vendors. It is likely that this food has not been properly refrigerated or cooked.

■ Stay away from food that is reheated or not thoroughly cooked. Use extra caution in areas of the world that lack refrigeration.

■ Shun salads and raw vegetables and other foods (except some fruits—see below) in any area where the water is not considered safe.

■ In developing countries, vegetables must be thoroughly washed, first with soapy water and then with boiled or treated water (see "Purifying Water").

■ Avoid dairy products in rural areas or developing countries that don't require pasteurization. These products include milk, cheese, ice cream, and cream-based sauces. Canned milk is generally safe, as is powdered milk mixed with boiled water or bottled water. Boiling fresh unpasteurized milk also makes it safe, but be sure to refrigerate it immediately after boiling.

■ Skip products made with uncooked or lightly cooked eggs, such as fresh mayonnaise, ice cream, milk shakes, some sauces, and mousses. Raw eggs are a major source of salmonella, the organism that causes most food poisoning.

■ Fruit that you peel yourself is generally safe—especially citrus fruits, which have acids that discourage bacterial growth. Don't eat fruits that are difficult to wash.

■ Avoid raw shellfish, especially oysters and clams, and make sure that all other seafood is thoroughly cooked.

Some people must be especially careful: raw oysters may contain bacteria that can cause life-threatening infections in those whose immune systems are impaired, which sometimes occurs with liver disease and other chronic illnesses.

■ Eat sushi only in developed countries, in restaurants that cater to business travelers and foreigners.

■ Do not eat rice in the evening unless you are sure it has been freshly prepared. Many small restaurants cook a large pot of rice in the morning and leave it over low heat all day, providing an environment in which bacteria flourish.

At a smorgasbord or buffet, avoid food that has been left out for more than 30 minutes without a heating or cooling apparatus and adequate protection from flies.

PREVENTING TRAVELER'S DIARRHEA

Diarrhea is a common travel ailment. Most cases last only two to three days, but it can leave you feeling drained for a week or more. Besides infective organisms, many factors can contribute to diarrhea—including stress, climate change, and simply eating different foods. Here are more hints for preventing diarrhea.

■ Check out restaurants before sitting down to a meal. Are counters and tabletops clean? Are there screens on the windows? Are the bathrooms clean? Is there open trash? Do you see evidence of

rodents, flies, or mosquitoes? If things look dirty, choose another establishment.

■ Clean and dry your hands before touching food. If soap and water are not available, use disinfectant towelettes.

■ If you are unsure about whether a restaurant cleans its dishes sufficiently, order a pot of hot tea with your meal. Use the hot water and a clean cloth to rinse off plates, glasses, and utensils before eating or drinking.

■ Another safeguard is to carry a swab of cotton soaked with alcohol or hydrogen peroxide (or packaged alcohol swipes). Use it to wipe off utensils before eating. This is particularly important with reusable wooden chopsticks, which may be more difficult to clean than metal utensils. Be aware, however, that alcohol is not 100 percent effective in cleaning utensils.

■ If you tend to develop diarrhea even when taking precautions, talk to your physician about preventive drugs. Some doctors recommend

two bismuth subsalicylate tablets four times a day to prevent diarrhea. This dosage causes black stools, but this is not serious. Treatment should not continue for more than two weeks, and if you are sensitive to aspirin or have a kidney disorder, do not use this method.

TREATING INTESTINAL DISTRESS

Although diarrhea is the body's way of eliminating a harmful organism, most travelers are reluctant to wait it out. Here are some tips for overcoming diarrhea quickly:

■ Begin treatment with the first symptoms, such as a loose stool, abdominal cramps, and perhaps nausea or weakness. Loperamide hydrochloride acts faster than bismuth subsalicylate, but the latter may be safer, especially for treating children.

■ Even a mild case of diarrhea can cause dehydration, so drink plenty of fluids, such as boiled or bottled water and broth. Avoid alcohol and caffeine; they can irritate the intestinal tract.

■ Watch for signs of dehydration, especially in infants, children, and elderly people. Symptoms include a dry mouth and tongue, reduced urine output, listlessness, and a weak pulse. Seek medical attention immediately if symptoms develop.

■ For mild dehydration, use an oral-rehydration or electrolyte-replacement solution; these are available in drugstores, sporting-goods stores, and even grocery stores. You can also make your own rehydrating formula by mixing four heaping teaspoons of sugar with one-half teaspoon of salt, and dissolving the mixture in a quart of water.

■ If diarrhea persists, or if other symptoms (bloody stools, vomiting) develop, see a doctor. If this is impossible, start taking the antibiotics in your travel medicine kit (see page 260).

■ Eat only light, bland foods for a day or two to help settle your stomach. Follow the BRAT diet: Bananas, Rice, Applesauce, and Toast.

■ Once you start to feel better, plain potatoes and pasta are good choices. Avoid dairy products, meat, vegetables, high-fat or spicy dishes, and other hard-to-digest foods until you have completely recovered.

If symptoms develop or persist after you return home, see your doctor as soon as possible. You may have contracted giardiasis or some other parasitic disorder.

HANDLING OTHER INTESTINAL UPSETS

■ Changes in time zone, diet, exercise routine, and sleep patterns can result in irregularity. Avoid constipation by making sure you get enough fiber. Bran cereal or dried fruit can help, especially in areas where such high-fiber foods as raw fruit and vegetables are regarded as potential health hazards.

■ Exercise whenever possible, and drink at least eight glasses of nonalcoholic, caffeine-free liquids a day.

■ If you are susceptible to indigestion, heartburn, or gas, travel with a supply of antacids or another preferred remedy (see "Intestinal Disorders," page 348). Avoid foods that tend to exacerbate the problem.

ROUGHING IT

You may sometimes have to rely on prepackaged foods— for example, when you are miles away from a restaurant, grocery store, or market, or when you travel to a region that is regarded as having low sanitation standards. When this is the case, the following suggestions may help:

■ For breakfast, bring along granola bars, cold cereal, or single-serving packets of instant oatmeal or another quick-cooking cereal. Dried food comes in handy at any meal and for snacks.

■ For lunch, pack some crackers, peanut and other nut butters, and hard cheese, such as Gouda or Swiss (preferably low-fat varieties). Cocktail-size rye or pumpernickel breads, bagels, and tortillas come in handy for lunch and other occasions when you want good sources of low-fat carbohydrates.

■ For dinner, buy dried soups in foil packets. Pour the mix into a plastic bag, add boiling water (and dry milk powder if you wish), and stir. Camping-supply stores often provide an assortment of prepackaged meals that require little or no preparation.

When to Take along Antibiotics

Taking antibiotics to prevent traveler's diarrhea during a two-week trip may be advisable under the following circumstances. Talk to your doctor if one or more of these apply to you.

You will be in a remote area where food and water are likely to be contaminated and medical care is not readily available.

You have a heart condition, diabetes, kidney disease, or other chronic illness that makes a case of diarrhea more serious.

You are traveling on business and it is crucial that you be at your peak every day.

You take ulcer medication that changes the acid content of the stomach and makes diarrhea more likely.

VACATIONING WITH CHILDREN

You want your children to enjoy traveling while staying healthy and safe. When you use car seats, pack the right clothes, and add some ingenuity, everyone enjoys the trip.

PLAN AHEAD

■ Check in advance to ensure that the hotels or motels you want to stay in are equipped to deal with children. Do they have cribs? Window safety guards? Babysitters or other child-care services?

■ Make a list of essential things to take with you, especially if you're going abroad. Formula, disposable diapers, and other baby-care items are hard to find in some countries. You will also want to supply your travel medical kit with special items (see box on page 289).

■ Bring along a nightlight, cereal bowl, or other reminder of home to help ease the strangeness of the new environment for a young child. Let your child choose the object if he or she is old enough.

■ Keep children's schedules in mind when planning departure times.

■ Stick with familiar napping routines (cuddling a favorite blanket, reading a story). Put such sleep aids in a tote bag or other accessible place.

■ Talk to older children about your destination. Show them brochures or books about the places you intend to visit and the activities you've planned. Ask for suggestions on what they'd like to do or see.

■ Arrange your itinerary to include some recreational activities, especially if you plan on visiting a lot of historical sites or art museums. Depending on the children's ages, you may want to spend time at a playground or a pool after every one or two historical sites or museums.

■ If you are traveling by car, pack a cooler with favorite foods. It can help tide children over when meals are delayed or when they don't like restaurant food. When traveling by plane or train, keep handy some dry, lightweight foods, such as cereal, crackers, and trail mix.

> If your child takes a favorite toy along, be sure to check for it each time you leave a restaurant, hotel, or other stop. Consider buying a duplicate to leave at home in case the original is lost in transit.

PREVENTING ILLNESS

■ Wait until your infant is at least a month old to take him or her on an airplane. Babies less than two weeks old can experience respiratory problems from the changes in air pressure on an airplane, and the recirculated air means an increased risk of infections.

■ Before leaving on a vacation, make sure your child's immunizations are up-to-date.

■ If you are planning a trip abroad, schedule a full pediatric checkup at least six weeks before leaving (to allow enough time for any immunizations to take effect). Ask the doctor for advice on medications and special precautions.

■ Try to keep your child's eating and sleeping routines as normal as possible.

■ To help prevent motion sickness and other stomach problems, feed your child light foods on planes and when traveling by car. Avoid such high-fat items as hamburgers, french fries, and hot dogs. Try not to eat on the run.

■ Traveler's diarrhea can be especially dangerous for infants and children. Bring along pre-mixed formula for infants and make sure that older children follow the same food and water precautions as adults (see "Eating and Drinking Here and Abroad," page 282).

■ Since breast-feeding is the safest way to feed an infant during travel, nursing mothers should never plan to switch an infant to formula immediately before a trip.

■ Pack clothing for the climate you'll be in, but allow for an occasional cool day in Florida or warm spell up north. For colder climates, choose clothes that can be layered: T-shirts, turtlenecks, sweaters, and windproof jackets.

■ Children are more susceptible to heat injuries than adults, especially when exercising in extremely hot weather. On very hot days, don't plan a lot of sightseeing on foot.

■ Frequent handwashing is important for preventing infections. Bring along disposable wipes for quick cleanups, and make sure children wash their hands at rest stops.

> **If a child gets a fever, give him or her acetaminophen and then a bath in lukewarm water a half hour later. Water evaporation on the skin can help bring down a temperature.**

CHILD CARE

■ If the resort or hotel you have chosen offers babysitting services and children's activities, find out the qualifications of the staff. Also ask whether the children are cared for in a large room with other children or in your own hotel room. If children will play together in a group, check out the play area for safety and cleanliness.

■ When you hire a new babysitter in an unfamiliar place, let the child get to know the sitter before you leave them alone. Ask the sitter to come at least an hour before your departure.

SAFETY TIPS

■ A lost and frightened toddler may not be able to give strangers your names or the name of your hotel. Before you go on vacation, ask your pediatrician or local police where you can buy an identification tag that attaches to the tongue of a child's shoe.

■ Instruct your child about what to do when approached by a stranger (see "Protecting Your Kids," page 174). If you're still concerned, give him or her a police whistle to wear on a neck chain, and work out a signal, such as two short blasts.

■ Make a quick inspection when visiting relatives or friends. Check to see that medicines, vitamin supplements, and other hazardous items are out of a small child's reach. This is especially important during holidays, when bowls of nuts and hard candies, as well as alcoholic drinks, may be offered to guests (see "Child-proofing Your Home," page 198).

■ When you check into a hotel room or rented vacation property, take the time to child-proof before settling in. Remove matches, breakables, and other potential hazards. Cover electrical outlets not in use (you can carry along some extra covers or use electric tape). If tables, dressers, and other furniture have sharp corners, ask for extra blankets to cover them. If necessary, move furniture to make the room safer.

■ Don't overlook window latches and guards. If there's a balcony, make sure that the child cannot climb over or slip through its railing.

■ Check the drapery cords. If they are hanging down, free them from their track and tie the cords together high enough so that a child can't become entangled in them.

■ Lock the wet bar and put the key in a safe place. Similarly, keep your medicines out of your child's reach.

■ Make sure your room has a smoke alarm and that you know where the fire exits are. Teach older children what to do if a fire alarm sounds.

■ Supervise children's showers at hotels (or relatives' houses), where water temperature may be higher than usual.

■ Use a halter to keep a young child from wandering off when your attention is diverted.

PLANES AND TRAINS

■ If your child seems apprehensive before a trip, try taking the child to the airport or train station for a visit before the departure date. Talk about what it's like to ride on planes or trains. Point out other children who seem to be having fun. At home, read young children stories about airplane or train travel.

■ When flying, plan to arrive early at the airport to take advantage of an airline's preboarding for travelers with young children. This gives you a chance to get your child and gear settled before the rush of boarding other passengers.

■ In a plane, children over the age of two must be buckled into their own seats. Airlines permit adults to hold infants less than two years old in their laps. However, it is safer to buy a seat for your infant, put your car seat in it, and buckle him or her in. A rear-facing car seat is recommended for children weighing 25 pounds or less. Make sure the seat has passed federal safety standards for use in motor vehicles and aircraft.

■ The change in air pressure during takeoff can be especially uncomfortable for a small child, especially if he or she has an ear infection. Swallowing eases ear discomfort by equalizing air pressure in the eustachian tube. However, some doctors recommend withholding feeding or pacifiers on ascent because the air swallowed with the sucking will ex-

pand at higher altitudes and might cause abdominal discomfort. Nursing, bottle-feeding, or sucking a pacifier during the plane's descent appears to be beneficial in preventing ear pain. Consult your pediatrician for the latest advice.

■ Provide chewing gum or hard candy for older children to help keep their ears clear.

■ When making airline reservations, ask for a bulkhead seat. This row of seats generally has more leg room, which means more space for children to play or stretch out in. Bring a blanket to put on the floor to ensure that your child's play area is as clean as possible.

Never buckle an infant into a seat with you in a plane or car. In case of a collision (or severe turbulence on an airplane), the child may be sandwiched between your body and the belt—leading to serious injury.

CAR SAFETY SEATS

■ Infants and young children (generally those weighing under 40 pounds) legally require car safety seats. The seats must be certified for use in Canada and have a CMVSS (Canadian Motor Vehicle Safety Standards) label.

■ Many hospitals provide free or low-cost car safety seats for their newborn babies. If you're pregnant, check with your hospital in advance. If it does not provide this service, buy a car seat for your newborn for the drive home from the hospital.

■ When buying a new safety seat, bring your car and your child and try out the seat before buying (or ask if you can return the seat if it doesn't fit or isn't comfortable). Make sure that the seat you buy is right for your child's height and weight and that it's wide enough to accommodate coats and other bulky clothes.

■ When buying a new car, bring your safety seat with you to ensure that it fits in the new model.

■ If you are renting a car, inquire in advance about which models will accommodate your car seat. Never try to jury-rig a seat to fit in a car.

■ Children are generally safer in the backseat, in the center, than in the front seat. Infants (up to 20 pounds, or about one year) should face backward. (Children under two do not generally get motion sickness from facing backward.)

■ If you're driving alone and you have a newborn baby, you will want to keep an eye on him or her, especially if the baby was premature or has a medical problem. In this situation, you can place the infant seat in the front, *unless* the passenger side has an air bag. Air bags do not work with rear-facing safety seats, and your baby could be injured by an air bag that inflates. Check your car owner's manual concerning air bags and children.

■ Never use an indoor baby seat, or booster, as a car seat.

■ Tuck tightly rolled, small blankets on each side of your baby if there are spaces between the infant and the sides of the safety seat.

■ When a child has outgrown the safety seat, he or she can use the regular safety belt, unless the shoulder belt crosses the face or neck. In this case, the child needs a booster seat. Never use a pillow or cushion as a booster; the child will not be secure. And never put the shoulder belt under the child's arm.

■ Do not hold a child on your lap while riding in a car—it's extremely unsafe, even if you're belted in.

■ If your child complains about being strapped in, check that no buckles or straps are causing pain. Then try to distract the child with books or soft toys.

■ Replace a seat that has restrained a child in an accident.

■ For more information on safety seats, contact the Child Restraint Information Program, C.A.A., 1775 Courtwood Crescent, Ottawa, Ontario, K2C 3J2.

TRAVEL GAMES FOR KIDS

The whole family can play games that require only imagination and curiosity.

■ When driving, count farm animals, billboards, out-of-province license plates, and other sights along the way.

■ Make up words or phrases using the letters of license plates on passing cars. For instance, the license number YLW 686 may suggest the word *yellow* or the phrase "young love works."

■ Help one another to learn more about cities, provinces, countries, lakes, and rivers. One person thinks of a place. The others ask questions that can be answered with yes or no to help identify the place. The first one who guesses the place wins.

■ Try a more difficult variation of the geography game with older children. The first player names a place, and the next one has three seconds to come up with another place in the same category that begins with the last letter of the first. For example, the first player might name Toronto, the second Ottawa, the third Annandale, the fourth Edmonton, and so forth.

■ Use the car's odometer to make up games. Here's one game: Select a landmark on the road up ahead. Everyone guesses the distance to the landmark. Whoever comes closest to the odometer reading wins.

■ Make up a story by taking turns contributing sentences. For example, the first person comes up with the title "Molly Goes to the Beach." The second person provides the first sentence: "Molly goes to the beach every summer, but this summer there was something different." The next person takes it from there, and so on.

When traveling by car, take a break about every two hours at rest stops and encourage young children to run around.

Medical Kit for Children

Vacationing with children necessitates adding to your travel medicine kit (see page 260). Here are suggestions on what to include:

1. Children's acetaminophen
2. Children's cough and cold remedies
3. Extra bandages and dressings for minor cuts and scrapes
4. Pediatric rehydration solution, especially if you will be traveling where traveler's diarrhea may be a problem
5. Child-safe motion-sickness preparation (ask your pediatrician)
6. Antibiotics if your child is prone to ear infections or other recurrent problems (ask your pediatrician)
7. Syrup of ipecac to treat certain poisonings
8. Low-concentration insect repellent
9. An antihistamine to treat bug bites and other allergic reactions
10. Disposable wipes, for quick cleanups
11. Nose aspirator (for babies under 12 months), in case of cold or congestion
12. Water-resistant sunscreen formulated for sensitive skin
13. Children's sunglasses
14. Children's wide-brimmed hat

TRAVELERS WITH SPECIAL NEEDS

Disability or chronic illness does not preclude travel. With careful planning, people with special health needs can enjoy a wide variety of destinations and activities.

GETTING READY

■ A pre-trip checkup is essential, especially if you're heading to an out-of-the-way destination or a developing country (see "Getting Medical Care Abroad," page 280).

■ Discuss your travel plans with your doctor. He or she may suggest vacation places, advise you about special precautions, and give you a list of physicians or health facilities at your destination.

■ If your regular doctor advises against travel, consider getting a second opinion. Doctors who are not experienced travelers may be overly cautious.

■ Enlist the help of a travel agent who is sensitive to your needs. For referrals to travel agents and tour groups that specialize in travel for the disabled, contact your provincial office of the Canadian Paraplegic Association. Or contact Kéroul, which provides details on travel in Canada and Europe: 4545 Pierre de Coubertin, P.O. Box 1000, Station M, Montreal, Que., H1V 3R2.

> **The likelihood of travel-related illness or injury actually goes down with age. So take a tip from senior citizens: be well prepared and take precautions when traveling.**

■ Try to talk to someone with a similar disability or illness who has traveled to the same area.

■ For a list of guidebooks for travelers with special needs, write to The President's Committee on Employment of the Handicapped, Washington, DC 20210.

■ Consider traveling with a companion, especially if your travel plans include stopovers and transfers. Some airlines require that people with certain health conditions be accompanied.

■ If you plan to take a group tour, talk to the tour leader before making your reservation. Some tours are designed to meet individual requirements, providing an appropriate pace along with the security of companionship.

■ Allow time in your schedule for frequent rests, if necessary, so you can get the most out of the time you spend on the go.

■ Be aware that the stress of travel may exacerbate some medical conditions, such as asthma, angina, diabetes, and high blood pressure. Begin your trip well rested, and practice relaxation exercises to help minimize stress.

■ Get a medical identification card, bracelet, or pendant to alert medical personnel in case of an emergency.

■ Carry your doctor's name and address, a letter from your doctor that explains your health needs, and the names of one or two relatives or friends to contact in case of an emergency.

■ Learn the name of your illness in the languages of countries you will be visiting.

■ If you have any condition that weakens the immune system, consider getting a flu shot and pneumococcal vaccine before traveling. This is especially important for people with diabetes, heart conditions, and respiratory diseases, as well as those undergoing chemotherapy or radiation therapy.

■ Bring along any equipment you use regularly to make yourself more comfortable.

■ Arthritis patients can prevent stiffness during long hours in transit by doing range-of-motion exercises, such as leg lifts and shoulder and ankle circles (see "Controlling Arthritis," page 360).

USING A WHEELCHAIR

■ Most airplanes and airports are now wheelchair-accessible in North America and Western Europe. Call ahead to let the airline know that you will be traveling in a wheelchair. Airlines generally require 48 hours' notice so that they can provide a special wheelchair that fits in the aisle of the aircraft.

■ Consider purchasing a "wheelchair tightener," a device that helps squeeze a wheelchair through narrow doorways.

■ Battery-operated chairs are easily damaged in flight, and some airlines do not allow batteries to be carried on board. Check with the airline in advance. You may also need to buy an adapter for recharging the battery in foreign countries.

■ When booking a room at a hotel or on a cruise ship, ask for one close to the elevator. Also look for the international symbol of accessibility: a drawing of a person in a wheelchair.

■ Choose off-peak travel times. Book nonstop flights whenever possible.

■ With some conditions, such as arthritis, using a wheelchair while traveling may be helpful even if you do not normally need one. It can make getting around the airport and sightseeing much easier.

Call ahead before setting out to a restaurant, museum, or tourist attraction. Find out if there is an entrance with a ramp or just a few steps.

HEART CONDITIONS

■ Air travel, or reaching an altitude above 5,000 feet, may not be recommended for some people with heart disease, since reduced oxygen at high altitudes can exacerbate angina.

■ Bring a copy of your most recent EKG (or ECG) with you, along with a list of your medications. In case of an emergency, this can help physicians treat you more effectively.

■ Check the expiration date of your nitroglycerine to make sure that it's fresh. Since nitroglycerine tablets deteriorate after about one month, bring a prescription with you to refill at pharmacies abroad, if you plan a lengthy stay.

■ High blood pressure and the medications prescribed for it increase the likelihood of heat exhaustion and fatigue. Plan several rest stops on active days and layovers on days spent in transit, especially when your itinerary takes you to hot climates.

DIABETES

■ Time-zone changes of more than one or two hours can cause problems with the timing of insulin injections. Adjust your schedule with your doctor before you leave. In general, when a time-zone change leads to a shorter day, you may have to reduce your dosage. A longer day may require an extra dose of insulin.

■ To maintain a regular eating schedule when flying, call the airline at least 24 hours in advance and order a special meal to be served at a certain time. Also bring along plenty of snacks so that you won't have to skip a meal in case of delays. Include candy or some other sugar source for hypoglycemia.

■ The insulin used in Canada is not available in every country. If possible, bring your own. If you must buy insulin abroad, make sure you take the right dosage.

■ If your trip involves extensive walking, make sure your shoes and socks fit properly. Even so, check your feet carefully every day for injuries. To minimize the risk of foot infections, treat blisters and scratches immediately.

■ Motion sickness, traveler's diarrhea, stress, and fatigue affect insulin needs. Be extra diligent about food and water (see "Eating and Drinking Here and Abroad," page 282), and ask your doctor about other precautions. Step up your self-testing of blood sugar levels so you can adjust your insulin dosage as needed.

■ Carry a note from your doctor describing your need for syringes, as well as a prescription allowing you to buy new ones. Many customs agents automatically associate syringes with illegal drug use and confiscate them.

Blind airline passengers should ask a flight attendant about the number of seats to the lavatories and emergency exits, and any safety instructions.

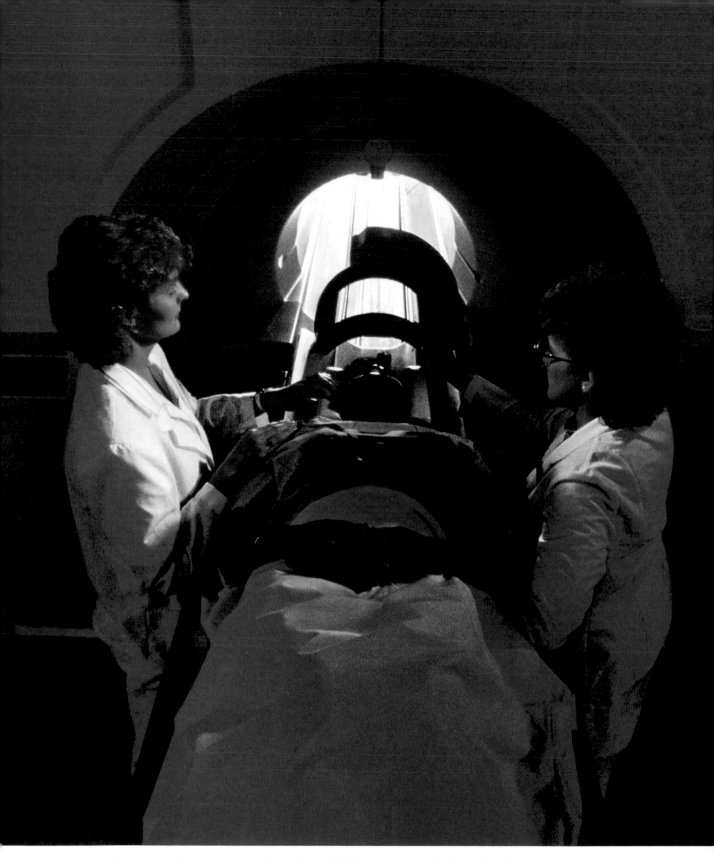

In magnetic resonance imaging *(MRI), a magnetic field and radio waves cause atom-ic particles to emit signals, which translate into computer images. Patients who are bothered by such enclosed spaces should notify their doctors—a mild sedative may help.*

CHAPTER 9

YOU AND YOUR DOCTOR

Gone are the days of the family doctor making house calls in the middle of the night. The old country physician, who often took farm animals or produce as payment, has given way to a complex and sometimes overwhelming medical network. Today we have to deal with specialists for every part of the body—as well as technicians, laboratory assistants, and a variety of other health professionals. Indeed, today "family practice" is itself a specialty.

The challenge to us as patients is to understand the health-care system ahead of time, before we need it. We have certain responsibilities—and rights—within that system. Decide now: Do you have the proper insurance? Are you getting timely examinations? Have you chosen a doctor with whom you feel comfortable? The more you take care of now, the less you'll have to worry about in the event of an illness. You'll be doing the best thing: taking control of your own health.

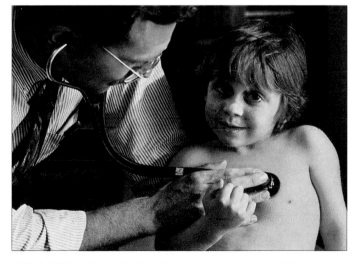

This little boy obviously trusts his doctor. No matter how much the medical system changes, the doctor-patient relationship remains important.

THE INFORMED PATIENT

Patients who are active participants in their own care tend to get the best results. Here's how to ensure that you get the kind of medical attention you deserve.

VISITING THE DOCTOR

■ Before you visit a doctor for a specific complaint, write down your symptoms, what triggers them, and other pertinent facts. This way, you won't forget important details. If you have questions, list the most important ones first.

■ Be as specific as possible. Saying you have a stomachache won't tell the doctor nearly as much as describing "a sharp pain on the left side of the abdomen when I walk."

■ If the doctor begins winding up the conversation before you have asked all your questions or understand the responses, say so. You should insist on knowing the nature of your illness and the steps in diagnosis and treatment.

■ Make sure you understand your doctor's instructions. Ask questions, and write down the answers. If you are still uncertain about what to do when you get home, call for further clarification.

■ To avoid being kept waiting, ask for the first appointment of the day or after lunch.

Emergencies do happen that preempt your doctor's appointments. Call the office before leaving home to see if the doctor is running late.

FINDING A NEW DOCTOR

When looking for a new doctor—perhaps a specialist— most people rely on the recommendations of their present physician, pharmacist, dentist, or friends and family members. Tell them the kind of doctor you are seeking. Are you most comfortable with the take-charge type who likes to try the newest drugs or medical technology? Or do you prefer a conservative physician who follows a cautious "wait and see" approach?

■ If your company has a staff physician or nurse, ask him or her for recommendations.

■ If you are moving to a new location and have no referrals from your doctor or others, here's what to do:

■ Start by analyzing your needs. Your age, sex, and medical history are critical. If you are a young woman starting a family, look for a gynecologist and a Family Medicine specialist who will be able to care for you and your growing family. If you have heart disease, diabetes, or any other chronic condition, look for an internist who specializes in your disorder.

DIGGING DEEPER

■ Call hospitals in your area and ask whether they have physician referral services. Be sure to tell the referral service what kind of doctor you're seeking (family physician, internist, gynecologist).

■ If the hospital does not have a referral service, call the office of the chief of medicine (surgery, obstetrics, etc.) and ask for the administrative assistant. This person usually knows the qualifications of department physicians and can provide helpful leads.

■ When you have a list of names, do some research. At your local library, look for the Canadian Medical Association's *Canadian Medical Directory*. This book lists physicians by name and geographical region, and gives other useful information such as their specialties, affiliations and education history.

■ After paring down your list to three or four candidates, call their offices. Tell the receptionist why you're calling; be prepared to call back when someone has enough time to answer all your questions, which should include:

■ What hospital or hospitals is the doctor affiliated with?

■ What are the doctor's hours?

■ Who covers for the doctor when he or she is not available?

■ How does the doctor feel about treating other members of your family?

■ Does the doctor have a pre-

294

ferred time for receiving and returning phone calls?

■ If you want the care of social workers as well, look for a community health center.

KEEPING YOUR FAMILY'S MEDICAL RECORDS

■ Start with a notebook for the whole family, with a section for each family member. A looseleaf binder allows you to add pages easily, but any notebook will do.

■ Record vital statistics at birth, including the child's length, weight, birthplace, birth-certificate number, and blood type.

■ Update the notebook, keeping track of checkups, immunizations, screening tests, illnesses, prescriptions, etc. Such a log can be turned over to your children as they assume responsibility for their own health care.

■ Keep a list of anything that seems to provoke an allergic reaction—pollen, an animal, fumes, food. Note the date and type of reaction, such as a rash, sneezing, or wheezing.

■ When a family member is hospitalized, write down the attending doctor and hospital or other facility. Also note the medical problem, length of stay, patient's chart number, treatment, and any medication that is prescribed.

■ Bring this log when you see a doctor for the first time.

TRACING YOUR FAMILY'S HEALTH HISTORY

Tracking your family's health history can literally save your life when it alerts your doctor and you to possible illness.

Prepare cards, like the ones below, for all family members.

■ Concentrate on first-degree relatives—parents, siblings, and children—because they have 50 percent of their genes in common with yours. Then move on to grandparents, uncles, aunts, nieces, and nephews, with whom you share 25 percent of your genes. Later you may want to add cousins and more distant ancestors. The more detailed your history, the better.

■ Don't limit your investigation only to diseases and other illnesses that have proved

fatal. A relative may have hypertension, for example, and it may not be life-threatening for him or her, but it may be a serious problem for you.

■ Don't assume that you'll get a disease or condition just because it runs in the family. For example, if family members tend to develop adult-onset diabetes, you can lower your susceptibility by exercising and avoiding obesity.

■ Hereditary risks vary with the disease and the age at which it strikes; therefore, get an expert to interpret your family's health data.

What Your Family's Medical History Reveals

A physician might urge the patient ("Self") to lower her risk of stroke, heart attack, and diabetes. Colon cancer is also a concern.

Family Health Tree

This Relative is My _Maternal Grandfather_
Relative's Name _John Kelly_
Birth Date _1899_   Date of Death _1951_ (if applicable)
Cause of Death _Colon Cancer_
Blood Type and RH _____
Occupation _____

Family Health Tree

This Relative is My _Maternal Grandmother_
Relative's Name _Sarah Samuels Kelly_
Birth Date _1902_   Date of Death _1954_ (if applicable)
Cause of Death _Stroke_
Blood Type and RH _____
Occupation _____
Diseases and Infirmities _Diabetes_

Family Health Tree

This Relative is My _Father_
Relative's Name _Allen Larson_
Birth Date _8/15/22_   Date of Death _1982_ (if applicable)
Cause of Death _Kidney Failure_
Blood Type and RH _____
Occupation _Building Contractor_
Diseases and Infirmities _Diabetes_
Weight: ☐ Underweight ☒ Average

Family Health Tree

This Relative is My _Mother_
's Name _Martha Kelly Larson_
te _4/3/25_   Date of Death _11/16/92_ (if applicable)
f Death _Heart Attack_
ype and RH _B+_
tion _Housewife_
s and Infirmities _High blood pressure_
                   Arthritis
☐ Underweight ☐ Average ☒ Overweight

	Never	Moderate	Heavy
	☐	☐	☒
	☐	☐	☐

Family Health Tree

This Relative is My _Self_
Relative's Name _Anne Larson-Jones_
Birth Date _5/6/52_   Date of Death ___ (if applicable)
Cause of Death _____
Blood Type and RH _B+_
Occupation _Teacher_
Diseases and Infirmities _High blood pressure_

Weight:	☐ Underweight	☒ Average	☐ Overweight
Habits:	Never	Moderate	Heavy
Tobacco	☒	☐	☐
Alcohol	☐	☒	☐

TAKING MEDICATIONS

To get the greatest benefit from any medication—and to minimize the chance of side effects—it's important to follow instructions carefully. Your pharmacist can be an ally in this aspect of your medical care.

NEW PRESCRIPTIONS

■ When you have a doctor's appointment, bring all the drugs that you take regularly: prescriptions, over-the-counter drugs, vitamins, and other supplements. Your physician can then determine if you are taking too many medications and if any drug or supplement is interfering with the action of another.

■ Listen carefully when your doctor or pharmacist tells you how to take medication. When you get the prescription filled, make sure the instructions are affixed to the drug container.

■ Take the full course of medication, even if symptoms disappear, unless your doctor says you can stop sooner.

■ Find out what to do if you miss one or more doses. This can be especially important for women who take oral contraceptives.

■ If you have trouble keeping track of multiple drugs with different dosages, use a medication calendar. Set an alarm clock or watch timer as an extra reminder.

■ Shake the bottle before measuring a dose of liquid medication. This ensures that the active ingredient is evenly distributed.

■ Place nighttime medicines far enough from your bed that you'll have to get up to reach them.

■ Don't fumble around in the dark when you interrupt your sleep: turn on a light. This way, you'll be aware enough to make sure you are taking the right dosage of medication.

■ Ask your doctor how to stop a medication. Such drugs as steroids and heart medications must be tapered off slowly to avoid severe reactions that abrupt withdrawal may produce.

CHOOSING A PHARMACY

■ Select a pharmacy that keeps a medication profile for its regular customers. This should include the physician's name, as well as any drug allergies, adverse reactions, and chronic diseases.

■ Chain pharmacies and mail-order services, which generally offer lower prices than in-

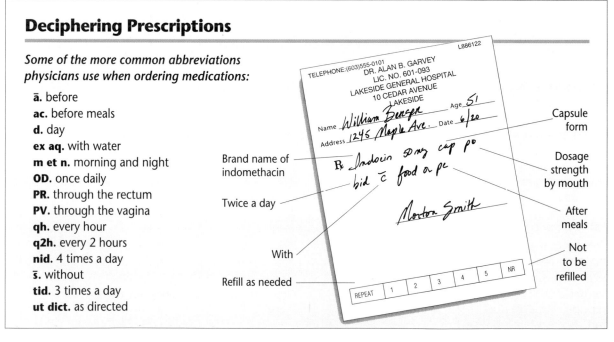

Deciphering Prescriptions

Some of the more common abbreviations physicians use when ordering medications:

ā. before
ac. before meals
d. day
ex aq. with water
m et n. morning and night
OD. once daily
PR. through the rectum
PV. through the vagina
qh. every hour
q2h. every 2 hours
nid. 4 times a day
s̄. without
tid. 3 times a day
ut dict. as directed

Brand name of indomethacin

Twice a day

With

Refill as needed

Capsule form

Dosage strength by mouth

After meals

Not to be refilled

dependent pharmacies, can be quite satisfactory for predictable needs, such as medications for chronic conditions. However, it is a good idea also to have a local pharmacist for emergencies. When you suddenly become ill and can't get to your doctor's office, a neighborhood pharmacist can take a prescription by phone from your doctor and deliver it—or have it ready for pickup—the same day.

■ Make sure that the staff is willing to spend time explaining how to take a drug.

■ Ask the pharmacist how long it takes for delivery of medications that are out of stock. If it's more than one or two days, it may be best to try another pharmacy.

■ The Canadian Medical Association advises against physicians dispensing pharmaceuticals even though they can legally do so. Only if the drugs cannot be provided within a reasonable distance by a pharmacy does the CMA consider it proper for a physician to dispense drugs.

Whenever you fill a new prescription, ask for the package insert from the manufacturer. It may offer useful information about the medication, especially its side effects.

GENERIC DRUGS

Prescription drugs are of two kinds, either brand name or generic (a copy of the brand-name drug that is usually less expensive). The doctor notes on the prescription whether a generic drug can be substituted or if the drug should be dispensed as written (DAW) with a brand-name product.

■ Generic drugs contain the same active ingredients as brand-name products, but their inactive ingredients may differ, which can alter the way the drug works in the body. If you don't seem to be getting the expected result from a generic drug, tell your doctor so that he or she can decide whether to switch to a brand-name product. If you take a generic medication regularly, ask your pharmacist to inform you of a change of supplier.

FORMS OF MEDICATION

Most drugs act by subtly changing the activities of certain cells, tissues, or organs in the body. Some drugs act outside the cells, some act on receptors on the cells' surface, and some act inside the cells.

■ The common forms are tablet, capsule, liquid, powder, injection, intravenous infusion, suppository, inhaler, drops, ointment or cream, and transdermal patch. How fast the drug will work depends on your age, weight, health status, dosage, and other factors.

■ Oral medications—tablets, capsules, and liquids—are absorbed from the gastrointestinal tract into the bloodstream. They are filtered through the liver before they reach the rest of the body through general circulation.

■ When a patient is seriously ill, drugs may be injected into a vein or muscle or infused into a vein so that the medication reaches the bloodstream more quickly than when it is taken by mouth.

■ Take capsules or tablets with fluid while in an upright position if you can. Otherwise, the capsule or tablet may get stuck in your throat, delaying its action and possibly damaging the esophagus.

■ If you have trouble swallowing pills, try placing the pill in your mouth and taking a long drink from a bottle—not a can—of soda or mineral water.

SIDE EFFECTS

All medications, including nonprescription drugs, can produce side effects. Before taking any drug, ask about possible adverse effects and what to do if they occur. Always let your doctor know if you stop taking a drug because of side effects.

■ Ask whether you should avoid alcohol while on medication. Alcohol compromises the effectiveness of some drugs, especially antibiotics, and it compounds the adverse effects of others.

■ Ask your doctor or pharmacist about foods that don't mix with the medication you're

WHAT TO DO ABOUT COMMON SIDE EFFECTS

Side Effect	Possible Causes	Action to Take
Bloodshot or dry eyes	Antipsychotics, oral contraceptives	Use saline drops to moisten eyes. Contact physician if condition doesn't improve
Changes in urination pattern	Bronchodilators, digitalis, antihistamines	Contact physician
Confusion	Sleeping aids, anti-anxiety drugs, anticonvulsant drugs	Contact physician
Constipation	Antiarrythmics, antacids	Increase intake of high-fiber foods and fluids
Diarrhea	Cholesterol-lowering drugs, antacids, gallstone drugs	Contact physician if symptoms persist
Dizziness	Antibiotics and drugs to treat anxiety, psychosis, angina, and hypertension	Contact physician if symptoms persist
Drowsiness	Antihistamines, pain relievers, muscle relaxers	Contact physician for another formulation. Do not drive, drink alcohol, or operate machinery
Dry mouth	Antihistamines, antihypertensives, antipsychotics, diuretics, tranquilizers	Drink plenty of water. Avoid sweets to prevent tooth decay. See your dentist regularly
Headache	Antidepressant drugs, migraine medications, anti-angina drugs, fertility drugs	Contact physician
Heart palpitations	Bronchodilators, decongestants	Contact physician if symptoms persist
Insomnia	Antihistamines (especially nondrowsy formulations), pain relievers containing caffeine (especially migraine medications)	Contact physician for another formulation or medication
Moodiness	Anti-anxiety drugs, fertility drugs	Contact physician. A change in dosage may relieve symptoms
Muscle cramps	Migraine medications	Contact physician if symptoms persist
Nausea, vomiting	Antibiotics, aspirin, pain relievers, chemotherapeutic drugs, nonsteroidal anti-inflammatory drugs, antidepressant drugs, cholesterol-lowering drugs, fertility drugs	Contact physician
Ringing in ears (Tinnitus)	Long-term aspirin use	Contact physician
Skin rashes (Hives)	Antibiotics (especially penicillin derivatives), aspirin, barbiturates, codeine, diuretics, sulfa drugs	Stop taking and contact physician
Sun sensitivity	Antibiotics, antidepressants, antidiabetic drugs, antihistamines, oral contraceptives	Avoid exposure to sunlight
Vision problems	Corticosteroids, digitalis, sulfa drugs, antiarrhythmic drugs	Contact physician

taking. For example, acidic foods increase the chance of stomach upset when you take aspirin and arthritis medications. Coffee, cola, and other drinks with caffeine, by contrast, increase the effectiveness of aspirin.

■ Eating before taking medication can often minimize side effects. Whether or not food is recommended before taking drugs, drinking a glass of water is always a good idea. Water also washes away any unpleasant aftertaste.

■ If you develop hives, mouth sores, vision problems, or ringing in the ears while on medication, call your doctor immediately. Go to an emergency room if you have difficulty breathing, swelling in your mouth or throat, or uncontrolled vomiting (see "What Is a Medical Emergency?" page 280).

■ If a drug upsets your stomach or produces other adverse effects, ask your doctor if you can take it in an alternative form. Some side effects can be remedied by taking the drug as a suppository, medicated patch, or an inhalant.

■ If you have minor side effects, such as drowsiness or slight dizziness, wait a day or two to see if they subside. If they persist, call your doctor.

■ The time at which you take a drug can sometimes make side effects more tolerable. For example, if a drug causes drowsiness, try to take it before going to bed. In any event, avoid such drugs before driving or performing any other tasks that require full alertness.

SAVING MONEY

■ Check your provincial or territorial health plan. It probably provides drug benefits for seniors over 65 years old. Many also provide benefits for people with chronic diseases, AIDS, and other conditions. Several plans help low-income families, too. In addition, many employee benefit packages provide drug plans. Make sure you take full advantage of such a benefit.

■ For some expensive drugs, it pays to shop around. Call several pharmacies and ask the price of the drug. Your regular pharmacist may be able to match the price. If you do buy a drug elsewhere, make sure that it is entered on your regular pharmacist's client profile of you.

■ If you have to personally meet the cost of expensive drugs, take advantage of tax-saving provisions set by Revenue Canada. Save all your receipts for medications and other allowable medical expenses. If your total medical expenses in a 12-month period ending during the taxation year were more than 3 percent of your net income (or a specified amount, determined by Revenue Canada), you can make a claim for them. This provision

takes the form of a non-refundable tax credit.

■ If you cannot afford a needed medication, tell your doctor and pharmacist. Many drug companies offer low-cost or free drugs to needy patients.

STORING MEDICATIONS

■ Your bathroom medicine cabinet is the worst place in the house to store medications. They deteriorate more rapidly in such warm, damp places. Try to find a cool, dry place in a closet or cabinet outside the bathroom.

■ If you have young children or grandchildren, avoid any risk of accidental poisoning by placing medicines and vitamin and mineral supplements where they are inaccessible, such as in a locked box or locked closet.

■ Store medicines in the original containers. If you must remove some pills, label them.

■ Replace caps and lids of medicine containers. However, you can discard the cotton packing after opening a new bottle of pills.

■ If circumstances make proper storage impossible, such as not having a refrigerator at work in which to keep antibiotics, ask your doctor for an alternative drug that doesn't require special storage.

■ Regularly check expiry dates of medications. Dispose of old medicines by taking them back to the pharmacy.

Discard any medicines that have a strange smell, as well as pills that have disintegrated.

EXAMINATIONS AND TESTS

More than two billion dollars are spent in Canada each year on diagnostic tests. Yet consumer advocates say that at least a third of all tests are unnecessary and that test results are too often misinterpreted. Here's what you should know about tests.

THE COMPLETE PHYSICAL

An annual physical is no longer recommended for healthy adults under 65. Instead, most doctors now suggest that a healthy adult requires a physical examination no more than every two to five years. However, such screening tests as Pap smears and breast and prostate examinations should be done more often. After age 65, an annual checkup is usually recommended.

■ Schedule a complete physical for the early morning, and don't eat beforehand (unless your doctor tells you to). This ensures more accurate blood and urine tests.

■ Try to relax! If you are nervous or tense, let your doctor know because this can raise blood pressure and alter results of other tests. Feel free to ask the doctor to explain what's happening, which may allay fears.

■ Caffeine, nicotine, and alcohol raise blood pressure temporarily. Refrain from all three for at least three hours before having your blood pressure measured.

■ The blood test that is part of a routine physical gives you your cholesterol level. In many instances, a single reading for cholesterol is not accurate because the levels vary from one day to the next and are influenced by stress and diet. If there is concern about your cholesterol, several readings may be necessary to ensure accuracy.

■ Don't use a deodorant or talcum powder before you have a mammogram or chest X-ray. Chemicals in these products can show up as suspicious-looking spots on an X-ray.

What Should Be Included in a Complete Physical

Both Men and Women

Medical history

Vital statistics (height, weight, blood pressure, heart rate, etc.)

Routine blood and urine tests (chemical profile)

Skin examination (check for suspicious moles and growths)

Slit-lamp eye examination (check exposed blood vessels)

Ear examination (check for wax buildup and signs of infection)

Heart exam (including EKG, or ECG)

Abdominal exam (check liver and spleen size, listen to bowel sounds)

Neck exam (listen for bruits, abnormal sounds indicating reduced blood flow, and check thyroid gland)

Lymph node exam (check for tenderness and abnormal swelling)

Nerve reflexes (by tapping knee, ankle, and other points)

Stool test for hidden (occult) blood

Possible chest X-ray, depending upon circumstances (e.g., history of heart or lung disease, tobacco use)

After 50: Sigmoidoscopy to examine lower 12 to 24 inches of the colon. Recent research indicates that screening by sigmoidoscopy (using a viewing device to examine the lower bowel) could lead to a nearly 60 percent reduction in the risk of dying from cancer of the rectum or lower colon. Mammograms should be performed on women every two years.

Men Only
Testicular exam
Digital prostate exam

Women Only
Breast examination
Pelvic exam and Pap smear

■ Many drugs alter test results. Be prepared to give the doctor or technician performing the test a list of all medications that you take regularly, including vitamins, aspirin, and other nonprescription drugs. Ask if you should bring the medication bottles.

■ Some foods alter test results. Ask your doctor about any dietary restrictions you should observe before undergoing a test.

■ Allow ample time for a test. The test itself may take only five minutes, but the waiting and prep work can add hours.

■ Before you leave home, call to make sure the testing center is on schedule.

Request a copy of your lab report. When you see a new doctor or specialist, take the most recent one with you.

QUESTIONS ABOUT TESTS

Answers to the following questions can help you decide if the test is really needed:

■ Why am I having this test? Will the results make a difference in my treatment?

■ Are there other ways of getting the information? What are the risks in not having the test?

■ Who does the actual lab work and who analyzes the results? (In general, this should be done by a specialist in the procedure; for example, an angiographer working with a nuclear cardiologist should review coronary angiograms.)

■ How useful are the results? Am I likely to need additional tests?

■ How accurate is the test? What factors affect the results?

■ Will it hurt? What are the risks of permanent injury?

■ How much does it cost? Does my insurance cover it?

ALLERGY TESTS

■ Some allergies are detected by skin-prick tests, in which small amounts of allergens are injected into the skin. Expect 30 or more allergen extracts to be tested in a single session.

■ Patch tests are used to find causes of contact dermatitis, which is a skin rash caused by direct contact with chemicals, a metal, or another substance. Strips impregnated with suspected allergens are taped to your back for two days. For accurate results, don't shower or get the patches wet.

■ Typically, an allergic response develops in 15 minutes, feels like a mosquito bite, and lasts 15 to 30 minutes. If you're allergic to several of the extracts, you may feel like you've been attacked by a swarm of mosquitoes. Failure to react to any of the extracts means you'll probably have to return for more skin tests.

■ Allergy skin tests use extracts of the suspected allergens. In unusual cases, this can provoke a severe response. Therefore, allergy skin tests should always be done in the allergist's office, hospital outpatient clinic, or other medical setting in case of an emergency.

■ If you have a moderate to severe reaction, your allergist will give you an antihistamine or other medication. These drugs will make you drowsy, so don't attempt to drive home yourself.

RISKY RAYS

Radiation has a cumulative effect. Your risk of cancer from this source rises with the number of X-rays you have.

■ Avoid duplication. If you have had X-rays recently, ask for your film and take it to any new doctor.

■ X-rays should be avoided during pregnancy unless absolutely necessary. If you do have them while pregnant, be sure the fetus is protected with a lead covering.

■ When you have a mammogram, ask if the unit is accredited by the Canadian Association of Radiologists.

■ Ask if an alternative test can substitute for an X-ray. For example, ultrasound can sometimes be used instead of fluoroscopy, a type of video X-ray that delivers relatively high doses of radiation.

Most modern X-ray equipment uses low-dose radiation. If the X-ray equipment looks old, ask to see proof that it has been recently accredited to make sure it is safe.

BREAST SELF-EXAMINATION

In about 80 percent of all breast cancers, it's the woman herself who first finds the breast lump or other warning sign. The Canadian Cancer Society recommends that by the age of 40 all women should practice monthly breast self-examination, a simple, 10-minute procedure. Do it during the week after your menstrual period, when breasts are unlikely to be swollen or tender.

After menopause, pick an easy-to-remember date, such as the first of the month. A woman in a high-risk group should discuss the need for earlier and more frequent examinations with her doctor. It's a good idea to have your doctor or a nurse check your technique. Here are the three basic steps.

VISUAL EXAMINATION

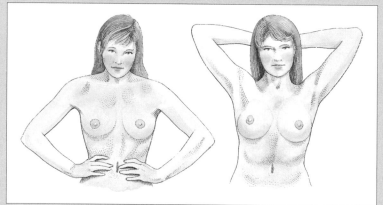

1. Stand in front of a mirror, with the arms in the positions shown here. Inspect the breasts for any changes in shape, unusual dimpling, and skin puckering, redness, or scaling.

PALPATION WHILE STANDING OR SITTING

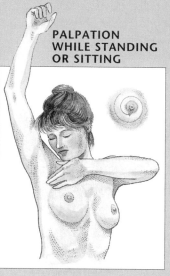

2. It's best to do this step while showering or bathing—fingers glide more easily over the breast when it is wet and soapy. Raise one arm, then use three or four fingers of the other hand to examine the breast. Move in circles, beginning at the outer edge and working your way toward the nipple. Also examine the armpit. Feel for any lump, thickening, or mass that is not part of your normal breast anatomy. Repeat on the other breast.

PALPATION WHILE LYING DOWN

3. With a pillow or rolled towel tucked under your shoulder, raise one arm over your head. Using the same finger technique described in Step 2, again examine each breast for any lumps or other changes.

SEE YOUR DOCTOR AS SOON AS POSSIBLE IF YOU DETECT:

Any unusual lump, swelling, thickening, or asymmetry. Any skin change, such as scaling, dimpling, inflammation, or pitting that resembles an orange peel. Any nipple change, including a bloody or milky discharge unrelated to breast-feeding. Any sore or ulceration that does not heal.

PRESURGERY AND OTHER TESTS

Most invasive tests that require anesthesia (such as coronary angiography, dilation and curettage, and biopsies) are performed in a hospital or special testing center. After fasting (both food and fluids) for 8 to 10 hours, you undergo the test early in the morning, then spend several hours in a special recovery area. You can usually go home after the anesthesia has worn off and your condition is stable.

■ Most routine tests before elective (nonemergency) surgery are now done on an outpatient basis. Filling out forms and going from place to place for different tests can take an entire day.

■ Standard pre-admission tests generally include a complete blood count, a urinalysis, and a chest X-ray if you have not had one recently. Patients older than 35 may be given an electrocardiogram.

■ If you took a drug to prevent gagging, do not eat or drink until the gag reflex returns to normal. Otherwise, you may choke or inhale food into your lungs.

■ Increase your fluid intake after any test that uses a dye. Try to drink at least two quarts in the 8 to 10 hours following the test to help your kidneys clear the substance from your body. Plain water is preferred, but apple juice and weak tea are acceptable.

■ Don't be alarmed if your urine is a strange color. It should return to normal in a couple of days.

Do not drive for four to six hours after having certain medications, such as antihistamines, or eye examinations that use drops. Have a friend do the driving until your eyes return to normal.

FOR WOMEN ONLY

■ Avoid douching, tub baths, and sexual intercourse for 24 hours before having a pelvic examination and Pap smear.

■ All women should undergo a regular clinical breast examination, and from age 50 this should include mammography every two years. If you are at risk for breast cancer, discuss with your doctor the need for earlier mammography.

■ Schedule routine breast examinations for the week after your menstrual period. This is when your breasts are least likely to be swollen. For self-examinations, see the box on the facing page.

■ When doctors compare mammograms for possible breast changes, remember that your last two are the most important. The baseline mammogram you had at age 35 or 40 probably is not relevant when you are 50 or 55.

FOR MEN ONLY

■ Be diligent about scheduling a prostate examination annually after age 50. Your doctor examines the prostate by feeling it through the rectum; suspicious findings require blood tests, X-rays, and perhaps an ultrasound or CT examination and biopsy.

■ Perform testicular self-examination on a monthly basis. To do this, hold a testicle with one hand and use the fingers of the other to feel carefully for any hard nodules, masses, or enlargement. If you find any of these symptoms, see your doctor as soon as possible to rule out testicular cancer.

EXERCISE STRESS TESTS

■ A stress test should be done in a doctor's office, hospital lab, or medical testing center, with a doctor in attendance.

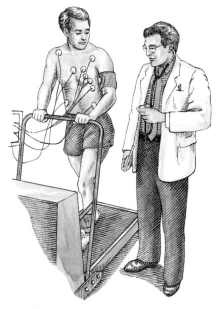

■ Wear comfortable clothing—shorts or sweat pants, sneakers or walking shoes. Don't eat for at least four hours before the test.

■ Ask your doctor about discontinuing medication before a test. For example, beta-blockers slow your heart rate and, if present in your system, can distort the test results.

■ Don't smoke for at least four hours or consume alcohol or caffeine for three hours before the test.

Scoping for an Inside View

Your doctor can now view almost every internal organ with the aid of an endoscope—a small tube equipped with fiberoptic lights and magnifying devices. Although endoscopic procedures cause some discomfort and pose a risk of infection and perforation, they are generally safer and less invasive than exploratory surgery. The most commonly used scopes are:

Arthroscope: Inserted through a small incision to examine a joint.
Bronchoscope: Inserted through the mouth to examine the upper portion of the lungs.
Colonoscope: Inserted through the rectum to examine the entire large intestine.
Colposcope: Used to examine the vagina and cervix, although it is not actually inserted into the body cavity.
Cystoscope: Inserted through the urethra to examine the bladder.
Gastrointestinal endoscope: Inserted through the mouth to examine the esophagus, stomach, and upper portion of the small intestine.
Laparoscope: Inserted into the abdomen through an incision near the navel to examine the female reproductive organs and gallbladder.
Sigmoidoscope: Inserted through the anus to examine the lower portion of the colon. (Insist on a flexible one—a rigid device is very uncomfortable.)
Surgical procedures performed through special scopes with the aid of magnifying video cameras are often called Band-aid surgery because they do not require large incisions. There is little bleeding, and recovery time is much shorter. However, special training is needed, so make sure your doctor is experienced in this type of surgery.

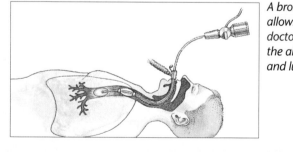

A bronchoscope allows a doctor to view the airways and lungs.

■ Stop the test immediately if you develop chest pain, faintness, or extreme fatigue.

SCANNING TESTS

The use of CT (computerized tomography) and MRI (magnetic resonance imaging) scans has proved invaluable in diagnosing illness, particularly in the brain. CT scans involve X-rays; MRI scans do not.

■ CT and MRI scans are painless, but the machinery can be intimidating. Let the examiner know if you cannot stand being in an enclosed place; a mild sedative can help ease your claustrophobia.

■ You must lie very still during a CT or any other scanning procedure. A child or very anxious person may need to be heavily sedated.

■ Many special X-ray studies and scans require injection of a dye to make internal organs show up on film. Most patients feel stinging, burning, or a hot flush when the dye is injected. Allergic reactions are uncommon, but be sure to tell the examiner if you have allergies, especially to iodine, shellfish, or specific medications.

■ Ask for foam earplugs or earphones when undergoing an MRI. For 30 to 45 minutes, you will be enclosed in a small, noisy doughnut-shaped machine. You won't feel a thing, but it will sound as if you are surrounded by a dozen jackhammers.

■ You don't need to undress unless your clothing contains metal—a zipper, hooks or eyes, etc.

■ Make sure that the examiner is aware of any metal on or in your body. Tooth fillings and artificial joints are generally okay, but metal clips or pins are not. Above all, a cardiac pacemaker cannot withstand MRI—if you have one, a CT scan is usually an acceptable alternative to MRI.

EYE TESTS

When doctors peer into your eyes, they are looking for more than vision problems— they are also seeking clues to diabetes and other diseases. Here's what to expect at a

routine eye examination:
- Physical observation of your eyes as you move them.

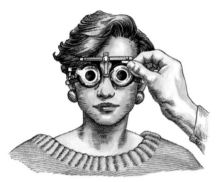

- Vision tests, usually using the Snellen eye chart. You will be asked to read letters of various sizes, usually through an instrument fitted with different lenses. The doctor can also view your retina through this instrument.
- Ophthalmoscope inspection using a hand-held magnifying device with a bright light that is directed into the eye's interior. With this device, a doctor can detect structural abnormalities and inspect the tiny blood vessels of the eye for signs of circulatory disorders. In some cases, dilating drops will be inserted.
- Slit-lamp microscope examination, during which you watch a point of light while the doctor examines your eyes with a magnifying device.
- Tonometry, to measure pressure within the eyeball.

WHEN YOU SEE AN EYE DOCTOR
- If you wear glasses or contact lenses, bring them with you whenever you visit the ophthalmologist or optometrist so that they can be checked. After age 40, you may need

new glasses more often than when you were younger.
- Some eye exams require the use of special drops to widen, or dilate, the pupil, allowing the doctor to examine the retina. These drops make your eyes more sensitive to light—wear sunglasses until your eyes return to normal. Also, it takes hours before you can focus your eyes enough to drive, so arrange for transportation home.
- If you are given anesthetic eyedrops, be extra careful not to rub your eyes for a while— you won't be able to tell if you're rubbing too hard until the anesthetic wears off.
- If your job poses a risk to your eyes, ask your doctor about protective measures and how often you should have your eyes checked.
- Dilating eyedrops should not be used if you have glaucoma. Make sure your doctor screens for glaucoma before inserting drops.

SCHEDULING EYE EXAMS
See an ophthalmologist promptly for such symptoms as eye pain, redness, blurring, seeing flashing lights, or any other vision changes. Otherwise, follow this schedule:
- A child's first eye exam should occur at six months. New tests allow for diagnoses of vision problems in infancy. As a rule, the sooner problems are diagnosed, the better.
- For children without vision problems, the next screening should occur at age 3, again at 5, and annually for those in school up to age 19.
- An adult 20 to 64 should be

> ## Eye-Care Professionals
>
> **Ophthalmologists** are M.D.'s trained to diagnose and treat eye disorders, test vision, and prescribe corrective lenses.
> **Optometrists** are trained to test vision, prescribe lenses, and screen for common eye disorders, such as glaucoma and cataracts, but they cannot diagnose or treat eye diseases.
> **Opticians** are trained to grind and fit eyeglasses or contact lenses but are not qualified to examine eyes or prescribe glasses or medications.

examined every two years if vision is normal, and every 18 months for those who wear glasses. A change in vision calls for a checkup.
- From age 65 on, have your eyes examined annually.
- Checkups for adults 40 or older should include a glaucoma screening.
- A diabetic needs an eye exam every six months.
- A hypertensive needs an exam every 6 to 12 months.
- A glaucoma patient needs an exam every 6 to 9 months.

"Eat carrots for good eyesight" has taken on a new meaning. Preliminary research links beta-carotene, a chemical in carrots, to prevention of macular degeneration, which is the loss of central vision that often affects older people.

THE HOSPITAL

In an emergency, you'll probably go to the nearest hospital. Otherwise, expect to be admitted to the hospital that your doctor or surgeon uses. Some medical problems will require a specific kind of hospital.

CHOOSING THE BEST HOSPITAL

■ Investigate privately run hospitals, the local general hospital, and other facilities, such as veterans' hospitals. Many general hospitals are affiliated with medical schools, and some offer special programs for high-risk pregnancies, trauma, mental illness, and chronic disorders.

■ Check to see that the facility you choose is accredited by the Canadian Council on Health Facilities Accreditation. This means that the facility has met national standards and guidelines. If a facility is not accredited by the Council, ask why. Teaching hospitals must be accredited by the Council, as a requirement of provincial licensing. To check the status of a hospital, contact the Canadian Council on Health Facilities Accreditation, 1730 St. Laurent Blvd., Suite 430, Ottawa, Ont., K1G 5L1. Or look for the directory *Guide to Canadian Health Care Facilities* in your public library.

■ If your treatment requires state-of-the-art equipment, hard-to-find specialists, or other special needs, consider a teaching hospital. These facilities are associated with a medical school and usually have a highly trained staff with access to the latest medical research and technology.

■ If you choose a teaching hospital, be prepared for multiple examinations by groups of residents and medical students. Dealing with these visits can be trying, but the quality of care can make up for the inconvenience. If, however, you find the recurring visits objectionable, ask your doctor whether they can be reduced.

■ For routine illness, try your community hospital. In general, community hospitals offer more personalized care and are more convenient for visits by friends and relatives, which can be especially important to elderly or terminally ill patients. Many community hospitals, linked by computer to major medical centers, can provide specialized care.

■ If complications arise while you're in a community hospital, your doctor may order you to be transferred to a larger medical center. However, if you feel you are not getting adequate care, you don't need to wait for your physician; you can ask to be transferred.

. . . .

If your child has to undergo surgery, try to arrange for the child to visit the hospital before the operation. Familiarity can ease a youngster's anxiety.

. . . .

WHAT TO BRING WITH YOU

■ Valid identification.

■ Your Medicare card, proof of private insurance, such as Blue Cross, and a hospital card if you have one.

■ The name, address, and telephone number of your employer.

■ The name, address, and telephone number of a relative or friend for the hospital to contact in case of an emergency or a change in your condition.

Be sure to pack the following items in a small overnight bag:

■ Toiletries (toothbrush, toothpaste, shaving kit, hand cream or lotion).

■ One or two changes of pajamas, a robe, slippers (unless you prefer those supplied by the hospital).

■ A list of the drugs you are taking, giving information about brand or generic name and dosage.

■ Reading materials and reading glasses (if needed).

■ A family photograph or picture of someone dear to you.

■ Change and a few dollars in

small bills for newspapers and other incidentals.

• •

Leave at home any items of value, such as jewelry or large amounts of cash. Also, most hospitals ban smoking, so don't bring cigarettes. Now is a good time to quit.

• •

GETTING ADMITTED

There are several steps you can take to make admission to a hospital as smooth as possible.

■ Before you go to the hospital, complete a preadmission form in your doctor's office, giving also your room preference and information about your insurance coverage. The hospital will probably call you prior to your admission to verify the information and arrange a visit to the pre-admission unit.

■ Routine tests, such as a chest X-ray and blood and urine analyses, are done on an out-patient basis before admission.

■ In your doctor's office, and in the presence of your physician, you will also sign a Consent to Surgery, indicating that you have received an informed explanation of the surgical procedure and agree to it. This is forwarded to the hospital and becomes part of your chart.

■ Call the hospital the morning of your expected admission to find out when your bed will be ready. This way you can avoid an unnecessary wait.

■ At the hospital, you fill out and sign admissions forms.

The hospital will explain your financial responsibilities and hospital policies. Have a friend or relative accompany you through the admissions process.

■ Extras such as a private room, or private-duty nurse, will be covered by your private insurance and are requested in advance. Telephones are usually provided free, but some hospitals may charge for them.

WHO'S WHO AT THE HOSPITAL

Here's a quick guide to the various caregivers you may encounter during your hospital stay. Titles and responsibilities may vary from hospital to hospital.

Title	What they do
Admissions clerks or officers	Guide patient through the admissions process, including filling out papers, taking insurance information, and explaining hospital routines and regulations.
Attending physicians	Hospital doctors assigned to oversee a patient's treatment.
Consultants	Specialists called in by the attending physicians for an opinion or to perform a specific test or procedure.
House staff (Interns and residents)	Medical students or graduates completing their training with actual patient care.
Primary nurses	Monitor physical condition, coordinate tests, procedures and treatment, provide liaison with physicians.
Registered nursing assistants	Assist nurses in monitoring physical condition and administering medications.
Private-duty nurses	Registered Nurses (R.N.'s) employed by a patient; not a member of the hospital staff.
Nurses' aides or orderlies	Help patients with personal care, change bed linen, help them get around the hospital.
Social workers	Work with patients and their families to address emotional and financial issues and arrange for home care if needed.
Medical technologists	Specialists who conduct laboratory tests, administer some diagnostic tests and assist with other tests.
Therapists	Specialists in physiotherapy, occupational or speech therapy, who help patients recover their physical strength, flexibility and skills.

SETTLING IN

After completing the paperwork, you will be accompanied to your room. There you should expect several routine procedures before treatment begins. These will include:

■ A medical history and complete physical examination, including blood pressure measurement, urine analysis, electrocardiogram, a complete blood workup, and a chest X-ray. (Some of these procedures will be omitted if you had them done just before entering the hospital.)

■ Other tests and procedures, depending on the reason for your being in the hospital. These tests confirm that you are able to undergo the prescribed treatment.

■ A nurse's assessment, which may repeat questions from your medical history but will also include inquiries about your medication, home situation, and support systems. This information is used in planning care in the hospital and after your discharge.

■ If an operation is planned, your chart will contain the Consent to Surgery form you signed in your doctor's office. Check the chart and the form to see that the proper parts of your body, including left and right, are specified on the form. This helps prevent mistakes (see "Your Rights as a Patient," page 310).

■ Most hospitals have patient lounges, sun rooms, and other areas that are more cheerful and interesting than your room. If your condition permits, explore these areas.

Pleasant surroundings could help you recover faster.

■ Bring a radio with headphones to help pass the time and keep you in touch with the outside world. Also, studies show that music can reduce your perception of pain and, thus, your need for pain medication.

HOSPITAL DIETS

■ Inquire in advance about a special diet if you need one. Some hospitals provide kosher, vegetarian, and other diets, but many do not. When they are unable to meet such dietary needs, most hospitals will let outside sources provide the food.

■ If you plan to provide some or all of your food, ask your doctor or hospital dietitian about any dietary restrictions you should observe.

■ If you do provide your own food, the hospital should not charge you for meals.

VISITING FRIENDS IN THE HOSPITAL

■ Call to find out the hospital's visiting hours and the policy on gifts (flowers are not permitted in some departments; food may not be recommended for some patients). Also check with the patient to see what time would be best for you to come by.

■ Keep it short. A visit lasting 5 minutes is plenty for a patient who is very ill; 20 minutes is appropriate for other patients. If someone else comes to visit the patient, cut your visit short.

■ Avoid mob scenes. At most, visit with one other person.

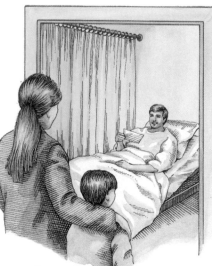

■ Some hospitals permit children to visit, but most do not. Call ahead to ask before bringing a child to the hospital.

■ Don't expect to be entertained or to entertain the patient. Sharing a few tidbits of good news from friends and family is enough.

■ Take your lead from the patient. Let the patient discuss his or her illness, but if the topic brings uneasiness, switch to a more cheerful subject.

■ Don't discuss your own illness or declining health.

■ Don't let more than one conversation get started.

■ Actions speak louder than words. A hug or a squeeze of the hand can let the patient know you care.

Your visit can actually help shorten a patient's hospital stay. Doctors have long noted that a patient's emotional outlook improves after a visit from a friend or relative, and this can speed recovery.

BIRTHING CENTERS

"The nurse-midwives gave me all the time I needed, and they really got to know me and my family. It was a great experience."
—Sidney Stevens, mother of two

• • • • • • •

As recently as the early 1970's, most mothers-to-be entered the hospital early in labor and spent the hours before delivery lying flat in a hospital bed. Few fathers ventured past the hospital waiting room during their wives' labor and delivery.

Today hospitals have changed. Almost all have at least one comfortably furnished birthing room where women and their partners stay before, during, and after their babies are born. Medications and painkillers for women in labor are kept to a minimum. During labor, expectant mothers are encouraged to walk around.

But the birthing revolution is far from over. Growing numbers of women are choosing to have their babies in the homey setting of a birthing center. There they are attended by a nurse-midwife, rather than an obstetrician.

A midwife (who may be a Registered Midwife) gets involved early, providing prenatal care. During labor the midwife monitors the mother-to-be and assists with childbirth. Midwives are trained to recognize possible complications, and quick transfer to a hospital is always available.

Procedures vary among centers, but most permit women to walk around and bathe as labor progresses. Stays in birthing centers are usually shorter than in hospitals,

from 12 to 48 hours. This factor, as well as the reduced need for expensive machinery, means that birthing centers cost the health-care system considerably less, despite the added features these centers offer.

A crucial distinction. Besides relying chiefly on midwives, the major difference between birthing centers and hospitals is philosophical: pregnancy and birth are viewed as natural, healthy processes, so much so that they can be a family event in birthing centers. Many of them even encourage older children and grandparents to be present during the birth itself.

Sidney Stevens, a freelance journalist, had her first child in a hospital and her second in a birthing center. "My first baby was born in a big, impersonal city hospital," she says. But her second pregnancy and birth were vastly different.

"On my first visit to the midwife, she talked to me for a full hour about what to expect," Stevens recalls. "When I developed a kidney infection and had to be hospitalized, the staff spent time with me to explain things and calm my fears."

Better bonding. When she went into labor with her second child, Stevens says, "I was in a big private room decorated with flowers and pictures. There was a pullout couch where my husband could sleep, and we were allowed to keep the baby with us."

Birthing centers and midwives are still regarded with a great deal of suspicion in Canada. But studies have shown that maternal and neonatal mortality rates are comparable for low-risk births in hospitals and birthing centers. And birthing centers have about half the rate of cesarean sections.❑

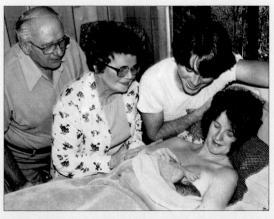

Birthing centers are a popular option for families who want to share the experience of birth.

YOUR RIGHTS AS A PATIENT

You are entitled not only to ask questions but also to be treated with respect, honesty, and fairness. Even so, it is up to you to know your rights and the proper channels to go through if you have a grievance.

YOU HAVE A RIGHT

Organizations may have different ways of expressing patients' rights, but, basically, you deserve the following from the health-care system:

■ To be treated with respect and dignity. If a practitioner makes you feel uncomfortable, let him or her know. For example, if you object to being called by your first name, politely request that you be addressed as Miss (Mr., Mrs.).

■ To know and understand the diagnosis as well as the benefits and risks of a recommended treatment or procedure. Ask your doctor to explain these in simple language.

■ To be informed about alternative medical or surgical treatments.

■ To be informed of the consequences of not going ahead with treatment.

■ To refuse treatment. You can decline to have an operation or procedure and you can leave the hospital at any time. However, rather than refusing treatment altogether, seek a second opinion or discuss alternative therapies with your doctor.

■ To be treated at a hospital in an emergency.

■ To receive an adequate standard of care consistent with your needs.

■ To receive treatment free of discrimination.

■ To choose your doctor, or at least know who is handling your care. If you are hospitalized in an emergency or by someone other than your doctor, ask the name of the doctor assigned to oversee your care. This physician is obliged to keep you fully informed.

■ To switch doctors. If you are hospitalized, however, the doctor you want to treat you must have staff privileges at that facility.

■ Confidentiality. In most cases, doctors are obliged to keep patient conversations and medical records confidential. However, you waive this right each time you file an insurance claim or apply for life or health insurance.

■ To be informed of continuing health-care requirements following discharge from the hospital. If the instructions are complicated, ask that they be written out. Read them to make sure they are clear. Ask for a number to call for more information if questions arise after you go home.

■ To discuss the cost of treatment that is not covered by your provincial or territorial health insurance. If you believe you are being charged unfairly, you have a right to contest the fees in court.

■ To speak up without fear of reprisal if you feel your rights have been violated by a hospital or by a member of the medical profession.

■ To refuse to be examined by medical students or anyone other than your doctor. If you plan to exercise this right, let your doctor know.

■ To be informed if you are participating in a research project. If you object to participating, you have the right to refuse.

WHAT IS A RESEARCH PROTOCOL?

Clinical trials to determine the safety and effectiveness of a new drug or medical device are often held in hospitals. The plan for such trials is called a protocol. Before agreeing to take part in a study, you may want to ask your physician if the research protocol requires the following:

■ An institutional review board must approve the project, verifying that risks to participants are minimal and that participants were chosen fairly and equitably.

■ A researcher must explain the purpose of the study orally and in writing and get your written consent to take part in the project.

■ You do not waive your legal right to privacy by participating in the study.

■ Results are continually monitored to ensure your safety.

■ You can drop out of the clinical trial at any time if you get anxious, experience serious discomfort, or just have second thoughts.

> **If possible, ask a friend or family member to act as your advocate while you are in the hospital. Then, if you are too weak or ill to fight for your rights, you know someone else will.**

EXERCISING YOUR RIGHTS

■ Some health-care organizations have set guidelines for patient's rights. If they have, they should be posted up where you can see them.

■ Many hospitals employ patient advocates to act as liaisons between patients and hospital administrators or physicians. However, since these advocates are on the hospital's payroll, some may not adequately represent you.

■ In some matters, such as access to medical records, you may get better results by having someone outside the hospital staff looking after your rights. Talk to a lawyer or a representative of a consumer advocate group.

■ Be assertive—it can pay off. Studies show that patients who demand their rights usually get the best treatment.

RETRIEVING YOUR MEDICAL RECORDS

■ Your medical records belong to your doctor or health care facility. But since the information is about you, you are entitled to inspect and copy the documents in your file.

■ You should write to the doctor or hospital asking for copies, or give your lawyer a signed authorization to get

hold of the document copies.

■ The onus is on the doctor or hospital to justify any denial of access. In cases where psychiatric records are concerned, access may be refused in the patient's interest.

■ If you do not need the entire file, specify what information you want, such as lab tests, X-rays, ECG's, and hospital discharge summaries. You may be able to avoid tests that duplicate previous results.

■ Some doctors fear that the information in a patient's file will be used in a malpractice suit; others hesitate, fearing that a patient will misinterpret the information. If you encounter resistance getting your records, be persistent.

CHECKING WHAT'S IN THE COMPUTERS

■ Insurance companies keep files on all policyholders, and share this information with each other through the Medical Information Bureau. These files store information obtained from doctors, hospitals, and past insurance applications and claims. You have a right to see at least some of this information. Here's how to gain access to your records:

■ Contact the Medical Information Bureau, 330 University Avenue, Room 506, Toronto, Ont., M5G 1R7. Ask for a form to request that your full file be sent to you.

■ Review your file with your doctor and ask for explanations of anything you do not understand.

■ If you find any inaccuracies, write to the bureau, asking

that the information be corrected. Document your claim with copies of your medical records. If the agency declines to change the information, submit a letter of dispute that will be included in your file.

ADVANCED HEALTH CARE DIRECTIVES

■ If you feel strongly about life-support systems and other right-to-die issues, spell out these wishes in a living will. This document and a durable power of attorney for health care form what are known as advanced health care directives. The Canadian Medical Association has advised that all physicians honor them.

■ Give copies of your living will and durable power of attorney for health care to your doctor and lawyer. Keep the original in an accessible location. Date and initial the living will every year so that others will know it is consistent with your most recent wishes.

■ A sample living will is available from Dying with Dignity, 600 Eglinton Avenue East, Suite 401, Toronto, Ont., M4P 1P3.

SURGERY AND A SECOND OPINION

Even the simplest operation carries some risk. To get the best and most appropriate treatment available, you must pick a competent surgeon and know when to get a second opinion.

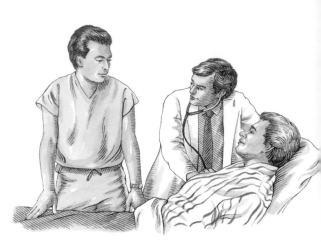

QUESTIONS TO ASK BEFORE SURGERY

Unless you are in an emergency situation, you are the one who decides whether to have surgery. Before any operation, you must sign an informed consent form, and you shouldn't sign it until all of your questions are answered. These include:

■ Why do I need this operation at this time?

■ Are there alternatives that do not involve hospitalization or surgery?

■ What are the risks of having the operation? What are the risks of not having it?

■ How long will I be in the hospital?

■ What can I expect during the recovery period?

■ What residual effects will there be from the operation?

■ Do most patients who undergo such surgery require physical rehabilitation?

■ When should I be able to resume my normal routine?

■ Can the procedure be done on an outpatient basis? What are the risks and benefits associated with doing this?

■ Are there risks if I postpone the operation until I get a second opinion?

CHOOSING A SURGEON

When you're facing surgery, you want a surgeon who has had extensive experience and a good track record in the procedure. This requires advance checking on your part.

■ Ask your primary-care physician for at least two recommendations for surgeons, and then ask the reasons that each is suitable for your situation.

■ Make sure the surgeon you choose is certified by the Royal College of Physicians and Surgeons of Canada in a surgical specialty, such as general surgery, orthopedic surgery, etc. For more specialized surgical practices, the surgeon should have a Certificate of Special Competence. Both indicate that the doctor has undergone advanced training and passed a rigorous examination in his or her specialty.

■ Find out what hospital the surgeon is affiliated with. It should be one that is accredited by the Canadian Council on Health Facilities Accreditation. This commission conducts a program to promote high levels of patient care in hospitals and other health-care facilities. The Canadian Association for Accreditation of Ambulatory Surgery Facilities Incorporated is a nationally recognized organization that seeks to assure high professional standards for ambulatory or outpatient surgery centers.

■ Ask about the doctor's success rate. If it is below average, find out if he or she specializes in high-risk cases. If so, a high failure rate does not necessarily indicate work that is substandard.

■ If you are undergoing a complicated or unusual operation, find out how many such procedures have been performed at the hospital and by the surgeon you have chosen. If the surgeon hesitates or seems insulted by your question, look for another surgeon.

■ If your operation is being performed in a teaching hospital, determine if a surgical resident will assist in the operation and how much of the operation he or she will be doing. If you are uncomfortable with the answer, insist that the surgeon perform more of the operation—or choose another surgeon.

■ Although microsurgery and lasers have changed the way many operations are performed, these innovations are not right for all situations. Have the surgeon explain the technique he or she has chosen and why it's best for you.

Remember, you're choosing a surgeon, not a dinner companion. It's important to choose the best person for the job, not just someone you like. It is essential that you have confidence in your surgeon's skills.

SECOND OPINIONS

■ When your doctor advises surgery—of any kind—it is time to get a second opinion, preferably from a nonsurgical specialist. If you have been told you need a heart operation, for example, consult a cardiologist, who treats heart conditions medically rather than surgically.

■ If you have any misgivings about the accuracy of a diagnosis, or the appropriateness of a treatment, get a second opinion, if only to reassure yourself.

■ If your doctor tells you you have a rare or serious disease, seek out a specialist for a second opinion.

■ If your doctor tells you your symptoms are being created by your imagination or attributes them to nerves, consult another doctor. Other reasons for seeking out a second opinion are given in the summary of "Second Opinions," right.

■ Ask your family doctor for a referral. Many specialists will not see a patient without a referral from a family physician. But beware of the old-boy network. Although most doctors provide the names of competent, impartial specialists, some recommend a friend or colleague simply to confirm his or her opinion. If you are not happy with the specialist your doctor has referred you to, say so and ask for another.

■ To find a specialist on your own, ask for a referral from a hospital that your doctor is not affiliated with. If there is a teaching hospital or medical school nearby, call the department of surgery. Ask the administrative assistant if the department has referral lists for second opinions.

■ The Canadian Cancer Society and your local or provincial health department can also help you find qualified physicians or hospitals.

■ The national or provincial association of surgical specialties may be able to provide you with a list of certified surgeons in your area.

■ Let your doctor know that you are seeking a second opinion. The second physician you consult will need your medical records, and you can frequently avoid duplicate testing if the first physician sends the second your medical records.

■ Be sure to ask the second physician the same questions you asked the first (see "Questions to Ask Before Surgery," on the facing page).

■ If the two opinions you get conflict, you may have to seek a third or fourth opinion. Remember, however, that at some point you must decide for yourself. List all the pros and cons, and determine whether the benefits outweigh the risks.

Second Opinions

There are valid and important reasons for seeking a second opinion. Some are given on this page (opposite). You may also want a second opinion if:

Your doctor recommends major elective surgery, such as a coronary artery bypass operation.

Previous surgery or treatment has failed to produce improvement.

Your doctor cannot determine what is wrong.

Your doctor says the condition cannot be treated.

Your doctor is not a specialist in your condition.

Your current treatment is risky or has undesirable side effects.

You're told that you have cancer, AIDS, or another chronic, progressive disease.

Some forms of surgery in particular should be questioned, and a second opinion obtained:

Angioplasty (use of a balloon to unclog a blocked artery)

Back surgery

Cataract removal

Cesarian section

Coronary artery bypass

Gallbladder removal

Hernia repair

Hysterectomy

Knee surgery

Prostate reduction or removal

Tonsillectomy

In Canada, insurance companies generally do not ask for second opinions. However, if major dental surgery is proposed, a company may request a second opinion. And, if a company has reason to doubt a claim for injury, it may request a second opinion from its own doctor.

■ If you decide to go through with the procedure, usually the first physician you consulted will do the operation. If you feel more comfortable with the surgeon who gave the second opinion, however, ask if he or she will take your case.

DEALING WITH POST-OPERATIVE PAIN

After the anesthesia wears off, most surgery patients experience varying degrees of pain, especially in and around the incision. The worst is usually over in 48 to 72 hours; until then, pain can be minimized by taking painkillers.

■ Don't hesitate to ask for pain medication as soon as you begin to feel discomfort.

■ Let your doctor or nurse know if you need medication more often or in a stronger dose. Pain can be controlled more effectively if medication is given early rather than waiting until it becomes intense.

■ To minimize pain when turning or moving, use the bed side rails for support. Use a slow, steady motion, avoiding fast or jerky movements. If

moving on your own is difficult, ask a nurse or aide to help you.

■ Whenever possible, wait until your pain medication takes effect before moving about, such as getting out of bed.

■ As much as possible, move parts of your body that were not affected by the operation. This improves circulation, prevents stiffness, and distracts your attention from the pain of your incision.

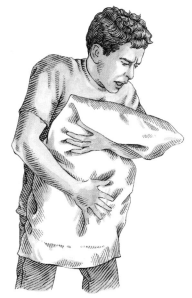

■ If you have a chest or abdominal incision, apply pressure to it when moving or coughing. You can do this by firmly hugging a pillow or by placing one hand above and the other below the incision.

GETTING BACK ON YOUR FEET

Many operations require extensive physical therapy or other forms of rehabilitation. Ask your surgeon what to expect, and plan for your rehabilitation before the operation.

■ Find out what you can do before the operation to speed your rehabilitation. For example, arthritis patients may be advised to start muscle-strengthening exercises before a joint replacement.

■ Ask your surgeon to describe what is involved in post-surgery rehabilitation. Are you likely to need physical or occupational therapy? If so, who does the surgeon recommend? A pre-surgery consultation with a therapist is often advisable, especially if extensive physical therapy is likely.

■ Various types of equipment may be used for physical therapy, including exercise mats, practice stairs, ramps, parallel bars, and pulleys and weights.

■ Heat is often used in therapy, applied with compresses or infrared lamps. Your physician may recommend ice packs for cold therapy.

■ If you are undergoing a radical procedure, such as a mastectomy or laryngectomy, consider joining a support group of patients who have had the same operation. Although this is usually done after the operation, talking to someone who has recovered from a similar procedure can be reassuring and helpful in planning your own rehabilitation.

■ Inquire whether your rehabilitation can be carried out at home or whether you will need to go to a rehabilitation center or other such facility.

■ Determine in advance if your insurance covers rehabilitation. Usually, a doctor's recommendation for a specific rehabilitation program is needed for coverage.

LONG-DISTANCE MEDICINE

"This technology gives patients in the most isolated areas instantaneous access to every medical specialty."
—Jay H. Sanders, M.D.

• • • • • • •

Doctors can use telemedicine centers like this one to examine patients hundreds of miles away.

After suffering several frightening episodes of chest pain, Shirley Wallace, a homemaker living in a rural area, took an exercise stress test. The results of the test, often used to evaluate coronary artery disease, were inconclusive.

Ordinarily, Dr. Charles Walker, Shirley Wallace's physician, would have sent his patient to a cardiologist at the nearest medical center, a medical college, 130 miles away. Wallace might then have had to return to her town for an angiogram or other tests. But thanks to the college's telecommunications link with the nearby county hospital, Wallace didn't have to make two trips.

While Dr. Walker examined his patient at the county hospital and discussed her symptoms, a detailed image appeared on a video monitor at the medical college's Telemedicine Center. There a cardiologist watched the monitor, asked some questions, and listened to the patient's heart and lungs through an electronic stethoscope. The specialist was able to study an electrocardiogram—a printout showing the electrical pattern of the patient's heartbeat—that had been transmitted over telephone lines. Based on what he saw and heard, the cardiologist recommended that Wallace have an angiogram in her home town.

Diagnosis from afar. Doctors can use telemedicine technology for a wide range of purposes. Nowadays they diagnose illnesses and carry out treatments without ever seeing the patient in person. This can make a crucial difference for those too ill to be transferred between hospitals.

The uses of telemedicine aren't confined to the hospital. Several products have been developed that let patients stay home while a doctor monitors their heart rate, blood pressure, and temperature over the phone.

The electronic age. Telemedicine centers were not possible until technology brought about major improvements in the quality of the video picture. There are now three hospitals in remote areas of Newfoundland that regularly use this technology. They are able to consult specialists in radiology, ultrasound (for pregnancy, heart conditions, gallbladder disease), nuclear medicine and other medical specialties, through the Telemedicine Centre at Memorial University in St. John's. The University of Western Ontario is linked to Sioux Look-Out in the north of the province for the transmission of X-rays. Other provinces, too, practice some telemedecine, although nowhere is there a program as comprehensive as in Newfoundland.

High-tech medicine will eventually spread to various nonmedical locations as well. Telemedicine centers could soon turn up in correctional facilities, so that prisoners won't have to be moved when they need medical treatment. Long-distance medicine could also be applied in national parks where a clinic "phones" X-rays of hikers' injuries to radiologists at a hospital. ❑

ALTERNATIVES TO HOSPITALS

Although our hospitals are ranked among the world's best, there are times when you may be better off at home, in a nursing home, a one-day surgical center, or another type of health-care facility.

THERE'S NO PLACE LIKE HOME

Home care provides an alternative to the high cost of hospitalization and the often impersonal atmosphere of nursing homes. Here's how to use at-home health services:

■ Talk to your doctor about the feasibility of home care. Many services that are provided in hospitals can be carried out at home—some cancer chemotherapy, oxygen therapy, tube feedings, rehabilitation exercises, and round-the-clock nursing, among others.

■ To find reliable home health services, check with your local department of social services, local agency for the aging, or visiting-nurse association. For example, in Quebec, local community health centers (CLSC's) provide extensive home care services, and in New Brunswick, home health care is provided through the Extra-Mural Hospital system.

■ Review your provincial health plan and private insurance policy to see if home care is covered.

■ Find out if physical therapy and other rehabilitation programs can be carried out at home. If so, ask your doctor to suggest a therapist who will come to your home.

■ Check with a local social services agency for the aging about community or provincial programs, such as a visiting-nurse association. Many communities have Meals on Wheels programs that bring nutritious meals to the homebound. Wheels to Meals programs transport clients from home to a community center where a meal is served.

■ Look into engaging a private geriatric-care manager. These are typically social workers or nurses who hire home aides, pay bills, and arrange nursing home placement.

Some provincial extended health-care services even make homemaking services available. Ask your local social services department if you are eligible for such assistance.

Elder-Care Options

For the elderly with few health problems who are able to live independently but need housing, these are among the alternatives to skilled-care nursing homes.

Accessory apartment. Private living unit set up within a single-family residence.

Assisted-care facility. Private apartments or rooms, with aid in managing everyday tasks, meal service, and some protective supervision.

Board-and-care home. Usually a group home providing supervision and personal care.

Congregate housing. Specially designed and managed multi-unit rented housing, typically with self-contained apartments. Provides supportive services, such as meals, housekeeping, transportation, and social and recreational activities.

Continuing care. A combination housing development and retirement community that provides a full range of accommodations and services for older adults, including independent living, congregate housing, assisted living, and nursing-home care. Residents move from one level to another as their needs change.

ECHO (Elder Cottage Housing Opportunity) Housing. Separate, self-contained living unit situated beside an existing home as a residence for a relative or unrelated tenant. Also called a granny flat.

DAY AND AMBULATORY SURGERY CENTERS

Many operations and procedures that formerly required a hospital stay are now done in hospital outpatient departments or ambulatory surgery centers. It's wise to take certain precautions before deciding on an outpatient facility.

■ Ask what type of anesthesia will be used, and how long you should expect to stay at the center following the procedure. In general, you can go home as soon as the anesthesia wears off and all vital signs (blood pressure, heart rate, and so forth) are stable.

■ In considering an ambulatory surgery center, ask about back-up emergency services. Is the center affiliated with a hospital that can admit you immediately if the need arises?

■ Make arrangements for someone to take you home. Chances are that after even a simple procedure you should not drive for a day or so, and you are not likely to feel up to

walking or taking public transportation.

■ Before going home, make sure you know what to do if complications arise. Ask specifically what signs indicate that you should seek emergency help. Heavy bleeding, a high fever, inflammation, and increasing pain are the most common signs of serious post-surgery complications.

WALK-IN MEDICAL CLINICS

These freestanding clinics offer many of the same services as hospital emergency rooms, usually without a long wait, and they usually provide a 24-hour service. Many can provide a full range of health care services, although some are not as well equipped as emergency rooms. They can admit you directly to a hospital if the need arises.

■ Ask what arrangements the center has for transferring seriously ill or injured patients to a hospital.

■ Some people choose to get their primary health care from such clinics. If you use the clinics for emergencies only, you can receive appropriate follow-up care when you go to your regular doctor.

MAKING A NURSING HOME DECISION

Whether you have a relative who needs medical attention while recovering from surgery or an elderly family member who has a chronic, debilitating illness, you may need to investigate nursing homes.

■ Determine first whether the person could remain at home

with sufficient support services provided by provincial and private health insurance plans. These can include visiting nurses, meals, housekeeping, and even respite care for a family member who is caring for an elderly person.

■ Convene a family meeting when a decision is imminent. Tactfully ask about income, life insurance, pension, and other financial resources.

■ Before a relative or friend enters a nursing home, try to persuade him or her to give durable power of attorney to someone to make legal, financial, and medical decisions; ordinary power of attorney ends when a person becomes incapacitated. Also find out if the person can benefit from extended care insurance.

■ Ask a trusted doctor to recommend a nursing home based on the patient's specific needs. When a doctor is unable to make a referral, consult your clergyman or the social-services department of your local hospital. They regularly work with staffs and residents of nursing homes.

■ Contact your local medical society, community services or health departments for suggestions.

■ Talk to the staff at senior-citizen centers, United Way offices, and local agencies for the aging, which may also be familiar with homes.

■ Ask friends and neighbors for recommendations.

■ Drop in unannounced on a weekday at a nursing home that is under consideration. Tell the receptionist that you want to look at the facility for

Consumer Checklist

Here are some features you should check out when considering a nursing home for a family member, friend, or yourself.

Does the nursing home have accreditation from the province? Is the license on display?

Does it have a formal quality-assurance program?

Is the administrator available to answer questions, hear complaints, discuss problems?

Does the facility have a written description of patients' rights and responsibilities?

Is it near a cooperating hospital and the patient's physician?

Is a physician readily available when medical attention is needed?

Are patients and families involved in treatment plans?

Is it clean, welcoming, and free of unpleasant odors?

Is the kitchen clean and free of flies and other insects?

Is perishable food refrigerated or is it left out on tables or counters?

Does a dietitian plan menus for those on special diets? Are personal likes and dislikes considered?

Are there provisions for special dietary needs, such as kosher or vegetarian diets?

Are visitors welcome at mealtimes?

What are the visiting hours? (They should last 10 to 12 hours daily.)

Are patients alert and engaged in interesting activities? Or do they appear sedated and dozing in front of a TV?

Are rooms set aside for physical exams and therapy, patient activities, and private visits with family and friends?

Is there a chapel or other facility for residents who may want to attend religious services?

Is there an isolation room for patients with contagious illnesses?

Is the facility well lighted and free of hazards underfoot?

Are there handrails in hallways?

Are fire exits clearly marked and unobstructed? Are fire drills conducted regularly?

Do toilets, bathtubs, and showers have hand grips and call bells or buttons? Are the bathrooms convenient to bedrooms?

Is the staff friendly, courteous, and well trained?

What is the ratio of nurses to patients? How much staff turnover is there annually?

a prospective patient.

■ Walk around, posing questions to both the staff and the residents. Use the accompanying consumer checklist to assess the home's pros and cons.

Many provinces inspect nursing homes to ensure they meet standards of care and comply with health and building codes. Ask to see copies of the evaluations, which are available on request.

EASING THE ADJUSTMENT

■ Bring some belongings—books and tapes, family photos, quilts, or throw pillows—that will make the new room feel homey.

■ Plan to spend several hours with a patient on admission day. Help to arrange the room, learn the way around, and meet staff and residents. You might also consider staying for a meal or planned activity.

■ Reassure the patient that you plan to maintain the same close relationship you have had in the past.

■ Invite the nursing home resident to get-togethers outside the facility whenever possible.

■ Call and visit often. Urge friends and relatives to write and phone.

■ Join the nursing home's family council, or form one if none exists. Such councils address concerns of patients and families and can provide a valuable support group for relatives.

Don't promise your parents or grandparents that you will never send them to a nursing home. And don't ask your children to make such a promise to you.

THE ART OF VISITING

■ Call in advance to find out when it's convenient for the patient to have a guest.

■ Resume some of the activities that you enjoyed together, such as listening to music or playing cards.

■ Bring videos or photos of family events—graduation ceremonies, Little League games, school plays—as well as photo albums you can leave behind.

■ Pack a special food treat. Whenever possible, bring enough for the resident and roommates or other visitors.

■ Keep nursing home residents informed of what's happening in the outside world. Bring news of friends and family. Collect newspaper clippings, magazine articles,

and other items of interest.

■ Begin making an oral history of the family. Tape-record the resident's memories of events and people when you visit. Leave a tape recorder at the home and encourage him or her to use it often.

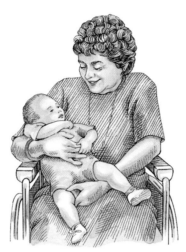

■ Once in a while, bring an unusual guest—a baby, child, pet (with the administrator's approval), or an old acquaintance. Or bring a musical instrument to play.

■ Holidays, birthdays, anniversaries, and other special occasions can be especially lonely for nursing home residents. Try to arrange a home leave for the patient. If this is impossible, look into celebrating the occasion at the nursing home.

■ Offer to do a shopping errand, read aloud a book or magazine, or write a letter.

■ Bring something you can work on together—puzzles, games, or crafts projects.

■ Give a back, hand, or foot rub. Touching is a way to show your affection and communicate things that words may not convey.

Knock before entering the room. It's important for nursing home residents to retain a measure of privacy.

PALLIATIVE CARE

Palliative care units provide supportive nursing care without medical intervention for the terminally ill. Growing numbers of patients with end-stage cancer, AIDS, and other conditions are choosing this option. Here are a few things to consider when investigating palliative care.

■ First make sure that palliative care is what you want. Remember, too, that you have a right to change your mind, even after you enter a palliative care unit.

■ Ask about the policy on managing pain. Most palliative care units want residents to be as comfortable as possible.

■ Many communities offer at-home palliative care services. Look into this if you or your loved one would prefer to die at home.

■ Ask about the policy regarding visitors. Many allow adult visitors at any time, especially as death approaches. Most allow visits from children. Some even permit pets.

■ When facing the death of a loved one, family members need extra emotional support. Ask if the unit offers grief counseling and other such services.

■ Designate a family member or friend to work with the staff to make decisions if you cannot do so.

HEALTH CENTERS AND OTHER COMMUNITY CARE

Traditionally, we seek the help of a doctor or hospital when we need medical help. But with the health-care system overstretched financially, there is a move away from institutional treatment and back to the community.

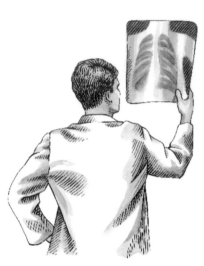

BASIC DISTINCTIONS
■ The system of payment that most of us use is called "fee for service." This means that patients go to the health-care providers they choose—doctors and hospitals—and the provincial and territorial medical and hospital plans pay fees on the basis of each medical service rendered. But cheaper ways of providing efficient health care are being examined.

■ The philosophy behind the new alternatives is preventive medicine, or self-care, aimed at making the population healthier and so reducing the burden on the health-care system. To this end, more and more provincial health departments are emphasizing health education and support services that aim to keep people as independent of costly institutionalization as possible.

HEALTH SERVICE ORGANIZATIONS (HSO'S)
■ These organizations, set up in Ontario only, are in fact general practices, much like the traditional doctor's office. The difference is in the way they are funded, which is reflected in the doctor's approach to the patient. HSO doctors are paid an amount per patient by the provincial government, rather than a fee

for each service. But the doctor receives the full amount only as long as the patient does not go elsewhere for services the HSO is expected to provide. This means that:

■ HSO's are encouraged to become group practices, so that if your doctor is not there, another doctor in the practice is able to see you. In theory, you the patient are inconvenienced as little as possible by your doctor's absence.

■ HSO's are also encouraged to provide a wide range of medical specialties. Those that do are even more convenient for their patients, who end up spending less time traveling to see specialists, and receive faster diagnosis and treatment.

■ Since HSO doctors are given an incentive payment if their patients use ambulatory care, or outpatient services, rather than taking up hospital beds, they encourage preventive medicine and non-institutionalized care. This approach is particularly attractive to patients who prefer to recuperate at home rather than in a hospital. Studies have also shown that people often recover faster in their home environment than in a hospital.

COMMUNITY HEALTH CENTERS (CHC'S)
■ In some parts of the country, health care is provided by community health centers, which offer social services as well, based on community needs. The doctors and other professionals who work there are paid salaries by the provincial government, not fees for service. And they cover a broad range of specialties. You still get to choose your own doctor, but you may also receive regular care from a nurse, a physiotherapist, or a social worker. Like the health service organizations, community health centers emphasize preventive medicine and public health.

■ Because the staff members of the CHC's are salaried, they are not under as much pressure to get patients in through the door as doctors in the traditional health-care system are, which means that they tend to spend more time attending to their patients.

■ CHC's are usually set up by members of a community, who are represented on the board of directors of the CHC, which means that they are in touch with individual community needs and can address these issues.

■ They aim to provide health care to those who cannot gain access to it due to linguistic and cultural barriers, physical disabilities, poverty, isolation, or other special needs. For example, some CHC's have a walk-in medical clinic for the homeless and psychiatrically disabled.

■ Most CHC's provide a special clinic for seniors, including home visits and assessments, and nursing care at home. They also offer exercise classes for seniors, and discussions on subjects such as coping with arthritis, grieving and how to improve the memory.

■ Other programs provided by these centers include discussions on healthy eating, pre- and post-natal care, and health education in day-care centers and schools.

■ CHC's are proactive in the community in other ways. For example, one community identified that no course in English as a second language was available for immigrants, and so it helped to set up one.

■ Quebec has the most extensive system of community health centers, called CLSC's, in the country. Primary health care is a main component of their services, but they also consider other factors that affect your well-being. A doctor at the CLSC may refer you to a social worker, for example, if you are having family problems.

■ Each CLSC decides with its board what public health concerns it wishes to address. There may be prenatal courses, child development courses, teen clinics or suicide prevention programs.

■ CLSC's also run a program called Home Care, in which seniors and the chronically ill who are confined to their homes benefit from home visits by nurses, homemakers and other professionals. Some CLSC's have found that admissions to nursing homes have dropped since they began providing extended home care.

■ In addition to medical and social services staff, CLSC's employ community organizers who work with local groups around issues such as tenants' rights and barrier-free housing.

■ If you personally have particular needs or concerns, ask your CLSC or CHC if it can address them.

■ If there is no community health center in your area, consider forming a group to begin one. For help in making a proposal, contact your provincial health department. In Ontario, contact the Association of Ontario Health Centres, Suite 401, 5233 Dundas St. West, Islington, Ont., M9B 1A6.

NURSING STATIONS

■ In remote First Nations reservations, health care is provided by specially trained nursing staff working in nursing stations. The nurses have studied "Outpost Nursing," or have followed a "Northern Clinical Program."

They have the skills to provide primary health care— with telephone backup in emergencies.

■ Most of the care in nursing stations is routine—medical examinations, prenatal care, well-baby clinics, laboratory and diagnostic work, setting broken bones, etc. It may also include surgery for gunshot wounds.

■ Public health is a concern of these stations. The nurses often lead groups to discuss tuberculosis prevention and treatment, good nutrition, and parenting.

■ Emergencies are evacuated by plane or helicopter to larger medical centers.

ADULT DAY CARE

■ Most provinces provide an adult day support program as part of their home-care plans. The programs are aimed at helping people who are physically or mentally impaired to maintain or restore their capacity for self-care.

■ These programs provide transportation when it is needed, meals or transportation to community meals, and socialization and recreational activities. In this way, people who would otherwise be housebound can remain integrated in the community. They are also more likely to be stimulated, which will have a beneficial effect on their well-being.

■ Although the facilities offered are subsidized by the provincial health plans, people using them are charged a daily rate.

HEALTH-CARE INSURANCE

Soaring health-care costs have reached crisis proportions. Federal and provincial health-care funding are being cut back. Since this is leaving you with more to pay out of your own pocket, you have a strong motivation to save wherever you can.

WHAT THE HEALTH-CARE SYSTEM PROVIDES

■ Canada provides universal medical coverage to all its residents through provincial and territorial health-care plans that are jointly financed by the federal and provincial or territorial authorities. The basic elements of the plans are coverage for ward-rate hospitalization (and hospital services) and medically necessary services. The provinces are free to provide any extra medical services they choose and include them as benefits in their health-care packages. This means that coverage varies from province to province.

■ What all the provincial and territorial plans share is: they are comprehensive, in that they cover all medically necessary services; they are portable, from one province or territory to another; and they are publicly funded.

■ But these health-care plans are being reexamined to see how their cost can be reduced. One result is that some provinces have delisted some of their extended coverage. For instance, Ontario's medicare plan (OHIP) no longer pays the cost of medical examinations and paperwork associated with applications for insurance benefits and motor vehicle accident claims. And

Ontario and other provinces have reduced their coverage for out-of-country medical services.

■ Keep informed about changes in your provincial health insurance. Become an expert on the benefits of your provincial plan. Take advantage of extended coverage for which you are eligible.

PRIVATE HEALTH INSURANCE

■ Private insurance companies are not allowed to cover services already provided under provincial and territorial plans. But they can cover health services not fully insured by these plans.

■ If you are employed, it is a good idea to purchase basic supplemental health care through a group plan at work. Group insurance may include extended health care (paying the additional costs of a semi-private or private hospital room, dental care, vision care, and other services), disability, and life insurance.

■ If you are not covered by an employee's group plan, you should purchase extended health care privately. If you belong to a group (like a professional association) it may be able to negotiate a group plan for its members and make it available to you at a more affordable cost.

■ Group plans provide a basic coverage for all members and may make additional features available as options, at an additional cost. Study the benefits of your group plan and consider purchasing optional benefits that are important to you and your family. For instance, if dental care is not part of your group plan, compare the cost of the added benefit with your yearly dental bills to determine if it is worth the price.

DISABILITY INSURANCE

■ This is an expensive policy if you purchase it privately. But if you have a young family dependent on your continued earnings, it can be an important feature of your insurance plan.

■ Some disability insurance is already a feature of Unemployment Insurance (for short-term illness), Workmen's Compensation (for employment-related injuries and conditions); and Canada and Quebec pension plans.

■ An employer's group disability plan is attractive because it usually has few or no restrictions about where or how the sickness or injury occurred. In the event of an injury or prolonged illness, contact the administrator of your group plan for advice about how to proceed with a claim.

■ If an injury occurs at work, give notice immediately to your insurance company, even if you are covered by Workmen's Compensation. This could be important if you fall ill while you are off work because of a work-related injury. For instance, if a person with a work-related back injury suffered a heart attack during the period he was covered by Workmen's Compensation, the Workmen's Compensation Board would continue coverage until the end of the total claim period. But a group disability plan might do so only if it was notified of the initial injury before the heart attack.

■ If you are disabled, you may be eligible for assistance from the Canada Mortgage and Housing Corporation's Residential Rehabilitation Assistance Program (RRAP). Grants and loans are available to adapt housing for special needs, for new barrier-free housing, and to adapt public and private transportation for disabled people.

■ In Quebec, Newfoundland and New Brunswick, contact your provincial housing agency for funding. In other provinces, call your nearest CMHC office.

DRUG PLANS

■ Even if your group health insurance plan provides a drug plan, there are ways you can save money. And if you save your insurance company money, this could translate into better coverage in the long run or reduced premiums.

■ Ask your pharmacist if there is a lower cost alternative to the prescribed drug. Generic drugs are usually cheaper than brand-name drugs. If the doctor has specified "No substitutes," however, this will not be possible.

■ The dispensing fee, charged to cover the cost of filling the prescription, is often more expensive than the cost of the drug. Shop around for a pharmacy that charges a lower dispensing fee.

■ Some group plans take advantage of mail-order offers from drug companies, which charge a low dispensing fee for prescriptions ordered by phone or fax, and deliver the drugs to you the next day. Any consumer can use the service, even if not a member of a group health plan. However, if your doctor wants you to begin medication immediately, this service is not suitable. But when you can anticipate renewing a prescription, it is an effective way to save money.

OUT-OF-COUNTRY HEALTH INSURANCE

■ This is essential. Provincial health departments recommend you purchase coverage even if you are traveling to the U.S. for a weekend, because costs for out-of-country care can be exorbitant if hospitalization is needed, and could financially ruin you.

■ Review the coverage for travel insurance in your group plan, or buy it as an individual or family for each trip. Some Gold credit cards may offer

out-of-country coverage, but limits always apply.

■ For questions to ask and an idea of the kind of coverage you should be seeking, see "Buying Travel Insurance," above.

Buying Travel Insurance

Before you travel out of Canada, make sure you take out travel insurance. Here are some facts to establish.

Your policy should cover you for the entire duration of your trip. Make sure you can renew the policy if you decide to extend your trip.

Find out what restrictions and limitations your policy has, e.g. preexisting medical conditions, sports, destinations.

Does the policy pay for services provided in out-patient clinics or doctors' offices?

What is the toll-free or collect telephone number for emergency assistance? This is important because hospitals (particularly those in the U.S.) need proof of your ability to pay bills. With a toll-free service, they can verify your coverage.

Does the policy pay for an emergency return home?

Does it provide for trip cancellation, baggage loss and other damages?

What maximums or deductibles apply in the event of a claim?

If you are traveling with your family, does the policy cover them all or does each person need a separate policy?

ALTERNATIVE MEDICINE

Increasingly, North Americans are using alternative medicine for ailments ranging from asthma to backaches. Popularity aside, it is still important to get a doctor's diagnosis of an ailment before you choose any of these healing methods.

ACUPUNCTURE

■ The technique most often associated with Chinese medicine, acupuncture involves the insertion of extremely fine needles into strategic points on the body. These points are located along meridians, which are said to relate to organs and bodily functions.

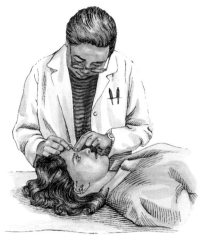

■ Each acupuncture point is said to have a specific therapeutic effect. The goal of acupuncture is to restore the smooth flow of qi (energy) throughout the body. When this is accomplished, the body is in balance and can begin to heal itself.
■ Among Western practitioners, acupuncture is most commonly used in the case of chronic pain, including such conditions as arthritis and back problems. Acupuncture has also been used to treat addiction to drugs, alcohol, and nicotine.
■ Acupressure, which is based

on the same principles as acupuncture, uses finger and thumb pressure in place of needles. Common applications include relief of backaches, headaches, and nausea.

AROMATHERAPY

■ For centuries, people have claimed that scents have a beneficial effect on the mind and body. Orthodox scientists know that odor molecules breathed in through the nose activate receptors in the nose, which convert into nerve impulses that travel to the olfactory bulbs in the brain. These bulbs are connected to the limbic system, the seat of memory and emotion. Aromatherapists use the same principle, applying fragrant oils extracted from plants.
■ Some 40 aromatic oils are used, to relieve pain, headaches, nervousness and irritability, ease bronchial problems, arthritis, and skin disorders, and generally relax the patient. They are usually applied during a massage, and inhaled, or added to a bath.

AYURVEDIC MEDICINE

■ A traditional Indian medicine, Ayurveda is one of the oldest and most complete systems in the world. Disease is seen as an imbalance in the life force. Healers may use tonics, herbal medicines, exercise, dietary guidance, and other methods.

■ Preventing disease and taking responsibility for one's own health get high priority. In Canada its most familiar aspects are Yogic exercise and meditation.
■ Yogic exercise combines stylized poses with deep, relaxed breathing and meditation. The poses strengthen muscles and improve the body's flexibility. The diaphragmatic breathing increases the oxygen flow throughout the body, boosting its energy and relieving stress. Practitioners claim that yoga eases complaints such as back pain, migraine, insomnia and high blood pressure.

Steer clear of so-called secret or miracle cures, especially for incurable diseases, such as arthritis, cancer, and diabetes.

BEHAVIORAL MEDICINE

■ Biofeedback, imagery or visualization, behavior modification, and counseling fit into this category. Stress is seen as a major cause of disease. Behavioral therapists emphasize stress-reduction techniques to treat people with intractable pain, heart disease, cancer, and other chronic conditions.
■ To learn biofeedback, you will be hooked up with sensors to a machine that monitors one or more of your vital signs, then translates them into audio

or visual cues. The purpose is to use the cues to regulate such functions as breathing rate, blood flow, and muscle tension to relieve pain and ease other symptoms of stress.

■ Once you have learned the technique, you may be able to practice biofeedback on your own. Patients who achieve the greatest success usually combine biofeedback with medication, lifestyle changes, and other relaxation techniques.

■ Other forms of behavioral medicine include encounter groups and Gestalt therapy. Both aim to improve self-awareness, confidence and the ability to form fruitful, lasting relationships. Both also help people suffering from anxiety and tension.

BODYWORK

■ This term embraces a range of body-healing techniques. Some practitioners concentrate on just one method, while others employ several techniques. The methods include:

■ Swedish massage, which rubs, kneads, and taps the muscles.

■ Tragerwork, which focuses on rocking, cradling, and gently moving the body to increase flexibility and range of movement and promote relaxation.

■ The Alexander technique, which combines body realignment with visualization and relaxation exercises.

■ Polarity therapy, based on the Chinese and Ayurvedic concept of keeping the body's energy flow balanced in order to stay healthy. By means of gentle massage, yogic stretching and exercise, and a special diet, any blockages to the flow of energy through and around

Group therapy provides a forum in which people can work out their anxieties or emotional problems and pave the way to an improvement in their overall well-being.

the body are removed. Advocates of this therapy claim it bolsters the nervous system, promotes emotional and mental stability, and relieves headaches, backache, muscle cramps, indigestion, constipation and stress.

■ Hellerwork is a method of deep tissue manipulation that aims to realign the body and teach the patient how to move in the most efficient way. It also involves discussion of emotional issues. A preventive form of therapy, it helps avoid pain and joint stiffness, as well as improving general health.

CHINESE MEDICINE

■ An ancient system in which disease represents a lack of harmony with the natural order. Treatment aims at reestablishing a balance of mind, body, and spirit.

■ The traditional Chinese tools include extensive herbal treatments, massage, acupuncture, and nutritional guidance, as well as the balancing exercises of t'ai chi ch'uan.

■ T'ai chi is a series of postures created in specific sequences called forms. A form can have as few as 18 postures or as many as 100. The movement from one posture to another is slow and flowing. The benefits of this gentle martial art are increased agility and stamina, boosted energy and improved muscle tone and poise. It is said to ease arthritis and lower back pain, and the controlled breathing necessary may improve asthma.

CHIROPRACTIC

■ The theory of chiropractic holds that spinal misalignment is the cause of innumerable diseases. Chiropractors aim to cure disease by restoring normal function to organs, muscles, and joints through manipulation of the spinal vertebrae and other joints.

■ Most often, chiropractors treat patients with back and neck pain. However, practitioners may also treat arthritis, hormonal imbalances, and digestive disorders.

Dancing can be a superb form of medicine. Many people are learning what this couple already knows—ballroom dancing can provide a good workout that keeps your body fit and your spirits high.

CREATIVE THERAPIES

■ Music, art, drama, dance—even keeping a diary—can be therapeutic. Music therapy uses rhythm and sound to improve mental and physical function. Recent studies show that listening to music prompts the brain to create more endorphins, which are body chemicals that blunt pain and promote well-being.

■ When music is played in an operating room or dentist's office, patients can be given lower dosages of anesthetics.

■ Music therapy has other medical uses, including improving the coordination and walking rhythm of patients with Parkinson's disease or those recovering from a stroke. Singing helps overcome stuttering. Playing a wind instrument can improve lung function.

■ Art and drama therapies provide a way to express feelings that are too painful or frightening to put into words. Therapists often use art and drama to help victims of child abuse come to terms with the traumatic events.

■ Dance, often used with music therapy, provides both exercise and a means of self-expression. Dance therapy is popularly used in nursing homes. "Chair dancing," which uses only the upper body, is done by those confined to wheelchairs.

FLOTATION THERAPY

■ A form of Restricted Environmental Stimulation Therapy (REST), or isolation therapy, this technique involves placing the patient in a dark chamber or room in a shallow pool of water. The water is saturated with Epsom

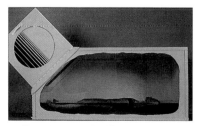

A flotation tank offers a quiet and extremely relaxing environment that relieves stress and muscle tension.

salts, which causes the patient to float, and is maintained at skin temperature—34°C (93.5°F). A session of flotation therapy may last from half an hour to two hours.

■ The relaxation experienced is said to lower blood pressure, relieve muscle tension, pain, and stress-related problems, such as insomnia. Claims have also been made that flotation therapy can help smokers and heavy drinkers to cut down.

GUIDED IMAGERY

■ This technique, also called visualization or waking-dream therapy, strives to harness the mind's healing powers. Psychiatrists have used imagery for nearly a century, but its value in treating organic disease has only recently been recognized.

■ Medical research has documented improved immune-system responses among HIV-positive patients using imagery and increased survival rates among people with advanced cancers. Today leading cancer centers, pain clinics, and other mainstream medical institutions teach guided imagery.

■ Advocates stress that even when a cure is not possible, imagery adds to the quality of life by fostering a sense of control. It also offers a way for patients to ease their pain and achieve a sense of well-being without resorting to drugs.

■ To use imagery, define your goal, for example, short-circuiting a headache, then develop a mental image of how to accomplish the goal. To stop a headache, you may visualize the source of your pain—hot, tensed, knotted muscles. You may then try to picture a gently flowing river and imagine how peaceful you feel sitting on its banks. Finally, visualize the river running through your head, relaxing tensed muscles.

HOMEOPATHY

■ A major force in North American medicine just before the turn of the century, homeopathy is based on the doctrine that "like cures like." The guiding principle is that substances that can produce certain symptoms in a healthy person can cure a sick person who shows the same symptoms. When the correct remedy is chosen, it can assist the natural healing process.

■ Homeopaths are considered holistic practitioners because they aim to treat the whole patient instead of just a specific disorder or disease.

HYDROTHERAPY

■ For centuries, many peoples —from American Indians to Scandinavians to Turks—have recognized the beneficial effects of water applied to the body at varying temperatures and pressures. The heat of steam or hot water dilates the blood vessels and increases circulation. It also relaxes muscles and eases stiffness and pain. The cold makes blood vessels contract, reducing the blood flow and any swelling or inflammation. The contrast between the two relieves muscle cramps and inflamed tissues.

■ A sitz bath, in which the patient sits in a small bath filled with warm water, his feet out of the bath or in another filled with cold water, is said to improve abdominal injuries and disorders.

■ Hydromassage, in which whirlpools and underwater jets massage the skin, can relieve the pain of sore or injured muscles and joints.

■ Warm water is also used as a medium in which people with weakened or injured limbs can exercise, and strengthen their muscles without risking injury or excessive strain.

HYPNOTHERAPY

■ Subjects enter a trancelike state that may help them work out emotional problems or cope with illness and physical disorders. A person's willingness to be hypnotized and an ability to shut out distractions can aid in hypnotizability. Some practitioners of hypnosis tell of using self-hypnosis to anesthetize themselves during surgery. However, hypnosis

more commonly aids those with chronic or recurring ailments like arthritis and skin diseases. It has also been used to break such habits as smoking, overeating, and nail-biting.

■ To perform self-hypnosis, learn the basic technique from a professional, then practice it on your own, using a method like that described in the accompanying box. It may take weeks or months before you are able to reach a hypnotic state through self-hypnosis.

IRIDOLOGY

■ This study of the marks, colors and textures on the iris of the eye is used to diagnose physical and mental ailments. Iridologists observe the changes in these markings, through which they claim to be able to identify dietary deficiencies and the presence of toxins in the body. To many people this is preferable to the more invasive techniques of blood tests and X-rays. However, orthodox doctors do not accept the efficacy of this technique, and

Hydrotherapy involves different treatments, all with the aid of water. The buoyancy of water allows patients to move their limbs and teach their bodies to be flexible again, without risk of muscle strain.

Relax With Self-Hypnosis

Self-hypnosis is relatively easy to learn. Once you have mastered the basic steps, you can tailor it to your needs. Self-hypnosis is used to promote relaxation, reduce stress, and relieve pain.

1. Sit in a comfortable position with your legs uncrossed.

2. Choose a small object or spot to focus on. A flickering candle works well for some people; a picture or a spot on the wall will do. Make sure that the object you pick is in front of you and just slightly above your line of sight. Focus all your attention on this spot.

3. Breathe slowly and deeply in a comfortable rhythm. As you relax, think, "My eyelids are feeling heavier and heavier. They feel like weights are dragging them down. They are almost heavy enough to close. In a little while I will be so relaxed that they will close."

4. With your eyes closed, visualize a real or fantasy place, one that is peaceful and comforting, far away from all concerns and distractions.

5. With these images in mind, relax the muscles in your arms, legs, and the rest of your body. Imagine feelings of coolness, numbness, warmth, heaviness, or lightness. Focus on these sensations, letting your mind expand on them.

6. To bring yourself out of a state of hypnosis, think, "Now I am going to wake up." Pause, count to three, and open your eyes.

7. The difference between waking consciousness and hypnotic consciousness can be subtle. You may not notice it at first, but be patient.

are concerned that it may fail to diagnose a condition that requires surgery or medication.

NATIVE AMERICAN MEDICINE

■ Healers practice according to different tribal customs. Disease is often attributed to a disharmony in the cosmic order, as well as to hexing, breaking a taboo, fright, or soul loss. Healing methods include chanting and drumming and the use of sweat lodges, crystals, and herbs.

NATUROPATHY

■ Naturopaths draw on the entire spectrum of alternative, or natural, medicine. In 19th-century Europe, naturopathy evolved as a separate discipline from traditional medicine, relying heavily on exercise, fresh air, hydrotherapy, herbal remedies, and diet. This form of treatment flourished in North America in the early years of the 20th century, until the rise of modern, more scientific medicine.

■ Today it is making a comeback, with practitioners emphasizing a healthy diet and lifestyle, including abstinence from tobacco and alcohol. Many naturopaths are trained in other alternative therapies, especially massage, chiropractic, homeopathy, and Eastern medicine.

OSTEOPATHY

■ A practice invented in the United States in the late 19th century, osteopathy has a large following there, but remains restricted to a few provinces in Canada—Alberta, British Columbia, Ontario and Quebec. It is based on the theory that all the body's systems are interdependent, and therefore if one part is not functioning well, this affects all the others. Since the musculoskeletal system forms more than 60 percent of the body, osteopaths believe that it plays a central role in a body's health and this is where they should start in diagnosing an ailment.

■ During an introductory session with an osteopath he will observe how you sit, stand, walk and hold your head, check your leg length, shoulder height, hip alignment and curvature of the spine. He will manipulate and palpate joints and tissues to assess their range of movement and seek diagnostic clues. By means of a range of hands-on techniques this treatment has successfully relieved back pain, knee problems, respiratory problems such as asthma, circulatory and digestive problems, migraines and sinusitis.

REFLEXOLOGY

■ Practitioners believe that specific points on the hands, ears, and feet correspond to major organs, glands, and other parts of the body. By pressing, massaging, and otherwise manipulating these points, practitioners aim to direct the body's energies along channels that lead to the corresponding areas. In so doing, the reflexologist works to improve circulation, eliminate toxins, and reduce stress, besides alleviating specific disorders.

HERBAL MEDICINE

■ Herbal healing may appeal to those who fear that physicians overmedicate or who have experienced adverse reactions to prescribed medicines. In fact, there's a long tradition worldwide of using herbs to ease symptoms and cure ailments. Though many doctors who trained at medical schools in North America remain skeptical, the use of herbs is becoming increasingly common in Canada.

■ Consult an experienced herbalist for the appropriate selection and dosage. Like drugs, herbs can produce side effects. For example, herbal teas may contain chemicals that cause rapid heartbeat and double vision in some people.

■ It is possible to grow and dry your own herbs, but use extra caution if you gather wild herbs. Many plants look alike, and what you think is a beneficial herb may turn out to be a deadly poison. And because pesticides are so widely used in the countryside and to control weeds on highways, there is a

Herbal Remedies

The following are safe and easy herbal recipes that can be made with ingredients you may already have in your kitchen pantry.

GINGER

Recommended for colds, flu, relief of gas pains, and motion sickness. Recent research supports its use for motion sickness, but sources dispute its effectiveness for other problems. No reports of toxicity.

1 oz. grated gingerroot
1 pt. water

Mix one ounce of grated gingerroot per pint of boiled water. Drink as much as you wish.

PEPPERMINT

Recommended for coughs, colds, flu, congestion, and as a digestive aid. Peppermint is an FDA-approved cold, cough, and congestion medicine. Research also supports its use as a digestive aid. No reports of toxicity.

1/2 oz. peppermint leaves
1 pt. water

Mix 1/2 ounce of peppermint per pint of boiled water. Steep 5 to 20 minutes. Drink as much as you wish.

EUCALYPTUS

Recommended to clear the nose and bronchial tubes.

2 oz. eucalyptus leaves
1 qt. water

Boil fresh eucalyptus leaves in water, then inhale the steam with a towel over the head.

GARLIC

Recommended for colds, flu, cough, and bacterial infections, and as a diuretic. This herb contains a chemical that acts as an antibiotic. Garlic may occasionally produce allergic reactions.

8 oz. minced garlic
Olive oil

Place peeled, minced garlic cloves in a jar. Cover with olive oil, let stand for three days, shaking occasionally. Strain and store in a cool place. Take one teaspoon hourly for symptoms.

Herbal Glossary

When you patronize an herbalist, pharmacy, or health-food store, you may want to know the meanings of the following terms.

Active principle or ingredient: The chemical or chemical compound in a plant that has a medicinal effect.

Analgesic: Pain reliever.

Antiseptic: A substance that fights infection by destroying or halting the growth of bacteria.

Astringent: A substance that causes soft tissue to draw together, or pucker. In herbal medicine, astringents are used externally to check minor bleeding and internally to control diarrhea.

Decoction: An extract made by boiling or simmering a plant or plant parts, usually the stem or root, to extract the active ingredient. When it cools down, the liquid is strained for drinking.

Elixir: A sweetened liquid that contains alcohol and a medicinal substance.

Essence: A preparation of an herbal medicine in concentrate form, such as an ounce of herbal product dissolved in a pint of alcohol.

Essential oil: Any of the many volatile, readily vaporizing plant oils that are constituents of various herbal medications.

Extract: The key elements withdrawn from a plant by physical means, chemical means, or both.

Infusion: The liquid from steeping an herb in water to extract its active ingredient; similar to a tea.

Herb: A plant lacking permanent woody tissue that dies down after its growing season ends. Many regrow annually or every two years.

Tincture: A medication whose medicinal agent is dissolved in alcohol.

Tisane: An infusion or weak tea prepared with one or more herbs and spices.

should be approached with the same care. For example, herbalists often recommend white willow, which contains salicylate—the active ingredient in aspirin—for pain. But observe the same precautions as with aspirin. Don't give white willow to anyone under the age of 18 who has the flu or other viral infection because of the risk of Reye's syndrome.

■ Other herbs (shown below, from left) and their suggested uses include elecampane for asthma and bronchitis; catnip for insomnia and menstrual pain; chamomile as a mild sedative; wintergreen for temporary pain relief; echinacea to fight infections; witch hazel for skin problems; marshmallow to soothe skin abrasions; cascara sagrada for constipation; and dandelion as a laxative, diuretic, and appetite stimulant.

■ Be wary of herbal products promising to boost your immune system. Such products may not be what your system needs at the time to work more effectively.

■ Take only the recommended amount of the herb and no more.

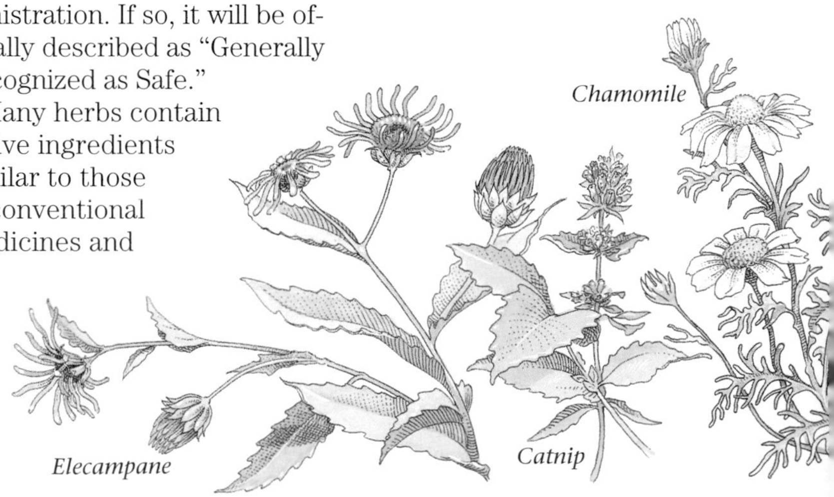

real danger of contamination of this source.

■ Choose the most reliable sources. Among the best are products whose labels describe the active ingredient in the herb and tell how much of it each dose contains.

■ When reading labels or promotional material, remember that "natural" does not mean harmless.

■ Ask a knowledgeable herbalist whether an herb you intend to take has been reviewed and approved by Health Canada or the U.S. Food and Drug Administration. If so, it will be officially described as "Generally Recognized as Safe."

■ Many herbs contain active ingredients similar to those in conventional medicines and

Chamomile

Elecampane

Catnip

■ Tell your physician what herb or herbs you are taking so that your doctor can help monitor its effectiveness.

■ Be alert to such allergic reactions as skin eruptions and breathing difficulties. Stop using the herb and contact a physician if you have such reactions.

■ Know the limitations of herbal medicine. Life-threatening illnesses, high fever, breathing difficulties, and serious injuries call for treatment by a physician or hospital emergency room staff.

Pregnant and lactating women, the very young, and the elderly should consult a physician before choosing to take herbal remedies.

THE RIGHT BALANCE

■ If you have a bacterial infection, suffer a traumatic injury, or develop such chronic conditions as diabetes, asthma, or heart disease, consider alternative therapies as an adjunct to conventional medicine, not a substitute for it.

■ Get a diagnosis before "doctoring" yourself with herbal, homeopathic, or other remedies. Self-care is important in medicine, but any persistent or worsening symptom requires a physician's diagnosis and recommendations.

■ Don't be too quick to discount the power of the mind in healing. The more you believe that a treatment will work, the more likely it is to do just that.

■ Similarly, don't expect miracles from either conventional or alternative therapies. If you don't see an improvement after a fair trial, it may be time to try a different remedy.

■ Let your doctor know if you are also using an alternative practitioner.

■ A pregnant woman should take extra care to safeguard herself and her fetus. Consult your obstetrician before choosing any alternative therapy.

PROTECT YOURSELF

■ Check alternative practitioners as carefully as you would a doctor. Ask about their training, licensing, and affiliations with professional societies.

■ Consult friends and family members about their experiences with alternative therapies. Be sure you know what ailments they sought relief from, how long treatment took, and whether they would consult the practitioner again for similar or other problems.

■ Inquire in advance about fees and the usual number of treatments.

■ Find out if the practitioner demands that you buy nutrition supplements, medical devices, or other items as part of the therapy. If so, ask if you must buy them from him or her exclusively or whether a pharmacy or other store stocks them.

■ Consider asking your doctor for a referral. Many alternative practitioners work with mainstream doctors.

■ Natural remedies sold as nutritional supplements do not have to undergo testing or meet the same safety standards as prescription or nonprescription drugs. If in doubt, first check the supplements' safety with your doctor or pharmacist.

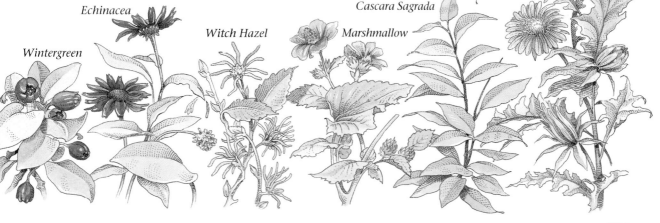

Dandelion

Echinacea

Witch Hazel

Cascara Sagrada

Marshmallow

Wintergreen

Physical therapists are effective in helping people regain their strength and recover from heart attacks, strokes, and other debilitating illnesses. This therapist is using water exercises to help her patient gain muscle strength and relearn how to walk.

CHAPTER 10

ILLNESS AND RECOVERY

Whether it's as simple as a sore throat or as complex as heart disease, illness is frightening. And while modern medicine has made great advances, being an informed patient is still one of the best ways to take charge of your health. Knowledge can help us to ease our fears, and it allows us to help sick family members or friends when illness strikes.

With the proper instruction, we can handle many illnesses ourselves. It takes only a little knowledge to ease a baby's croup or our own heartburn. More severe problems—such as breast cancer, high blood pressure, or a heart attack—always require immediate medical care. Even in serious cases, though, involvement in our own treatment can greatly speed our recovery. Some wellness strategies—things as simple as exercising, eating right, or even getting a pet—will help us stay physically and emotionally healthy. Treat yourself with care, and remember that trustworthy information is as important to good health as any medicine.

Working on crafts *is therapeutic for both the mind and the muscles. By concentrating on small achievements, many patients are able to get well faster.*

COPING WITH PAIN

Pain is the body's way of telling you that something is amiss, but it is often hard to pin down. No two people experience pain in the same way, and controlling it is frequently a matter of trial and error. Still, most people can find relief.

THE NATURE OF PAIN

Pain occurs when certain nerve endings are stimulated to send pain messages to the brain. In general, widespread chronic pain is usually due to an illness, such as arthritis or cancer, or to a structural problem, such as a ruptured spinal disc. Localized acute pain, such as a headache, heartburn, toothache, or cramps, may stem from temporary ailments. Injuries also can trigger pain.

■ Although pain is usually a symptom of an underlying disease, it has its own harmful effects, such as inflammation and muscle spasms. Note any other problems that could provide telling clues to what's causing the pain.

■ Does stress bring on the pain? If so, consider a psychological rather than a physical source. Even if the pain turns out to be psychosomatic, don't discount it. Psychosomatic pain is just as real and stressful as organic pain and should be dealt with.

■ Does rest bring relief? Poor circulation may be the problem, because tissue that does not get enough oxygen sends out pain messages. Common examples include angina, which is chest pains that develop when the heart muscle is starved for oxygen, and intermittent claudication, which is calf pain due to clogged arteries in the legs.

• • • • • • • • • • • • • • • • • • •

Pain that is unusually intense, lasts for more than a few days, grows steadily worse, or is accompanied by fever, vomiting, and other symptoms warrants prompt medical attention.

• • • • • • • • • • • • • • • • • • •

NONPRESCRIPTION PAINKILLERS

Most pain can be controlled with nonprescription drugs. Here's what you should know to make the best choice.

■ Aspirin, the most common painkiller, also lowers a fever, and, because it counters inflammation, it is especially effective against arthritis and other inflammatory disorders.

■ Ibuprofen, like aspirin, is a

Count Down to Pain Relief

Progressive muscle relaxation eases tension and often alleviates pain. The following routine takes about 15 minutes.

1. Get comfortable in a chair, with your hands in your lap and feet resting on the floor. Loosen your belt, tie, and other tight clothing, and take a deep breath, letting it out slowly.

2. Start by extending one arm in front of you. Make a tight fist, and tense the muscles as hard as you can. Hold for a count of five, concentrating on how the tense hand feels.

3. Relax your hand. Then clench your fist again for a count of five.

4. Now release the tension completely, allowing your hand to feel completely relaxed. Take a deep breath, and slowly exhale.

5. Repeat this sequence for the other hand, then for your arms, shoulders, and facial muscles, taking deep breaths between each muscle group until the entire upper body is relaxed.

6. Using the same routine of tensing and then relaxing muscles, go on to your stomach, buttocks, legs, and feet.

7. After tensing and relaxing your entire body, close your eyes and sit quietly for at least five minutes. Breathe deeply, and concentrate on a word, number, or pleasant scene.

nonsteroidal anti-inflammatory drug. It is stronger than aspirin but less likely to cause stomach upset and bleeding.

■ Acetaminophen also controls pain and lowers a fever, but it does not fight inflammation. It is easier on the stomach than aspirin and ibuprofen, and it does not cause bleeding. Chronic use, however, can damage the kidneys.

■ To minimize stomach upset, take aspirin or ibuprofen with food or an antacid. Buffered aspirin contains an antacid, but it's more expensive than ordinary aspirin.

■ Coated, or enteric, aspirin dissolves in the small intestine rather than the stomach. It can be used as an alternative if other forms of aspirin cause stomach upset.

■ Caffeine increases the effectiveness of aspirin. Some brands contain caffeine; you can achieve the same effect by taking two regular aspirin with a cup of coffee, cola, or other caffeinated beverage.

■ Never give aspirin to anyone under the age of 18 who has a cold, flu, chicken pox, or other viral infection. In this setting, aspirin has been linked to Reye's syndrome, a potentially fatal childhood brain and liver disorder. Acetaminophen is a safe alternative, but check with your doctor before giving it to a baby.

■ When taking any painkiller, always follow instructions and be alert for side effects, especially stomach pain, dark, tarry stools, or other signs of intestinal bleeding. If these occur, see your doctor as soon as possible.

■ Try standard dosages first. Extra-strength painkillers often are not more effective than the regular dosage, but they are more likely to produce unwanted side effects owing to added ingredients. Taking more than the recommended dosage of a painkiller may cause a rebound effect, in which the pain becomes greater once the medication wears off.

■ Avoid analgesics that combine aspirin and acetaminophen. These are more likely to cause kidney disease than acetaminophen alone.

■ Does aspirin bring on a runny nose, sneezing, itching, or difficulty breathing? If so, you are probably allergic to salicylate, which is the major ingredient in aspirin. Switch to another painkiller, such as acetaminophen.

BY PRESCRIPTION ONLY

For more serious pain, your doctor may prescribe a stronger analgesic. Many of these analgesics contain narcotics, and long-term use can produce addiction.

■ Codeine, often combined with aspirin or acetaminophen, can cause severe constipation. When taking these medications, increase your fiber and fluid intake; if this is not enough, add a stool softener.

■ For chronic or recurrent pain, try varied methods of reducing pain instead of relying on narcotic prescription drugs.

Alternative therapies, such as acupuncture, acupressure, meditation, yoga, and biofeedback, are gaining increased recognition as effective approaches to pain control. In fact, most orthodox pain clinics employ these and other alternative therapies.

RELIEVING PAIN WITHOUT MEDICATION

There are numerous self-help techniques and alternative therapies that alleviate pain without drugs. Here are a few approaches.

■ Take a brisk walk or engage in some other form of vigorous exercise. During exercise, the brain steps up production of endorphins, hormones that are chemically similar to opium. Regular exercise can also prevent menstrual cramps, migraine headaches, and other pain syndromes.

■ Heat relieves pain by relaxing the muscles and reducing nerve sensitivity. Take several hot baths or showers a day. A hot water bottle or hydrocolator (a type of wet heating pad) may also help.

■ If heat alone doesn't work, try contrast bathing. Soak in a hot tub for 10 minutes, then stand under a cold shower for a minute or so.

■ In some cases of acute pain, cold may be more effective than heat in reducing inflammation, relaxing muscles, and relieving pain. Try moist cold compresses or ice packs.

■ Massaging or rubbing a painful area helps block the pain message before it has a chance to reach the brain. Because massage combines rubbing and relaxation, it can be doubly effective.

■ Look for any distractions. Many people forget their aches and pains while watching a movie, reading a good book, or listening to music. Singing along may be even better. As the pain increases, sing louder; as it lessens, sing more softly.

■ Try to get enough sleep every night. Fatigue often adds to muscle tension and pain perception.

■ Use your imagination. Think of a pleasant place and imagine being there. What sounds would you hear? What would the place smell like? Describing your imaginary place to someone else may also be helpful.

■ For intractable pain, ask your doctor for information about TENS, or transcutaneous electrical nerve stimulation. With this therapy, a special device delivers small amounts of electrical current just under the skin, short-circuiting the nerves' pain messages.

Migraine sufferers may be especially sensitive to a component of food and drink called tyramine. To minimize attacks, avoid cheese, chocolate, peanuts, and red wine.

THE SPECIAL CASE OF BACK PAIN

Most backaches are due to muscle spasms and clear up in a few days with no treatment. Without preventive action, however, the pain is likely to recur.

■ Evaluate your daily activities and habits. Is stress aggravating the problem? Poor posture, wearing high heels, bending from the waist, sitting for long periods of time, and inadequate exercise can all contribute to back pain.

■ Sleep on your side or on your back (as shown below), not on your stomach. Placing a pillow between your knees (if you sleep on your side) or under your knees (if you sleep on your back) helps stabilize your back as you sleep.

■ Apply a cold pack during the first day or two of back pain to reduce any tissue swelling. After that, switch to a heating pad to help relax tensed muscles. Aspirin or ibuprofen may be used to help ease the pain as well. Consult your physician.

■ Two days of bed rest is usually enough for most backaches. More than that may weaken muscles, making recurrent pain more likely.

■ A backache accompanied by

If you prefer sleeping on your back, minimize back pain by placing pillows under your head and your knees.

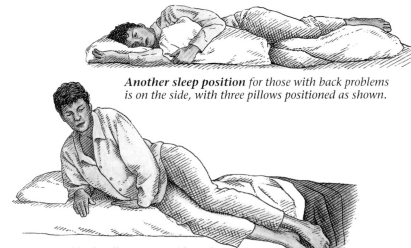

Another sleep position for those with back problems is on the side, with three pillows positioned as shown.

To get out of bed, roll onto your side and bend your knees. Using your arms, sit up, then stand up.

sciatica—throbbing or shooting pains in the buttocks or down one leg or both legs—may signal a ruptured disc. Most disc problems are best treated with rest and special exercises. If a doctor suggests disc-removal surgery, get a second opinion to make sure it is necessary.

■ After seeing a physician to rule out possible nerve damage, consider a chiropractor to treat acute lower back pain. Studies have shown that one or two chiropractic adjustments bring relief to some patients.

■ Massage may also alleviate back pain, especially if it is due to muscle spasms. Avoid very deep or vigorous massage, such as rolfing, which can worsen a disc problem.

BACK-STRENGTHENING TIPS

■ Maintain your ideal body weight. Excess poundage strains back and abdominal muscles, increasing the chance of back pain.

■ When working out, concentrate on the abdominal muscles, which support the back. Try low-impact exercise, such as walking, swimming, or bicycling, to increase back strength. If you have back problems, see a doctor before undertaking an exercise program to strengthen your back.

■ To lift an object from the floor, first bend at the knees, then at the hips. Hold the object close to your body and raise yourself to an upright position.

■ If you swim, choose the crawl over the breaststroke or butterfly, which may strain the back. Better yet, swim one lap with the crawl, then one with the backstroke. The variety promotes flexibility.

■ Consider a consultation with an Alexander-technique instructor. Many back problems are due to faulty posture, and practicing the Alexander technique can correct posture.

Some types of back pain require immediate medical attention. See a doctor if, in addition to a backache, there is fever, stiff neck, headache, loss of bladder control, nausea, or pain or numbness in the legs. Consult a doctor if back pain is the result of an accident.

DEALING WITH HEADACHES

Being able to identify what types of headaches you get may help you prevent or alleviate them. Besides the categories below, other causes include toothaches, eyestrain, jaw misalignment, and head injuries.

Type of headache	What it feels like	What to try
Tension Headaches	Persistent pain characterized by tightness around the forehead, often accompanied by taut muscles in the neck and shoulders.	Massage neck and shoulders, try relaxation exercises, and use over-the-counter pain relievers in moderation. Warm compresses and rest may also help.
Cluster Headaches	Sharp pain, often behind one eye, that lasts from a few minutes to several hours. May recur at the same time each day, accompanied by nasal stuffiness and redness in the eyes.	Identify and eliminate triggering factors, which may include certain foods, tobacco smoke, and alcohol. Ask a doctor about preventive use of lithium or vasoconstrictive drugs, such as calcium-channel or beta-blockers.
Migraine Headaches	Intense, pulsating pain, sometimes in one section of the head, often accompanied by nausea and/or vomiting and sensitivity to bright light. Some migraines are preceded by mood swings, vision disturbances, and other symptoms.	Identify and avoid triggering factors. Mild migraines may be relieved by over-the-counter medications and resting in a dark room. However, most migraines require prescription analgesics; several may be tried before finding one that works.
Sinus Headaches	Throbbing pain around the eyes with nasal congestion. Fever and yellow or green mucus may indicate infection. If you suspect infection, see your doctor, who may prescribe an antibiotic.	Over-the-counter decongestants for stuffiness and painkillers.

VIRUSES AND OTHER INFECTIONS

Most people catch at least one cold a year, and many also suffer from other infectious diseases. Therefore, it is important to know how to protect yourself, as well as what to do once you have been infected.

RELIEVING THE SYMPTOMS OF COLDS AND FLU

Some 200 viruses cause upper respiratory infections, explaining why colds are so common.

■ Be aware of the symptoms of a cold: a runny nose, cough, and fever are all clear signs that your body is fighting off a cold virus.

■ To soothe a sore throat, suck on hard candy or gargle with warm salt water (one-half teaspoon of salt in eight ounces of water). These remedies are better than most cough drops, which may cause an upset stomach when used too often.

■ To loosen phlegm, drink 8 to 10 glasses of water or other nonalcoholic liquids a day. Warm drinks may be more soothing than cold.

■ Try chicken soup. Researchers have finally confirmed what mothers have long observed—chicken stock really does alleviate cold symptoms. In addition, breathing in the hot steam rising off the soup soothes raw nasal passages and the throat, and also loosens mucus.

■ Increase your intake of supplements that provide vitamin C. Although the effectiveness and safety of megadoses of vitamin C are still debated, some doctors recommend dosages of 500 to 2,000 milligrams a day. However, check with your doctor before taking vitamins in large quantities. Alternatively,

drink extra orange juice, which is high in vitamin C.

■ Blow your nose gently, both nostrils simultaneously. Blowing hard or compressing one nostril stresses the eustachian tubes, the passages between the ears and throat, increasing the risk of an ear infection.

....

Whispering won't help your laryngitis. In fact, it may make it worse. Whispering actually strains the vocal cords as much as yelling. If it hurts to talk, use a pad and pencil.

....

COLD MEDICATIONS

■ Use over-the-counter decongestants, analgesics, and cough medicines judiciously. They cannot cure a cold any faster; in fact, they may make it last longer by drying out the secretions that rid your body of invading viruses.

■ Choose decongestant drops or inhalers rather than oral medications. Oral decongestants can dry out the body's

other mucous membranes. However, don't use inhaled decongestants for more than three consecutive days, because they can cause a rebound effect when stopped.

■ Choose preparations that ease one or two symptoms, rather than medications that claim to treat a dozen or more. You'll get more of the medication you need and avoid the risk of side effects from ingredients you don't need.

■ The federal Department of Health has found that oxymetazoline, phenylephrine, and xylometazoline are safe and effective for treating nasal congestion. However, avoid chlorpheniramine maleate, belladonna alkaloids, and atropine sulfate, which have not been proven effective and may cause serious side effects.

■ Avoid antihistamines in treating a cold or flu. Although they alleviate sneezing and a runny nose caused by allergies, antihistamines are generally not effective against the same symptoms when they are produced by a virus.

■ If you have heart disease, high blood pressure, diabetes, or a thyroid condition, consult your doctor before taking nasal decongestants, which may increase the heart rate and raise blood pressure.

■ Never share nose drops or inhalers. The droppers and

containers are likely to transmit viruses and bacteria from one person to another.

AN OUNCE OF PREVENTION

Viral infections can spread quickly. Here are steps you can take to protect yourself.

■ Avoid touching your face unless you've washed your hands. Always wash your hands after coughing, sneezing, or blowing your nose into a tissue, after caring for a sick person, and before preparing food or eating. Although plain running water can wash away most germs, use soap for extra protection.

■ Use a solution containing chlorine or disinfectant alcohol to kill germs on such surfaces as countertops, telephones, and doorknobs.

■ Throw tissues away immediately after use; do not stuff them in your pocket or purse.

■ Leave windows open a crack when possible to circulate air and remove germs. This is especially important in today's super-insulated houses. Colds and flu are more easily spread when people are indoors and windows are closed.

■ Moisturize your home's air with a humidifier, plants, or a kettle on the stove.

■ Don't smoke, and don't allow smoking in your home. Exposure to cigarette smoke weakens the immune system and immobilizes the tiny hairlike cells that clear nasal passages of germs, increasing your risk of colds and other infections.

■ Get plenty of rest, drink lots of liquids, eat a nutritious diet, avoid excess stress, and get enough exercise.

■ Get a flu shot. People over the age of 65 or anyone with a weakened immune system, diabetes, heart disease, or respiratory disorders should have a flu shot each fall.

. . . .

A handshake is more likely to spread a virus than a pat on the shoulder or a peck on the cheek.

. . . .

TAKING A TEMPERATURE

Although 37°C (98.6°F) is considered normal, a person's temperature increases through the day, starting at about 36°C (97°F) in the morning and often rising to just over 37°C (99°F) by midday. So, a slightly elevated temperature is not necessarily a sign of illness.

■ Old-fashioned mercury thermometers are the least expensive devices and are accurate enough for most purposes. (After you have used such a thermometer, be sure to rinse it in cold water and then clean it with alcohol to kill any germs.) Digital thermometers, which display the tempera-

ture electronically, similar to the time display on a digital wristwatch, work faster and are easier to read than an ordinary mercury thermometer.

■ Consider buying an electronic ear thermometer, which instantly registers the temperature. Such devices are relatively expensive, but they are a boon if you're caring for an invalid or someone with a serious illness. And you can take a child's temperature while he or she sleeps.

■ An oral thermometer has a long slender bulb, while a rectal one has a round bulb.

■ For older children and adults, an oral thermometer will do. Make sure the mercury is below the 35°C (95°F) mark before taking the temperature. Hold the thermometer firmly between your thumb and forefinger at the end opposite the bulb. Shake it a few times with a vigorous movement. Place the oral thermometer under the tongue, toward one side and as far back as possible. Use lips or fingers (not the teeth) to hold it in place for three to four minutes. While the thermometer is in place, breathe through the nose.

■ For children under five years old, a rectal thermometer is most accurate. Use petroleum jelly to lubricate the bulb end of the thermometer. Place it in the rectum, gently inserting it about one inch. Hold it still with one hand and keep your other hand on the child for about two to three minutes. The rectal temperature will be about 0.5°C (1°F) higher than the oral temperature.

■ If a child will not tolerate a rectal thermometer, you can take the temperature under the armpit with an oral thermometer. Have the child cross his or her arms to hold the thermometer in place for about 5 minutes. Add 1 degree to the reading.

WHEN TO SEE A DOCTOR

Colds and flu can develop into more serious infections, such as bronchitis and pneumonia. In other cases, what you might think is a cold or flu may actually be strep throat or another condition that requires antibiotics. Look out for these danger signs and call your doctor if:

■ The fever victim has a chronic condition, such as diabetes or lung or kidney disease.

■ A cough lasts more than two weeks, indicating a possible bacterial respiratory infection.

■ A cough produces green, yellow, brown, or bloody phlegm, signaling possible bronchitis or pneumonia.

■ A fever exceeds 39°C (102°F), or stays over 38°C (101°F) for more than three days, or a lower fever persists for more than a week.

■ A fever develops toward the end of a cold. Or a temperature that is already elevated

suddenly increases. Or a fever of over 39°C (102°F) occurs with other such symptoms as chest pain or wheezing, which are signs of pneumonia.

■ A persistent fever is accompanied by swollen glands or a persistent sore throat, indicating a possible smoldering infection.

■ A fever is accompanied by a stiff neck, headache, and confusion, which may indicate meningitis, an inflammation of the brain or spinal cord.

■ Ear pain and sudden hearing loss develop, indicating an ear infection or ruptured eardrum.

■ Difficulty swallowing or a sore throat lasts more than a week, indicating mononucleosis, strep throat, or tonsillitis.

PNEUMONIA

All types of pneumonia result in lung inflammation, but the disease has many different causes, including viruses, bacteria, parasites, chemicals, and inhaled pollutants, such as coal dust. Here are tips for avoiding pneumonia.

■ Always wear a face mask when working with potentially harmful materials that can be inhaled, including chemicals, asbestos, and substances that

produce dust.

■ Be especially careful when handling materials that may contain bird or bat droppings, such as the dirt that accumulates on outdoor ledges and sills. Droppings are a common source of fungi that cause pneumonia. The same goes for rodent droppings, which are linked to a fatal form of flu.

■ If you have a chronic lung disorder or your immunity is low, talk to your doctor about inhaled preventive antibiotics. Immunization against pneumococcal pneumonia may also be advisable. If you do develop a cold or flu, prophylactic antibiotics help prevent pneumonia from developing.

■ If you live or work in an older building with central air-conditioning, contact your public health department about inspecting the ducts for the *Legionella* bacterium, the organism that causes Legionnaires' disease. Or ask the building management to install a special antiseptic system to keep the air-conditioning ducts clean.

■ Avoid crowded, smoke-filled environments as much as possible, especially if you have a condition that predisposes you to pneumonia. Above all, do not smoke yourself—smokers have a much higher incidence of pneumonia and other lung disorders than nonsmokers.

Wait a half hour before taking the temperature of anyone who has had hot or cold liquids or who has smoked, all of which can cause inaccurate readings.

MONONUCLEOSIS

Mononucleosis is often called the kissing disease because it is especially common among adolescents and is easily spread by physical contact. The symptoms of mononucleosis—fatigue, headache, persistent fever, sore throat, and swollen lymph nodes—are similar to other, more serious conditions, including leukemia. See your doctor for a blood test to confirm the diagnosis.

■ Bed rest is the best course of treatment while symptoms are active. Continue to take it easy for several weeks until your energy levels return to normal or your physician gives you the green light.

■ Watch for complications of mononucleosis. In some cases, the disease can affect the liver, spleen, and other organs. Difficulty breathing, yellowing of the skin and eyes, or any neurological change requires prompt medical attention.

OTHER INFECTIOUS DISEASES

If an adult has not been immunized and has not been exposed previously to such childhood diseases as mumps or measles, the effects can be more serious than in young people.

■ A woman planning to become pregnant should be tested for immunity against German measles, which can cause

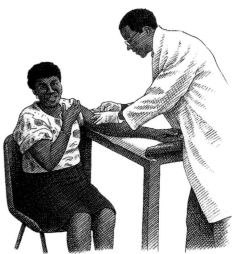

a miscarriage or birth defects. If she lacks immunity, she should be immunized.

■ Men who have not had mumps or were not immunized should talk to their doctor about being vaccinated.

DO YOU HAVE ALL YOUR SHOTS?

The following booster shots, as well as new immunizations, are recommended for adults.

Vaccine	Booster or immunization schedule	Exceptions
Hepatitis	Immunization especially recommended for high-risk individuals, including health-care workers, male homosexuals, hemophiliac patients, and others who receive blood transfusions, as well as family members and sexual partners of persons with hepatitis B	
Influenza	Annual flu shots for all persons over 65, adults of any age who have chronic heart or lung diseases, health-care workers, and people with compromised immune systems	Anyone allergic to eggs and pregnant women during the first trimester
Measles	Unimmunized persons born in 1957 or later or those vaccinated between 1963 and 1967 should get the vaccine. Young adults should receive a measles booster if they have not had one since 1980	Pregnant women; persons with compromised immune systems
Pneumococcal pneumonia	Single immunization for adults of any age who have diabetes or chronic heart or lung diseases, and for all adults over age 65	Pregnant women
Polio	Vaccine recommended for any unimmunized adult planning to travel to areas where polio is endemic	Pregnant women; persons with compromised immune systems
Rubella and Mumps	Unimmunized adults who lack immunity, especially men who lack immunity to mumps and women planning a pregnancy whose rubella antibody tests are negative	Pregnant women; persons with compromised immune systems
Tetanus/ Diphtheria	Booster shots every 10 years. However, patients with punctures or wounds contaminated by dirt should get tetanus immune globulin if their prior vaccination is in doubt or is more than five years old.	Pregnant women during the first trimester

PROTECTING YOUR EARS, NOSE, AND THROAT

Although the ears, nose, and throat have distinctly different functions, their close anatomical proximity means that a problem in one is likely to affect the other organs. Self-care techniques may help.

EARACHES AND OTHER EAR DISORDERS

Most earaches are due to infections, but symptoms vary according to the site. Infections in the ear canal, commonly referred to as swimmer's ear, can cause an ear discharge, pain that is intensified by tugging the earlobe, and temporary hearing loss. A middle-ear infection—otitis media—produces a feeling of pressure inside the ear, while inner-ear infections cause ringing in the ears, dizziness, and nausea. Ear infections are most common in childhood, but prompt treatment is needed at any age to prevent hearing loss.

■ Refrain from blowing your nose when you have an ear infection. Blowing increases pressure against the eardrum and may cause it to rupture.

■ If you have swimmer's ear, keep the ear canal as dry as possible. Insert a ball of cotton in the outer part of your ears when showering or washing your hair, and don't swim until the infection clears up. If an ear does get wet, dry it out with a hair dryer—use a low setting, and hold it several inches from your ear.

■ A ruptured eardrum produces sudden pain, hearing loss, a bloody discharge from the affected ear, dizziness, and ringing in the ears. See a doctor as soon as possible. Antibiotics can clear up any underlying infection, and a temporary patch over the eardrum can improve hearing while the ear heals. To ease pain, place a heating pad set on low over the ear.

HEARING LOSS

There are two types of hearing loss: sensory, in which sound impulses cannot be processed properly by the nervous system, and conductive, in which earwax or another, structural problem blocks sound waves.

■ Loud noise causes hearing loss because it damages the cochlea, the snail-shaped structure that transmits sound waves. Wear earplugs when working with noisy machinery or appliances. Turn down the volume when listening to music.

■ Don't try to dislodge an object in the ear with a swab or any pointed or sharp objects (see "First Aid," page 408).

NOSE AND SINUS PROBLEMS

The nose houses our sense of smell and allows air to flow in and out of the body. The sinuses are air-filled cavities surrounding the nose. Most nasal and sinus problems are

---

Removing Earwax

Earwax usually does not require removal—it flows naturally out of the ear canal and can be washed away. Some people, however, have especially sticky earwax that builds up inside the ear, resulting in hearing loss. Here's how to remove it.

1. Use an eyedropper to insert a few drops of mineral oil or glycerin into the ear twice a day for four or five days to soften the wax.

2. When the wax is sufficiently soft, some will be visible in the outer ear. Warm some water to body temperature. (Water that is warmer or colder can cause dizziness.) Use a rubber bulb syringe to squirt water gently into the ear canal, then turn your head to allow the water to flow out of the ear. Repeat until the wax plug falls out.

3. Gently dry the outer ear with a soft towel, and use a hair dryer on a low setting to dry the ear canal.

If you are unable to remove the wax yourself, see an ear specialist, who may use an electric suction device or special probe. Not all hearing loss is a result of wax buildup. If your ears are clear of wax and you continue to experience hearing loss, see a doctor.

---

temporary, often due to a cold, hay fever, or other allergies, but even so, they can make life miserable (see "Viruses and Other Infections," page 338).

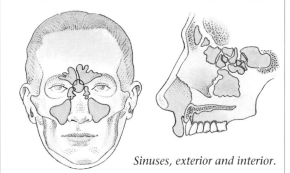

Sinuses, exterior and interior.

■ Sinus infections generally develop in the aftermath of a cold. Consult a physician if you have throbbing pain in the sinus cavities, fever, or a nasal discharge of pus, or if you lose your sense of smell.

■ Occasionally, sinusitis may arise independent of a cold. It may result from an abscess in an upper tooth, severe facial injury, or from jumping feet-first into a pool or body of water without covering the nose. An antibiotic drug is usually prescribed.

■ When blowing your nose, do so gently. And don't try to clear your nose by sniffing—this can force mucus into the sinuses and the eustachian tube connecting the throat and ears.

■ Don't use decongestant nasal sprays or nose drops for more than three or four days at a time. Prolonged use irritates the nasal mucous membranes.

■ See a doctor for persistent nasal congestion unrelated to a cold or allergies. Nasal polyps may be the problem.

■ Don't pick your nose or poke at it with a sharp object; such actions often result in nosebleeds (see "First Aid," page 420).

■ Your sense of smell diminishes with age, accounting for the complaint, common among older people, that "food has no taste." Add lemon juice or extra herbs and spices to emphasize the basic bitter, sweet, salty, and sour flavors that do not require a sense of smell.

THROAT PROBLEMS

The throat never rests for more than a few seconds—every time you swallow, breathe, or speak, one of its parts goes into action.

■ Rest your voice now and then, especially if your job demands a lot of talking, singing, or projecting of your voice. Otherwise, you may develop polyps or nodules on the vocal cords, resulting in a hoarse or raspy voice.

■ If you do develop vocal-cord nodules or ulcers, try speaking or singing at a lower pitch, a tactic that voice therapists often recommend to professional singers.

■ Gargling with salt water can alleviate a sore throat. For a soothing sore throat gargle, try apple cider vinegar or lemon juice.

■ For a homemade cough remedy, add a tablespoon each of fresh-squeezed lemon juice and honey to a cup of hot water, and sip slowly. Other folk medicine cough antidotes include eating a spoonful of prepared horseradish from time to time and consuming chopped raw onions and garlic.

■ Consult a doctor if self-help methods do not bring improvement. You may need antibiotics to cure strep throat, tonsillitis, or other bacterial infections.

■ If you suffer from chronic laryngitis, review your personal habits for a possible cause. Smoking, heavy drinking, and eating highly spiced foods all irritate the throat and can cause inflamed vocal cords.

■ See a doctor promptly if you develop a severe sore throat that comes on suddenly and is localized on one side. You may have quinsy, an abscess that forms between the tonsils (or a bit of tonsillar tissue left over after a tonsillectomy) and surrounding soft tissue.

■ Throat irritation from a nagging cough can be alleviated by taking a long, hot shower or inhaling steam from a vaporizer. To improvise, take a towel and fill a sink or bowl with very hot water. Form a tent with the towel, bend over, and inhale. Just be sure that you don't get so close that the steam burns you.

MANAGING ASTHMA AND ALLERGIES

At their worst, asthma and allergies can be life-threatening. But treatment and sensible behavior can relieve even severe cases once you identify the causes.

IDENTIFYING ALLERGENS

■ Keep a diary of allergy or asthma attacks. Note the time and place of the attack, the symptoms, and possible causes, such as mowing the lawn, coming in contact with a cat, or eating a certain food.

■ Inspect your yard and garden. Pollen allergies are well known, but there are many other possibilities: Decaying leaves and compost heaps harbor mold spores. Pyrethrum, a natural pesticide, contains pulverized chrysanthemums, a common allergen. Common fertilizers and other garden chemicals can provoke allergic reactions.

■ If you are allergic to ragweed but experience symptoms outside of ragweed season, the cause may be in your kitchen. Honey often contains ragweed pollen, as do bee pollen capsules (sold in health-food stores). Mangoes and watermelons contain substances that are chemically similar to ragweed.

■ If you have allergies or asthma during the week but not on the weekends, suspect occupational asthma, which may be due to workplace chemicals or indoor pollution.

■ If you have an asthma or allergy attack soon after eating dried fruit or drinking wine, you may be sensitive to the sulfites used to preserve natural food color.

■ If you suspect you have a food allergy but haven't identified the offending foods, try eliminating from your diet foods that are often a cause, such as shellfish, citrus fruits, tomatoes, berries, milk, eggs, nuts, corn, wheat, and food additives. Eat only foods that you know are safe until you have been symptom-free for 10 days. Then gradually add foods one at a time at intervals of a week or so. If you start having symptoms, you may be allergic to the most recently reintroduced food.

> **Allergies around the winter holidays may indicate a reaction to Christmas trees. Many people are allergic to mountain cedars, a favorite species for Christmas trees, as well as tree molds and chemicals used to treat the trees.**

LIVING WITH ASTHMA

In asthma, the lungs' protection mechanism goes awry, closing the airways against ordinarily harmless substances and resulting in wheezing and difficulty breathing. When properly treated, asthma should not interfere with daily activities, including exercise, sleep, and work. However, be prepared to play a major role in controlling the disease.

■ Cold air causes the airways to tighten and can precipitate an attack. On cold days, breathe through your nose rather than your mouth. The nasal passages warm the air before it reaches the lungs. A scarf over the mouth also warms the air.

■ Reduce stress when possible. Although stress is not the underlying cause of asthma, it can trigger or worsen an attack. And having asthma can certainly cause stress.

■ Stay indoors as much as possible when pollution levels or pollen counts are high or when it is cold and windy. On days when you must be out despite the weather, use preventive medication to ward off an attack.

■ Treat yourself to a relaxing hot bath to relieve asthma symptoms and alleviate stress. Inhaling the moist, hot air from a sink filled with hot water also helps clear the lungs of mucus.

■ Join a health club, YMCA, or YWCA, or develop an indoor exercise routine so that you can keep up with your workouts despite the weather. Swimming indoors in a heated pool is the safest type of exercise for asthma sufferers. A stationary exercise cycle is another good choice. Use an inhaled medication, such as cromolyn sodium, to prevent exercise-induced asthma.

■ Consider joining a support group, such as those sponsored by the Canadian Lung Association. Talking with other asthma patients can boost confidence and provide new insight into the disease.

■ Take a vacation from allergic asthma. Experts say that an environmental change is occasionally helpful. Since cold air is a trigger for asthma, if you can afford it, go south in winter—say to Florida. However, they also say that no permanent move anywhere is going to cure asthma.

USING MEDICATIONS

■ For the most effective treatment of asthma and allergies, see an allergist, immunologist, or a primary-care physician who has been trained in treating allergic disorders.

■ Reducing airway inflammation is the key to controlling asthma. Anti-inflammatory drugs, such as inhaled steroids and cromolyn sodium, are usually prescribed to prevent asthma attacks and seasonal allergies. They take several days to start working, however, so start the medication before the pollen season.

■ In general, inhaled bronchodilator drugs should be reserved for alleviating symptoms rather than chronic use.

■ Learn the warning signs of an asthma attack, which may

include coughing, wheezing, shortness of breath, chest tightness, or a sore throat. Taking medication at this stage can often abort a more serious attack.

■ Talk to your doctor about using a peak flow meter, which measures lung function. It can help identify asthma triggers and also determine if your medication is working.

■ Ask your doctor to identify antihistamines that relieve symptoms without causing excessive drowsiness or nervousness. Some people take medications that make them drowsy at bedtime but choose a different medication during the day. Using antihistamines preventively—about an hour before exposure to an allergen—may work best.

■ Use an inhaled beta agonist no more than three times during an asthma attack. Steroid sprays are generally more effective. If symptoms persist or worsen, you **must** call your doctor or go to the emergency room.

■ Don't leave asthma or allergy medications in the glove compartment of a car. High temperatures in the glove compartment can render medications ineffective.

If you use an inhaler, try adding a nebulizer, or "spacer," to it. A spacer helps the medication form a mist before you inhale it, allowing the drug to penetrate the smallest airways.

ALLERGY-PROOFING YOUR HOME

■ Enclose mattresses and pillows in plastic casing, and wash sheets and other bedding in hot water weekly to eliminate dust mites, which are the most common trigger of allergic asthma. Don't hang sheets to dry outside; they can collect pollens that cause allergies.

■ Remove wall-to-wall carpeting, which can trap allergens. Replace with tile or polished floors. Remove draperies and venetian blinds, plush upholstery, and furniture stuffed with kapok, a highly allergenic tree product. Even ornately carved wood furniture, knick-knacks, lamp shades, and books can trap dust and other allergens.

■ Use a humidifier (or dehumidifier) that is designed to keep the humidity level in the house at about 45 percent. Clean the apparatus regularly to prevent a buildup of mold and bacteria in the water reservoir.

■ Use air-conditioning to dry and cool overly humid air in summer. Use hot water or steam heat to moisten and warm the air in winter.

■ Eliminate mold and mildew with ammonia, chlorine, or

another strong cleanser. Open windows and use fans to ventilate the room. The person with asthma should not be in the house during this cleaning or for several hours afterward.

■ Keep the basement and garage dry. Leaving on a light-bulb in the basement may prevent the growth of mold and mildew. If not, use an electric space heater once or twice a week.

■ Strong-smelling cleaning preparations can aggravate your allergies. Use baking soda, vinegar, mild soaps, and other products that contain no petro-chemicals or ammonia.

■ Vacuum daily, using a water-trap, double-filter vacuum. Wear a mask during vacuuming and for at least 15 minutes afterward. Or leave the premises and have someone else do the cleaning.

ALLERGY-PROOFING PETS

Since there is no such thing as a totally nonallergenic furry or feathered pet, they are not recommended for people with asthma. Animal dander and saliva are among the most common allergens. However, for people with mild allergies, there are measures you can take short of banning pets.

■ Try washing and brushing your pet frequently to reduce dander. Special pet shampoos reduce dander and saliva allergens, although plain water works just as well.

■ Train animals to stay off furniture and out of the bedroom. You can buy special electronic training pads that give the animal a mild shock.

■ Investigate different breeds and genders. Female cats may be less allergenic than males. Non-shedding dogs, such as poodles, are often tolerated better than dogs that shed.

■ Spend some time with the animal of your choice before committing yourself to buying or adopting it. For example, take the animal on approval to the home of a friend. If you don't experience symptoms after a few hours of close contact, chances are you won't when you bring the pet home.

If you are allergic to cats, use extra caution when renting or buying a home. Cat dander and saliva remain in a house—even a tidy one—long after the animal moves out.

ANAPHYLACTIC SHOCK

This is the most serious type of allergic reaction, and it can be fatal unless reversed immediately with adrenaline and antihistamines.

■ Anaphylactic shock is most often touched off by bee venom, penicillin, aspirin, nuts, shellfish, and eggs. If you have ever had even a mild reaction to any of these allergens, it is best to avoid them. The next reaction may be more serious.

■ Widespread swelling and difficulty breathing during an allergic reaction is a medical emergency. Get immediate help.

■ If you have ever experienced anaphylaxis or any other severe allergic reactions, always carry an adrenaline kit.

ALLERGIC REACTIONS

Allergies can trigger many annoying symptoms and conditions. Here are common reactions and what you can do about them.

Organs Affected	Symptoms	Likely Cause	What to Do
Gastro-intestinal system	Nausea, vomiting, diarrhea, cramps	Food allergens	Take nonprescription medications; eat bland foods until symptoms subside
Mouth and throat	Itching, swelling	Foods or drugs	Seek immediate emergency treatment if swelling impedes breathing
Brain and nervous system	Fatigue, mood swings, irritability	Additives in foods and wine	Keep a diary to identify offending substances and avoid them
Skin	Itching, hives, swelling	Chemicals, insect stings, foods	Treat mild itching with antihistamines, cortisone cream, or soothing lotion

ATHLETES WITH ASTHMA

"All asthmatics should exercise, and can do so with proper medication."
—*Michael Kaliner, M.D.*

• • • • • • •

Jackie Joyner-Kersee is widely regarded as America's top female athlete—an accolade she has earned through dedication and hard work. In the 1984 Olympics, Jackie won a silver medal in the heptathlon, a grueling seven-part event spread over two days. She returned in 1988, taking the gold in the heptathlon and setting an Olympic record in the long jump. In the 1992 summer games in Barcelona, she made Olympic history when she took the gold medal in the heptathlon, becoming the first woman to win successive Olympic multi-event titles and the first athlete ever to win multi-event medals in three Olympics.

Canada's Susan Auch won a silver medal at the 1994 Winter Olympics at Lillehammer. Her event was the punishing 500-m long track speed skating. What makes these accomplishments so remarkable is that both Jackie and Susan are asthmatics and must take medication before and after their races.

But they are only two of scores of world-class athletes with asthma. Three to 11 percent of the world's top athletes have exercise-induced asthma (67 of the 597 members of the 1984 U.S. Olympic team, for example, were asthmatic).

Exercise as an asthma trigger. Physical activity is one of the most common triggers of asthma attacks, affecting about 80 percent of all asthmatics. What's more, exercise can induce asthma symptoms in healthy people as well. According to Dr. Donald A. Mahler, a lung specialist at Dartmouth-Hitchcock Medical Center in Lebanon, New Hampshire, 12 to 15 percent of Americans develop asthma symptoms during vigorous exercise, but most think their coughing and shortness of breath are normal responses to a strenuous workout. Others cut back their exercise to avoid breathing problems, but asthma specialists discourage this tactic; instead, they recommend medically prescribed exercise to increase the lungs' stamina.

Benefits of exercise. While the exact cause of exercise-induced asthma is not known, many experts believe it is brought on by the drying and cooling effects of air moving rapidly in and out of the lungs. Breathing through the mouth, which is necessary during any vigorous aerobic exercise, also reduces the warming of air in the nasal passages.

In general, long-distance running, cross-country skiing, and other endurance activities are the most likely to trigger asthma. Exercising when it's cold doubles the chances of an attack because cold air is also a major asthma trigger. Swimming in a heated pool is one of the best activities for asthmatics; other good choices include tennis and other stop-and-go activities, such as baseball and football.

At Denver's National Jewish Center for Immunology and Respiratory Medicine, exercise is an important part of the asthma treatment program. "Virtually every asthma patient can benefit from exercise conditioning," says Dr. Robert C. Strunk, himself an asthmatic who enjoys running and mountain climbing. "The trick is to pick an appropriate activity and learn to use medication to prevent an attack of exercise-induced asthma." ❑

Asthma didn't stop Jackie Joyner-Kersee from becoming a champion.

INTESTINAL DISORDERS

Indigestion, heartburn, diarrhea, and constipation are very common problems. However, most cases can be avoided by a commonsense approach to eating and managing stress.

INDIGESTION

■ Stress is a major factor in indigestion—take a few minutes to relax before eating. Make family meals an enjoyable time. Save reprimands and unpleasant topics for later.

■ Avoid eating on the run. Eat small, frequent meals, and don't gulp your food. Eating too fast promotes overeating, which leads to indigestion.

■ Identify foods or beverages that seem to trigger an attack. Onions, cabbage, beans, and other gas-producing foods are common offenders. Also make a note of medications—aspirin, ibuprofen, certain antibiotics, and many others may cause stomach problems.

■ If you tend to get indigestion, cut down on mealtime beverages. Fluids dilute digestive juices, which slows digestion. Also avoid alcohol, caffeine, and carbonated drinks, which commonly cause indigestion.

■ If indigestion becomes a chronic problem, see your doctor. Digestive disturbances may be a symptom of more serious conditions, including colon disorders, ulcers, and gallbladder disease.

TAKING THE BURN OUT OF HEARTBURN

Heartburn, which is a burning sensation in the center of the chest from the breastbone to the throat, occurs when the stomach's digestive juices invade the esophagus, a condition called acid reflux.

■ Try antacids. These over-the-counter medications usually alleviate ordinary heartburn. However, overuse of antacids can mask the symptoms of serious disorders. So use them judiciously.

■ Cut down on caffeine, chocolate, alcohol, and fats, which tend to relax the esophageal sphincter, allowing the reflux of stomach acids.

■ Red peppers and other hot, spicy foods irritate the membranes lining the throat and esophagus, producing pain similar to heartburn. If you eat such foods, switch to bland foods for a while to give the membranes a chance to heal.

■ To prevent heartburn, don't bend over or lie down for at least two hours after a meal. If you must rest, sit in a reclining chair.

■ If you frequently awaken with heartburn, try elevating the head of your bed by about six inches, using a couple of bricks or thick books.

■ Wear loose-fitting clothes. Tight pants and belts can put pressure on the stomach, increasing the chances of reflux.

■ Lose excess weight, especially if you have a bulging abdomen. Extra pressure on the stomach encourages reflux.

> **Heartburn is often mistaken for a heart attack because the pain is similar. If in doubt, seek emergency medical help. It's better to overreact to heartburn than to underreact to a heart attack.**

HICCUPS

Hiccups are sudden, involuntary contractions of the diaphragm that develop when the stomach is distended. To prevent hiccups, eat slowly and avoid fatty foods.

■ If you often develop hiccups, avoid carbonated beverages and chewing gum. They promote the swallowing of air, causing hiccups.

■ Cut back on alcohol; heavy drinking often produces a bout of hiccups.

■ Everyone has a favorite hiccup remedy, but if yours doesn't work, try this: Hold your breath as long as you can, and then breathe out. Repeat this two or three times. This exercise stretches the diaphragm, which contracts during a hiccup.

FIGHTING FLATULENCE

Flatulence, or intestinal gas, is usually caused by swallowing too much air or by bacterial fermentation of undigested food in the colon. Though experiencing some gas is normal, excessive gas can be annoying and even painful.

■ Chew your food slowly and thoroughly.

■ Eat fewer gas-producing foods, such as dried beans, broccoli, cabbage, and bran.

■ Limit intake of soda and other carbonated beverages.

■ Eliminate milk from your diet. If the problem goes away, you may be lactose-intolerant. Check with your doctor.

STAYING REGULAR

Constipation is very common among older people because of reduced colon function, but it can occur at any age.

■ Increase physical activity. Regular exercise helps stimulate the bowels and promotes regularity.

■ Add fiber to your diet, but do so gradually. An abrupt increase can cause diarrhea, bloating, and gas.

■ Drink more fluids to produce a softer stool.

■ If hemorrhoids are a problem, redouble your efforts to avoid constipation and straining. Do not read while going to the toilet; sitting overly long on the toilet seat increases pressure on the rectum and exacerbates hemorrhoids.

■ Be wary of over-the-counter hemorrhoid preparations that have an ingredient ending in "-caine." These contain a local anesthetic, which can irritate the swollen tissue.

■ Review your medications with your physician—many drugs promote constipation. Offenders include codeine, antacids, diarrhea medications, sleeping pills, antidepressants, tranquilizers, heart medications, such as beta-blockers and calcium-channel blockers, and calcium and iron pills.

■ Avoid prolonged use of laxatives. An occasional high-fiber stool softener is not harmful, but overuse of laxatives disrupts normal bowel function, leading to chronic constipation.

■ Establish a regular time for bowel movements. Since eating stimulates the colon, after breakfast is usually a good time. Some people find that drinking a cup of tea or warm water with a bit of lemon when they first get up stimulates a bowel movement.

Always see a doctor if blood appears in your stool. It's probably due to excessive straining, hemorrhoids, or another relatively harmless cause. But it may be a sign of colon cancer.

TAKING ACTION TO STOP DIARRHEA

See a doctor if diarrhea persists for more than a few days. Don't delay if it is accompanied by a fever or severe abdominal pain or if there is blood in the stool.

Type of diarrhea	Possible causes	Remedies
Chronic but intermittent	Irritable bowel syndrome	Reduce stress
Chronic but intermittent	Chronic inflammatory disorder, such as Crohn's disease	Take medications to halt the inflammatory process
Diarrhea alternating with constipation; blood or pus in stools	Colon polyps or tumor, diabetes, diverticulosis	See a doctor for treatment of the underlying disorder
Chronic diarrhea accompanied by excessive sweating	Overactive thyroid	See a doctor for anti-thyroid treatment
Greasy, foul-smelling stools	Malabsorption syndrome	Diet to avoid offending foods or replacement of missing enzymes
Chronic diarrhea and cramps, with bloating	Lactose intolerance	Eliminate milk from diet or take lactase supplements
Sudden onset of severe diarrhea with greenish tinge	Food poisoning or viral infection	Switch to clear fluids and gradually reintroduce bland foods, such as toast and rice

COMMON SKIN DISORDERS

In addition to providing a protective armor against outside invaders, the skin regulates body temperature, holds in body fluids, and manufactures vitamin D. This largest organ of the human body has great recuperative powers.

WARTS

Warts, which are caused by viruses, are often highly contagious. Most are benign and disappear without treatment. Genital warts are an exception; their presence greatly increases the risk of genital cancers and so should be treated by a doctor at once. Otherwise, warts don't have to be removed unless they become irritated or unsightly.

■ Over-the-counter preparations work in some cases, but follow directions carefully. Some contain salicylic acid, which can burn the skin. Never apply these preparations to the genital area or the face.

■ Plantar warts, which develop on the soles of the feet and toes, are sometimes difficult to differentiate from calluses. In general, a callus hurts when touched directly, while plantar warts produce pain from the pressure of walking or standing. Don't try to treat plantar warts yourself. A physician should remove them surgically or with liquid nitrogen or an electric needle.

ECZEMA AND DERMATITIS

Eczema and dermatitis both refer to inflamed, scaly, itchy skin. Eczema typically occurs in babies, produces symmetrical patches on the face and limbs, and is often associated with allergies and asthma. Dermatitis, a variation of

eczema, is triggered by exposure to an irritant (see "Itchy Skin," page 124).

■ Although eczema and dermatitis can cause intense itching, try not to scratch. Scratching only intensifies the problem and may also lead to infection. If a baby develops eczema, keep his or her nails cut short to prevent scratching, and if necessary, cover the hands with cotton socks or mittens.

■ If you have dermatitis, look around the house for possible irritants. Common offenders include nail polish remover, makeup, dyes, soap, and household cleansers. Some substances—such as ingredients in sunscreen and shaving lotion—cause dermatitis only when exposed to the sun.

■ Look at the rash pattern for clues to the cause. Dermatitis of the wrist, neck, or earlobe may be caused by nickel, an alloy in jewelry. A rash around the waist or on the feet may be from chemicals in a leather belt or shoes.

■ Eliminating eggs or milk may improve childhood

eczema. But check with your doctor before eliminating milk from a child's diet, especially if the child is under age two.

■ Such medications as over-the-counter hydrocortisone creams and lotions may cause dermatitis. Use a hydrocortisone product on itchy skin for only four or five days. If the condition persists, see a doctor.

■ Babies commonly develop diaper rash, a form of dermatitis. When this happens, change the baby more frequently, and expose the diaper area to air whenever possible. If you use disposable diapers, switch brands or try cloth diapers. Some babies are sensitive to the plastic covering or chemicals in disposable diapers.

PSORIASIS

Patches of red, scaly skin with silvery scales are a sign of psoriasis, which develops when skin cells reproduce too fast. The elbows, knees, torso, and scalp are most commonly affected, and some people also develop arthritis. There is no cure for psoriasis, but the disease usually can be controlled.

■ Stress does not cause psoriasis, but it can trigger a flare-up. To improve your stress-coping ability, increase your exercise or learn relaxation techniques, such as deep-breathing exercises, meditation, or yoga.

■ Abstain from alcohol or drink only small amounts occasionally. Excessive alcohol consumption tends to aggravate psoriasis.

■ There is some evidence linking psoriasis to faulty metabolism of a fatty acid in animal fats. Eliminate red meat and other animal fats from your diet and see if your symptoms improve.

■ Psoriasis of the scalp can produce severe dandruff. Use shampoos and soaps containing coal tar. If the dandruff continues, see a dermatologist for a prescription shampoo.

■ Psoriasis tends to develop where skin rubs against skin. Maintain ideal weight and apply cornstarch to skin creases to reduce friction.

- - - - - - - - - - - - - - - - - - -

Psoriasis improves when the skin is exposed to the sun's ultraviolet rays, which explains why scaling often disappears during the summer. Moderation is important, however; a sunburn can trigger a psoriasis flare-up.

- - - - - - - - - - - - - - - - - - -

IMPETIGO

Impetigo is a bacterial skin infection characterized by itchy, blistering eruptions that form a crust, usually on the face, legs, and arms. Impetigo spreads easily through direct contact and is most common in children and young adults, especially in warm weather.

■ If impetigo develops, see a doctor promptly. Antibiotics clear up the infection within a few days. Both pills and an antibiotic skin cream may be prescribed.

■ To remove the skin crusts of impetigo and prevent the spread of bacteria, wash the affected areas with warm water and antibacterial soap several times a day.

■ Do not share towels or clothing with a person who has impetigo or any other skin disorder.

■ Biting flies sometimes carry the bacteria that cause impetigo. Use window screens to keep flies out, and cover a baby's crib with mosquito netting during the fly season.

■ After someone with a skin disorder uses a washcloth, launder it in hot water and chlorine bleach.

FUNGAL SKIN INFECTIONS

Fungi are yeastlike organisms that thrive in moist areas of the skin and mucous membranes. Jock itch and athlete's foot are common examples of fungal skin infections; thrush, or candidiasis, usually affects the mouth and genital area.

■ Avoid going barefoot in public locker rooms and showers; these are prime breeding places for the fungi that cause athlete's foot.

■ If you are prone to fungal infections, try changing your shoes, socks, and underwear at least once during the day. Allow sufficient time between wearings to let shoes dry out.

■ After bathing, dry your feet well, then sprinkle cornstarch on them.

■ If you develop a fungal infection, try an over-the-counter spray or cream containing miconazole, clotrimazole, Whitfield's ointment, or Castallani paint. Avoid products with cortisone or other steroids—these can make the infection worse. If the infection persists after a week of treatment, see a doctor. You may need an oral antifungal prescription.

■ Oral thrush is often mistaken for fever blisters and other mouth sores. Try scraping away some of the pustules—thrush comes off easily, exposing a red, bleeding sore underneath.

■ Keep the feet clean and dry. Bathe them frequently, and use a hair dryer to dry thoroughly between your toes. Wear cotton socks that draw moisture away from the feet, and change them often. Select shoes that are well ventilated, especially when exercising.

- - - - - - - - - - - - - - - - - - -

Poorly fitted dental bridges or improperly cleaned dentures promote oral thrush, especially among the elderly and other people with low immunity.

- - - - - - - - - - - - - - - - - - -

HIGH BLOOD PRESSURE AND STROKE

High blood pressure, our most common chronic disease, greatly increases the risk of a heart attack. Stroke, our third leading cause of death, is also a consequence of uncontrolled high blood pressure.

MEASURING BLOOD PRESSURE

Hypertension, the medical term for high blood pressure, is often called a silent killer because it does not produce obvious symptoms until it reaches an advanced stage. However, early detection and treatment can prevent its dire consequences.

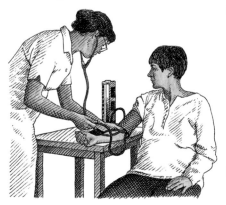

■ Have your blood pressure measured at least every other year, and more often if it is elevated (above 140/90) or in a borderline range (140/85–89).

■ Blood pressure varies markedly during the course of a day. A diagnosis of hypertension requires at least three elevated readings taken at different times, unless the first measurement is dangerously high (above 160/115).

■ Nicotine and caffeine both raise blood pressure. Don't smoke or consume a beverage containing caffeine for at least four hours before a blood pressure measurement.

■ Oral contraceptives and many other prescription drugs tend to raise blood pressure. So do some nonprescription cold and allergy pills. Give your doctor a complete list of all your medications. You may be instructed to stop one or more and to return for a follow-up measurement.

■ If hypertension is diagnosed, expect to undergo a battery of other tests. Some of these will look for an underlying cause — such as a narrowed renal artery or a hormonal disorder. Others—such as a chest X-ray, eye examination, and kidney studies—look for signs of damage from the high blood pressure.

■ Automated blood pressure machines for home use generally are not as accurate as the ones used by a doctor. If you monitor your blood pressure at home, have your doctor check your machine during routine check-ups to make sure it is properly calibrated.

· ·

Take blood pressure readings at home or work and compare the results with those obtained in a doctor's office. This can rule out white-coat hypertension, in which blood pressure is elevated when you are in a doctor's office and normal at other times.

· ·

CONTROLLING HIGH BLOOD PRESSURE

Although a doctor prescribes the course of treatment, the patient is responsible for the day-to-day management of the disease. This often requires basic lifestyle changes.

■ Control your weight. Excess weight raises blood pressure and forces the heart to work harder. Losing weight often restores normal blood pressure.

■ Go easy on salt. About one-third of North Americans are salt-sensitive—they have a tendency to conserve sodium, which increases body fluids and raises blood pressure.

■ Smoking, alcohol, and caffeine raise blood pressure. So, do not smoke, and cut back on alcohol and caffeine.

■ If you are sedentary, start a cardiovascular exercise conditioning program. Check with your doctor first to see if you need an exercise stress test.

■ Remove unnecessary stress from your life, and adopt stress-coping techniques, such as relaxation exercises and meditation.

■ If you don't have a pet, consider getting one. Studies show that petting and caring for an animal can lower blood pressure (see "Pet Therapy," page 377).

■ Diabetes often prompts a rise in blood pressure. If you have diabetes, strive to keep it in check.

TAKING ANTIHYPER-TENSIVE DRUGS

Although lifestyle changes are an important component of controlling high blood pressure, antihypertensive medications are usually needed.

■ Some medications cause a sudden drop in blood pressure when you stand up abruptly, resulting in dizziness or fainting. Avoid sudden changes in position. Get out of bed in stages, sitting at the side of the bed for a few moments before standing.

■ Diuretics increase urine output. Reduce fluid intake in the evening to avoid having to get up during the night.

■ Thiazide diuretics promote excretion of potassium, an electrolyte needed to maintain proper body chemistry.

Increase your intake of potassium-rich foods, such as citrus fruits, bananas, whole-grain products, and green, leafy vegetables. If signs of potassium deficiency—muscle weakness, tremors, irregular heartbeat—develop, see your doctor. Potassium supplements or a potassium-sparing diuretic may be prescribed.

■ Avoid using salt substitutes, which are often high in potassium, while taking a potassium-sparing diuretic. The combination can lead to dangerous potassium toxicity.

■ Some antihypertensive drugs increase sun sensitivity. Cover up when going outdoors, and apply a sunscreen to all exposed skin (see "Sun Sense," page 126).

■ Beta-blockers can cause cold hands and feet because of reduced circulation. Avoid handling cold objects, such as an iced drink or frozen foods, and wear warm gloves and woolen socks outdoors in the winter.

WARNINGS OF A STROKE OR MINI-STROKE (TIA)

See a doctor or go to the nearest emergency room if you experience any of the following:

■ Sudden weakness or numbness of the face, arm, and leg on one side of the body.

■ Loss of speech or trouble speaking or understanding speech.

■ Dimness or loss of vision, especially in one eye or half of both eyes.

■ Sudden onset of blurred or double vision.

■ Sudden onset of unsteadiness,

MAJOR BLOOD PRESSURE MEDICATIONS

Type of Drug	Examples	Potential Problems and What to Do
Thiazide Diuretics	Chlorothiazide, metolazone, hydrochlorothiazide	Weakness, muscle cramps, sun sensitivity, impotence, frequent urination. Increase potassium intake; talk to your doctor
Beta-Blockers	Atenolol, acebutolol, metoprolol, nadolol, propanolol, timolol	Insomnia, nightmares, weakness, dizziness, cold hands and feet, impotence, worsening of asthma. Ask your doctor for alternative drug, especially if you have asthma or a history of depression
Angiotensin Converting Enzyme (ACE) Inhibitors	Captopril, enalapril, lisinopril	Loss of taste, cough, headaches, palpitations, rashes. Dosage may be too high; talk to your doctor
Calcium-Channel Blockers	Diltiazem, nifedipine, verapamil	Swelling of legs, dizziness, headaches, hot flashes, constipation. Try wearing support hose; increase exercise, fiber, and fluid intake
Vasodilators	Hydralazine, minoxidil	Headaches, rapid heartbeat, excessive hair growth (minoxidil). Talk to your doctor; these drugs are usually taken with other medications and dosages may be too high
Centrally Acting Alpha Blockers	Clonidine, guanabenz, methyldopa	Dry mouth, drowsiness, constipation, fatigue. Increase fluid intake. Clonidine skin patch may reduce side effects
Alpha Blockers	Prazosin, terazosin	Faintness when beginning therapy. Avoid abrupt movements
Peripheral-Acting Adrenergic Antagonists	Guanethidine, rauwolfia (wholeroot), reserpine	Depression, nightmares, stuffy nose, impotence. Ask for alternative drug, especially if you have a history of depression

lack of coordination, dizziness, difficulty walking, or falling.

■ A sudden, excruciating headache.

■ Recent change in personality or mental function, including memory loss.

DEALING WITH A STROKE

A stroke occurs when the blood supply to part of the brain is interrupted, either by a blockage (ischemic stroke) or by a burst blood vessel (cerebral hemorrhage).

■ Many strokes are heralded by mini-strokes, or transient ischemic attacks (TIA's). To prevent a full-blown stroke, seek immediate medical attention if a TIA occurs.

■ If you suspect a stroke, immediately take the patient to an emergency room, preferably in a hospital with a stroke unit.

COMEBACK AFTER A STROKE

■ Stroke rehabilitation should begin as soon as the patient is stable. Family members can help by working with nurses and physical therapists to exercise paralyzed limbs. Passive exercises maintain muscle tone and strength (see box below).

■ As nerve function returns, encourage the patient to move about and attempt as much self-care as possible. Remember, the degree of function varies according to the severity of the stroke and the part of the brain affected. Don't worry about things like spills and messy eating—it's more important that the patient strives for independence.

■ After the patient goes home, family members must assume much of the caregiving and rehabilitation. Seek guidance from physical, occupational, and speech therapists. If possible, arrange for home visits from therapists to monitor the patient's progress and prescribe new routines.

■ Memory loss and speech difficulties are common consequences of a stroke. Prod the patient's memory with photo albums, music that recalls a special event, or a scent associated with a place or person.

■ Encourage the patient to speak, starting with asking questions that can be answered with a simple yes or no. Some stroke patients never regain normal speech, and others must relearn the language process. Repeat words, and use pictures and other visual aids, much as you would teach a child to speak.

Stroke patients often require physical changes in their home to facilitate getting around. If the patient is in a wheelchair, install ramps as needed, and make other necessary changes, such as widening doors, lowering counters, and lowering light switches.

PASSIVE EXERCISE TO RETAIN MUSCLE TONE

After getting a physician's authorization, a stroke victim may be able to perform physical therapy several times a day. Try to put each limb through its full range of motion.

To exercise the shoulders and arms, begin by straightening one arm and supporting it.

Raise the arm above the head. If you cannot lift it that high, raise it as much as possible.

To exercise the elbow, bend the arm, trying to bring the hand to the ear.

SURVIVING A STROKE

"My stroke taught me to love, to appreciate my family more, and to savor little successes—one at a time."
—Jacquelyn Mayer Townsend, former Miss America

• • • • • • •

Jacquelyn Mayer Townsend, in 1963 and today.

At the age of 28, Jacquelyn Mayer Townsend was the epitome of the American dream. She had enjoyed a glamorous singing career with Fred Waring and the Pennsylvanians, in 1963 she was crowned Miss America, and she was now a wife and mother of two. Then, on November 27, 1970, Jacquelyn awoke to the terrifying realization that she was paralyzed and unable to speak. A severe stroke had turned her fairy-tale life into a nightmare. But this former tomboy and beauty queen was a fighter, and with the help of family and friends she would win her most terrifying battle.

"My husband, John, and my son, Bill, were excellent teachers," she recalls. "My dear friend Fred Waring also encouraged me to talk. He called me every day and gave me three more words that I would learn. He kept telling me that when I could say 'juxtaposition,' I would be able to say any word.

"My daughter, Kelly, was nine months old when I had my stroke, so we learned to talk and read together," she adds.

The years of laborious physical and speech therapy paid off, and Jacquelyn now declares herself nearly recovered. As a spokesperson for the National Stroke Association in the United States, she devotes much of her time to helping other survivors. "I learned the healing power of love and faith," she says, "and I'm grateful I can pass that message on."

Life-saving treatments. Great strides are being made in stroke prevention, treatment, and rehabilitation. The incidence of strokes has been cut in half since Townsend was stricken, thanks largely to improved treatment of high blood pressure, the leading risk factor of stroke.

Many strokes, or "brain attacks," are preceded by warning attacks, or mini-strokes. Prompt treatment with drugs or surgery often prevents a full-blown stroke. On the horizon are powerful clot-dissolving drugs, which, given early, will stop some strokes before there is permanent brain damage. Research has also found that brain cells can survive hours or even days with minimal blood flow.

New therapies. The realization that brain cells can survive a stroke has led to an emphasis on rehabilitation, which often begins as soon as the patient is stable. "We now know how important it is for stroke patients to be up and about as soon as possible," says Dr. Matthew H.M. Lee, director of New York University's Rusk Institute of Rehabilitation Medicine. Programs at Rusk use music and recreation therapy, along with traditional physical and speech therapies.

Perhaps the most encouraging words come from Dr. Fletcher McDowell, president of the National Stroke Association: "The majority of strokes are now preventable. Everyone should learn how to reduce their risks." ❑

HEART DISEASE

A heart attack doesn't necessarily mean the end of a normal life. In fact, most heart-attack survivors return to work and continue to pursue their usual activities. And because many patients make positive changes in their lifestyle, some enjoy even better health.

ADOPTING A PRUDENT LIFESTYLE

Experts agree that lifestyle is important in both treating and preventing heart attacks and other manifestations of heart disease. Here are a few starting points.

■ Add physical activity to your daily routine by walking whenever possible. If there are stairs in your home, you have a head start. At work, walk up two or three flights of stairs instead of taking the elevator. Walk to neighborhood stores instead of driving.
■ Make a list of your cardiovascular risk factors (family history of early heart attacks, cigarette smoking, high blood pressure, elevated cholesterol, diabetes, obesity, sedentary lifestyle), and develop a plan for change.
■ Concentrate on one or two goals at a time. When you have them under control, go to the next ones on your list.
■ Start with a major risk factor that can make a big difference to all the rest. For example, if you smoke, put quitting at the top of your list. Not only is it the leading cause of heart attacks, but it also damages every other organ system.

One of the most important heart medications may be in your medicine chest—ordinary aspirin. Check with your doctor to see if you should take a daily dose to reduce the risk of another heart attack. Generally, the best time to take it is after breakfast.

A HEART-HEALTHY DIET

Diet is a critical factor in fighting heart disease. It is vital to follow a diet that controls weight, lowers elevated blood cholesterol, and maintains normal blood sugar.
■ Cut out the fat. The Heart and Stroke Foundation of Canada urges all people to restrict their saturated fat intake to 10 percent of their energy intake, or of the calories they consume in a day. However, some specialists in heart-recovery programs recommend this limit only for

When to Call the Doctor

Summon an ambulance or emergency medical service immediately if you experience any of the following symptoms of a heart attack:

Chest pains or uncomfortable sensation of pressure, fullness, or squeezing in the center of the chest that lasts more than two minutes.

Pain originating in the chest and spreading to the shoulders, arms, stomach, back, neck, jaw, or mouth. The pain usually originates on the left side, but either side may be involved.

Light-headedness, fainting, sweating, nausea, shortness of breath, or unusual heaviness in the legs.

Call your doctor for guidance if you experience:

Unusual fatigue.

Palpitations or other abnormal heartbeats.

Increasingly frequent angina attacks, or angina that develops during rest.

Swelling of ankles and feet.

Waking in the middle of the night short of breath, or inability to sleep lying down.

heart patients, and recommend that healthy people restrict their intake to 20 percent.

■ Increase your fiber intake. Soluble fiber, such as oat bran and the pectin in fruits, may lower blood cholesterol; insoluble fiber helps prevent overeating by making you feel full without adding calories to the diet.

■ Include servings of dried beans, lentils, or other legumes in your diet several times a week. These high-fiber foods appear to have cholesterol-lowering properties.

■ Reduce your salt intake, especially if you have high blood pressure, congestive heart failure, or edema.

■ Switch to decaffeinated beverages. Excessive caffeine—more than five or six cups of coffee a day—increases the tendency to develop cardiac arrhythmias, especially among patients with heart-valve disease. If you have heart disease, it's a good idea to limit your caffeine consumption to a wake-up cup of coffee in the morning and perhaps an occasional pick-me-up when your energy flags.

A growing body of research indicates that vitamin E may help prevent atherosclerosis, the clogging of the coronary arteries and other blood vessels with fatty deposits. Ask your doctor about high-dose supplements; the usual recommended dosage is 200 to 400 milligrams a day.

STRESS REDUCTION

A certain amount of stress is inescapable, but the way we respond to it can affect the heart and other organs.

■ Are you a Type A personality —impatient, aggressive, driven, compelled to win, always on the go? If so, you are likely to overrespond to stress, making you vulnerable to a heart attack.

■ Consider meditation, yoga, t'ai chi, or some other alternative therapy that teaches mind-body control. These therapies can lower blood pressure and promote an enhanced sense of well-being.

TAKING HEART MEDICATIONS

Most heart patients require medications to control symptoms and reduce the risk of heart attack. Always use heart drugs exactly as instructed, and report adverse reactions to your doctor.

■ Nitroglycerin, the oldest heart medication, is still the most widely used. It opens the blood vessels, thus reducing blood pressure and the heart's workload. It is often used to stop an attack of angina.

■ Doctors sometimes prescribe a prophylactic nitroglycerin pill in order to prevent angina. Or a patient may wear a medicated patch that releases a constant small dose of the drug into the bloodstream through the skin, thus preventing angina. The doctor may tell a patient to use these patches intermittently in order to avoid developing a tolerance to nitroglycerin. For example, the doctor may recommend removing the patch during the night.

■ Calcium-channel blockers, a class of drugs that work by interfering with muscle contraction, can cause swelling of the lower legs and feet. Avoid elastic garters and other constrictive clothing.

■ Cholestyramine, a common cholesterol-lowering drug, can cause constipation. If your doctor prescribes this drug, increase your fluid and fiber intake, and, when needed, use a stool softener.

■ Because cholestyramine interferes with the body's absorption of other heart drugs, including thiazide diuretics, digoxin, and beta-blockers, these drugs are generally taken several hours before cholestyramine.

■ Many doctors recommend high-dose niacin to lower blood cholesterol. Although niacin does not require a prescription, it should be taken only as the doctor directs. Make sure it's labeled niacin or nicotinic acid, and not nicotinamide, a niacin derivative that does not have the same cholesterol-lowering effect. Time-released niacin is less likely to cause flushing and hot flashes.

■ Digitalis drugs, which are derived from foxglove plants, have long been used to treat heart failure and control some kinds of cardiac arrhythmias. Always check with a doctor before taking any other medication, since many interact with digitalis. Also avoid products containing bicarbonate of soda, which can lead to toxicity.

AFTER A HEART ATTACK

Two out of three Canadians who have heart attacks survive. Most leave the hospital after a week to 10 days and then recuperate at home.

■ As recuperation begins, it is essential that the patient understand the doctor's instructions. Most hospitals offer discharge education classes for both the heart patient and spouse. Attend such classes, take notes, and read pamphlets and other educational materials.

■ Don't be afraid to call your doctor if you have troubling symptoms or questions. Many people hesitate to "bother the doctor," but after a heart attack, it's important to check in regularly.

■ The patient should avoid any type of straining until he or she is fully recovered. If constipation is a problem, use a stool softener until a normal diet and exercise routine can be resumed.

THE EXERCISE PRESCRIPTION

Exercise is critical to recovery from a heart attack. Before leaving the hospital, most patients undergo a modified exercise stress test to determine a safe level of activity. After observing how you do during the test, your doctor can write specific instructions for exercising.

■ Look into a cardiac rehabilitation exercise program. Many community hospitals, Y's, and some exercise clubs offer special supervised exercises for heart patients. Participating in such a program eases the fear of having a heart attack while exercising. It also lets you safely gauge your own limits. Having peers to exercise with can provide the motivation to continue working out.

■ Go easy at the beginning of your exercise program. You may be instructed to walk only two or three blocks at a time for the first few weeks. Gradually extend your distance according to your doctor's instructions. Don't worry about speed—walk at a pace that is comfortable for you.

■ Take your pulse before exercising, immediately after stopping, and again five minutes later. Your pulse should rise during exercise but return to normal within five minutes of stopping.

■ Chart your progress. Keep a daily log showing distance or duration of exercise, pulse rates, and any symptoms. Show the log to your doctor, and ask if you should make any changes, either cutting back or speeding up.

People who exercise regularly have 40 percent fewer heart attacks than their sedentary peers.

THE QUESTION OF SEX

Doctors and patients alike are reluctant to bring up the question of sex after a heart attack, more out of embarrassment than for any medical reason. Establishing an open dialogue about all aspects of normal life, including sex, is an important aspect of recovery.

■ There are no set rules for resuming sex after a heart attack, but most doctors advise waiting at least two weeks after hospital discharge.

■ If sex provokes angina, inform your doctor. He or she may recommend taking nitroglycerin beforehand.

■ In many cases, the healthy spouse is reluctant to engage in sexual activity, fearing it will provoke a heart attack. Be assured that sex rarely brings on a heart attack.

A patient who can climb 20 stairs in 10 to 15 seconds without symptoms or without the heart rate increasing more than 20 to 30 beats a minute should be able to engage in moderate sexual activity.

AFTER CORONARY BYPASS SURGERY

This open-heart operation entails using grafts of healthy blood vessels—usually an artery from the chest wall or a vein from the leg—to bypass blocked segments of coronary arteries. The operation improves symptoms, but it does not cure the underlying disease. Hence, lifestyle changes are needed to keep the grafts from clogging.

■ Even though it hurts, breathe as deeply as possible to inflate the lungs. Using a lung-exercise device can help you gauge your progress. Coughing several times a day and doing deep-breathing exercises are essential to keeping the lungs inflated.

■ If a portion of vein was removed from the leg, wear surgical elastic stockings for several weeks. To make it easier to put these stockings on, lightly dust your foot and ankle with talcum powder first. Turn the stocking inside out, ease it over your feet, and stretch it as you pull it up.

■ Although doctors order exercise as soon as possible following a bypass operation, some activities are dangerous in the early weeks following the operation. Avoid weight lifting or upper-body exercises that place stress on the chest incision. Such activities are usually fine after the incision and breastbone have healed.

LIFE WITH A PACEMAKER

Pacemakers are implantable devices that stabilize the heartbeat in patients whose heartbeat is abnormally slow or fast.

■ For the first eight weeks after implantation, avoid strenuous or abrupt movements, which can dislodge the leads attached to the heart muscle. Don't raise your arm above your head on the side that has the pacemaker except to wash or dress. Other activities that are barred for the first eight weeks include swimming, bowling, tennis, vacuum cleaning, carrying heavy loads, mowing or raking the lawn, and shoveling snow. After this period, the doctor is usually able to tell if such activities can be resumed.

■ Call your doctor if you experience shortness of breath, dizziness, chest pain, muscle twitching, prolonged hiccuping, unusual weakness or fatigue, or swelling of the lower legs or arms. These may be signs of a pacemaker problem.

■ Pacemakers require checking periodically. Ask your doctor about enrolling in a telephone-monitoring program, which is available at most hospitals and cardiology clinics. You can then have your pacemaker checked via the telephone hookup, rather than going to the doctor's office (see page 315).

■ Magnets can reprogram a pacemaker. Avoid exposure to any magnetic metal detector, such as those used at airport security checkpoints. Carry a letter from your doctor and request a hand check, rather than one using a magnetic device. Also, do not undergo a magnetic resonance imaging (MRI) scan while wearing a pacemaker. If you are exposed inadvertently to a magnetic field, see your doctor as soon as possible to reprogram your pacemaker.

■ Electrical household appliances and office equipment usually do not interfere with a pacemaker, with the exception of older microwave ovens that are not well insulated. Do not stand in front of such an oven while it is operating. Avoid sources of high-voltage electricity like radio transmitters.

■ Many doctors instruct their pacemaker patients to monitor their own pulse daily; others feel it is not necessary. If you do monitor your pulse, take it for one minute while resting, as well as at the end of any prolonged exercise session. Contact your doctor or telephone-monitoring unit if the pulse is five or more beats slower than the low end of your normal range. A pulse that is faster than normal usually is not a cause for concern unless it is consistently above 100 beats per minute.

Most pacemakers now run on lithium batteries that usually last 8 to 10 years. Replacing the battery can be done in a simple outpatient procedure that requires only local anesthesia.

CONTROLLING ARTHRITIS

When joints and muscles are painful or inflamed, even the simplest task can seem overwhelming. Here are ways to deal with the symptoms and consequences of arthritis.

TYPES OF ARTHRITIS

The term *arthritis* refers to more than 100 related illnesses known as rheumatic diseases. All are characterized by joint inflammation, decreased flexibility, and other symptoms. As the cartilage that covers the bone erodes, bones begin to rub together. The result is often pain, stiffness, and reduced function.

■ Osteoarthritis is the most common form. Heredity, obesity, injury to joints, and the wear and tear of daily life may cause it. Osteoarthritis tends to develop slowly over the years, beginning after age 40. At first, it may affect a joint or joints on only one side of the body.

■ Rheumatoid arthritis, the most severe form of arthritis, usually develops between the ages of 25 and 50, and affects more women than men. Heredity may play a role, but its causes are mostly unknown. It has been labeled an autoimmune disease, which means that one part of the body attacks another part. Rheumatoid arthritis tends to develop within a few weeks or months and affects joints bilaterally.

LIVING WITH ARTHRITIS

■ Start the day with a warm shower or bath, followed by gentle stretching and range-of-motion exercises. The warm water alleviates pain, and the exercise, in which you bend or move each joint fully, helps dispel morning stiffness.

■ Schedule your work so that you can perform the most demanding tasks when you feel your best. For most arthritis patients, this is midday, after morning stiffness has worn off and before afternoon fatigue sets in. Rest between tasks.

■ Whenever possible, use a larger joint to spare smaller ones from excessive strain. For example, use your shoulder to help your hand and wrist push open a door. When twisting off a bottle cap, use your whole hand, not just your fingers.

■ Keep moving. Shift positions while seated, take breaks from desk work, and get up and walk around on planes and trains. Movement keeps joints limber and lubricated.

■ If you're overweight, losing excess pounds may alleviate the stress on your joints and increase your mobility.

■ Keep a diary to identify factors that trigger increased pain and stiffness. Some people find that certain foods—especially red meat, green peppers, eggplant, and tomatoes—provoke a flare-up of arthritis. Eliminating them may help.

■ Remove from closets and drawers the items you use most, then put them within easy reach.

■ Use oven mitts instead of potholders if arthritis makes gripping pot and pan handles difficult when you are cooking. The padding in mitts allows you to grasp the pot handles with the palm of your hand, not just with your fingers.

■ Use a cane or even a wheelchair when you're in pain to conserve your energy.

■ Gadgets designed for arthritics can make life easier: special combs, toothbrushes, eating and cooking utensils, shoehorns, and other devices.

■ It's good to be able to save steps, especially during a flare-up. For example, install extension telephones in each room in your home or buy a cordless phone.

EXERCISING WITH ARTHRITIS

■ Work with a doctor or physical therapist to design an exercise program of stretching and strengthening specific muscles. Exercise may not only help you achieve a greater range of motion in affected joints, but it may also prevent arthritis from occurring in other joints.

■ A warm bath or shower before exercising can help limber up joints, although some people prefer applying ice to the joints before exercising.

■ For improving muscle tone and overall conditioning, choose such activities as swimming, walking, biking, and low-impact aerobics.

■ If an exercise or a motion hurts, stop doing it. Pain is a sign that the activity is aggravating your condition.

■ Time your exercise for about half an hour after taking your regular medicine, when the medication is at peak effectiveness. But don't increase pain medication in order to exercise—suppressing pain excessively can lead to overuse injuries and damage inflamed joints.

■ Find a yoga teacher experienced in working with arthritics. The gentle stretching and toning exercises of yoga can increase mobility. You may also find that yoga relaxes you and helps relieve the stress that often accompanies a chronic ailment.

RELIEVING ARTHRITIS PAIN

■ Once your physician has diagnosed your condition, you will get anti-inflammatory medications, probably aspirin and prescription drugs, to suppress inflammation and alleviate pain. Be sure to take the recommended doses.

■ Alternative remedies include evening primrose and salmon-oil capsules. Consult your physician before trying treatments such as these.

■ Natural medicine therapies to relieve pain include acupuncture, the insertion of thin needles at strategic points on the body, and acupressure, which relies on thumb pressure in place of

EXERCISES FOR ARTHRITIC HANDS

The hands, knees, and other heavily used joints may become arthritic as you age. Do these exercises to keep hands limber.

Place a large rubber band *around your fingers. Open and close your hand against the resistance.*

Hold a tennis ball, *sponge, or piece of foam rubber in your palm. Squeeze your fingers around it, then release.*

Place your palm *on a table. Slowly raise and then lower each finger and your thumb, one at a time.*

Form a zero *with your index finger and thumb. Then stretch your fingers apart. Repeat, using all your fingers.*

needles (see "Alternative Medicine," page 324). Consult your physician about these.

■ Sleep in flannel pajamas under a down comforter, which is warmer and lighter than blankets.

■ To ease joint pain in the fingers and hands, wear nylon or spandex gloves. Wearing them to bed at night may reduce morning pain, swelling, and stiffness.

■ When joints feel hot and inflamed, place an ice pack on the affected joint for 20 minutes to alleviate the pain and regain flexibility.

■ Ask your doctor about taking vitamin supplements with prescription arthritis drugs. Some anti-inflammatory drugs, for example, boost your need for vitamin C.

■ Wear athletic shoes or other lightweight supportive shoes to protect feet and ankles.

Stress often produces a flare-up, so people with arthritis may want to enroll in a stress-reduction program. Learning to say no to unnecessary demands can help.

LIVING WITH DIABETES

Diligent self-care—including watching your diet, exercising regularly, and not smoking—is critical to maintaining normal blood sugar levels. So are regular visits to a diabetes specialist or clinic.

A MATTER OF CONTROL

Diabetes is a metabolic disorder in which the body cannot metabolize glucose, its major fuel. Type I, or insulin-dependent, diabetes is due to a lack of insulin, the hormone that controls glucose metabolism. Type II, or non–insulin-dependent, diabetes develops when the body cannot use insulin effectively. Symptoms include excessive urination, hunger, thirst, and fatigue.

■ If diabetes is diagnosed, follow your physician's instructions, especially when it comes to maintaining normal blood sugar levels. Keeping diabetes under control greatly reduces the risk of heart attacks, blindness, kidney failure, skin infections, and urinary tract infections, among other complications.

■ Home medical test kits let you measure your blood glucose levels, which are considered more reliable than urine tests. You prick your finger and apply a drop of blood to a sensitized color strip. Some kits offer a color chart that helps you determine your glucose level by comparing the strip to the chart, while other kits provide digital readouts.

■ Encourage children with diabetes to take responsibility for managing the disease. Even children as young as eight can learn to measure their blood sugar and inject themselves with insulin.

■ Frequent testing through the day shows the exact effect of insulin dosage, diet, and exercise on blood sugar levels: you can tell immediately if corrective action is needed.

■ Self-management is especially important during adolescence, when control over the disease is a key to building self-confidence. What's more, research shows that achieving control of diabetes early prevents complications.

■ Do not smoke. Smoking is a health risk for anyone, but for a person with diabetes, smoking increases the risk of blindness, heart disease, and circulatory problems.

■ When traveling by plane, order a special meal. If timing is important to your self-care regimen, find out when the food will be served so you can time your insulin shot.

■ Begin preparing for time-zone changes a couple of days before departure. For example, if you are traveling to a later time zone, go to sleep an hour earlier than usual the day before the trip. This will help adjust your body rhythms and will help you manage blood sugar levels.

■ Wear a medical identification bracelet or necklace at all times. This allows emergency medical personnel to respond correctly if they find you in a diabetic coma (see page 405).

■ Diabetes is the leading cause of adult blindness in Canada. See an ophthalmologist at least annually for an eye examination, more often if needed.

Medical advances now make it possible for most women with diabetes to have healthy babies. However, a diabetic woman should seek prenatal care from a specialist in high-risk pregnancies.

DIET AND DIABETES

Diet is a key factor in treating diabetes, but the rules differ according to the type of the disease. People with Type I diabetes must match their food intake to their insulin dosage, whereas cutting calories is the key to controlling most cases of Type II diabetes.

■ Maintain normal body weight for your height and stature. Although the predisposition to diabetes is genetic, excess body fat increases the likelihood of developing Type II diabetes. In fact, weight loss is the only treatment needed by most patients with Type II diabetes.

■ Eating low-fat, high-fiber, high-carbohydrate food is the key to dietary control of diabetes. This diet not only helps lower blood sugar but promotes weight loss without making you feel hungry.

■ Consult a dietitian referred by your hospital or doctor for an appropriate diet.

■ Eat four to six small meals a day rather than three larger ones. This helps maintain normal blood sugar levels over the course of the day.

■ Sugar is not the only sweetener that sends blood glucose soaring—corn syrup, honey, fructose, and many other sweeteners have the same effect. Check labels, and be wary of any ingredient that ends in "ose," which is the suffix for a simple carbohydrate, or sugar.

■ Drink in moderation, if at all. Alcohol can impair circulation, which is a problem for diabetics.

EXERCISE AND DIABETES

Exercise is particularly important for people with diabetes. Not only can it help in managing blood sugar levels, but it can also help prevent cardiovascular disease, which is often a complication of diabetes.

■ Check with your physician before starting a vigorous exercise regimen. Besides a physical examination, you may want to have an exercise-

tolerance test to determine a safe exercise level.

■ Ask your doctor's advice on the timing of meals and insulin injections. Exercise burns up excess sugar, and poor timing (for example, an insulin injection prior to exercise) can lead to dangerously low blood sugar.

Exercise speeds up insulin absorption. Inject pre-exercise insulin in an area that will not be intensely exercised. For example, if you are going to jog, inject yourself in the arm or the abdomen, rather than the leg.

PROPER FOOT CARE

The feet are especially vulnerable to diabetes complications because of reduced circulation and susceptibility to infection. Here are measures to protect your feet.

■ Inspect your feet carefully each day, especially when you exercise. Look for red or discolored skin, blisters, corns, calluses, and other signs of irritation or infection. Cracking, dryness, and such fungal infections as athlete's foot can also become troublesome.

■ Choose well-fitting cotton or wool socks or stockings. Avoid garters and other constricting leg wear.

■ Wear shoes and socks rather than sandals whenever possible.

■ When breaking in new shoes, wear them for just an hour or two at a time during the first week. Inspect your feet after each wearing. If you notice blisters or other

irritations, choose another style or type of shoe. If the irritated places do not heal in a few days, see your doctor.

■ Wash your feet in lukewarm water and a mild soap. Don't soak them for more than 10 minutes. Be sure to clean between the toes. Dry the feet carefully, blotting them with a soft towel.

■ Don't cut corns or calluses with a knife or razor. Instead, rub them gently with a fine (not coarse) emery board or pumice stone. Have a doctor check any redness or discoloration around a corn or callus for infection.

■ To improve circulation to your feet, gently massage them two or three times a day. Use moisturizing lotion or oil regularly to prevent dry skin.

■ Using nail clippers, clip toenails straight across and then smooth them with an emery board or file. Moisten the cuticles with oil.

■ Don't leave the doctor's office until he or she checks your feet.

If you have bad eyesight, have a friend, relative, or podiatrist inspect your feet for you. Some manicurists also have experience caring for the feet of people with diabetes.

COMMON CHILDHOOD PROBLEMS

Here's help for parents who want to blend medical knowledge with commonsense approaches to handling a child's illness, managing tantrums, and toilet training.

SURVIVING THE COLIC STAGE

Infant colic is defined as inconsolable crying that has no apparent cause and lasts anywhere from a few minutes to several hours. It usually begins in the third week or so of life, tapers off at about two months, and ends during the third month. Here are suggestions for preventing colic and soothing a colicky baby.

■ See your pediatrician to rule out an organic cause for the crying. Some babies are born with allergies to milk or other substances in infant formulas. If so, your doctor may suggest switching to a soy formula.

■ Don't assume that all crying in early infancy is colic. If the baby has a fever or other symptoms, he or she may have an ear infection or other disorder. Call the doctor.

■ Experiment with your baby's feeding schedule. Some babies drink too much too quickly, which causes gas and discomfort. Smaller, more frequent feedings may help.

■ Placing a lukewarm water bottle on the baby's abdomen may soothe him or her. So can sucking on a pacifier.

Some colicky babies are comforted by vibrations—place the baby in a car seat and take him or her for a car ride.

■ If you are breast-feeding, try nursing in a more soothing environment, such as a quiet, darkened room. If you are tense and nervous, practice deep breathing or another relaxation technique before breast-feeding. Some experts believe that colic develops when a baby is overstimulated or senses that the mother is tense.

■ If you are bottle-feeding, don't overheat the formula; instead, give it at room temperature or even on the cool side. Also, test the size of the nipple holes by filling the bottle with cold formula and turning it upside down. Without shaking, a drop of milk should drip out each second. If the holes are too small or too large, the baby is likely to swallow more air, leading to gas.

■ Burp the baby after each ounce of formula consumed or every two or three minutes while breast-feeding. Hold or prop the baby upright for 15 minutes after each feeding to prevent regurgitation.

■ Often a colic attack ends when the infant passes rectal gas or has a bowel movement. Sometimes the insertion of a thermometer into the baby's rectum will elicit gas or a bowel movement.

■ Have both parents take turns comforting the baby; now and then, find an alternative caregiver so you can both take a break.

■ Body contact and rhythmic or rocking motion often work wonders in soothing a wailing infant. Try carrying the baby in an infant carrier as you go about your household chores. Or lay the infant stomach down across your lap and rub his or her back.

CHICKEN POX

By adolescence, almost all children get chicken pox, a highly contagious viral disease. It rarely causes serious problems, but it makes many children very irritable and uncomfortable. A child is most contagious from the day before the rash appears until five days afterward.

■ To alleviate itching, bathe the child every few hours. Add a few tablespoons of baking soda or a cup of finely ground oatmeal to lukewarm water. (You can buy preground colloidal oatmeal at a pharmacy.) Pat dry, apply calamine lotion to the rash, and dress the child as lightly as possible.

■ Discourage the child from scratching. Clip fingernails short, and cover a baby's hands with cotton mittens or baby socks. To help prevent infection, wash the child's hands frequently with an antibacterial soap.

■ Use a saltwater gargle if the child develops mouth or throat blisters. Encourage him or her to drink extra fluids, such as apple juice or diluted grape juice, which soothe mouth sores and also prevent dehydration.

■ If itching is so intense that the child is unable to sleep, talk to your pediatrician about prescribing an anti histamine. This medication alleviates itching and also induces drowsiness.

■ Keeping the child in bed is usually not necessary, but isolate him or her from adults who have not had chicken pox, as well as from other children who have not yet had it. Provide pleasant activities, such as games, books, and music, to detract from the isolation and general discomfort.

Never give aspirin to a child with chicken pox or any other viral infection. In this setting, aspirin increases the risk of Reye's syndrome, a rare but potentially fatal disease affecting the liver and brain.

CROUP

The wheezing and tight, barking cough of croup are frightening to parents and child alike, but this common viral disease, which affects children chiefly between the ages of six months and three years,

seldom causes complications. Still, it bears watching and requires home treatment to calm the child and alleviate the coughing.

■ Keep the air as moist as possible. Put a cool-mist vaporizer in the child's bedroom. Do not add camphor or menthol; these aromatic oils can further irritate inflamed nose and throat tissues.

■ At the onset of an attack, turn the bathroom into a steam room by closing the

door and turning on the hot shower. Take the child into the steamy room. Assure the youngster that the steam will help him or her breathe easier. The coughing should subside within 30 minutes.

■ Reduce milk and milk products, substituting apple juice, broth, and frequent sips of water to help loosen mucus and prevent dehydration.

■ Crying can trigger a coughing spell. Spend extra time cuddling and comforting the child to prevent crying.

IMMUNIZATION SCHEDULE OF THE CANADIAN PAEDIATRIC SOCIETY

Age	DPT	Polio	Hepatitis B	Measles	Mumps	Rubella	HBCV*	Tetanus Diphtheria
Birth			✔					
2 months	✔	✔					✔	
4 months	✔	✔					✔	
6 months	✔	✔						
6–18 months				✔	✔	✔		
12–15 months				✔	✔	✔		
15 months				✔	✔	✔		
15–18 months	✔	✔					✔	
4–6 years	✔	✔						
11–12 years				✔	✔	✔		
14–16 years		✔						✔

* Haemophilus B conjugate vaccine, previously called Hib, is a new vaccine against *Haemophilus influenzae B* bacteria.

Tobacco smoke can turn croup into a medical emergency. Don't allow anyone to smoke in the house when a child has croup.

EAR INFECTIONS

Ear infections are second only to the common cold on the list of childhood ailments. Middle-ear infections, or otitis media, are the most common because a child's eustachian tube is small and narrow, allowing bacteria from the throat to travel into the middle ear. Although ear infections always require medical treatment, here are measures you can take to make the child more comfortable and to prevent future bouts.

■ Be alert for early signs of an infection, such as fussiness, fever, and tugging or rubbing an ear. Early treatment is important in preventing a ruptured eardrum and other complications.

■ To ease ear pain, apply a heating pad or warm washcloth to the affected ear. Make sure the heating pad is on a low setting, and don't let a child fall asleep with a heating pad in the bed or crib.

■ Don't apply eardrops or a cotton earplug unless instructed to do so by the child's doctor.

■ Encourage the child to sleep on the side opposite the affected ear, especially if the infection is in the outer ear. Pressure on the swollen ear canal increases pain.

■ Teach the proper nose-blowing techniques. Blowing too hard or constant sniffling can send bacteria into the eustachian tube, increasing the risk of an ear infection.

■ To prevent recurrent swimmer's ear, tilt the child's head to each side to allow water to drain from the ears after bathing or swimming. Use a hair dryer on a low setting to dry the ear canal.

■ If your child has recurrent ear infections, consider buying an otoscope so that you can look for inflammation and other signs of an infection yourself. Inexpensive models are available at medical supply houses and many pharmacies. Ask your pediatrician to instruct you in how to use the device.

■ To prevent milk from entering the eustachian tube, always feed an infant in an upright position, and don't allow a baby to fall asleep with a bottle.

Give the child the full course of antibiotics, even if all symptoms have disappeared. A follow-up visit to the doctor is important to make sure that the eardrum is clear of pus and fluid.

TAMING TEMPER TANTRUMS

At some point, even the most easygoing child is likely to throw a temper tantrum; for others, tantrums are a regular, almost predictable response to any frustration. Remember, tantrums are not a reflection of poor parenting skills; instead, they are part of normal development. Here are suggestions for handling them with equanimity.

■ Heed early-warning signs. Take care to notice when your toddler is fatigued, hungry, or overwhelmed. Encourage the child to switch to a more restful activity, such as looking at a book.

■ Make sure that toys are appropriate to the child's age, so that he or she will not be overwhelmed or bored.

■ Offer simple choices rather than directives that may invite defiance. For example, ask the child if he or she wants oatmeal or cold cereal for breakfast, or would prefer to wear sneakers or sandals. This approach allows a child to retain some control and still do what you want.

■ Include the child in family conversations. Toddlers often feel frustrated and left out when adults talk only to each other.

■ Head off problems with advance planning. If, for example, you plan to shop at a store that sells every child's favorite designer sneakers, warn your child in advance that you will not splurge on such footwear.

■ Be consistent. If your child realizes that "no" means "no," he or she is less likely to try manipulating you with an outburst of temper and tears.

■ If a child repeatedly whines before launching a tantrum, set aside a "whining chair," stool, or corner. Whenever the child starts to whine, have him or her sit in the designated spot until the episode resolves itself.

■ During a tantrum, first try to ignore the outburst. Though you instinctively want to offer physical comfort, experts say it's better to go about your normal activities unless the child is in danger of physically harming himself.

■ Refrain from spanking or other physical punishment. If a time-out is needed, take the youngster to a quiet room where he or she can regain composure.

■ When a toddler picks a public place, such as the supermarket, to throw a tantrum, quietly and calmly lead the child to a private place until the emotional storm is over.

■ Don't threaten or bribe the child to gain silence or compliance. Such actions establish patterns that are hard for both of you to break.

■ Offer the child a choice, such as, "If you quiet down, we can continue shopping for the food we need or else we can return to the car and you can cry there."

. . . .

The tantrum stage seldom lasts more than a few months. However, if tantrums persist, seek help from a child or family therapist.

. . . .

TOILET TRAINING

Somewhere between 18 months and 3 years of age, your toddler is ready to be toilet trained. Patience and time are critical factors in passing this important hurdle in child development.

■ Don't start toilet training too early. Wait until the child starts referring to bowel movements or urination while doing one or both of them. This is an indication that he or she has developed some understanding of bodily functions and has the necessary bladder and sphincter control.

■ Approach toilet training in stages. Begin by putting a potty-chair in the bathroom or playroom, and answer any questions about it. Let the child throw toilet paper into the potty and sit on it as much as he or she wants. If the toddler seems motivated and interested, suggest that he or she give it a try.

■ Don't expect immediate results, and don't encourage the child to spend an inordinate amount of time on the potty. You might, however, spend a few minutes reading to or chatting with the child; this helps relax the sphincter muscles to prompt a bowel movement.

■ Focus first on gaining daytime bowel control before bladder control. Refrain from criticizing accidents, but be sure to praise successes. Show the toddler the bowel movement or urine, but don't be overly eager to flush it away in the child's presence. Young children are likely to consider their feces an extension of themselves, and many are fearful of being sucked down the drain.

■ Switch to training pants when your toddler begins to stay dry for several hours at a time. Bedtime diapers may still be needed, however, because night control takes longer. In fact, occasional episodes of bed-wetting may persist long after toilet training has been achieved.

■ A toilet-trained youngster may resort to stool holding for many reasons. If your child repeatedly refuses to go to the bathroom, consult your pediatrician. There may be a physical problem, such as an anal fissure, that is discouraging normal bowel movements.

FEMALE AND MALE PHYSICAL ILLS

Most women and men experience some problem related to their sexual function or their reproductive and urinary tracts. Many such conditions are amenable to treatment.

PERIOD PROBLEMS

Although menstruation is a perfectly normal function, it produces many symptoms that can disrupt a woman's life. Here are suggestions for dealing with them.

■ Increase exercise to relieve fluid retention, depression, and other premenstrual symptoms. Exercise speeds up body metabolism and increases sweating and urination, alleviating abdominal bloating and swelling.
■ Try changing your diet to reduce premenstrual symptoms. Cut down on salt to help ease fluid retention. Watermelon, cucumbers, and parsley act as diuretics and may reduce bloating. Avoiding caffeine may help relieve breast discomfort and anxiety. Turn to starchy foods—

such as pasta, potatoes, and breads—to help satisfy the craving for sweets that many women experience.
■ Abstain from alcohol during your premenstrual phase. Premenstrual hormonal and metabolic changes lower your tolerance to alcohol.
■ Ask your doctor about high-dose calcium supplements. Some women taking 1,300 milligrams of calcium daily report fewer mood swings and less fluid retention before their periods. Magnesium and vitamin B_6 may also help.
■ To relieve menstrual cramps, take ibuprofen or aspirin rather than acetaminophen. Generic products are just as effective as the more costly brands for menstrual cramps.
■ Keep warm, especially in winter. Cold weather may worsen menstrual cramps. A hot water bottle or heating pad on the abdomen helps relieve the pain. Add aromatic herbs to a warm bath to make it even more relaxing.
■ Consider switching to sanitary pads from tampons. Some women report fewer cramps when using pads. Be sure to change pads frequently to prevent urinary tract infections and vaginitis.
■ Experiment with herbal teas. For example, raspberry-leaf tea is said to help relax the uterine muscles and relieve menstrual cramps.

See a doctor if your menstrual cramps become more severe in the latter days of a period. They may be due to endometriosis, the abnormal development of uterine tissue elsewhere in the pelvic cavity.

VAGINITIS

At some time, most women experience vaginitis, which is characterized by intense itching and a vaginal discharge that may have an unpleasant odor.
■ If this is your first case of vaginitis, see a doctor. Although yeast infections are the most common type, other organisms also cause vaginitis, and effective treatment requires an accurate diagnosis.
■ If you are sure you have a recurrent yeast infection, try the anti-yeast preparations available over the counter. If one course of the medication does not relieve your symptoms, see a doctor; you may have some other condition.
■ When you first notice symptoms, try douching with a mixture of one to three tablespoons vinegar in one quart of water. Although regular douching is not recommended, it can help clear the vaginal tract of excess bacteria. However, don't douche or take

a tub bath for 24 hours before seeing a gynecologist.

■ Antibiotic therapy often kills the vaginal bacteria that keep yeast in check. When taking antibiotics, eat yogurt that has live *Lactobacillus acidophilus* culture, which promotes the regrowth of beneficial bacteria and restores the balance of vaginal organisms.

■ Try inserting lactobacillus capsules or granules directly into the vagina. This is more effective than inserting plain yogurt, which is sometimes recommended. Capsules and powder are available at health food stores and pharmacies.

■ To remove yeast spores, wash a diaphragm or cervical cap in soapy water, rinse thoroughly, and make sure it is dry before putting it away. If you suffer a recurrent bout of vaginitis, replace the diaphragm or cap.

■ Wear loose-fitting, white cotton underwear. To kill yeast spores, wash underclothes in hot water with chlorine bleach. If the bleach irritates your skin, placing freshly washed underwear in a microwave oven set on high for 30 seconds will also kill any remaining spores.

MENOPAUSE

Menopause marks the end of menstruation and a woman's reproductive years. The age when it occurs varies, but by their late forties, most women have irregular periods, hot flashes, and other symptoms. By age 55, virtually all women have completed menopause.

■ When you first experience the menstrual changes that herald the onset of menopause, see your gynecologist to confirm that the symptoms are not related to some other medical problem.

■ To prevent or reduce hot flashes, drink plenty of fluids, including water and fruit juice. Limit your intake of spicy foods, caffeine, and alcohol— they can actually increase the frequency of hot flashes.

■ Maintain the room temperature at 20°C (68°F) or lower. Dress in layers of light clothing that are easy to remove.

■ To help cool off during a hot flash, keep a fan nearby. Close your eyes and imagine being at the seashore in autumn or on a high mountain, feeling the wind on your face. Slow, deep breathing may also help.

■ The lack of estrogen after menopause promotes osteoporosis, a thinning of the bones. To help prevent bone loss, increase your consumption of high-calcium foods, such as skim milk, yogurt, and green, leafy vegetables. Regular weight-bearing exercise, such as running and walking, may prevent bone loss.

■ Talk to your doctor about estrogen replacement therapy.

Although it is still somewhat controversial, an increasing number of doctors advocate estrogen therapy, especially for those at high risk of osteoporosis. These include thin, small-boned women of Northern European extraction, smokers, and women who enter menopause early, naturally or from a hysterectomy.

Don't become unduly alarmed by a modest weight gain during menopause. The added body fat may actually protect against osteoporosis because androgens, male hormones produced by the adrenal glands, are converted to estrogen by fat cells.

BREAST CANCER

Breast cancer is the most common female malignancy, and the leading cause of cancer death in women. Still, most breast cancers are curable if they are detected and treated while the tumor is small and confined to the breast.

■ See a doctor as soon as possible if you develop any of the following: a new breast lump or any lump or thickening that persists through a menstrual cycle; any change in breast contour or symmetry; skin dimpling, reddening, or pitting; and a nipple discharge, scaling, or bleeding.

■ Be diligent about monthly breast self-examination (see "Examinations and Tests," page 300). In addition, have a doctor examine your breasts annually. The National Cancer

Institute recommends mammography every two years after age 50. Younger women at high risk need more frequent examinations. Mammography can detect tumors that are too small to be felt.

■ If cancer is diagnosed, review the treatment options. These range from a lumpectomy, which removes only the tumor, followed by radiation therapy, to a mastectomy, the removal of all or part of a breast, combined with radiation and chemotherapy. If in doubt, seek a second opinion from a specialist at a cancer center or teaching hospital.

■ Consider joining a support group, such as Reach to Recovery. Every province has one. Ask your doctor or hospital, or the Cancer Information Service, to request that a volunteer visit you while you are still in the hospital. These trained volunteers have had breast cancer themselves and can offer practical advice as well as a temporary breast prosthesis to wear when you go home from the hospital.

Don't assume that any lump you find is cancerous—the vast majority turn out to be benign. In fact, most breast lumps are cysts that disappear completely when a doctor uses a hollow needle to withdraw fluid.

URINARY TRACT INFECTIONS

Both men and women can contract urinary tract infections, commonly called cystitis, but women are much more vulnerable than men because of their short urethra, the tube that carries urine from the body, and the close proximity of the urethral opening to the vagina and anus, which harbor bacteria.

■ Be alert for early symptoms: frequent urge to urinate, pain or burning during urination, scant urine that sometimes contains blood or pus, and possible pain in the pubic area.

■ Increase your intake of fluids, especially water and cranberry juice, to about 10 or more glasses a day. The extra liquid helps wash bacteria from the bladder. Although experts disagree about the value of cranberry juice, many doctors recommend it to prevent recurring cystitis, and many people plagued by cystitis are convinced it works.

■ To relieve cystitis pain, drink a glass of water containing a teaspoon of baking soda. However, don't use this treatment if you have high blood pressure (baking soda is high in sodium) or if you are drinking cranberry juice (baking soda cancels out the benefits of cranberry juice).

■ Pay attention to personal hygiene. Use a mild soap and water to keep the vagina and anus clean. Wipe from front to back to prevent transporting bacteria around the anus or vagina to the urethra.

■ If the symptoms persist or worsen, see a physician for antibiotics. To eradicate bacteria, take the full course, even if your symptoms disappear within a few days.

■ A diaphragm can press against the bladder, increasing the risk of cystitis. Try another form of birth control or ask your doctor about being fitted with a smaller diaphragm.

■ After menopause, many women experience increased urinary urgency and continence problems. See a urologist; special exercises and medication may help. If not, surgery often restores urinary control.

Sexual activity promotes cystitis, especially in women. To prevent recurrent infections, urinate before sexual activity. Afterward, drink a glass of water, wait for the bladder to fill, and urinate again.

MALE URINARY PROBLEMS

Urination problems in men over the age of 50 usually indicate an enlarged prostate, also known as benign prostatic hypertrophy. Symptoms include frequent, urgent urination, night and day, and delayed or interrupted stream. An enlarged prostate gland is not serious in itself, but difficulty emptying the bladder may lead to urinary tract infections and sometimes even damage to the kidneys. The following steps can help ease the symptoms of an enlarged prostate.

■ Do not put off urinating. This can aggravate symptoms.

■ Try to empty your bladder each time you urinate, even if it takes several minutes.

■ Cut down on caffeine and alcohol, which stimulate urination. Drink plenty of fluids during the day but reduce intake in the evening to avoid waking to urinate.

■ Certain medications can exacerbate urinary problems. Avoid antihistamines and decongestants. Ask your doctor if any antispasmodics, antidepressants, diuretics, or tranquilizers he or she prescribed could be causing the trouble.

■ Although surgery was once the most common treatment for enlarged prostate, there are now medications that may alleviate the symptoms or the problem. Consult your doctor.

PROSTATE CANCER

Prostate cancer is the most common male malignancy. About half of all men over 50 are believed to have cancerous cells in their prostate glands, but most will not experience symptoms or spread of the cancer, because, unlike other cancers, prostate tumors tend to grow very slowly and most do not cause problems. However, those cancers that grow do so rapidly and spread quickly, explaining why prostate cancer is the second leading cause of cancer deaths among men.

■ After age 40, all men should undergo an annual digital rec-

tal examination. See your doctor promptly if you develop warning signs, such as difficulty in urinating, blood in the urine, or pain in the lower back, pelvis, or upper thighs.

■ Many doctors recommend that all men over age 50 have an annual blood test to screen for possible prostate cancer. Before undergoing this test, talk to your doctor about its ramifications. The test detects prostate specific antigen (PSA), a substance that is elevated in prostate cancer. But benign prostate enlargement and inflammation also raise PSA levels, resulting in false-positive results.

■ If prostate cancer is diagnosed, talk to your doctor about surgical options. New procedures are less likely to cause impotence, incontinence, and other complications. Also consider going to a support group such as Us Too, for prostate cancer victims.

■ A normal reading on a prostate-specific-antigen test does not rule out prostate cancer. About 40 percent of men with prostate cancer have normal PSA levels.

IMPOTENCE

■ There is no age limit on sexuality. A healthy man can remain sexually active well into his nineties. Still, impotence is a common, often curable problem that increases with age.

■ An occasional episode of im-

potence is usually nothing to worry about. Stress, physical exhaustion, temporary illness, and many other factors can influence sexual performance.

■ If stress or another psychological problem seems to be implicated, psychotherapy may help. Also, working with your partner, you may be able to use "sensate focus" exercises to regain sexual function. Developed by the noted sex therapists Dr. William Masters and Virginia Johnson, these exercises involve massage, touching, and other sensual activities. The goal is to achieve arousal without feeling pressured to engage in sexual intercourse.

■ Talk to your doctor if you are on medication. Many drugs—especially those prescribed for high blood pressure, ulcers, migraines and other headaches, and depression—can cause impotence. Often, lowering the dosage or changing prescriptions solves the problem. You may also want to have a clinical examination to rule out any physical disorder.

■ Review your drinking habits. Alcohol has been implicated in cases of impotence. (So, too, have marijuana and cocaine.)

THE SIDE EFFECTS OF CANCER TREATMENT

Although treatment of cancer can certainly pay off, it often makes the patient feel ill. Fortunately, the effects usually stop when the treatment is over. Meanwhile, many effects can be minimized.

NAUSEA AND VOMITING

Potent anticancer drugs and radiation treatments commonly cause nausea and vomiting. You may want to try the following strategies, which have worked for many patients.

■ Avoid fatty, sweet, and spicy foods. A clear, liquid diet or bland foods—such as apple sauce, cottage cheese, and custard—are often tolerated. Sour foods, such as pickles and lemon sherbet, can reduce nausea, as can a little nutmeg sprinkled over bland food.

■ Chemotherapy will sometimes produce an unpleasant metallic taste in the mouth; try overcoming it with a mint or a piece of sour candy. Rinse with a flavored mouthwash before eating.

■ Strong food odors can provoke nausea. If possible, the patient should stay out of the kitchen when food is being prepared, and eat foods served cold or at room temperature, which renders foods less odorous.

■ Vary meal patterns to find one that minimizes nausea. Some patients avoid food and drink for an hour or two before and after treatments; others have a large meal three or four hours before, and then liquids or light meals the rest of the day. Putting off chemotherapy until the evening may also help.

■ Try the distraction of music, a conversation, or a movie. This is especially effective in countering the anticipatory nausea that many patients experience before a treatment.

MOUTH AND SKIN PROBLEMS

■ Suck on sour sugarless candy or chew on sugar-free gum to stimulate saliva flow.

■ Lubricate lips with cocoa butter or petroleum jelly.

■ To alleviate dry skin and inflammation from radiation therapy, gently apply skin cream or lotion containing vitamins A, D, and E.

■ Chemotherapy and radiation increase the skin's sensitivity to sunlight. Wear protective clothing and a sunscreen with an SPF of 15 or higher when in the sun.

■ To combat skin itchiness, use a mild cortisone spray or cream, but refrain from scratching or massaging the skin, which can result in increased skin inflammation and peeling.

■ Use a humidifier to keep the air moist and alleviate dryness of the nasal membranes. Be sure to clean the humidifier's filter frequently to reduce the risk of airborne infection.

Mouth sores and inflamed mucous membranes lining the esophagus can cause swallowing problems. Coat inflamed membranes by drinking milk or eating yogurt at the beginning of a meal, or switch to pureed foods. Drink nonirritating liquids, such as apple juice or peach nectar.

BLEEDING PROBLEMS

Chemotherapy, radiation treatments, and sometimes the cancer itself can suppress clotting and cause bleeding problems, resulting in anemia. Here are some ways to minimize bleeding.

■ Avoid any activity that puts pressure on a part of the body. Wear loose-fitting clothing, and shift positions often when in bed or sitting down.

■ To avoid nicks and cuts, use an electric razor for shaving and an emery board to file nails instead of trimming.

■ Substitute acetaminophen

for aspirin or ibuprofen, painkillers that also increase bleeding tendencies.

■ Constipation and straining can cause rectal bleeding. Your doctor may recommend increased fiber and fluid intake. A stool softener may be needed, but avoid strong laxatives and enemas.

■ Mucous membranes lining the mouth, airways, and intestines are especially vulnerable to bleeding. Drink at least 8 to 10 glasses of fluid a day to prevent drying of the membranes. Eat soft, bland foods, avoiding hard foods like pretzels and potato chips that can cut your gums.

■ Use a soft-bristle toothbrush and floss carefully to avoid gum irritation. If even this causes bleeding gums, clean the teeth with a sponge-tipped applicator or a gauze pad dipped in salt water.

Premenopausal women may experience exceptionally heavy menstrual periods during cancer chemotherapy. This blood loss can be minimized by taking oral contraceptives during chemotherapy—with your doctor's approval.

HAIR LOSS

Balding may seem trivial compared to the other effects of cancer, but to many patients, especially women, hair loss is one of the most traumatic aspects of treatment. Although loss is often inevitable, it sometimes can be minimized by these tactics.

■ Plan ahead. Consider buying a wig and even wearing it occasionally before balding begins. Alternatively, invest in a variety of stylish turbans and scarves to mask the hair loss.

■ Reduce stress on hair. Have it cut in a short, manageable style before beginning treatment. Avoid dyes, perming, excessive shampooing and brushing, hair dryers, electric curlers, and elastic bands.

■ When sleeping, wear a hairnet and use a satin pillowcase to decrease hair tangles.

■ Try not to despair over hair loss during chemotherapy. The hair eventually grows back, sometimes thicker and a different color than before. For example, gray hair may grow back in its original color.

FIGHTING WEIGHT LOSS

Cancer itself reduces appetite and causes weight loss, and the side effects of treatment compound the problem. Still, it is important to maintain weight and good nutrition.

■ Eat several small meals during the day. Do not limit yourself to three main meals. A few bites of the right foods or a few sips of the right liquids every hour or so can help you get more protein and calories.

■ Increase protein intake. The body needs extra protein to repair itself. Many cancer patients find they can no longer tolerate red meat because of an unpleasant taste. Milk, cheese, eggs, fish, and poultry are high-protein alternatives. A combination of grains and legumes also provides complete protein.

■ Enrich foods whenever possible. Make double-strength milk by mixing dry skim milk with milk instead of water. For even more nutrition, add this mixture to breakfast drinks. Also use double-strength milk to make custards, milk shakes, and sauces.

■ Snack on nutritious, high-calorie foods, such as cheese and whole-grain crackers.

■ Add beans, poultry, seafood, or other high-protein foods to your salads.

■ Use herbs to make foods tastier. For example, ginger perks up soups and sauces.

■ Make meals look more appetizing with an appealing presentation. Place a bud vase with a fresh flower on a table or tray and arrange food attractively on a pretty plate.

■ Patients suffering from bouts of diarrhea may lose vital nutrients. Increase your intake of foods and liquids that contain sodium and potassium, which are often lost during diarrhea.

■ If the patient is losing weight, talk to the doctor about special nutrition supplements. Patients with severe diarrhea, nausea, and vomiting may require intravenous feeding, which can be administered at home with the help of a nutrition therapist.

MENTAL HEALTH

Everyone experiences emotional ups and downs. But when anxiety, depression, insomnia, and other psychological problems interfere with day-to-day life, it's time to take action.

CONQUERING INSOMNIA

Although some illnesses and medications cause insomnia, most sleep problems can be traced to anxiety, depression, or other emotional concerns.

■ If worries or disturbing thoughts preclude restful sleep, teach yourself to switch them off. Meditation, relaxation exercises, and imagery can take your mind off pressing problems and induce sleep. Or try a variation of the age-old counting-sheep remedy. For example, go through the alphabet, naming a city or country for each letter. Chances are you'll fall asleep before reaching the tough Q's or X's.

■ Follow a bedtime routine. When you feel sleepy, start your sequence of checking locked doors, brushing your teeth, putting on night-clothes, and getting into bed. After a while, the body begins to associate these activities with going to sleep.

■ Set your alarm for the same time each morning, regardless of what time you went to bed or how well you slept. Avoid napping during the day. By nighttime, you'll be more than ready to sleep.

■ Regular physical activity promotes sleep, but avoid working out in the late evening. Instead, exercise before dinner—you'll eat less and sleep better.

■ Don't stay in the bed for more than 15 minutes if you haven't fallen asleep. Get up and read a good (but not too engrossing) book. Return to bed when you feel sleepy.

■ Avoid reading, watching TV, or eating in bed—save the bed for sleeping and love-making only.

■ As much as possible, avoid late-day use of substances that can cause insomnia. These include alcohol, caffeine, antidepressants, bronchodilator asthma medications, blood pressure medications, decongestants, and diuretics.

■ Relax in a warm bath before going to bed. Try adding a few drops of lavender, marjoram, or other aromatic oils, which aromatherapists recommend to induce sleep.

■ Foods high in the amino acid tryptophan promote sleep. Try bedtime snacks of yogurt, almonds, dates, dried figs, or bananas. A glass of milk or chamomile tea may also help.

Perhaps you need less sleep than other people. To determine your sleep needs, go to bed at the same time each night for a week. Each morning, get up spontaneously, without an alarm clock. Add up the hours you slept, and divide by seven. That's your normal night's sleep.

SEEKING HELP FOR DEPRESSION

Clinical depression is an illness, not a state of mind. Unlike the feelings of sadness accompanying a major loss, such as the death of a loved one or loss of a job, clinical depression is all-pervasive, unrelieved, and disruptive of family life, work, and normal routines.

■ Recognize the symptoms of depression: persistent feelings of sadness, anxiety, irritability, worthlessness or hopelessness; loss of interest in ordinarily pleasurable activities; fatigue and sleep disturbances; change in appetite or significant weight change; difficulty concentrating and making decisions; crying, and thoughts of suicide or dying. If you experience four or more of these symptoms for two weeks, seek treatment.

■ When self-treatment does not help ease feelings of depression, seek help first from your family physician. Depression can be a symptom of several different disorders, including thyroid disease. A thorough examination and a discussion of other symptoms should help the doctor determine whether the depression is due to an underlying disorder.

■ If an organic cause for your depression cannot be found, ask for referral to a psychiatrist or mental health clinic. Although many cases of depression clear up in about six months on their own, treatment with antidepressant medication speeds recovery and reduces the chances of recurrence.

■ A combination of antidepressant medication and psychiatry is more effective than either one alone. But don't expect immediate results; recovery from clinical depression takes time. Some of the new antidepressant medications start to work in two to three weeks, but older ones may take six weeks or longer. Psychotherapy usually takes 10 to 20 weeks before much improvement occurs.

The risk of suicide actually increases during the early stages of recovery from depression. Patients who were unable to make decisions while in the depths of depression can now do so, but they may not have recovered enough to feel that life is worthwhile.

OVERCOMING THE BLUES

Although serious clinical depression requires medical treatment, mild cases may improve with self-care. Here are a few mood-lifting tactics.

■ Listen to music or read a poem that reminds you of happier times. Sometimes an old movie (Fred Astaire and Ginger Rogers flicks are a good choice), an amusing book, or a favorite song brings back a smile.

■ Keep yourself busy, especially around the holidays, when many people feel sad. Schedule a visit with friends, a trip to a museum, a night at the movies, or a day at a shopping mall.

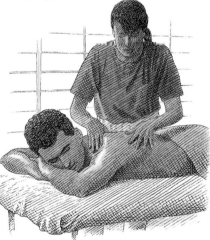

■ Treat yourself to a massage with a scented oil—geranium, orange, and broom are said to fight depression.

■ Exercise prompts the brain to release endorphins, natural mood elevators. Psychiatrists routinely recommend an exercise regimen as part of depression treatment.

■ Put the blues to work for you. Feeling down-in-the-dumps serves a worthy purpose if it causes you to exam-

ine what's bothering you. Then, when you understand the problem, you are better able to formulate a solution.

■ Many medications, including drugs commonly prescribed for heart disease, contribute to depression. Ask your doctor or pharmacist if any of the drugs you are taking cause depression. If so, ask for an alternative medicine. Before starting a new drug, talk to your doctor about your tendency to be depressed—this may influence his or her choice of medication.

■ Volunteer to help out at a local community organization. Helping a child learn to read or talking with an elderly person can help you feel positive about yourself and take your mind off your own problems.

■ Do something you've always dreamed of. Plan a trip to an exotic place, or learn a new language or hobby. New skills and challenges help increase self-esteem.

THE WINTER BLUES

Winter depression is often due to seasonal affective disorder (SAD), a consequence of the shortened days of bright sunlight. People who live in northern climates are especially vulnerable to SAD.

■ Let in the light. Remove dark or heavy drapes, paint walls white or yellow, and move your desk or favorite chair to the brightest part of the room.

■ Plan a winter trip to a warm, sunny place.

■ Take a long walk. Some studies have found that an

hour-long morning walk alleviates SAD symptoms in 50 percent of patients. Exercising outdoors—even on a cloudy day—seems to help.

■ Visit a greenhouse at a local botanical garden or garden shop. The warmth, brightness, and beautiful flowers are natural mood lifters.

● ●

Light therapy is now the preferred treatment for SAD that does not respond to self-help measures. Sitting under extremely bright lights (from 2,500 to 10,000 lux—5 to 20 times the level of ordinary artificial light) between 30 minutes and 2 hours a day can alleviate symptoms in just a few days.

● ●

ANXIETY AND PANIC ATTACKS

Anxiety and fear often lead to panic attacks, frightening episodes that strike out of the blue and are often mistaken for a heart attack. Symptoms include shortness of breath, chest pains, dizziness or faintness, and an overwhelming fear and sense of impending doom.

■ Break the anxiety-producing task into manageable steps. If you have a fear of driving, start by just sitting in the driver's seat. The next day, turn on the motor. On the third day, move the car to the end of the driveway. Each day thereafter, increase the distance you drive until you overcome the fear.

■ The rapid, shallow breathing of a panic attack changes the body's balance of oxygen and carbon dioxide, producing dizziness and other symptoms. Restore the balance by breathing into a paper bag to reduce the blood oxygen level and increase carbon dioxide.

■ Use relaxation exercises and visualization techniques to overcome fear of an activity. For example, if you have a fear of flying, take a few slow, deep breaths, close your eyes, and imagine yourself at the airport—waving good-bye to your friends, approaching the gate, and so forth. Concentrate on a happy landing. If you start to picture a negative outcome, stop the visualization, repeat the relaxation exercises, and try again.

■ Change the tapes that you play in your mind. Instead of telling yourself "I can't speak to a group," switch to "I have valuable knowledge to share."

■ Don't resort to alcohol or nicotine to calm jittery nerves. Any benefit from these substances is short-lived, and both increase, rather than ease, feelings of anxiety.

● ●

Don't automatically assume that chest pains and other symptoms are due to anxiety and a panic attack—a heart attack produces similar symptoms. If in doubt, seek emergency care to rule out a heart attack.

● ●

HELPING A LOVED ONE

Helping a person with a mental disorder demands patience and persistence, but the knowledge that you are making a difference can be very satisfying.

■ Don't expect much in the way of thanks or cooperation. Instead, realize that your loved one is suffering from an illness, rather than being deliberately difficult.

■ Urge the person to get help. Obtain names of some qualified professionals who treat depression from your primary-care physician, a nearby hospital, or a mental illness hotline. Then work to persuade the person to seek help.

■ Assist with treatment where appropriate. Family members and friends can help by supplying the physician or other practitioner with observations about the effectiveness of medications, changes in the patient's behavior, and eating and sleeping habits.

■ Let the person know you are available for outings—perhaps a picnic in the park, a shopping excursion, or an evening at a concert. Just having someone to be with and to talk to can help a person with mental illness immeasurably.

PET THERAPY

"Thanks to Giacomo, I have my health again—and the pure joy of his companionship."
—Shawn Stephen Riley

• • • • • • •

Shawn Stephen Riley, a writer, fondly remembers how he became involved with pet therapy. It was a beautiful fall day in 1988, and, although he was still recovering from a bone marrow transplant 13 months earlier, his doctor had just given him the go-ahead to get a kitten. An ad in the local paper read, "We're three little kittens, but only one of us has mittens."

Riley recalls, "When my wife and I arrived at the farm, I fell head over heels in love with one of the males, and we named him Giacomo after a character in Danny Kaye's movie *The Court Jester*." Six months later, Riley's wife filed for divorce. "Giacomo proved to be a source of constancy during this rough spot in my life," Riley says. "Thanks to Giacomo, I recovered completely from the bone marrow transplant and the divorce."

Riley is not alone in enjoying the benefits of pet therapy. Dr. Erika Friedmann, a psychiatrist at the University of Pennsylvania, was one of the first medical researchers to document the effects of pet therapy. She studied 96 patients who had been hospitalized with heart disease and found that pet ownership increased the chances of survival even more than having a spouse or supportive family. Only 3 of the 53 pet owners died in the year following hospitalization, compared with 11 deaths among the 39 who did not have animals.

Giacomo brought comfort and friendship to his owner at a critical time.

Impressive results. In a more recent study, cardiologists gathered data on 8,000 men and women with similar lifestyles. When the pet owners were compared to those without pets, the researchers found some amazing differences. All of the subjects over age 40 who had pets had lower blood pressure than those without pets, and the men in the study aged 30 to 60 who had pets also had lower cholesterol levels.

Doctors, social workers, educators, and mental health workers are among the growing number of professionals who are using pet therapy. Many nursing homes now have resident pets; others regularly bring animals in for lonely and withdrawn patients to cuddle. Autistic and other developmentally handicapped children also seem to benefit from interacting with animals.

Horses too. Cats and dogs are the animals used most often in pet therapy, but some programs employ unusual or large animals. The Human-Animal Bond Association of Canada offers Visits that Heal, and Therapeutic Riding, as well as Hearing-Ear Dogs. The Lanark County Therapeutic Riding Association specializes in therapeutic horseback riding. Terri Kramer, a physical therapist who coordinates the equestrian-therapy program between the Thorncroft Equestrian Center and the Bryn Mawr Rehabilitation Hospital in Malvern, Pennsylvania, explains its success: "The horse's gait is three-dimensional, just like our own, so it is the best thing we can find to mimic walking."

Laura Hervey, a quadriplegic, is one of the most severely impaired riders at Thorncroft. After two years of riding lessons, the 30-year-old has made a great stride by learning to lift her right leg. Just as important, she has found a new source of joy. "I love to ride," she says. ❏

DEALING WITH ADDICTION

Alcohol, drug, and nicotine addictions are major causes of illness and premature death. Here are some ways to start breaking the grip of addiction.

HELPING AN ALCOHOLIC

Although alcoholism is a disease, many people, including some doctors, still view it as a moral issue. Therefore, seek out a doctor experienced in treating alcoholism.

■ Educate yourself about the nature of addiction so that you will be able to deal with the behavior of someone close to you. Alcoholics or Narcotics Anonymous, Al-Anon, and the Addiction Research Foundation are good information sources.

■ If an alcoholic can't go to work or gets sick because of drinking, don't cover up for him or her. Only when alcoholics are forced to deal with the consequences of their drinking will they be able to do something about it.

■ Don't let hurtful, offensive, or embarrassing actions go unheeded. When the person is sober, tell him or her what happened. Talk objectively about the offensive behavior; speak subjectively only about how you felt. Focus on the behavior, not on the personality.

. . . .

Members of Al-Anon, a self-help organization for friends and families of alcoholics, say that the only difference between a problem drinker and an alcoholic is that a problem drinker is someone you love.

. . . .

■ Let the person know you are worried about his or her alcohol use. Choose a time when the person is sober, and perhaps regretting his or her actions. Don't be surprised if you get an angry response or an attempt to turn the argument back on you. Denial is part of the disease.

THE ROAD TO RECOVERY

■ Make use of employee-assistance programs, which many large companies offer. Under federal law, employers cannot discriminate against a worker for alcohol or drug use if the employee voluntarily stops such behavior and seeks counseling or treatment.

■ Enlist the support of friends and family members. They have probably been worried about you and will gladly help with your recovery.

■ Attend an Alcoholics Anonymous meeting or other self-help groups. Meetings are free, and both alcoholics and nonalcoholics are welcome at open meetings. People will talk about how they started their own road to recovery and can provide many helpful suggestions to others.

■ Detoxification from long-term alcoholism usually requires medical supervision in an in-patient clinic or other facility to prevent delirium tremens and other serious withdrawal symptoms. Drugs are usually given to help the alcoholic through detoxification. Once alcohol is out of the system, treatment of the addiction can begin.

QUITTING SMOKING

Nicotine is by far our number one addictive substance, and smoking is the leading cause of premature death in Canada. Try these stop-smoking strategies.

■ Make a list of the benefits of stopping smoking: money saved, fresher breath, less coughing, fewer headaches and stomachaches, more energy, and reduced risks of a heart attack, stroke, cancer, gum disease, and other ailments. Keep this list handy. Review it whenever you feel the urge to smoke.

■ Choose a day to quit. Find a time when you will feel relaxed, such as during a vacation. Tell your friends and co-workers of your plan and ask for their help.

■ Take note of your smoking habits. Do you especially look forward to the first cigarette of the day, or do you smoke only in the afternoons? Are there situations in which you would feel uncomfortable not smoking? Do you smoke when you need to relax or because it gives you a lift? Armed with these observations, come up with substitutions.

■ If you smoke when you're depressed, call a friend or work out instead of lighting up. If you enjoy the routine of smoking, find another, healthier routine, such as going to the water fountain or practicing breathing exercises.

■ Prepare to quit by cutting down on cigarettes and nicotine. Buy only one pack at a time to make smoking less convenient. Switch to a low-nicotine brand that doesn't taste as good as your regular brand. The week before your anticipated quit date, halve the number of cigarettes you smoke and halve the number again two days later.

■ Prepare healthful snacks, such as celery, carrot sticks, or fresh fruit, to quell cravings.

■ On the day you quit, throw away all remaining cigarettes and discard all ashtrays, matches, lighters, and other smoking paraphernalia.

■ Avoid temptation. Ask friends and colleagues not to smoke in your presence, sit in the nonsmoking section of restaurants, and schedule some events at which smoking is prohibited, such as a concert or a movie, especially for the first few days after you've quit.

■ Develop an exercise plan or increase the amount you exercise. After quitting, stamina increases, making exercise more enjoyable. Exercise also curbs your appetite.

■ Be prepared for withdrawal symptoms. About half of all smokers experience headaches, irritability, jittery nerves, and muscle aches when they first quit. These symptoms usually subside in two or three days, but they can last longer in some cases.

■ Don't be concerned if you feel a bit light-headed or if your smoker's cough worsens. Within a few hours of stopping, the body starts healing itself. You may feel slightly dizzy because more oxygen is reaching the brain, and coughing clears the lungs of the residue of smoking.

■ Nicotine is a powerful stimulant, but it's also a deadly poison when taken in large amounts. Although nicotine gum or a nicotine patch makes quitting easier for some people, they can cause serious cardiac arrythmias when combined with smoking.

Resolve to put aside the money you save by not smoking, and use it to buy something you really want or need.

Spotting Drug Abuse

Behavior usually offers clues to someone's addiction to drugs. Some common tipoffs:

Are they often late for work and need to leave early?

Do they often call in sick?

Have family members found hidden drug paraphernalia, such as rolling papers, small glass bottles, or eyedrops?

Are there signs of physical deterioration or indifference to hygiene and grooming?

Do they have mood swings, going from irritable one moment to overly affectionate the next?

Do they have large amounts of cash one moment and cash shortages the next?

Have their eating habits changed significantly?

Do they seem to be unusually uncoordinated or have slower-than-normal reflexes?

Have they been arrested for driving or other actions while under the influence of drugs?

Do they have trouble sleeping?

Do they worry that people are spying on them or persecuting them?

Do they seem depressed or distracted?

Do they make phone calls or visit friends at odd hours?

Are there other unexplained behavior changes?

For information on dealing with drug abuse, contact the Addiction Research Foundation, 33 Russell Street, Toronto, Ontario, M5S 2S1.

An emergency can happen anywhere—*on a street, in a restaurant, or, as in this case, on a playing field. Although most rescue teams respond quickly, what you do before they arrive—literally, the first aid—can mean the difference between life and death.*

GUIDE TO FIRST AID

GUIDE TO FIRST AID

Protecting yourself and your family in an emergency means being alert and prepared at all times. It means thinking clearly and not panicking. It also means reading this emergency guide before you need it.

This chapter tells you how to provide first-aid care. Read it carefully, but don't be too concerned about memorizing the information. You'll be surprised how much of it will come back to you in an emergency.

Review the information with your children, as well. You don't need to go through it page by page with them, but they should know basic first-aid measures. Even three-year-olds can dial an emergency number or learn how to control bleeding.

The entries in this chapter are generally directed toward someone who is alone with the victim. If you're advised to call for medical help, have someone else do this, if anyone is available; you can then start treatment more quickly.

If possible, at least one adult in your family should take a course in first aid at a qualified training center, such as one run by the Red Cross.

GENERAL RULES

When dealing with a medical emergency, follow these basic guidelines:

■ Try to remain calm so that you can properly assess the situation and treat the victim.

■ Call for emergency help or ask someone else to do so.

■ Know the order of priorities when caring for an unconscious person:

Check breathing and apply artificial respiration, if necessary (see page 386).

Check pulse and administer CPR, if necessary (page 403).

Stop any severe bleeding (page 392).

Treat any burns (page 396) and fractures (page 412).

■ If there is any possibility of a head, neck, or back injury, do not move the person unless he or she is in danger—for example, from oncoming traffic (see page 416).

■ Check to see if an injured person is wearing medical identification—a bracelet, pendant, or card—that will tell you of any allergies or chronic conditions.

■ Loosen any tight clothing, and cover the person to guard against shock.

■ Treat for shock, if necessary (see page 422).

Know the shortest route from your home to your local hospital before an emergency occurs. When taking someone in, call ahead if time permits. It will help the staff to know in advance the victim's problem, as well as the name and telephone number of his or her doctor.

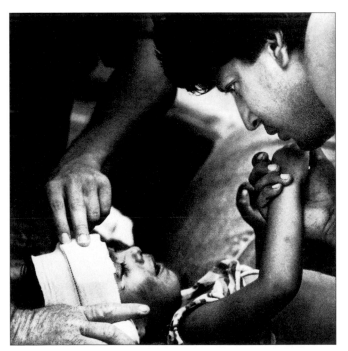

When someone, whether a child or an adult, has been injured, he or she needs comforting words along with first aid.

The Recovery Position

You and the other members of your family should know about the recovery position. In cases of unconsciousness or serious injury, this is the best way to position a breathing adult until help arrives. It's designed to keep anything—such as blood, vomit, or the tongue—from blocking the windpipe and choking the victim. Place the person in the recovery position as soon as

possible. However, first make sure that he is breathing. If he is not, apply artificial respiration (see page 386). If necessary, check his pulse and give CPR (page 403). Significant bleeding should also be controlled (page 392). Once you have placed someone in the recovery position, it's important to check frequently to be certain he is still breathing.

Caution: Do not use this position for someone who has sustained a head, neck, or back injury; in that case, the victim should not be moved at all (see page 416). Also, do not use the position for a child; instead, let an injured but breathing child lie as he is.

(see page 386). (page 403). (page 392). (see page 416).

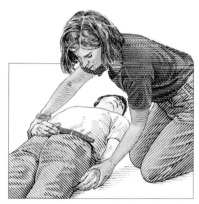

1. Kneel beside the victim and turn his head toward you. Keeping the closer arm straight, tuck it under the body. Put the other arm across the chest.

2. Lift the ankle that is farther from you over the other ankle, so that the legs are crossed.

3. Roll the victim onto his stomach: grasp his clothing at the far hip and pull while cushioning the head with your other hand and supporting the body with your knees. Tilt the victim's head back to open the airway.

Making an Emergency Call

Your local emergency number should be listed at the front of your telephone book; post it near every phone in your home and office. If you are using a public phone, you do not need to pay when calling this number. When the operator answers, give the following information:

1. The site of the emergency (include names of cross streets, if possible)

2. The number of the telephone you are using

3. Your name (if you wish)

4. What happened to the victim—for example, a fire or car accident

5. The number of people injured

6. The victim's condition, including any obvious injuries

7. Any first aid currently being given

Caution: Do not hang up until the operator tells you to. This way, you will be sure that you have answered all questions.

4. Bend the arm near you to prop up the victim's upper body. Bend the leg near you to prop up the lower body. Pull the other arm out from under the victim and lay it straight beside his body.

383

HOW TO STOCK YOUR FIRST-AID KIT

A first-aid kit will prepare you to treat minor illnesses and injuries and to deal with more serious injuries until the victim can receive medical help.

When you have assembled the items listed at right, put them in a sturdy container with a lid, such as a toolbox or a fishing-tackle box. Attach a strip of masking tape to the outside of the box, and write on it your local emergency telephone number and the number of your poison control center.

Keep the kit in a room other than the bathroom (too damp for some drugs) and out of the reach of small children. Babysitters and all household members—except small children—should know the location.

For suggestions on first-aid and health-care items to take with you when traveling, see "Your Travel Medicine Kit," page 260, and "Vacationing with Children," page 287.

Check your kit periodically to be sure any used items or expired medications are replaced. One way to remember to do this is to check your kit on the same day you adjust your clocks for daylight saving time.

Supplies for Your First-Aid Kit

1. Rolls of gauze bandages, 2-inch and 4-inch widths
2. Sterile gauze pads, packed individually
3. Adhesive bandages, various sizes
4. Butterfly bandages
5. Roll of adhesive tape, 1-inch width
6. Scissors
7. Elastic bandage, 3-inch width
8. Cotton-tipped swabs
9. Roll of absorbent cotton
10. Small bottles of aspirin and acetaminophen
11. Small bottle of children's acetaminophen for those younger than 12
12. Oral and rectal thermometers
13. Petroleum jelly
14. Syrup of ipecac
15. Powdered activated charcoal
16. Tweezers and sewing needles
17. Hydrogen peroxide
18. Calamine lotion
19. Bar of plain soap
20. Flashlight and extra batteries
21. Large triangular bandages
22. Large safety pins
23. Antacid
24. Antibiotic ointment
25. Antiseptic wipes
26. Antihistamine
27. Dosage spoon or eye-dropper
28. Safety matches
29. Paper tissues
30. First-aid manual

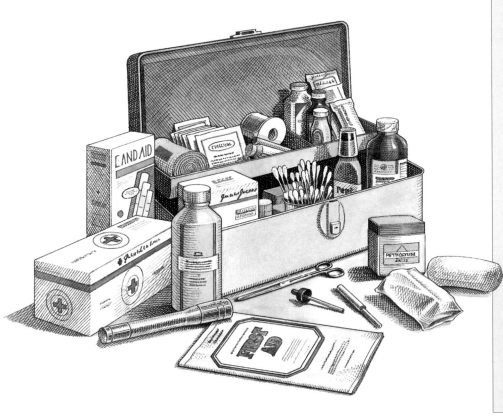

Abdominal Injuries

The abdomen is often injured in falls and in automobile accidents in which the driver is thrown against the steering wheel. An injury to this area—the lower two-thirds of the trunk—can be serious because the abdomen holds the bladder, intestines, and other internal organs, which are richly supplied with blood. If the victim has also sustained a head, neck, or back injury, do not move him unless he is in a perilous situation; see pages 416–418 for instructions. See also: *Bleeding and Bruises*.

External Injuries

Abdominal injuries often bleed heavily, so it is essential to stop the blood flow as quickly as possible. However, before doing this you should check the victim's breathing and perform artificial respiration, if necessary (see page 386). You may also need to check the pulse and apply CPR (page 403).

■ If the victim is conscious, lay him on his back and bend his knees. Place clothing or a folded blanket under his knees to keep them propped up. This position may help to keep the wound closed. If the victim is unconscious, leave him in his current position, if possible, while you treat major bleeding (ignore minor bleeding).

■ Carefully remove the victim's clothing from around the injured area. Do not breathe on the wound, as this will increase the risk of infection.

Also, do not touch the wound or try to push any protruding organs back into the body.

■ Cover any exposed organs with a pad—sterile, if possible—soaked in clean water. Then place a clean dressing (see page 394) over the pad and the entire wound. For a wound with no exposed organs, apply the dressing only.

■ Tape the dressing in place, or tie a bandage firmly around the torso to secure the dressing. Be sure, however, that the bandage does not put pressure on the wound. Tie the knot away from the wound. If the dressing or bandage becomes saturated with blood, place a new bandage over it.

■ If the victim is unconscious but breathing, support his abdomen while moving him into the recovery position (see page 383).

■ Cover the person with a blanket to help prevent shock (see page 422).

■ Call for immediate medical aid and reassure the victim that help is on the way.

> **Do not give the victim anything to eat or drink, as he may need immediate surgery. If he is thirsty, moisten his lips with water.**

Internal Injuries

Injuries to the abdomen that do not break the skin are more common than those that do. Though not as obvious, they can be very serious—for example, a forceful blow can damage the kidneys or

rupture the liver or spleen. The victim may be suffering from internal bleeding. If so, he needs medical help as soon as possible.

WARNING SIGNS

Internal bleeding may not be readily apparent. If a blow to the abdomen has occurred—or has even possibly occurred—look for any of the following symptoms:

■ Bleeding from the nose, mouth, or ears
■ Pain and tenderness in the abdomen
■ Tightening of abdominal muscles
■ Bruising or discoloration in the area
■ Nausea, vomiting (possibly of blood)
■ Muscle spasms
■ Faintness, weakness, or dizziness
■ Restlessness, confusion
■ Thirst
■ Rapid, weak pulse
■ Quick and shallow breathing
■ Cold, clammy, pale skin; sometimes sweat on the forehead
■ Pain at the end of the shoulders (caused by injuries below the diaphragm)

ACTIONS TO TAKE

■ If the victim is conscious, place him on his back. Bend his knees and put clothing or a rolled blanket underneath to keep them in the bent position. Use the recovery position for someone who is unconscious but breathing (see page 383).
■ Call for medical help.
■ Try to make the victim comfortable; if necessary, cover him to keep him warm.

Appendicitis

The appendix is a narrow tube that attaches to the large intestine on one end and is closed on the other. When it becomes kinked or blocked with hard waste, an inflammation—or appendicitis—can occur. The first warning sign of appendicitis is usually abdominal pain. This pain may increase until the tube ruptures, spreading infection within the body. A burst appendix requires immediate surgery. Because of this danger, a doctor should be seen as soon as appendicitis is suspected.

WARNING SIGNS
Any or all of these signs may be present:
■ Recurring spasms of pain—first near the navel, then moving to the lower right side of the abdomen
■ Pain becomes a constant ache after a few hours
■ Tenderness in the lower right side of the abdomen
■ Loss of appetite
■ Nausea, vomiting
■ Pain when walking or urinating
Symptoms of appendicitis take from 4 to 48 hours to develop; they also vary greatly, which can make the condition hard to diagnose. Children and the elderly often show only a few symptoms, such as a tender abdomen and a loss of appetite.

ACTIONS TO TAKE
■ Seek medical assistance if abdominal pain increases, be-comes continuous, keeps the victim awake, or lasts more than four hours.
■ Keep the victim lying down. If it makes him feel better, place an ice pack or cold compress on the sore area.
■ If he is thirsty, let him rinse his mouth with water—without swallowing. Do not let him eat or drink.
■ Do not administer purgatives, laxatives, or any medications, including such over-the-counter remedies as antacids.

Artificial Respiration

Artificial respiration (or mouth-to-mouth resuscitation) allows a person to breathe air into the lungs of someone whose own breathing has stopped or become dangerously weak. Breathing problems may be caused by many diseases or conditions, including a heart attack, a stroke, or an airway blockage. A person who stops breathing may die within six minutes; after only four minutes, he may suffer irreversible brain damage. Therefore, artificial respiration should be given as quickly as possible.

To find out if someone's breathing has stopped, put your ear next to his mouth and nose, listening and feeling for breath. At the same time, see if his chest and abdomen are rising and falling. If you do not detect breathing, call for medical help immediately—unless the victim is under eight years old. With a child under eight, call only after you have tried the following steps for one minute; after calling, start the procedure from the beginning, continuing until help arrives.

CLEARING THE AIRWAY
■ Lay the victim on his back on the floor or another firm surface, unless he has suffered a head, neck, or back injury. (If such an injury is suspected, follow the instructions in "Head, Neck, and Back Injuries," page 416.)

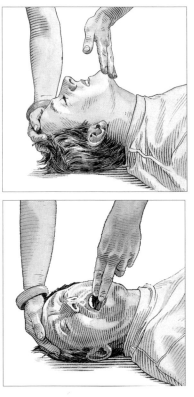

■ Place your hand on the victim's forehead. Tilt the head back and lift the chin.
■ If the victim does not begin breathing, turn his head to the side. Place your hand on his forehead to keep the head tilted. Clear his mouth of any

foreign matter with your fingers. (Do not put your fingers into a child's mouth, however, unless you can see the foreign material.) Then move his head back, lifting the chin and tilting the head.

■ The tongue may have slipped back into the victim's throat. If this is the case, do not try to move the tongue with your fingers, as you may get bitten. Instead, open the airway as you would for someone who has suffered a head, neck, or back injury (see page 416).

■ Place your ear close to the victim's nose and mouth, listening for breathing and feeling for exhaled air. See if his chest rises and falls.

■ Opening the airway may be enough to cause breathing to start. Once breathing is normal, put an adult victim in the recovery position (see page 383) until an ambulance arrives. Make sure he continues to breathe, as a change in position may cause an obstruction in the airway. As long as a child continues to breathe, do not move or change his position unless he begins to vomit or choke.

ARTIFICIAL RESPIRATION

If the victim does not begin breathing after the airway is opened, begin artificial respiration. (The procedure for infants differs in certain ways; see next page.)

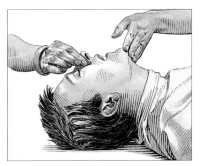

■ Pinch the victim's nose shut with your index finger and your thumb. Open your mouth wide and take a deep breath. Placing your lips tightly around the victim's open mouth, exhale a full breath for 1 1/2 to 2 seconds. Remove your mouth and take another deep breath. Pinch the nose again and exhale a second breath—it should also be for 1 1/2 to 2 seconds—into the victim's open mouth.

■ When you remove your mouth, turn your head toward the victim's chest so that your ear is over his mouth. As you listen and feel for exhaled air,

also watch for the chest to rise and fall.

■ If the chest does not move, there may be an obstruction. Reposition the head and give two more breaths. If the chest still does not move, follow instructions for an unconscious choking victim (see page 401).

■ If the chest does move, check the carotid pulse by placing your index and middle fingers in the hollow between the Adam's apple and the neck muscle at the side. If you do not feel a pulse, start chest compressions if you are trained to do so (see "CPR," page 403).

■ If there is a pulse but the victim is not breathing, continue with artificial respiration, giving one vigorous breath every five seconds—or every four seconds if the victim is a child. Remove your mouth each time to allow the victim to exhale, and turn your head to watch for the rise and fall of the chest. Continue until the victim breathes by himself or until medical help arrives.

The risk of transmitting an infectious disease during artificial respiration is very low. There are no documented cases of human immunodeficiency virus (HIV) being transmitted this way; however, hepatitis and bacterial meningitis can be contracted. If you are concerned, purchase a mask with a one-way valve at a drugstore or medical-supply house.

ARTIFICIAL RESPIRATION FOR INFANTS

This technique is the same as the preceding description, except for a few differences:

■ After placing the baby (less than one year old) on a firm surface and clearing the airway, cover *both nose and mouth* with your mouth. Puff in gently for 1 to 1 1/2 seconds, making the chest rise. Remove your mouth, inhale, and breathe into the infant's nose and mouth again.

■ If the chest does not rise, reposition the head and give two more breaths. If it still does not rise, follow instructions for choking on page 401.
■ If it does move, check the pulse at the brachial artery, on the inside of the arm between the elbow and the shoulder.
■ If there is a pulse, continue puffs at a rate of one every three seconds. If there is no pulse, use CPR (see page 404).

WHEN MOUTH-TO-MOUTH IS IMPOSSIBLE

Poison residue or a facial injury may prevent you from breathing into a victim's mouth. In such cases, use the method already described but breathe only into the victim's nose, holding the mouth shut.

Remove your mouth, and hold the victim's mouth open with your hand. Repeat every three to five seconds (depending on the victim's age).

Bites & Stings

This section covers the treatment of injuries caused by mammals, snakes, spiders, ticks, mosquitoes, flies, bees, wasps, ants, and jellyfish.

Animal Bites

Bites from many animals, including humans, will spread germs from the animal's mouth to the wound, where they can cause infection. Report bites to your local animal-control agency.

ACTIONS TO TAKE

■ Wash the area thoroughly for at least five minutes with soap and warm water—running water, if available.
■ Dry the wound gently with a sterile cloth, wiping down and away from the wound.
■ Stop any bleeding.
■ Cover the wound with a clean dressing.
■ Take the victim to a doctor if the skin has been broken. Tetanus shots or antibiotics may be needed.

Snakebites

Every year thousands of cases of poisonous snakebite occur in North America. Although few people die from snakebite, some do suffer crippling injuries to the

affected limbs. With quick medical attention, however, damage is generally minimal.

SIGNS OF POISONOUS SNAKEBITE

Most snakebites are not venomous, but you should assume that a bite is poisonous unless you are certain it is not. The victim may show one or more of the following signs:

■ One or two small puncture wounds (fang marks)
■ Sharp pain, bruising, or swelling around the bite
■ Blurred vision
■ Nausea, vomiting, diarrhea
■ Slurred speech
■ Difficulty swallowing
■ Difficulty breathing
■ Convulsions
■ Onset of paralysis

ACTIONS TO TAKE

If you are sure the snake was not poisonous, wash the wound with soap and warm water. Then apply an antibiotic cream and a bandage. If possible, position the wound below the heart and have the victim seek medical attention.

Unless you know the snake was not poisonous, get the victim to a hospital as quickly as possible. In the meantime, take the following steps:

Snakebite kits, sold in American drugstores, are meant for use when medical help cannot be reached. The kits contain instruments for drawing venom from a bite, and should be used only by those trained to deal with snakebite.

Guarding against Rabies

The rabies virus is carried by infected animals— usually cattle, skunks, raccoons, bats, foxes, dogs, and cats—and transmitted to humans by a bite or scratch. The virus travels from the wound to the brain. Since rabies symptoms do not develop until it is too late for treatment, it is crucial to consult a physician as soon as possible concerning any animal bites. Untreated rabies is generally fatal.

After cleaning and dressing the wound as described under "Animal Bites," seek medical help immediately if the victim has been bitten by a wild animal, a stray pet, or any pet other than a cat or dog. On the way to the doctor, the victim should not move the affected part. The doctor may

Rabies in raccoons has recently spread in the eastern seaboard.

start the antirabies treatment—a series of injections— right away, or she may wait to see if the animal develops rabies symptoms.

Call your local health or police department about capturing the animal. It should be observed by a veterinarian for 7 to 10 days for rabies symptoms, such as agitation, viciousness, and paralysis. If the animal escapes, notify police immediately. Inform them of its behavior, identifying marks, and last known location.

If the animal is a cat or dog whose owner is known, find out if its immunizations are up-to-date. Even if they are, make sure the owner observes the pet for 10 days for rabies symptoms.

To prevent rabies, make sure your pets are vaccinated against it, since they may come in contact with wild animals. Many provincial and local governments require these vaccinations. Check with your veterinarian if you're not sure of your pet's last immunization. Also, teach your children to stay away from any unfamiliar animal, even if it appears to be normal.

■ Note the snake's size, coloring, and skin pattern to help the doctor identify it and choose a treatment, but stay away from the snake.
■ If possible, call the hospital so that the proper antidote can be prepared.
■ Keep the victim calm and still, either sitting or lying down. She should not move.
■ Wash the wound under warm running water with soap, if possible, and apply a clean dressing.
■ Remove all bracelets and rings if the hand or arm has been bitten.
■ If possible, immobilize a bitten area by splinting it (see page 413). Position it below the heart.
■ If you must transport the

victim and the bite is on one of her feet, keep her completely off the bitten foot. Carry her if you can.
■ If the victim can swallow, give her nonalcoholic liquids to drink. Do not give her aspirin or sedatives, and do not give her anything to drink if she is nauseated, vomiting, or having convulsions.
■ If the victim becomes unconscious but is breathing normally, place her in the recovery position until help arrives (see page 383).
■ If breathing stops, administer artificial respiration (see page 386) and, if necessary, CPR (page 403).
■ If the victim becomes weak and pale, treat her for shock (see page 422).

Spider Bites

All spiders inject venom when they bite, but only a few species—most notably, the black widow and the brown recluse—can injure human beings. Young children, the elderly, and the chronically ill are particularly at risk.

SYMPTOMS OF SERIOUS SPIDER BITE
■ Redness and swelling around the bite
■ Intense pain around the bite
■ Sweating
■ Nausea, vomiting
■ Muscle cramps
■ Joint pains
■ Chills
■ Fever
■ Difficulty breathing

ACTIONS TO TAKE

Get medical help promptly. If someone has killed the spider, take it with you for identification. In the meantime:

■ Keep the bitten area lower than the heart.

■ Apply a paste of baking soda and water to relieve pain.

■ Apply an ice pack (ice wrapped in a cloth or put into a plastic bag) or a cold compress to the area. Do not put ice directly on the skin.

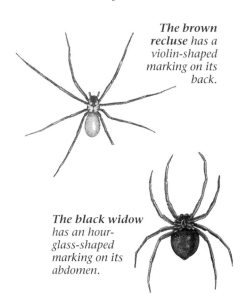

The brown recluse has a violin-shaped marking on its back.

The black widow has an hour-glass-shaped marking on its abdomen.

Tick Bites

Once on human skin, a tick bites, embeds its head, and feeds from a blood vessel. Most of these bites are harmless, but certain ticks can transmit viral or bacterial diseases, such as Rocky Mountain spotted fever, Colorado tick fever, and Lyme disease.

■ Without touching the tick, cover it with oil or petroleum jelly.

■ Using tweezers, grip the tick as close to the victim's skin as possible.

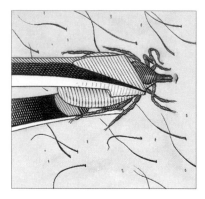

■ Gently but firmly pull the tick straight out, making sure that the head and all mouth parts are removed.

■ Drop the tick into a container of alcohol to kill it. Take it with you if you seek medical help; the doctor may need to identify it.

■ If the tick head remains embedded, the victim should see a doctor right away. Otherwise, wash your hands and disinfect the area of the bite with antiseptic.

■ If no tweezers are available, get medical assistance.

SYMPTOMS OF LYME DISEASE

Lyme disease is a dangerous bacterial infection, but it can be treated with antibiotics. If the victim has any of the following symptoms coupled with a possible tick bite, he should seek medical help immediately. (Remember that he may not be able to feel or see the bite.)

■ Localized redness or a circular rash

■ Flulike symptoms: headaches, muscle aches, fever, chills

■ Fatigue

■ Joint pain (usually in the knee)

Mosquito and Fly Bites

In Canada, bites from mosquitoes—as well as horseflies, deerflies, and blackflies—generally produce only minor irritations, unless an allergic reaction occurs (see facing page). Try not to scratch a bite, however, as this may cause infection by opening the wound and letting in bacteria.

■ Wash the bite with soap and cold water.

■ Apply ice, calamine lotion, or a baking-soda paste made with water.

Bee and Wasp Stings, Ant Bites

Although stings and bites from these insects may be painful, they are usually not dangerous. Exceptions are multiple stings or bites, stings in the throat or mouth, and attacks that cause allergic reactions (see facing page).

■ If the victim has been stung by a bee, remove the stinger—wasps do not leave stingers—by gently scraping the skin with a clean knife blade. If a clean knife is not available, use your fingernail. Do not press down or squeeze the stinger with tweezers; this may force more venom into the body.

■ Apply ice, a baking-soda paste, or calamine lotion to the affected area.

■ For several bites or stings, add baking soda to bathwater —four tablespoons per gallon of water.

STINGS IN THE MOUTH OR THROAT

The danger of a sting in the mouth or throat is that the throat may swell rapidly and block the airway.

■ If the victim has difficulty breathing, call for emergency help. If needed, use artificial respiration (see page 386).

■ Otherwise, give the victim an ice cube to suck on or cold water to swish around in his mouth and then spit out. This will lessen the swelling.

Jellyfish and Portuguese Man-of-war Stings

Some sea creatures carry venom in their tentacles. Jellyfish stings are seldom very harmful, but Portuguese man-of-war stings can be serious.

SYMPTOMS

■ Burning, stinging
■ Long red welts
■ Muscle cramps
■ Nausea, vomiting
■ Difficulty breathing
■ Shock

ACTIONS TO TAKE

■ Wrap a cloth around your hands (to prevent contact with the poison) and remove any attached tentacles.

■ Pour seawater—not fresh-water—over the affected area.

■ Wash the area with vinegar, rubbing alcohol, witch hazel, or diluted ammonia.

■ Apply a sand-and-mud paste or one made of seawater mixed with talcum powder, baking soda, flour, or sand. After a few moments, scrape off the paste. You can also use shaving cream.

■ If pain continues, apply a mild topical antihistamine or steroid.

■ If necessary, treat for shock (see page 422).

■ Seek medical help. The victim may need a tetanus shot if it has been five years or more since he last had one.

Allergic Reactions

Known as anaphylactic shock, a massive allergic reaction to a sting or bite (or to certain drugs and foods) can occur within seconds or be delayed 30 minutes or more. This life-threatening condition should be treated immediately.

SYMPTOMS

■ Swelling in areas other than the sting or bite site, especially the face or tongue

■ Weakness
■ Tightness in the chest
■ Sneezing or wheezing
■ Hives or rash
■ Severe itching
■ Difficulty breathing
■ Loss of consciousness

ACTIONS TO TAKE

■ Call for medical help at once. You may need to treat the victim for unconsciousness (see page 427) or shock (page 422).

■ If an emergency kit for insect bites is available, carefully follow the instructions in the kit.

■ Lay the victim on his back. Raise his feet onto a cushion, blanket, or folded coat. Keep his head low and turn it to one side in case he vomits. Maintain an open airway and, if necessary, give artificial respiration (see page 386) or CPR (page 403).

■ Keep the victim warm with a blanket or other covering.

■ Remove any stinger (see "Bee and Wasp Stings," on facing page).

■ Loosen tight clothing around the neck and waist to make breathing easier.

■ Apply a cold compress to the injured area, but do not put ice directly on the skin, as it may cause frostbite.

■ Do not give the victim anything to eat or drink. Do not let him smoke.

■ Give the victim an antihistamine, if one is available.

■ If the victim is having difficulty breathing, put him in the recovery position (see page 383) unless, as sometimes happens with respiratory problems, he insists on sitting up.

Bleeding & Bruises

Severe bleeding, when left untreated, may lead to shock or even death; therefore, stopping the bleeding from an injury is crucial. Bleeding can usually be controlled by pressing down on the wound for at least five minutes. This will stop the flow of blood and will help the wound form a clot. Raising the injured area above the heart also slows blood flow, but doing this is safe only if the victim has no broken bones.

The sight of blood can be distressing, but don't let it distract you from your first priority. Although it is very important to control the bleeding, you should first check the victim's breathing and apply artificial respiration, if necessary (see page 386). You may also need to check the pulse and administer CPR (page 403).

See also: *Abdominal Injuries; Nosebleed; Shock; Skin Problems.*

Severe Bleeding

■ Lay the victim down and remove any clothing from around the wound, if you can do so without wasting time or causing pain. If nothing sharp or large is embedded in the wound, press down hard on it with absorbent material or with your bare hands.

PRESSURE POINTS

It may be possible to stop severe bleeding at one of the body's main pressure points—places where arteries can be pressed against underlying bone to stop blood flow. Use this technique only as a last resort and with extreme care. Alternate five minutes of maximum pressure with five minutes of reduced pressure. After doing this once, call for medical help. Then continue the technique—changing the amount of pressure every five minutes—for as long as necessary.

Hold the victim's arm at a right angle to the body. With your thumb on the outside of the upper arm and your fingers on the inside, press your fingers hard against the bone.

LOWER-ARM WOUND

LEG WOUND

Lay the victim down and bend the injured leg at the knee. Press down firmly in the center of the fold of the groin, one thumb on top of the other, against the rim of the pelvis.

1. Brachial artery: for bleeding from the lower arm
2. Radial artery: for bleeding from the hand
3. Femoral artery: for bleeding from the leg

■ If possible, raise the wounded area above the level of the heart. If the bleeding continues, keep adding to the absorbent material. If the bleeding stops, tape the material in place and put a sterile dressing over it. Use any clean, thick cloth if you do not have a sterile dressing.

■ Do not remove the dressing. If blood seeps through it, put another dressing on top and tape or tie it in place.

■ Keep the victim as still as possible. Do not give him anything to eat or drink.

■ If severe bleeding from a hand, arm, or leg continues longer than five minutes, you may be able to stop the bleeding from one of the body's main pressure points (see box on facing page).

Large Wound

Press the sides of a large wound together gently but firmly and maintain the pressure for up to 10 minutes. Then treat as described under "Severe Bleeding."

Object in Wound

■ Do not try to remove a large or sharp object, such as a piece of glass, from a wound. It may be plugging the wound and slowing the blood flow. Also, removing the object may cause further damage to the surrounding tissue.

■ Press down on the sides of the wound to make the bleeding stop. You may need to press for a long time.

■ Make a ring-pad (see page 395) and place it around

the object.

■ Bandage the wound with diagonal strips, but do not cover the object.

Bleeding from Nose, Mouth, or Ear

If a person has been in an accident or received a severe blow, she may bleed from the nose, mouth, or ear. This often indicates a serious internal injury to the head, chest, or abdomen.

■ Call for medical help.

■ If the victim has a neck or back injury, do not move her (see pages 416–418). Otherwise, place her in a half-sitting position with her head tilted toward the bleeding side.

■ Cover the bleeding area with a clean, folded handkerchief or any cloth pad, but do not apply pressure to the ear.

■ Do not give the victim anything to eat or drink.

■ If the victim loses consciousness but is still breathing, place her in the recovery position (see page 383).

The human immunodeficiency virus (HIV) and viruses causing some types of hepatitis may be transmitted when the blood of an infected person enters a cut or abrasion on another person's skin. It is possible to contract a disease when performing first aid on someone who is bleeding. Therefore, if feasible, avoid direct contact by using latex gloves, plastic wrap, or several dressings.

Bruises

Bruises are external signs of bleeding beneath the skin. When blood seeps into the tissues, it causes swelling, soreness, and discoloration. Before you treat a minor bruise, check to see whether there are any more serious injuries, especially fractures (see page 412).

ACTIONS TO TAKE

■ Apply a cold compress to the bruised area to reduce the swelling. To make a compress, soak a small towel in cold water and wring it out, or fill a plastic bag with crushed ice and then wrap the bag in a cloth. The victim should keep the compress on the bruise for at least 30 minutes—if necessary, fix the compress in place with an elastic bandage. Be sure that the victim does not fall asleep with the ice pack on, as prolonged use may damage the skin.

■ Instead of using a compress, you can hold the bruised area under cold, running water.

■ If a bruise develops on an arm or leg, elevate the limb above heart level.

CONSULT A DOCTOR IF:

■ The bruise does not start to fade within a week.

■ The pain is severe or limits normal movement.

■ The bruise is large and occurs on or near the abdomen or on the back.

■ The victim has difficulty moving the bruised area 24 hours after the injury.

■ Bruises occur without any apparent reason.

■ An elderly person or a person suffering from poor circulation has a bruised lower leg.
■ The victim has a black eye, especially if vision is affected (see page 410).

Bandages and Dressings

A bandage is a piece of fabric—usually gauze, muslin, or elastic—with three basic uses: keeping a dressing in place over a wound, stopping bleeding, and supporting or immobilizing an injured part of the body.

If an emergency occurs and you have no bandages on hand, make them out of clean sheets, pillowcases, diapers, towels, table linens, handkerchiefs, scarves, garments, or any other suitable material.

A dressing, generally made of several layers of sterile material covered with gauze, absorbs blood and prevents infection. In an emergency, make a dressing by forming a pad of any clean, dry, absorbent cloth or paper. (Do not use cotton balls or any other fluffy materials unless they are sandwiched between two nonfluffy layers; the fibers may stick to the wound.) Combinations of bandages and dressings are available commercially in the form of bandage compresses.

USING ROLLED BANDAGES

Traditional nonstretch, open-weave gauze bandages are sold in rolls of various widths. They are inexpensive and convenient but require a little practice to use correctly.

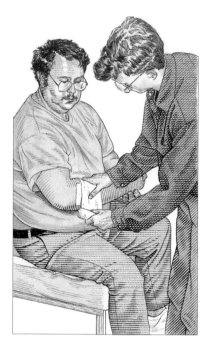

■ To apply a bandage to an arm or leg: Put the end of the bandage on the limb a few inches below the wound. Moving outward from the body, make a firm turn to hold the bandage in place. Press the bandage against the skin so that you can unroll it easily.

While maintaining even pressure, bandage the limb in the position in which it is to remain. Having started two or three turns below the wound, you should finish two or three turns above it. Fold in the end and fix it securely with a safety pin or adhesive tape. Or you can tie a knot.

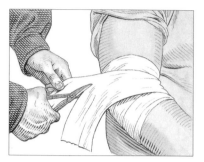

■ To make a knot: If you do not have a safety pin or adhesive tape, leave a piece of bandage free. The length will depend on the thickness of the area being bandaged. Cut the end of the bandage in half lengthwise.

Tie the two strips together with a single knot, pulling the ends but not allowing the knot to rest near the wound. This knot will keep the cut you have made from tearing any further.

Take the two ends around the limb again and tie them in a square knot, but not near the wound: Twist the left end over, under, and over the right end, then pull taut. Again take the left end over, under, and through the loop. Pull taut.

■ To make a ring-pad: A ring-pad protects a wound that has glass or another object in it. Wind one end of a narrow bandage once or twice around your fingers to make a loop. Bring the other end through the loop, under, and back through again.

Continue winding the free end of the bandage around the loop until you have used most of the bandage. Finish the end with a slipknot, as shown.

USING ELASTIC BANDAGES

Stretchy crepe or elastic bandages are easy to put on, and because they follow the body's contours, the pressure they exert on the wound is well distributed. Even though they

---

Is the Bandage Too Tight?

Leave the victim's fingers or toes exposed when wrapping a limb. After applying the bandage, and again 10 minutes later, check for signals that the bandage is too snug. If any appear, remove the bandage and put on another more loosely.

The following are signs that circulation has been impaired:

1. The victim has a tingling feeling or numbness in his fingers or toes.

2. The victim cannot move his fingers or toes.

3. The tips of the fingers or toes are very cold.

4. The fingernail or toenail beds appear blue or unusually pale.

5. An injured arm has no pulse or a weaker pulse than the other arm.

---

have give, however, be careful not to put them on too tightly. Elastic bandages are expensive but can be washed and used again.

USING TRIANGULAR BANDAGES

Unfolded triangular bandages are ideal for making slings (see page 413). They can also be folded into broad bandages, for tying limbs to splints, or into narrow bandages, for holding dressings in place. You can improvise one by cutting a piece of three-foot-square linen or cotton in half diagonally. For a sling, tie the knot on the shoulder and not behind the neck.

■ To make a broad bandage, spread the triangular bandage

out on a flat, clean surface. Fold the top of the triangle to the center of the base and then fold it once more in the same direction.

■ To make a narrow bandage, fold the top of the triangle to the center of the base, fold it again in the same direction, and then add a third fold in the same direction.

■ A folded triangular bandage can also be used instead of rolled bandages to make a ring-pad.

Burns

Burns are categorized by their degree of severity, but these first-aid guidelines apply to all types:

▪ Do not put ice or butter on a burn. Use other preparations only if a doctor advises you to do so.

▪ Remove jewelry and tight clothing from the burned area before swelling occurs.

▪ Keep the burn site above the heart. If the burn is on the face, have the victim sit up.

▪ Any dressing should be sterile, if possible, and made of a nonfluffy material to prevent it from sticking to the wound (see page 394).

First-Degree Burns

These burns harm only the outer layer of skin. They commonly result from briefly touching a hot object, scalding the skin, or staying in the sun too long.

SYMPTOMS
▪ Red skin
▪ Pain
▪ Swelling

ACTIONS TO TAKE

▪ Hold the burn under cold running water, or immerse it in cold (but not iced) water for 15 to 30 minutes. If this is not possible, apply a cold-water compress.

▪ Apply a dressing if the burn might be rubbed by clothing or otherwise irritated.

▪ If she asks for it, give the victim aspirin or aspirin substitute for pain.

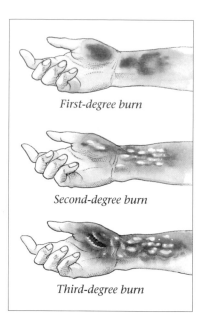

First-degree burn

Second-degree burn

Third-degree burn

▪ If the burn covers more than two inches, the victim should see a doctor immediately. For a sunburn, consult a doctor only if at-home remedies provide no relief (see page 424).

Second-Degree Burns

These burns damage not only the first layer of skin but also the one beneath it. Severe sunburn is a second-degree burn. Another cause is contact with hot liquids and flash burns from gasoline.

SYMPTOMS
Second-degree burns share the symptoms of first-degree burns, but the pain is more severe and the swelling lasts for several days. The skin, which may be red and blotchy, generally develops blisters.

ACTIONS TO TAKE

▪ Use the cold-water technique described for first-degree burns, but do not use running water.

▪ Without breaking the blisters, apply a dressing.

▪ If mouth or throat burns occur, seek medical care. Do not give the victim anything to drink. She may rinse her mouth without swallowing.

▪ Also see a doctor if the burn covers more than two inches or if it becomes infected. Signs of infection include increasing pain, redness, or warmth in the area.

▪ Take the victim for a tetanus shot if she has not had one in the past five years.

Third-Degree Burns

These destroy all layers of skin and sometimes damage fat cells, muscles, and bones. Frequent causes of third-degree burns are fire, electric shock, and prolonged contact with hot liquids.

SYMPTOMS
▪ White or charred skin
▪ Severe pain or little pain (from nerve damage)
▪ Possible shock

ACTIONS TO TAKE

▪ Call your local emergency number. In cases of electric shock, see page 409.

▪ Check to see if the victim is breathing; if not, give artificial respiration (see page 386). If no pulse is present, apply CPR (page 403).

▪ Put an unconscious person who is breathing in the recovery position (see page 383).

▪ Do not put water on the burn.

▪ Cover exposed burned areas with a nonfluffy dressing—sterile, if possible—but do not remove pieces of clothing adhering to the burn.

■ If necessary, treat for shock (see page 422).

■ The victim needs a tetanus shot if she has not been immunized in the past five years.

Clothes on Fire: Stop, Drop, and Roll

If your own or someone else's clothing catches fire, remember this: stop, drop, and roll.

Stop: Running will only feed the fire. When the victim is someone else, hold a cotton or wool (not synthetic) blanket or coat in front of you; then wrap it around the person.

Drop: The victim should lie flat to keep the flames from rising to her head.

Roll: The victim should roll on the ground. You can also douse the fire with water or any nonflammable liquid (not alcohol).

When the fire is out, remove any hot clothing that can easily be taken off the victim, but leave any fragments that are stuck to the skin. Give the first aid appropriate to the severity of the burn.

Chemical Burns

Contact with caustic liquids, dry lime, and some other chemicals can cause serious injury to the tissues. Do not attempt to neutralize the chemical; the best treatment is to flush the area with plenty of water.

■ While wearing gloves (to protect your hands), flush the burned area heavily with water for 5 to 20 minutes. (If the injury is an eye burn, see page 410.)

■ Remove the victim's contaminated clothing.

■ Make sure that the victim is not lying in the chemical.

■ Cover the burned area with a nonfluffy sterile or clean dressing.

■ Get medical help.

Chest Wounds

Chest wounds are especially dangerous when the lungs are damaged. An injury that penetrates a lung is known as a "sucking chest wound": when the victim inhales, air is pulled through the wound rather than the airway, creating a sucking sound and preventing the lung from inflating. As the victim exhales, bubbles of blood-stained liquid emerge from the wound. It is essential to seal the wound so that the victim can breathe properly.

ACTIONS TO TAKE

■ Call for medical help.

■ Cover the wound with a clean cloth or a piece of airtight kitchen plastic wrap big enough to cover the entire opening. If necessary, you can use other types of plastic, but the material should be clean.

■ If no cloth or plastic is available, place a hand on each side of the wound and push the skin together firmly to close the wound.

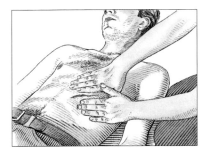

■ Apply a dressing and secure it with adhesive tape. If the person has difficulty breathing, untape one side of the dressing and pull it and the cloth or plastic away from the wound so that air trapped in the chest can escape.

■ Maintain an open airway; if the victim stops breathing, use artificial respiration (see page 386).

■ Rest the victim in a comfortable position. Using cushions or blankets, lean him toward the injured side. Loosen his belt. Do not give him anything to eat or drink.

■ If necessary, treat for shock (see page 422). Instead of laying the victim on his back, however, you may need to use a semi-reclining position, with the head slightly propped up.

Childbirth

As soon as a pregnant woman goes into labor, her doctor should be notified. Depending on the duration of her contractions and their frequency, the woman may be told to wait at home for several hours or to go immediately to a hospital or other care facility. If labor progresses quickly, however, she may begin to give birth before she can reach the hospital. After calling for medical help, use the following procedure if you need to assist in a birth. Do not attempt to delay delivery.

ACTIONS TO TAKE

■ Wash your hands and fingernails with soap and water; then let them air-dry.

■ Place clean linens on a bed. If time permits, protect the mattress by placing a plastic tablecloth beneath the sheets. (If there is no bed, put clean cloths or newspapers on the floor or any large surface.)

■ Have the expectant mother undress from the waist down and lie with her back propped up against several pillows. Her knees should be bent, her feet flat, and her thighs wide apart.

■ At the start of each contraction, the woman should grasp her knees and tilt her head forward. She may want to hold her breath and push downward. Urge her to relax as much as possible between contractions. Take note of the color of expelled fluid so that you can tell the doctor; a dark color may indicate that the baby will need special help.

■ When the baby's head has fully emerged, support it on both sides with cupped hands. If the umbilical cord is wrapped around the infant's neck, quickly and carefully slip it over the head. If the amniotic sac, a fluid-filled bag, surrounds the head, gently tear the bag with your fingernail and re-

move any residue from the baby's face with your hand or a clean cloth.

■ Keep holding the head as the infant turns to allow the shoulders to come forth. (The head will be slippery, making a firm grip difficult.) If the upper shoulder appears first, gently direct the head downward. Then carefully raise the head so that the other shoulder and the rest of the body can emerge. If possible, note the time of delivery.

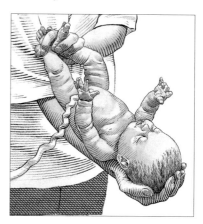

■ After the child is born, gently wipe out the nose with a cloth; then use one of your fingers to clear the mouth. Holding the head and trunk with your hand and forearm and the ankles with your other hand, tilt the body so that the infant's head is lower than the feet, allowing secretions to drain.

■ If the baby is not breathing, place him on his side, keeping the head lower than the feet. Firmly tap the soles of the feet with an index finger. If this does not work, rub the infant vigorously with a clean blanket. If the baby is still not breathing, use the artificial respiration technique for infants (see page 388). If you should need to perform CPR (page 404), you must tie the umbilical cord before performing chest compressions; follow the description that appears later on this page for tying the cord only.

■ Once the infant begins breathing, wrap him in a blanket. Cover the top and back of the head but not the face. It is very important to keep the baby dry and warm. Place him on his side next to the mother, but do not pull on the umbilical cord. The baby's head should be slightly lower than the rest of his body.

■ If possible, get the mother and baby to the hospital. Otherwise, prepare for the placenta, or afterbirth, to be delivered. This commonly occurs between 5 and 20 minutes after childbirth. Place a bowl between the mother's legs to collect the placenta. Use sanitary napkins or clean cloths to absorb the blood at the openings of the vagina and rectum. Do *not* pull on the cord to hasten delivery of the placenta. If it has not emerged after 20 minutes, gently massage the mother's abdomen just below the navel, pressing downward. Be sure to wait 20 minutes; early massage can be dangerous. Gentle massage is also helpful after the placenta has been delivered.

■ If the placenta has not emerged 30 minutes after the birth, the mother needs immediate medical care. Keep the baby, still attached to the cord, at the same level as the mother's vagina to prevent blood from being drained from either individual. Tie the cord, using the instructions that appear in the next column.

■ When the placenta has emerged, keep it slightly above the level of the baby.

■ If the placenta has been delivered and transportation to the hospital is significantly delayed, you may need to cut the cord:

Tie the cord, if you have not already done so, with pieces of clean string or narrow cloth in two places: about six and eight inches from the newborn's body. Knot the strings tightly enough to stop circulation.

Sever the cord between the two knotted strings with scissors. If possible, sterilize them first by boiling them for five minutes. There should be no further bleeding from either end of the cord. If there is, tighten the string where the bleeding is occurring or tie another one next to it.

Store the umbilical cord and placenta in a plastic bag or other container so that a physician can examine them.

■ If the cord has been cut, place the baby on the mother's abdomen and lay a blanket across both of them. Let the mother hold the infant while traveling to the hospital.

A new mother gazes joyfully at her baby, whose head is still damp.

Choking

A person chokes when a piece of food or another object obstructs his airway. This obstruction keeps the oxygen in the lungs from reaching the brain, and the person stops breathing. Unless he receives immediate first aid, he can die within minutes.

Choking is the sixth most common cause of accidental death today. Children under four are especially vulnerable, often choking on hot dogs, peanuts, hard candies, or parts of toys. Adults put themselves at risk when they fail to chew food thoroughly, drink alcohol in quantities great enough to affect their judgment, or let their dentures become dislodged.

WARNING SIGNS
■ Gasping or noisy breathing; breathing may stop
■ Clutching the throat
■ Inability to speak or cough
■ Bluish or ashen skin color
■ Swelling of veins in head and neck

The Heimlich Maneuver

If an adult or child is choking, use the Heimlich maneuver—an emergency procedure designed to expel an obstruction from the victim's airway by producing an artificial cough. If this is not successful, call for medical help.

Caution: A baby requires a different technique; see "First Aid for a Choking Infant," on the facing page.

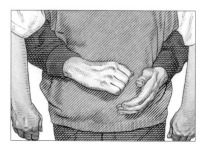

■ Stand behind the victim. Put your arms around his waist. Place your fist with the thumb side against the abdomen, just above the navel but below the ribs and breastbone.

■ Holding your fist with your other hand, give up to five quick, forceful, upward-and-inward thrusts. Do not squeeze the ribs with your arms; use only your fist. Pause briefly between thrusts to check for signs from the victim that the object has come up—coughing, speaking, deeply inhaling.
■ After five thrusts, check the victim's mouth to see if the obstruction has come up. If so, remove the matter from the mouth. If not, repeat the sequence until the person coughs up the object or becomes unconscious (see "First Aid for an Unconscious Victim," on the facing page).
■ Even if the thrusts have been successful, the victim may be winded by their force and unable to breathe at first. When he does begin to breathe again, have him sit quietly and, if he wants, let him sip water.
■ While the Heimlich maneuver may be necessary to restore a victim's breathing, abdominal thrusts can damage the liver and other internal organs. Therefore, anyone who has been revived by this technique should see a physician.

SELF-ADMINISTERED HEIMLICH MANEUVER

■ If you are alone and choking, place your fist on your stomach slightly above your navel and below your ribs. Put your other hand on top of your fist. Give up to five quick, forceful, upward-and-inward thrusts.

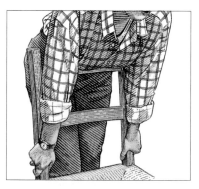

■ If this procedure does not work, press your stomach forcefully over the back of a chair.

■ Repeat until the object is expelled.

First Aid for a Pregnant or Obese Choking Victim

When the victim is pregnant or obese, use chest thrusts.
■ Stand behind the victim, and place your arms under the armpits and around the chest. Put the thumb side of your fist on the middle of the breastbone.

■ Grab your fist with your other hand. Give up to five quick, forceful, upward-and-inward thrusts—squeezing your fist but not your arms. Then check the victim's mouth to see if the obstruction has come up.
■ Repeat until the person coughs up the object or loses consciousness (see "First Aid for an Unconscious Victim").

First Aid for a Choking Infant

To dislodge an obstruction in the airway of an infant (less than one year old), use the following technique:

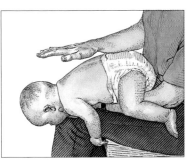

■ While sitting down, rest the back of one arm on your thigh. Place the infant face down along the forearm, with the head lower than the chest. Support the head by firmly holding the chin. Give up to five back blows between the infant's shoulder blades with the heel of your hand. Thump the child's back more gently than you would an adult's but hard enough to dislodge the blockage.

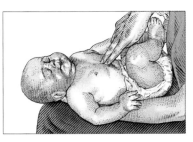

■ If this does not work, turn the baby over, and using only two fingers, give up to five quick, gentle, downward thrusts to the center of the chest, just below the nipples. Check the mouth to see if the object has come up.
■ Repeat the procedure— alternating up to five back blows with up to five chest thrusts—until the child coughs up the object or becomes unconscious.
■ If the baby loses consciousness, open the airway and give artificial respiration (see page 388) for one minute, then call for medical aid. After calling, open the airway again and give two breaths of artificial respiration. If the chest does not rise, keep repeating the sequence—back blows, chest thrusts, artificial respiration—until the object becomes dislodged or help arrives.

First Aid for an Unconscious Victim

Suspect choking if a person is found unconscious and not breathing after she has been eating, or if someone suddenly loses consciousness for no apparent reason.
■ Call for medical help immediately, unless the victim is between one and eight years old. In that case, proceed with the techniques below for one minute; then make the emergency call. After calling, start the procedure again. (For an unconscious infant, see the preceding section.)
■ Place the victim on her back and open the airway by tilting the head back and lifting the chin (see page 386).
■ Check for breathing. If there is none, try to remove the obstruction with your fingers. With your thumb on the tongue and your fingers under the chin, lift the victim's lower jaw while, with your other hand, you perform a sweeping movement along the cheeks and deep into the throat. (Do not sweep the mouth of a child unless the object is visible.) Try to hook and remove the obstruction, but be very careful not to push it deeper into the throat.

■ If the victim is still not breathing, place her head in the correct position for artificial respiration (see page 386). If the lungs do not inflate with the first two breaths, tilt the head back again and give another two breaths. Then check to see whether the victim has a pulse. If there is no pulse, CPR will be necessary to circulate blood to the brain (see page 403).

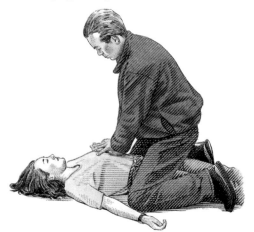

■ If the victim does have a pulse but is not breathing, perform the Heimlich maneuver with the person stretched out on the floor or ground. To do this, first turn the victim so that she is lying face up. Then, while kneeling astride her hips, put the heel of your hand slightly above the navel and well below the bottom of the breastbone. Cover this hand with the other hand and, with your arms held straight, perform up to five quick, upward thrusts.

■ After the first five thrusts, check the victim's mouth. If the object has not been expelled, try artificial respiration again. If the lungs do not ex-

pand after two breaths, repeat the sequence of thrusts, finger sweep of the mouth, and artificial respiration. Continue until the object has been dislodged or help arrives.

. . . .

How can you tell whether someone is choking? A person is not choking if he is able to cough freely and has normal skin color. When in doubt, ask the victim if he can talk. If he can, the windpipe is not completely blocked and oxygen is reaching the lungs. As long as the person can cough or talk, do not perform any first-aid procedures.

. . . .

Convulsions

Convulsions are triggered by electrical disturbances in the brain. These disturbances may result from a head injury, a brain tumor, epilepsy, high fever, electric shock, or other illnesses or injuries.

Convulsions usually last only a minute or two and are generally not life-threatening. The main danger comes from falls.

SYMPTOMS
One or more of the following may occur:
■ Loss of consciousness
■ Rolling of the eyes
■ Twitching or stiffening muscles
■ Drooling
■ Lack of bladder or bowel control
■ Bluish cast to face, especially around the mouth, caused

when victim temporarily stops breathing

ACTIONS TO TAKE
■ Try to support the victim if he falls and move any sharp objects and furniture out of his way.
■ If the victim's breathing stops and does not resume quickly after the convulsions have subsided, check to see whether his tongue is blocking his throat. If it is, put one hand on the victim's forehead and the other under the bony part of the chin, tilting the head back to open the airway.
■ Do not put a wallet, finger, or any other object between the victim's teeth.
■ Loosen any tight clothing around the victim's neck.
■ Do not try to stop convulsive twitching or hold the victim down.
■ Do not throw water at the victim or force him to drink anything.
■ When the episode ends, keep the victim lying down, since he may be dazed and confused. If he vomits, turn his head to the side to prevent him from choking. Place him in the recovery position (see page 383).

CONSULT A DOCTOR IF:
■ The victim sustains injuries.
■ The victim is pregnant or very young.
■ The active part of the seizure lasts longer than five minutes.
■ The person has a series of convulsions without regaining consciousness (see page 427).
■ The cause of the seizure is unknown.

CPR (Cardio-pulmonary Resuscitation)

CPR is a technique that alternates artificial respiration and chest compressions to revive victims who have no pulse. The artificial respiration allows oxygen into the blood, while the chest compressions force the blood through the circulatory system. When a person's heart stops beating, blood no longer carries oxygen to the brain. Serious damage may occur within minutes. The victim therefore needs to be treated as quickly as possible.

Be prepared in advance for this type of emergency. Make sure that at least one adult in your household takes a course in CPR. See also: *Artificial Respiration.*

Caution: Only someone formally trained in CPR should carry out this technique, because chest compressions can cause injury to ribs and internal organs. The information provided here should be used only as a memory aid for trained people. A person who has been trained in CPR needs to be certain that there is no pulse before compressing the chest; otherwise, a faintly beating heart may stop. For treatment of infants and small children, see the next page.

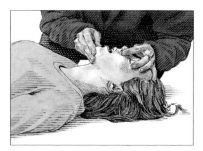

1. Open the airway (see page 386). Then use artificial respiration: Pinch the victim's nose shut and inhale. Sealing your lips around her open mouth, exhale for 1 1/2 to 2 seconds. Repeat the procedure, then release the nose. With your ear above her mouth, feel for exhaled air and watch for the chest to move. If the chest does not move, reposition the head and repeat breaths. If this does not work, there may be an airway obstruction (see "Choking," page 400).

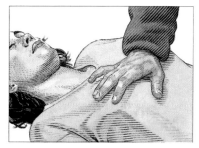

2. If the chest does move, check the carotid pulse by placing your index and middle fingers in the hollow between the Adam's apple and the neck muscle at the side. If you do not feel a pulse, start chest compressions.

3. Kneeling beside the victim's chest, locate the place above the waist where the ribs meet the base of the breastbone. Measure two finger-widths above this spot and place the heel of your hand there.

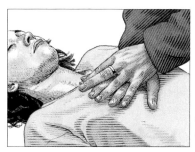

4. Lay your other hand on the first and interlace the fingers. Push down hard and quickly with the heel of your hand, depressing the chest 1 1/2 to 2 inches. Do not move your hands once they are in position.

5. Do this 15 times, counting as you press: "one and two and..."—up to 15. Then release your hands and resume artificial respiration, giving two breaths. After 4 cycles of compressions and breaths (which take about 1 minute), check the pulse. Continue the cycles until you feel a pulse—check every 12 cycles or 3 minutes.

CPR For Infants

Before deciding that an infant (less than a year old) needs help, make sure that he isn't just sleeping. Gently shake the baby. If there is no response, follow the instructions below for one minute, then call for help.

▪ Place the infant on a firm surface and clear the airway (see page 386). Apply artificial respiration: Cover both nose and mouth with your mouth, and puff in gently for 1 to 1 1/2 seconds. Remove your mouth, inhale, and give another breath. If the chest does not move, reposition the head and give two more breaths. If the chest still does not rise, follow instructions for choking (page 401).

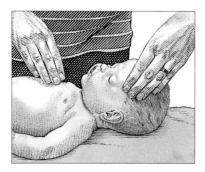

▪ If the chest does move, check the pulse at the brachial artery, on the inside of the arm between the elbow and the shoulder. If there is no pulse, place two fingers in the center of the chest a finger-width below the level of the nipples.

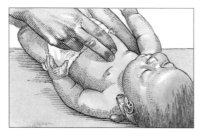

▪ Press down no more than an inch. Do this five times, counting "one and two and three and four and five." Then release your hands and resume artificial respiration, giving one breath. Keep repeating this procedure, but check the pulse after one minute the first time, then after every three minutes.

For Children Under Eight Years Old

With this age group, the problem often involves an airway obstruction. Use the techniques in "Artificial Respiration" (page 386) for one minute before calling for help. After calling, apply the techniques again from the beginning.

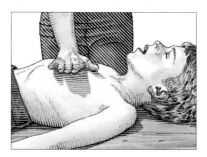

▪ If you do need to perform chest compressions, follow the instructions for an adult (see the preceding page), with these differences: Depress the chest 1 to 1 1/2 inches with only the heel of one hand, holding the fingers off the ribs. Give five compressions, then one breath. Check the pulse after performing this procedure for one minute, then after every three minutes.

Dental Emergencies

Someone who has received a serious injury to the teeth or mouth needs to see a dentist or doctor immediately. Make sure that the victim is able to breathe properly. Clear her mouth of any blood and broken teeth. Have her sit or stand upright to prevent her from choking.

KNOCKED-OUT TOOTH

▪ It may be possible for a tooth to be reinserted, especially if you can get to a dentist quickly. Handle the tooth only by the crown (nonroot area) and rinse it lightly in warm tap water. Do not scrub the tooth. Either place it in the victim's mouth (in the empty socket, under the tongue, or against the cheek), or carry it in a cup of cold milk. (Saliva or milk will help keep the tooth alive.) Put the tooth in the victim's mouth only if she is fully conscious. If you replace the tooth in the socket, the victim should bite down on gauze, or a piece of cloth, to keep it in place.
▪ Unless you are placing the tooth back in the socket,

control the bleeding by putting a sterile gauze pad or handkerchief over the empty socket and applying pressure.

LOOSENED TOOTH

If the tooth is merely loosened, have the victim keep it in its socket by biting down on a gauze pad. Get medical care as soon as possible.

TOOTHACHE

■ Take aspirin or another pain reliever. Do not apply aspirin to the gum, as it can burn the tissue.
■ For relief of a severe toothache, some respond to cold (an ice pack against the jaw or rinsing out the mouth with very cold water), and others respond to heat (hot compresses or rinsing out the mouth with warm, salty water).
■ If the pain is accompanied by a fever, swollen glands, or a boil on the gums, the cause may be an abscessed tooth. Go to the dentist's office or hospital immediately.

Diabetic Coma and Insulin Reaction

Diabetics may need first-aid treatment for two related but very different conditions— diabetic coma and insulin reaction. A diabetic coma, which involves a potentially life-threatening loss of consciousness, develops over a period of several hours or days. It often occurs when the diabetic doesn't take her prescribed dosage of insulin, and may also result from stress, an infection, or excessive sugar consumption. An insulin reaction usually occurs when a diabetic who has taken insulin as directed has not eaten properly. Exercise can also trigger an insulin reaction, which is sometimes called insulin shock or hypoglycemia.

When giving first aid to an unconscious person, check for medical identification—a card or bracelet—that will inform you of a chronic condition, such as diabetes. Do this after treating any breathing or circulation problems. See also: *Shock; Unconsciousness.*

SYMPTOMS OF DIABETIC COMA

One or more of the following symptoms may exist:
■ Thirst
■ Nausea, vomiting
■ Weakness
■ Fast, deep breathing
■ Breath that smells oddly sweet or fruity
■ Gradual loss of consciousness

SYMPTOMS OF INSULIN REACTION

One or more of the following symptoms may exist:
■ Hunger
■ Nervousness
■ Confusion
■ Sweating
■ Convulsions
■ Loss of consciousness

ACTIONS TO TAKE

■ If the victim is conscious, feed her something containing sugar or other carbohydrates, such as candy, fruit, nondiet soda, or fruit juice. (This will help in the case of an insulin reaction and will not hurt in the case of a diabetic coma.) It may take up to 30 minutes for the sugar to take effect and the symptoms to abate. After you have given the victim food, call her physician or seek other medical care.
■ If the person is unconscious, call your local emergency number; then check breathing and pulse. Administer artificial respiration (see page 386) or CPR (page 403), if necessary. Place the victim in the recovery position (page 383), and again check her breathing. Wait for help to arrive.

If You Have Diabetes

To find out about correct foods, substitutes, and portions, get a food-exchange list from your doctor or the Canadian Diabetes Association.

If you alter your calorie intake (because of dieting or illness), remember that your insulin amount will need to be adjusted.

Exercise regularly, but check with your doctor before embarking on any program. Always eat something before exercising.

Take good care of your feet to avoid nerve damage and infections. Buy only shoes that fit properly.

Schedule regular eye exams. Diabetic retinopathy can occur without symptoms, but laser treatment may slow its progression.

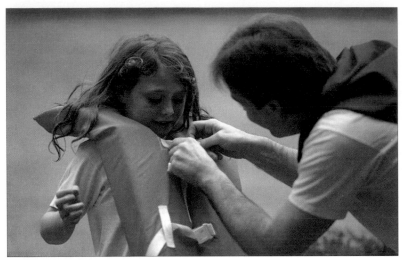

*A **personal flotation device** helps ensure that this child will be safe while sailing. Thinking ahead and taking precautions can prevent drownings.*

Drowning

Many drownings occur within 15 feet of a boat, dock, or shore. More than 80 percent of the victims are male, and alcohol is often a factor. See also: *Artificial Respiration; CPR; Head, Neck, and Back Injuries.*

WARNING SIGNS

Assume that anyone in the water fully clothed may be drowning. A swimmer experiencing cramps or exhaustion is more difficult to recognize; if he is having trouble breathing, he may be unable to shout for help. Look for any of the following signs:

▪ The victim's strokes become erratic and his movements appear jerky or simply stop.
▪ The victim's body sinks, so that only his head shows above the water.
▪ The victim's face—particularly the lips and ears—turns a bluish-purple color.

ACTIONS TO TAKE

▪ Call your local emergency number if a phone is immediately available, or send someone for help before you attempt a rescue.
▪ Do not overestimate your swimming skills or your strength; a panicky victim can easily pull a rescuer down with him.
▪ If the person drowning is close enough, reach out to him with an oar, a pole, or a lifesaver attached to a rope. When he grabs the object, try to pull him to shore. Watch out for your own safety: Stand as far away from the water as possible and hold on to something secure, if anything is available. If you feel yourself being pulled in by the swimmer, quickly release the object.
▪ If the victim is far away, take a rowboat. Pulling someone into a rowboat is difficult, and you risk capsizing the boat. Therefore, if possible, have

the victim hold on to the back of the boat, or a lifesaver attached to the boat, while you row to shore.
▪ Do not attempt a deep-water swimming rescue unless you are experienced in Red Cross lifesaving techniques. If you do swim out to a drowning person, you should be secured to shore by a rope.
▪ If you suspect a head, neck, or back injury, as in a diving accident, slide a board (for example, a surfboard or table leaf) under the victim's head, back, and buttocks and pull him out of the water on it. Be very careful—any movement of the head may cause paralysis or death. If no board is available, have the victim attempt to float on his back until help arrives. If you must move the victim to shallow water, keep his head and spine in vertical alignment as you support him and then pull him straight back (not sideways) by the armpits or legs (see "Head, Neck, and Back Injuries," pages 416–418).

REVIVING THE VICTIM

▪ If the victim has stopped breathing, begin artificial respiration immediately (see page 386), and if the heart has stopped, perform CPR (page 403). Do not try to drain swallowed water from the lungs at this point. Instead, clear any debris out of the victim's mouth with your index and middle fingers before starting artificial respiration. If the victim brings up food and water, turn his head to one side to expel fluids and prevent choking. Resume artificial respiration as soon as possible. If you suspect a head, neck, or back injury, do *not* turn the head. Turn the whole body to the side, and keep the head and spine in alignment. If you are alone, concentrate on supporting the neck to keep it from bending as you turn the victim.

■ Once breathing has resumed, place the victim in the recovery position (page 383)—unless there is a head, neck, or back injury—and cover him with a blanket or whatever is available. As you wait for medical help, check frequently to make sure that the victim is still breathing.

When lying down *for a rescue, anchor your feet as firmly as possible.*

With a rowboat *rescue, pull the victim toward the boat with an oar.*

If a diver sustains a head, neck, or back injury, you'll need to move her on a board. Carefully follow the instructions on the facing page.

Drug Overdose

An accidental or intentional overdose of drugs—whether over-the-counter, prescription, or illicit—requires immediate action. Call for medical assistance first, then call your local poison control center for instructions. Save any vomit, pills, or containers so that you or the hospital can identify the substance. See also: *Artificial Respiration; Poisoning; Shock.*

ACTIONS TO TAKE

■ If the victim stops breathing, give her artificial respiration (see page 386). If her pulse stops, apply CPR (page 403).

■ If she is breathing but unconscious, roll her onto her stomach in the recovery position (see page 383).

■ Do not induce vomiting unless the poison control center advises it. If you are told to do so, use two tablespoons of syrup of ipecac (one tablespoon for a child, two teaspoons for an infant) followed by two glasses—each glass should be eight ounces or more—of water. Repeat if the victim has not vomited after 20 minutes. If ipecac syrup is not at hand, put a tablespoon to the back of the victim's throat.

■ If you know that the victim has swallowed tranquilizers or sleeping pills, rouse her by slapping her lightly with a cold, wet towel and try to keep her awake.

■ Do not give the victim coffee or walk her around.

Ear Injuries

Head injuries, loud noises, explosions, changes in air pressure, and objects pushed into the ear can all cause damage to the middle or inner ear. The most potentially serious ear injury is a perforated eardrum. See also: *Head, Neck, and Back Injuries.*

SYMPTOMS

One or more of the following symptoms may exist with an ear injury:
▪ Severe earache
▪ Dizziness and loss of balance
▪ Hearing loss
▪ Headache
▪ Discharge from the ear of blood or watery fluid (also a possible sign of a fractured skull)

ACTIONS TO TAKE

▪ If you suspect a neck or back injury, do not move the victim. Otherwise, sit him up with his head tilted toward the injured side so that blood or fluid can drain out.
▪ Protect the injured ear by covering it with a piece of clean cotton or gauze. Tape the covering in place. Do not attempt to plug the ear or put anything in the canal; this can build up pressure in the middle ear and cause damage.
▪ Do not allow the victim to strike the side of his head to try to restore hearing, as this can worsen the damage.
▪ If the victim is unconscious but breathing, place him in the recovery position (see page 383) with the injured ear downward, resting on a clean towel to absorb fluids. Call for immediate medical assistance.
▪ If the victim's breathing stops, begin artificial respiration (see page 386).

An Object in the Ear

Children often push things into their ears. This usually causes nothing more serious than temporary deafness. If the object is pushed deep into the ear, however, the eardrum may be perforated.

SYMPTOMS

One or more of the following may be present:
▪ Discharge from the ear (clear, cloudy, bloody, or foul-smelling)
▪ Pain or buzzing in the ear
▪ Hearing loss

ACTIONS TO TAKE

▪ Have the victim tilt the affected ear downward. Hold his head and shake it very carefully. The object may fall out.
▪ If this does not work, attempt to remove the object only if it is clearly visible and can be grasped easily. (Otherwise, you risk pushing it farther into the ear and damaging the fragile structures of the inner ear.) Keeping the victim's head still, remove the foreign body with tweezers.
▪ Do not try to flush the object out with water, and do not make more than two attempts to remove it.
▪ If you are unable to remove the object, get immediate medical help. Also see a doctor if the victim experiences a discharge or decreased hearing after you have removed the object.

An Insect in the Ear

If an insect crawls or flies into someone's ear, its buzzing can sound frighteningly loud and its movements can be very distressing. You may need to calm and reassure the victim. Make sure that he does not put his finger in his ear, as this may provoke the insect to sting or to bite.
▪ Turn out all the lights in the room except for one. Have the victim move the affected ear toward that source of light. Gently pull the earlobe back and up to straighten the ear canal, and the insect may fly out toward the light. You can also try shining a flashlight in the ear.

▪ If these procedures do not work, put several drops of mineral or vegetable oil into the affected ear. Pull the earlobe back and up to straighten the ear canal; then hold the victim's head still with the ear angled toward the ground. Even if the insect does not suffocate, it might float out in the oil.
▪ If this fails to remove the insect, or if the insect stings

408

or bites the victim in the ear, seek immediate medical help.

Caution: Do not use oil or other liquids to remove anything except an insect. Liquids may cause some objects, such as beans and beads, to swell, making removal more difficult.

Electric Shock

Electricity kills hundreds of people every year and causes severe internal and external injuries—such as burns, broken bones, and damaged tissue—to many others. When rescuing an electric-shock victim, you need to be especially careful. Treatments will differ according to the cause of the accident.

From an Appliance

■ If the victim has received an electric shock from a household appliance, switch off the current only at its source—the main fuse box or breaker panel. Do not unplug the machine or use the switch on the appliance or you risk electrocution.

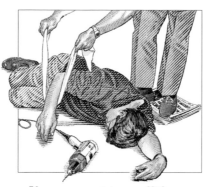

■ If you cannot turn off the power at its main source, do not touch the victim until you have separated him from the source of electricity. To do this, first stand on a nonconducting surface—rubber mats or a stack of newspapers—if possible. Then use a wooden broom handle or another *dry, nonmetallic* object to move the person. You can also use a rope or makeshift rope (made from a pair of tights or a dry towel). Without touching the victim, loop the rope around an arm or foot and pull him away from the source of electricity.

Caution: Do not choose anything even slightly damp, or anything that has been in a damp place, to stand on or to reach the victim. If you use a broom handle, a stack of newspapers, or any other object that has absorbed even a small amount of moisture, you risk electrocution.
■ Call for medical aid.
■ Check breathing and pulse. Apply artificial respiration (see page 386) or CPR (page 403), if necessary. Place an unconscious person who is breathing in the recovery position (page 383).
■ Treat any burns (see page 396). If the impact of the shock has thrown the person

to the floor or against another hard surface, check for fractures and treat as needed (see page 412).

From High-Voltage Electricity

Someone who has been injured by high-voltage electricity, as from a power line, needs immediate help.
■ Call your emergency number and tell the operator that high-voltage electricity is involved, so that he can dispatch both medical and utility crews.
■ Stay at least 20 feet away from the source of electricity (and from the victim, as long as she remains in contact with that source) to avoid the risk of electrocution.
■ If you are able to treat the victim, use the instructions given in the next section. Remember, however, that the person may have sustained a head, neck, or back injury; in this event, she should not be moved (see pages 416–418).

From Lightning

Unlike other victims of electric shock, someone struck by lightning is not electrically "live" and can be treated immediately after the incident.
■ Call for medical help.
■ If the person is not breathing, use artificial respiration (see page 386). If she has no pulse, apply CPR (page 403).
■ If the person has lost consciousness but is breathing, place her in the recovery position (see page 383).
■ Treat any burns (see page 396) or fractures (page 412).

Eye Injuries

An eyelash or a piece of dirt caught in the eye is the most common eye problem, but corrosive chemicals and sharp objects, such as glass, cause more serious injuries.

AN OBJECT IN THE EYE

The cardinal rule when anything gets in the eye is not to rub: the pressure may cause scratches.

▪ Wash your hands with soap and water before touching your eyes or anyone else's.

▪ You can often flush out eyelashes, dirt, and the like. Pull the upper lid down over the lower to produce tears, or squeeze warm water over the eye with a medicine dropper.

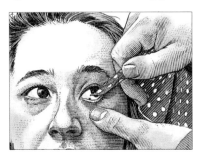

▪ If that does not work, ease the lower lid down. If you see the speck, gently remove it with the tip of a moistened clean cloth. Only the tip of the cloth should contact the eye surface.

▪ After one or two failed attempts, assume that the object is deeply embedded and seek medical attention.

▪ If something, such as a splinter or shard of glass, is embedded in the eye, do not attempt to remove it. Instead, cover the eye with a paper or

plastic cup to protect it; be careful not to touch the eye or apply any pressure to it. If no cup is available, use sunglasses. Place a bandage very lightly over both eyes (movement by one eye causes reciprocal motion in the other) and take the victim to the hospital.

OTHER INJURIES

▪ For chemical burns caused by household cleansers, insecticides, and other substances, quick treatment is crucial.

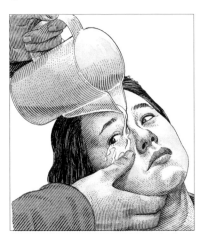

Tilt the victim's head sideways, with the injured eye downward. Hold the lids open and flush the eyeball with gently running water from a faucet or pitcher. The water should flow from the bridge of the nose outward over the entire eyeball continuously for 10 minutes or more. Then loosely bandage the eye and seek immediate medical help.

▪ Cuts to the eye or eyelid can have serious consequences. Being careful not to apply pressure, lightly bandage both eyes before taking the victim to the hospital.

▪ Treat a black eye with an ice pack or a cold compress,

and have the victim see a physician to determine whether any severe damage has occurred.

▪ If a contact lens becomes displaced or sticks to the eyeball, get medical help rather than risk damaging the eye.

Fainting

When the blood supply to the brain suddenly diminishes, a person may faint—that is, briefly lose consciousness. The causes for this vary. Shock, pain, or acute stress can cause fainting, as can ordinary events, such as being in a stuffy room, getting winded, or skipping meals.

WARNING SIGNS

One or more of the following may indicate that someone is about to faint:

▪ Pale or greenish-white skin that feels cold and clammy, though the victim may complain of being hot

▪ Beads of sweat on face, neck, hands

▪ Frequent yawning

▪ Dizziness

▪ Nausea

▪ Double or tunnel vision

▪ Fatigue

ACTIONS TO TAKE

▪ If someone has fainted, check to see if he is breathing. If he is, raise his feet above the level of his head to increase the circulation to his brain. Do not prop his head up; this could obstruct breathing. If he is not breathing, begin artificial respiration (see page 386). Check his pulse and apply CPR (page 403), if necessary.

■ If the victim vomits, turn his head to the side to prevent choking; then make sure he is still breathing.

■ Loosen tight clothing at the neck and waist.

■ If possible, use smelling salts to revive the victim, waving them beneath his nose. Do not splash him with water, but gently wipe his face with a cool, wet cloth.

■ The victim will probably revive quickly. When he does, tell him to remain lying down or seated for a few minutes. Do not give him anything to eat or drink except sips of cold water. (Alcohol is especially dangerous, as it lowers the rate of the body's vital functions and may make the condition worse.) Make sure he gets up slowly.

■ If someone is about to faint, have him lie down on his back with his legs raised about 10 inches—hold his legs or prop them up. If space is limited, have him sit with his head between his knees. Loosen any tight clothing.

CONSULT A DOCTOR IF:

■ The cause of the fainting is illness, an injury, or unknown.

■ The victim is old or has a heart problem.

■ Fainting is a recurring problem for the victim.

■ The victim's fall results in any type of head injury, even if slight; a concussion may have occurred.

■ The victim's level of alertness does not return to normal within 10 minutes or he remains confused.

If you need to stand still for a long time, reduce the risk of fainting by rocking gently from the heels to the balls of your feet or by squeezing your calf muscles when you shift weight from one leg to the other.

Fishhook Removal

Removing a fishhook is best left to a physician, but you may be able to do it yourself if the hook isn't caught on any part of the face.

ACTIONS TO TAKE

■ If only the hook's point has gone into the skin and the barb is still visible, gently back the hook out the way it went in.

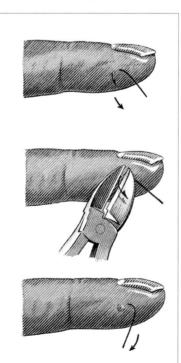

■ Otherwise, anesthetize the area with ice, then push the hook forward, in the direction of the curve, until the barb breaks through the skin. Snip off the barb with wire cutters and pull the shaft out from the other direction.

■ Wash the area thoroughly with soap and water. Apply an antiseptic and then bandage.

■ Seek medical attention if the victim has not had a tetanus shot in the past five years.

Food Poisoning

Diarrhea, vomiting, and stomach cramps may occur 2 to 96 hours after eating contaminated foods. See also: *Poisoning, Vomiting.*

ACTIONS TO TAKE

■ Keep the victim on a liquid diet for several hours, then move to bland foods. Do not offer tea, coffee, acidic drinks, or any dairy products. If vomiting recurs, start again with a liquid diet.

■ Adults may be given an antidiarrheal medicine.

■ Call a doctor if the symptoms are severe or persistent, or if the victim is less than three years old.

■ Botulism is a rare but life-threatening form of food poisoning, usually caused by improperly processed home-canned foods. Dizziness, muscle weakness, and blurred vision set in 24 to 48 hours after eating contaminated food. The victim should be taken to a hospital immediately.

Fractures & Dislocations

A fracture may be a cracked or broken bone. In a closed fracture, the broken bone does not pierce the skin, whereas in an open fracture the skin is broken. Incomplete breaks usually occur in children, whose soft bones still bend. Most fractures are not life-threatening. See also: *Bleeding and Bruises; Head, Neck, and Back Injuries; Shock; Sprains and Strains.*

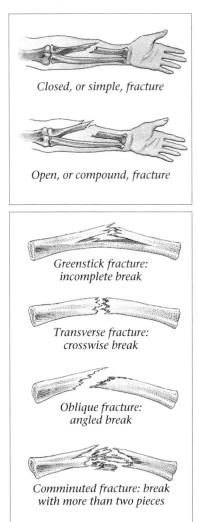

Closed, or simple, fracture

Open, or compound, fracture

Greenstick fracture: incomplete break

Transverse fracture: crosswise break

Oblique fracture: angled break

Comminuted fracture: break with more than two pieces

SYMPTOMS

The victim may experience any or all of the following:
- Sensation or sound of a bone snapping and, possibly, of the ends of the bone grating together
- Inability to use the injured part of the body without feeling pain
- Deformed appearance of the injured part when compared with the unharmed side
- Swelling in the injured area
- Bruising in the area
- Tenderness in the area

ACTIONS TO TAKE

- If the fracture involves a head, neck, or back injury (see page 416), do not move the victim unless she is in imminent danger. Call for emergency help.
- Do not let the victim put weight on a broken leg or foot.
- Do not move the fractured bone unnecessarily or try to push it back into place.
- Take care of any breathing problems (see page 386), severe bleeding (page 392), unconsciousness (page 427), or shock (page 422).
- Make the victim as comfortable as possible, supporting the injured area with cushions or a rolled-up blanket.
- Do not give the victim anything to eat or drink.
- Gently apply a dressing to any wound (see page 394), taking care not to move the fractured area unnecessarily.
- Place a cold compress on a closed (but not an open) fracture to help prevent swelling. The compress can be a small towel soaked in cold water and wrung out or a plastic bag of crushed ice wrapped in a towel.
- If you must move the victim, splint the injured limb first, if time allows (see facing page). Do not, however, use a splint on a broken knee; instead, simply stabilize the knee in a comfortable position.

If you have an itch beneath a cast, resist scratching it with such items as wire hangers, as this may cause infection. Instead, aim a hair dryer under the cast and blow warm air or baby powder onto the skin.

Broken Jaw

The symptoms and treatment of a broken jaw differ from those of other fractures.

SYMPTOMS

The victim may have one or more of the following:
- A wound inside the mouth
- Difficulty speaking or an inability to open the mouth fully
- Excessive flow of saliva, often tinged with blood
- Broken teeth
- An abnormal bite

ACTIONS TO TAKE

- Get immediate medical care.
- Have the victim cup her jaw in her hands on the way to the hospital. If she is unable to do so, support the jaw for her.
- Do not tie the jaw, as the victim may need to vomit or clear her mouth of secretions.
- Watch the victim to make sure she has not stopped breathing. If she has, use

mouth-to-nose artificial respiration (see page 388). Noisy breathing may occur if the victim is unable to swallow secretions.

Broken Rib

A fall or a blow to the chest may result in a fractured rib, which causes intense pain when the victim coughs or inhales deeply. A person with a cracked rib may be driven to the hospital, but leave him where he is if he has a serious chest wound (see page 397). Call for immediate medical help if the victim cannot breathe sufficiently, becomes restless and thirsty, or has frothy blood issuing from his mouth. If necessary, treat the victim for shock (page 422).

Dislocations

A bone becomes dislocated when it is forced out of place at a joint. This happens most often with shoulders, jaws, elbows, fingers, hips, kneecaps, and toes. A sprain usually accompanies a dislocation; sometimes a fracture will also take place.

SYMPTOMS
Any or all of the following may be present:
■ Severe pain
■ Swelling, bruising
■ Deformity of the joint
■ Difficulty moving the joint

ACTIONS TO TAKE
■ Treat a dislocation as you would a fracture (see facing page). Take the victim to the hospital, or call your local

emergency number.
■ Do not try to push the dislocated bone back into place.
■ If you need to immobilize a limb, splint it in its current position (see below).

Be careful not to pull on a child's arm too hard. Children can easily suffer "nursemaid's elbow," a partial dislocation.

Slings and Splints

If you have to take someone with a fracture to the hospital, use a sling or splint to secure the broken bone. Do not change the position of the bone, but secure it in its current position. You can make effective splints from boards, umbrellas, or pillows, and also from rolled-up blankets or newspapers. You may want to use blankets or towels as padding between the splint and the body.

After applying a splint, check the limb every 15 minutes to make sure that circulation is good. The victim's fingers or toes should be warm and pink, responsive to your touch, and able to wiggle.

ARM SLINGS
You can buy a ready-made sling or a triangular bandage to use as a sling, or you can make one (see page 395). Use a sling only if the injured arm will bend easily. Never bend a broken arm by force. If the arm does not readily bend, place it in a splint, as explained under "Arm Splints," on the next page.

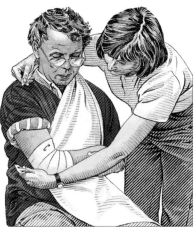

■ While the victim holds his arm, place an open triangular bandage between his chest and forearm. Bring the upper end over the shoulder on the uninjured side and around the back of the neck to the front of the injured side.

■ Bring the lower end of the bandage up over the hand and forearm, and tie it to the upper end just above the collarbone. The hand should be slightly higher than the elbow, and the fingertips should extend from the sling.

■ Pin the apex of the triangular bandage near the elbow, or twist and tuck it in.

413

You can also improvise an arm sling. Take a tie, belt, narrow scarf, or roll of gauze, and do the following:

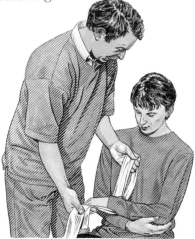

▪ Fold the strip of cloth in half lengthwise and bring the middle section behind the injured arm's wrist, where it will form a loop.

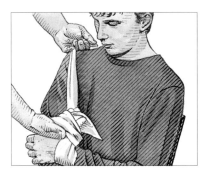

▪ Wind the ends over the injured arm and through the loop. Separate the ends, bring them around the neck, and tie a knot at the collarbone.

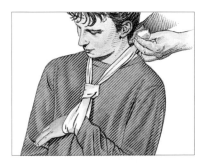

▪ When tying the ends, make sure that the hand is elevated just above elbow level or a bit higher—so that the fingertips point to the opposite shoulder—for hand or forearm wounds.

If you have nothing on hand, you may be able to use the victim's jacket:

▪ Turn up the bottom edge of the victim's jacket and pin it securely to the front of the jacket at chest level. The fold will support the arm.

▪ Or pin the sleeve of the injured arm to the front of the jacket.

▪ Or gently put the hand inside the fastened jacket at chest level, so that a button or zipper supports it.

ARM SPLINTS

The type of arm splint you should use depends on whether the victim's arm will bend. Never try to manipulate a broken bone—do not forcibly move the arm.

▪ If the arm will bend easily, position it across the chest and put padding (towels, diapers, clothing, or rolled-up newspapers or magazines) between the fractured area and the chest.

Support the arm with a sling (see previous page), then secure it to the chest by tying a broad bandage around the arm and torso—a technique called body splinting.

▪ If the arm will not bend, have the victim lie down, and put padding between the fracture and the body. To immobilize the arm, wrap broad bandages around it and the torso, but keep them away from the injured area.

ELBOW SPLINTS

▪ If the broken elbow is bent, follow the instructions in the preceding section for an arm that bends.

▪ If the elbow won't bend, have the victim sit down, and place a folded newspaper along the back of the arm. While the victim holds the paper, tie it in place with one bandage at the top and one at the bottom.

FINGER OR TOE SPLINTS

Use a flat piece of wood or plastic, such as an ice-cream stick or tongue depressor, to splint a finger or toe. Secure it to the finger or toe with strips of cloth or tape. If wood or plastic is unavailable, try "buddy taping": use the digit next to the injured one as a splint by putting cotton or other soft material between the digits and taping them together.

LEG SPLINTS

The easiest way to immobilize a broken leg is by bandaging it to the other leg:
■ Put padding between the legs, especially at the knees and ankles.

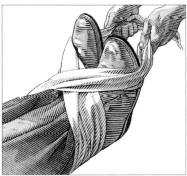

■ Tie the feet together with any cloth (a necktie will do); use a figure-eight pattern, as in the illustration. Knot the material on the outer edge of the shoe on the uninjured side.

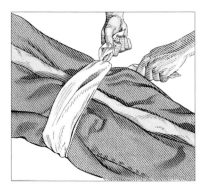

■ Tie the knees together with a bandage, knotting it on the uninjured side. Tie extra bandages above and below the fracture.

If you must transport a person with a broken leg, improvise a splint with a blanket:
■ Roll the blanket lengthwise as tight as you can. Place one end between the victim's legs at the crotch. Then bring the blanket down the inside of the injured leg, around the foot, and along the outer side up to the thigh.
■ Bind the feet and ankles together with a bandage in a figure-eight pattern (see illustration, above left). Use a square knot.
■ Wrap a wide bandage around the victim's knees and tie it on the uninjured side, again using a square knot.
■ Tie additional bandages above and below the fracture.
■ Finally, tie a bandage around the thigh or calf, making sure to avoid the fracture.

ANKLE OR FOOT SPLINTS

Remove the victim's shoe. Mold a pillow or rolled towel around the leg and foot, starting at the calf and extending well beyond the heel. Tie strips of cloth around the pillow or towel to secure it.

Frostbite

Exposure to cold can cause ice crystals to form in the skin's fluid and tissue. Uncovered parts of the body are vulnerable, and the hands and feet may be vulnerable even when protected. Left untreated, frostbite can cause severe damage to the affected areas. People particularly at risk include newborns, the elderly, diabetics, and those taking certain medications.

WARNING SIGNS

■ The affected part feels cold and hard, with an aching pain.
■ The skin becomes white or grayish in those with fair complexions and a lighter shade than normal in those with dark complexions.
■ The area becomes numb.

ACTIONS TO TAKE

■ Get the victim indoors.
■ Remove any clothing and jewelry from the affected area.
■ Warm the frostbitten part with your own skin—for example, have the victim put his foot under your armpit. You can also immerse the frozen part in tepid water, but do not rub or massage it.

  Caution: If there is any chance of further damage from the cold, leave the affected area alone, except for skin-to-skin warming. It is dangerous to "thaw" an area temporarily only to have it refreeze. Do not let the victim walk if his feet are frostbitten.
■ Immersing the frostbitten area in a basin of lukewarm water may be helpful if the

frostbite is superficial, but use this technique only if the skin is still soft and pliable, and be sure the water is not hot—40.6°C to 43.3°C (105°F to 110°F) is best. Do not use other heat sources, such as a campfire; the frostbitten part may burn before the victim's feeling has returned.

■ When skin color returns, wrap loose cloths around the area and then cover the cloths with a blanket or sleeping bag.

■ Have the victim move his fingers and toes to help restore circulation. Place sterile gauze or a cloth between the digits to keep them separated.

■ Raise the affected part above the heart.

■ The area may develop blood-filled blisters as it thaws. Do not break them or put anything on them.

■ Seek medical attention as soon as possible for all frostbite cases, as they are often more severe than they seem. Immediate care is especially important if numbness remains or if there is obvious tissue damage.

Head, Neck, & Back Injuries

An injury to the head, neck, or back may result from a car or sports accident or from taking a bad fall. No matter what the cause, these injuries should always be considered emergencies, with potential for lasting damage to the brain and spinal cord. It is essential to get the victim medical help immediately.

Caution: A person who has sustained a head, neck, or back injury should not be moved unless she is in a dangerous situation, as from fire or possible drowning. If she is vomiting, turn her on her side (preferably with the help of others) while supporting the head and neck. Keep the head, neck, and back in alignment; do not allow the body to bend at the waist. See also: *Artificial Respiration; Shock; Unconsciousness.*

Head Injuries

SYMPTOMS

One or more of the following may occur:

■ Bleeding from the nose, ears, or mouth; clear fluids from the nose or ears
■ Cuts, bruises, swellings on the face, scalp, or behind ears
■ Eye pupils may be different sizes
■ Double vision
■ Headache
■ Vomiting
■ Confusion or drowsiness, possibly preceded or followed by unconsciousness
■ Convulsions
■ Memory loss
■ Weak pulse or a change in pulse rate
■ Shallow or noisy breathing
■ Combative behavior
■ Paralysis or weakness

ACTIONS TO TAKE

■ If the injury was not severe enough to knock the person off her feet, carefully help her to lie down.
■ If the victim has stopped breathing, provide artificial respiration, taking care not to

twist or rotate the head. Instead of tilting the head backward, sit or kneel behind the victim's head. Put your thumbs on either side of her mouth and grasp her jaw with your fingertips. Lift the lower jaw with your index fingers as you push your thumbs downward. The jaw will jut forward so that you can begin artificial respiration (see page 387).

■ If part of the skull moves when you touch it, or a portion is obviously depressed below the surface, there may be a skull fracture. In this case, place a dressing on the wound without applying any pressure. Place additional layers as needed on top of the first dressing.

■ If there is no obvious skull fracture, stop any bleeding by pressing a clean cloth pad on the wound. Then place a second dressing on top of the first. If you suspect that there is also a neck injury, see "Neck and Back Injuries" on the facing page. Otherwise, wrap the head in a bandage (see illustrations on facing page).

■ Insist that anyone who loses consciousness from a head injury, no matter how briefly, gets medical attention.

■ Even if a blow to the head appears minor, monitor the victim over the next 24 hours. Awaken her from sleep every hour to check to see whether she is confused—ask her to identify familiar people or objects. If she should exhibit confusion or any of the symptoms listed, call the doctor or hospital immediately; this could be a sign that a serious head injury has occurred.

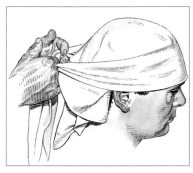

1. Secure a head dressing *with a triangular bandage. Put the long edge across the forehead so that the point is at the back of the head. Bring the two long ends around to the back and cross them at the neck.*

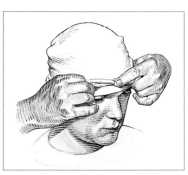

2. Now bring the two ends *around to the front. Tie them together at the forehead, away from the wound, to secure the bandage. Keep the victim's head as steady as possible while you're working.*

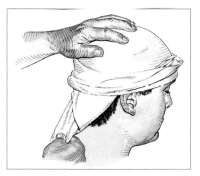

3. Gently place one hand *on the bandage to keep it from slipping. With the other, draw the point downward, parallel with the back of the neck, so that the bandage fits snugly.*

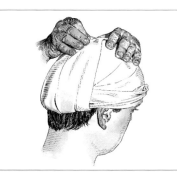

4. Lift the point *of the bandage up to the crown and fix it lightly in place with a safety pin or adhesive tape. Or tuck the point into the edge of the bandage at the front.*

Is It a Concussion?

A concussion occurs when sudden impact causes the brain to strike the inside of the skull. It may result from a fall, a blow to the head, or even landing on the feet too hard.

The concussion victim generally loses consciousness, though often only briefly. Call for medical help, and treat for unconsciousness as described on page 427.

Upon awakening, the victim may experience headache, dizziness, nausea, vomiting, and memory loss. He may also become agitated or combative.

A simple concussion will usually require no special care other than close observation, but a doctor should be consulted to determine whether a skull fracture or other severe injury has taken place.

Neck and Back Injuries

SYMPTOMS
Any or all of the following may be present:
- Difficulty moving fingers, toes, or limbs
- Numbness or tingling in arms, legs or shoulders
- Pain in neck or back
- Difficulty breathing

ACTIONS TO TAKE
- Provide artificial respiration if the victim stops breathing (see page 386) or CPR if the pulse stops (page 403).
- Treat head wounds as described earlier, but wrap the entire head only if the bleeding was not slowed with the first bandage and if someone else can support the victim's neck as you work.
- Keep the victim immobilized until medical help arrives. Place pillows or rolled blankets on both sides of the head to hold it still.
- Cover the victim from the neck down with a blanket or coat.
- If you need to move the victim to prevent further injuries, use a wide board or door as a makeshift stretcher. The ideal board would reach from the victim's head to his feet, but head-to shoulder support may be enough for someone with a neck injury, and head-to-knee support may be enough for someone with a neck or back injury.
- Hold the victim's head still. Remember that with some injuries even the slightest movement of the head can cause paralysis or death.

▪ With the help of several people, roll the victim onto her side while you support the head and neck. The head, neck, and back should be in alignment, and the body should not twist at the waist. Have someone slide the board close to the victim's side. When you are ready to place the victim on the board, count "one, two, three"—at which point everyone should gently roll the victim onto the board; be sure to keep supporting her head and neck.

▪ Using large strips of cloth, tie the person to the board in several places.

▪ With a neck injury, brace the neck if you can: Put sandbags on both sides of the head and secure them by placing tape (if available) across the forehead and around the bags. If no sandbags are at hand, use bags of flour or sugar.

Heart Attack & Stroke

A heart attack may occur when blood and oxygen fail to reach the heart. When they fail to reach the brain, a stroke may occur. Both of these emergencies are life-threatening.

Heart Attack

WARNING SIGNS

Any or all of the following may be present:

▪ A crushing, persistent chest pain, which often begins under the breastbone and radiates to one or both shoulders, the arms, neck, jaw, stomach, or back

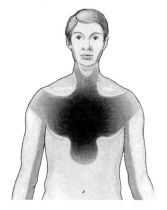

▪ Shortness of breath
▪ Pale skin or a bluish tint to the lips, skin, and fingernail beds
▪ Profuse sweating
▪ Shock
▪ Physical collapse
▪ Indigestion
▪ Nausea
▪ Vomiting
▪ Weakness
▪ Restlessness
▪ Anxiety

ACTIONS TO TAKE

▪ Call for medical help, making it clear that you suspect a heart attack. If the victim has a history of heart disease, tell the ambulance team.

▪ To aid a heart attack victim who is conscious, ease him into a sitting position or use pillows to prop him into a half-sitting position. Place a folded towel or pillow beneath the knees.

▪ Loosen clothing to ease breathing and aid circulation.

▪ Cover the victim with a blanket or coat for warmth.

▪ Keep him from moving or exerting himself in any way until help arrives.

▪ Do not give him anything to eat or drink.

▪ If the victim is unconscious or becomes unconscious, put him in the recovery position if he is breathing (see page 383). Frequently check for breathing and pulse. If necessary, administer artificial respiration (page 386) or CPR (page 403).

Stroke

WARNING SIGNS

The victim may experience one or more of the following:
▪ Sudden blurred vision or loss of vision
▪ Numbness, weakness, or paralysis of the face, arm, or leg
▪ Dizziness, loss of balance
▪ Difficulty swallowing
▪ Sudden severe headache
▪ Confusion, drowsiness
▪ Difficulty speaking
▪ Loss of bladder or bowel control
▪ Loss of consciousness

ACTIONS TO TAKE

■ Summon medical help immediately.

■ If the victim is conscious, have him lie down with head and shoulders raised slightly, using a pillow for support. Turn his head toward his weak side so that any mouth secretions can drain. Loosen his clothing.

■ If he is unconscious, check to see that the mouth and airway are not obstructed—the tongue may have slipped back (see page 386). Perform artificial respiration if the victim's breathing has stopped, and use CPR if the victim has no pulse (page 403).

■ If he is unconscious but breathing, place him in the recovery position (see page 383), but turn his head toward the weak side so that mouth secretions can drain.

Heat Exhaustion & Heatstroke

Being exposed to high temperatures for a long time or exercising on hot, humid days can lead to heat exhaustion or the life-threatening heatstroke. A victim of heat exhaustion sweats profusely—losing vital fluids and minerals—but the evaporation of sweat prevents an extreme temperature rise. With heatstroke, however, sweating diminishes or stops and body temperature soars. Heat exhaustion often precedes heatstroke. Particularly susceptible to these disorders are the obese, the very young and the very old, the chronically ill, and those taking certain medications.

Heat Exhaustion

SYMPTOMS

Besides the abundant sweating, a victim may experience any of the following:
■ Pale, clammy skin
■ Dilated pupils
■ Weakness, dizziness
■ Nausea, vomiting
■ Muscle cramps
■ Headache
■ Slight rise in temperature

ACTIONS TO TAKE

■ Cool the person off by moving him to the shade or an air-conditioned room. Lay him down, loosening his clothing and elevating his feet.

■ Unless he has been vomiting, give the victim cold—but not iced—liquids to drink, such as juice or salted water (one teaspoon of salt per quart of water). If the person vomits, stop administering fluids and seek medical assistance.

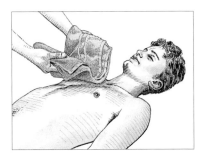

■ Apply cool, wet towels to the skin. If air-conditioning is not available, direct a fan toward the victim.

■ Consult a physician to be sure there is no serious underlying cause for the condition.

■ If the victim passes out, put him in the recovery position (see page 383) and call for immediate medical aid. If necessary, apply artificial respiration (page 386) or CPR (page 403).

Heatstroke

SYMPTOMS

Any or all of the following may occur:
■ Flushed, hot skin, often dry
■ Rapid pulse
■ Dizziness, confusion
■ Irritability, combativeness
■ Hallucinations
■ Loss of consciousness
■ Sudden rise in temperature to 40°C (104°F) or more

ACTIONS TO TAKE

■ Call for medical help; the victim's life is in danger.

■ Remove the victim's clothing and place him in a tub filled with cold water (do not use ice) or spray him with cool water. If neither option is available, wrap him in wet sheets or towels or use cold packs (place a sheet between the cold packs and the skin).

■ Fan the victim, or use an electric fan, but do not induce shivering.

■ Constantly monitor body temperature. When it drops to 38.3°C (101°F) or 38.9°C (102°F), dry the victim off, but keep fanning him. If his temperature rises, repeat the cold-bath procedure.

■ If the victim loses consciousness, put him in the recovery position (see page 383), but continue the cooling treatments after checking his breathing (page 386) and pulse (page 403).

Hypothermia

Prolonged exposure to the cold may cause someone's body temperature to drop below 35°C (95°F), resulting in the dangerous condition called hypothermia (meaning "low heat"). Hypothermia can lead to brain damage and even death. Those at greatest risk include infants (especially when premature or ill), the elderly, people who are intoxicated, and those who suffer from heart disease or malnutrition. See also: *Frostbite.*

SYMPTOMS

Besides a low body temperature, the victim may exhibit one or more of the following signs. She herself, however, may not be aware of her symptoms.
▪ Drowsiness
▪ Lethargy
▪ Irritability
▪ Unsteady gait
▪ Slurred speech
▪ Confusion
▪ Shivering
▪ Stiff muscles
▪ Red skin (especially common with babies)
▪ Loss of consciousness

ACTIONS TO TAKE

▪ Call for medical help.
▪ Check breathing and pulse; if necessary, apply artificial respiration (see page 386) or CPR (page 403).
▪ Take the victim into a warm room, if possible. Remove any wet clothing and wrap her in blankets, coats, or other coverings; however, do not use an electric blanket. Make sure her head is covered.
▪ Have the victim lie down. If she is unconscious but breathing, place her in the recovery position (see page 383). She should remain still, since physical activity would draw blood away from her vital organs. Do not massage her limbs, as this would have the same effect.
▪ If the victim must remain outside, put a sleeping bag or some kind of material between her and the ground. Lie down next to her so that your body heat can help keep her warm, and put blankets or other coverings over her. Be sure her head is covered.

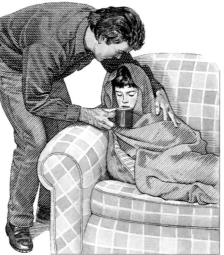

▪ Give a conscious victim warm liquids, such as tea, coffee, broth, or warmed milk. Do not give alcohol.
▪ Wrap a hot-water bottle or electric heating pad, set on its lowest setting, in a towel or cloth. Place it on the victim's torso (not on her arms or legs). Do not put a heating device directly on her skin.

HOW TO PREVENT

▪ Wear the proper clothing to help you stay warm and dry.
▪ If you begin to shiver while swimming, get out of the water, dry off, cover up, and exercise until you feel warm.
▪ With an infant, do not let a room get so cold that the baby's skin feels cold when you touch it.
▪ Be sure that an elderly person has adequate food, clothing, and heat during the winter. Take seriously any complaints about the cold.

Nosebleed

Because the capillaries inside the nose are so close to the surface, they can easily rupture. A jolt to the nose, a cold or sinus infection, exposure to dry air or high altitudes—all these can cause nosebleeds.

Although most nosebleeds are more of an inconvenience than a health emergency, there are exceptions. If the nosebleed results from a head injury with a suspected skull fracture, call for medical help but do not try to stop the bleeding (see page 416). If a nose injury causes bleeding, apply an ice pack and seek hospital treatment. When the nosebleed is a simple one and not the result of trauma, follow the steps below. See also: *Bleeding and Bruises.*

ACTIONS TO TAKE

▪ Have the victim sit up unless he feels dizzy.
▪ Tilt his head forward slightly, tell him to breathe through his mouth, and pinch the nostrils firmly (or have him do so).

■ Hold the nostrils shut for 10 to 15 minutes without interruption. Then remove your fingers to see if the bleeding has stopped. If it has, make sure the victim does not blow his nose. If the bleeding continues, pinch the nostrils for a few more minutes.

■ If the bleeding does not stop, gently insert into the nostrils sterile gauze or a clean cloth lightly covered with petroleum jelly. Pinch the nostrils for another 5 minutes and leave the gauze or cloth in place for at least 30 minutes.

■ Get medical attention if these measures do not stop the bleeding or if the victim has recurring nosebleeds, is taking a blood thinner, or has had radiation treatment or chemotherapy.

If a child gets frequent nosebleeds and his doctor has determined that there is no serious cause, take two preventive measures: daub petroleum jelly into his nostrils once or twice a day, and run a humidifier in his bedroom at night.

Poisoning

First aid for poisoning varies, depending on the substance involved and whether it has been ingested, inhaled, or absorbed by the skin. See also: *Artificial Respiration; Drug Overdose; Food Poisoning.*

ACTIONS TO TAKE

■ Call a poison control center or hospital immediately for instructions. If you live in a large city, a poison control center may be listed in the front of your telephone directory, along with other emergency numbers. If you know the poison source, have the container in front of you when you call so that you can identify the substance.

■ If the victim stops breathing, give her artificial respiration (see page 386). Use the mouth-to-nose method if you see or taste poison residue on her mouth.

■ If she is breathing but unconscious, put her in the recovery position (see page 383).

■ Give a conscious victim a glass of milk or water to dilute the poison only if you are instructed to do so by the poison control center.

Caution: Induce vomiting only if the poison control center tells you to do so. Vomiting can do more harm than good if the victim has swallowed a petroleum product or anything corrosive, such as bleach. It is also dangerous if the victim is unconscious or drowsy.

■ If you are told to induce vomiting, use two tablespoons of syrup of ipecac for an adult, one tablespoon for a child, or two teaspoons for an infant (under one year old). Follow this with at least eight ounces of water or milk. Administer again if vomiting does not occur within 20 minutes. If the second dose does not work, get the victim to a hospital.

Poisonous Mushrooms

Although most mushrooms are edible, some are toxic. Never eat a wild mushroom unless you can positively identify it as safe.

Poisonous mushrooms can cause severe illness and even death, particularly in children. Symptoms of poisoning include abdominal pain, vomiting, and diarrhea. They usually occur at least six hours after eating the mushroom, but with the *Amanita muscaria,* symptoms develop much more quickly. The *Amanita phalloides,* or death cap, causes most fatal cases of mushroom poisoning.

Amanita muscaria

Amanita phalloides

▪ If you do not have syrup of ipecac, put a tablespoon to the back of the victim's throat to induce vomiting.

▪ For inhalation of carbon monoxide, chemical fumes, and the like, call your local emergency number for help and advise the operator that oxygen will be needed. Then take the victim outdoors and loosen any tight clothing around her neck and waist.

▪ When insecticides, weed killers, or other poisonous chemicals get on the skin, wash the area immediately with soap and lukewarm water, letting the water run on the area for at least 10 minutes. If possible, the victim should stand under a shower. Use gloves to remove contaminated clothing, and seal the clothing in a plastic bag. Call a doctor (see "Chemical Burns," page 397). If the eyes are affected, refer to "Eye Injuries," page 410.

▪ Every poisoning victim should see a physician. When you take the victim to the hospital or office, bring along the poison container and a sample of the vomit, if any. If the poison was a chemical, take along the product or at least have the name written down.

For exposure to poison ivy, oak, or sumac, wash the area thoroughly with soap and water, followed by rubbing alcohol to remove the irritating oils. To treat the rash, apply cold compresses, then calamine lotion. Wash any contaminated clothing or tools.

Severed Digits

The most frequent cause of severed fingers and toes is carelessness around chain saws, power saws, and lawn mowers. Severed digits—and even limbs—can sometimes be reattached by micro-surgery; therefore, you should save the severed part if you can. See also: *Bleeding and Bruises; Shock.*

ACTIONS TO TAKE

▪ Lay the victim down, with his head lower than his heart, and elevate the injured limb. If the victim is vomiting, turn his head to the side to keep him from choking.

▪ Place a clean cloth pad, such as the inside of a folded handkerchief, over the wound. Hold it there, adding more layers if necessary. When the bleeding diminishes, bandage the cloth in place (see page 394).

▪ If bleeding continues, follow the instructions on page 392. Do not attempt to apply a tourniquet—unless you are an expert, you may do more harm than good.

▪ Do not try to tape the amputated digit back in place; this may cause tissue damage as well as pain. Instead, wrap the severed part in a clean cloth and put it in a plastic bag. Seal the bag and either pack it in ice or place it in another bag filled with cold water. Make sure that the ice or cold water does not directly touch the amputated digit. Take the bag to the hospital with the victim.

Shock

Serious injuries that involve a great deal of blood loss may lead to shock. When the body loses too much of its blood supply, it directs the remaining blood away from the extremities and to the internal organs. The danger of this life-threatening condition is that too little blood may reach the brain or the skin tissues or that circulation may stop altogether.

Shock may also be caused by such injuries as serious bites and stings, burns, electric shocks, and fractures. See also: *Bites and Stings ("Allergic Reactions"); Unconsciousness.*

SYMPTOMS

The victim may experience one or more of the following symptoms:

▪ Pale or bluish lips, fingernails, and skin
▪ Enlarged pupils
▪ Weakness
▪ Fainting
▪ Restlessness, anxiety
▪ Nausea, vomiting
▪ Sweating
▪ Confusion
▪ Thirst
▪ Shallow, rapid breathing
▪ Very fast but weak pulse

ACTIONS TO TAKE

■ If a head, neck, or back injury has occurred, do not move the victim unless he is in danger (see page 416). If he has not sustained a head, neck, or back injury, have him lie down on his back. To improve the victim's circulation, prop up his lower legs, if possible, so that they are 8 to 12 inches off the ground.

■ If the victim is bleeding, try to stop the blood flow (see page 392).

■ Get medical help as quickly as possible.

■ If the victim loses consciousness (see page 427), make sure his legs are elevated above his head; improved circulation can help him regain consciousness.

■ If the victim starts to vomit, turn his head to the side. Be prepared to clear the mouth and airway and apply artificial respiration if he stops breathing (see page 386).

■ Check the pulse regularly. If there is none, use CPR (see page 403).

■ Loosen any belts, ties, shirt collars, and other tight apparel.

■ In cool weather, keep the victim warm with a blanket or other covering, but do not overheat. In hot weather, have him lie down in the shade. In either case, place a blanket or towel between the victim and the ground.

■ Do not give the victim anything to eat or drink. If he complains of thirst, wet his lips with water.

■ Offer words of reassurance and comfort to the victim, and stay with him until medical help arrives.

Skin Problems

Though usually of only minor concern, blisters, cuts, scrapes, and sunburns should be treated properly. See also: *Bleeding and Bruises; Burns.*

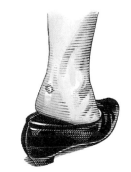

Blisters

Try not to rub or irritate a blister; unbroken blisters will usually absorb the accumulated fluid. If friction is unavoidable, however, you may need to puncture the blister. Sterilize a needle—hold it over an open flame (then let it cool), or clean it with rubbing alcohol. Insert the needle at the blister's base, and gently squeeze the blister to drain it. Care for a drained or burst blister with these steps:

■ Wash with soap and water.

■ Remove any loose skin fragments, being careful not to tear any skin, and daub on an antibacterial ointment.

■ Cover with clean gauze or a sterile bandage.

Cuts and Scrapes

Most minor wounds, such as scrapes and small cuts, need very little attention once the bleeding has stopped, as they tend to heal themselves. A superficial break in the skin usually bleeds for only a few minutes. Afterward, clean the area with soap and lukewarm water (after washing your own hands), then run cold water over it. Blot dry with a clean cloth or sterile gauze pad, wiping away from the cut itself. Though usually not essential once the bleeding has stopped, a bandage can protect a cut if clothing or other objects are likely to rub against it. When a cut requires greater attention, follow the appropriate measures below.

ACTIONS TO TAKE

■ If bleeding continues, press on the wound with a gauze pad or clean cloth.

■ If the cut is a puncture wound, as from a nail, try to encourage the flow of blood to remove bacteria. Wash the area with soap and water; then take the victim to a physician or hospital.

■ If a small object is in the wound, you can attempt to remove it with tweezers that have been sterilized over an open flame or boiled for five minutes and then cooled. Large or deeply embedded objects should be removed only by a medical specialist. To control bleeding from a wound with a protruding object still in it, press on both sides of the wound.

Do not put vitamin E oil on a cut. It will not heal the wound, and any effect it has may camouflage an infection. Instead, use an antibiotic ointment.

CONSULT A DOCTOR IF:
▪ A cut is more than half an inch long or very deep, or occurs on the face or on a joint.
▪ Bleeding does not stop.
▪ There is numbness in the area or difficulty in moving the wounded part.
▪ You suspect an infection (which may develop within a few days of the injury) because of fever, swelling, redness (possibly streaks), pus, pain, warmth in the area, or enlarged lymph glands.
▪ The wound was caused by a dirty object, and the victim has not had a tetanus shot within the past five years.

Sunburn

If you have a sunburn that involves considerable pain and inflammation, consult a physician. For a relatively mild sunburn, use the following basic techniques:
▪ Take a cool bath or shower.
▪ Soothe the skin with compresses of very cold water, but stop if you begin to shiver or feel cold. You can also try used, cooled tea bags that are still damp.
▪ Apply a hydrocortisone cream to control itching and inflammation.
▪ If your arms and legs swell, elevate them above the level of your heart.
▪ Take aspirin or ibuprofen for pain relief.
▪ If blisters develop, do not break them; opening blisters can increase the risk of infection and slow healing. If blisters break on their own, follow the guidelines under "Blisters," on the previous page.

Splinter Removal

A splinter is a piece of wood, glass, or other material lodged under the surface of the skin. If not carefully removed, it can cause infection.

ACTIONS TO TAKE
▪ Seek medical attention for a deeply embedded or very large splinter.

▪ Before removing a small splinter, wash your hands, then wash the skin around the splinter with warm, soapy water. With a clean washcloth, wipe downward and outward from the wound to avoid carrying dirt to it. Pat the skin dry with a clean towel.
▪ Remove splinters with sterilized tweezers and, if necessary, a needle. To sterilize, place the tweezers and needle in boiling water for about five minutes, or hold their ends over a flame for a few seconds. Do not wipe off any soot or touch the sterilized parts of the implements.

▪ If the splinter protrudes from the skin, pull it out with the sterilized tweezers at the same angle at which it entered the skin. A magnifying glass may help.
▪ If the splinter is visible below the skin but is not protruding, you will need to expose the end of the splinter so that you can grasp it with the tweezers. First put an ice cube over the area to anesthetize it. Then, using the sterilized needle, slit the skin just over the end of the splinter. Carefully lift up the skin, and pull the splinter out at the same angle at which it entered the skin.
▪ Squeeze a little blood from the wound to help clean it.

▪ Wash the wound with a mild antiseptic or with soap and water, and apply an adhesive bandage.
▪ See a physician if pain or swelling occurs after removal, or if the splinter breaks and part remains embedded. The victim may need a tetanus shot if he has not had one in the past five years, and he'll need to receive it within 72 hours of the injury.

When you know you have a splinter (or an embedded cactus spine) but you can't see it, put adhesive tape over the sore spot, then pull it off; the splinter may be lifted out.

The Danger of Tetanus

A piece of a splinter left in a wound—or a dirty splinter, even if it has been removed—can lead to tetanus, as can any dirty wound.

Tetanus is a very serious infection that can cause fever, irritability, profuse sweating, difficulty swallowing, and stiffness in the jaw and neck. Eventually, muscle spasms develop, beginning in the jaw or face. Because the victim often has trouble opening his mouth, the disease is also called lockjaw.

Make sure that everyone in your family is regularly vaccinated against tetanus. If you suspect a tetanus infection after an injury, take the victim to a hospital immediately.

Sprains & Strains

A sprain occurs when the ligaments and tendons around a joint are stretched or torn. This injury happens most often to ankles, although knees, wrists, elbows, hips, shoulders, and fingers can also suffer sprains. See also: *Fractures and Dislocations.*

Ankle Sprains

Twisting the foot when walking or running may cause an ankle sprain, which frequently occurs when playing such sports as basketball and tennis. An ankle sprain is often hard to distinguish from a fracture. If you have any doubt, assume that the ankle is broken and get medical help right away (see page 412).

SYMPTOMS
With an ankle sprain, any or all of the following may take place:
- Severe pain
- Swelling
- Bruising
- Inability to stand on foot

ACTIONS TO TAKE
- Remove the shoe and elevate the foot above the heart.
- Do not let the victim put weight on the injured ankle.
- Apply a cold compress to the ankle for 20 to 30 minutes. The compress can be a small towel soaked in cold water and wrung out or a plastic bag filled with crushed ice and wrapped in a cloth.
- Bandage the ankle in a figure-eight pattern: Wrap the bandage around the instep once or twice, then stretch it diagonally upward over the foot. Bring it around the ankle and heel to the front of the foot and then diagonally across the instep and under the arch.

Continue wrapping the bandage in figure-eight turns; each turn should overlap the previous one by about three-fourths of the bandage's width. Stop and secure with tape, clips, or a knot when the foot and ankle are covered. Leave the toes uncovered (see box, page 395).
- Apply a cold compress over the bandage several times a day for 15 to 20 minutes at a time during the first 48 hours.
- If pain and swelling persist, seek medical attention.
- If you sprain your ankle when you're alone and far from any help, leave your shoe on. Using strips of bandage or cloth, bind your ankle in a figure-eight pattern. Put as little weight as possible on the foot as you make your way to a place where the sprain can be treated properly.

No ice for a compress? You can instead use a bag of frozen vegetables wrapped in a towel.

Other Sprains

SYMPTOMS
One or more of the following may be present:
- Pain
- Swelling
- Bruising
- Tenderness

425

ACTIONS TO TAKE

▪ Apply cold compresses to the sprained joint.

▪ Bandage so that there is support above and below the injury; use a figure-eight pattern for a sprained knee, wrist, or elbow. Support a wrist, elbow, or shoulder with a sling (see page 413).

▪ If pain and swelling persist, seek medical attention.

Strains

A strain, or "pulled muscle," occurs when a muscle is overexerted—as from falling or lifting something improperly—causing it to stretch or tear.

SYMPTOMS

Any or all of the following may occur:

▪ Sudden, sharp pain

▪ Stiffness or cramp develops in the muscle

▪ Swelling

▪ Discoloration

▪ Loss of motion or power

ACTIONS TO TAKE

▪ Help the victim into the most comfortable position possible. Elevate the injured limb so that it is above the level of the heart.

MUSCLE CRAMPS

A cramp, or charley horse—a sudden spasm of muscles—causes acute pain. Cramps may occur as a result of an unusual amount of exertion or from a loss of fluids or nutrients caused by severe sweating, vomiting, or diarrhea. They may also happen during sleep, for no apparent reason.

Massaging or kneading the affected muscles will lengthen them so that they can be stretched, and stretching them will generally relieve a cramp. These maneuvers can be done by the victim alone or, preferably, with the help of another person. Someone who has prolonged pain or recurrent cramps should see a doctor.

CRAMP IN THE HAND

Straighten your fingers, using gentle force, if necessary. Then spread the fingers and push the outstretched tips back. Massage the muscles as you stretch them.

CRAMP IN THE CALF

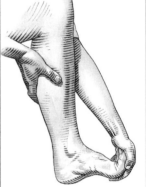

To stretch the calf muscle, pull up on the front of your foot with one hand. At the same time, use your other hand to squeeze your calf.

WHEN SOMEONE ELSE HAS A CRAMP

Have the victim lie down. For a cramp in the calf, foot, or hamstring (back of the thigh), straighten the knee and toes, and press the foot firmly up toward the shin. For a hamstring cramp, also press down on the knee. Massage the affected muscles.

CRAMP IN THE BACK OF THE THIGH

Sit on the floor and straighten your leg. Press your knee to stretch the hamstring muscle. Massage the muscle.

CRAMP IN THE FOOT

Sit down and pull your toes up toward the shin with your hand. Massage the muscles as you stretch them.

■ Apply a cold compress to the strained muscle, and bandage it in place. The compress can be a small towel soaked in cold water and wrung out or a plastic bag full of crushed ice wrapped in a cloth.

■ After 20 to 30 minutes, remove the compress.

■ Bandage the area, but not too tightly since the muscle may swell (see page 394).

■ Use a sling to support a strained arm (see page 413).

■ For back strain, the victim should avoid lifting and bending and should rest in bed for a couple of days.

■ If the pain or swelling is intense or lasts longer than 48 hours, seek medical attention.

Unconsciousness

Someone may lose consciousness for a variety of reasons, such as poisoning, insulin shock, or a head injury. Because his reflexes have stopped working normally, the victim is in danger of choking to death. Vomit, saliva, or blood may block the top of the windpipe, or the tongue may fall back over it. See also: *Artificial Respiration; Bleeding; CPR; Shock.*

ACTIONS TO TAKE

■ If you are not sure whether a collapsed person is conscious or unconscious, shout "Are you okay?" If he does not respond, try tapping his shoulder.

■ If the person is unconscious, call for medical help at once, unless the victim is a child

under eight years old. For someone under eight, check the breathing first. If the child is not breathing, perform artificial respiration (see page 386) for one minute, then call for help. After calling, start artificial respiration again, continuing until help arrives.

■ Unless he is in a dangerous situation or not breathing, do not move the person. If a head, neck, or back injury is possible, as with a serious fall, refer to page 416. Otherwise, try to open the victim's airway by raising his chin slightly and clearing foreign matter from his mouth with your fingers.

■ With all unconscious persons, be prepared to clear the airway and apply artificial respiration (see page 386) or CPR (page 403), if necessary.

■ If an adult victim is breathing normally and not vomiting, roll him into the recovery position (see page 383), but take care to move the entire body as a unit—cradling the head so as not to twist the neck. If he is vomiting, roll him onto his side so that he does not choke; again, move the body as a unit.

■ If an unconscious child is breathing normally, do not move him at all, since changing his position may cause a problem with his airway.

■ Check for a medical identification card, bracelet, or pendant that might explain the cause of the unconsciousness.

■ Loosen tight clothing, and open doors and windows to let in air.

■ Keep the victim warm. Do not give him anything to eat or drink when he awakens.

Vomiting

Vomiting is usually a symptom of another condition, such as intestinal flu, excessive eating or drinking, or motion sickness. The main goal of treatment in these cases is to prevent dehydration. See also: *Food Poisoning; Unconsciousness.*

ACTIONS TO TAKE

■ Encourage the victim to replace lost fluids by sucking on chipped ice or by taking frequent sips of water, juice, tea, or flat ginger ale.

■ Once the victim is feeling better, offer him only bland foods—such as dry toast, crackers, and flavored gelatin —until he is ready to resume a normal diet and several hours have elapsed since he last vomited.

CONSULT A DOCTOR IF:

■ The vomiting continues for more than a day or two.

■ Severe abdominal pain, fever, or other unusual symptoms occur.

■ The vomit contains blood or dark, gritty matter.

■ A young child is vomiting and also crying a lot or sleeping excessively or at unusual times.

If an unconscious person is vomiting, he is in danger of choking. Roll him onto his side, moving his entire body as a unit and carefully supporting his head and neck so that the neck does not twist.

Consulates, 281
Consultants, 307
Contact lenses, 150–151
    bifocal, 149–150
    swimming with, 104
    travel with, 259
Continuing care, 316
Contractions, in childbirth, 398
Contracts, 20
Contrast bathing, 336
Convenience foods, 79
Convulsions, 402
Cooking
    good posture and, 119
    low-fat, 54
    techniques for, 74–81
Copper, 45
Copperhead snakes, 237
Coral snakes, 237
Corn, 65
Corns, 143
Cornstarch, 123, 192
Coronary bypass surgery, 144, 359
Coronary heart disease. *See* Heart
    disease.
Corporal punishment, 163
Cosmetic dentistry, 147
Cosmetic surgery, hotline for, 19
Cosmetics, 122, 124
    for eyes, 149, 151
    as sunscreen, 128
Cougars, 236–237
Cough, 340
Counseling, 324
Country line dancing, 95, **95**
Cover letters, 28
CPE (Certified Professional
    Electrologist), 135
CPR (cardiopulmonary resuscita-
    tion), 403–404, **403**
Cramps
    menstrual, 368
    muscle. *See* Muscle cramps.
Cranberries, 65
Cranberry juice, for cystitis, 370
Crawl stroke, 102
Creative therapies, 326
Creative thinking, 32
Credit-card statements, 20
Creme rinses, 132, 133
Cribs, 199, 206
Cross-country skiing, 106–107, 112
    in cross training, 111
Cross training, 87, 110, 111–112
Croup, 365–366
Cruise ships, 263
Crunches, abdominal, **109,** 119
Crying, 364
CSA-approved seals, 211
CT (computerized tomography),
    304

CTS (carpal tunnel syndrome),
    26, 27
Cucumbers, 65
Curling bars, 112
Curling irons, 130
Currents, 243
Cuticles, hair, **130**
Cuts, 423
    See also Bleeding and
    bruises.
Cutting boards, 75–76
Cystitis, 370
Cystoscopes, 304

D

Dairy products, 68, 38, 39
Dance, 92, 95
Dance therapy, 326, **326**
Dandruff, 132, 133, 351
Dark
    fear of, 164
    SAD and, 375–376
Day care, 169–170, 171
    adult, 182–184
    in the workplace, 171
Debt statements, 20
Decks, 217
Decoctions, 330
Decongestants, 338
Deeds, 20
Deer, 229
Deerfly bites, 390
DEET (insect repellent), 233
Dehydration, 121
    in babies, 41
    diarrhea and, 284–285
    during exercise, 85
Deli food, 70, 71
Delivery, of babies, 398–399
Dental care
    for bridges, 351
    brushing teeth, 144–146, **144**
    emergency, 404–405
    implants, 147
    orthodontics, 147
Dentures, 146
Deodorants, 122, 123
Depilatory preparations, 123, 135
Depression, 374–375
    in children, 166
    in disabled persons,
    memory loss and, 33
    from unemployment, 29–30
Dermatitis, 122, 130, 301, 350
Designated driver, 267
Desserts, 70
    dieter's (recipes), 55

Detergents
    dish, as pesticide, 194, 196, 197
    for laundry, 125
    in soap, 120
Detoxification, 378
Diabetes, 352, 362–363
    air travel and, 275, 291
    contact lenses and, 150
    exercise and, 85
    hotline for, 19
Diabetic coma, 405
Diaper rash, 350
Diaphragms, 370
Diarrhea, 349
    as side effect of medication, 298
    traveler's, 281, 282–283, 284–285,
    286
Diatomaceous earth, 194–196
Diet
    arthritis and, 360
    for athletes, 39
    BRAT (Bananas, Rice,
    Applesauce, Toast), 285
    calcium intake and, 40–41
    in cancer treatment, 372, 373
    cardiovascular health and,
    356–357
    cooking techniques and, 74–81
    diabetes and, 362–363
    dining out and, 56–59
    eczema and, 350
    fiber in, 41
    food allergies and, 344
    hair care and, 130
    heart disease and, 357
    high blood pressure and, 352
    hospital, 308
    hyperactivity and, 166
    meal planning and, 46–51
    migraine headaches and, 336
    organic foods and, 41–42
    premenstrual symptoms and, 368
    skin care and, 125
    tooth care and, 145
    travel and, 282–285
    vegetarian, 60–61
    water consumption and, 41
    See also Nutrition.
Dieting
    eating habits and, 55
    exercise and, 54, 85, 100
    fat consumption and, 40, 53–54
    food bingeing and, 53
    strategies for, 52–53
    ten rules for, 53
Digestion, 39
Digitalis, 357
Digital thermometers, 339
Digits, severed, 422
Dinner, 49, 56–59
Diphtheria, 341, 365

I

IAMAT (International Association for Medical Assistance to Travelers), 281
Ibuprofen, 334–335
Ice packs, 336
ID cards, 174
Illness and recovery, **332**, 333–379
  addiction, 378–379
  arthritis, 360–361
  asthma and allergies, 344–346, 347
  common childhood problems, 364–367
  coping with pain, 334–337
  diabetes, 362–363
  ear, nose, and throat problems, 342–343
  for females and males, 368 371
  heart disease, 356–359
  high blood pressure and stroke, 352–354, 355
  intestinal disorders, 348–349
  mental health, 374–376, 377
  side effects of cancer treatment, 372–373
  skin disorders, 350–351
  viruses and other infections, 338–341
Imagery, 324, 326
Immunization
  for adults, 341
  for children, 365
  for travel, 261
Impetigo, 351
Implants, tooth, 147
Impotence, 371
Incandescent lights, 126, 189
Incontinence, hotline for, 19
Independence, in elderly, 201
Indian food, 58
Indigestion, 348
  See also Intestinal disorders.
Indonesian food, 58
Indoor air pollution, 204–206, 344
Infant care
  air travel and, 275
  artificial respiration and, 388
  babysitters and, 168–169
  bedtime safety, 199
  bottle-feeding, 145–146, 364, 366
  CPR and, 404
  cribs for, 199
  dehydration and, 41
  first aid for, 401
  See also Babies.
Infant colic, 364

Infections and viruses, 338–341
Influenza, immunization against, 339, 341, 365
Informed consent, 312
Infrared light, 127
Infusions, 330
Ingrown hair, 123
Ingrown toenails, 143
Inhalers, 338, 345
Inheritance, 179, 185
Injuries
  avoidance of, 86–87, 110
  care for, 114, **115**
  See also Emergencies.
Ink stains, removal of, 191
In-laws, 184–185
Inner-ear infection, 342
Inoculation
  for adults, 341
  for children, 365
  for travel, 261
Insects,
  bites from, 232–234, 389–391
  repelling and exterminating of, 194–197, 195
Insoluble fiber, 38
Insomnia, 374
  as side effect of medication, 298
Installment purchases, 20
Instant-Calming Sequence, 14
Insulation, 205, 216, 217
Insulin-dependent diabetes, 362
Insulin reactions, 405
Insurance
  health, 307, 310, 314, 317, 322–323
  travel, 280, 323
Internal injuries, 385
International Association for Medical Assistance to Travelers (IAMAT), 281
Interns, 307
Interviews, job, 29
Intestinal bleeding, 335
Intestinal disorders, 41, 348–349
Intruders, 222–223
Inventory, household, 20
Iodides, 124
Iodine, 45
  water purified with, 283
Ionizing smoke detectors, 206
Iridology, 327
Iron, 45, 81, 198
Irregularity, 349
Ischemic stroke, 354
Isolation therapy, 326
Isometric exercise, 91, 259
Italian food, 58
Itchy skin, 124–125

J

Japanese food, 58–59
Jaw problems, 91, 146, 412–413
Jellyfish stings, 245, 391
Jet lag, 276
Job loss and search, 28–30
Jock itch, 351
Jogging, 86, 98–99
  in cross training, 111
  and massage, 88
Joint dislocation, 413–415
Journal writing, 16
Jumping jacks, 93–94
Jumping rope, 94
Junk food, 50
Juvenile Diabetes Foundation Canada, 19
  hotline for, 19

K

Kayaking, 272–273
Kerosene space heaters, 205
Kéroul, 290
Keyboard strain, 26, 27
Kidney diseases, 335
  hotline for, 19
Kidney Foundation of Canada, 19
Kids Help Phone, 19
Kissing disease, 341
Kitchen
  cleaning of, 192–193
  ergonomics of, 24, 119
  fires in, 220–221
  lighting in, 188
  noise control and, 23
  safety in, 198, 200–201
Knee injuries, 87, 114
Knee-to-chest pull, single, 87
Knots, 394–395
Korean food, 59

L

Labels
  food, 72, 73
  pesticide, 227
  for shampoo and conditioner products, 134
  UL-approval seals, 211
Labor, in childbirth, 398
Lactic acid, 88, 122
Lactobacillus, 369

Mildew, 193, 345–346
Military press, **109**
Milk
    allergies to, 364
    in bathwater, 125
    calcium in, 40
    selection and storage of, 68
Milk paint, 213
Millet, 60
Mineral oil, 121
Minerals, 40, 45
Mini-stroke, 353–354, 355
Minoxidil, 135
Mirrored lenses, 152
Miscarriage, 341
Missing children, 175
Mock predators, 229
Mock sour cream (recipe), 77
Moisturizers, 122, 134
Molars, 146
Mold, 345–346
Moles, 129
Molybdenum, 45
Money
    boomerang kids and, 181
    family stress and, 159, 161
    health care costs, 322–323
Mononucleosis, 340, 341
Monosodium glutamate (MSG), 57
Monovision, 149–150
Moodiness, 298
Mood swings, 368
"More" (food label), 73
MORE. *See* Multiple Organ Retrieval
    and Exchange Program of
    Ontario
Morning breath, 146
Morning stress, 13
Mosquitoes, 195, 197, 232–233, 390
Mothballs, 204
Moths, 195
Motion sickness, 262–263, **263,** 286
Mouth problems
    bleeding from, 393
    in cancer treatment, 372
    insect stings in, 391
    oral thrush, 351
    sores, 351
Mouth-to-mouth resuscitation,
    386–388
Mouthwash, 146
MRI (magnetic resonance imaging),
    292, 304, 359
MSG (monosodium glutamate), 57
Mudslides, 254–255
Multiple Organ Retrieval and
    Exchange Program of Ontario
    (MORE), 19
Multiple sclerosis, 134
Multiple Sclerosis Society of
    Canada, 19

Mumps, immunization against, 341,
    365
Muscle building, 108–109
    in cross training, 110, 111
Muscle cramps, 115, 426, **426**
    massage for relief of, 88,
    as side effect of medication, 298
Muscle relaxation, progressive, 17,
    334
Muscular Dystrophy Association of
    Canada, 19
    hotline for, 19
Mushrooms
    poisonous, 421
    selection and storage of, 66
Music
    noise control and, 22
    relaxation with, 16
    therapy, 327

N

Nail-biting, 138
Names, memory for, 32–33
Napping, 16
Narcotics Anonymous, 378
Nasal sprays, 343
National Organization for Rare
    Disorders, 19
National Tuberous Sclerosis
    Association, 19
Native American medicine, 328
Natural childbirth, 398–399
Nature tours, 16
Naturopathy, 328
Nausea, 298, 356, 372
Nebulizers, 345
Neck
    exercises for, 87, 91
    injuries to, 417–418
Nectarines, 66
Nervousness, 376
Newlyweds, money management
    for, 159
Niacin, 44, 357–358
Nickel, allergies to, 122, 350
Nicotinic acid, 44
Nightmares, 164
Night terrors, 164
Night vision, 265
Nitrogen dioxide, 239
Nitroglycerin, 357
No-cream whipped cream (recipe),
    77
Noise
    at home, 22–23
    at work, 24–25
Noncomedogenic products, 124

Non-impact aerobics, 92
Non-insulin-dependent diabetes,
    362
Nonprescription painkillers,
    334–335
North American Chronic Pain
    Association of Canada, 19
Nose, 342–343
    blowing of, 338, 366
Nosebleeds, 393, 420–421
Nose drops, 343
Numbness, 353
Nurse-midwives, 309
Nurses, 307
Nursing homes, 316–319
    alternatives to, 316
Nursing stations, 321
Nutrition
    in carbohydrates, 39
    fat and, 39–40
    food groups, 42, 43
    in minerals, 40, 45
    in protein, 38–39
    skin care and, 120, 121
    vitamins as source of, 40, 44
    See also Diet; Food.
Nuts, as source of protein, 39

O

Oatmeal, and skin care, 124–125
Obesity, 52, 84
    as cardiovascular risk factor, 356
Occupational hazards, 90–91, 344
Odor, removal of
    from carpets, 192
    from painting, 213
    from refrigerators, 193
Office
    ergonomics of, 24
    noise in, 24–25
    stress in, 15
    working out in, 90–91
Office chairs, 25
Oil-based paints, 213
Oils,
    for cooking, 77–78
    in hair care products, 134
Oily hair, 131
Oily skin, 121, 122
Ointments, for eyes, 153
Onions, 66
Onycholysis, 138
Operations, 312–314, 315
    abroad, 281
    air travel and, 275
    ambulatory surgery centers for,
    317

in fruit juices, 46
prevention of cancer with, 38
Vitamin D, 39, 40, 44, 128, 134
Vitamin E, 40, 44, 121, 134, 423
atherosclerosis prevention with,
357
cancer prevention with, 38
cataract prevention with, 148
in fat, 39
heart disease prevention with,
357
Vitamin K, 39, 44
Vocal cords, 343
Vocational education, 34
Volunteering, 13, 35
Vomiting, 372, 427
as side effect of medication, 298

W

Walk-in medical clinics, 317
Walking, 96–97, 111
Wall coverings, 216, 217
and noise control, 23
Wardrobe. *See* Clothing.
Warning signs
abdominal injuries, 385
appendicitis, 386
drowning, 406
frostbite, 415
heart attack, 418
motion sickness, 262
stroke, 418
Warranties, 20, 21
Warts, 350
Wasps, 195, 232, 390–391
Waste disposal, 190
Water
healthful benefits of, 41
lead in, 207–208
purification of, 240, 283
skin moisture from, 121
travel and consumption of,
282–283
See also Dehydration.
Water aerobics, 93–94
Water-based paints, 213

Watercress, 68
Watermelons, 68
Water moccasins, 237
Water pollution, 240
Waterproof products, 127
Waterskiing, 272, 273
hand signals for, **273**
Water-soluble vitamins, 44
Water sports
canoeing and kayaking, 272–273
safety of, 242–245, 272
sailing and boardsailing, 273
swimming, 102, 111
waterskiing, 273, **273**
Waterwalking, 97
Wax, in ears, 342
Wax, paraffin, 136
Weather emergencies, 246
avalanches, 255
blizzards, 249–250
driving through, 266
earthquakes, 251–252
floods, 250–251, 253
hurricanes, 248
lightning and thunderstorms,
246–247
mudslides and landslides,
254–255
tornadoes, 247–248
wildfires, 252–254
Weather stripping, 23, 217
Weevils, 195
Weight cuffs, 112
Weight loss. *See* Dieting.
Weight training, 108–109
in cross training, 110, 111
Well water, 208, 240
Wheat germ, 78
Wheelchairs, 180, 290–291
Whipped cream, no-cream (recipe),
77
Whirlpool baths, 17
Whiteners, tooth, 145
Whitewater, 272, 273
Wild animals, 236–237
Wildfires, 252–254
Wills, 20, 179, 185
living, 21, 311
Wind, dry skin and, 120
Windbreaks, 23

Window guards, 198
Windows, 126
Windshields, 127
Winter blues, 375–376
Winter itch, 123
Witch hazel, 122
Withdrawal, from smoking, 379
"Without" (food label), 73
Women
body fat of, 39
common health problems of,
368–370
injuries to, 114
with osteoporosis, 40
physicals for, 300
surgery for, 303
See also Pregnancy.
Wood, in home renovation and
repair, 213–214, 217
Wood stoves, 204–205
air pollution from, 239
Working parents, 172–173
Workmen's Compensation, 322
Workplace
day care centers in, 171, **171**
ergonomics of, 24
exercising in, 15, 90–91
noise in, 24–25
stress in, 15
Wounds. *See* Emergencies.
Wrinkles, 120, 127
Wrist strains, 26, 27

X, Y, Z

X-rays, 300, 301, 304
breast, 300, 301, 369–370
dental, 145
Yard safety, 226–229
Yeast infections, 368–369
Yellow jacket stings, 232
Yellow nail syndrome, 138
Yoga, 17, 111, 324, 325, 335, 357,
361
Yogurt, 48, 369
Zen meditation, 17
Zinc, 45, 78

*Grateful acknowledgment is made for permission to excerpt or adapt
featured material taken from the following works:*

Arthritis Foundation *Overcoming Rheumatoid Arthritis,* printed in September 1983. Used by permission of the Arthritis Foundation. **Avon Books** *Sylvia Porter's Love and Money* by Sylvia Porter. Copyright © 1983, 1984, 1985 by Davis Publications, Inc. Reprinted with permission of William Morrow and Company, Inc. **Bantam Books** *Tiny Game Hunting* by Hilary Dole Klein and Adrian M. Wenner. Copyright © 1991 by Hilary Dole Klein and Adrian M. Wenner. Used by permission of Bantam Books, a division of Doubleday Dell Publishing Group, Inc. **Christian Herald** "Can Two Families Be One?" by Marion Duckworth. *Christian Herald,* June 1986. Copyright © 1986 by Christian Herald Association, Inc. **Consumers Union** "Fitness Update: Shoulder Stretch, Hamstring Stretch, Trunk Twist, Calf Stretch," Copyright © 1991 by Consumers Union of U.S., Inc. Reprinted with permission of *Consumer Reports on Health,* November 1991. **Dorling Kindersley Ltd.** *The Complete Book of Massage* by Clare Maxwell-Hudson. Copyright © 1988 by Dorling Kindersley Ltd. Text copyright © 1988 by Clare Maxwell-Hudson. **Doubleday** *The Relaxed Body Book* by Daniel Goleman, Ph.D., and Tara Bennett-Goleman, M.A. Copyright © 1986 by American Health Partners. Used by permission of Doubleday, a division of Bantam Doubleday Dell Publishing Group, Inc. **Facts on File** *The W.E.T. Workout.* Copyright © 1985 by Jane Katz. Reprinted with permission of Facts on File. **Health Letter Associates** "Back to the Woods," from the *University of California at Berkeley Wellness Letter,* May 1993. Copyright © 1993 by Health Letter Associates; "Better Walking Workouts," from the *University of California at Berkeley Wellness Letter,* September 1992. Copyright © 1992 by Health Letter Associates; "Ask the Experts: What's a Safe Way to Remove Earwax?" from the *University of California at Berkeley Wellness Letter,* February 1993. Copyright © 1993 by Health Letter Associates; "Myth: 'Energy Bars' Boost Your Athletic Performance," from the *University of California at Berkeley Wellness Letter,* October 1992. Copyright © 1992 by Health Letter Associates; "Home Exercise Equipment," from the *University of California at Berkeley Wellness Letter,* December 1992. Copyright © 1992 by Health Letter Associates. Reprinted with permission of the *University of California at Berkeley Wellness Letter* and Health Letter Associates. **The Hearst Corporation** Excerpt from *A Guide to Super Snacks for Kids* by Jo-Ann Heslin, M.A., R.D., and Annette B. Natow, Ph.D., R.D. *Redbook,* October 1986. Copyright © 1986 by The Hearst Corporation. "100 Great Little Nutrition Tips," *Redbook,* February 1988. Copyright © 1988 by The Hearst Corporation; "But He Started It" by Roberta Israeloff. *Redbook,* July 1992. Copyright © 1992. Reprinted with permission of Roberta Israeloff. **Hippocrates Partners** "World's Fare" by John Hastings, *Health,* September 1993, Volume 7, Number 5. Copyright © 1993 by Hippocrates Partners. **Houghton Mifflin Company** Excerpt from *Health & Fitness Excellence: The Scientific Action Plan* by Robert K. Cooper, Ph.D. Copyright © 1989 by Robert K. Cooper. **Little, Brown and Company** from *The Athlete Within* by Harvey B. Simon, M.D., and Steven R. Levisohn, M.D. Copyright © 1987 by Charter Oak Trust and Harvey B. Simon Family Trust. **Medletter Associates** "How to Make Food Taste Better" excerpted from *The Johns Hopkins Medical Letter Health After 50.* Copyright © Medletter Associates, 1992. **William Morrow & Company, Inc.** "Jet Lag" condensed, with approval, from *Traveler's Medical Companion* by Eden Graber and Paula M. Siegel. Copyright © 1990 by Eden Graber and Paula M. Siegel. Reprinted with permission of Fielding's Travel Books, an imprint of William Morrow and Company, Inc. **Newsweek** "Typing Without Keys," excerpted from February 21, 1994, interview with Susan Harrigan. Copyright © 1994 Newsweek Inc. **PADI** *Open Water Manual.* Copyright © 1980 Int'l PADI, Inc. **Public Citizen's Health Research Group** *Medical Records: Getting Yours. A State-by-State Survey of Laws Governing Access to Medical Records.* Copyright © 1992 Public Citizen's Health Research Group. **The Reader's Digest Association, Inc.** "Avoiding Dog Bites," adapted from "Should You Trust A Tail-Wagging Dog?" by Jane Mattern Vachon, *Reader's Digest,* November 1992. Copyright © 1992 The Reader's Digest Association, Inc. **RD Publications, Inc.** "Frostbite: Dangerous Myths, Useful Facts," from *American Health,* November/December 1982. Copyright © 1982 by American Health. Reprinted with permission of Kent Dannen; "A Buyer's Guide: What to Look for—and Avoid—in Fresh Produce," *American Health,* July/August 1986; "Know Your Sport" by Rick Sharp, from *American Health,* January/February 1991. Copyright © 1991 by American Health. **Retirement Living Publishing Co., Inc.** "Charting Your Health" excerpt from *New Choices for the Best Years,* June 1991. Copyright © 1991 by Retirement Living Publishing Co., Inc. **Southern Illinois University** *Evolution of Federal Dietary Guidance Policy: From Food Adequacy to Chronic Disease Prevention* by Marion Nestle and Donna V. Porter. *Caduceus,* Summer 1990, Volume VI, Number 2, Copyright © 1990 by Southern Illinois University. **The New York Times** "Limbering Up: Exercises for the Hands, Wrists and Fingers" by John Kella, Ph.D., *The New York Times, Health,* Wednesday, March 4, 1992. Reprinted with permission of John J. Kella, Ph.D.; "A Guide to Massage," by Amy Singer, September 28, 1986, *The Good Health Magazine.* "Relieving Stress: Mind Over Muscle" by Daniel Goleman and Tara Bennett-Goleman, September 28, 1986, *The Good Health Magazine.* **Times Mirror/Mosby** *Rehabilitation Techniques in Sports Medicine* by William E. Prentis, Ph.D. Copyright © 1990 by Times Mirror/Mosby College Publishing. **Weekly Reader Corporation** "Tornadoes, Lightning, Hurricanes, and Earthquakes" from *Current Health,* September 1990. Copyright © 1990 by Weekly Reader Corporation. **Workman Publishing** *60 Ways to Relieve Stress in 60 Seconds* by Manning Rubin. Copyright © 1993 by Manning Rubin.

ILLUSTRATIONS

10–18, 20, 22–26, 28–35 Lane Dupont. **39** Nick Hardcastle. **40** Laszlo Kubinyi. **41, 42** *top* Nick Hardcastle. **42** *bottom* Laszlo Kubinyi. **46** Nick Hardcastle. **47** Karin Kretschmann. **48–49** Nick Hardcastle. **50–51** Karin Kretschmann. **52** Nick Hardcastle. **54, 56–59** Karin Kretschmann. **60** *top* Laszlo Kubinyi. **60** *bottom* Nick Hardcastle. **62–64, 66–67, 68** *top* Laszlo Kubinyi. **68** *bottom* Nick Hardcastle. **69** Laszlo Kubinyi. **70** Ray Skibinski. **73–74** Nick Hardcastle. **75** *top* Karin Kretschmann. **75** *bottom,* **76–79** Nick Hardcastle. **80** Laszlo Kubinyi. **81** Nick Hardcastle. **84–94, 96–98, 100–104, 107–110, 112–114** Laszlo Kubinyi. **118–122** Nick Hardcastle. **123** Laszlo Kubinyi. **124, 126, 127, 130** *top* Nick Hardcastle. **130** *bottom* Laszlo Kubinyi. **135, 137, 139–142, 144** Nick Hardcastle. **147** Laszlo Kubinyi. **148, 151, 153** Nick Hardcastle. **156–167, 169, 170, 172–173, 175–178, 180, 182, 184–185** Lane Dupont. **188–189, 192** Karin Kretschmann. **194** Ray Skibinski. **196** Karin Kretschmann. **197–198** Ray Skibinski. **199** Karin Kretschmann. **200** Ray Skibinski. **201, 203** Karin Kretschmann. **204–206** Ray Skibinski. **207** Karin Kretschmann. **208** Ray Skibinski. **210–214, 216** Karin Kretschmann. **217** Ray Skibinski. **218–221** Karin Kretschmann. **222, 223** Ray Skibinski. **226** *top* Karin

Kretschmann. **226** *bottom*, **228–230, 232** *top* Ray Skibinski. **232** *bottom* Karin Kretschmann. **233** Ray Skibinski. **234, 237** Laszlo Kubinyi. **238** Ray Skibinski. **239, 240** Karin Kretschmann. **241** Ray Skibinski. **242–243** Laszlo Kubinyi. **244** Karin Kretschmann. **245** Laszlo Kubinyi. **246, 248–250** Karin Kretschmann. **252, 254, 255** Ray Skibinski. **258, 259** Lane Dupont. **260, 261** Ray Skibinski. **262–268, 270–274, 276, 278, 281–284, 286–288, 291** Lane Dupont. **294, 299** Karin Kretschmann. **301** Ray Skibinski. **302** Laszlo Kubinyi. **303** Karin Kretschmann. **304** Laszlo Kubinyi. **305, 306, 308, 311, 312, 314, 316–320, 324, 328** Karin Kretschmann. **330, 331** Laszlo Kubinyi. **334–336, 338–341** Nick Hardcastle. **343** *top*

Laszlo Kubinyi. **343** *bottom*, **344, 345, 348–352** Nick Hardcastle. **354** Laszlo Kubinyi. **356–359, 361, 363, 364, 366–376, 378, 379** Nick Hardcastle. **383** Roy Knipe. **384** Laszlo Kubinyi. **386–388** Roy Knipe. **389, 390** *left* Laszlo Kubinyi. **390** *middle & right*, **392** *left & middle* Roy Knipe. **392** *right* Laszlo Kubinyi. **394, 395** Roy Knipe. **396** Laszlo Kubinyi. **397–404** Roy Knipe. **407** Laszlo Kubinyi. **408–411** Roy Knipe. **412** Laszlo Kubinyi. **413–415, 417, 418** *top* Roy Knipe. **418** *bottom* Laszlo Kubinyi. **419–421** *top* Roy Knipe. **421** *bottom* Laszlo Kubinyi. **422–426** Roy Knipe. **19, 38, 44, 45, 61, 71, 99, 111, 115, 134, 138, 298, 307, 325, 337, 341, 346** Chart illustrations by Ray Vella.

PHOTOGRAPHS

Title page spread: *Top (l. to r.)* Chuck Savage/The Stock Market; Steven Mark Needham; Rick Friedman/Black Star; Chris Harvey/Tony Stone Worldwide; Jay Maisel. *Bottom (l. to r.)* Jeff Hunter/The Image Bank; Rich Clarkson; H.P. Merten/The Stock Market; Charles Gupton/Uniphoto; Burton McNeely/The Image Bank; Melchior Di Giacomo/The Image Bank. **8** Chuck Savage/The Stock Market. **9** Michael A. Keller Studios, Ltd./The Stock Market. **27** James A. McInnis. **36** Steven Mark Needham. **37** Mark Ferri. **43** Culver Pictures. **56** Leong Ka Tai/*Bon Appétit*. **78** Jack Reznicki. **82** Rick Friedman/Black Star. **83** Phil Schofield/AllStock **95** Blake Little/Onyx Enterprises, Inc. **105** David Barry. **106** Michael Keller/FPG International. **116** Chris Harvey/Tony Stone Worldwide. **117** Rosanne Olson/AllStock. **126** Tim Brown/Tony Stone Worldwide. **129** Neke Carson/NYT Pictures. **140** Mitchel Gray. **147** Implant Dentistry of North Carolina. **148** Ken Browar/Tony Stone Worldwide. **154** Jay Maisel. **155** Ricardo De Aratanha/The Image Bank. **159** Illustration based on a photo by Ron Chapple/FPG International. **168** Comstock Inc. **171** Goldman, Sachs. **172** Rob Goldman/FPG International. **179** Dana Fineman/Sygma. **183** Cathleen Curtiss/The Washington Times. **186** Jeff Hunter/The Image Bank. **187** Andy Sacks/Tony Stone Worldwide. **190** Craig Hammell/The Stock Market. **202** Anette Sørensen. **209** Steven Goldblatt. **215** Dee Breger/Phototake. **224** Rich Clarkson. **225** SuperStock. **235** Roger Payne. **236** Warren Garst/Tom Stack & Associates. **246** A. & J. Verkaik/The Stock Market. **253** John Schultz. **256** H.P. Merten/The Stock Market. **257** Leonard McCombe, *Life Magazine* © Time Warner. **277** Ken Graham Photography. **279** William R. Sallaz/Duomo Photography, Inc. **285** Jack Reznicki. **290** Georges Bosio/Gamma Liaison. **292** Charles Gupton/Uniphoto. **293** Lynn Johnson/Black Star. **297** Jack Reznicki. **309** National Association of Childbearing Centers. **315** Medical College of Georgia. **324** Based on a photo by Matt Meadows/Peter Arnold, Inc. **325** © Joe Lynch/Medichrome. **326** *top*, Nancy Sicsel/NYT Pictures, **326** *bottom*, Courtesy The Flotation Tank Association. **327** © Joe Lynch/Medichrome. **332** Burton McNeely/The Image Bank. **333** Mitch Kezar/Uniphoto Picture Agency. **347** Steven E. Sutton/Duomo Photography, Inc. **355** *left* Miss America Pageant; *right* Collection of Jacquelyn Mayer Townsend. **360** Jack Reznicki. **362** American Diabetes Association. **377** Shawn Stephen Riley. **380** Melchior Di Giacomo/The Image Bank. **382** Gary Kanadjian/gfk Images. **391** Dave B. Fleetham/Visuals Unlimited. **399** Penny Gentieu/Black Star. **406** David Madison/Bruce Coleman Inc.

SPECIAL THANKS

Access Foundation, Malverne, NY; Accessible Tours of Directions Unlimited, Bedford Hills, NY; Air Pollution Control Association, Pittsburgh, PA; Denise Albrecht, Sandy Hill Community Health Center, Ottawa, Ont; American Academy of Otolaryngology–Head & Neck Surgery, Alexandria, VA; Dr. Drew Allbritten, Executive Director, American Association for Adult and Continuing Education, Washington, DC; American Academy of Dermatology, Schaumburg, IL; American Academy of Pediatrics, Elk Grove Village, IL; American Association of Retired Persons, Washington, DC; American Cancer Society, National Headquarters, Atlanta, GA; American Chronic Pain Association, Rocklin, CA; American Institute for Cancer Research, Washington, DC; American Massage Therapy Association, Evanston, IL; American Optometric Association, St. Louis, MO; American Red Cross, Washington, DC; American Water Ski Association, Winter Haven, FL; The Arthritis Foundation, Atlanta, GA; Asbestos Information Center, Tufts University, Medford, MA; Association of Home Appliance Manufacturers, Chicago, IL; Asthma and Allergy Foundation of America, Washington, DC; Lynn Atkinson; Susan Auch, Olympic speed skater; Mary Bush, Health Canada; Donna Campbell, Ottawa Civic Hospital, Ont.; Canadian Association of Radiologists; Canadian Automobile Association; Canadian Breast Cancer Foundation; Canadian Diabetes Association; Canadian Massage Therapist Alliance; Canadian Medical Association; Canadian Paraplegic Association; Canadian Society for International Health; Centers for Safety Commission, Corporation for National Service, Washington, DC; Club Society, New York, NY; Sue Oliver Cressy, Lanark County Therapeutic Riding Association, Almonte, Ont.; Pat Cruikshank, Health Canada; Department of Foreign Affairs; Dr. Yvan Deslauriers, Health Canada; Dr. Alan Drummond, Canadian Association of Emergency Physicians; Burt W. Dubow, O.D., F.A.A.O., St. Cloud, MN, Chairman, Contact Lens Section, American Optometric Association; Ecologically Safe Homes, Unionville, IN; Elderhostel; Environment Canada; Environmental Construction Outfitters, New York, NY; Dr. Brian Gillespie; Heart and Stroke Foundation of Canada; Micheline Ho; Paul A. Homoly, D.D.S., Charlotte, NC; Vonnie Hunter; ICS Books, Merrillville, IN; International Association for Medical Assistance to Travelers; International SOS Assistance, Philadelphia, PA; Dr. William Jeanes; Dr. Elizabeth Kaegi, Canadian Cancer Society; Terry Kaufman, NDG-Montreal West CLSC; Erin Keough, Telemedicine Centre, Memorial University of Newfoundland; Kéroul; Robert K. King, Co-Director, Chicago School of Massage Therapy, Chicago, IL; Irene Klatt, Canadian Life and Health Insurance Association; Anne-Marie LaFleche, Canadian

Council on Health Facilities Accreditation; Constable Nicole Lauzon, RCMP; Living With Cancer, Inc., Long Island City, NY; Merrill Lochhead, Dover Court Community Centre, Ottawa, Ont.; The Male Sexual Dysfunction Clinic, Baltimore, MD; Teresa Maloney, Gatineau Birthing Centre, Que.; Ronald Marchant, Canada Safety Council; Dr. Leonard Marcus, American Society of Tropical Medicine and Hygiene, Newton, MA; Mended Hearts Club, American Heart Association, Dallas, TX; Mike Morris, Home Hardware, Ottawa, Ont.; National Clearinghouse for Alcohol and Drug Information, Rockville, MD; National Coalition Against the Misuse of Pesticides, Washington, DC; National Fire Protection Association, Quincy, MA; National Pesticide Telecommunications Network, 800-858-7378; National Stroke Association, Inglewood, CO; Chien Nghiem, IDA-Carver's Pharmacy, Ottawa, Ont.; Diana Parkin, freelance midwife; PMS and Menopause Self-Help Center, Los Altos, CA; Pelican Environmental Corp., Holliston, MA; The Points of Light Foundation, Washington, DC; Richard Pope, Canada Parks Service; Professional Association of Diving Instructors, Santa Ana, CA; Profile Women's Fitness Center, New York, NY; Sheryl Ralph-Williams, Diabetes Educational Unit, Ottawa Civic Hospital, Ottawa, Ont.; R.M. Rankin, herpologist, Canadian Museum of Nature; Selma and Ted Roach; Samsum Medical Research Foundation and Clinic, Santa Barbara, CA; Marilynne Seguin, Dying with Dignity; Transport Canada; U.S. Coast Guard, Public Information Office, Washington, DC; U.S. Department of Agriculture, Human Nutrition Information Service, Food and Consumer Services, Hyattsville, MD; U.S. Environmental Protection Agency, Washington, DC; U.S. Food and Drug Administration, Washington, DC; U.S. Department of Transportation, National Highway Traffic Safety Administration, Washington, DC; Jim White, Canada Mortgage and Housing Corporation; Nanette Whitwam, Rideau Trail Association; Wilderness Medical Society, Indianapolis, IN; Cathryn Wright, Executive Director, James Bay Community Health Project; Barbara Yawn, M.D., M.S.C., Director of Clinical Research, Olmsted Medical Group, Rochester, MN.